A Tour of the StringBuffer Class . . . .
   StringBuffer Constructors. 81
   A Brief Look at the Method toString 81
   Manipulating StringBuffer Data. 82
   Length and Capacity of the StringBuffer 84
A Tour of the StringTokenizer Class 85
Summary 87

Chapter 4   **Multiple Classes** **89**
Introduction 89
Creating Main Class Objects 89
The Keyword this. 91
Using Multiple Classes 92
   Nested Classes. 92
      Inner Classes 92
      Static Nested Classes 95
   Multiple Classes 97
   Controlling Data Access (Public, Protected, Private). . . . 100
      Why Use Access Attributes? 101
   The Static Block 101
Inheritance. 102
   The Object Class 103
   The toString Method 103
   Inheriting Your Own Classes. 105
   Inheritance Depending on Access Attribute 108
The Keyword super 109
The Keyword final with Classes and Methods 110
Polymorphism 110
   Casting Objects. 110
   Polymorphism in Action 112
   Abstract Classes 113
   Abstract Methods. 114
Interfaces 115
   Defining Interfaces 115
   Using Interfaces 117
   Interface Objects (well, sort of!). 118
   Does My Object Implement that Interface? 119
Defining on the Fly 120
Summary. 121

Chapter 5   **Packages, Utilities, and Error Handling** **123**
Introduction 123
What is a Package? 123
Importing Packages 124
Creating Your Own Packages 125

Using JARs. 128
   Running an Application from a JAR 128
   Running an Applet from a JAR 129
Exploring Useful Classes 132
   Useful java.lang Classes 132
      Primitive Data Type Wrappers 132
      The Math Class 133
      The System Class 133
   Useful java.util Classes. 134
      The ArrayList Class. 134
      The LinkedList Class 139
      The Stack Class 140
      The Random Class 142
Error Handling. 143
   Exceptions 143
      Using try/catch and finally 144
      Using the finally Block 147
      Throwing Exceptions 147
      Throwing Your Own Exceptions 148
   Errors 150
   Assertions 150
      Assertions in Control Flow 151
      Assertions in Internal Invariants 152
      Other Useful Notes 152
   Summary. 153

Chapter 6   **Stream I/O** **155**
Introduction 155
Introduction to Streams 155
Console Input 155
   Console Game Example—Tic-Tac-Toe 157
Writing Data to a File 166
Reading Data from a File 168
Object Serialization 170
Summary. 175

Chapter 7   **Threads.** **177**
Introduction 177
What Is a Thread? 177
Creating a Thread 178
Extending a Thread 178
Using the Runnable Interface 180
Stopping a Thread 181
Synchronization 183
   Synchronized Methods 185

This book is to be returned on or before the
last date stamped below.
You may have this book renewed for a further
period if it is not required by another reader.

Java
Programming

Andrew Mulholland and
Glenn Murphy

A CD-ROM OR DVD ACCOMPANY
THIS BOOK – SEE WALLET ON
INSIDE LEFT COVER

Library of Congress Cataloging-in-Publication Data

Mulholland, Andrew.
    Java 1.4 game programming / by Andrew Mulholland and Glenn Murphy.
      p. cm.
    ISBN 1-55622-963-1
    1. Java (Computer program language)   2. Computer games—Programming.
    I. Murphy, Glenn, 1908-   II. Title.
    QA76.73.J38 M849 2003
    794.8'152762—dc21

                                        2002155485
                                              CIP

ISBN 1-55622-963-1

10 9 8 7 6 5 4 3 2 1
0301

Java is a trademark of Sun Microsystems, Inc.
All brand names and product names mentioned in this book are trademarks or service marks
of their respective companies. Any omission or misuse (of any kind) of service marks or
trademarks should not be regarded as intent to infringe on the property of others. The
publisher recognizes and respects all marks used by companies, manufacturers, and
developers as a means to distinguish their products.

All inquiries for volume purchases of this book should be addressed to Wordware
Publishing, Inc., at the above address. Telephone inquiries may be made by calling:

(972) 423-0090

Contents

Chapter 1 **Introduction to Java 1.4** **1**
  Introduction. 1
  Introduction to the Java Platform 1
  Introduction to Java 2 Standard Edition 1.4 2
  What the Future Holds. 2
  What This Book Covers 3
  Who Is This Book For?. 3
  Installing the J2SE 1.4 SDK 4
  A Word on Integrated Development Environments (IDEs) . . . 5
  Useful Web Sites 5
  Summary 6

Chapter 2 **Basics of Java Programming** **7**
  Introduction. 7
  Introduction to Object-Oriented Programming (OOP) 7
    What Is an Object? 7
    Object-Oriented Programming in Java 8
    Constructors 9
    Class Members and Object Members—The static Keyword 11
    References 12
  HelloJavaWorld—A Simple Console Program 13
    Printing Text to the Console Screen 14
    Comments 15
  Primitive Data Types 16
    Numeric Data Types. 16
      Integers 16
      Floating-Point Data Types 19
  Simple Arithmetic Operators. 22
  Operator Precedence 23
  Unary, Binary, and Ternary Operators 24
  Oh No, More Operators! 25
  Arithmetic Assignment Operators 26
  The boolean Data Type 27
  Bitwise Operators. 27
  Bit Manipulation 29
  Bit Shifting 30
  Bit Flags. 31

The char Data Type 32
Character Escape Sequences. 32
Defining Unicode Characters. 33
Constants 33
Conditional Statements and Loops. 34
   Conditional Statements 34
      Simple if Statements 34
      The if with else Statements 36
      Logical Operators. 36
      The Conditional Operator 37
      Switch Statements 37
   Loops. 40
      Using the while Loop. 40
      Using the do while Loop 41
      Using the for Loop 42
      An Advanced Look at the for Loop. 44
      Using break and continue 45
      Jumping to Labels 46
   Methods. 47
      Parameter Passing. 49
      Method Signatures. 50
   Variable Scope. 51
   Summary 52

Chapter 3   **Arrays and Strings. 53**
Introduction 53
Arrays 53
   Accessing Array Elements 54
   Arrays Are Objects 56
   Setting Values from Array to Array. 56
   Arrays with for Loops 57
   Passing Arrays as Parameters. 59
   Multi-dimensional Arrays 60
   Multi-dimensional Multi-length Arrays. 62
Strings. 65
   String Concatenation 66
   Strings with Character Escape Sequences 67
   Arrays of Strings. 69
   Program Arguments. 70
A Tour of the String Class 72
   Comparing Two String Values. 72
   Retrieving String Data. 74
   Manipulating String Data 76
A Word on Regular Expressions 78
Invocation Chaining. 79

Object and Class Monitor 187
Synchronized Static Methods 187
Synchronized Blocks with Objects. 188
Wait and Notify 189
Sleeping Threads 191
Interrupting a Thread 193
Daemon Threads 194
Thread Priorities 195
A Final Word on Deadlock. 195
Summary. 196

Chapter 8   Applications and Applets 197
Introduction 197
A Brief Note on Components and Containers 197
Heavyweight and Lightweight Components 197
Introduction to AWT and Swing. 198
What Is an Application? 198
A Simple Java Application 199
What Is an Applet?. 201
A Simple Java Applet. 202
Viewing an Applet with AppletViewer. 204
Specifying Program Arguments for Applets in HTML . . . 205
Applet Security. 207
Look and Feel 208
Summary. 210

Chapter 9   Graphics 211
Introduction 211
Template Graphics Windowed Application 211
Introducing the Event Dispatch Thread 212
Creation and Initialization. 213
Disabling the Layout Manager 213
Pixel Coordinates 214
Sizing with the Window Border. 215
Let's See That in an Applet 219
AWT Notice 1 220
Closing a Window 222
Adding Components. 223
AWT Notice 2 225
Graphics and Graphics2D Overview 226
Graphics Class Basics. 226
setColor(Color col) 226
dispose() 227
drawLine(int x1, int y1, int x2, int y2) 227

drawRect(int x, int y, int width, int height) and
fillRect(int x, int y, int width, int height). 227
drawString(String s, int x, int y) 228
Drawing Shapes 228
Affined Transformations. 230
Fonts 234
Font Objects Are Immutable. 234
Understanding the Fonts Coordinates. 235
Getting the Available Fonts 238
Off-Screen Images. 239
The Image Class 239
Drawing to an Off-Screen Image. 240
The drawImage Method 242
Creating Transparency for a Sprite 245
Clearing the Sprite Background 250
The BufferedImage Class 251
Loading Images. 253
Supported Image Formats 253
Loading Images with the MediaTracker Class 254
Loading Images with the ImageIO Class. 258
Rendering 261
The Main Game Loop 264
Passive Rendering 264
Introducing the Main Loop. 268
Reducing Flickering 270
Overriding the Update Method. 270
Double Buffering 271
Synchronized Drawing with the Main Loop. 272
Let's See That in an Applet. 276
Synchronized Painting Using Threads. 278
Using a VolatileImage Back Buffer 284
VolatileImage in its Current State 286
Active Rendering and Full-Screen Exclusive Mode 286
Introducing the BufferStrategy Class 287
Page Flipping 287
The FullScreenDemo Example. 288
Summary. 296

Chapter 10 **Using the Mouse and Keyboard** **297**
Introduction 297
Using Listeners 297
KeyListener 298
MouseListener 298
MouseMotionListener 298
Reading Keyboard Input. 298

Adapter Classes 302
Reading Mouse Input 303
Integrating Mouse Events with the Main Loop 310
Creating the MouseProcessor 312
   Adding Events to the MouseProcessor 314
   Processing Events in the MouseProcessor 314
   The MouseProcessor in Action 314
Handling Repetitive Key Input 319
An All-Purpose Event Queue 326
Losing Focus 328
Changes for an Application 336
Where's My Tab Key? 337
Summary 337

Chapter 11 Using Sound and Music **339**
Introduction 339
Supported Sound Formats 339
Applet Simple Sound Example 339
Application Simple Sound Example 342
Using the Java Sound API 343
   Playing Sampled Sound 343
   Streaming Audio 347
   Playing MIDI Music 354
Creating a Sound Manager 357
Using the Sound Manager 368
Summary 371

Chapter 12 Game Programming Techniques **373**
Introduction 373
Animation 373
   Animation with One-Dimensional Image Sheets 373
   Animation with Two-Dimensional Image Sheets 380
   Mapping One Dimension to Two 386
Timing in Java 387
   Using a Native High-Resolution Timer in Windows 389
   About the JNI 389
   Creating a Java Timer 389
   Creating WinClock.dll 393
   Using the High-Resolution Timer 395
Garbage Collection and Creating Objects 397
   Object Pooling 399
Collision Detection 401
   Bounding Circle 402
   Bounding Box 408
Creating a Game Framework 412

Contents

A Framework Demo 430
Integrating the Screens into the Framework 436
Tile Scroller Example 439
Tile Walker Example 449
Changing the Player Size 465
Changing the Application Size 466
Changing the Map Size 466
Summary 467

Chapter 13 Introduction to GUI 469
Introduction 469
Using Buttons 469
Using Text Fields 474
GUI Extra Section 476
Setting Images for Buttons 477
Extending the GUI 479
A Recap on the Event Dispatch Thread 480
Creating Your Own GUI System 480
Using Our New GUI System 494
Summary 501

Chapter 14 Introduction to Databases 503
Introduction 503
What Is a Database? 503
Why Do I Need To Know about Databases? 506
Database Packages 506
Introduction to SQL 507
Summary 509

Chapter 15 Using SQL with MySQL 511
Introduction 511
What Is MySQL? 511
Installing MySQL 512
Starting the MySQL Server Automatically 515
SQL Statements 518
Data Definition Language 518
Creating and Dropping Databases 518
Creating a Database 518
Dropping a Database 519
Column (Field) Types in MySQL 520
Creating, Modifying, and Dropping Tables 521
Creating Tables 521
Modifying Tables 524
Dropping (Removing) Tables 526
Data Manipulation Language (DML) 527

Inserting Data 528
Modifying Data 530
Removing (Deleting) Data 531
Using SELECT Statements 533
Relational Databases 537
Joining Tables 541
Data Import Methods 542
Importing from a Text File 542
Importing from a Native Source 543
Backing Up and Restoring Data 544
Backing Up a Database to a File 544
Restoring a Backed Up Database 546
Summary 547

Chapter 16 **Using the JDBC** **549**
Introduction 549
What Is the JDBC? 549
Getting the MySQL Driver for the JDBC 549
Creating a Connection to a Database 550
Inserting Data into a Table 552
Retrieving Data from a Table 554
A Sample Windowed Database Application 557
Accessing Database Metadata from a ResultSet 565
Prepared Statements 567
Summary 569

Chapter 17 **Introduction to Networking** **571**
Introduction 571
Fundamentals of Networking 571
Protocols 571
TCP: Transmission Control Protocol 572
UDP: User Datagram Protocol 572
IP Addresses 572
Ports 573
Sockets 573
Stream and Datagram Sockets 574
Networking Applets 574
Example: TCP Echo Server 574
Example: TCP Echo Client 577
Example: UDP Echo Server/Client 581
Creating a Network Framework 587
Multiplayer "I'm a circle!" —A Sample Network Game 588
Creating the Server 588
Creating the Client 604
Summary 621

Contents

Chapter 18 **Introduction to NIO Networking 623**

    Introduction 623

    Why Use NIO? 623

    Channels 623

    The ByteBuffer Class 624

    Creating a Blocking Server 626

    Creating a Non-Blocking Server 631

    Summary 638

    Index 639

About the Authors

This for me is probably the easiest part of the book to write. I really have a liking for writing about myself as I always feel it will sound boastful and conceited, which I am.

Well, I started life as a baby and I'm afraid that's where it all began. I started programming at around 16 years of age while attending college in my hometown of Manchester, England. I use the term "attended" loosely, however, because as soon as the programming began, I was hooked, and ducked out of many a lecture to create a variety of games, albeit on an 80x25 ASCII character resolution and a useful gotoxy(x, y) method. In the second year of college, a friend and programming buddy, Nick Kitson, and I co-wrote a 16,000-line soccer management game in Pascal called ESM European Soccer Manager, where you could actually watch the matches in an overhead view. Working on this taught me more than anything about programming. My advice—pick a goal and go for it.

After college, I made it into the Computer Games Technology program at the University of Abertay Dundee and am now midway through the (honours) 4th year. While "attending" university I have furthered my knowledge from Pascal to C/C++ and then on to Java. The ability to make web games playable in a browser (applets) was what originally made Java so appealing to me, and had been a mystery to me for long enough. There began my introduction to Java. Before Java, I was mainly a procedural programmer, and not that well tuned to object-oriented programming (OOP). The good thing about Java, in this sense, is that it is completely OOP, so there was no choice but to program in this style. For this I think learning Java is the best guide to OOP you can get. And then came the book.

After working on a Java game over the summer of 2000, I teamed up with my now co-author Andrew, who has been my flatmate and friend since the first year of university. The university's random accommodation allocation for freshers can take the credit for us meeting in the student halls. We began work on the book in late 2001, while both juggling our honours degree courses at the same time. Besides losing my virginity and trying to complete Jet Set Willy, this book has been the most grueling experience of my life, but it was all worth it in the end. (I hope this last sentence makes it to publication.)

My primary hope for this book is that it makes me as much money as possible. My secondary hope, besides programming games in Java, is that the book indicates the difficulties that we came across when researching Java for games programming in a clear manner, especially those surrounding threads, input, and graphics that we put a lot of work into. I think to become a good programmer you have to enjoy it; otherwise it's little use. Most of the enjoyment I find is in showing off what I have done, which there is no harm in now and again (and again and again ☺). One thing I am aware of is that in actually challenging yourself to do something, and believing that you can do it, there seems to be a fear factor where you often do not even attempt to code something, because you have never done it before. In buying this book, you have made a solid move in conquering this fear.

My interests mostly revolve around playing pool, watching films, and occasionally programming the night away, and there is still no better feeling than "7-balling" someone in a crowded club. I also collect Star Wars costumes and wear them out clubbing regularly.

As a final word, I hope this book is as useful to you as it was for me in writing it, and wish you luck in your quest of knowledge.

Glenn Murphy
glenn@chopsewage.com

This for me is probably one of the hardest parts of the book to write. I really have a dislike for writing about myself as I always feel it will sound boastful or conceited. Nevertheless, here goes...

Well, I am currently 21 years old and halfway through my 4th (honours) year of university studying BSc (Hons) Computer Games Technology at the University of Abertay in Dundee, Scotland. I would say I have been coding for around six years now and have obtained quite a broad range of skills within this time.

My first real stab at game programming was about a year and a half before I left home to go to university when I downloaded the DJGPP DOS compiler (http://www.delorie.com/djgpp) and the Allegro game library (http://www.talula.demon.co.uk/allegro) originally started by Shawn Hargreaves. After starting and never finishing a few projects, the next logical step was to move onto looking at OpenGL and DirectX. As well as looking at the 3D side of games programming however, I also invested time in learning Perl and MySQL, although I have recently switched to using PHP4 as it is sooo much nicer than Perl. ;)

From there, I then progressed onto Java and to be honest it is probably the best thing I have ever done. Java really is such a great language. Don't get me wrong—it does have some issues, but the structure of the language and also the documentation is really excellent (ever tried using MSDN? Urgh.).

One thing that deceived me, however, when I started to use Java was the simplicity. When you start looking into Java properly, you think—ah great, all the libraries have been written for me. However, as you will see as you progress through the book, these libraries are excellent for business application development, but there are some pitfalls and serious issues to consider when looking at the language and libraries (packages) from a game development point of view.

Probably now is a good time for a plug. Previously to this book, I coauthored *Developer's Guide to Multiplayer Games*, which focuses in detail on using sockets in C/C++ to create client-server games. That book has a large tutorial section that takes you through the process of writing a reusable network library and a multiplayer game, which also includes a signup/login and lobby system. What the book does not cover, however, is DirectPlay as we remain platform independent throughout the book, so your game server will compile as easily on the Linux platform as it will on the Windows platform. If you are interested, you can find out more information (and buy it ☺) at the following Amazon.com link: http://www.amazon.com/exec/obidos/tg/detail/-/1556228686

On a final note, I hope you enjoy reading this book and find the information within it useful. If you have any questions or problems with anything in the book, do not hesitate to e-mail either myself or Glenn and we will try to help you as best we can!

Andrew Mulholland
andrew@hfplimited.com

Chapter 1

Introduction to Java 1.4

"Everywhere is walking distance if you have the time."

—Steven Wright

Introduction

In this chapter we will get started with Java 2 Standard Edition 1.4 by getting it set up and ready to enter the world of Java game programming. We will also look at what you can expect from this book and learn a little about Java as a whole.

Introduction to the Java Platform

The Java platform consists of the Java language, Java bytecodes, and the Java Virtual Machine (generally termed the JVM). The analogy behind the Java platform is that when you compile your Java code, it is translated into Java bytecodes, which can then be interpreted by the Java Virtual Machine. In practical terms you may enter your source code into a ".java" file (the Java language), which will then be compiled into a ".class" file (the Java bytecodes). The class file can then be run on the Java Virtual Machine, which runs on your computer. This means that your single compilation will run on many platforms, at least in theory, as each has its own version of the JVM interpreting the bytecodes on the particular platform. There are many implementations of the JVM on various operating systems, such as Windows, Mac OS, Solaris, Linux, etc.

In addition to having platform independence, Java can seriously reduce coding time because it is a very well-structured language. If you do not understand object-oriented programming, do not worry about this for now, as we will explain OOP in the following chapters.

 NOTE: All the individual parts of Java, such as the Java language, the Java Virtual Machine, and the Java bytecodes, are collectively known as the Java platform.

Another key element to Java is the ability to create small programs known as *applets* that run within a web browser, which run independently by means of the Java Virtual Machine (yes, web games that run inside a browser). What's more, it is easy to include an applet in a web page using the <APPLET> tag (we will learn about this in Chapter 8, "Applications and Applets"). There is also little difference between creating games as traditional stand-alone applications or as applets, as we will see later in the book.

Introduction to Java 2 Standard Edition 1.4

The Java 2 Standard Edition has seen many positive moves for creating professional games with the release of J2SE 1.4. The ability of full-screen exclusivity means that you can now make full-screen games, whereas in earlier editions programmers were forced to fake full-screen mode. This simply entailed removing a window's decorations and sizing it to the dimensions of the screen. This technique obviously has none of the real advantages of full-screen exclusivity. With the new full-screen mode, you can take advantage of such things as page flipping and switching display modes, just like DirectX can do. Another important new feature to J2SE 1.4 is hardware-accelerated graphics, making your graphics processing run at great speed. There has also been an improvement on the networking side of things with the introduction of NIO (New IO), as is discussed in Chapter 18 (in a galaxy far, far away).

It is important to note that throughout the lifetime of the Java Standard Edition, the aspect of backward compatibility is maintained to ensure that programs compiled using older versions of Java (e.g., 1.1, 1.2, 1.3) will still run on the latest JVM. However, the internal implementations can change, become defunct, and are said to be deprecated, which means that they are still in existence to support older code but should not be used for whatever reason; in general they have been found to be unsafe. Don't worry though; when compiling your code, you will be alerted if you are using something that is deprecated.

What the Future Holds

The future of the Java language for professional games programming has great potential with its platform independence and ease of use. In the best-case scenario, the future could see versions of the Java Virtual Machine running on the latest game consoles, with code being compiled to work on each of the machines with little or no major portability issues involved. This advantage could see developers switching to Java as their language of choice for game programming in the future.

What This Book Covers

The aim of this book is to first introduce you to the Java programming language and then build upon that knowledge by looking at the key elements required to make games, such as graphics, input, sound, and networking. This book discusses the following three topics:

- Introduction to the Java language—The book provides a complete guide to getting started using Java 2 Standard Edition 1.4 and looks at all of the major elements that make up the language. No previous knowledge of Java or programming in general is required, as we start from the very beginning. A simple text-based game of tic-tac-toe demonstrates these concepts.

- Game programming in Java—We look at the major areas associated with game programming in Java. In this tome you will find all of the important technical information for creating games in Java, including the newest features of Java 1.4, such as full-screen exclusive mode. The development of a game framework merges all your knowledge into a powerful, reusable base for making your own games in Java.

- Programming network games in Java—We discuss programming networked games in Java, covering topics such as client-server and database connectivity (for high-score lists and storing data on an online server) in Java. This book also covers the "new to J2SE 1.4" networking package NIO (New I/O). Key elements are building a solid network frame and a sample network game ("game" used loosely here :)).

Who Is This Book For?

This book is aimed at people who are new to programming and also programmers new to the Java language as a whole who want to learn how to make games using Java 1.4. The aim of this book is to teach you the technical aspects of programming games using Java 1.4. Although we cover the basics of game programming theory in this book, we do not delve into the theory at an advanced level, as this book is designed to teach games programming using Java 1.4 and not specifically general games programming theory. For example, we look at the basics of collision detection, such as sphere and bounding box collisions, but do not delve into advanced techniques such as pixel perfect collision testing. However, we do look into important technical features of Java for game programming, such as full-screen mode, thread synchronization issues, and using the JNI (Java Native Interface) to implement a high-resolution timer in Java, to name but a few. Don't worry, all this will be explained as you progress through the book…

```
if(purchasedBook == false)
    System.out.println("should you choose to purchase it,
        please and thank you.");
```

Installing the J2SE 1.4 SDK

In this section we will look at installing J2SE 1.4 for Microsoft Windows as an example; however, the installation process should be similar on other platforms, as the concepts remain the same.

To install the Java 2 Standard Edition, you can either use the companion CD-ROM that comes with this book or download it from the Sun Microsystems, Inc. web site. Here is the direct link to download the Java 1.4 SDK for all applicable platforms: http://java.sun.com/j2se/1.4.1/index.html.

For Microsoft Windows, once you have obtained the file (which will be called j2sdk-1_4_1_01-windows-i586.exe) you can then simply double-click it to begin the installation process.

Once you have accepted the Java software license agreement, you will be asked in which directory it should be installed. We will assume that you have installed to the default directory. After clicking Next, you will be presented with a list of options and, as with the directory, we recommend that you leave the options as they stand.

If you then continue by clicking Next, you will be asked on which browsers you wish to make the Java plug-in default. The most common browser for the plug-in is Microsoft Internet Explorer; however, if you also wish to use the plug-in with Netscape, check the Netscape 6 box also. Note that these options are only for using Java applets within a browser, not for Java applications (see Chapter 8, "Applications and Applets" for more details on the differences).

After clicking Next, the Java SDK will install, and you will be ready to begin making your first simple Java applications and applets.

 NOTE: Although as a developer you need the rather large Java SDK to create Java applications and applets, the end user only requires the JRE 1.4 (Java Runtime Environment). If this is required, perhaps for your mates to be able to play your latest applet games on the web, the Java 1.4 Runtime Environment is available on the companion CD and from the Sun Microsystems, Inc. web site (http://java.sun.com).

You should be aware that the tools, such as the Java compiler javac.exe and the interpreter java.exe, are contained within the bin/ directory of the installation directory of the SDK. We will look at using these features in the next chapter when we begin programming.

A Word on Integrated Development Environments (IDEs)

Although it is possible to compile Java applications and applets from the command line (which is the method we have chosen for this book), it is a good idea to use an integrated development environment (IDE). The main reason for this is that it gives you everything in one place (i.e., a text editor, compiler/interpreter linkage, help system, and sometimes even more useful features such as code auto-complete).

Our development tool of choice is JCreator, as it provides a reasonably simple IDE that maintains some great features. The freeware version is available on the companion CD; however, we highly recommend upgrading to the professional version. More information can be found on the web site http://www.jcreator.com.

 NOTE: The IDE that our technical editor Mika likes is IntelliJ IDE. It is quite easy to use and has many very powerful features in it: http://www.intellij.com/idea/.

 NOTE: (From technical editor Joel) If you have a few extra megabytes of RAM, definitely give Eclipse a try. This free open-source Java editor built by IBM is better than many professional level IDEs and is gaining a large contributing user community, as well as industry support (including Borland, Rational, Togethersoft, and Webgain). It allows for clean, straightforward navigation and advanced debugging of code, with tools and wizards to build and refactor your code. Incremental compiling allows you to modify your program while it is running. It is useful for writing game servers for a network: http://www.eclipse.org.

Useful Web Sites

- http://java.sun.com—This site is the home of the Java platform and provides all of the latest news and updates about Java. Among its vast amount of features, this site includes the latest releases of the J2SDK for downloading, a large developer's community (which you may sign up to), and many useful online tutorials.
- http://www.javagaming.org—This site is supported by Sun Microsystems and is designed to support the making of games using Java technology for any range of programmer. This site includes tutorials and maintains a large community of forums full of experienced Java programmers who will answer your questions in no time. In saying that, the current forums are so vast that they should cover a lot of your questions already. (We won't give you our usernames on this site to save us from embarrassment, in case you happen to notice some of the questions that we might have posted to the boards.)
- http://www.javaworld.com—This site includes many tutorials and columns covering a wide range of topics with contributions from programmers all around the world; it also contains many forums for you

to post questions. You could one day post a useful column on this site, if you become good enough.

■ http://www.mysql.com—This is the home site for the MySQL open source database. This site includes important downloads that we will discuss in Chapter 15 when we look at using databases for storing online information and connecting to it via JDBC (Java Database Connectivity).

Summary

In this chapter, we found out about Java and then followed that by setting up the Java SDK. In the next chapter we will take a look at the basics of Java programming. Now that Java has become more games oriented, we can only presume that it will get better and better. As more developers use it, there will be more demand for new features, which will strengthen this already great language even more in the future.

Chapter 2

Basics of Java Programming

"All the world will be your enemy, prince of a thousand enemies."

—Watership Down

Introduction

Hopefully you are all set up now and ready to execute some code of your own. In this chapter you will learn about the structure of the Java language with a variety of simple console programs. A *console program* is a program that is text based and looks similar to text entered in a command prompt window. The example programs in the early chapters of this book are console programs and are not visually attractive windowed applications or applets. We will keep it simple to start off with until you understand the nuts and bolts of the Java language.

Introduction to Object-Oriented Programming (OOP)

The transition from a procedural programming (non-OOP) language to an object-oriented programming language is a large step for many programmers. It is true that both methods of programming can ultimately achieve the same goals, but you will find OOP is a neater and faster way to program, it is more suitable for teamwork, and programs are usually easier to design using the object-oriented approach. With OOP in Java, you will find that programming is challenging to begin with, yet very easy and very rewarding once you master it.

What Is an Object?

Objects are the building blocks that make up a program. It is difficult to explain exactly what an object is because an object can be anything you want. For example, you can create an object that represents an alien that can hold all information related to the alien and also contain functionality associated with it. You can include data such as the number of lives the alien has and also the functionality to affect the data, such as code to kill the alien, which could remove one of the lives.

The essential elements that make up an object are variables and methods. *Variables* are data members, or attributes, that contain data relating to the object, such as a text string or numeric value. *Methods* provide the functionality of the object and can be used to interact with the attributes. Methods are also known as functions or procedures in various other programming languages.

Object-Oriented Programming in Java

The Java language is completely object oriented. This means that there are no global statements whatsoever (although static members can be conceived as being somewhat global—we will discuss static members later). Any attributes or methods must be defined as part of a class or interface. We will discuss interfaces in Chapter 4, "Multiple Classes," so do not worry about them for the time being.

A *class* in Java is used to define the structure of an object. A class can be broken down into three main parts: constructors, attributes (properties), and methods.

Let's now look at an example of a very simple class structure containing these three parts before we go any further. An example of a class could be a person, which could describe the attributes and methods that a person could have associated with them. An object can then be created from the person class, like you or me, or even your partner (if you do not have a partner, then well done; you are a true programmer).

In order to create an object, we must first create a class. Do not worry about compiling any of the code right now; just sit back, grab a coffee, and try to understand some basics.

Here is the beginning of our "Person" class:

```
class Person
{

}
```

Now, at the moment, we have the outline code for a Person class. First we should add some attributes. Let's add a numeric attribute to the class to store the age of a person.

```
class Person
{
    int age;
}
```

The keyword `int` stands for integer, representing a numeric data type, which is explained in more detail later on in the chapter. At this point, the `Person` class is all attributes and no functionality (clearly pointing to a career in politics). We can add a method to the class as follows, which can be used to change the value in `age`:

```
class Person
{
    public void setAge(int newAge)
    {
        // set the age to the value stored in newAge
        age = newAge;
    }

    int age;
}
```

Now we have a class called `Person`, containing one method called `setAge` and one attribute called `age`. The method `setAge` can be used to assign a new value to the age of the person. Again, do not worry too much about how methods work for the time being; your coffee should just be cool enough to drink about now.

In order to create an object (or an instance, as it is also known) from the `Person` class, a constructor must be invoked. All classes contain a default constructor, which does nothing and can be overloaded with many constructor types, as we shall see.

Constructors

The *constructor* is a method that is called when the object is created and used to initialize the state of the object. The constructor must be declared with the same name as the class in which it is contained and cannot have a return value (we will look at return values in the "Methods" section toward the end of this chapter). We will now add two constructors to the `Person` class:

```
class Person
{
    public Person()
    {
        // basic constructor age is set to 0 by default
    }

    public Person(int newAge)
    {
        // contructor that sets the age to a specified value
        setAge(newAge);
    }

    public void setAge(int newAge)
    {
        // set the age to the value stored in newAge
        age = newAge;
    }

    int age;
}
```

You can declare a reference to a `Person` object as follows:

```
Person billyGate;
```

At the moment, you have a reference to an object of type `Person`, which currently does not reference any object. The members of the object cannot be accessed, like the attribute `age`, because no object has been created. Note that the reference variable `billyGate` is actually equal to null at this point; the keyword `null` is discussed in the next chapter.

A call to a constructor must be made to create a new object of type `Person`, assigning the variable `billyGate` to reference the new object.

If no constructors are declared for a class, a default constructor is available that takes no parameters and simply creates a default object of the class when invoked. In our code snippet we have created our own default constructor `Person()`, which contains no code, and a second constructor also called `Person(int newAge)`, which contains code that sets the value `age` in the `Person` object to a new age specified by a parameter value. We will look at parameters in the "Methods" section near the end of this chapter, so do not worry if you do not fully understand them.

 NOTE: Had we only declared the second constructor and omitted the first constructor, there would no longer be a default constructor available that takes no parameters, as the default constructor only exists if the class doesn't contain any user-defined constructors.

To create an object from the `Person` class, we could use the following line of code:

```
// using second constructor, set age value to 21
Person billyGate = new Person(21);
```

This line of code declares an identifier called `billyGate` of type `Person` and creates a "new" `Person` object using the second constructor in the `Person` class to initialize the object, setting the `age` value in the new `Person` object to 21.

We could also use the following code instead, this time using the first (default) constructor to initialize the object and then set the value of `age` using the `setAge` method, which is a member of the newly created object.

```
// use first constructor
Person billyGate = new Person();

// use setAge member to set age to 21
billyGate.setAge(21);     // set the value of age to 21
```

We can also access the `age` variable and set its value directly, as follows:

```
billyGate.age = 21;
```

 NOTE: You cannot have two constructors with the same signature. We will see about method signatures in the "Methods" section toward the end of this chapter.

So far we have seen *instantiation*, which is the term used to describe the creation of an object or instance of a class. The following diagram will hopefully help you understand this a little better, as it shows the relationship between the `Person` class and objects created from it.

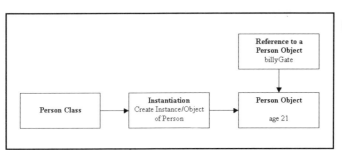

Figure 2-1

Class Members and Object Members—The static Keyword

I promise that this is the last bit before we start making some code that we can actually run, but it does need explaining. An *object member* is a member that is created when the object is created. This means it can only be accessed once the object has been created because otherwise it does not exist. The example we have just seen creates an instance of the class Person referenced by billyGate. We could have also created many more instances of the Person class. Suppose we said that the billyGate object was the only person that we would ever need or want to create; then we could scrap the Person class altogether and simply create a new class called BillyGate instead.

```java
class BillyGate
{
    public static void setAge(int newAge)
    {
        // set the age to the value stored in newAge
        age = newAge;
    }

    int static age;
}
```

Notice that we have removed the constructors and added the static keyword to the two defined members. This is because we no longer need to create an instance of this class. We can just access the static members using the class name. For example:

```java
BillyGate.setAge(21);
```

These static members are known as class members, whereas before we had object members.

The examples that we have used so far only contain either object members or class members; you can of course use both. Let's return to our Person class now and add a static attribute. The static attribute must be something that is going to be the same for all Person objects that we create. So we could add an integer variable called daysInAYear.

```java
class Person
{
    // code as before
```

```
    static int daysInAYear;
}
```

We can access the attribute `daysInAYear` before we create any objects from the `Person` class. For example:

```
Person.daysInAYear = 365;
```

If we create new instances of `Person`, then they too can access the static variable `daysInAYear`.

```
Person glennMurphy = new Person(21);
Person andrewMulholland = new Person(20);
glennMurphy.daysInAYear = 366;      // it is a leap year
System.out.println(andrewMullholland.daysInAYear);
```

This code will create two new instances of `Person`, referenced by `glennMurphy` and `andrewMulholland`. The `glennMurphy` object then sets the static variable `daysInAYear` to `366`, and the `andrew-Mulholland` object will access `daysInAYear`, printing its value to the console window (this printing code will be explained later in the chapter). The number that will be printed to the console window is `366`, which means that `daysInAYear` does not belong to any of the objects alone; it belongs to all of them, and changes made from one affect the other. There is only one part of memory containing the value `366` to which they all refer. In short, it is the same attribute however it is accessed. Figure 2-2 illustrates the relationship between the `Person` class containing class members and object members and the objects created from it.

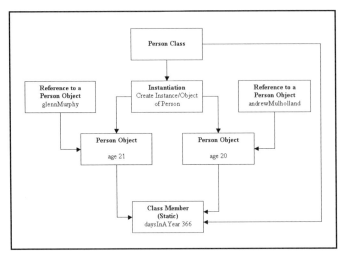

Figure 2-2

References

To access objects (remember they are instances of classes) in Java, we use what are known as *references*. We have used three references so far in our code examples: `billyGate`, `glennMurphy`, and `andrew-Mulholland`. These were not the actual objects that we created but merely references (also known as *handles*) to the objects created. Take the following code for example:

```
andrewMulholland = glennMurphy; // he'll never be my equal
```

This code simply makes `andrewMulholland` reference the same object that `glennMurphy` references; hence you could then access the same object using either of the two references. This is best illustrated in Figure 2-3 by seeing what Figure 2-2 would look like after the above code is implemented.

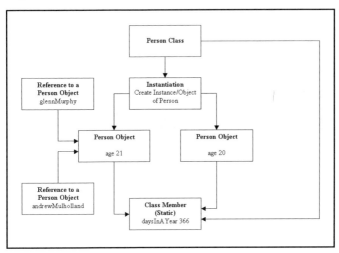

Figure 2-3

The object with the age equal to `20` that `andrewMulholland` once referenced is now lost, but do not worry about freeing the memory; this is taken care of by Java's garbage collector (see the "Garbage Collection and Creating Objects" section in Chapter 12 for more detail).

Now let's get something compiling, finally!

HelloJavaWorld—A Simple Console Program

Well, you should have finished that cup of coffee by now, so let's get cracking with our first example program, `HelloJavaWorld.java`. You must first create a source file called `HelloJavaWorld.java` and then enter the following source code into it:

```
public class HelloJavaWorld
{
    public static void main(String args[])
    {
        System.out.println("Hello Java World");
    }
}
```

Now compile your source code by going to the command prompt and entering the following command (ensuring that you are in the same directory as your code):

```
C:\j2sdk1.4.0\bin\javac HelloJavaWorld.java
```

Note that you may need to change the C:\j2sdk1.4.0\bin part if you have installed Java to a directory other than the default suggested.

Once you have compiled the source code without any errors, you will notice that a new file called `HelloJavaWorld.class` has been created in the source directory. This file is the program file that is used with the `Java.exe` interpreter to run your program. Here is the command that you need to execute the .class file that was created:

```
C:\j2sdk1.4.0\bin\java HelloJavaWorld
```

When you run this program, the words "Hello Java World" should be displayed in a console window. This can be seen in the following screen shot:

Figure 2-4

All Java application programs begin executing code in the method called `main`, as shown in the HelloJavaWorld example. Inside the `main` method is a line of code that prints our chosen text to the screen. The program is basically a class containing one method, `main`, which is static and contains one line of code to print some text to the console window. To contain a block of code, you simply use curly brackets to begin and end the block. In this example, the first opened curly bracket and the last closed curly bracket specify the code segment for the class `HelloJavaWorld`, whereas the middle two curly brackets specify the code segment for the method `main`. Most of you know the phrase "what goes up must come down"; well there is another phrase, which is not so popular, that goes "for every opened curly bracket, there must be a closed curly bracket."

Do not worry about the keyword `public` for the time being; this keyword concerns the control of attribute and method access, which is explained in more detail in Chapter 4, "Multiple Classes," where its usage becomes more topical along with the `private` and `protected` keywords and package level access.

We will gradually learn about all of the bits of code that go into making this simple example as the book progresses. It is important to realize that all aspects of the code are there for a reason, and all of these reasons will be explained one step at a time.

Printing Text to the Console Screen

In our first example, `HelloJavaWorld.java`, we used one line of code to print a text string to the console window.

```
System.out.println("Some text here");
```

The text string is entered between double quotation characters. The actual method that is invoked is `println`, which is a member of a static object called `out`, which in turn is a member of the class `System`. The `System` class provides facilities for standard input and output, among other things, and is included by default in all of your programs as part of the `java.lang` package. We will look in detail at packages in Chapter 5.

Whenever we require output to the console window, we will use this command with which we can also print the value of variables. In this chapter, you will occasionally see variable values specified with a text string separated by the "+" operator as follows:

```
System.out.println("The value = " + value);
```

As well as being an arithmetic operator, which we will look at very soon, the + operator is also used in Java for string concatenation (joining a string onto the end of another one). The value of the variable `value`, in the case of the previous line of code, is converted by Java into a string value and appended to the end of the specified string. Do not concern yourself with this too much for the time being; we will discuss this in more detail in the next chapter when we start using strings.

Comments

Adding comments to your code is very important. Comments allow you to add sentences among your code that will be ignored by the compiler. This is important in many ways, like for setting reminders, reporting bug errors, and describing what the code actually does. You can add comments to your code using two basic methods: by line or by block. The following is an example of a comment in a line of code:

```
// none of my code is working, ARRRGGHH!!!
```

Any text entered on a line of code after the two forward slashes (//) is a comment and will not interfere with the functionality of your program. You can also use this method on the same line that you have code, but this type of comment must be entered to the right-hand side of any code.

```
Do some code;     // this is on the right-hand side
```

The other method for adding comments to your code is to specify a block area. This is implemented by specifying the beginning and end of the comment, using /* to begin the block and */ to end it. The following are examples of using the comment blocks:

```
/* You can enter text information here */

/*
    This is some text to describe what my program does.
    You can use as many lines as the statements enclose.
*/

Some code /* they can be added between code */ More Code;
// Although this makes your code messy/less readable
```

Primitive Data Types

Java supports a variety of primitive data types, from numeric to character based. These data types allow the storage of data in many different forms that use different amounts of memory. You will use these different data types to store many different values (such as someone's age, as we have already seen).

Numeric Data Types

The numeric data types can be split up into two areas: integers and floating-point.

Integers

Integers are data values used for explicitly storing whole numbers, such as 3, 7022, or –99. The value 3.14, for example, is not an integer value but is known as a floating-point value, as we shall see a little later in this chapter. The following table shows the four integer type variables available in Java, their range, and the amount of memory they use.

Integer Type	Range	Memory (bytes)
byte	–128 to 127	1
short	–32768 to 32767	2
int	–2147483648 to 2147483647	4
long	–9223372036854775808 to 9223372036854775807	8

NOTE: There are no unsigned types available explicitly in Java. In many other programming languages, the use of unsigned numeric data types indicates that the value stored will only be positive, meaning the positive value range is doubled. For instance, an unsigned `byte` would have the range 0 to 255 instead of –128 to 127.

In order to use a variable, it must be declared, which simply states that you are creating the variable of a specified data type. There are a number of ways in which you can declare a variable. The simplest way is as follows:

```
int numberA;
```

This is the standard way in which all variables are declared—by entering the type of data followed by a name that you must specify. Java is a case-sensitive language. This means that if we have just declared the variable numberA, trying to access this variable by typing NUMBERA will not work. In other languages, such as Pascal, this would be okay.

 NOTE: Variable names must begin with a letter or an underscore (_) character (not a number). Also, you cannot use any of the reserved keywords as variable names.

The previous code creates a variable of type `int` called `numberA`. If you want to declare another variable, you can repeat this code, specifying a different name instead of `numberA`, as follows:

```
int numberA;
int numberB;
```

Conveniently, you can also do this in one line using a comma (,) to separate the variables.

```
int numberA, numberB;
```

The value of a variable can also be assigned when the variable is declared.

```
int numberA = 128, numberB = -64;
```

You do not have to set values for both if you do not want to.

```
// set numberA's value only
int numberA = 128, numberB;

// or set numberB's value only
int numberA, numberB = -64;
```

Then you can assign values later on in the code now that the variables have been declared.

```
// set numberA to 77
numberA = 77;

// set the value of numberB to the value of numberA.
numberB = numberA;
```

We talked before about objects and references to objects, and that the primitive data types are not references; if you set `numberB` equal to `numberA`, the value of `numberB` will be set equal to that of the value of `numberA`. They will not reference the same memory, so changes made to one will not affect the other later on in the code.

```
numberA = 77;
numberB = numberA;
numberA = 101;
// numberB remains equal to 77
```

Converting between Integer Data Types

Integer values are of type `int` by default. That is, any number that you hard-code, like the value `77` that we just assigned to the variable `numberA`, will have the range of the data type `int`, as shown in the integer range table on the previous page. This means that when declaring values to variables of type `long`, you must specify in the code that the number entered is also of type `long` and not of type `int`. For example, an attempt to set a variable of type `long` to a value exceeding the limit of an `int` (either less than –2147483648 or greater than 2147483647) will cause a compiler error.

```
long myNumber = 3000000000;      // this will not compile
```

In order to tell the compiler that you want the value 3000000000 (that is, 3 with nine zeros) to be of type `long`, you must add the letter L (or the unadvisable lowercase l, as this looks like the number 1) onto the end of the number.

```
long myNumber = 3000000000L;    // this will compile
```

Another problem is setting the value of one integer data type from the value of another integer data type that is larger in range. Let's say we have the following four variables:

```
byte numberByte = 27;
short numberShort = 2001;
int numberInt = 55000;
long numberLong = 30000000000L;
```

The following statements will be fine:

```
numberShort = numberByte;    // short has greater range than byte
numberLong = numberShort;    // long has greater range than short
```

The variable being assigned a value must be of a data type smaller than or equal to the data type of the variable from which it is being assigned; otherwise, a method called *typecasting* must be used to tell the compiler to convert the assigned value to that of an acceptable data type. In actual fact, when we converted the previous valid data type values, this was known as *implicit casting*, where we know that the data can be validly assigned. The real typecasting that we refer to is known as *explicit casting*. This is where the cast must be defined in the code itself to alert you of the dangers involved in the cast (e.g., possible loss of data), allowing you to make sure you are prepared to lose data if that is the case.

```
numberShort = numberLong;              // this will not compile

// using typecasting
numberShort = (short)numberLong;       // this will compile

// byte is acceptable for a short value too
numberShort = (byte)numberLong;        // this will compile also
```

To typecast a value, simply specify the type enclosed in parentheses, writing it to the left of the value in question.

It is important that you choose the correct data types when programming; otherwise you could lose values because the size of the value may be too large to be stored in the specified data type.

```
short numberShort = 2001;
byte numberByte = (byte)numberShort;
// byte cannot store a positive integer value larger than 127
```

This code typecasts the value of `numberShort` to type `byte`, which will set the value of `numberByte` to a seemingly random number because `2001` is out of its storage range. The value of `numberByte` will actually set the value of the lowest 8 bits of `numberShort`. The value of `numberShort` is unaffected by the typecasting code; it remains equal to `2001`.

So when assigning a variable from a variable with a larger data type, be sure that the value is within the assigned variable's storage range; otherwise, use a larger data type in the first place. Sometimes it is simply more convenient to always use the `int` data type and not have to worry about typecasting and possible data loss.

Let's look at an example for you to play around with: `Using-Integers.java`.

```java
public class UsingIntegers
{
    public static void main(String args[])
    {
        byte numberByte = 27;
        short numberShort = 2001;
        int numberInt = 50000;
        long numberLong = 3000000000L;

        // typecasting not needed as a long is larger than an int
        numberLong = numberInt;
        System.out.println("numberLong should equal " + numberLong);
        System.out.println("numberLong actually equals "+numberLong);

        // typecast numberShort's short value to a byte value
        numberByte = (byte)numberShort;
        System.out.println("numberByte should equal "+numberShort);
        System.out.println("numberByte actually equals "+numberByte);
    }
}
```

This basic example makes two assignments as examples of converting values between integer data types. The first assignment works fine, but the second requires typecasting. Run the code and see what values are actually assigned from the conversions. The output from the program should look similar to this screen shot.

Figure 2-5

As you can see, the value of `50000` was assigned successfully from an `int` data type to a `long` data type, but the value of `2001` was not assigned successfully from a `short` data type to a `byte` data type. The actual answer of `-47` was assigned because of the methods used to convert between the data types, which in this case involved ignoring relative information on storage bits that a `byte` value cannot contain. If the value was not `2001` but a value within the range that a `byte` could store, the assignment would have been successful.

Floating-Point Data Types

You should now understand how to declare and assign variables with specified data types. We can now look at two new data types, `float` and `double`, which are known as floating-point data types. Floating-point data types allow for more accurate storage than integers and store values with decimal places (for example, 0.25, 3.99, or –12.55555).

F-Point Type	Range	Memory (bytes)
float	±3.4E+38 (Approx 7 significant figures)	4
double	±1.7E+308 (15 significant figures)	8

Declaring floating-point type variables is the same as declaring integer type variables.

```
float floatNumber;
double doubleNumber;
```

Assigning values for floating-point variables is the same also, but the value you assign can contain a decimal point.

```
double Pi = 3.141592653589793;
```

The assigned values do not require a decimal place, but if they are whole numbers, it sometimes makes your code clearer.

```
double flatPi = 3;        // this will work
double flatPi = 3.0;      // or this will work too
```

As we already know, the default value for a whole number is of type `int`. The default value for a floating-point value is of type `double`, which means that numeric values assigned to variables of type `float` must be cast to a `float` value. This can be done either by adding the letter F (or preferred lowercase f) to the end of the value or by using the typecasting method that we saw earlier.

```
float floatNumber = 3.1415;          // this will not compile

// add the 'f' letter to the end of the number
float floatNumber = 3.1415f;         // this will compile

// using typecasting
float floatNumber = (float)3.1414;   // this will compile also
```

Converting between Floating-Point Data Types

You can also use the typecasting method to convert from a `double` to a `float` variable, and there is no danger of getting drastically wrong conversions like with integers when converting from a `double` to a `float` data type, though some of the accuracy of the original `double` number could be lost when it is converted into a less accurate `float` value. There is no point typecasting a `float` value to a `double` because a `double` can store any value that a `float` can anyway. The following example, `SliceOfPi.java`, illustrates this perfectly, declaring and setting the value of `bigPi`, a variable of type `double`, and then declaring a `float` variable, `smallPi`, and assigning its value to the value of `Pi`, typecasting the value to a `float`.

```
public class SliceOfPi
{
    public static void main(String args[])
    {
```

```
        double bigPi = 3.141592653589793;
        float smallPi = (float)bigPi; // using typecasting

        System.out.println("bigPi = " + bigPi);
        System.out.println("smallPi = " + smallPi);
    }
}
```

When you compile this code, you should get output similar to this screen shot.

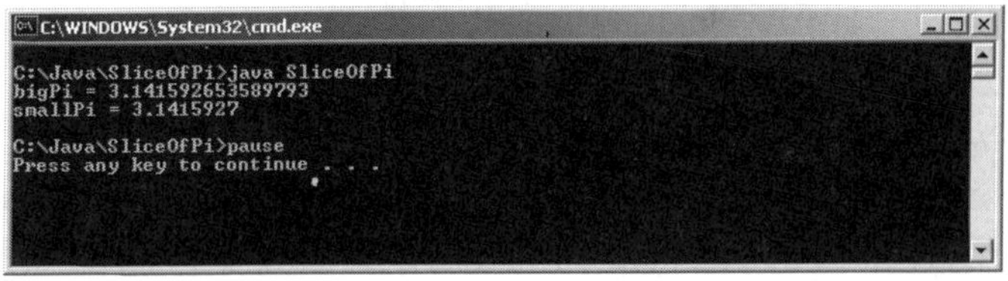

Figure 2-6

As you can see from Figure 2-6, the accuracy of `bigPi`'s value when converted to a `float` value and assigned to the `float` variable `smallPi` is considerably less than its original `double` value. You may find it better to just use the `double` data type if you require very accurate floating-point data storage and are not overly concerned with memory usage.

Converting between Integers and Floating-Point Data Types

This is not as bad as it might sound; you just have to look at it logically. An integer cannot contain any values after a decimal place, so it will represent the value 3.14 as 3 and it will also represent the value 3.9 as 3, rounding the value down to the highest integer that is less than or equal to its `float` value by standard conversions. A floating-point variable can be assigned the value of an integer without any typecasting required.

```
int intNumber = 50000;
float floatNumber = intNumber;
```

Remember that you need to add the letter "f" to floating-point values in order to assign them to a `float` variable. However, this is not required if the value you specify is an integer value.

```
// no 'f' is required as integers convert straight to floating-point
float floatNumber = 50000;
```

To convert from floating-point values to integer values, simply use typecasting.

```
float floatNumber = 50000.6f;

// using typecasting
int intNumber = (int)floatNumber;
```

The value of the variable `intNumber` will be set to `50000`, and the 0.6 will be chopped off; the original value is still stored in the floating-point variable `floatNumber` of course.

Simple Arithmetic Operators

Now that we know how to declare and assign values to integer and floating-point data types, we can now take a look at manipulating these values using numeric operators. The standard numeric operators are shown in the table below, along with a description.

Operator	Description
*	Multiplication
/	Division
+	Addition
−	Subtraction

A simple example of a numeric expression is an operator, like the ones in the operator table above, with an operand on either side of the operator (for example, 5 + 2).

The value of a variable can be assigned a numeric expression using the same assignment methods that we have already seen simply using the "=" assignment operator.

```
int singleNumber = 4;
int doubleNumber = 4 + 4;
int trebleNumber = 4 + 4 + 4;
```

The variables `doubleNumber` and `trebleNumber` could also have been assigned using the already declared variable `singleNumber` with the multiplication operator.

```
int singleNumber = 4;
int doubleNumber = singleNumber * 2;     // 4 * 2 = 8
int trebleNumber = singleNumber * 3;     // 4 * 3 = 12
```

You could even define the value of `trebleNumber` using the variables `singleNumber` and `doubleNumber` with the addition operator.

```
int trebleNumber = singleNumber + doubleNumber;     // 4 + 8 = 12
```

Subtraction is the same as addition.

```
int positiveNumber = 7;
int negativeNumber = 0 - 7;     // or just use = -7
```

Or, you could make `negativeNumber` the negative value of the value stored in the variable `positiveNumber`.

```
int negative = -positive;     // equals -7 also
```

Dividing two integer values will give the answer as an integer value (that is, the actual value rounded down to the highest integer that is less than or equal to the actual value—basically cutting off anything after the decimal place).

```
int number = 9 / 2;               // equals 4, it does not equal 4.5
```

Floating-point variables use these operators in exactly the same way as integers.

```
double doubleNumber = 9.0 / 2.0;     // equals 4.5
float floatNumber = 9.0f / 2.0f;     // equals 4.5
```

If you are assigning the value from an integer calculation to a floating-point variable, you must typecast the integer calculation to a floating-point calculation. For example, the following line of code will set the variable `doubleNumber` to 4 when the actual answer should be 4.5, but the calculation is an integer calculation.

```
double doubleNumber = 9 / 2; integer calculation equals 4
```

The following three lines of code all assign a value of 4.5 to the variable `doubleNumber`.

```
/* divide two double values */
double doubleNumber = 9.0 / 2.0;

/* divide two integer values casting the integer value 9 to a
double, then dividing a double by the integer value 2 giving an
answer of type double */
double doubleNumber = (double)9 / 2;

/* divide two integer values casting the integer value 2 to a double,
then dividing the integer 9 by this double value giving the answer
of type double */
double doubleNumber = 9 / (double)2;
```

Parentheses can be used to specify the order in which the values of an expression are to be calculated; this is mostly useful when you have a numeric expression that contains more than one operator (for example, 3 + 4 * 6) allowing you to choose the order in which the calculations occur. Let's now take a quick look at operator precedence.

Operator Precedence

Operator precedence deciphers the order in which calculations in an expression occur. Looking at the calculation example 3 + 4 * 6, the answer could be calculated by adding 3 and 4, which gives 7, and then multiplying 7 by 6, giving the answer of 42. However, we could also multiply 4 and 6 first, which gives 24, and then add on the 3, giving an answer of 27. The multiplication operator (*) actually has a higher precedence than the addition operator (+). This means that the numeric expression 3 + 4 * 6 would actually give the answer 27 and not 42, executing the multiplication first and then the addition. In order to specify the order in which calculations occur you can simply use parentheses. If we want the addition calculation to be executed before the multiplication, we can enclose the addition calculation in parentheses (e.g., (3 + 4) * 6, which will give us the answer 42). When in doubt, it is recommended that you use parentheses to specify the order of operations. It is often best to use parentheses anyway to make your code more understandable.

The following table shows an operator list containing operators with a higher precedence at the top and thoses with a lower precedence at the bottom. The table also shows the *associativity* of grouped operators that are of equal precedence. The associativity deciphers the order of operators of equal precedence. For example, division has a "left" associativity,

Chapter 2

which you may look upon as being left to right. This means that the expression 24 / 4 / 2 would be the same as (24 / 4) / 2, equaling 3, and would not be the same as the expression 24 / (4 /2), which gives a result of 12. Here is the operator precedence table and the associativity of operators of equal precedence.

Operator Group	Associativity
(), [], ., postfix++, postfix--	Left
+ unary, − unary, ++prefix, −−prefix, ~, !	Right
new, (cast)	Left
*, /, %	Left
+, −	Left
<<, >>, >>>	Left
<, <=, >, >=, instanceof	Left
==, !=	Left
&	Left
^	Left
|	Left
&&	Left
||	Left
?:	Left
=, *=, /=, %=, +=, -=, <<=, >>=, >>>=, &=, |=, ^=	Right

Thinking back to the two examples that we have looked at so far, we can first see that the multiplication operator is higher up the table than the addition operator, meaning it has a higher precedence. We can also see that the division operator has a left (left to right) associativity, as we previously discussed.

Don't worry about this amass of operators; we will cover them all throughout the book.

Unary, Binary, and Ternary Operators

Quite simply, a unary operator is one that is used with one operand. For example, in the operator precedence table we see the second row contains the + and − unary operators, which may, for the unary minus operator, be used as follows:

```
int a = 10;
int b = -a;
```

Hence, the minus sign preceding the variable a in the second line is a unary operator, used with one operator—the variable a.

Binary operators are used to perform an operation on two operands, such as the * operator for multiplying two numbers together.

There is only one ternary operator, which is the ?: conditional operator that uses three operands and is discussed a little later in this chapter.

Oh No, More Operators!

Yes there are many more operators, but they are all very useful. Here is a table of three more operators.

Operator	Description
++	Increment operator
--	Decrement operator
%	Modulus — This is the remainder from a division calculation

The increment and decrement operators will add or subtract a value of one from a variable of a numeric data type. They can be used with both integers and floating-point variables.

The increment and decrement operators are simply neater implementations of the following code:

```
int counter = 0;
counter = counter + 1;
int countdown = 10.0;
countdown = countdown - 1;
```

Instead, we can use this code:

```
int counter = 0;
counter++;
double countdown = 10.0;
countdown--;
```

This method of using these operators is the postfix method, which means they are entered on the right-hand side of their associated operand. You can use the increment and decrement operators in a postfix or prefix form, giving different results each time.

Take the following segments of code as an example:

```
int numberA = 10;
int numberB = numberA++;
```

This code assigns the current value in numberA to numberB and then increments the value of numberA after that. So the result of this code leaves numberA equal to 11 and numberB equal to 10.

If we wanted the increment code to execute first and then the assignment of numberB afterwards, we would use the prefix increment operator instead. The code would now be as follows:

```
int numberA = 10;
int numberB = ++numberA;
```

As you can see, the increment (++) operator is now entered on the left-hand side of its associated operand. This code first increments the value of numberA by 1 and then assigns the new value of numberA to numberB. The result is that both variables are equal to 11.

The modulus operator % is used to calculate the remainder value of a division calculation. We can see the use of the modulus operator in the following example: Eggsample.java.

Chapter 2

```java
public class Eggsample
{
    public static void main(String args[])
    {
        int totalEggs = 15;
        int eggsPerBox = 6;
        int filledBoxes = totalEggs / eggsPerBox;
        int remainingEggs = totalEggs % eggsPerBox;

        System.out.println("Number Of Eggs = " + totalEggs);
        System.out.println("Eggs Per Box = " + eggsPerBox);
        System.out.println("Filled Boxes = " + filledBoxes);
        System.out.println("Remaining Eggs = " + remainingEggs);
    }
}
```

When you compile and run `Eggsample.java`, you should get output similar to the following screen shot.

Figure 2-7

As you can see from the console output, there are two filled boxes of eggs, calculated using integer division, which will ignore any remainder values. The amount of remaining eggs is given using the modulus operator.

Arithmetic Assignment Operators

The following assignment operators are similar to the increment and decrement operators that we have just seen. They are used so that you do not need to enter the source variable twice when assigning a value to a variable based on its current value. The following table shows a list of arithmetic assignment operators for the arithmetic operators that we have used so far in this chapter.

Operator	Description
*=	Multiplication assignment
/=	Division assignment
+=	Addition assignment
-=	Subtraction assignment
%=	Remainder assignment

So we can set a value to a variable and then double its current value as follows:

```
int number = 22;
number *= 2;          // all the fours, 44
```

In fact, it is possible to assign values to variables using the assignment operators wherever the value type is valid, even in mid-code, so to speak.

```
int numberA = 30;
int numberB = 7;
numberA /= numberB -= 4;
```

The last line of code first subtracts 4 from `numberB`, setting it to the value of 3. Then `numberA`, which equals 30, is divided by the new value of `numberB`, which now equals 3, giving `numberA` the value of 10, which is the result of 30 divided by 3. This conforms to the operator precedence table shown earlier.

The boolean Data Type

A variable of type `boolean` can contain one of only two values, true or false. These values are also generally known as 1 and 0, with 1 representing true and 0 representing false. However, in Java the value of a `boolean` type variable is either true or false only; they are not numeric and therefore cannot be assigned from numeric values. The default value for a `boolean` type variable is false. The keywords `true` and `false` can be used to assign values to `boolean` type variables. For example:

```
boolean bookIsOnFire = false;      // hopefully
boolean thisBookIsGreat = true;    // hopefully you agree
```

Bitwise Operators

The following table shows the standard bitwise operators in Java and a description of them.

Operator	Description
&	Bitwise AND
|	Bitwise inclusive-OR (generally known as OR)
^	Bitwise exclusive-OR (generally known as XOR)
~	Bitwise NOT

To illustrate the function of these bitwise operators, we can use two byte values, A and B, which in java could be represented by a variable of type `byte`. The following table shows the binary notation of A and B (as there are 8 bits in a byte).

Byte	Binary Value
A	01101010
B	11110000

Chapter 2

The AND (&) operator tests two bits and returns the resulting bit true if both test bits are true; otherwise, the return bit is false. The following table shows the result of A AND B.

Byte	Bits							
A	0	1	1	0	1	0	1	0
B	1	1	1	1	0	0	0	0
A AND B	0	1	1	0	0	0	0	0

The OR (|) operator tests two bits and returns the resulting bit true if any or both of the test bits are true; if they are both false, the return bit is also false. The following table shows the result of A OR B.

Byte	Bits							
A	0	1	1	0	1	0	1	0
B	1	1	1	1	0	0	0	0
A OR B	1	1	1	1	1	0	1	0

The XOR (^) operator tests two bits and returns the resulting bit true if one, and only one, of the bits is true; otherwise, if the two values are equal, the return bit is false. The following table shows the result of A XOR B.

Byte	Bits							
A	0	1	1	0	1	0	1	0
B	1	1	1	1	0	0	0	0
A XOR B	1	0	0	1	1	0	1	0

The NOT (~) operator will invert all of the bits, where ones becomes zeros and zeros become ones, and is therefore a unary operator used with only one operand, whereas the other bitwise operators we have just seen were tested against two operands (binary operators), A and B. The following table shows the result of a NOT operation on byte A.

Byte	Bits							
A	0	1	1	0	1	0	1	0
NOT A	1	0	0	1	0	1	0	0

The bitwise AND, OR, and XOR operators can also be used with `boolean` expressions, as Boolean values effectively only contain one bit that is either true or false. This can be implemented in Java as follows:

```
boolean musicOn = true;
boolean televisionOn = true;
boolean areBothOn = musicOn & televisionOn;      // true
boolean areAnyOn = musicOn | televisionOn;       // true
boolean isOnlyOneOn = musicOn ^ televisionOn;    // false
```

There are also assignment operators for these three bitwise operators, as shown in the following table.

Operator	Description
&=	Bitwise AND assignment
|=	Bitwise inclusive-OR assignment
^=	Bitwise exclusive-XOR assignment

These assignment operators can be used in the same way that we used the previous set of assignment operators.

Bit Manipulation

In order to understand how to manipulate bits, you must first understand how numbers of the decimal notation, those numbers that we are used to using, are stored in the binary notation. The following table shows a list of decimal numbers and their binary representations.

Decimal	Binary
0	0
1	1
2	10
3	11
4	100
5	101
11	1011
15	1111
212	11010100

Decimal numbers are base 10 numbers, whereas binary numbers are base 2. If we look at how we perceive the value of a decimal number, we can then understand how to convert these numbers to their binary notation. So imagine the following number: 574. We know what this number is because it is familiar to us, but we can also look upon its value in the following way.

Base 10^n	10^2	10^1	10^0
Value	100	10	1

Note that just in case you don't understand the term 10^2, it translates as 10 * 10, equaling 100. So, for example, 10^5 would be 10 * 10 * 10 * 10 * 10, equaling 100000, and 4^3 would be 4 * 4 * 4, equaling 64.

We can then look at the value of 574 in the following way as a decimal notation:

$(10^2 * 5) + (10^1 * 7) + (10^0 * 4) = 500 + 70 + 4 = 574$

This is a bit pointless but only because our perception of the value in the decimal notation is immediately understandable. Now take the following table:

Base 2^n	2^2	2^1	2^0
Value	4	2	1

Now the binary base is 2 and the decimal base is 10. This means that decimal values range from 0 to 9 and binary values range from 0 to 1. So the binary value 101 can be worked out in the following way, similar to the way we looked at the decimal notation:

$(2^2 * 1) + (2^1 * 0) + (2^0 * 1) = 4 + 0 + 1 = 5$

If we look back to the decimal/binary table on the previous page, we can now work out the larger bit value of 11010100 as follows:

$(2^7 * 1) + (2^6 * 1) + (2^5 * 0) + (2^4 * 1) + (2^3 * 0) + (2^2 * 1) +$
$(2^1 * 0) + (2^0 * 0) =$
$128 + 64 + 0 + 16 + 0 + 4 + 0 + 0 =$
212

Bit Shifting

Bit shifting allows you to shift the bits of an integer value to the left or right. The following is a table of bit shifting operators and a description of what they do.

Operator	Description
<<	Shifts bits to the left, adding zeros from the right
>>	Shifts bits to the right, copying the sign bit (leftmost bit) from the left
>>>	Shifts bits to the right, adding zeros from the left

These operators are binary and take two operands. The left operand is the integer value on which to perform the shift, and the right operand is the number of bits to shift. Left-shifting by powers of two will perform an integer division, and right-shifting by powers of two will multiply the value. For example, let's say we had the decimal value 2, which would be represented in binary by the value 00000010 in a byte. An alternative to directly multiplying this value by 8 would be to bit shift the value three places to the left.

```
byte number = 2; // binary 00000010
```

We could then left-shift the bits three places, as follows:

```
number = number << 3;
```

When shifting the bits three places to the left and filling in zeros from the right, our binary notation would be 00010000, which is the decimal value of 2^4, equaling 16. This is the same as multiplying 2 by 2^3.

 NOTE: The previous code of bit shifting the value of the variable `number` could have also been performed using the assignment left-shift operator, as follows:

```
number <<= 3;
```

Bit Flags

It is possible to store many `boolean` states in a single integer value and test the values quickly using bit testing. For example, we could have a variable of type `byte`, which can then be used to represent eight states for the eight bits it contains. First of all, we can declare our eight mask values. We would first need to specify the values for the masks to represent the position of the bits that we want to test.

```
byte ROCKETS = 1;
byte LASERS = 2;
byte SHIELDS = 4;
byte INVINCIBLE = 8;
byte AUTO_PILOT = 16;
byte AIR_CONDITIONING = 32;
byte TRACTOR_BEAM = 64;
byte WINDOW_WIPERS_ON = 128;
```

The values are all powers of two to represent each bit in the 8-bit value. For example, the `AUTO_PILOT` mask has a value of 16, which in binary form is the value 10000, to which we can then test the fifth bit in our state variable to see whether it is true or false and also set this value. So for example, let's say we have a variable, `state`, and we want to initialize this value to represent data indicating that the ship's rockets are on, the shields are active, and the air conditioning is on too, as it can get awfully hot in there. We can set these flags as follows:

```
byte state = ROCKETS | SHIELDS | AIR_CONDITIONING;
```

As you can see it is a neat and easy-to-read system, saves memory, and is fast too. Here we have effectively set the variable `state` to the binary value `00100101`. You can see that these bits correspond to the masks that we have used. We may then want to turn off the air conditioning, which we would perform as follows:

```
state &= ~AIR_CONDITIONING;
```

You can set the state, say, of invincibility of the ship to true/on, as follows:

```
state |= INVINCIBLE;
```

You can test the individual states as follows:

```
if((state & ROCKETS) > 0)
    System.out.println("Fire when ready");
```

You can also combine the masks and create new masks for given scenarios. For instance, we could say that if we have rockets and window wipers on at the same time, we are unbeatable. We would then create a new mask for the unbeatable scenario.

```
byte UNBEATABLE = ROCKETS | WINDOW_WIPERS_ON;

if((state & UNBEATABLE) > 0)
    System.out.println("We can see the danger, lemony fresh");
```

Well, that's enough playing with my bits, as my mother used to say.

Chapter 2

The char Data Type

The `char` data type is used to represent a single character. In Java, characters are stored using 2 bytes of memory. The reason for this is that Java allows for the storage of many more characters than just the ASCII character set, which only contains 256 individual characters. Java uses a 16-bit character set called Unicode, which is the worldwide character encoding standard. Ideally, the low-order byte of the Unicode representation can be used to store the ASCII representation of characters, which means that a character with a value from 0 to 255 will be an ASCII character. The following line of code shows the declaration of `char` variables.

```
char firstLowercaseLetter = 'a';
char firstUppercaseLetter = 'A';
char ampersand = '&';
```

As you can see, the character must be specified between single quotation characters. A `char` is effectively the same as a `short` in that it is the same size and can be assigned its value numerically, which can then be altered with an arithmetic expression. For example, the ASCII numeric value of the letter "A" is 65, which means that the following line of code will also assign the character value "A" to a `char` variable and then increment the value by one, giving the variable the value of 66, which is the value of the letter "B" character.

```
char letter = 65;      // value equals 'A'
letter++;              // next value is 'B'
```

Character Escape Sequences

Character escape sequences allow for a character to be interpreted differently than its literal value. Character escape sequences are defined using the backslash (\) character, followed by the escape sequence code. The following table shows a list of character escape sequences with a description of what they do.

Character Escape Sequence	Description
\b	Backspace
\f	Form feed
\n	New line
\r	Carriage return
\t	Tab
\u{hex}	Unicode escape sequence (see the next section for details)
\\	Backslash character. This is how a backslash can be treated as just an actual backslash character.
\'	Single quote. Define a single quote character so it is not treated as a character delimiter.
\"	Double quote. Define a double quote character so it is not treated as a string delimiter.

The aforementioned escape sequences are used with string notations and will be discussed in more detail in the "Strings" section of Chapter 3.

Defining Unicode Characters

Unicode characters can be defined using the "\u" character escape sequence, followed by the hexadecimal notation of that character. For example, the hexadecimal notation for the number 65 is 0041, which is (4*16) + 1. So the following code would assign the letter A to the character variable letter.

```
char letter = '\u0041';
```

Constants

Constants are values that are declared with an initial value and cannot be altered thereafter. The standard naming convention for constants is for the variable name to be all in capital letters with multiple words being separated by an underscore character (_). Declaring constants is very simple. Here we use a new keyword, final, to create a constant variable.

```
static final byte MAX_DAILY_HOURS = 24;
```

The static keyword is used with the final keyword because you may not require multiple instances of a constant variable when you create multiple objects of the class to which the constant attribute belongs, as they will only share the same unchangeable value anyway. However, you can declare a constant with the keyword final alone (omitting the keyword static). The advantage of this lies in not specifying the value of the constant immediately.

```
final byte MAX_DAILY_HOURS;
```

The value of MAX_DAILY_HOURS must now be assigned a value in every constructor that is defined in the class to which it belongs; the value must be assigned once and only once and will then stay and cannot be changed from then on. This is useful if you want each object to have its own copy of a constant variable, with each constant being set to its own unique value in the constructor(s).

 NOTE: A final value cannot be initialized in any other method; it must be initialized either at the declaration point or in all of the constructors of the class to which it belongs. It must be implemented in all of the constructors because any one, but only one, of them could be used when creating the object where the constant must be initialized.

Chapter 2

Conditional Statements and Loops

So far, we have looked at storing values in our programs, which isn't the most exciting thing in the world. We will now look at how to manipulate the data using conditional statements and loops, the key ingredients to adding functionality to your games and spicing them up a little. *Conditional statements* are used to test values and execute different sections of code based on the result of the test. *Loops* are used to repeatedly execute a section of code, meaning you can use the same piece of code to perform a task multiple times, an essential implementation for many circumstances.

Conditional Statements

The ability to choose the path that your program takes, based on any given data, is the key to all functionality in programming. In order to create conditional statements, we must first learn about the relational operators that we will use with these statements. The following table is a list of the relational operators in Java.

Operator	Returns true if...
<	Left operand is less than the right operand
<=	Left operand is less than or equal to the right operand
==	Operands are equal
>=	Left operand is greater than or equal to right operand
>	Left operand is greater than right operand
!=	Operands are not equal

The equality operator (==) is different from the other relational operators in that it can be used to test the value of any similar data types, such as two integer expressions, two Boolean expressions, or even two objects.

NOTE: When testing the value of two objects, we are not actually testing the data within the objects, but rather we are testing to see if both references refer to the same object. For example, remember back when we created two `Person` objects referenced by `glennMurphy` and `andrewMulholland`. A test between these two references using the equality operator (==) would simply return true if they both referred to the same object, like they do in Figure 2-3 but do not in Figure 2-2. We will look at comparing objects in more detail later in the book.

Simple if Statements

An `if` statement is rather self explanatory; it contains a Boolean expression and is followed by a line or block of code that it will execute if the Boolean expression returns `true`. The following code shows an example of an `if` statement with one line that it will execute if the Boolean expression returns `true`.

```
boolean televisionOn = true;
if(televisionOn == true)
    System.out.println("The TV is on");
```

This `if` statement will execute the one line of code that is immediately after it, provided the Boolean expression returns `true`. If there was another statement after the screen printing code, it would execute regardless of the result of the `if` statement. You must specify a code block for the `if` statement if you wish to have more than one line of code executed when its test is `true`.

```
if(televisionOn)
{
    System.out.println("The TV is on");
    System.out.println("Turn it off and get back to work");
}
```

Notice that the Boolean expression merely specifies the `boolean` data type `televisionOn` on its own. This is another way to test if the Boolean value is true just without the "`== true`" part, which is a neater way to do it, although it is also less readable and less like pseudocode. You may implement this test in whatever way you feel the most comfortable. Similarly, you can also write the test like this:

```
//    not false is the same as equal to true
if(televisionOn != false)
    System.out.println("I said turn it off!");
```

Using the other relational operators is the same as using the `==` and `!=` operators, although you cannot use them with Boolean expressions, as you cannot say that one Boolean value is, for example, greater than or equal to another. The other relational operators must be used with values with a comparable scope that exceeds just equality testing, such as numeric values.

```
int numberOfLions = 5;
int numberOfWildebeest = 2;

if(numberOfLions > numberOfWildebeest)
    numberOfWildebeest--;
```

Those poor wildebeest; they have a heck of a time! You can also have `if` statements nested inside one another quite simply.

```
if(numberOfLions > numberOfWildebeest)
{
    numberOfWildebeest--;
    if(numberOfWildebeest == 1)
    {
        System.out.println("Oh no, there is only one left");
    }
}
```

This code will first check to see if there are a greater number of lions than wildebeests. If this is `false`, none of the nested code will be executed at all. If it is `true`, the value of `numberOfWildebeest` is decremented by one and followed by another `if` statement, which tests to see if there is only one wildebeest left. If this is `true`, some text is printed to the console screen stating this unfortunate fact.

Chapter 2

The if with else Statements

Suppose we wanted to execute some code for either of the two possible results of a Boolean expression, `true` or `false`. We can perform this task easily using an `else` statement along with an `if` statement, basically giving the option of performing one task if a test is satisfied or else perform another task.

```
int personsAge = 21;

if(personsAge == 0)
    System.out.println("Get me one of those cool door swings");
else
    System.out.println("Old enough to start programming :)");
```

This code simply says that if the value of the `personsAge` variable is equal to 0, then perform the first task; otherwise, if this is false, perform the `else` task. The problem with this code, and in many other situations, is that we may need to check more than just two possible outcomes. In this code, we do not check to see if the value of `personsAge` is less than zero, presuming that any value other than zero is a positive integer. To test more than two different outcomes, we can use an `else if` statement. An initial `else if` statement needs to appear after an `if` statement and can then be followed by more `else if` statements, each performed in the same way as `if` statements with a Boolean test.

```
if(personsAge == 0)
    System.out.println("Get me one of those cool door swings");
else if(personsAge > 0)
    System.out.println("Old enough to start programming :)");
else    // must be negative
    System.out.println("On the way, perhaps");
```

You can have as many `else if` branches after an initial `if` statement as you require but only one `else` statement at the end. Note the `else` statement is optional and not required after using `else if` statements.

Logical Operators

Logical operators are used to test Boolean expressions, similar to the bit-wise operators that we saw earlier. The following table shows the full list of logical operators:

Operator	Description
!	Logical NOT (also known as logical-negation)
&&	Logical AND
||	Logical OR

These operators can be used in conjunction with `if` statements to add more complex tests.

```
if(houseOnFire && haveNoWater)
    System.out.println("Call the fire brigade");
```

These operators are not only used with conditional statements. They can be used wherever a Boolean expression is required, such as assigning a value to a Boolean variable or specifying a condition for terminating a loop, which we shall see later in this chapter.

The Conditional Operator

The conditional operator is used to return one of two possible values, based on a Boolean test, using the question mark (?) and colon (:) characters. As we mentioned earlier, this is a ternary operator involving three operand arguments. The following shows the conditional operator in action:

```
int number = 4;
boolean isEven = (number % 2 == 0) ? true : false;
```

This statement will return the value of `true` to the variable `isEven` because the remainder of `number`, which is equal to 4, from 2 is 0. If the Boolean expression before the question mark is true, the first value after the question mark is returned; otherwise the value specified after the colon character is returned instead. You can return any value in this statement, not just Boolean values, and you can even return object references. We will look in detail at objects in the next two chapters.

The code that we have just seen would be performed similarly using `if` statements in the following way:

```
int number = 4;
boolean isEven = false;
if (number % 2 == 0)
    isEven = true;
```

As you can see, the conditional statement can make your code neater, but an `if` statement makes it more obvious as to what the code does.

Switch Statements

If you have one value that you need to test for equality with a variety of different outcomes (known as cases), you can use a switch statement. A switch statement introduces us to four new keywords: `switch`, `case`, `break`, and `default`. A basic switch statement would look as follows:

```
int number = 1;
switch (number)
{
    case 0:
        System.out.println("Number is zero");
        break;

    case 1:
        System.out.println("Number is one");
        break;

    default:
        System.out.println("Number not found");
        break;
}
```

The value that you are testing is enclosed in brackets after the `switch` keyword is entered. To specify a case statement, you must enter the `case` keyword followed by a constant value that it will be compared with, followed by a colon character (:). From here, any lines of code after the colon will be executed until a `break` statement is reached, which will then exit out of the whole switch statement block.

The `default` keyword is used to specify an area of code that can be executed if none of the `case` values match the `switch` statement test value. A `default` statement does not need to be included in a `switch` statement if it is not required, but it is useful for debugging.

NOTE: You can only use values that are compatible with the data type `int` as the test and case values for `switch` statements; that is, the compiler will look for an `int` value. This means that you can test characters, as they are also numeric values. Finally, the case values must be constant values, as in hard-coded numbers (e.g., 17, 2288, etc.) or constant variable values.

The example `DaysOfTheMonth.java` uses a `switch` statement to assign the number of days to a variable based on the current month and year. Here is the code:

```java
public class DaysOfTheMonth
{
    public static void main(String args[])
    {
        int month = 7;
        int year = 2002;
        int totalDays = 0;

        switch(month)
        {
            case 1: case 3: case 5: case 7:
            case 8: case 10: case 12:           //  31 days
                totalDays = 31;
                break;

            case 4: case 6: case 9: case 11:  //  30 days
                totalDays = 30;
                break;

            case 2:                             //  28 or 29 days

                if(year % 4 != 0)
                    totalDays = 28;
                else if(year % 400 == 0)
                    totalDays = 29;
                else if(year % 100 == 0)
                    totalDays = 28;
                else
                    totalDays = 29;

            default:
                System.out.println("Error, Invalid month index =
                    " + month);
                break;
        }

        if(totalDays != 0)
        {
```

```
        System.out.println("Month = " + month);
        System.out.println("Year = " + year);
        System.out.println("There are " + totalDays + "
        days in this month");
    }
  }
}
```

When you run this program, you should get output similar to this console screen shot:

Figure 2-8

This example shows us a new feature of using `case` statements inside the `switch` statement, which is using many `case` statements that all lead to the same code segment. This example is ideal for showing this feature because there are multiple months that share the same amount of days. So, for example, the months of April, June, September, and November all contain 30 days and are represented in the `DaysOfTheMonth.java` example as month numbers 4, 6, 9, and 11, respectively. The `case` statements and values can therefore simply be written one after another, separated by a colon after each value. This is functionally the same as the following code.

```
if(month == 4 || month == 6 || month == 9 || month == 11)
    totalDays = 30;
```

The `case 2:` statement represents the month of February. Here we need to test if it is a leap year or not in order to accurately assign the number of days for the month of February. The definition of a leap year can be worked out with four steps.

1. If the year is not divisible by 4 (that is, the remainder of the year divided by 4 is not zero, e.g., 1997, 2002), then it is definitely not a leap year. Assign `totalDays` the value of `28`. Otherwise go to step 2.
2. If the year is divisible by 400 (that is, the remainder of the year divided by 400 is zero, e.g., 1600, 2000), then it is a leap year. Assign `totalDays` the value of `29`. Otherwise go to step 3.
3. If the year is divisible by 100 (that is, the remainder of the year divided by 100 is zero, e.g., 1900, 2100), then it is not a leap year. Assign `totalDays` the value of `28`. Otherwise, go to step 4.
4. It must be a leap year, so assign `totalDays` the value of `29`.

The code for these four steps is simple; we can use the modulus operator (`%`) to find the remainder values and the `if`, `else if`, and `else` statements to test the values.

```
if(year % 4 != 0)
    totalDays = 28;        // not leap year
else if(year % 400 == 0)
    totalDays = 29;        // leap year
else if(year % 100 == 0)
    totalDays = 28;        // not leap year
else
    totalDays = 29;        // leap year
```

NOTE: It is a common mistake with `switch` statements to forget to add a `break` statement at the end of your `case` block. If this is omitted, the code will simply continue to execute the next line of code. For example, the following code will print all three words to the console window regardless of the fact that only the first case is true.

```
switch(1)
{
    case 1:
        System.out.println("Forgot");
    case 2:
        System.out.println("the");
    case 3:
        System.out.println("breaks");
}
```

The first `case` statement will be executed because the switch test value is equal to 1 also, but then the other case statements will also be executed because there are no break statements to tell your program to exit from the switch block altogether. Sometimes, you may actually wish to execute the code from one case block and then continue to execute the code in the next case block also, although this can lead to unseen errors later on.

Loops

Loops are used to execute code repeatedly, meaning that you only need to enter code once and then execute it a specified number of times. In order for a loop to stop, at least one condition for termination should go with it; otherwise, the loop could be infinite, running forever (that is, until you find some way of crashing out of it, like pressing Ctrl+Alt+Del or buying a shotgun, but it won't come to that).

Let's say we want to write the value of all of the positive integers that are less than 10 to the console window, which is 0 to 9. A loop can be used to perform this task in just a few lines of code instead of manually coding ten `System.out.println...` statements, which would be too tedious a task for someone of your intelligence. The basic loops are the `while` loop, the `do while` loop, and the `for` loop.

Using the while Loop

A `while` loop is implemented in exactly the same way as an `if` statement. It must specify a Boolean expression test for itself and be followed by a line or block of code that it will execute if the Boolean expression test is true. The following example, `WhileCounter.java`, will perform the task of printing the numbers 0 to 9 to the console window using a `while` loop. Here is the code:

```
public class WhileCounter
{
    public static void main(String args[])
    {
        int counter = 0;
        while(counter < 10)
        {
            System.out.println("Value = " + counter);
            counter++;
        }
    }
}
```

The screen output in a console window should be similar to the following:

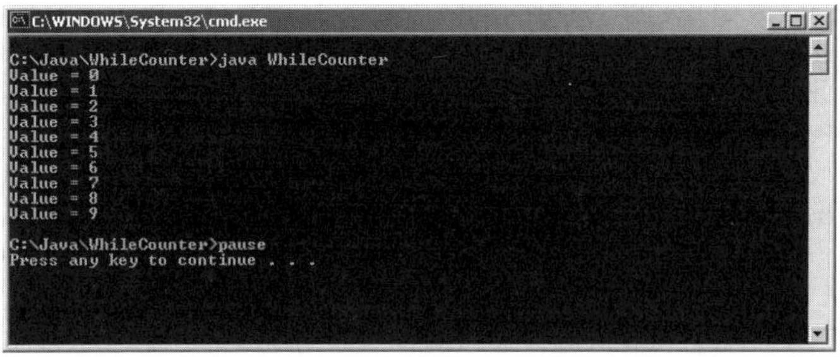

Figure 2-9

Inside the code block of the `while` loop is a line of code to increment the value of the variable `counter` by 1, which eventually causes the loop to terminate. When the `while` loop begins, and every time the code block of the `while` loop completes its execution after that, there is a test to see if the condition `counter < 10` is true. The `while` loop will continue to execute while the conditional statement test returns `true` and terminate when it returns `false`, which in this case is when the variable `counter` is equal to `10`.

Using the do while Loop

A `do while` loop is very similar to a `while` loop. The difference is that a `do while` loop will execute its code block at least once and then test for termination, whereas the `while` loop tests for termination at the beginning before entering its code block.

```
int counter = 11;
do
{
    System.out.println("Value = " + counter);
    counter++;
} while(counter < 10);
```

Here, the code block of the `do while` loop is entered, first of all, where the value of `counter` is printed to the console screen and then incremented by 1 to the value `12`. The loop is then terminated, as `12` is not less than 10. This code will only print the value of `11` to the console, a wrongly written program if you wanted to print only numbers that are less than 10 to the console screen. So be aware of the fact that there is no condition for entering the `do while` loop for the first time. They are advantageous for situations where you want to execute code at least once and maybe more times.

Using the for Loop

The `for` loop is the most convenient of the loops. The standard implementation for a `for` loop is to specify a start value, a termination condition, and an action to be performed. A standard `for` loop looks like this:

```
for(int counter=0; counter<10; counter++)
    System.out.println("Value = " + counter);
```

This will do the same as the previous `WhileCounter.java` example, only in a neater fashion. For the `for` loop an integer `counter` is declared and initialized to 0. This is done once at the start of the `for` loop. The next statement is the termination condition for the loop, which in this case is if the value of `counter` is less than 10. The last statement is an action that will be performed per loop, which is to increment `counter` by one.

The following `MultiTable.java` example shows a multiplication table of values from 1 to 5 using two `for` loops.

```
public class MultiTable
{
    public static void main(String args[])
    {
        final int TABLE_SIZE = 5;

        for(int j=1; j<=TABLE_SIZE; j++)
        {
            for(int i=1; i<=TABLE_SIZE; i++)
            {
                int value = i * j;
                if(value < 10)
                    System.out.print(" ");

                System.out.print(value + " ");
            }

            System.out.println();        // move to new line
        }
    }
}
```

The output for this program should look like the following screen shot.

Figure 2-10

This example contains two `for` loops, one nested inside the other. After the first `for` loop is entered, the second `for` loop is executed straight away. The code block for the second `for` loop is where the important code is implemented; this block of code prints a value to the console window, which is the multiplication of the current values of the variables i and j. The first time that the code block for the second `for` loop is entered, j is equal to 1. From here, the value of i will run from 1 to 5, with j always equal to 1. This gives us the first output line of 1, 2, 3, 4, and 5. These are the calculations of `(1*1)`, `(1*2)`, `(1*3)`, `(1*4)`, and `(1*5)`, where j is the first operand (always 1) and the second operand is i (incremented by one each time). After this, there is a call to the `System.out.println()` method to move the console carat position onto the next line. This procedure is then repeated with the value of j incremented each time until it is equal to 5.

NOTE: The printing method that was used to print the multiplication values was `System.out.print()`. This method leaves the cursor position at the point where the last character was output, not moving it onto the next line, whereas `System.out.println()` will move the cursor to the start of the next line.

The purpose of the `final int` variable `TABLE_SIZE` is to define the limit of the `for` loop counter variables i and j and is a good technique for making reusable code. It means that changes made to the value of this variable at a later time will influence the outcome of the table sufficiently, so you only need to make the change once. If you change the value of `TABLE_SIZE` from 5 to the value 10, for example, you will get output similar to the following screen shot:

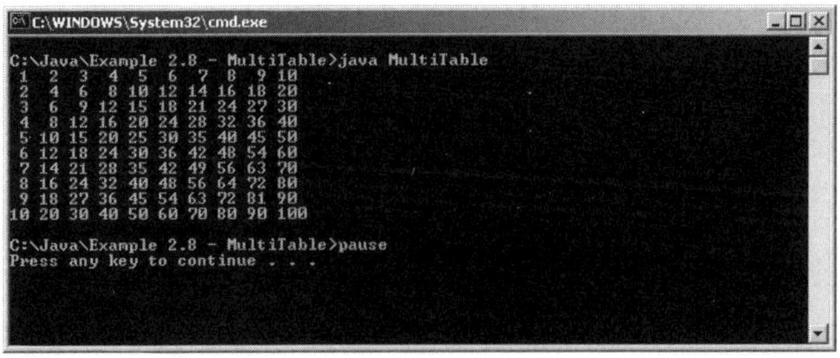

Figure 2-11

Here the dimension of the table is now 10, where the last calculated value is 10 multiplied by 10, giving the value 100 in the bottom-right corner of the table. You could specify the width and the height of the table as two separate variables, giving you a table of any dimension, such as 5 by 9 or 200 by 310 (although the latter dimension would not fit in the console window properly).

NOTE: Notice that when declaring the constant variable `TABLE_SIZE`, it is only declared as `final` and not `static` and `final`. This is simply because the method `main` that it belongs to is already static, which means that variables declared inside it are static also.

An Advanced Look at the for Loop

The first statement in a `for` loop is most often used to declare a variable and assign it a value. It is also possible to declare more than one variable of the same specified data type in the same declaration. For example, the following code declares two variables, `i` and `j`:

```
for(int i=0, j; i<10; i++)
    System.out.println("i = " + i);
```

We can also add more actions to the third statement of the `for` loop separated by commas, as follows.

```
for(int i = 0, j = 0; i<10; i++, j=i*i)
{
    System.out.println("i = " + i);
    System.out.println("i squared = " + j);
}
```

This code will add one to the variable `i` per loop cycle and assign to the variable `j` the value of `i*i`, printing the value each time.

The statements in a `for` loop do not need to be implemented if it is unnecessary to do so. Suppose you have a previously declared variable that you want to use as the counter in the `for` loop. This means that you do not need to implement a declaration statement for the `for` loop at all, as you want to use a previously declared variable instead.

```
int counter = 0;

// later on in code (within scope of variable counter)

for(; counter<10; counter++)
    System.out.println("Value = " + counter);
```

Note that you must still add a semicolon (;) where the statement should be. You may still initialize an existing variable in a `for` loop.

```
int counter = 0;

// later on in code

// Counts down from 10 to 0
for(counter = 10; counter>=0; counter--)
    System.out.println("Value = " + counter);
```

Similar to removing the first statement, you may remove the last statement and simply implement the code inside the code block for the `for` loop, as follows:

```
int counter = 0;

// later on in code

for(; counter<10;)
{
    counter++;
    System.out.println("Value = " + counter);
}
```

You can omit the second conditional statement also, which would leave you with the following code:

```
for(;;)
    System.out.println("This loops infinitely");
```

The loop statement `for(;;)` performs the same way as `while(true)` as a loop declaration, looping continuously. You can exit out of an infinite loop (or a loop that already has a condition to terminate early) using break statements, which we will now discuss.

Using break and continue

We have already seen the `break` statement, using it to exit out of `case` statements inside a `switch` statement. Similarly, the `break` statement can also be used to exit from loops; this can replace or supplement existing termination conditions, which means that you can have multiple termination conditions for loops at different stages in the code block.

```
int number = 0;
while(true)
{
    number++;
    if(number > 9)
        break;
}
```

This slice of code again will count from 0 to 9, "breaking" out of the `while` loop when the value of the variable `number` is greater than 9. Notice that we have replaced the condition statement with the Boolean value of `true`; this will simply make the loop repeat forever, which means you must add code to jump out of the loop yourself using a `break` statement.

The `continue` statement is very useful with loops. It allows you to jump through the loop's code block, basically jumping from the current position and past the rest of the code block to start off the next loop stage. A good example of this is shown in `OddNumbers.java`. This example uses the `continue` statement to jump past the remaining code in the loop's code block when the value of the loop counter is found to be even. The result is that only odd numbers are printed to the console screen.

```
public class OddNumbers
{
    public static void main(String args[])
    {
        for(int counter=0; counter<10; counter++)
        {
            System.out.print("Value of counter =  " + counter);

            if(counter % 2 == 0)      //  counter is even
            {
                System.out.println(", counter is even so continue");
                continue;             // jump to next loop step
            }

            System.out.println(", odd number found, hurray");
```

```
        }
    }
}
```

When you run this code, the output should be similar to the following screen shot.

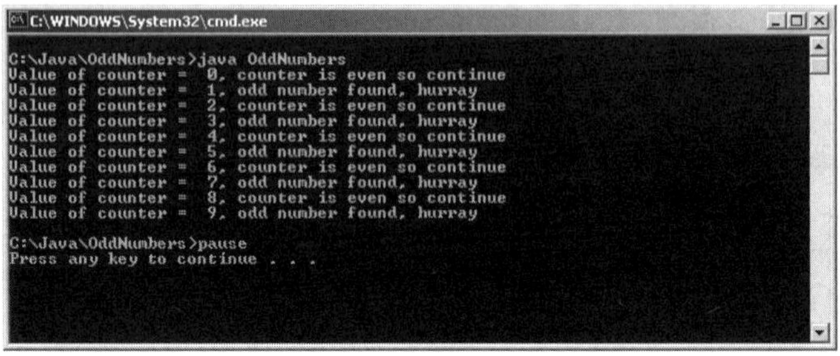

Figure 2-12

The previous example was structured merely to illustrate the use of the `continue` statement. In order to get a list of odd numbers, the following code is a simpler and more suitable implementation.

```
for(int counter=1; counter<10; counter+=2)
{
    System.out.println("Odd number = " + counter);
}
```

Instead of testing to see if the value of `counter` is an even or odd number, we can simply ensure that all of the numbers are odd. To do this, the value of `counter` is initialized to 1 and is incremented by 2 every loop cycle. This means that by continually adding values of 2 per loop cycle, the value of `counter` is always the next odd number, as it started as an odd number.

Jumping to Labels

The ability to jump to labels can be a very useful tool when using nested loops. Let's consider the following section of code:

```
for(int i=0; i<5; i++)          // first loop
{
    for(int j=0; j<5; j++)      // second/nested loop
    {
        break;
    }
}
```

Here we have two loops, one nested inside another. If you are in the second/nested loop, there is no instant way that you can break out of both loops altogether. The `break` statement will only "break out" of the nested loop but continue performing the first loop until it terminates when the value of `i` is not less than 5.

We can give the first loop a label and then break out of both loops entirely by specifying the label with the `break` statement, as follows.

```
firstLoop:
for(int i=0; i<5; i++)          // first loop
```

```
{
    for(int j=0; j<5; j++)    // second/nested loop
    {
        break firstLoop;
    }
}
// breaking from firstLoopLabel will go to here
```

Here we specify the first loop with the label firstLoop, followed by a colon. It is almost like giving the first loop an identifier or variable name so that you can differentiate between it and the nested loop from within the nested loop. You can then specify which one of the loops that you want the break statement to affect by adding the label after the break keyword.

Now that we are able to choose the loop that we want the break statement to "break," we can look at using the continue statement in exactly the same way.

The following example code illustrates the use of the break and continue statements using labels with two loops, one nested inside the other. They are manipulated from within the second/nested loop.

```
firstLoop:
for(int i=0; i<10; i++)
{
    for(int j=0; j<10; j++)
    {
      if(i!=7)
          continue firstLoop;  //  or just break this loop
      else if(j!=7)
          continue;            //  continue this loop

      //  if this is reached both i and j equal 7

      System.out.println("i = " + i);
      System.out.println("j = " + j);

      break firstLoop;         // this will exit both loops
    }
}
```

This code only prints to the console the values of the variables i and j when they are both equal to 7, using the label firstLoop to manipulate the first loop from inside the second/nested loop.

Methods

Methods are used as the building blocks of your program, performing tasks that can be called again and again and using the same code to perform the task each time. The basic but fundamental parts of a method's declaration are its name, its return type, parameter signature, and code segment curly brackets. The following lines of code are an example of a method declaration.

```
static void doSomething()
{
```

```
    // add code here
}
```

This method is called `doSomething` and has a return type of `void`, which simply indicates that the method does not return a value. We have seen the keyword `void` already, which is the return type of the method `main`. If the method `doSomething` were added to your main program class, then in the `main` method of the class you would call the method `doSomething` by entering the following code:

```
doSomething();
```

 NOTE: The method `doSomething` needs to be static at the moment because the method `main`, from which we are assuming the method `doSomething` is going to be called, is also static. The method `doSomething` would not need to be static if we created an instance of the class to which `doSomething` would belong. We will look at this in more detail in Chapter 4, "Multiple Classes."

If you want a method that returns a value, you must specify the return type of the method, and then you must use the keyword `return` in the method code block to specify the returned value.

```
static int getFiveDoubled()
{
    return 10;
}
```

The following method will simply return the value of `10` to wherever it was called from. The following line of code could be added, for example, in your `main` method to assign this value to a variable:

```
int myNumber = getFiveDoubled();
```

This line of code will assign the value of `10` to the variable `myNumber`.

 NOTE: Just because the method `getFiveDoubled` now has a return type, it does not mean that it cannot be called on its own.

```
getFiveDoubled();
```

This method will essentially do nothing, but you may have a method that performs a required task and then returns a value, which you want to ignore.

A method that has a return value (not void) must have a return statement at every possible exit point from the method. The compiler will pick up if a path without a return value is possible. On the other hand, if you have a method with return type void and then want to exit out of the method early, you can use the keyword `return` on its own. For example, take the following code:

```
public void doSomething()
{
    if(leaveEarly == true)
        return;

    // else continue with the rest of the code
}
```

This is similar to how the break statement is used to exit out of certain code blocks, such as switch cases and loops, as we saw earlier. The example we have just seen is a very basic example, but the use of the keyword `return` in this instance can be very useful for immediately exiting out of complicated code clusters in a given method.

Parameter Passing

The previous method, `getFiveDoubled`, is pretty pointless and very inconvenient because it will only return one value, `10`. However, we could create a method that will take in any number, double it, and then return the doubled value. This can be achieved using parameter passing. *Parameter passing* allows you to pass values to a method that the method can then manipulate. The following method contains one parameter, which is doubled and the new value is returned.

```
int doubleNumber(int number)
{
    number *= 2;
    return number;
}
```

As you can see, the parameter is a variable called `number` of type `int` and is specified between the brackets that follow the name of the method. To call this method, you could, for example, use the following code:

```
// double of 2 equals 4
int myNumber = doubleNumber(2);

// then double its current number of 4 equals 8
myNumber = doubleNumber(myNumber);

// then quadruple its current number to equal 32
myNumber = doubleNumber(doubleNumber(myNumber));
```

This last line of code will call the method `doubleNumber` twice, first returning a value that is double the value of `myNumber`, which in turn is then passed as a parameter to the second call to `doubleNumber` that eventually returns the final value of `32`, assigning it to the variable `myNumber`.

To reiterate what we mentioned earlier, if the value that you pass as a parameter is of a primitive data type variable, the variable itself is not passed to the method. A new variable with that value is created in the method and then used. This means that changes made to this value inside the called method will not affect the value of the original variable. (This is not the case for objects, however, which can also be passed as parameters. This is discussed in Chapter 4.)

You can also have more than one parameter, using a comma to separate consecutive parameters. The following simple example, `Spiders-Eyes.java`, contains the method `multiply`, which contains two parameters that are both of type `int` and returns the value of the two parameters multiplied together. Here is the code:

```java
public class SpidersEyes
{
    public static int multiply(int valueA, int valueB)
    {
        return valueA * valueB;
    }

    public static void main(String args[])
    {
        int numberOfSpiders = 10;
        int eyesPerSpider = 8;
        int totalEyes = multiply(numberOfSpiders, eyesPerSpider);

        System.out.println("Total Eyes = " + totalEyes);
    }
}
```

When you run this code, the output should look similar to the following screen shot.

Figure 2-13

There are two things to note from this example. First, we have used the keyword `static` for the method `multiply`. This is because there is no instance of the class `SpidersEyes` currently created, so in order for `main`, which is static, to be able to access the method `multiply`, it must be static also. (If this is confusing, do not worry about it for the time being. It will all become clear in Chapter 4 when we start looking at using classes fully.) The second thing to notice is that the method `main` also takes a parameter, which is an array of `Strings`. We will learn about these in the next chapter.

Method Signatures

It is possible to have two methods that share the same name. However, they must have different signatures because otherwise when you wish to call one of the methods, the compiler has no way of differentiating one from the other, as the invocation of the method is based on the compiler recognizing the signature. Having methods of the same name but with different signatures is known as *overloading* the method.

The name of the method and the parameter signature of that method determine a method's signature. The return type of a method does not influence its signature. Hence you cannot have two methods with the same name with two different return values with the same parameter signature.

In the previous example, `SpidersEyes.java`, we had a method called `multiply`, which took two parameter values of type `int`, returning the value of the parameter values multiplied together. If we also included a method that did the same thing but used values of type `dou-ble` instead, we could create another method with the same name but with a different parameter signature.

```
public static int multiply(int a, int b)
{
    return a * b;
}

public static double multiply(double a, double b)
{
    return a * b;
}
```

The parameter signature is determined by the data types of the parameters and therefore the number of parameters also. Let's say that we now added the following method together with the previous two methods:

```
public static long multiply(int a, int b)
{
    return (long)(a * b);
}
```

The program would no longer compile because this method and the original `multiply` method share the same signature. They have the same name and also the same parameter signature—two parameters both of type `int`. The most obvious solution is to change the parameter signature of the latter method to take two parameters of type `long`.

```
public static long multiply(long a, long b)
{
    return a * b;
}
```

This will now work because the parameter signatures are different. If you are unable to alter the parameter signature in a reasonable manner, do not bother; just give the methods different names (e.g., `multiplyInt`, `multiplyDouble`, `multiplyLong`, etc.).

Variable Scope

So far in this chapter we have used variables as soon as they have been declared, without really encountering problems with the scope of the variables. The *scope* of a variable is the area in which a variable belongs, specified by the area in which it is declared. The following example code contains two declared variables, one inside a code block and one outside of that code block (imagine that the code is entered into a method, like `main` for example).

```
int outside = 10;

{
    int inside = 5;
    // outside is valid inside this code block
    inside = outside;
```

```
}

outside = 5;
// inside cannot be accessed here
```

The variable `inside` cannot be accessed anywhere outside the code block in which it was declared because it is out of the variable's scope. The variable `inside` simply does not exist outside of the code block. Therefore, this is true of all code blocks, like the ones belonging to `while` and `for` loops and `if` and `else` statements and methods.

For example, look at this `for` loop:

```
for(int counter=0; counter<5; counter++)
{
    System.out.println("counter = " + counter);
}
```

The variable `counter` is declared in the scope of the `for` loop code block; it only exists inside this code block and cannot be accessed further on in the code outside of the code block. If you want to access the `counter` variable later in the code, implement your code like this:

```
int counter;

for(counter=0; counter<5; counter++)
{
    System.out.println("counter = " + counter);
}

System.out.println("counter final value = " + counter);
```

Here we simply declare the variable `counter` before the `for` loop and then use it with the `for` loop in the same way but this time we do not declare it at the first stage of the `for` loop. Later, outside of the `for` loop code block, we can still access the variable `counter` because it has been declared within the scope of this area.

A variable declared inside a method is known as a local variable to that method and does not exist outside of the method. So far, we have only declared variables inside methods. In the next chapter, we will start declaring class variables declared within the class code block only and not local to any method, meaning you will be able to access and manipulate these variables from any method. We will see this notably in Chapter 4.

Summary

In this chapter we delved into the basics of programming in Java. We can now create simple console applications using primitive data types in combination with logical decision making and loops. These aspects provide us with the fundamentals for making a class structure for defining objects, data, and functionality. At the start of this chapter, we briefly looked at classes and objects. In the next chapter, we will look at arrays and strings, two very important aspects of the Java language that will provide us with a good introduction to objects in preparation for Chapter 4.

Chapter 3

Arrays and Strings

"First things first, but not necessarily in that order."

—Doctor Who

Introduction

Hopefully, you now have a reasonably good understanding of the basics of Java programming and are fairly comfortable using primitive data types, conditional statements, loops, and methods. In this chapter we first take a look at arrays, their importance in programming, and how they are used in Java. We then delve into strings, where you will learn about the `String` class and other useful string-related classes, such as the `StringBuffer` and `StringTokenizer`. We have already looked very briefly at objects at the beginning of the previous chapter with the `Person` class but have yet to use objects properly in any code examples. In Java, arrays and strings are objects, which means we are now about to start using objects for the first time. This should also provide us with a solid introduction in preparation for Chapter 4, "Multiple Classes."

Arrays

An *array* is a list of variables (or elements, as they are generally known). Every element in an array is of the same specified type (this statement is not entirely true, as objects can be cast to different types, but do not worry about this for now; we will discuss this in detail in the next chapter). You can have an array of `int` variables, just as you can have an array of `boolean` variables or you can have an array of objects—like an array of `String` objects, as we shall see later on in this chapter. Arrays are generally used for creating lists of a finite length (finite meaning the array has a specific number of elements or length, hence it is not infinite). So for example, we may want to create ten variables of type `int` to store ten numeric values. What we would not want to do is declare ten variable names, such as:

```
int firstValue, secondValue;     // and so on, tedious, doh
```

Of course, what we would do is create an array of length `10` and of type `int`. We can declare an array as follows:

```
int[] myArray;
```

We can also declare the same array with the following code:

```
int myArray[];
```

The square brackets can be placed either after the data type or after the variable identifier name; it is up to you, as they both do the same thing, which is declare an array. However, you may have a number of arrays that you want to declare of the same type in the same line of code, so the brackets next to the data type may be preferred.

```
int[] listA, listB;
```

Or you may prefer to declare an array and also a single data type in the same line of code that are both of the same data type.

```
int list[], number;
```

This will declare an array reference `list` and a single variable called `number` that are both of type `int`. Referring back to the original task of creating 10 variables of type `int`, the following code will do just that:

```
int[] myArray = new int[10];
```

We now have ten individual `int` variables that each have their individual memory places to store individual values. We use the keyword `new` to specify that we are creating a new array object. You will use the keyword `new` to explicitly create all objects in Java, so get used to it. If you want to create the array object at a later point and not when it is declared, you can do so by using single variables, as follows.

```
int[] myArray;        // just declare for now

// later in the code
myArray = new int[10];
```

When you declare an array variable but do not assign it to an array, such as `myArray`, its value is null. We shall see about this in a moment when discussing arrays as objects.

 NOTE: Just in case this concerns you at this time, if you declare the array with the square brackets after the identifier, like `int myArray[];`, then assigning `myArray` later on is done the same way, as `myArray = new int[10];`, without the square brackets.

Accessing Array Elements

So how do we access these variables? Well, we access one of the variables in the array using a positive integer regarding its position in the array, known as the *index*. We can print the value of the first element in `myArray`, as follows.

```
int myArray = new int[10];
// print the value of the first element
System.out.println("Element 0 = " + myArray[0]);
```

When an array is first initialized, the values of its elements are set to the default value for the type of the array. So for `myArray`, which is an array of type `int`, its elements are all equal to 0. We can assign desired values to the individual element, as follows.

```
myArray[0] = 369;
```

Notice that the index number used to access the first element in the array is zero. In computing in general, you might have heard that the first number to a computer is zero, not one ("one" is the obvious equivalent to the word "first"). This is something that you should be aware of from the beginning and at the end for that matter, with the end of an array being where the most common array error occurs. At first you might try to access the last element in the array of length 10 with the following code:

```
myArray[10] = 911;       // hmmm, alert the police
// this variable does not exist
// there is no variable at index 10
```

The array may be of length 10, but the index of the last element is not; it is 9, as the first element was 0. Just imagine that you have an array of size 2; the first element is accessed using the index value 0, so the second element, which is also the last, must therefore be accessed using the index value 1. So the index value of the last variable in an array is the length of the array minus 1. You should stamp this fact in your mind if you are new to arrays, as this is a common misconception.

So far, we have initialized the array using the keyword `new` specifying the size of the array numerically. You may want to specify values to be stored in an array at the point of declaration. The following code shows how this can be done:

```
int[] myArray = {71, 76, 69, 78, 78, 73, 83, 71, 79, 68};

// ASCII codes?
```

Instead of explicitly specifying the length of the array and using the keyword `new`, defining this list of values assigns these values to the individual array elements and also defines the size of the array, which is the number of values in the list and in this case is 10.

 NOTE: This assignment technique can only be implemented when the array is declared.

So you could have a list that states whether three lights are switched on or off. If you knew this information when the array was declared, then you originally would have entered the following code.

```
boolean[] lightOn = new boolean[3];
lightOn[0] = true;
lightOn[1] = false;
lightOn[2] = true;
```

A less tedious way to program this when the variable is declared is as follows:

```
boolean[] lightOn = {true, false, true};
```

Arrays Are Objects

We should backtrack a little at this time and return to when we first declared an array—remember when we declared the array `myArray` of type `int` without initializing it?

```
int[] myArray;
```

At the moment, we actually have a reference to an `int` array object called `myArray` which is currently equal to `null` because it has not been assigned to reference an array object, which first needs to be created.

```
if(myArray == null)
    System.out.println("myArray refers to no object");
else
    System.out.println("myArray refers to an object");
```

At the very beginning of Chapter 2, we looked at the `Person` class and objects derived from it with references such as `glennMurphy` and `andrewMulholland`. Similarly, `myArray` is used to reference an array object of type `int`. We can set `myArray` to reference one array object at one time and then another at a later place in the code.

```
int[] myArray = new int[10];

// later on in the code
myArray = new int[5];
```

The array reference value is declared and initialized to reference an array object of length `10`, and somewhere later on, `myArray` is set to reference a new array object of length `5`. The originally created array object of length `10` is no longer referenced and the data is lost (though the Java Virtual Machine will handle deallocating this memory with the garbage collector (see Chapter 12) for you).

Setting Values from Array to Array

Imagine we have two arrays, `listA` and `listB`, both of type `int` and length 5.

```
int[] listA = {1, 1, 2, 3, 5};
int[] listB = {0, 1, 4, 9, 16};
```

The following diagram represents this code with `listA` and `listB` referring to separate array objects.

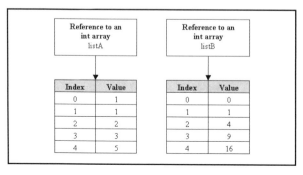

Figure 3-1

If we want to set all of the values from one array object to the other, the obvious choice may be the following code:

```
listA = listB;      // warning, warning!!!
```

We have already realized that arrays are objects in Java and that listA and listB are references. This means that this method will actually make listA reference the same object that listB references, meaning from now on using either reference will affect the same object. The following diagram is an updated illustration of Figure 3-1 after the above code is added.

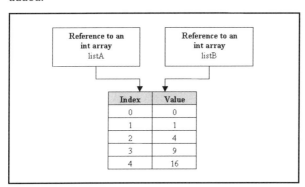

Figure 3-2

If you want listA and listB to continue to reference individual objects and just make the value of one set of elements equal to another, you can cycle through each element of both arrays assigning the values one at a time. The following code will perform this task:

```
for(int counter=0; counter<listA.length; counter++)
    listA[counter] = listB[counter];
```

 NOTE: This code assumes that both listA and listB are of equal length.

We will now take a closer look at using for loops to access array elements and find out what the length member of an array object is.

Arrays with for Loops

The best way of "cycling" through all of the elements of an array is using a for loop using the loop's counter variable as the index value to access each of the array elements. For example, imagine that we wanted to set the value of all of the elements in the aforementioned array lightOn to false. We would use a for loop to perform this operation as follows.

```
boolean[] lightOn = {true, false, true};

// turn out the lights, turn out the lights
for(int counter=0; counter<lightOn.length; counter++)
    lightOn[counter] = false;
```

This code introduces us to a new area, the length member of the array. This variable is a member of all array objects and contains the value that is

the length of the array, which is 3 for the array object that `lightOn` references. Using the `length` member in the termination condition for the
`for` loop means that later alterations to the size of the array object that
`lightOn` references will not affect the code that sets all of the elements
to false. The only thing that may be different is the number of elements in
the array that are to be set to false, which the `for` loop will adapt to
accordingly with the new array length.

The following example called `FreelanceProgrammer.java` imag-
ines that you are a freelance programmer who wants to work out the
average amount of money earned per month in a single year. In it we create an array of type `double` of length `12`. Each array element (of 12)
represents the amount of money earned in that respective month. This
example is used not only to highlight the use of arrays but also to show
some new implementation techniques when using classes, as we shall see.
Let's first take a look at the code.

```java
public class FreelanceProgrammer
{
    public static void printEarnings()
    {
        for(int i=0; i<earnings.length; i++)
            System.out.println(earnings[i]);
    }

    public static void printAverageMonthlyEarnings()
    {
        double totalEarnings = 0.0;

        for(int i=0; i<earnings.length; i++)
            totalEarnings += earnings[i];

        double average = totalEarnings / earnings.length;

        System.out.println("Average Monthly Earnings = " + average);
    }

    public static void main(String argv[])
    {
        printEarnings();
        printAverageMonthlyEarnings();
    }

    static final double earnings[] = {   20,  80,  640, 1200,
                                         300, 900,  800,  680,
                                        1200, 480, 2000, 1300
                                      };
}
```

When you run the program, you should get an output similar to the screen
shot on the following page.

The immediate thing to note from this example is that the array variable `earnings` has been declared as a class member and is not local to
any methods. This means that the three defined methods (`main`,
`printEarnings`, and `printAverageMonthlyEarnings`) have
access to this variable. The remainder of the code is quite self-explanatory.

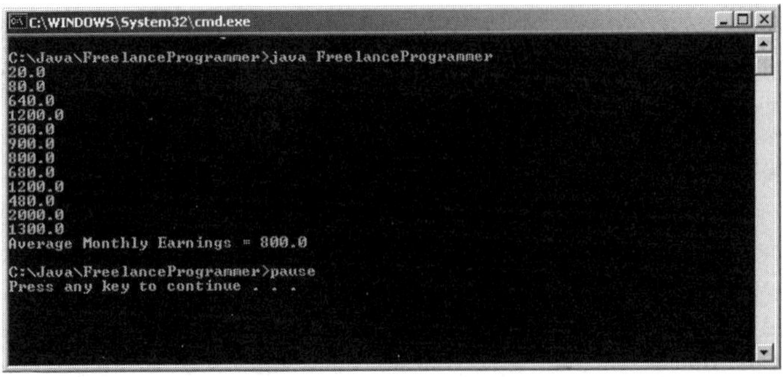

Figure 3-3

The method `main` is entered where the method `printEarnings` is invoked, which simply prints all of the values in the array to the console screen. Then the method `printAverageMonthlyEarnings` is invoked. This method first cycles through the array, adding up all of the earnings per month to get the total earned for the year. Then the average monthly earnings are printed to the console screen, which is the total earnings (`9600`) divided by the number of months (`12`), giving the answer (`800`).

NOTE: Accessing an element that does not exist, such as array element number 12 in the previous example, would cause an `ArrayIndexOutOfBoundsException` exception to be thrown. Exceptions are objects that are "thrown" by the Java Virtual Machine when an "undesired" event occurs in your program. Exceptions are discussed in detail in Chapter 5, so try not to throw any as best you can for now, and we'll try not to as well.

Passing Arrays as Parameters

Passing arrays as parameters can sometimes be a stumbling block and needs to be pointed out. As we have seen when we assign one array reference to another using the = operator, we do not copy the element values themselves but just reference the new object instead. Passing arrays as parameters works similarly. For example, set up a method to take an array parameter, as follows.

```
public void gimmeSomeNumbers(int[] list)
{
    // affects the original array
    for(int i=0; i<list.length; i++)
        list[i] = 0;

    // does not affect the original array
    list = null;
}
```

Then we can declare an array, passing it to this method as follows.

```
int[] myArray = {3, 1, 4, 1, 5, 9, 2, 6};
gimmeSomeNumbers(myArray);
```

Now, the reason for the strange code in the `gimmeSomeNumbers` method was to illustrate an important part of passing the object to the array. In the first bit of code, we set all of the array elements to 0. As you have merely passed a reference to the method `gimmeSomeNumbers`, the variable parameter `list` will now access the same array object that `myArray` refers to. This basically means that changes made to `list` will affect the same object that `myArray` refers to. The second thing to note is that by setting `list` to `null` at the end of the method `gimmeSome-Numbers`, we do not affect the original variable `myArray`, which still references the array object. We are merely stating that `list` itself no longer refers to the array object, so `myArray` is safe.

These highlighted facts are true for any objects passed as parameters. It is always important to be aware of whether you are altering your original values when using parameters. When passing primitive data values to a method, a new value is created in the method; this was discussed at the end of the previous chapter.

Another thing you may stumble across when using arrays is when you have a group of numbers that you want to pass as an array object to a method, but the numbers are not currently in an array. A neat way to implement this is by using the previous method, `gimmeSomeNumbers`, as the example method to call.

```
int numA = 1;
int numB = 14;
int numC = 147;

gimmeSomeNumbers(new int[] {numA, numB, numC});
```

That's just one of those freakish-looking anomalies that works, but it is probably most useful when you have just a single variable value and you want to pass the value as an array argument with just the one element.

Multi-dimensional Arrays

It is often the case that you will require arrays of more than one dimension—not just a list of elements but a table of elements with two dimensions, or as many dimensions as you require. The game board for the game tic-tac-toe is ideal for illustrating a two-dimensional array, storing the data (which is 3x3 squares, nine in total, for the players to place their "O" or "X") and using a two-dimensional array where both dimensions are three elements in length. This can be implemented as follows.

```
char board[][] = new char[3][3];
```

You now have nine elements of type `char` (3 x 3 = 9), which can be accessed by defining the position of the array element with two index values. The following table illustrates graphically the two-dimensional array for the tic-tac-toe game board and the indices of the array elements ("indices" is simply the plural for index). This should give you a good insight into how arrays are structured.

Board Indices	0	1	2
0	Element [0][0]	Element [1][0]	Element [2][0]
1	Element [0][1]	Element [1][1]	Element [2][1]
2	Element [0][2]	Element [1][2]	Element [2][2]

You could then place an X character value in the middle square on the game board, setting the value of the element at indices (1, 1) for the respective dimensions, as follows.

```
board[1][1] = 'X';
```

So let's draw a game board for tic-tac-toe using this two-dimensional array and make some pretend moves for the game, showing Os winning the game with a diagonal line of three. Here is the source code for Pretend-TicTacToe.java.

```java
public class PretendTicTacToe
{
    public static void drawBoard()
    {
        System.out.println();           // new line
        System.out.print("  ");

        for(int i=0; i<BOARD_SIZE; i++)
            System.out.print(" " + i);

        System.out.println();           // new line

        for(int j=0; j<BOARD_SIZE; j++)
        {
            System.out.print(j + " |");

            for(int i=0; i<BOARD_SIZE; i++)
                System.out.print(board[i][j] + "|");

            System.out.println();       // new line
        }
        System.out.println();           // new line
    }

    public static void main(String args[])
    {
        board[0][0] = 'O';  //  move 1
        board[1][0] = 'X';  //  move 2
        board[1][1] = 'O';  //  move 3
        board[2][2] = 'X';  //  move 4
        board[0][2] = 'O';  //  move 5
        board[0][1] = 'X';  //  move 6
        board[2][0] = 'O';  //  move 7

        drawBoard();

        System.out.println("O's have won the game");
    }

    static int BOARD_SIZE = 3;
    static char[][] board = new char[BOARD_SIZE][BOARD_SIZE];
}
```

Here is a screen shot of the output that you should expect when you compile this source code:

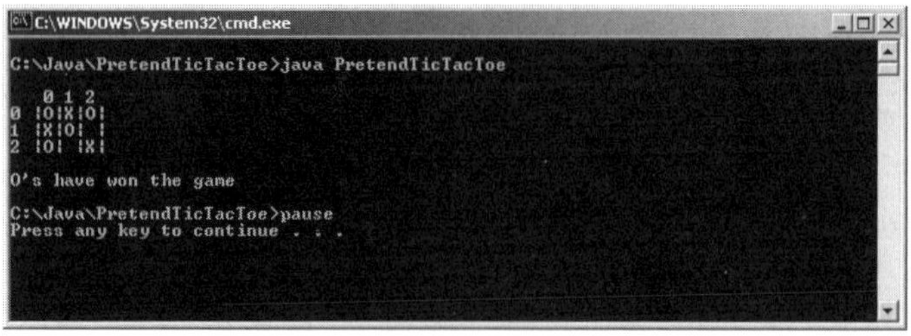

Figure 3-4

At the beginning of `main`, seven `char` values are assigned to elements of the two-dimensional array `board`, representing moves made in a game of tic-tac-toe at specified board positions. Then the method `drawBoard` is invoked. This method draws the data stored in the array `board` to the console screen by using two `for` loops to cycle through the array, with one `for` loop nested inside the other.

```
for(int i=0; i<3; i++)
    for(int j=0; j<3; j++)
        System.out.println(board[i][j]);
```

This code is a basic example of how two `for` loops work together, cycling through all of the elements in the two-dimensional array `board`.

In Chapter 6, "Stream I/O," we will learn about reading input from the keyboard, where we will make a complete working game of tic-tac-toe.

Multi-dimensional Multi-length Arrays

There may come a time when you do not want to create a completely rectangular two-dimensional array, like the game board for the tic-tac-toe game. For instance, you may want the second array to contain only two elements and the third array to contain only one. Using a 3x3 array for this would therefore allocate memory for three more elements than you require.

It is possible in Java to declare a two-dimensional array by specifying only the length of the first dimension and omitting the length of the second.

```
char[][] board = new char[3][];
```

We now have a two-dimensional array with three elements defined in the first dimension. Each of these three elements is a reference to a single-dimensional array object, and each of these references does not currently reference a single-dimensional array object. So we can therefore create new single-dimensional array objects of varying lengths and assign these references to them, as follows:

```
board[0] = new char[3];
board[1] = new char[2];
board[2] = new char[1];
```

The table we used earlier to illustrate the two-dimensional array for the tic-tac-toe game board would now look like this for the new game board:

Board Indices	0	1	2
0	Element [0][0]	Element [1][0]	Element [2][0]
1	Element [0][1]	Element [1][1]	No element
2	Element [0][2]	No element	No element

So how do we get the length of these individual arrays by accessing the `length` attribute? The length of the first dimension of the array is accessed as usual using `board.length`. The length of the arrays of the second dimension can be accessed similarly.

```
for(int counter=0; counter<board.length; counter++)
    System.out.println(board[counter].length);
```

The point to note is that `board[0]`, `board[1]`, and `board[2]` all reference array objects, just like `board` does. The difference is that `board` is a reference to a two-dimensional array object whereas `board[0]`, `board[1]`, and `board[2]` are references to one-dimensional array objects (you can see that `board` represents the table and `board[0]`, `board[1]`, and `board[2]` represent the columns of the table).

A good example of where you may require arrays of varying lengths is if you wanted to create a variable for every day of the year. Maybe each element, say of type `int`, could store the number of hours you have spent on your computer for a day in that year (what's 365 multiplied by 24 again?). You could just create an array as follows.

```
int[] hoursOnComputer = new int[365];
```

The problem with this would be if you wanted to access the days of the year based on what month it was. You would need to accumulate all of the days in the months up until the target month and then add to this figure the day of the target month, eventually giving you the index value for the element representing the day that you require. Preferably, you would implement each day as a two-dimensional array.

```
int[][] hoursOnComputer = new int[12][31];
```

Here we specify the maximum possible days in any of the months, which is 31. However, there are some months with less than 31 days in them, which means we allocate memory that is not required for the months with 30 days and February (which has 28 or 29 days, depending on whether it is a leap year).

The example `ComputerHours.java` creates a two-dimensional array, allocating the correct number of elements for each month in the year specified. Here we can use the `switch` statement that we created in Chapter 2, which returns the number of days in a given month and year.

```
public class ComputerHours
{
    public static int getTotalDays(int month, int year)
    {
        switch(month)
        {
            case 0: case 2: case 4: case 6:
            case 7: case 9: case 11:          // 31 days
```

Chapter 3

```
                    return 31;

          case 3: case 5: case 8: case 10:    //  30 days
               return 30;

          case 1:                             //  28 or 29 days

               if(year % 4 != 0)
                    return 28;
               else if(year % 400 == 0)
                    return 29;
               else if(year % 100 == 0)
                    return 28;
               else
                    return 29;

          default:
               System.out.println("Error, Invalid month
                    index = " + month);
               return -1;
     }
}

public static void main(String args[])
{
     int year = 2002;
     int totalElements = 0;
     int[][] hours = new int[12][];

     System.out.println("The year is " + year);

     for(int i=0; i<hours.length; i++)
          hours[i] = new int[getTotalDays(i, year)];

     for(int i=0; i<hours.length; i++)
     {
          System.out.println("Month "+i+" contains
               "+hours[i].length+" days");
          for(int j=0; j<hours[i].length; j++)
          {
               hours[i][j] = 24;
               totalElements++;
          }
     }

     System.out.println("Total elements allocated = " +
          totalElements);
     }
}
```

When you run this program, the output should be similar to the screen shot on the following page.

First, we declare and initialize a two-dimensional array, only specifying that it contains 12 elements that are empty references to undefined array objects of one dimension.

```
int[][] hours = new int[12][];
```

Then we can initialize these 12 array elements to reference one-dimensional array objects of a specified length on the fly. These lengths are

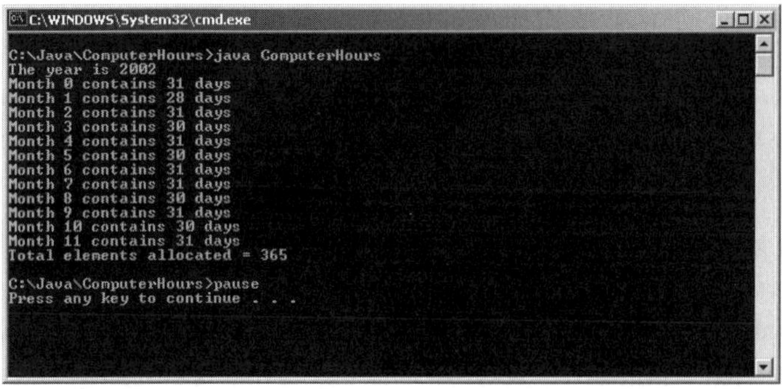

Figure 3-5

retrieved from the method `getTotalDays(int month, int year)`. This method returns the number of days in the month and year, defined as arguments to the method.

```
for(int i=0; i<hours.length; i++)
    hours[i] = new int[getTotalDays(i, year)];
```

Finally, all of the array data elements are assigned the value of `24`, and each time the variable `totalElements` is incremented by 1.

```
for(int i=0; i<hours.length; i++)
{
    System.out.println("Month "+i+" contains
        "+hours[i].length+" days");
    for(int j=0; j<hours[i].length; j++)
    {
        hours[i][j] = 24;
        totalElements++;
    }
}
```

The total number of elements assigned a value is printed to the console screen. In this case it is `365` (as you will see when compiling and running the program), which is the correct number of days for the year 2002. Try setting the year to a leap year, like the year 2004. The total elements allocated should change to `366`.

As we have seen, arrays are very useful for listing data of a finite length; that is, you know what the length is going to be when the array object is created. Arrays are not always ideal for listing though. In Chapter 5 we will look at more dynamic means of data storage with classes such as `LinkedList` and `ArrayList`.

Strings

A *string* is simply a collection of characters. In other programming languages, a string is often implemented manually by the programmer using an array of characters. It also often requires a great deal of time writing code to support an array of characters, like allocating memory for them, searching for sub-strings, etc. Arrays of characters can still be programmed in Java.

```
char[] myCharArray = {'U', 's', 'e', ' ', 'a', ' ', 'c', 'l',
    'a', 's', 's'};
```

However, the Java language includes a `String` class as the standard for storing string data. This `String` class is a member of the `java.lang` package and is readily available for you to use in your Java code. We will look at packages in detail in Chapter 5, so don't worry about them for now; all you need to know now is that you may start using the `String` class in your code right away, like this:

```
String myString;
```

Here we have a reference to a `String` object that is currently equal to `null`, ready to be assigned to a `String` object. There are two ways in which you can create a `String` object. The simplest way is to specify a character string enclosed in double quotation marks; this is known as a *string literal*.

```
myString = "String literal";

// you may create a string with no text also
myString = "";
```

We have been using string literals so far in this book as parameters to the method `System.out.println` to print text to the console screen. All string literals are implemented as instances of the `String` class.

The other method for creating a `String` object is the method used to create most other objects in Java: calling a constructor.

```
// constructor that takes a string literal argument
myString = new String("String literal");

// or create a string object with no text
myString = new String("");

// or the default constructor does the same
myString = new String();
```

There is also a constructor that takes an array of characters as a parameter, creating a `String` object with the value of the characters stored in the array.

```
char[] myCharArray = {'c', 'h', 'a', 'r', 's'};
myString = new String(myCharArray);
```

The character string data held in a `String` object is constant; its value cannot be changed once it has been defined. String objects are therefore known as being immutable. The `StringBuffer` class is used for defining character strings that are mutable—the character string data in the object can be changed. We will discuss the `StringBuffer` class a little later in this chapter.

String Concatenation

In Java the + operator, as well as being used for numeric addition, is also used for string concatenation (i.e., joining two string values to create one combined value). In fact, when using the + operator for string concatenation in Java, the `append` method of the `StringBuffer` class is actually used to create a new `String` object with the value of the operands combined.

```
String sentence = "Hello" + " World";
```

Here the two string values are joined together, creating a new `String` object containing the data `"Hello World"`.

You can also use the assignment operator (+=) for string concatenation. The following `SimpleStrings.java` example is a very simple example to get you started using strings.

```
public class SimpleStrings
{
    public static void main(String args[])
    {
        String sentence = "Hello ";
        String word = "World";

        sentence += word;

        System.out.println(sentence);
    }
}
```

When compiling and running this example, you should get output like the following screen shot.

Figure 3-6

When the string concatenation takes place, a new `String` object is created containing the text `"Hello World"` to which the variable `sentence` references. The `String` object with the text `"World"` is still referenced by the variable `word`, and the `String` object with the text `"Hello"` is no longer referenced by `sentence` and is lost.

Strings with Character Escape Sequences

In Chapter 2 we mentioned character escape sequences (please return to that chapter to view a table showing the list of character escape sequences). These character escape sequences are used with strings to perform special printing tasks at the point in which they appear in the text. Let's take for example the newline character escape sequence \n. This escape sequence moves the print caret onto a new line; it is not two characters like \ and n but one.

```
System.out.println("Move to a new line");
System.out.print("Also move to a new line\n");
```

The first line of code here uses the method `println`, which is a member of the object `out` that in turn is a static member of the class `System`.

This method prints whatever value is passed to it to the console screen and moves the caret position to the beginning of the next line. The method `print` in the second line of code only prints text to the console screen, leaving the caret position where it is after the given text is printed without moving onto the next line. However, we include the newline \n character escape sequence onto the end of the printed string. This will move the caret position to a new line similarly to the first line of code.

The character escape sequences are actually characters themselves, in case you have not yet realized. This means they all have numeric values, just like the letter A has the numeric value 65 and \n has the value 10.

```
System.out.print("New line here too" + (char)10);
```

Here we typecast the value 10 to a type char, which, when appended to the string literal "New line here too", creates a new String object with the newline character escape sequence as the end character.

You can therefore set any character in the string as a character escape sequence.

```
String quote = "Well I've had a wonderful time,\n but
     this wasn't it";

System.out.println(quote);
```

This code will print all of the text up until the character escape sequence \n, and at this point, the caret position is moved onto the new line, where the remaining (hopefully untrue) text is printed.

There may be a time where you need to print out the text that makes up a character escape sequence; we may try the following code.

```
System.out.println("You use \n to go to a new line");
```

This text will move the caret onto a new line after the text "You use " has been printed to the console and then only the text after the \n is printed. What you need to do is include another preceding backslash character (\) with the escape sequence text as follows.

```
System.out.println("You use \\n to go to a new line");
```

This code will print the text that we initially intended. It's quite ironic actually that we change the text by adding a backslash character (\) in order to ensure that the text is printed as it was before we changed it (by doing this, we are actually escaping the \ character). Anyway, you may add the backslash character to any of the character escape sequences if you want to print the actual text.

Printing special characters is also implemented using character escape sequences such as single and double quotation marks. For example, the double quotation marks in Java are used to delimit the text for a string literal. What if we want to enclose a quote in double quotation marks followed by the person who said the quote? We could not just type out the text as it is read. We would need to add a backslash character (\) to any special characters in the text that we just wanted to be treated as normal characters.

```
String quote = "\"I find television very educating. Every time
somebody turns on the set, I go into the other room and read
a book.\", Groucho Marx";
```

You may want to set the value of a character variable to the single quotation character ('). To do this, you must precede the character symbol with a backslash character (\) as follows.

```
char normalCharacter = 'A';
char singleQuotation = '\'';
```

You should take a break from programming now and go in search of Groucho Marx's most famous quotes, which are very funny.

Arrays of Strings

So far we have looked at arrays of primitive data types, like int and boolean. Here we look at arrays of Strings, which are objects. The code is mostly the same; the problem is adapting your mind to understanding that Strings are different because they are objects, and therefore the array elements reference other objects of type String; they are not actually the data itself, like they are for primitive data types. We can declare an array of Strings, as follows.

```
String[] names;
```

We can initialize the array similar to the way we learned in the "Arrays" section earlier.

```
names = new String[5];
```

This code creates an array of length 5 and of type String. Each element in the array is a reference to a String object, each of which currently is equal to null; hence, they do not currently reference a String object.

We can then create String objects and assign them to be referenced by elements in the array.

```
names[0] = "Glenn";              // string literal
names[1] = new String("Andrew"); // constructor
```

Remember, there are two ways to create String objects, defining a String as a string literal or by using a constructor of the String class. Here, the first two elements in the array reference objects, whereas the other three elements (with indices 2, 3, and 4, respectively) remain equal to null (not referencing a String object).

As the elements in the array are just references, we could swap the references of the first two elements, as follows.

```
String saveString = names[0];
names[0] = names[1];
names[1] = saveString;
```

Now the first element references the String object containing the text "Andrew" and the second element references the String containing the text "Glenn". No new String objects are created in these three lines of code; the references are simply swapped.

We can also use the alternate method for initializing the string array.

```
names = {"Glenn", "Andrew", "Jim", "Wes", "Leeloo"};
// who is the fifth element?
```

Or more importantly, you can create a `String` object using constructors also.

```
names = {new String("Glenn"), new String("Andrew"),
    new String("Jim"), new String("Wes"),
    new String("Leeloo")
    };
```

This technique is more important to note because most other objects are created using their constructors like we have used above, whereas `String` objects can also be created specially using string literals.

Program Arguments

In case you haven't realized it thus far, we have already been declaring an array of `String` objects, from the first example until now, as a parameter to the method `main`.

```
public static void main(String[] args)
{
    // code here
}
```

The parameter `args` is a parameter variable just like we used before when declaring our own methods with parameters, like in Chapter 2. You can call this parameter whatever you like, as it is just an identifier like any other variable you declare, although the type, an array of `String` objects, must remain the same.

```
public static void main(String[] programArguments)
{
    // code here
}
```

A *program argument* is a text value (of which there may be many) that is passed to the program at run time. In Java, program arguments are defined as `String` objects that are passed to the method `main` in the aforementioned `String` array. We must first define program arguments and then write a program to take a look at the arguments. We can create what is known as an echo program, echoing the program arguments to the console screen.

Defining program arguments is very simple. Append text separated by spaces onto the original command line that you have been using to run your programs. Each section of text separated by a space represents one element in the `String` array argument of `main`. We have already looked at the command line used to run Java programs in Chapter 2 and have been using them since, perhaps in the batch file `.bat` that you created for convenience. Let's imagine that we have a program called `Echo.java`, which has been compiled to create a class file called `Echo.class`. This command line assumes also that the program is situated in the directory `c:\java\Echoapp\` and that the `java.exe` program is situated in the directory `c:\j2sdk1.4.1_01\bin\`. The following command line would be entered in order to run the program `Echo.class`.

```
c:\j2sdk1.4.1_01\bin\java.exe c:\java\Echoapp\Echo
```

You can enter this text in the command prompt or in a batch file and then run the batch file. Ideally, if all of your paths were set, this command would be entered as follows.

```
java Echo
```

For more details on this, please refer back to Chapter 2.

Now you need to add some text onto the end of the command, like so.

```
java Echo who what where when why
```

 NOTE: If you are using an integrated development environment (IDE) to execute your Java programs, there should be an option somewhere to specify program arguments for your program. Try the `Project` menu item and then `Settings` or `Options`. There should be a text dialog somewhere for you to enter the arguments. Otherwise, you will just have to run the program manually using the command line.

Now we need to create an echo program to test that the program arguments are working. Here is the code for the example `Echo.java`.

```java
public class Echo
{
    public static void main(String args[])
    {
        System.out.println("There are " + args.length +
            " arguments:");

        for(int i=0; i<args.length; i++)
            System.out.println(args[i]);
    }
}
```

When specifying the program arguments `who`, `what`, `where`, `when`, and `why` when running the program `Echo.java`, you should get output similar to the following screen shot.

Chapter 3

```
C:\WINDOWS\System32\cmd.exe

C:\Java\Echo>java Echo who what where when why
There are 5 arguments:
who
what
where
when
why

C:\Java\Echo>pause
Press any key to continue . . .
```

Figure 3-7

The `length` member of the array object is used to control which array elements are accessed. In other programming languages, the number of program arguments needs to be specified as a separate variable using a second parameter of `main`; in Java it does not, as the array object itself stores this information.

A Tour of the String Class

The String class provides a variety of useful methods for manipulating String objects. Remember that the text of a String object cannot be changed, which means that many of its methods are read-oriented or return a new String object of the required changes.

Comparing Two String Values

In order to compare the text values of one String object to another, you cannot just use the equality operator (==) because this will test if two variables reference the same object. The method equals, a member of the String class, can be used to compare two string values, where you may specify a String object as a parameter to test against, returning true if the text values of the two strings are equal and false if they are not.

```
String a = "hello";
String b = "hello";

if(a.equals(b) == true)
    System.out.println("The string values are equal");
```

 NOTE: You may actually specify any object as an argument to the method equals, not just String objects, as all objects contain the method toString, which returns a String object representation of that object. We will look at this in Chapter 4 when we start creating our own classes/objects and can take a proper look at the method toString().

 NOTE: As you can see in the previous example, we have added "== true" after the method call, but this is really not essential; we could equally have the following if statement.

```
if(a.equals(b))
```

If we were checking if "a" was not equal to "b", we may have...

```
if(a.equals(b) == false)
```

In our shortened form, we can use the ! operator to create the following if statement, which would also check if the statement was false.

```
if(!a.equals(b))
```

This if statement would return the value true, as both of the text values of strings a and b are equal. However, the method equals is case sensitive. If you want to ignore case sensitivity when testing if two strings are equal in value, you can use the method equalsIgnoreCase.

```
String a = "hELLo";
String b = "Hello";

if(a.equalsIgnoreCase(b) == true)
    System.out.println("Ignoring case, they are equal");
```

The equals methods are used to test if two string values are equal or not equal, with the return type being boolean, true or false. You may want to compare two string values lexicographically, testing if one string is greater than or less than the other. This can be seen as similar to an alphabetical test, but instead of comparing letters in the alphabet, the letters to compare are the Unicode values of the characters in each string, which is fine for alphabetical letters since their Unicode/ASCII values are sequentially ordered anyway.

The method `compareTo` returns an `int` value after comparing two string values lexicographically. The method returns 0 if the characters in the `String` object are equal to those in the argument parameter, a negative number if the characters in the `String` object are less than the string argument parameter, and a positive number if the characters in the `String` object are greater than the string argument parameter.

Similar to the method `equals`, the method `compareTo` is case sensitive. There is another method called `compareToIgnoreCase` that is not case sensitive. The following example, `StringSorter.java`, arranges a list of names into alphabetical order using the method `compareTo` to compare the string values, implementing a well-known sorting algorithm called bubble sort.

```java
public class StringSorter
{
    public static void main(String args[])
    {
        String list[] = {"Glenn", "Andrew", "Jim", "Wes", "Brendan"};
        String saveString;

        for(int i=0; i<list.length-1; i++)
        {
            for(int j=0; j<list.length-1-i; j++)
            {
                if(list[j].compareTo(list[j+1]) > 0)
                {
                    saveString = list[j];
                    list[j] = list[j+1];
                    list[j+1] = saveString;
                }
            }
        }

        System.out.println("In Alphabetical Order...");

        for(int i=0; i<list.length; i++)
            System.out.println(list[i]);
    }
}
```

Chapter 3

When you compile and run this code, you should get output displaying the list of names in alphabetical order, similar to the following screen shot.

Figure 3-8

The bubble-sort algorithm is one of the simplest and therefore one of the slowest sorting algorithms. For future reference, the quick-sort algorithm is a much faster sorting algorithm, yet more difficult to implement.

Retrieving String Data

The simplest data to retrieve from a string value is a single character at a specified location or index in the string. The following code will run through the string `str`, printing each character individually, one per line.

```
String str = "Super String";

for(int i=0; i<str.length(); i++)
    System.out.print(str.charAt(i));
```

This code introduces us to two new methods. The first is the method `length`, which simply returns the number of characters in the string. The second method is `charAt`, which takes an index parameter of type `int` and returns the `char` value of the character in the string at the index position specified.

You can also retrieve a sub-string of a string using the method `sub-string`. The method has two forms, one taking the beginning index as a parameter of type `int` and the other taking two parameters: the beginning and end indices, both of type `int`. Both methods do not change the current string to which they belong, as string values cannot be changed, but they return a newly created `String` object.

```
String str = "This is interesting";
String sub = str.substring(8);
// sub value is "interesting";

sub = str.substring(8,11);
// sub value is "int";
```

You may want to search an array for characters and sub-strings. The method `indexOf` can be used to check if a sub-string exists inside of a string value at a given index position. For example, you would say that the sub-string "`lo Wor`" exists in the string "`Hello World`" at index position 3 in the source string. This is because the character `l` is at index 3 in the source string just as the first character `H` is at index 0 in the source string. The code to check for this sub-string is as follows:

```
String str = "Hello World";
String sub = "lo Wor";
int returnValue = str.indexOf(sub);

if(returnValue != -1)
    System.out.println("sub-string found at index " + returnValue);
else
    System.out.println("sub-string not found");
```

The method `indexOf` returns an `int` value that is the index position in the string where the sub-string closest to the start of the string is found. If no sub-string is found, the method returns the value −1. It is possible that you may want to find the index position of further sub-strings inside a string. For example, the string "`she sells sea shells on the` sea shore" contains two instances of the sub-string "she." Another method called `indexOf` takes two parameters; the first is again the sub-string to test, and the second is the index position to begin searching from. Therefore, we can test for many instances of a sub-string in a string, as follows:

```
String str = "she sells sea shells on the sea shore";
String sub = "she";
int index = 0;

do
{
    index = str.indexOf(sub, index);
    if(index !=-1)
    {
        System.out.println("sub-string found at index " + index);
        index++;
    }
} while(index !=-1);
```

In the `do while` loop, the value of the variable `index` is assigned the return value from the method `indexOf`. This method is passed the sub-string value `she` to search for and also the current value of `index`, which is the index position to start searching from. Each time we find a sub-string, the value of index is incremented by 1. This is because we don't want to find the same sub-string over and over again; we want to search from the position in the string after the last position where a sub-string was found.

The following example, `LetterCounter.java`, checks every letter in a string, calculates how many of each letter exists in the string, and prints the amounts to the console screen.

```
public class LetterCounter
{
    public static void main(String args[])
    {
        String str = "making games requires knowledge of boring
            things too";
        int index;
        int totalChars;

        System.out.println(str + "\n");

        for(int i=(int)'a'; i<(int)'z'+1; i++)
        {
            index = 0;
            totalChars = 0;
            do
            {
                index = str.indexOf((char)i, index);
                if(index !=-1)
                {
                    totalChars++;
                    index++;
                }
            } while(index != -1);
```

```
        if(totalChars != 0)
            System.out.println(totalChars + " letter " +
                (char)i + "'s found");
    }
}
```

When running this code, you should get output similar to the following screen shot.

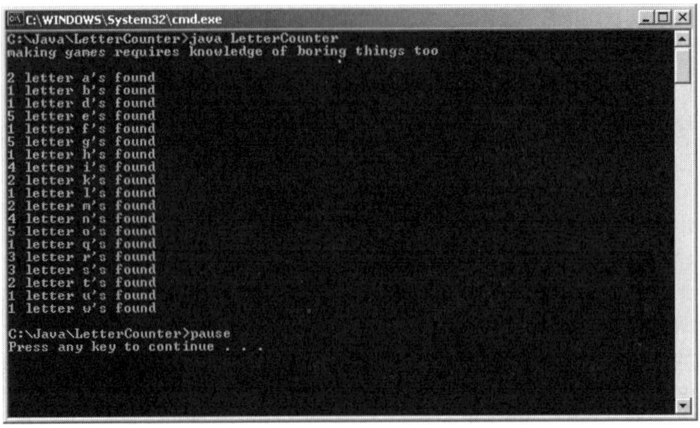

Figure 3-9

Here we use another alternative to the method `indexOf`, where the first parameter is a `char` value instead of a `String` sub-string value. There is also a method called `lastIndexOf` that will find the last instance of a sub-string or character inside a given string. It has all of the parameter variations of the method `indexOf`. The difference between the methods `indexOf` and `lastIndexOf` is that `lastIndexOf` searches from the end of the string to the beginning, whereas `indexOf` searches from beginning to end. Instead of specifying a second parameter as the start index to begin searching from, specify the end index to begin searching from. For example, finding the index of the last `o` in the string "`Hello World`," you would use the following code.

```
String str = "Hello World";
int lastIndex = str.lastIndexOf('o');
```

To find the index position of the second to last `o` in the string "`Hello World`," which is also the first, you would add the following code:

```
int nextLastIndex = str.lastIndexOf('o', lastIndex - 1);
```

This search will find the next `o` character from the index position where the last `o` character was found, less one, searching from the letter `W` to the beginning of the string.

Manipulating String Data

There are several useful methods that can be used to create new string objects that are modified versions of the original string in some way. The methods `toLowerCase` and `toUpperCase` will return newly created

`String` objects containing text with characters all in lowercase and uppercase, respectively.

```
String str = "Hello World";
String lowerCase = str.toLowerCase();
String upperCase  = str.toUpperCase();
```

The method `toLowerCase` does not change the characters in the `String` object that `str` references to all lowercase characters, but returns a new `String` object containing this value. If you wanted `str` to reference a `String` object that was a version of itself but with all its characters changed to lowercase, you could implement the code as follows.

```
String str = "Hello World";
str = str.toLowerCase();
```

The methods `indexOf` and `lastIndexOf` are case sensitive when searching for characters and sub-strings of a string. This is where the methods `toLowerCase` and `toUpperCase` come in handy. If you want to ignore the case of characters, it is often useful to create versions of the source string and test strings that are all of equal case, either all lowercase or all uppercase. You can then perform the search without worrying about case sensitivity, as you have (maybe just temporarily) fixed all characters to the same case anyway.

Another useful method is `trim`. This method will simply remove any spaces from the start and end of a string.

```
String str = "    Hello World    ";
str = str.trim(); // str now equals "Hello World";
```

Again, this method does not change the `String` object it belongs to but returns a new `String` object with the changes.

The method `valueOf` is used to convert a data value into its `String` representation. This method is overloaded to accept all of the data types, namely values of primitive data types. All of the primitive data types can be passed as parameters to the method `valueOf` in its various overloaded forms.

```
int number = 1234567;
String str = String.valueOf(number);
```

This code creates a new `String` object with the value `1234567` converting the numeric value into a string value where the numbers in the string are now represented as characters. Furthermore, the method `valueOf`, which takes a parameter of type `int`, is static and can therefore be accessed without a `String` object being created, using the name of the class to access it: `String.valueOf`. Here are a few examples of the overloaded method `valueOf` accepting different data types.

```
char character = '&';
String str = String.valueOf(character);

double Pi = 3.141592653589793;
str = String.valueOf(Pi);

boolean isCorrect = true;
```

Chapter 3

```
str = String.valueOf(isCorrect);      // str equals "true"

String empty = null;
str = String.valueOf(empty);          // str equals "null"
```

There is also a `valueOf` method that takes an array of characters as a parameter and returns the `String` object representation of the characters.

```
char[] characters = {'S', 'e', 't', ' ', 't', 'o', ' ', 's', 't',
    'r', 'i', 'n', 'g'};
String str = String.valueOf(characters);
```

Converting from strings to primitive data types (for example, converting a string representation of a number to an actual number stored in, say, a variable of type `int`) is discussed in Chapter 5.

The method `replace` is another useful method that replaces all of a specified character with a new character, returning a new `String` object with the desired changes.

```
String str = "thi% do&% mak& %&n%& r&ally";
str = str.replace('%', 's');
str = str.replace('&', 'e');

// str equals "this does make sense really"
```

This code simply replaces all instances of the character % with the character s and all instances of the character & with the character e, with each call to the method `replace` returning a newly created `String` object.

A Word on Regular Expressions

In order to gain a complete understanding of regular expressions, it would take many pages which we sadly cannot spare in this book, as they are not overly essential to games programming. What we can do, however, is tell you what they are and give you some simple examples from which you can investigate further if you so wish. If, when you read this small subsection, you are completely baffled as to how they work or even what they are, worry not. It is quite likely you may never need to use them, but they can be useful in certain circumstances.

A *regular expression* is a code that is used to match a pattern in a given string and is new to Java 1.4. Regular expressions are made up of normal characters and metacharacters. Normal characters are like letters, numbers, underscores, etc., whereas metacharacters are characters that have a special function and are used in conjunction with normal characters in order to define a type of pattern to match to string data. In the `String` class, you can use the method `matches` to match a regular expression passed as a parameter of type `String` to the characters in a `String` object, returning `true` if the match was found and `false` if it was not.

One of the simplest metacharacters is the full-stop (.), which is treated as any character when attempting to match a pattern. So let's say you had the regular expression "b.tter" and wanted to test this against a string.

```
String str1 = new String("better");
String str2 = new String("butter");
String regex = "b.tter";

str1.matches(regex);      // returns true
str2.matches(regex);      // returns true
```

In this case, matches on both string values will be found as the "." meta-character simply matches the character at that index no matter what (for example, the string "bZtter" would match also).

You can use a regular expression to check if a string only contains alphabetical characters and spaces as follows:

```
String str1 = new String("Only letters and spaces");
String str2 = new String("Other chars :@%#5365");
String regex = "[A-Za-z ]{1,}";

str1.matches(regex);      // returns true
str2.matches(regex);      // returns false
```

The square brackets ([]) indicate that you want to match one of the characters specified between them. The A-Za-z means that the character can be any of the characters from A to Z or a to z, hence ignoring the case. Notice that there is a space after the lowercase z, which actually indicates that a space is included as one of the possible characters to match also. The {1,} code indicates that you want to match one or more instances of any of the characters between the square brackets. Thus, this regular expression finds matches of strings containing one or more characters, where any of the characters contained are either alphabetical or space characters, meaning a match on str1 is found but a match on str2 is not found.

There are many more features to regular expressions, which can be useful for searching and manipulating textual data, which is beyond the scope of this book. An example of its use could be to validate that an e-mail address is of a valid nature, perhaps for an online gaming site account setup. For more on using regular expressions in Java, you should take a look at the method split in the String class and also the classes Pattern and Matcher, which are members of the package java.util.regex. Packages are discussed later in the book in Chapter 5.

We will now take a look at the StringBuffer class, which gives us the ability to store and change the string data itself without having to create new String objects every time a different string value is needed.

Invocation Chaining

Invocation chaining means that you are not limited to merely accessing one class/object member in a given statement with the . operator but may continue to access further members in a given statement. For example, let's say that we wanted to convert an integer value to a String object representation and then retrieve the first digit from the string as a character. We might perform this task as follows:

```
int i = 72;
String str = String.valueOf(i);
char firstChar = str.charAt(0);
System.out.println(firstChar);    // prints 7
```

This code is perfectly fine, but we could have also implemented this code in a neater fashion using invocation chaining as follows.

```
int i = 72;
char firstChar = String.valueOf(i).charAt(0);
System.out.println(firstChar);    // prints 7 also
```

It's quite easy to see how this works. The . operator has a left (left to right) precedence, as seen in the operator precedence table in Chapter 2. With this in mind, we can see that the following statement is evaluated first of all:

```
String.valueOf(i)
```

This will return a new String object representation of the integer variable i passed to it. Then the method charAt is invoked on the new String object, returning the first character in the string to the variable firstChar. You should look at the statement String.valueOf(i) as a reference to the String object itself, which it is, as this is what the method returns. You can then access members of the String object like charAt that we accessed.

If we said that we had a Person object inside a Planet object that in turn was inside a SolarSystem object, and the SolarSystem object was inside a Universe object, we may access the Person object from a reference to the Universe object as follows.

```
Person bob = myUniverse.mySolarSystem.myPlanet.myPerson;
```

A Tour of the StringBuffer Class

Using the String class to represent string data is all very well. However, if you have a program that needs to run at a desired speed, like a game, then preferably all of the memory required would be allocated before the main game loop begins, as allocating new memory and deallocating old memory can use up processor time/power. This can affect the speed of your programs. In many circumstances you cannot help but create new objects on the fly that are required for a dynamically running program, but sometimes there are alternatives. Creating new instances of objects is something that you will come across when programming in Java. The key is to know when to create a new object and when it is more efficient to keep the one you have and simply change the data inside it, which is important for processor-intensive programs, such as games.

When using a String object, any changes to the data mean creating a new String object containing the required changes. The String-Buffer is mutable (the data can be modified), which means that you can use the same object and simply change its contents; you can also handle the amount of memory set aside for the data, as we shall see in due course. The `StringBuffer` class is a member of the package `java.lang` similar to the `String` class and is therefore also readily available for you to use in your code.

StringBuffer Constructors

There are three constructors for the `StringBuffer` class: `String-Buffer()`, `StringBuffer(int length)`, and `StringBuffer (String str)`.

The first constructor, `StringBuffer()`, takes no parameters, creating a new `StringBuffer` object with no string value and a buffer capacity of 16 characters. The string buffer is preallocated memory for the character data of the string to be stored. The buffer capacity is therefore the number of characters that memory is currently allocated to store.

```
StringBuffer myStrBuf = new StringBuffer();
```

The second constructor, `StringBuffer(int length)`, creates a new `StringBuffer` object containing no characters and allocates a buffer of the capacity equal to the value of the argument `length`.

```
StringBuffer myStrBuf = new StringBuffer(50);
```

This code creates a new `StringBuffer` object with a buffer capacity of 50.

The third constructor, `StringBuffer(String str)`, creates a new `StringBuffer` object containing the character values equal to those in the `String` argument `str`.

```
StringBuffer myStrBuf = new StringBuffer("Hello World");

System.out.println("Length = " + myStrBuf.length());
// length equals 11

System.out.println("Capacity = " + myStrBuf.capacity());
// capacity equals 11 + 16 = 27
```

This code first creates a new `StringBuffer` containing the character sequence "`Hello World`." Here the capacity of the string buffer is initialized to the length of the string argument `str`, plus 16.

The second line of code simply prints the length of the string data currently contained in the newly created `StringBuffer` object to the console screen. For this, the method `length`, a member of the `String-Buffer` object, is invoked with the value returned, as we saw for `String` objects that contain a similar method.

The last line of code prints out the current capacity of the string buffer by invoking the method `capacity`; we will look at the length and capacity of `StringBuffer` objects a little later in this section.

A Brief Look at the Method toString

The method `toString` returns a `String` object representing the data contained in the object to which it belongs. The method `toString` is a

member of all classes in Java, as all classes are derived from the class
`Object` from which the method `toString` belongs. Even the `String`
class contains the method `toString`, which simply returns itself. Do not
worry about this fact for now, as it will be fully explained in Chapter 4. For
the time being, all you need to know is that the method `toString` is a
member of the `StringBuffer` class, which returns a newly created
`String` object containing the text equal to that which is contained in the
`StringBuffer` object.

```
StringBuffer myStrBuf = new StringBuffer("Hello World");
String myStr = myStrBuf.toString();
```

By creating a `String` object representation of a `StringBuffer` object,
you can manipulate the data as a `String` object using `String` object
methods.

```
String anotherString = "Hello World";
if(myStr.equals(anotherString))
    System.out.println("string values are equal");
```

This code illustrates a solution if you have a `StringBuffer` object and
you want to test if its string data is equal to that of a `String` object. A
method that is new to Java 1.4 is the method `contentEquals`, a member of the `String` class, which returns `true` if the characters in the
`String` object are equal to those contained in the `StringBuffer` argument. So the previous code could also be implemented as follows:

```
StringBuffer myStrBuf = new StringBuffer("Hello World");
String anotherString = "Hello World";
if(anotherString.contentEquals(myStrBuf))
    System.out.println("string values are equal");
```

If you are looking to perform certain string operations on a `String-
Buffer` object and cannot find the method to perform this task in the
`StringBuffer` class, chances are you will need to create a `String`
object representation of the data and use a suitable method found in the
`String` class instead.

Manipulating StringBuffer Data

We will now look at altering the character values of a `StringBuffer`
object. The simplest method for this is the method `setCharAt`. This
method takes two parameters. The first is the index position of the character to be replaced and the second is the new replacement character.

```
StringBuffer myStrBuf = new StringBuffer("Beware of the beast");
myStrBuf.setCharAt(15, 'l');
// myStrBuf now equals "Beware of the blast"
```

The `StringBuffer` class contains the method `charAt` similar to the
`String` class for retrieving the character at a given index position that is
passed as a parameter to the method.

The method `append` is used to add a value onto the end of the current
value contained in the `StringBuffer` object and is overloaded to accept
all of the different data types.

```
StringBuffer myStrBuf = new StringBuffer("I hate");
myStrBuf.append(" broccoli");
myStrBuf.append(" a lot");
```

The value of the text contained in the `StringBuffer` object referenced by `myStrBuf` will now equal "I hate broccoli a lot." Variables of any data type can be added too.

```
int value = 22;
StringBuffer myStrBuf = new StringBuffer("Value = ");
myStrBuf.append(value);
```

The method `insert` will insert, at a specified position in the string buffer, a string representation of a specified value. Again, this method is over-loaded to accept all of the different data types.

```
StringBuffer myStrBuf = new StringBuffer("I ate broccoli");
myStrBuf.insert(2, 'h');
```

This code inserts the character h into the string buffer at index position 2, giving the `StringBuffer` object the string value "I hate broc-coli." The insertion does not replace characters but simply moves the remaining characters along. The methods `append` and `insert` both increase the capacity of the string buffer by the length, in characters, of the argument.

In order to replace characters, you can use the method `replace`, which takes three parameters: the start index of the region that is to be replaced, the end index of the region that is to be replaced (both of type `int`), and the replacement string of type `String`.

```
StringBuffer myStrBuf = new StringBuffer("I adore broccoli");
myStrBuf.replace(2, 7, "hate");
```

This code will replace the word "adore" with the word "hate." The words are of different lengths to illustrate that you may replace larger sections of text with smaller sections and vice versa.

If you just want to remove a section of characters from the string buffer, the methods `delete` and `deleteCharAt` can be used. The `delete` method simply takes two parameters: a start index and end index for the section of the string buffer that you wish to be removed.

```
StringBuffer myStrBuf = new StringBuffer("I do not hate broccoli");
myStrBuf.delete(2,9);
```

This code removes the characters "do not " (removing a space on the end also) from the string buffer, leaving the string value "I hate broc-coli" once again. The method `deleteCharAt` takes one parameter, which is simply the index position in the string buffer of the character that you wish to remove.

The `Broccoli.java` example continues to remove the first charac-ter from a `StringBuffer` object initially containing the text "I hate broccoli", each time printing the remaining characters in the string buffer to the console screen. Here is the code:

```
public class Broccoli
{
```

Chapter 3

```
public static void main(String args[])
{
    StringBuffer myStrBuf = new StringBuffer("I hate broccoli");
    while(myStrBuf.length() > 0)
    {
        System.out.println(myStrBuf);
        myStrBuf.deleteCharAt(0);
    }
}
```

When you compile and run this code, you should get output similar to the following screen shot.

Figure 3-10

As you can see, each time the code block for the `while` loop is executed, the first character in the string buffer is removed. When printed each time on a new line, the original text "`I hate broccoli`" eventually reads down, as well as across.

Length and Capacity of the StringBuffer

Just to differentiate, the length of a `StringBuffer` object refers to the number of characters, whereas the capacity refers to the size of the string buffer (the allocated memory slots where characters can be placed) in the `StringBuffer` object. The method `setLength` can be used to set the length of the character string in the `StringBuffer` object, taking a parameter of type `int` as the new length.

```
StringBuffer myStrBuf = new StringBuffer("Hello World");
myStrBuf.setLength(5);      // now equal to "Hello"
```

If the new length is less than the current length, the value is truncated to the specified size. If the length is increased, then for every new character, a null character (in Unicode, \u0000) is appended to the string.

The method `ensureCapacity` will set the capacity of the string buffer to a minimum capacity to which it will not fall under, taking a parameter of type `int` as the minimum capacity. This means that you can set up your `StringBuffer` object so that it will not need to allocate any more memory if you know the maximum amount of memory that you will require. Suppose you know that your string data will never exceed 100 characters; you can simply ensure that the capacity of the string buffer is always a minimum of 100 from the beginning.

 NOTE: When calling `ensureCapacity`, the capacity is actually set to the greater of either the argument value or the current capacity of the string buffer multiplied by 2, plus 2.

A Tour of the StringTokenizer Class

The `StringTokenizer` class is used to store and handle groups of strings, known as *tokens*, that are combined into one long string. An example of its advantage is when reading in data from a file. Let's say you store a high-score list in a file for a game that you have made; each line in the file consists of three data strings used to store information about the username, e-mail address, and high score, respectively, with any two of these strings being separated by a comma character. For example:

```
String line1 =
    new String("Glenn,glenn@chopsewage.com,12000");
String line2 =
    new String("Andrew,andrew@dreamcircle.co.uk,9000");
```

The individual data strings, such as the username, can then be treated as tokens of the full string, and the comma can be treated as the delimiter of the tokens. The delimiter is simply a character used to separate tokens. The `StringTokenizer` class belongs to the package `java.util` (which we will look at in detail in Chapter 5). For the time being, we will use the class by specifying its complete path name, including the package to which it belongs. (Again, we will learn about packages in Chapter 5, so do not worry about them for now.)

In the following example, `SimpleTokens.java`, we cycle through an array of strings. Each string is imagined to be a line of text read in from a file containing a username, e-mail address, and high score gained, with each value separated by a comma character. (We are not actually reading in from a file in this example but just creating an array of strings that may have been data read in from a file. We will look at reading in files for real in Chapter 6.) For each line of text, a new `StringTokenizer` object is created to handle extracting the individual string tokens and printing their values to the console screen. Here is the code:

```
public class SimpleTokens
{
    public static void main(String args[])
    {
        String[] data =
            {
                "Glenn,glenn@chopsewage.com,12000",
                "Andrew,andrew@dreamcircle.co.uk,9000"
            };

        String[] tokenType = {"username", "email", "high score"};
```

Chapter 3

```
for(int i=0; i<data.length; i++)
{
    int tokenIndex = 0;
    System.out.println("New line of data...");
    java.util.StringTokenizer tokenizer = new
        java.util.StringTokenizer(data[i],",");
    while(tokenizer.hasMoreTokens())
    {
        String token = tokenizer.nextToken();
        System.out.println("\t"+tokenType[tokenIndex]+"
            "+token);
        tokenIndex++;
    }
}
}
```

When you compile and run this example code, you should get output similar to the following screen shot.

Figure 3-11

In this example code, we use the most common constructor of the StringTokenizer class that takes two arguments.

```
java.util.StringTokenizer tokenizer =
    new java.util.StringTokenizer(data[i],",");
```

The first argument is the String object containing the data that we wish to "tokenize." The second is a string representing the delimiter of the tokens. The delimiter does not need to be one character but may be a number of characters in the string where each character acts as a delimiter. You should note if the delimiter consists of multiple characters; then the string value itself is not a delimiter, but its characters are all individual delimiters. Once the StringTokenizer object is created, we then extract the tokens using the methods hasMoreTokens and next-Token. StringTokenizer contains an index position, which moves along the string each time a token is found. The method hasMore-Tokens returns true if there is at least one more token available from the index position onward. From here, we use the method nextToken to get this next available token from the index position, which nextToken returns as a String object, moving the index position forward in the process.

To find out how many more tokens are left to get in the `String-Tokenizer` as a numeric value, you can use the method `countTokens` if necessary, which returns the number of tokens left from the index position to the end.

Summary

Thank goodness that's all over. I'm sure it wasn't that bad after all. Anyway, in this chapter you have cemented your learning of the basics of Java programming. From here on, it is not so basic, which does not mean that it is overly difficult, but some bits can get a bit tricky. In the next chapter we will start creating multiple classes and objects of our very own and try to learn what the heck polymorphism is all about.

Chapter 3

Chapter 4

Multiple Classes

"There are too many people and too few human beings."

—Robert Zend

Introduction

In order to truly understand object-oriented programming, we must define our own classes and derive objects from them. In the previous chapter you created objects from a variety of string-related classes, accessing their methods and attributes. In this chapter you will learn the fundamentals of making your own classes, using inheritance and interfaces, and you will learn about the structure of classes in the Java language.

 NOTE: If you are not sure about classes in general, you may want to refresh your memory by returning to the beginning of Chapter 2 where we discussed some important aspects of classes in relation to their members and constructors and objects in general.

Creating Main Class Objects

The only part of your code in an application that is required to be static is the method `main`, as this is invoked from the start. The method `main` is defined in the main class of your project. So far in this book, all of the examples have simply consisted of one solitary main class defining static members. For those of you who are not used to object-oriented programming, this may seem quite normal. Just start in `main`, declare global methods and variables in the main file, and then go from there, but this is merely escaping the point of OOP in general—using objects.

So let's say we want to make a class to represent a creature, like a human or alien or some other intelligent life form ("intelligent" used loosely). We could make an `Alien` class containing a string value for greeting us in its native language. The following class is an example of how we would implement this class, as we have been doing so far in this book.

```
public class Alien
{
    public static void main(String args[])
    {
        greeting = "Dak-Dak-DaDakDakDak";

        System.out.println("Alien says: "+greeting);
    }

    static String greeting;
}
```

Just enter this basic code for now into a source file `Alien.java`, and we will adapt it accordingly throughout this section.

The class `Alien` contains the `String` member `greeting`, which is static. The problem is that our `Alien` class basically represents one alien because `greeting` is static. We can still create objects of the `Alien` class at the moment, however, similar to when we created objects of the `String` class in the previous chapter. For example, we could add the following code somewhere in `main`.

```
Alien martian = new Alien();
```

This code declares a reference to an `Alien` object called `martian` and then assigns it to reference a newly created `Alien` object. The constructor invoked is a default constructor for the object, as the object does not define one of its own (this was discussed in detail in the constructor section at the beginning of Chapter 2).

However, we want to make many instances of the `Alien` class, each having its own copy of the variable `greeting`. So we need to make the variable `greeting` non-static. This simply entails removing the keyword `static` from the declaration of `greeting`. We can also create our own constructor for the `Alien` class that takes a `String` argument value to assign to `greeting`.

So in the example `Alien.java`, we can adapt the `Alien` class so that it is suitable for creating individual `Alien` objects, as follows.

```
public class Alien
{
    //  constructor
    public Alien(String greeting)
    {
        this.greeting = greeting;
    }

    public static void main(String args[])
    {
        // create two new aliens
        Alien martian = new Alien("Dak-Dak-DaDakDakDak");
        System.out.println("First alien says: " + martian.greeting);

        Alien plutonian = new Alien("Hi, erm... I'm from Pluto");
        System.out.println("Second alien says: " +
            plutonian.greeting);
    }
```

```
    String greeting;
}
```

When you run this code, you should get output similar to the following screen shot.

Figure 4-1

Here we create two new `Alien` objects from the entry point of the program in the method `main`. You should treat `main` as almost a separate method from the main class; it may seem strange that `main` is inside the main class and not separate, but in Java all code must be contained within the code block of a class or interface, even `main` (we shall see about interfaces toward the end of this chapter). The code for this example is quite straightforward apart from one new keyword, `this`, which we have used in the constructor.

The Keyword this

The keyword `this` is used inside non-static/object methods as a reference to the object to which the method belongs from within the object itself—a reference to itself. For example, take a look at the constructor for the `Alien` class that we have just declared where we used the keyword `this`.

```
public Alien(String greeting)
{
    this.greeting = greeting;
}
```

We have given the `String` parameter of the constructor the same name as one of the members of the class, calling both variables `greeting`. This is possible in Java and means that any use of the identifier will be in reference to the local variable `greeting` that is a parameter of the constructor. In this case, we need some way to access the greeting member of the class and not the parameter value, so we can use the keyword `this`, which will act as a reference to the current object to which the constructor belongs. The keyword `this` can be used in non-static methods in the same way as in the constructor of the `Alien` class.

NOTE: Just in case this has misled you slightly, the name of the parameter variable did not need to be called `greeting`. It is called `greeting` to illustrate a situation where you would need to use the keyword `this`, but it can be any name you like. Some people prefer to give parameters the same name as members of the class and then use the keyword `this` as appropriate, whereas others will give the parameter a different name altogether, maybe by using a naming convention, such as starting all

Chapter 4

parameter names with an underscore (_). The latter is obviously the least error-prone.

```
public Alien(String _greeting)
{
    greeting = _greeting;
}
```

Because there is no local variable called `greeting`, the keyword `this` is not required, though it can still be used anyway.

The keyword can be used in many areas. Another notable area is passing a reference for the current object you are in as a parameter to a method. For example, you may have a static method somewhere for printing to the console window the greeting of an `Alien` object, as follows.

```
public static void printGreeting(Alien alien)
{
    System.out.println(alien.greeting);
}
```

From inside an object method (an object method being a non-static method) of the `Alien` class, we could call this method as follows.

```
printGreeting(this);
```

Basically, we are in a method that belongs to the `Alien` object, and we need to send a reference to the method `printGreeting` of the object that we are currently in, which of course is of type `Alien`, so we use the keyword `this`, passing it as a parameter as shown.

Using Multiple Classes

In this section we will start off explaining nested classes before moving on to creating separate classes altogether. In our opinion, you should sit back and glance over the "Nested Classes" section and not get too involved with the code. Of much more interest and importance is creating individual classes and objects, which will come later in this chapter.

Nested Classes

A *nested class* is simply a class that is defined inside of another class, meaning that a nested class is a class that is a member of another class. A class that contains a nested class is known as the enclosing class of the nested class. Nested classes are used when their existence is dependent on another class to which there is a solid parent-child relationship. The use of nested classes can be split into two important areas: inner classes (non-static) and static nested classes.

Inner Classes

An *inner class* is a nested class that only exists within an instance of the enclosing class, which means by definition an inner class is a non-static nested class. To explain this effectively, we shall look at a case example. Let's say we wanted to make a program in which you created objects of type Human as well as objects of type Alien that were members of an instance of an enclosing class called Creatures. The idea is that an instance of the Creatures class is created, and in turn it will create instances of each of its nested classes. The following example, Creatures.java, is how we may implement this:

```java
public class Creatures
{
    public Creatures()
    {
        myAlien = new Alien("Dak-Dak-DaDakDakDak");
        myHuman = new Human("Hello, Bonjour, Hola");
    }

    public class Alien
    {
        public Alien(String greeting)
        {
            this.greeting = greeting;
        }

        String greeting;
    }

    public class Human
    {
        public Human(String greeting)
        {
            this.greeting = greeting;
        }

        String greeting;
    }


    public static void main(String[] args)
    {
        Creatures myCreatures = new Creatures();

        System.out.println("Alien says: " +
            myCreatures.myAlien.greeting);
        System.out.println("Human says: " +
            myCreatures.myHuman.greeting);
    }

    Alien myAlien;
    Human myHuman;
}
```

Chapter 4

When you compile and run this code, you should get output similar to the following screen shot.

Figure 4-2

In this example, we have created two inner classes: `Alien` and `Human`. These inner classes are non-static members of the `Creatures` class, which means that instances of these inner classes can only be created in association with an instance of `Creatures`. We create instances of the inner classes `Alien` and `Human` in the constructor of `Creatures`.

```
public Creatures()
{
    myAlien = new Alien("Dak-Dak-DaDakDakDak");
    myHuman = new Human("Hello, Bonjour, Hola");
}
```

This is perfectly valid because we are inside the object (an instance of the `Creatures` class) in its constructor and are therefore able to access non-static instance members of `Creatures`, like `myAlien` and `myHuman`. The inner classes have complete access to other non-static members of the enclosing class `Creatures`. For example, in the inner class `Human`, you could make a method to check if the variable `myAlien` references an instance of the inner class `Alien`, as follows:

```
public class Human
{
    public Human(String greeting)
    {
        this.greeting = greeting;
    }

    public boolean hasFriend()
    {
        if(myAlien==null)
            return false;
        else
            return true;
    }

    String greeting;
}
```

Then in `main`, the following code could be added to check if `myAlien` references an object.

```
if(myCreatures.myHuman.hasFriend())
    System.out.println("We have visitors, set your weapons to stun");
else
    System.out.println("Of course, earth is the center of the
        universe");
```

Note we could also just use the following `if` statement in `main` to achieve the same result.

```
if(myCreatures.myAlien==null)
```

If we wanted to create an instance of, say, the `Alien` class from outside an instance of `Creatures` (for example, in the `main` method), it would need to be created in association with an instance of `Creatures`. We could do this, as follows, in `main`:

```
public static void main(String[] args)
{
```

```
    Creatures myCreatures = new Creatures();
    Creatures.Alien martian =
        myCreatures.new Alien("DakDakDak");
}
```

The code `myCreatures.new Alien` is the same as using the code
`new Alien` from inside an instance of `Creatures` like `myCreatures`,
so we need to do this when we are in the static method `main`. However,
the new `Alien` object referenced by `martian` still maintains a reference
to its enclosing class (i.e., the object referenced by `myCreatures`, as it
can still access non-static members of its enclosing class). This means
that if we later set `myCreatures` to `null`, hence losing this reference to
that object, the inner class instance referenced by `martian` will still
maintain a reference to it, meaning the garbage collector cannot yet
destroy this data, and the data still exists in memory for the inner class to
access. Garbage collection is discussed in Chapter 12.

  If we want to create instances of the `Alien` and `Human` classes from
outside an instance of `Creatures` irrespective of the existence of a
`Creatures` object, declare the nested classes to be static.

Static Nested Classes

Nested classes are generally made static when they have a strong relationship with the enclosing class, but their existence is independent of an
instance of the enclosing class. Note that this means static nested classes
cannot access non-static members of their enclosing class. Note that a
static nested class does not mean that the members of the class are all
static.

  We might say that, for example, the `Alien` and `Human` classes are
strongly related to the `Creatures` class, but it should also be possible to
treat them independently from the `Creatures` class. This would mean
that, from outside the `Creatures` class when using the `Alien` and
`Human` classes, the word `Creatures` would act almost as a namespace
for the `Alien` and `Human` classes. A *namespace* is simply a keyword that
is used for grouping data, although in Java the best technique for grouping
classes is using packages, which we will discuss in the next chapter.

  The following code is an adapted version of the previous example,
`Creatures.java`, where we define the nested classes `Alien` and
`Human` as `static`. This means that we are able to create instances of
these classes irrespective of an existing instance of the `Creatures`
class.

```
public class Creatures
{
    public static class Alien
    {
        public Alien(String greeting)
        {
            this.greeting = greeting;
        }

        String greeting;
```

Chapter 4

```
    }

    public static class Human
    {
        public Human(String greeting)
        {
            this.greeting = greeting;
        }

        String greeting;
    }

    public static void main(String[] args)
    {
        Alien myAlien = new Alien("Dak-Dak-DaDakDakDak");
        Human myHuman = new Human("Hello, Bonjour, Hola");

        System.out.println("Alien says: " + myAlien.greeting);
        System.out.println("Human says: " + myHuman.greeting);
    }
}
```

This code will create the same output as the previous example seen in
Figure 4-2.

Here we create a new instance of each of the nested classes, `Alien`
and `Human`, which are now static and accessible without creating an
instance of `Creatures`. However, it is important to note that we are creating instances of these nested classes from `main`, which is still a member
of `Creatures`, static or not. If the `Creatures` class were a separate
class from the main class of which `main` is a member, we would access
the nested classes as members of the `Creatures` class, as follows.

```
//   when inside the Creatures class
Alien myAlien = new Alien("Dak-Dak-DaDakDakDak");

//   when outside the creatures class
Creatures.Alien myAlien =
    new Creatures.Alien("Dak-Dak-DaDakDakDak");
```

The use of nested classes is a design issue for the structure and reusability of your code, which is not that important if you are just making a
simple game but is important if you are building up a games library of
related classes.

You should also be aware that a nested class could itself contain a
nested class.

```
class TopLevelClass
{
    class NestedClass
    {
        class NestedNestedClass
        {
        }
    }
}
```

A class that contains a nested class but itself is not nested inside another class is known as the *top-level class*. We're getting a little complex now and should move on, as you will no doubt want to make classes that are independent of the main class.

Multiple Classes

When programming in Java, all completely independent classes should be entered into separate source files similar to how we have been entering the main class's source code so far in this book—into files of the same name as the class itself with a ".java" file extension. If you are a procedural programmer, this may seem quite strange, but give it time, you will soon see how neat and tidy it makes your code. Gone are the days of bunging up one main file with relatively unrelated methods that would be better placed in libraries for further use.

Using separate files for classes makes your project easier to design, as with object-oriented programming in general. Splitting a project up into smaller modules and then dealing with these modules is more efficient, especially for larger projects, and it is also easier for handling the code in a programming team.

So let's take the Alien class and put it into its own source file. We will remove the Human class completely for the time being to keep it as simple as possible, although we will bring it back when we look at inheritance later. In the upcoming example we will also change the name of our main class to MainApp and include another class named Universe as a more appropriate container for storing references to instances of Alien than Creatures in order to save confusion later when we look at inheritance and polymorphism with a Creature class. You should add all of the source files into the same directory as the main class.

The following example contains three classes—MainApp, Universe, and Alien—to be entered into the source files MainApp.java, Universe.java, and Alien.java, respectively. Simply copy these, compile, and run the main application, just like you have been doing. You need to compile the main file MainApp.java and then the compiler will compile the rest of the files that are used in the project automatically and produce a .class file for each of your classes used from there. You can then run the main class as you have been doing so far with the single class projects so far in the book. The other .class files used should also be loaded. Here is the code.

Code Listing 4-1: Alien.java

```
public class Alien
{
    public Alien(String greeting)
    {
        setGreeting(greeting);
    }

    public void setGreeting(String greeting)
    {
```

```
        this.greeting = greeting;
    }

    public String getGreeting()
    {
        return greeting;
    }

    public String toString()
    {
        return greeting;
    }

    private String greeting;
}
```

The Alien class represents an Alien object and is used to store a string value for a greeting from an Alien object. Here we are introduced to two important aspects of OOP in Java: the keyword private and the to-String method. We will discuss these new features after the rest of the code listings for this example.

Code Listing 4-2: Universe.java

```
public class Universe
{
    public Universe(int alienTotal)
    {
        alienList = new Alien[alienTotal];
    }

    public boolean setAlien(int index, Alien alien)
    {
        if(index>=0 && index < alienList.length)
        {
            alienList[index] = alien;
            return true;
        }
        else return false;
    }

    public Alien getAlien(int index)
    {
        if(index >=0 && index < alienList.length)
            return alienList[index];
        else return null;
    }


    public String toString()
    {
        String str = "Total aliens: " + alienList.length + "\n";
        for(int i=0; i< alienList.length; i++)
            str += "Alien " + i + ": " + alienList[i] + "\n";
        return str;
    }

    private Alien[] alienList;
}
```

An instance of the `Universe` class is used to store an array of a specified number of `Alien` objects. This number is passed as an argument to the constructor where a new array of type `Alien` is created of the specified length. Again, this class includes the keyword `private` and also the `toString` method, which will be discussed in a moment.

Code Listing 4-3: `MainApp.java`

```
public class MainApp
{
    public static void main(String[] args)
    {
        Universe universe = new Universe(4);
        universe.setAlien(0, new Alien("Dak-Dak-DaDakDakDak"));
        universe.setAlien(1, new Alien("Hi I'm from Pluto"));
        universe.setAlien(2, new Alien("But I'm from Pluto, I've
            never seen you there"));
        universe.setAlien(3, new Alien("Well I'm from Jupiter, I'll
            eat you all :)"));

        System.out.println(universe);
    }
}
```

When you compile `MainApp.java` and then run `MainApp.class`, you should get output similar to the following screen shot.

Figure 4-3

The main class `MainApp` first creates an instance of `Universe`, referenced by `universe`, passing the value 4 to the `Universe` constructor, which will in turn create an array of type `Alien` and length 4 inside the `universe` object, as you can see in the `Universe` class. We then create four new `Alien` objects, setting each of them to a specific array element index using the method `setAlien` of the `universe` object, which takes the index and `Alien` object reference as its parameters. This is an example of using the `Alien` class completely separated from the `Universe` class; we could simply make `Alien` objects in `MainApp` that have nothing to do with the `Universe` class whatsoever if we desired. We could have a `SolarSystem` class instead of a `Universe` class and create more than one `SolarSystem` object, to which `Alien` objects could be moved from one to another, make some `Planet` objects inside each `SolarSystem` object, and so on.

Anyway, the last bit of code in `MainApp` may seem quite strange, where we pass the reference `universe` to `System.out.println`,

Chapter 4

and then all of the relative information about the data in our program is printed to the screen. This will be explained in due time after we first look at the importance of the keyword `private`.

Controlling Data Access (Public, Protected, Private)

In the previous example, we used the keyword `private` for the very first time, both in the `Universe` class for the array variable `alienList` and in the `Alien` class for the variable `greeting`. The keyword `private` in this instance was used to restrict access from outside the respective classes. This allows you to add security to members of your classes, with any access to the data being handled using public methods in the class, which you make yourself. We have been using the keyword `public` throughout the book so far, which specifies that access be allowed from any other classes. On the other end of the scale, the keyword `private` restricts access from any other classes to that specific data, even from subclasses (subclasses are explained later in the "Inheritance" section). The keyword `protected` is somewhere between `public` and `private` access attributes.

There are actually four access attributes in Java: `public`, `private`, `protected`, and the default access attribute that is used when no access attribute keyword is specified. The default access attribute is very similar to being `public` but not identical, as we shall see below.

The following diagram shows the members of class A in package A that are accessible from a variety of other classes in various situations in respect to class A, based on the access attribute of a member of class A. You may not yet be familiar with some of these circumstances, such as packages and subclasses, but do not worry about this for now, as these will become familiar later in this chapter and in the next chapter. This diagram can act as a reference in the future when choosing your access attributes.

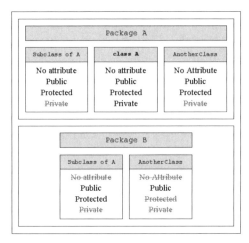

Figure 4-4

This diagram shows that the `public` access attribute means that public data is accessible from any class, anywhere. The `protected` access attribute means that access is allowed from any class inside the same package as class A and any subclasses of class A anywhere. The `private` access attribute means that access is restricted from anywhere outside of class A. "No attribute" simply means that an access attribute is not specified, which means that access is only allowed from classes in the same package as class A. Note that this diagram shows access levels from various classes in respect to class A members. For example, class A might contain the method `doSomething`, which has the access attribute `protected`, as follows:

```
public class A
{
    protected void doSomething()
    {
    }
}
```

This simply means that only classes in the same package as class A can access the method `doSomething`; any attempts from classes outside of package A where class A is in your code will cause a compiler error.

Why Use Access Attributes?

Access attributes are important for controlling access to data, which is important in many respects, not only for the security of your code but for preserving the efficiency too. An example of where you may want to prevent access to members of your classes is so that someone else using your class cannot manipulate the internal variables that make your class what it is. If you make these variables inaccessible, they can only influence changes in those variables via accessible methods that are safe because you have created them yourself, which means you can control what is done with your classes. This is not only suitable for other people using your classes but for you too. If you use methods to manipulate variables of a class, this is already efficient because it is easy to see where access is coming from, meaning it is easy to update code and chase bugs. It is perfectly fine to ignore the access attributes when you are knuckling down hacking away at your code, but it can vastly neaten your code and make it efficient and friendly.

The Static Block

Imagine the scenario: You declare a static variable member of a class, which needs to be assigned its value straight away when the class is loaded, but the code to create this assignment value cannot be made in an assignment statement alone. For example, the assignment value may require repetitive calculations, or it just might be neater on multiple lines. In this case, you can use a static block, which can be added to your code as follows:

```
public class MyClass
{
    public static int[] squares = new int[10];
```

Chapter 4

```
static
{
    //   values assigned
    for(int i=0; i<squares.length; i++)
        squares[i] = i*i;
}
}
```

NOTE: The reason we have declared the static block after the variable declaration of `squares` is because they are dealt with on a line-by-line basis when the class is first loaded to the Java Virtual Machine. If they were the other way around, the static block would not recognize the variable `squares` yet.

Here we have a static array of type `int` and length `10`. The array is initialized when the class is loaded. In order to actually define specified values for the elements of this array, we could have used the initialization block using curly brackets as follows:

```
public static int[] squares = {0, 1, 4, 9, 16, 25};
```

As you can see, entering many values is unsuitable when a simple algorithm could equally enter the code. This is why we can use a static block to perform this code. We could also have initialized the array in the static block and not at the declaration point.

```
public class MyClass
{
    public static int[] squares;

    static
    {
        // initialized
        squares = new int[10];

        // values assigned
        for(int i=0; i<squares.length; i++)
            squares[i] = i*i;
    }
}
```

NOTE: Remember when we discussed the use of `final` variables in Chapter 2, where we mentioned declaring `final` variables without a value and then assigning the value in one of the class constructors later on? Well, similarly, a `static final` value does not need to be assigned immediately at the declaration point but can also be assigned in a static block.

Inheritance

Inheritance is a very important part of object-oriented programming. It is often a worry for many programmers new to the subject. But fear not, as it is easy to understand in Java. *Inheritance* is the ability to derive a new class from an existing class. In this case, the existing class is known as the *base class*, or *super class*, and the new class is known as the *subclass*, or *derived class* of the base class. The subclass then inherits variables and methods from its base class that it can use as if they had been defined in the subclass. However, constructors of the base class are not inherited by its subclasses and neither are certain access attributes, depending on the circumstances. We will look at what is inherited and what isn't later in this section; for now we should understand the fundamentals of inheritance.

The Object Class

Before we begin making our own subclasses, we should understand an essential part of the Java language, the `Object` class, which should help us to understand inheritance a little better. What if I told you that you have been using inheritance all along in all of the classes that we have created so far? In Java, as we might have mentioned in passing before now, all classes are derived from the `Object` class by default, though this is hidden from you in your code. The `Object` class is a member of the `java.lang` package and is a super class of all classes. This means that all of your classes have inherited members of the `Object` class. All of the members inherited from `Object` are methods, and furthermore they are instance methods, which means they only exist when you create an object of your class. At this point, we should look at the most straightforward method inherited from the `Object` class by all classes in Java: the `toString` method.

The toString Method

The `toString` method is used to get a string representation of an object, returning this string representation value of type `String`. Remember back when we used the `toString` method in both the `Universe` class and the `Alien` class to return what was considered an ideal textual representation for the data stored in objects of those classes. So, for example, the `Alien` class's `toString` method returned the `Alien` string value `greeting`, as this was all that basically made our `Alien` objects different from any other `Alien` object.

The key thing to realize is that this method is initially inherited from the `Object` class, but in the `Universe` class and the `Alien` class we override the `toString` method, creating our own version of it. Then, when a string representation of an object of these types is required, the overriding `toString` method that we created is used instead of the `toString` method in `Object`. The string representation of the object is required when printing to the screen, where we appeared to be able to print the object.

```
System.out.println(universe);
```

This code simply invoked the `toString` method that we overrode in the `Universe` class, printing the return value from that method; otherwise it would have printed the value returned from the `toString` method of the `Object` class instead, which is a default textual representation of an object that actually consists of the class's name, followed by the hash code of the object, which we do not need to worry about.

We could similarly have printed this data as follows:

```
System.out.println(universe.toString());
```

The `toString` method is a method similar to any other method, but it is also handled as the default string representation of the object.

The following diagram shows the structure of the source code in Listings 4-1 through 4-3, which, in case you've forgotten, contained the classes `MainApp`, `Universe`, and `Alien`.

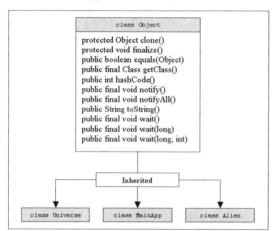

Figure 4-5

All classes inherit these methods from `Object`, as this is always the root class in any class's hierarchy. The following is a list of methods in the `Object` class with a description of what they do.

`protected Object clone()`	This method is used to create a copy of an object and returns it as type `Object`. Only classes that implement the interface `Cloneable` can be cloned. We will discuss interfaces later on in the chapter.
`public boolean equals(Object)`	This method returns `true` if this object is equal to one passed as a parameter. Hence, if this object is the same as that which the parameter currently references, then it returns `true`.
`protected void finalize()`	This method is called by the garbage collector when you are finished with your object, that is, when you no longer hold any references to it. Note that the garbage collector is likely not to call this method right away but when it's ready to, which can be some time after any references to this object no longer exist in your program and it is ready to be collected/removed. So if you override this method and provide code that needs to be handled in real time, it is recommended that you realize when your object is lost and handle this code then, instead of when this method is invoked by the JVM. For further information, see the "Garbage Collection and Creating Objects" section in Chapter 12.
`public final Class getClass()`	Returns a `Class` object of this object. An object of type `Class` can be used for such things as finding if an object is an instance of a given class.

`public int hashCode()`	This method returns a hash code value for the object.
`public string toString()`	As we mentioned earlier, this method is designed so that each object has a string representation of itself. In most cases this method is overridden in a class to return a desired value.

The methods `notify`, `notifyAll`, and the various overloaded `wait` methods concern the use of threads. These methods are discussed in Chapters 7 and 9, where we utilize these methods to help us make our passive rendering as active as possible. That is some way off, but it'll be worth the wait, so keep reading.

Inheriting Your Own Classes

To derive one of your own classes from another class, use the keyword `extends`, as in your class <u>extends</u> another class. Returning to our `Alien` and `Human` example, we could create a base class `Creature` and create `Alien` and `Human` classes that both <u>extend</u> the `Creature` class; that is, they are subclasses of the `Creature` class. In this case the base class must contain members that are true for both `Alien` and `Human` objects, as they will inherit these members and then the `Alien` and `Human` classes would include extra members that are specific to them and not to other `Creature` types. The following example (Listings 4-4 through 4-7) contains four classes: `Beings` (main class), `Creature`, `Alien`, and `Human`. Let's take a look at the code for this example.

 BIG NOTE: There is no multiple inheritance in Java. Any class can only extend one other class. A means of working around this issue is using interfaces, as we shall see toward the end of this chapter.

Code Listing 4-4: `Creatures.java`

```
public class Creature
{
    public Creature(String greeting)
    {
        setGreeting(greeting);
    }

    public void setGreeting(String greeting)
    {
        this.greeting = greeting;
    }

    public String getGreeting()
    {
        return greeting;
    }

    public void speak()
    {
        System.out.println("Creature says: " + greeting);
    }
}
```

```
    private String greeting;
}
```

This class is the base class for a creature in our program, as we assume that all varieties of creatures will require a greeting variable. In this class we require the public methods setGreeting and getGreeting, as the greeting variable is set to private, meaning that it is not itself inherited by any subclasses of Creature but those public methods are inherited and can be used to access greeting, which still exists but is just not inherited. We will discuss this a little later also.

Code Listing 4-5: `Alien.java`

```java
public class Alien extends Creature
{
    public Alien(String greeting)
    {
        super(greeting);
    }

    public void speak()
    {
        System.out.println("Alien says: " + getGreeting());
    }
}
```

As you can see, the Alien class uses the keyword extends after its name declaration followed by the base class Creature that it extends. The Alien class therefore inherits the public methods setGreeting and getGreeting from the Creature class. It does not inherit any constructors from the Creature class; constructors are never inherited.

The Alien class also overrides the method speak in the Creature class to use its own version of this method implementing its own specific code to speak as an Alien object.

We also use the keyword super in the Alien constructor. The keyword super indicates that we are accessing a member of the direct super class. In this case we are calling the constructor of the Creature class using the keyword super in a direct subclass of Creature – Alien. The keyword super is explained in detail a little later in the chapter.

 NOTE: The constructor call of the base class Creature in the Alien class constructor using super(greeting) is not required to actually create the inherited data. If this was not called, the data in Creature would still exist, where by default the value of the variable greeting would merely be set to null (unassigned to a String object). Call the constructor of the super class to initialize the state of the data defined in the Creature class from the constructor of the Alien object that we are creating, where we are basically calling the constructor of the super class as if it were simply a method to initialize the data. It is a common practice in a subclass constructor to make a call to the super class constructor to initialize the state of variables defined in the super class. It is a very useful technique. We will look at the keyword super a little later in the chapter. Furthermore, a call to the super class constructor using super() can only be called first in the constructor before any other code; otherwise, the code will not compile.

Code Listing 4-6: `Human.java`

```java
public class Human extends Creature
{
    public Human(String greeting)
    {
        super(greeting);
    }

    public void speak()
    {
        System.out.println("Human says: " + getGreeting());
    }
}
```

The `Human` class is almost identical to the `Alien` class, except for its implementation of the `speak` method, which is specific to a `Human` object with the text "`Human says: `", whereas an `Alien` object would have "`Alien says: `" before its greeting text. A `Creature` object would have "`Creature says: `" before its text greeting also, so we can distinguish which is which.

Code Listing 4-7: `Beings.java`

```java
public class Beings
{
    public static void main(String args[])
    {
        Creature myCreature = new Creature("blub-blub, what
            the heck am I then");
        Alien myAlien = new Alien("Dak-DakDakDak");
        Human myHuman = new Human("Hello there");

        myCreature.speak();
        myAlien.speak();
        myHuman.speak();
    }
}
```

In the main class `Beings`, create three objects. Each is an object of a different creature class. We have a `Creature`, an `Alien`, and a `Human` object. In the case of each, make a call to their respective `speak` methods. When you run this example, you should get output similar to the following figure.

Figure 4-6

Chapter 4

If this is a little confusing, added to the mix are any concerns about how the `Object` class is dealt with. Take a look at a hierarchical representation of the previous example in the following figure.

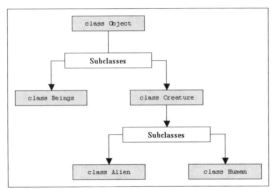

Figure 4-7

In terms of a class that extends another class (or a class that is extended by another class), the relationship between them is known as being *direct*. So in our example, you would say that the `Creature` class is a direct super class of the `Alien` and `Human` classes, and that `Object` is a direct super class of the `Beings` and `Creature` classes. Equally, you would also say that the `Alien` and `Human` classes are direct subclasses of the `Creature` class and `Beings` and `Creature` are direct subclasses of the `Object` class. Therefore, the `Object` class is an indirect super class of the `Alien` and `Human` classes, and they are indirect subclasses of the `Object` class.

In conclusion, any class that does not extend another is a direct subclass of the `Object` class by default. A class that does extend another class is part of a hierarchy of inherited classes, which will always lead to the root `Object` class.

Inheritance Depending on Access Attribute

When we create an `Alien` object, an object of type `Creature` and an object of type `Object` that go into making the `Alien` object what it is also exist. The members that are inherited from the super class depend on the access attribute of this member when defined in the super class. For example, look at the relationship between the `Creature` class and its subclass `Alien`. The `Alien` class inherits the public members of its super class `Creature`, but it does not inherit the private member `greeting` of the `Creature` class. This does not mean that this variable does not exist; it simply means that this variable is inaccessible from an `Alien` class. If you go back to Figure 4-4, a diagram of access attributes, you can see the accessibility relationship between a class and one of its subclasses from within the same package and also from a separate package. These access attributes are true for inheritance as well. Based on the diagram, we can see that private members are never inherited by any subclass and members with no access attribute are not inherited if the super class is in a different package to the subclass.

The Keyword super

The keyword `super` is used similarly to the keyword `this`. The keyword `this`, if you remember from the description earlier, provides us with a reference to the object we are currently in, which is useful for things such as accessing an instance variable instead of a local variable when they share the same identifier name. The keyword `super` is used to access the super class of the object that you are currently in. There are two ways that we can use the keyword `super`, one for calling a constructor of the super class and the other for accessing methods and attributes of the super class. As we saw in the previous example, we called the constructor of the `Creature` class from within the constructor of the `Alien` class.

```
//   default call to the super class constructor
super();
//   if a super class constructor took two parameters of type String
super("Thank you", "for all your support");
```

This is general practice, as it is most often the case that you need to initialize super class members also, as they form the base of your object. You may also need to access members of the super class, which you cannot access from the current object because there exists an overriding version of that member in the current object. For example, in the `Alien` class there is a `speak` method, but there is also a `speak` method in its super class `Creature`. The `speak` method in the `Alien` class replaces the `speak` method in the `Creature` class, but it does not remove it. What if we wanted to access this method instead? You would use the keyword `super` in the `Alien` object to access the `speak` method in the super class `Creature` instead of the `speak` method in its own class.

```
//   Inside an Alien object, use the speak method defined in
//   the Creature class instead
super.speak();
```

As you can see, we use the keyword `super` similarly to how we used the keyword `this` earlier. Note that you can only use the keyword `super` to access the immediate super class object of an object, and this access does not allow you to view inaccessible members of the super class, such as `private` members of the super class, under any circumstances. So using `super.greeting` in an `Alien` object will not work, and you will get a compiler error. The keyword `super` is for accessing constructors and overridden members of the super class of an object.

 NOTE: It is not possible to chain `super` keywords to access above one hierarchical class level. Calling `super.super.toString()` in the last defined `Alien` class would not call `Object.toString()`; it would not even compile.

The Keyword final with Classes and Methods

In Chapter 2 we looked at the keyword `final` for declaring constant variables, ones that could not be changed once initialized. The use of the keyword `final` also translates to use with classes and methods. Include the keyword `final` in the declaration of a class (for example, in the `Alien` class):

```
public final class Alien extends Creature
{
    //  Code here
}
```

This means that no other class can be derived from the `Alien` class. For example, the following class would not compile if our `Alien` class were declared as `final`.

```
public class Martian extends Alien
{
    //  Alien is final and that's final!
    //  No code here :( - will not compile
}
```

The keyword `final` when used with methods means that the method cannot be overridden in any subclass. For example, we could declare the `speak` method of the `Creature` class as `final`.

```
public class Creature
{
    public final void speak(String greeting)
    {
        System.out.println("Creature says: " + greeting);
    }
}
```

This means that the `Alien` and `Human` subclasses of `Creature` would not be able to implement their own versions of the speak method.

Polymorphism

Polymorphism by definition means the ability to take many forms. "Poly" means many, and "morph" means form. Now in terms of classes and objects in Java, this means the ability to use an object in a more general form. We can first look at this in terms of casting objects.

Casting Objects

We have already looked at casting in Chapter 2, where, for example, we cast a variable of type `int` to a variable of type `short`. We also mentioned implicit and explicit casting, where implicit casting means that the destination variable could safely hold the source value and explicit casting means the use of typecasting code explicitly.

```
int myInt = 10;
long myLong = myInt;              // implicit cast
short myShort = (short)myInt      // explicit cast
```

With the integer data types, there is a hierarchical relationship between them in terms of their storage sizes. Whether a cast needs to be explicit relies on this relationship. The same can be applied for casting objects. Casting an object to a super class type can be seen as an implicit cast, known generally as "casting up" through the class hierarchy, whereas casting an object to a subclass, known generally as "casting down" through the class hierarchy, can be seen as an explicit cast. For example, regarding the previous example, we can cast an `Alien` object implicitly to a reference of type `Creature`, as follows.

```
Alien myAlien = new Alien("Dak-DakDakDak");
Creature myCreature = myAlien; // implicit cast 'up'
```

Here we create an object of type `Alien`. This is the true type of the object. We then declare a reference of type `Creature`, called `myCreature`, and assign it to the new `Alien` object. We could also have simply entered the following code.

```
Creature myCreature = new Alien("Dak-DakDakDak");
```

This is an implicit cast because `Creature` is a super class of `Alien`. We know that the `Alien` object can be safely cast to a `Creature` object because `Alien` is derived from `Creature`, so any members of a `Creature` object exist as part of the `Alien` object also.

However, the casting of an object does not change the object itself; the object always remains exactly how it is. The only thing that changes is the reference to the object. For example, view the following line of code:

```
myCreature.speak();
```

The `speak` method that is invoked would be the one defined in the `Alien` class, not the one defined in the `Creature` class, as the true type of the object still remains of type `Alien`. Casting the object to any type does not alter the object; it doesn't even alter the type of object it is. It changes the way your program sees the object, as if it were a different type. When you access a member of the object, the member that is accessed is the member closest to the true type of the object, which is why the `speak` method in the `Alien` class is invoked and not that of the `Creature` class (even when we cast the object to type `Creature`).

Casting an object to a subclass type requires explicit casting. For example:

```
Creature myCreature = new Alien("Dak-DakDakDak");

//   Explicit cast back to type Alien
Alien myAlien = (Alien)myCreature;
```

You will need to cast down the class hierarchy when you need to access a member that is specific to the subclass type. For example, the `Alien` class may contain a method like `destroyPlanet`, which does not belong to the `Creature` class like the `speak` method does and therefore cannot be invoked from a reference of type `Creature`, like `myCreature`. It must be invoked from a reference of type `Alien`, like `myAlien`. You will more than likely need to cast objects down when using many of the classes in the package `java.util`. This package provides many classes that can be used for storing lists of objects. These lists contain objects of type `Object`, which any object can be cast to, casting up to the top of the class hierarchy. When you need to retrieve objects that you've added to these lists, you will need to explicitly cast your objects back to a more descriptive type, back down the class hierarchy, in order to use them properly. In Chapter 5 we will look at packages in general and pay particular attention to the `java.util` package.

Polymorphism in Action

In the previous example we had four classes: `Beings` (main class), `Creature`, `Alien`, and `Human`. In this example we are simply going to change the main class to `PolymorphicBeings`. The classes `Creature`, `Alien`, and `Human` remain exactly the same as they were defined in the previous example, so you will need to get the code for them from the previous example. The main class in this example is the important one, where we will take advantage of polymorphism. Here is the code for `PolymorphicBeings.java`:

```java
class PolymorphicBeings
{
    public static void main(String args[])
    {
        Creature creatureList[] =
            {
                new Creature("I'm a creature you know"),
                new Alien("Well I'm an alien, a more specific
                    creature"),
                new Creature("Ohh, he thinks he's special"),
                new Human("I'm a human and I know I'm special"),
                new Alien("Again I'm from Jupiter, and I'll eat
                    you all")
            };

        for(int i=0; i<creatureList.length; i++)
            creatureList[i].speak();
    }
}
```

When you run this code along with the classes `Creature`, `Alien`, and `Human` that we defined earlier, you should get output similar to the following figure.

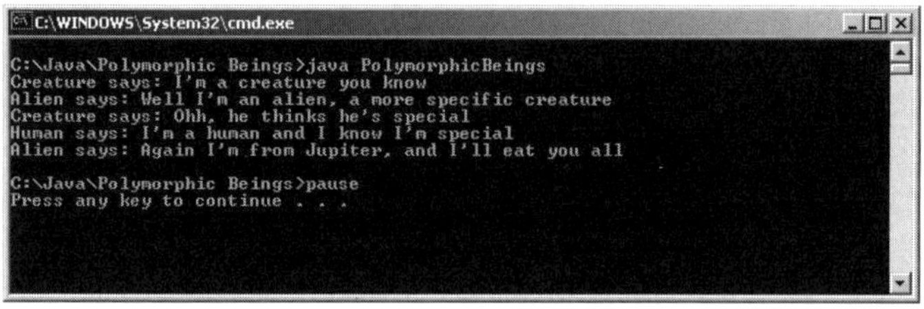

Figure 4-8

Here we have a list of many different types of objects, which are derived in some way by the `Creature` class. Two of the objects are instances of the `Creature` class themselves, whereas the other objects that are created are instances of subclasses of the `Creature` class. This means that it is safe to call the method `speak` on any of the objects, as this method belongs to the `Creature` class. The key is that this method can then be invoked specifically to its object, even though all of the objects are believed to be merely of type `Creature`. This is a great advantage for listing objects of varied types that you want to treat collectively. Imagine in a game that we had a list of many creatures of various subtypes of `Creature`, like `Alien` and `Human`, and in every game loop we wanted to call a `move` function on every object in the list. If the `move` method for an `Alien` differed from a `Human`, like the `speak` methods do, we could simply use a list like this and call the `move` method specific to the object automatically without needing to find out the exact type of the object that we are dealing with at the time.

Abstract Classes

> **Abstract:** Considered apart from any application to a particular object; separated from matter; existing in the mind only.
>
> —*Webster's Revised Unabridged Dictionary, © 1996, 1998 MICRA, Inc.*

That's a beautiful quote, as I'm sure you'll agree. In object-oriented programming there is often a time when a class is needed solely as the basis for being derived by another class, where it in itself should not be instantiated. In Java this would be an abstract class. An abstract class cannot be instantiated. In order to use an abstract class you must create another class, which extends the abstract class that can then be instantiated. For example, we could say that our `Creature` class may be declared as abstract if we wanted to prevent any instantiation of it. We would do this by entering the keyword `abstract` before the keyword `class` in the class declaration, as follows.

```
public abstract class Creature
{
    // code as normal here
}
```

The code encapsulated by the `Creature` class can stay the same. Making a class abstract simply means that it cannot be instantiated. It must be subclassed with an object derived from the subclass that inherited members of the abstract class from which it is derived. If in our previous example we did make the `Creature` class abstract, the code would not compile because we were trying to create objects of type `Creature` inside the main class `PolymorphicBeings`. If we removed these instantiations, the code would work fine. Polymorphism in that example would not be affected by the fact that the `Creature` class was abstract.

In the case of the `Creature` class, it is perfectly feasible that we should have made it an abstract class. This is because there is likely to be no actual object that would be defined as just a `Creature` but always detailed in a more specific subclass of Creature, like Alien or Human or Insect or whatever we wanted.

Abstract Methods

Abstract methods can only be defined within a class that has itself been declared as abstract. An abstract class does not need to contain an abstract method. However, a class with an abstract method is abstract, regardless of the class declaration. An *abstract method* is one that is defined but does not contain a code body, basically meaning that it is declared but not defined. So for example, if we are working on the premise of the Creature class being abstract, we could also declare a method in the class as abstract and omit the code body of the method. In the case of the example PolymorphicBeings, we could make the speak method of the Creature class abstract, as follows:

```
public abstract class Creature
{
    public Creature(String greeting)
    {
        setGreeting(greeting);
    }

    public void setGreeting(String greeting)
    {
        this.greeting = greeting;
    }

    public String getGreeting()
    {
        return greeting;
    }

    public abstract void speak();

    private String greeting;
}
```

As you can see, the method speak has been declared as abstract using the keyword abstract before the return type of the method. Also notice the semicolon at the end of the method signature, and the method does not define a code body.

Not only does the Creature class need to be extended in order to be instantiated, but any subclass of the Creature class must define the method speak with a supporting code body in place. Ideally the Alien and Human classes we have seen in previous examples do just this so it would be easy to plug this abstract version of the Creature class into these examples. Don't forget that a class defining an abstract method can call that method also, like the new Creature class can still call the abstract method speak polymorphically, provided that the actual type of the object that speak is invoked upon is of a subclass of Creature, such as Alien.

If you use an abstract class, you should be sure that you will never need an instance of that class. An abstract class can define normal methods to which it can provide suitable functionality, and should define abstract methods if it does not know how to handle those methods itself. Furthermore, a subclass of this class should be able to provide appropriate code for these abstract methods. If a class cannot provide a suitable implementation for a method, either the class should be abstract along with that method or the method does not belong in the class in the first place.

Note that one abstract class can be extended by another abstract class, where it too can choose whether or not to provide code bodies for inherited abstract methods, if any are inherited of course.

The use of abstract classes and methods is more of a design issue for well thought-out projects, and design issues for games often go out the window when you just want to get the thing working and then tweak the game code from there. This is perfectly normal, especially for programming games in Java. Awareness of all parts of the Java language is important in the long run, especially when you use the standard libraries provided in the Java SDK, which are full of abstract classes and interfaces, classes using those interfaces, and so forth. We're not saying designing games isn't extremely important, but we still like the idea of hacking away at things to learn and then tweaking the code, like the good old days.

The much-preferred alternative to using abstract classes in many respects is the use of interfaces, as we shall discuss now.

Interfaces

> **Interface:** a surface forming a common boundary between two things.

Chapter 4

A crap quote, as I'm sure you'll agree :). As you should have realized, there is no multiple inheritance in Java. In Java, multiple inheritance would mean that one class could extend more than another class, giving it multiple super classes. This is not possible in Java. Interfaces provide a solid workaround for multiple inheritance without the overhead involved with multiple inheritance and the added capabilities of using polymorphism with them, allowing you to add multiple identities to your classes.

The source code for an interface must be added to a file with the same name similar to classes. For example:

```
public interface MyInterface
{

}
```

This would be entered into the source file `MyInterface.java`.

Defining Interfaces

Interfaces can contain two different types of data, static final variables (constants) or method declarations, which are abstract methods without the need for the keyword `abstract` (interfaces can only contain methods that do not supply a code body anyway, so the need for the keyword abstract is, well, not needed).

```
public interface GameData
{
    public static final int SCREEN_WIDTH = 640;
    public static final int SCREEN_HEIGHT = 480;
    public static final int TOTAL_PLAYERS = 4;
}
```

We use the keyword interface for defining interfaces, just as we have used the keyword class to define our classes, followed by its name/identifier. The interface GameData simply defines three constant variables: SCREEN_WIDTH, SCREEN_HEIGHT, and TOTAL_PLAYERS. Interfaces can also define methods, as follows.

```
public interface Moveable
{
    public void move();
}
```

The Moveable interface declares one method, move, which as you can see does not actually implement code for the method itself. Note that an interface can contain constants and method declarations together; it is not restricted to one or the other. You can also declare one interface that inherits one or more other interfaces. For example, we could have the following two interfaces:

```
public interface LandMover
{
    public void walk();
}

public interface WaterMover
{
    public void swim();
}
```

We may also want to combine these interfaces to make an interface that supports both walk and swim methods. We could define this interface as follows.

```
public interface AmphibiousMover extends LandMover, WaterMover
{

}
```

The interface AmphibiousMover inherits all of the members defined in the interfaces LandMover and WaterMover, which in this example are the methods walk and swim from their respective interfaces.

 NOTE: Any of the overheads that are normally problematic when using multiple inheritance will be picked up by the compiler when inheriting multiple interfaces. For example, the interfaces LandMover and WaterMover could both contain a static final variable with the same name but different values. If you then implemented the Amphibious-Mover interface and tried to access this constant variable, the compiler will pick up the error because it cannot possibly decipher which of the two variables you wish to use. This doesn't necessarily mean that these interfaces could not still be used. They would themselves still compile because you can cast your object to an interface type and then access the appropriate constant variable that way. The compiler will then know what interface to access the constant from. We will see about casting objects to interface types shortly.

Using Interfaces

In order for a class to implement an interface, you need to use the keyword implements. For example, if we have a class, Alien, that needs to know the resolution of the displayable screen area, which is provided by constant variables in the GameData interface that we defined earlier, our Alien class could implement the GameData interface as follows.

```
public class Alien implements GameData
{
    public void printResolution()
    {
        System.out.println(SCREEN_WIDTH + ", "+ SCREEN_HEIGHT);
    }
}
```

The advantage in this case is that classes are not restricted to merely implementing one interface like they are restricted to only extending one other class. A class may still extend another class and implement multiple interfaces also. For example, we may declare the Alien class, which we could say extends the Creature class, like in previous examples, and implements the GameData and LandMover interfaces, as follows:

```
public class Alien extends Creature
        implements GameData, LandMover
{
    public Alien(String greeting)
    {
        super(greeting);
    }

    public void printResolution()
    {
        System.out.println(SCREEN_WIDTH + ", "+ SCREEN_HEIGHT);
    }

    public void walk()
    {
        // must supply code body for walk method
    }

    public void speak()
    {
        System.out.println("Alien says: " + getGreeting());
    }
}
```

As you can see, we have declared and implemented the method walk in the Alien class. Because the Alien class has implemented the LandMover interface, it must implement this method complete with code body. This is our first glimpse at the real advantages of using interfaces; we have the ability to give our classes different labels and are assured that the class implements the methods associated with that label.

Interface Objects (well, sort of!)

It is not possible to make an interface object. For starters, they do not provide an implementation for any methods that they declare, so to instantiate them would be completely unreasonable. You can, however, create an object of a class that implements an interface and then cast the object to a variable of the interface type. For example, take the Alien class that we have just defined. We can create an instance of the Alien class (the Alien class version that is implementing the LandMover interface previously defined), and then we can cast the Alien object to type LandMover.

```
public class MainClass
{
    public static void main(String[] args)
    {
        Alien myAlien = new Alien("DakDakDak-Dak");
        moveOnLand(myAlien);
    }

    public static void moveOnLand(LandMover landMover)
    {
        landMover.walk();
    }
}
```

As you can see, this gives us a great advantage; we are no longer just restricted to casting an object to a type that is within its acceptable class hierarchy where polymorphism could be used, but we are also now able to cast our objects to a type of an interface that its class implements, where we may also use polymorphism with the methods defined in the interface type to which we are casting. In the previous example, we passed the reference myAlien to the method moveOnLand, where it was received and cast to type LandMover. The method walk is then invoked from an object of type LandMover. This means we can use the method moveOnLand for any objects of classes that implement the LandMover interface. We are no longer restricted to objects that are subclasses of Creature. For example:

```
public class Submarine implements WaterMover
{
    public void swim()
    {
        // handle swimming
    }
}
```

If we had a method to handle a swimming object:

```
public void moveInWater(WaterMover waterMover)
{
    waterMover.swim();
}
```

...we could pass a Submarine object to this method, as well as a Human object or any object that also implemented the interface WaterMover.

Going back to what was initially discussed, we can now give our objects multiple identities, casting them within their class hierarchy or to any interface type they implement. But remember, the object is never changed when casting; it will always be the same. Access to members of the object is what actually changes, as it takes a different identity, be it a class or interface implementation.

Does My Object Implement that Interface?

There may be a time when you want to know if an object implements an interface or not. It's quite likely that you may have a list of related types, such as Alien and Human, that are all Creature derivatives, and you want to run through the list invoking methods on the object defined by an interface. Only certain objects in the list implement that interface and therefore contain that method, and others do not. For an array of Creature types, which could be Alien or Human objects, the Alien class may implement the LandMover interface, whereas the Human class may implement both the LandMover and WaterMover interfaces. You want to run through this array only invoking the swim method on any objects that implement this method. We all know aliens cannot swim (well, I think they can't), but the list does not know which objects can swim and which cannot.

The simplest way to perform this task is to use the keyword instanceof to check if an object is an "instance of" a class or interface. For example, let's say we have the Alien class that only implements the LandMover interface and not the WaterMover interface. Then we have an object of either type Alien or Human cast to a reference of type Creature, and we no longer know whether the true type of the object is an Alien or a Human. Or more to the point, we do not know which of the interfaces our object implements to which we want to invoke the appropriate method.

Using the instanceof operator, we could perform this check in two different ways. First, we could check to see if the object implements the appropriate interfaces and then implement its respective method, as follows:

```
Creature myCreature = new Alien("DakDakDak-Dak");

if(myCreature instanceof LandMover)
    ((LandMover)myCreature).walk();
```

The implementation of invoking the walk method is quite logical when you think about it. First, the reference myCreature is of type Creature. The Creature class does not implement any walk method, so any such method cannot be invoked in terms of a Creature type object. We also cannot cast the object back down to its true type, as we do not know its true type at this stage. What we can do, however, is cast the object to type LandMover, as we know it is an object of this type, implementing the `LandMover` interface as we just checked. We can then invoke the `walk` method in terms of a `LandMover` cast object.

Alternatively, also using the `instanceof` operator, we can check if our object is of a class type `Alien` and then work from there.

```
Creature myCreature = new Alien("DakDakDak-Dak");

if(myCreature instanceof Alien)
    ((Alien)myCreature).walk();
```

Both methods have their advantages. If you have a list of many different unknown objects all cast as type `Creature` and many implement the `LandMover` interface, the interface checking would be better because it would be one check, whereas the class check would mean checking all different types of `Creature` subclass types. The class method would be better simply because of the control it gives back to you in knowing the true type of the object again, accessing other members specific to it, etc.

You should take note that using `instanceof` checks if an object is not only an instance of the true type class but also if the object is an instance of any super classes of its true type. For example, testing `if(myAlien instanceof Creature)` will return `true` also. A better example is that `if(anyObject instanceof Object)` will always return `true`, as all objects are ultimately derived from the `Object` class at the very top of the class hierarchy.

Defining on the Fly

Although this aspect of programming is not completely conventional, it can make code neater for one-off defining implementations of members of a class. Okay, perhaps we should explain a little. Perhaps you want to have just a special type of alien that simply contains its own version of the `speak` method but only require one that might not be worth creating a whole new class for. In Java, you can create this new type of `Alien` object as follows.

```
Alien newAlien = new Alien("Dak-DakDakDak")
        {
            public void speak()
            {
                System.out.println("No comment");
            }
        };
```

This method is most notably used for supplying your own methods for event handling, which we will look at in Chapters 9 and 10. You should note that this method is just another way to define members of a class "on the fly" as opposed to perhaps declaring a nested class that would, in this example, extend the `Alien` class and then provide the defining method in there. This technique should simply be seen as an alternative way of doing this. Note that this can also be applied to defining interface methods on the fly for interface objects, though all interface methods would have to be defined in this case.

Summary

In this chapter we looked at nested classes and creating multiple classes in an application along with inheritance, polymorphism, interfaces, and a whole range of new keywords. In the next chapter you will learn about packages and the many useful supporting classes included in the Java SDK. You will also learn about error handling in Java, especially exceptions and assertions.

Chapter 4

Packages, Utilities, and Error Handling

"To err is human, but to really foul things up requires a computer."

—Farmers' Almanac, 1978

Introduction

In this chapter you will learn about the important packages that are included in Java to assist you, as well as how to create your own, reusable packages. We will delve into the way you handle errors in Java, and we will also take a look at assertions, which are new to the 1.4 release of the Java SDK.

What is a Package?

A Java *package* is a collection of related classes that can be imported into your program to support your software. They also provide namespace management, as well as access protection.

 NOTE: A namespace is the scope of the name of a variable.

The following table shows some of the main packages that are included in the recent Java 1.4 SDK (Software Development Kit) release along with a brief description of what they include.

Package	Description
java.lang	This is the fundamental Java package containing classes essential to the Java language. This package is included in your program by default and contains many useful classes, such as String, Thread, and the primitive data type support classes.
java.io	The I/O package contains classes that allow support for input and output operations. You can learn more about input/output in Chapter 6.
java.awt	This is the Abstract Window Toolkit package and contains all the necessary classes to create a GUI within your Java applications and applets.

Package	Description
java.awt.event	This package is used to support the Abstract Window Toolkit by containing classes for event handling.
java.awt.image	This package provides important classes for storing and manipulating images, most notably the BufferedImage and VolatileImage classes, which we will look at in Chapter 9, "Graphics."
javax.swing	The Swing package, as with the AWT package, is used to create a GUI. However, Swing is the newer of the two and, in our opinion, the best one to use (see Chapter 8, "Applications and Applets" for information on the differences regarding lightweight and heavyweight components).
javax.swing.event	As with the java.awt.event package, this includes extra event handling functionality to support the javax.swing package.
java.util	The utility package contains many useful classes, including storage classes such as ArrayList and Linked-List. We will look more into this package later in this chapter, as it is very important.
java.net	This package contains everything you need to handle basic networking in Java. You can find out more about how to use this package in Chapter 17, "Introduction to Networking."
java.nio	This is a new package to the 1.4 release and contains classes used to implement NIO (New I/O). More can be read about this subject in Chapter 18.
java.sql	Finally, we have the SQL package, which gives us database support within Java. We will use this when we take a look into databases in Chapter 14.

Although there are many other packages within the Java language, the above list is probably the most common that you will come across. Let's now take a look at how we can use and import these standard packages into our Java applications and applets.

Importing Packages

To use a package within our Java application or applet, we need to import it. We do this by means of the import keyword. So, for example, if we wish to include the I/O package, which is called java.io, we would have the following statement at the top of our code (before we define any classes):

```
import java.io.*;
```

Note how we have appended an extra decimal point and star to the end of the package name. This means that it will include all of the classes within the package (i.e., the asterisk is used as a wildcard).

Another example of this would be if we wished to include the utility package, which is called java.util. This would be done with the following statement:

```
import java.util.*;
```

Again, note the use of the asterisk to include all the classes from the package. However, if we only wished to include a single class from the package, we could do this too.

Within the utility package, there is an `ArrayList` class. If we simply wish to use the `ArrayList` class from the utility package and no others, we could import just the `ArrayList` class using the following statement at the top of our code.

```
import java.util.ArrayList;
```

Of course, if we used the asterisk, the `ArrayList` package would be included automatically. So once we do this, we could then create a reference to an `ArrayList` object within a class or method using the following statement:

```
ArrayList myArrayList;
```

Also, it is good to know that it is possible to access the `ArrayList` class (or any other class out of a package) by using its fully qualified name. For example, without any `import` statements, we could create the `myArrayList` object as we did before with the following line of code.

```
java.util.ArrayList myArrayList;
```

As we mentioned in the introduction, packages provide namespace management, so it is therefore possible that two packages could both have a class with the same name in it. Obviously, this could cause problems if both the packages were imported, so in this case it would make sense to use the fully qualified package name:

```
package1.MyClass firstReference;
package2.MyClass secondReference;
```

Creating Your Own Packages

Okay, so now you know how to include the standard packages. Let's look at how we can create our own packages.

By creating your own packages, it is possible for you to create collections of reusable classes, which is excellent from a game programmer's point of view, as many algorithms can be packaged and reused in many projects.

Let's now look at how to create a very simple mathematics package, which will contain two classes. One class will contain a static method for adding two integers, whereas the other class will contain a static method for subtracting two integers.

To create a package, we must first store it in its own directory, which must be named the same as the package. In this case, we will call our package `SimpleMaths` and the directory will be:

```
C:\MyPackages\simplemaths
```

To make a class part of a package, we need to use the `package` keyword, followed by the name of the package that we wish to make it a part of at the top of each of the source files in the package. We will need to include the following line of code at the top of any source (.java) files we wish to make part of our `simplemaths` package. (Also note that we need to ensure the files are all contained within the `simplemaths` directory.)

```
package simplemaths;
```

NOTE: It is convention to keep package names in lowercase.

Okay, now let's look at the source code for the two classes, `Addition` and `Subtraction`, we are going to make part of the package.

Code Listing 5-1: `Addition.java`

```java
package simplemaths;


public class Addition
{
    public static int add(int number1, int number2)
    {
        int result = number1 + number2;
        return result;
    }
}
```

Code Listing 5-2: `Subtraction.java`

```java
package simplemaths;


public class Subtraction
{
    public static int substract(int number1, int number2)
    {
        int result = number1 - number2;
        return result;
    }
}
```

As we mentioned before, both of these files should be placed within our `simplemaths` directory. The next step would be to compile the classes, which we can do by means of a batch file. Here is the listing of the batch file, which we have named `compile.bat`; it should be stored in the same directory as the source files.

Code Listing 5-3: `compile.bat`

```
C:\j2sdk1.4.1_01\bin\javac Addition.java
C:\j2sdk1.4.1_01\bin\javac Subtraction.java
pause
```

Obviously, if you have installed the 1.4 SDK to a different directory, you would need to change the paths in the `compile.bat` file.

When we execute the batch file, it will compile both the source files into the .class counterparts, which will then also be in the `simplemaths` directory.

That is our created package. Let's now create a simple console application to test the package out. We will first look at the complete source for the test application and then go into more detail as to how we compiled it.

Code Listing 5-4: The test application (`TestApp.java`)

```java
import simplemaths.*;


public class TestApp
{
    public static void main(String args[])
    {
        int num1 = 10;
        int num2 = 20;
        int res = 0;

        res = Addition.add(num1, num2);

        System.out.println(num1 + " + " + num2 + " = " + res);

        res = Subtraction.substract(num2, num1);

        System.out.println(num2 + " - " + num1 + " = " + res);
    }
}
```

When we run the example, the following output can be expected in the console.

Figure 5-1: Testing our own package

As you can see by using the `import` statement at the start of the code, we imported our own package `simplemaths`. This can be seen in the following line of code:

```java
import simplemaths.*;
```

Note how we used the asterisk so both the `Addition` and `Subtraction` classes were included from the package.

However, to include the package, we need to specify the classpath that the compiler should look in to find the package we are trying to include (as it will not be registered in the global environment). To do this, we use the `-classpath` parameter of both the compiler and interpreter when compiling and running the test application. The command line to compile the application can be seen here:

```
javac -classpath "c:\MyPackages" TestApp.java
```

For the above command to work, the `simplemaths` folder would need to be placed within the `c:\MyPackages` folder.

Chapter 5

To run the test application, you would use the following command:

```
java -classpath "c:\MyPackages" TestApp
```

Using JARs

A *JAR* is an archive that uses the ZIP file format to compress files stored within it. The great thing about using JARs is that it is possible to package up your applications and applets into a single JAR file and execute them directly from the compressed JAR archive. This is an excellent feature where applets are concerned, as the JAR is downloaded, decompressed, and executed from the browser (making the download smaller).

Running an Application from a JAR

Let's first look at how we can create an application that we can execute directly from the JAR archive. We will use a simple console application to output a line of text to the console for this example. The complete code listing for this application can be seen here:

Code Listing 5-5: `MyApp.java`

```
public class MyApp
{
    public static void main(String args[])
    {
        System.out.println("\n\nI was executed from the JAR!\n\n");
    }
}
```

Once we have our basic application in the file, we need to compile it in the usual way, leaving us with a `MyApp.class` file. Normally from here we would use the Java interpreter to execute the bytecode contained within the class file, but this time we wish to make it into a JAR archive.

To do this, we need to use the JAR tool, which comes with the Java SDK. The JAR tool is called `jar.exe` and can be found within the `/bin/` directory of the SDK.

Creating an actual JAR is a simple process. However, to make our application execute from the JAR, we also require a manifest file, which simply specifies the name of the main class that should be used when the JAR is executed. In this example we will call the manifest file `theManifest.txt` and it will only contain a single line of text (followed by a carriage return). The following line should be placed within this file:

```
Main-Class: MyApp
```

Now that we have the manifest file and our byte code contained within our `MyApp.class` file, we can proceed to create our JAR archive, which we will call `MyApp.jar`. Note that the JAR archive does not need to share the same name as its main class. The command used to create the archive can be seen here:

```
jar cmf theManifest.txt MyApp.jar MyApp.class
```

First we have the "jar" executable and we specify `cmf` as a parameter, where "c" stands for "create," "m" means we wish to modify the manifest, and "f" means we wish to output the archive to a file rather than the standard output (i.e., the screen). Next we specify the name of the file our manifest is stored in, which in this case is `theManifest.txt`. Then we state the name of the archive that we wish to create (i.e., `MyApp.jar`), and finally we specify the files and/or directories to include within the archive.

NOTE: Along with .class files, it is also possible to store any other type of media within a JAR file, including images and sounds. A useful thing to remember is that you can specify a directory name as a parameter and the JAR tool will then recursively add all the files within that directory and maintain the directory structure within the JAR archive.

When the command is executed, a file called `MyApp.jar` should then be visible in the same directory as your source and class file.

Now that we have the executable JAR file, we still need to use the Java interpreter to run it, but since we are using an archive, we need to specify the `-jar` parameter. The full command can be seen here:

```
java -jar MyApp.jar
```

Here is a screen shot of the output that we can expect when we execute the JAR archive that we have created.

Figure 5-2: Running an application from a JAR archive

Running an Applet from a JAR

Executing an applet from a JAR archive is equally as easy as running an application. First we will create a simple applet that we can use to package into a JAR file. Here is the complete code listing for the applet that we are going to archive into a JAR:

Code Listing 5-6: `MyApplet.java`

```java
import java.awt.*;
import javax.swing.*;

public class MyApplet extends JApplet
{
    public void init()
    {
```

```
    setSize(400, 300);
  }

  public void start()
  {

  }

  public void paint(Graphics g)
  {
    g.drawString("I was executed from a JAR!", 20, 20);
  }

  public void stop()
  {

  }

  public void destroy()
  {

  }
}
```

Once we compile the applet in the usual way, we can then archive it using the JAR tool, as we did in the previous application example. However, this time we do not require the manifest file, as we will specify the main class in the applet tag in the HTML page that we will look at soon. Here is the command we require to archive our applet into an archive called MyApplet.jar:

```
jar cf MyApplet.jar MyApplet.class
```

All that is different here is that we have excluded the m and manifest file-name parameters.

So we now have our applet in a JAR archive. We can then display the applet from the JAR in an HTML page by using the <APPLET> tag but this time add an extra parameter called archive in which we will specify the JAR file to load (note that the code parameter is then used to define the main class from within the JAR archive). Here is the complete HTML code listing for displaying the applet from the JAR file:

Code Listing 5-7: view.html

```
<HTML>

<HEAD>
    <TITLE>Applet JAR Example</TITLE>
</HEAD>

<BODY>
    <CENTER><B>Applet JAR Example</B>
    <BR>
    <APPLET CODE="MyApplet.class" ARCHIVE="MyApplet.jar" WIDTH=400
        HEIGHT=300>
    </APPLET>
    </CENTER>
</BODY>
```

```
</HTML>
```

So when we load the `view.html` file into a web browser (such as Internet Explorer or Opera), we can see that it will load from the archive and look like this:

Figure 5-3: Running an applet from a JAR archive

Note that we will look at applets in more detail in the chapters to follow.

The following table is a list of parameters that can be supplied to the JAR tool to perform various actions.

Action Parameters	Description
c	Used to create a JAR file, as we have seen in the previous examples
t	Used to list the contents of a JAR file
u	Used to alter an existing JAR by adding or replacing files
x	Used to extract files from the JAR

The following table is a list of optional parameters that can be used to affect the actions that you specify.

Optional Parameters	Description
v	Gives more detailed information output to the screen, such as file sizes. Note that the v stands for verbose.
f	Used to indicate that you will specify the name of the JAR file as the second command-line argument. Note that without specifying this option, it will be assumed that the input will come in from the standard input (the keyboard), and the output will be the standard output (the console screen).
m	Used to declare that a manifest file should be added and that you will specify the manifest filename as the third command-line parameter after the filename parameter
M	Tells the JAR file not to include a default manifest file
0 (zero)	Specifies that the JAR archive should not compress the data

For example, we could extract the archive that we created in the applet example with the following command-line argument:

Chapter 5

```
jar xf MyApplet.jar
```

The x action indicates that we wish to extract files, and the f option indicates that we wish to do this from the JAR file MyApplet.jar.

Exploring Useful Classes

Useful java.lang Classes

 NOTE: Remember that java.lang is imported by default and therefore does not need to be imported by your classes. However, note that it does not do any harm to import it anyway.

Primitive Data Type Wrappers

We learned in Chapter 2 that Java has many primitive data types, such as int, float, double, etc. In the java.lang package, there are wrapper classes for each of the primitive data types that include important functionality support, such as allowing them to be manipulated and converted to other formats easily.

The wrapper classes are named as follows:

Primitive Data Type	Wrapper Class
byte	Byte
short	Short
int	Integer
long	Long
float	Float
double	Double
boolean	Boolean
character	Character

These wrapper classes all contain a very useful method called parseX, where X is relative to the wrapper class. Here is a table showing the parse methods of each of the wrapper classes.

Wrapper Class	Parse Method
Byte	Byte.parseByte(String s)
Short	Short.parseShort(String s)
Integer	Integer.parseInteger(String s)
Long	Long.parseLong(String s)
Float	Float.parseFloat(String s)
Double	Double.parseDouble(String s)
Boolean	Boolean.getBoolean(String s)
Character	Character.toString(String s)

The parse method takes a string as a parameter and attempts to convert the string into the appropriate format. For example, let's say we have a string declared as follows:

```
String myString = "34.5";
```

If we then created a `double` variable and use the `parseDouble` method of the `Double` class, we could get the value as follows:

```
double myDouble = Double.parseDouble(myString);
```

The value of the `myDouble` variable would then be the floating-point value 34.5.

A special case, however, is the `Boolean` class, which has the `getBoolean` method that looks for the string `true` or `false` and then assigns it appropriately to the Boolean variable (i.e., the method returns a Boolean value).

Note that if the conversion is illegal from, say, the string notation to the primitive data type, then an exception will be thrown (e.g., `NumberFormatException`). We will discuss exceptions in detail toward the end of this chapter.

The Math Class

The `Math` class contains excellent static methods for performing useful mathematical functions. Here is a table of some of the most useful methods in the `Math` class, although you can find a complete overview within the Java 1.4 documentation.

Method Name	Use
`abs(float)`, `abs(double)`, `abs(int)`, `abs(long)`	Finds the absolute value of a number (i.e., the positive representation)
`ceil(double)`	Rounds the number up to the nearest integer
`floor(double)`	Rounds the number down to the nearest integer
`min(float, float)`, `min(double, double)`, `min(int, int)`, `min(long, long)`	Finds the smaller of two specified values
`max(float, float)`, `max(double, double)`, `max(int, int)`, `max(long, long)`	Finds the larger of two specified values
`pow(double, double)`	Returns the value of the first parameter raised to the power of the second parameter
`sin(double)`, `cos(double)`, `tan(double)`	Finds the trigonometric sine, cosine, and tangent of the specified angle. (Note that the angle is in radians.)
`asin(double)`, `acos(double)`, `atan(double)`	Finds the arc tangent (sine, cosine, and tangent, respectively)
`toDegrees(double)`	Converts radians to degrees
`toRadians(double)`	Converts degrees to radians
`random()`	Returns a positive random double within the range of 0.0 (inclusive) to 1.0 (exclusive)
`sqrt(double)`	Returns the square root of the specified number

Chapter 5

The System Class

The main use for the `System` class is data output and input from the console window (shown in Chapter 6, "Stream I/O"). It also contains a useful method for getting the current system time called `System.current-TimeMillis`, which returns the current system time in milliseconds and can be used to limit the frame rate of your application/applet. Note that we will discuss timing in Chapter 12 in much more detail.

Useful java.util Classes

The `java.util` package contains many excellent classes for storing data in a variety of different formats—such as linked lists and array lists. Let's look at the most useful of these classes now.

The ArrayList Class

The `ArrayList` class is used to store object references and is not dissimilar to an array. However, there are many advantages to using an `ArrayList` class over an array, depending on the situation of course.

The main advantage of using an ArrayList is that it is dynamic, whereas arrays are of a fixed length. This is useful in many circumstances for listing data where you do not know the exact size of the list and especially where the size of the list changes at run time.

An ArrayList manages its capacity automatically (i.e., if you add more object references than the ArrayList can hold, it will automatically double its size to accommodate the new reference(s)). It is also easy to cycle (iterate) through the list of object references by means of an iterator, which we will look at soon. Finally, it is also very easy to add, find, and remove objects within an ArrayList.

Let's see how we can use an ArrayList to store a list of names in this small example program. Here is the complete code listing.

Code Listing 5-8: `ArrayListExample.java`

```java
import java.util.*;


public class ArrayListExample
{
    public static void main(String args[])
    {
        // Create an ArrayList...
        ArrayList myArrayList = new ArrayList();

        // Add three 'String' objects to the ArrayList...
        myArrayList.add("Bob");
        myArrayList.add("Harry");
        myArrayList.add("Fred");

        // Print two blank lines...
        System.out.println("\n");

        // Iterate through the ArrayList to print its contents...
        Iterator i = myArrayList.iterator();
        while(i.hasNext())
        {
            String currentObject = (String) i.next();
```

```
        System.out.println(currentObject);
    }
  }
}
```

When we run this example, we can expect the following output in the console window:

Figure 5-4:
Using the
ArrayList
class

In the example, we first create an `ArrayList` object with the following line of code:

```
ArrayList myArrayList = new ArrayList();
```

Note as well that you can specify a parameter to state how many items you wish the `ArrayList` to initially be able to hold (remember that it will automatically increase to accommodate more objects though). Here is how we would have declared it to initially hold 25 object references.

```
ArrayList myArrayList = new ArrayList(25);
```

The advantage of preallocating required memory is that it is done first, and then no more memory needs allocating, provided you stay under the allocated limit, as allocating memory is relatively expensive and should be limited as much as possible when the game is in its playing stage.

Next, call the `add` method, which adds object references to the `ArrayList`. As all classes within Java are inherited from the `Object` class, it is safe to cast up to the `Object` class, so in this case the casting is done implicitly. Here is the `add` method where we add the string `"Bob"` to the `ArrayList` object:

```
myArrayList.add("Bob");
```

Now we want to print out all of the names from the list, so we need to create an `Iterator` object, which allows us to cycle through the `ArrayList` efficiently. Create the `Iterator` object and obtain the iterator from our instance of the `ArrayList` class by calling the `iterator()` method. This can be seen in the following line of code:

```
Iterator i = myArrayList.iterator();
```

Next, create a `while` loop, which checks for the condition of the iterator having more references in it. This is done by calling the `hasNext` method of our `Iterator` object and can be seen in the following line of code:

Chapter 5

```
while(i.hasNext())
```

So if there are references still available in the `ArrayList`, we need to get the next one and cast it to the appropriate type (remember all references within an ArrayList are of type `Object`). To get the next reference, call the `next()` method of the iterator and simply typecast it to a string. This can be seen in the following line of code:

```
String currentObject = (String) i.next();
```

Then from there, we can simply output the `String` object to the console using the following line of code:

```
System.out.println(currentObject);
```

Note that using an iterator at run time during a game involves creating an `Iterator` object each time that you wish to traverse a list in this way. The creation of many objects during the running of a game in Java can cause many problems involving garbage collection, notably pauses when the garbage collector takes processor time to handle memory that can cause pauses in other processing threads (e.g., your main loop). We will discuss garbage collection in detail in Chapter 12. Instead of using an iterator to traverse a list, the alternative is to use the `get` method of the `ArrayList` class (though this is not as efficient as using an iterator for traversal, but it does not require the creation of `Iterator` objects—say, for example, per frame in the main game loop). The `get` method takes one parameter of type `int`, specifying the index (position in the list) of the object that you are requesting, which is returned of type `Object` ready for you to cast down to whatever object you know it is. In the case of the current example, type `"String"`.

So instead of using the iterator technique, we can traverse the list with the `get` method as follows.

```
for(int i=0; i<myArrayList.size(); i++)
{
    String currentObject = (String)myArrayList.get(i);

    System.out.println(currentObject);
}
```

Note the use of the `size` method of the `ArrayList` class that simply returns the number of elements that it contains. If you try to access an index that is negative or greater than or equal to the size of the list, an `ArrayIndexOutOfBoundsException` exception will be thrown. Exceptions are discussed toward the end of this chapter.

Searching and Removing from an ArrayList

As well as adding and cycling through the references contained within an `ArrayList`, it is also possible to search for an object and remove objects. Let's now look at an extended version of the previous example where we search for a name and then remove it. Here is the complete code listing for this example.

Code Listing 5-9: `ArrayListSearchRemove.java`

```java
import java.util.*;


public class ArrayListSearchRemove
{
    public static void main(String args[])
    {
        // Create a ArrayList...
        ArrayList myArrayList = new ArrayList();

        // Add three 'String' objects to the ArrayList...
        myArrayList.add("Bob");
        myArrayList.add("Harry");
        myArrayList.add("Fred");

        // Find the position of the 'Harry' object..
        int position = myArrayList.indexOf("Harry");
        System.out.println("Harry was found at position
            "+position);

        // Now remove the object at that position...
        myArrayList.remove(position);

        // Print two blank lines...
        System.out.println("\n");

        // Iterate through the ArrayList to print its contents...
        Iterator i = myArrayList.iterator();
        while(i.hasNext())
        {
            String currentObject = (String) i.next();

            System.out.println(currentObject);
        }
    }
}
```

So when we run the example this time, we can expect the following output in the console window.

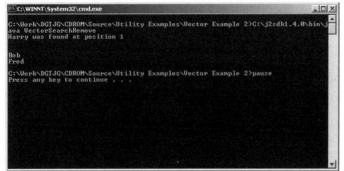

Figure 5-5: Finding and removing from an ArrayList

Chapter 5

So in this example, we created the `ArrayList` and added the string, as in the previous example, but this time we searched the `ArrayList` to find the `"Harry"` string. We did this by calling the `indexOf` method to find the position of the object within the `ArrayList`. This can be seen in the following line of code:

```
int position = my ArrayList.indexOf("Harry");
```

The `indexOf` method looks through the `ArrayList` using the specified `objects equals` method to make a comparison to each element in the `ArrayList`. You will note that the `equals` method is defined in the `Object` method and is therefore inherited by all classes (all classes being derived from the `Object` class). Therefore, in this example you can see that we have actually created two different Harry string objects. The reason that our code works, even though these are effectively two different `String` objects (one being the testing `"Harry"` string and the other the original `"Harry"` string that we passed to the `ArrayList`), is because the `String` class contains its own version of the `equals` method, overriding what would have been inherited from the `Object` class. Now, the `equals` method of the `String` class tests whether the string character representation of one string is equal to another object, thus our example still found a match, matching the data instead of whether they were the same object. We felt that the structure of this example may have been a bit misleading to begin with but decided to leave it in to illustrate this fact. If we were testing the equality of an actual object (that is, if the actual object parameter is the same as the one stored in the list and not its data values), we would need to both pass in the same object and provide a reference to it in the `indexOf` method also. For example, the following code shows us adding a `Person` object to the `ArrayList` and then searching for it.

```
Person peterWalsh = new Person();
myArrayList.add(peterWalsh);
int position = myArrayList.indexOf(peterWalsh);
```

Here we add and retrieve the same object, whereas before they were different. So as a final note, you should realize that the equality test is based on how the `equals` method of the parameter object is defined. For example, in the `java.awt` package there is a class named `Point` that simply represents an x and y coordinate. This method also overrides the `equals` method and defines that it will return `true` if the argument object is of type `Point` and also contains the same values for its x and y coordinates.

When it finds the object, it returns the index of the object that you may then pass to the `get` method for retrieving the object. Note that if the object could not be found, the method will return −1.

In our example, once we have the position of the object, we can then pass this position into the `remove` method of the `ArrayList` object, and the reference will be removed from the `ArrayList`. Also note that the `remove` method returns a reference to the object as well as removing it from the list. This method can be seen in the following line of code:

```
myArrayList.remove(position);
```

Note as well that we could have also just specified the object in the `remove` method that takes an `Object` parameter for the same effect:

```
myArrayList.remove("Harry");
```

 NOTE: There is also a very similar class to `ArrayList` called `Vector`. It has the same functionality as the `ArrayList` class. However, all of its methods are synchronized—see Chapter 7, "Threads" for a good explanation of synchronization. If synchronization is not an issue for your code, the best choice is the ArrayList, basically because it has faster access times.

The LinkedList Class

The `LinkedList` class is very valuable to us. You will especially like this class if you are familiar with the C programming language, as it makes linked lists very easy to implement and they are highly useful.

The `LinkedList` class is in fact very similar to the `ArrayList` class; however, it gives us optimized methods for adding elements to the beginning and end of the list. Let's look at a simple code example where we add the numbers 1 through 5 to a linked list and display them to the console using an iterator. We will define the integer values by creating instances of the integer wrapper class to store the values as an object so that they can be added to the linked list, as a primitive data type alone cannot be.

Code Listing 5-10: `LinkedListExample.java`

```java
import java.util.*;

public class LinkedListExample
{
    public static void main(String args[])
    {
        // Create a LinkedList...
        LinkedList myLinkedList = new LinkedList();

        // Add five 'Integer' objects to the LinkedList...
        Integer tempInt = new Integer(3);
        myLinkedList.add(tempInt);

        tempInt = new Integer(2);
        myLinkedList.addFirst(tempInt);

        tempInt = new Integer(1);
        myLinkedList.addFirst(tempInt);

        tempInt = new Integer(4);
        myLinkedList.addLast(tempInt);

        tempInt = new Integer(5);
        myLinkedList.addLast(tempInt);


        // Print two blank lines...
        System.out.println("\n");

        // Iterate through the LinkedList to print its contents...
        Iterator i = myLinkedList.iterator();
        while(i.hasNext())
```

Chapter 5

```
        {
            Integer currentObject = (Integer) i.next();

            System.out.println(currentObject);
        }
    }
}
```

When you compile and execute the example, you should see the following output in the console:

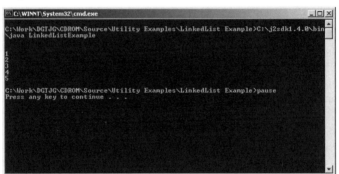

Figure 5-6: Using the LinkedList class

As you can see, using the `LinkedList` class is very similar to using the `ArrayList` class. The point of the example was to show how you can add elements to both the beginning and end of the list using the `addFirst` and `addLast` methods. In the example we do not add the numbers in order. However, by using the `addFirst` and `addLast` methods, we have added them to the list so they are in order in the list.

As well as `addFirst` and `addLast`, there is also `removeFirst` and `removeLast` to remove the first and last elements from the linked list.

The Stack Class

The `Stack` class allows you to maintain a stack (pile) of references, where the last reference to be added is taken off first by a technique called pushing and popping. Object references are "pushed" onto the top of the stack. Then you can "pop" the top reference off the top of the stack and regain the reference. Let's look at an example of this in action.

Code Listing 5-11: StackExample.java

```java
import java.util.*;


public class StackExample
{
    public static void main(String args[])
    {
        // Create a Stack..
        Stack myStack = new Stack();

        // Push three strings onto the stack...
        myStack.push("First");
        myStack.push("Second");
```

```
    myStack.push("Third");

    // Print two blank lines...
    System.out.println("\n");

    while(myStack.empty() == false)
    {
        String currentObject = (String) myStack.pop();

        System.out.println(currentObject);
    }
    }
}
```

When you run the stack example, the following should be visible in the console:

Figure 5-7: Using the Stack class

We "push" them onto the First, Second, and Third, and they are "popped" off in the reverse order of Third, Second, then finally First.

Okay, so we first create the `Stack` object called `myStack` using the following line of code:

```
Stack myStack = new Stack();
```

Then we call the `push` method of the `Stack` class to add three `String` objects. This can be seen here:

```
myStack.push("First");
myStack.push("Second");
myStack.push("Third");
```

Next, we create a `while` loop with the condition that the stack is not empty simply by calling the `empty` method of the `Stack` class, which returns `true` if the stack is empty and `false` otherwise. Here is the line of code that this can be seen in:

```
while(myStack.empty() == false)
```

Then within the `while` loop, we call the `pop` method of the `Stack` class, which returns the top reference from the stack and then removes it. As with the `ArrayList` and `LinkedList` classes, they store references of type `Object`, so we need to cast the reference back to begin a string. This can be seen in the following line of code:

```
String currentObject = (String) myStack.pop();
```

Chapter 5

As well as pushing into and popping from the stack, it is possible to use the `peek` method, which allows you to examine the top reference on the stack without actually popping it off the stack.

The Random Class

Although the `Random` class does not help with data storage, it provides a very useful means of generating random numbers (this class is far more flexible than the `random` method in the `Math` class). Let's look at a table of some of the useful methods that this class contains. (Note that the methods are not static, so you need to create an object from the class to use them.)

Method Name	Description
nextInt()	This method returns a random integer within the full range of the integer data type (negative and positive).
nextInt(int)	This method returns a random integer in the range of zero (inclusive) to a maximum of the integer parameter specified (exclusive).
nextLong()	This method returns a long value within the complete range of the long data type (positive and negative).
nextFloat()	This method returns a floating-point value within the range of 0.0 (inclusive) and 1.0 (exclusive).
nextDouble()	This method is the same as `nextFloat`, but with more accuracy due to being a double instead of a float.
nextBoolean()	This method returns either `true` or `false` randomly.
setSeed(long)	This method allows you to "seed" the random number. See below for an explanation of seeding.

Seeding Random Numbers

To generate a truly random sequence, a good idea is to seed a random number with the current system time, which you can get by calling the `currentTimeMillis` static method of the `System` class in Java, for example. However, there may be a time when you want to seed a random number to replicate random sequences of numbers. A good example of this is using a client-server system where you may have, for example, two clients and a server. If the server were to select a random seed, it could then send this seed to both clients to which they can then create the same random number sequence to perform calculations themselves, giving the same results yet still based on the initial random seed, provided you want to calculate the same random results on both clients, the result being that you reduce the server's workload.

Error Handling

> "Insanity: doing the same thing over and
> over again and expecting different results."
> —Albert Einstein (1879-1955)

The worst thing about programming has to be having bugs in your code. In most cases the bug is a simple error, which you spend ages looking for only to realize that you commented out the call to the method that you're attempting to debug about half an hour earlier. We will now look at exceptions and assertions and how they are used for handling errors in Java.

Exceptions

In Java, run-time errors are handled using exceptions. *Exceptions* are objects that are created when your program does something that is deemed to be irregular. When an exception occurs, it is said that an exception has been "thrown." When this happens, the exception must be handled, and it is said that the exception must be "caught." A common exception is the exception `ArrayIndexOutOfBoundsException`, which is thrown by the Java Virtual Machine when an attempt is made to access an illegal index in an array (where no element exists at the specified index).

So let's make a program that causes this exception to be thrown and then run it and see what happens. If you have not already seen what happens when an exception is thrown, you have either been very careful or very lucky. In any case, the following `BrokenArray.java` example is designed to cause an exception to be thrown. In it we create an array of type `int` of length `10`. We will then attempt to continually assign values to the elements of the array using a `for` loop without a termination condition. This means that the value of the counter variable in the `for` loop, which we will use as the array index value, will continue to increment until its value becomes the value of an invalid index in the array, causing an exception to be thrown. Here is the code for `BrokenArray.java`:

Code Listing 5-12: `BrokenArray.java`

```
public class BrokenArray
{
    public static void main(String args[])
    {
        int[] value = new int[10];
        for(int i=0;; i++)
        {
            System.out.println("index = " + i);
            value[i] = i;
        }
    }
}
```

When you compile and run this code, you should get output similar to the following figure.

Chapter 5

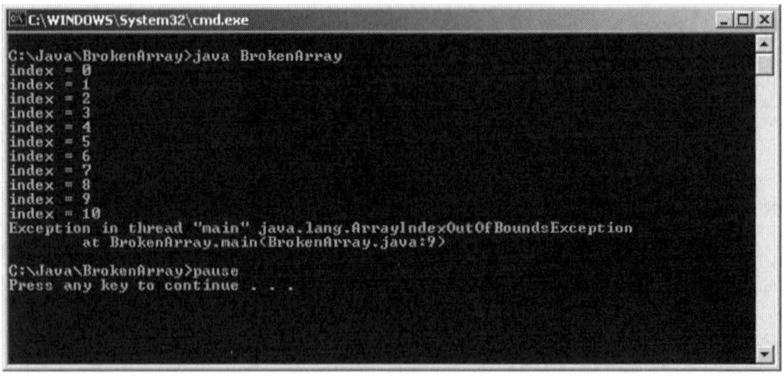

Figure 5-8: The exception is not caught

As you can see, when the example application attempts to access the tenth element of the array `value`, which does not exist, an `Array-IndexOutOfBoundsException` exception was thrown and the application was terminated. So how do we handle this sort of thing? We need to "catch" the exceptions that are "thrown" by the virtual machine.

Using try/catch and finally

Now that we have seen an exception being thrown by the JVM (Java Virtual Machine), let's make a modification to the previous array example so we can catch the exception. We catch the exception by using a `try/catch` block, which first tries to execute a section of code and, if an exception is thrown within the `try` statement, the interpreter then checks the `catch` statements to see if the exception has been caught. Let's look at the modified code listing for the previous example, where we now catch the `ArrayIndexOutOfBounds` exception.

Code Listing 5-13: `BrokenArrayHandled.java`

```
public class BrokenArrayHandled
{
    public static void main(String args[])
    {
        int[] value = new int[10];

        try
        {
            for(int i=0;; i++)
            {
                System.out.println("index = " + i);
                value[i] = i;
            }
        }
        catch(ArrayIndexOutOfBoundsException e)
        {
            System.out.println("Caught: "+e);
        }
    }
}
```

When we execute the example now with the `try/catch` block in it, we can expect the following output.

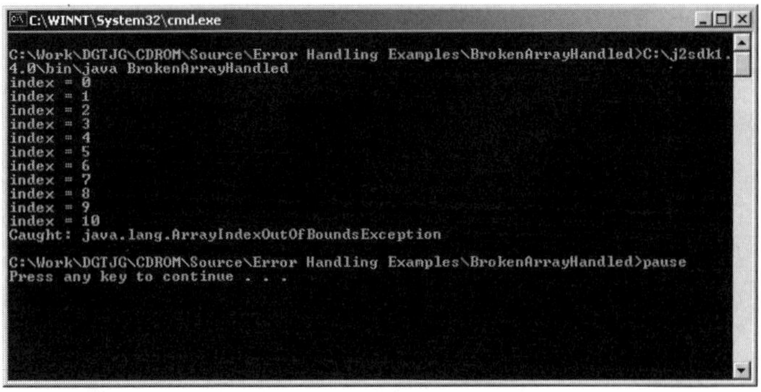

Figure 5-9:
The excep-
tion is now
caught by
the try/catch
block

So in this example, we placed our `for` loop within the `try` block, meaning that if any exceptions are thrown within this block, they will be caught in the `catch` block, provided that the `catch` block actually handles the exception. Note that it is also possible to have multiple `catch` blocks in case it is possible for more than one type of exception to be thrown within the `try` block. For example:

```
try
{

}
catch(Exception1 e)
{

}
catch(Exception2 e)
{

}
```

When an exception is thrown, it is then passed into the `catch` block as a parameter. The base class of all exceptions is the `java.lang.Exception` (readily available) class to which all other exceptions are derived.

```
catch(Exception e)
{
    System.out.println("Exception caught: "+ e);
}
```

In this code, when an exception is thrown, the `Exception` object referenced by "e" will then contain information about the exception, and calling the `toString` method of the `Exception` class (or by simply printing the object, which will call its `toString` method automatically) will give more detailed information about the exception and is a good technique for adding to `catch` blocks that are not expected to be reached.

As all exceptions are derived from the `Exception` class, it is sometimes useful when a number of classes can be thrown to just have one `catch` block, catching an exception of type `Exception` as we have just seen (all types of exceptions will be caught by this `catch` block). Note the following example:

```
int myArray[] = null;
```

Chapter 5

```
try
{
    myArray[7] = 77;
}
catch(Exception e1)
{
    System.out.println("Caught 1: "+ e1);
}
catch(ArrayIndexOutOfBoundsException e2)
{
    System.out.println("Caught 2: "+ e2);
}
```

This code will not compile because the first catch block will catch any exceptions, including the `ArrayIndexOutOfBoundsException` that is derived from `Exception`. However, if we swap these catch blocks around, we can first attempt to catch the more specific `ArrayIndex-OutOfBoundsException` and then attempt to catch any other types of exceptions that may have been thrown. The following code will now compile:

```
try
{
    myArray[7] = 77;
}
catch(ArrayIndexOutOfBoundsException e2)
{
    System.out.println("Caught 2: "+ e2);
}
catch(Exception e1)
{
    System.out.println("Caught 1: "+ e1);
}
```

An important distinction that you need to be aware of is that exceptions that are derived from the `RuntimeException` exception (which is itself a direct subclass of the `Exception` class) do not need to be caught if "declared to be thrown" by a given method. We will look at throwing exceptions in a moment.

For example, the `ArrayIndexOutOfBoundsException` exception is in fact derived from the `RuntimeException` class and does not need to be caught or "declared to be thrown" (we will see about this in a moment also).

When catching an exception, a very useful method that belongs to the `Exception` object passed to the catch block is the `printStackTrace` method, which prints out a back-trace of the error that can indicate the paths through the code where the exception came from. This obviously helps the debugging process. For example, we could use the following code in our catch block to print the stack trace:

```
catch(Exception e)
{
    e.printStackTrace();
}
```

If this code is invoked, it will print out information on the classes, methods, and error-causing lines in those methods, tracing the error through its invocation path, which is a great help for debugging when you can see the line of code where the error occurred.

Using the finally Block

There is also the `finally` block that we can add after the `catch` block(s). Regardless of whether the `try` block throws an exception or not, the `finally` block is <u>always</u> executed at the end, even if a `return` statement is present in either of the `try` or `catch` blocks.

A good example of a use for the `finally` block would be if you were to open and manipulate a file within the `try` block. It would then be possible for the `try` block to throw an exception at any time and miss the rest of the code within the `try` block, meaning the file could be left open. So in this case it would be a good idea to close the file within a `finally` block. Here is the pseudocode for this:

```
try
{
    // open and manipulate the file
}
catch(Exception e)
{
    // print an error message to the user
}
finally
{
    // close the file handle and perform any other cleanup
    // operations
}
```

Another thing to note regards the use of the keyword `return` where the `finally` block is involved. If we say that in the `try` block there is a scenario that can lead to a return being made, where the method we are in is exited, then in this case the method will not exit right away. Instead, before the return statement is executed, the `finally` block is first invoked and then the method returns. This is also the same for making a return call in a `catch` block with the `finally` block.

Another possible avenue to be aware of, as we are being ultra picky, is if you were to have not only a return call in the `try` block, but also a return call in the `finally` block. In this case the return call in the `try` block is never executed because when it is reached, the `finally` block is first executed and then the method returns from there before it is able to return to the original `return` statement within the `try` block.

Throwing Exceptions

Another useful piece of information is that you can throw an exception back from a method so that the method it was called from can handle it. Let's look at another modified version of the `BrokenArray` example where we created a new static method to print the array. The full code listing for this example can be seen here:

Code Listing 5-14: `BrokenArrayThrow.java`

```
public class BrokenArrayThrow
{
    public static void printArray() throws
        ArrayIndexOutOfBoundsException
    {
        int[] value = new int[10];

        for(int i=0;; i++)
        {
            System.out.println("index = " + i);
            value[i] = i;
        }
    }

    public static void main(String args[])
    {


        try
        {
            printArray();
        }
        catch(ArrayIndexOutOfBoundsException e)
        {
            System.out.println("Caught: "+e);
        }
    }
}
```

As you can see from the code, we have appended `throws Array-IndexOutOfBoundsException` to the declaration of our new static method `printArray`, meaning that if that exception is thrown within the method, it will throw it back to the method that called it. In this case it is the main method, where we handle the exception as we did before.

Throwing Your Own Exceptions

As well as catching the standard Java exceptions, you can also make and throw your own exceptions. Keep in mind, though, that throwing exceptions has many overheads and is best kept to a minimum.

First we need to create our exception class called `MyException`, which will extend the `Exception` class that is part of the `java.lang` package. The full source listing for the `MyException` class can be seen here:

Code Listing 5-15: `MyException.java`

```
public class MyException extends Exception
{
    public MyException(String theProblem)
    {
        super(theProblem);
    }
}
```

As you can see, all we do here is create a public class called `MyException`, which extends the `Exception` class. Then we create a constructor, which accepts a string as a parameter. We then pass this parameter to the constructor of the super class (`Exception`).

Next we need to create a small program to test our exception by throwing it using the `throw` keyword, and then we will attempt to catch it. The complete listing for this application can be seen here:

Code Listing 5-16: `TestApp.java`

```java
public class TestApp
{
    public static void main(String args[])
    {
        try
        {
            MyException myException = new MyException("My Error
                Message");
            throw myException;
        }
        catch(MyException e)
        {
            System.out.println("Caught: "+e);
        }
    }
}
```

When we run the code, we see the following output in the console window:

Figure 5-10: Catching our own exception

So within the `try` block, we first create an instance of our exception class using the following line of code.

```java
MyException myException = new MyException("My Error Message");
```

Once we have that, we can then "throw" the exception using the `throw` keyword, as can be seen in the following line of code.

```java
throw myException;
```

After it is thrown, the execution will then go to the `catch` statements and look for one that can handle a `MyException` exception. So we declare our `catch` block as follows:

```java
catch(MyException e)
{
    System.out.println("Caught: "+e);
}
```

This means that it will catch a `MyException` exception and reference it with the `e` object.

Chapter 5

NOTE: When creating your own exception, the `printStackTrace` method will work similarly with your exception objects as with the standard exceptions, as we discussed earlier.

Errors

Errors are similar to exceptions; however, you should not attempt to catch them. All errors are derived from the `java.lang.Error` class. The following table shows three of the most common types of error classes:

Error	When it occurs:
LinkageError	A LinkageError is caused by serious problems occurring within your application, such as trying to create an instance of a class that does not exist. It is pretty much impossible to recover from a LinkageError being thrown.
VirtualMachine-Error	As with the LinkageError, a VirtualMachineError is very serious and occurs in such events as running out of memory and resources.
ThreadDeath	A ThreadDeath error is the least important and is thrown on the termination of an executing thread, whether intentional or accidental.

It is possible to attempt to catch these errors, but there is really little point, as it will be very difficult if not impossible to recover from them. Your best bet is to read what the error was and go back to the code to try and work out what the problem was.

Assertions

Assertions are new to Java 1.4 and are an excellent tool to assist you in debugging your application and applet games. Assertions are simply a way to test situations where you would normally make assumptions as to the values of variables. For example, you could test that an age is not a negative number.

Let's look at a very simple example where we use the `assert` keyword to test if a Boolean variable called `testValue` is true or not.

Here is the complete code listing for this example:

Code Listing 5-17: `TestApp.java`

```
public class SimpleAssert
{
    public static void main(String args[])
    {
        boolean testValue = true;

        assert testValue;

        testValue = false;

        assert testValue;
    }
}
```

As the `assert` keyword is new to the Java language since the 1.4 release of the SDK, we need to compile the code using the `-source` parameter, where we specify 1.4. Here is the complete command we use to compile the code:

```
javac -source 1.4 SimpleAssert.java
```

Then when we execute the application, we need to enable assertions by using either the `-enableassertions` parameter or the `-ea` parameter. The complete command for executing the example is as follows:

```
java -enableassertions SimpleAssert
```

So when we run the application, we should expect to see the following output:

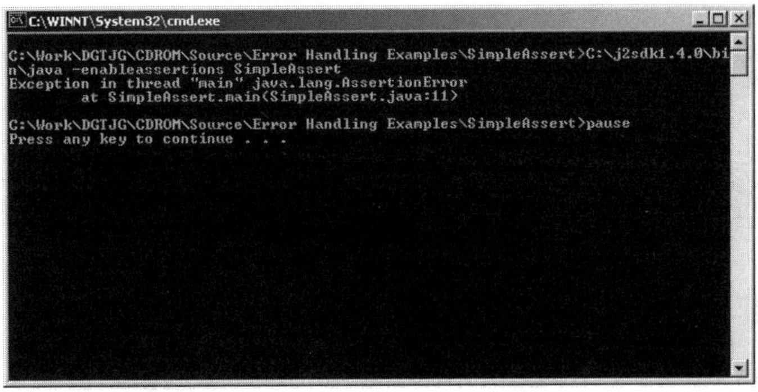

Figure 5-11:
Simple
assertion

As you can see from the screen shot, the `java.lang.Assertion-Error` error was thrown on line 11, which happens to be the line where we assert the `testValue` variable when it is false.

So an assertion will only throw an error if the test case turns out to be false. Let's look at some situations where using assertions is useful.

Assertions in Control Flow

Assertions can be used to detect if the execution is reaching areas that it should not be. For example, let's look at this simple method:

```
public int returnNumber(int myNumber)
{
    if(myNumber > 0)
    {
        return myNumber;
    }
    else
    {
        return 0;
    }

    assert false;
}
```

In the example above, you can see that the `assert` should never be reached, as the method returns from both the `if` statement and the `else` statement.

Think of assert as a sort of security blanket for you. In the previous example the execution would never reach the `assert`, but in more complex code there would be no reason not to put one there, just in case.

Assertions in Internal Invariants

Impressive section heading, eh? It is really nothing complicated. Basically, it is about using assertions to test assumptions, which are made within the `else` statements of `if/else` blocks and also within the default case of `switch` statements.

Let's say you have, for example, an `if` statement to test a condition like the following:

```
if(i > 0)
{
    // true statement code here...
}
```

Then if you append an `else` block to the end, you are making the assumption that the `i` variable will be less than or equal to zero.

```
if(i > 0)
{
    // true statement code here...
}
else
{
    // you assume that 'i' is equal or less than zero here
}
```

So, you could place an assertion in the `else` statement to ensure that `i` is equal to or less than zero. Our statement would then look as follows.

```
if(i > 0)
{
    // true statement code here...
}
else
{
    assert i <= 0;
}
```

Another useful part of assertions is that you can also store a numeric value within the assertion. If we use the previous example and store the `i` variable, the `assert` line would then look as follows:

```
assert i <= 0 : i;
```

Therefore, if the `AssertionError` is thrown, the value of `i` will also be printed. Also, note that where we add the `i` after the colon (:), we can also add other data types, such as string values for more informative error reporting.

Other Useful Notes

By default, assertions are turned off. If you remember in the previous assertion example that we compiled and ran, you were required to add the `-enableassertions` parameter so that the assertions would be used. If this parameter is omitted from the command line when running your program, the assertions will not be enabled. When assertions are not enabled, any assertion statements in your code will be ignored, so you need to be careful that you do not actually place any important code in the assertion statement. Here is an example of some bad assertion code:

```
assert i++ > 0;    // bad
```

If assertions were switched on, the assertion would test if `i` were greater than zero and increment `i`'s value by one. Of course, if assertions were off, the line would not be executed; therefore, `i` would not be incremented, which could have other implications within your program.

The best way around this is to create a Boolean variable to store the result and test the Boolean variable with the assertion. Here is a better way to perform the previous assertion:

```
boolean  result = i++ > 0;
assert result;    // good
```

Summary

In this chapter we learned how to use packages in Java as well as create our own packages. Then we looked over some of the useful classes within the standard packages. Finally we covered how to handle errors within your applications and applets. In the next chapter you will learn how streams and files work in Java. We will look at retrieving keyboard entries in the console window, allowing us to take a look at making a simple console game of tic-tac-toe.

Chapter 5

Stream I/O

"What goes in, must come out."
—Glenn and Andrew

Introduction

In this chapter, you will learn how to utilize streams and files in your games. Files are especially useful if you do not have access or simply do not wish to use a database for storing your data. In fact, for single-player games, it really makes more sense to use files to save (for example, players' saved games or high scores). An important use of files is for loading in specific game data, such as a file storing level data. The key aspects of this chapter cover writing data to a file, reading data in from a file, and then finally how to save and retrieve entire objects (classes) to and from a file by using serialization.

Introduction to Streams

A *stream* is simply an abstract representation of a physical input or output device. A stream can be thought of as a pipe that bytes of data flow through, and therefore data can be both read to and written from a stream.

As you have probably guessed, there are two forms of streams: *input streams* and *output streams*. Examples of input streams are a keyboard, disk file, or remote network application that is sending data. Examples of an output stream are a disk file, a console window, or even a printer.

Console Input

Now that we have a basic understanding of streams, let's see how we can get user input from the console window. In this example we will be using `System.in`, which is an instance of the `InputStream` class and is normally connected to the keyboard. However, to make use of the `InputStream`, we need to create a `BufferedReader` so that we can read lines of input from the console window. Let's now look at a complete example to see how we can get console input from the user.

Code Listing 6-1: Console input

```java
import java.io.*;

public class ConsoleInputExample
{
    public ConsoleInputExample()
    {
        BufferedReader keyboard = new BufferedReader(new
            InputStreamReader(System.in));

        String inputStr = new String();

        System.out.println("Type something and press enter...");
        System.out.println("Type \"quit\" to exit");

        try
        {
            while(!(inputStr=keyboard.readLine()).equalsIgnoreCase
                    ("quit"))
            {
                System.out.println("You typed in: "+inputStr);
            }
        }
        catch(IOException e)
        {
            System.out.println(e);
        }
    }

    public static void main(String args[])
    {
        ConsoleInputExample mainApp = new ConsoleInputExample();
    }
}
```

When we execute the example console application and then type in some
sample data (each followed by the Enter key), we can see that it will look
like the following figure.

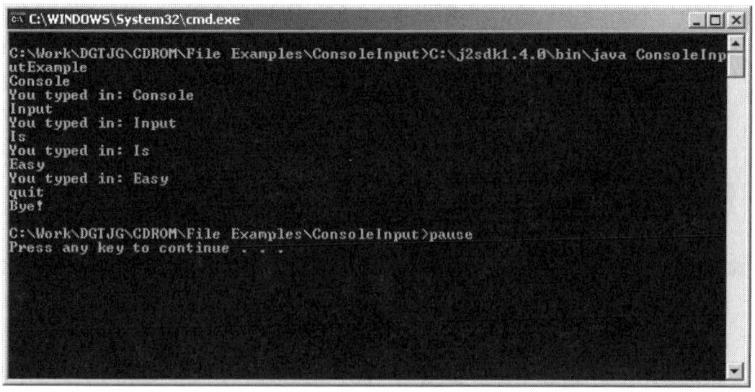

Figure 6-1:
Console
input
example

Our console application basically takes a line of input from the user, stores
it in a string, and finally outputs it back to the console. The only special
case is if the user types in "quit," in which case the application terminates.

Let's now look at the code and see how it works. First we include the `java.io.*` package so we have access to all the input classes (such as the `BufferedReader`).

Next we create a `BufferedReader` object, which we create by first creating an `InputStreamReader`, passing in our `System.in` stream as a parameter to its constructor. This can be seen in the following code:

```
BufferedReader keyboard = new BufferedReader(new
    InputStreamReader(System.in));
```

Once we have our `BufferedReader` object, which we have called `keyboard`, we then create a string called `inputStr` so we can store the data we read in.

Next, we create a `while` loop and then attempt to read a line of input from our `keyboard` object. Basically, this will wait until the user presses the Enter key, and then it will get all the characters that were pressed before the Enter key and store them in the `inputStr` string. Notice also how we check if the string is equal to the string `quit` (ignoring case). This is simply to allow the code to quit out of the program.

```
while(!(inputStr=keyboard.readLine()).equalsIgnoreCase("quit"))
```

This code might look a little strange, but it is quite straightforward. We first call the `readLine` method of the `keyboard` object, which blocks (waits) until the user enters the data and presses the Enter key. Once this is done, the entered string is assigned to `inputStr`, which is then the value used to compare with the string literal `quit` for testing if the `while` loop terminates or not.

If the user did not enter `quit`, simply output what the user entered.

All we are left to do now is catch the possible I/O exception and finish the `while` loop. Catching the exception can be seen here:

```
catch(IOException e)
{
    System.out.println(e);
}
```

The `IOException` exception is the base of all exceptions relating to problems with input and output. You will encounter this exception a lot, notably later on in the book when we utilize streams for networking in Chapter 17, "Introduction to Networking."

Console Game Example—Tic-Tac-Toe

Now that we know how to get input from the user via the console window, we are all set to produce some kind of logical game with user interaction and game logic, albeit from the perils of doom that is the ASCII console window. Let's look at a very simple console game called tic-tac-toe. In case you don't know how to play tic-tac-toe, the idea of the game is to get a line of three O's or X's (depending on which player you are) on a board consisting of 3x3 squares. Let's first look at the complete source code for this example, and then we will take a look at how the code works.

Code Listing 6-2: Tic-tac-toe example

```java
import java.io.*;

public class TicTacToe
{
    public void start()
    {
        char inputChar = ' ';
        String inputLine = null;
        initializeGame();
        drawGameState();

        BufferedReader reader =
          new BufferedReader(
             new InputStreamReader(System.in));

        do
        {
          try
          {
             //   wait for input from player
             inputLine = reader.readLine();
             if(inputLine.length() == 1)
               inputChar = inputLine.charAt(0);
             else
               inputChar = (char)-1;
          }
          catch(IOException e)
          {
             System.out.println(e);
          }

          //   handle the input
          handleInput(inputChar);

          //   print output
          drawGameState();
        } while(programRunning);
    }

    public void initializeGame()
    {
      //   clear the board
      for(int i=0; i<BOARD_SIZE; i++)
        for(int j=0; j<BOARD_SIZE; j++)
          board[i][j] = ' ';

      //   initialize move variables
      moveCounter = 0;
      turn = 0;
      moveType = COLUMN;

      System.out.println("Start playing Tic-Tac-Toe");
    }

    public boolean checkForWin()
    {
      char symbol = SYMBOL[turn];
```

```java
  // check vertical win
  Label1:
  for(int i=0; i<BOARD_SIZE; i++)
  {
    for(int j=0; j<BOARD_SIZE; j++)
      if(board[i][j] != symbol)
        continue Label1;

    // if reached, winning line found
    return true;
  }

  // check horizontal win
  Label2:
  for(int j=0; j<BOARD_SIZE; j++)
  {
    for(int i=0; i<BOARD_SIZE; i++)
      if(board[i][j] != symbol)
        continue Label2;

    // if reached, winning line found
    return true;
  }

  // check back slash diagonal win
  for(int i=0; i<BOARD_SIZE; i++)
    if(board[i][i] != symbol)
      break;
    else if(i == BOARD_SIZE-1)
      return true;    // winning line found

  // check forward slash diagonal win
  for(int i=0; i<BOARD_SIZE; i++)
    if(board[i][BOARD_SIZE - i - 1] != symbol)
      break;
    else if(i == BOARD_SIZE-1)
      return true;    // winning line found

  // if reach here then no win found
  return false;
}

public void makeMove()
{
  // is board position available
  if(board[moveCoords[COLUMN]][moveCoords[ROW]] == ' ')
  {
    // make move
    board[moveCoords[COLUMN]][moveCoords[ROW]] = SYMBOL[turn];
    moveCounter++;

    if(checkForWin() == true)
    {
      // player has won
      drawBoard();
      System.out.println("Congratulations, " + SYMBOL[turn]
            + "'s win the game");

      // start new game
      initializeGame();
```

```java
      }
      else if(moveCounter == (BOARD_SIZE * BOARD_SIZE))
      {
        // no win and board is full, so the game has been drawn
        System.out.println("Game drawn");
        drawBoard();

        // start new game
        initializeGame();
      }
      else    // else continue playing game, change turn
        turn = (turn + 1) % 2;
    }
    else
      System.out.println("Illegal move, board position already
            filled");
  }

  public void handleInput(char key)
  {
    switch(key)
    {
      case 'q': case 'Q':
        // quit the game
        programRunning = false;
        break;
      case '0': case '1': case '2':
        // move coordinate entered
        moveCoords[moveType] = Integer.valueOf(String.valueOf
                (key)).intValue();
        if(moveType == ROW)
        {
          makeMove();
          moveType = COLUMN;
        }
        else    // moveType is curently COLUMN coordinate
          moveType = ROW;
        break;

      default:
        // invalid input to game
        System.out.println("ERROR: Invalid entry, this input
                has no function");
        moveType = COLUMN;
    }
  }

  public void drawGameState()
  {
    if(moveType == COLUMN)
    {
      drawBoard();
      System.out.println("Type 'q' to quit program");
      System.out.println(SYMBOL[turn] + "'s move...");
      System.out.print("Enter column number ->> ");
    }
    else
      System.out.print("Enter row number ->> ");
  }
```

```
public void drawBoard()
{
  System.out.println();       //  new line
  System.out.print("  ");

  for(int i=0; i<BOARD_SIZE; i++)
    System.out.print(" " + i);

  System.out.println();        //  new line

  for(int j=0; j<BOARD_SIZE; j++)
  {
    System.out.print(j + " |");

    for(int i=0; i<BOARD_SIZE; i++)
      System.out.print(board[i][j] + "|");

    System.out.println();    //  new line
  }

  System.out.println();        //  new line
}

public static void main(String args[])
{
  TicTacToe game = new TicTacToe();
  game.start();
}

private final int BOARD_SIZE = 3;
private final int COLUMN = 0;
private final int ROW = 1;
private final char SYMBOL[] = {'O', 'X'};

private boolean programRunning = true;
private char board[][] = new char[BOARD_SIZE][BOARD_SIZE];
private int moveCoords[] = new int[2];

private int moveCounter;
private int turn;
private int moveType;
}
```

When we run the console example, we can see that it draws the board and then awaits input from the user. This can be seen here:

Figure 6-2:
The
tic-tac-toe
game

When a move is given, it then redraws the board showing the move that was made or it displays an error message if the move was invalid. Between moves, we work out the consequences of the move (i.e., who's won or if there is a tie). Let's look at the code that we used to create this simple (yet fun) game.

The first method that is called is of course the `main` method, so let's take a look at this method first:

```
public static void main(String args[])
{
    TicTacToe game = new TicTacToe();
    game.start();
}
```

All we do in the `main` method is create an instance of our `TicTacToe` class and then call its `start` method.

The `start` method is used to first set up the game and then goes into a `do/while` loop, known generally as the game loop, until the user requests that the game terminates. Let's look at the code we have used in the initialization part of the `start` method now.

First we create a variable called `inputChar` to hold the character that was entered by the player, which we will extract from the line the player inputs that will be held in a variable called `inputLine`. We create these two variables with the following two lines of code:

```
char inputChar = ' ';
String inputLine = null;
```

Next, we call the `initializeGame` method, which looks like the following:

```
public void initializeGame()
{
    //   clear the board
    for(int i=0; i<BOARD_SIZE; i++)
        for(int j=0; j<BOARD_SIZE; j++)
            board[i][j] = ' ';

    //   initialize move variables
    moveCounter = 0;
    turn = 0;
    moveType = COLUMN;

    System.out.println("Start playing Tic-Tac-Toe");
}
```

In this method, we first create an empty `board` array to store the positions where the players will place their Os or Xs, and then we initialize three variables that we will use to control the actual flow of the game, which will be discussed later.

After we have initialized the game, we call the `drawGameState` method to display the board and prompt the user for input. Note though that this function does not actually request any input from the user. It simply displays the board data and shows text on the screen asking the player for the input. This method can be seen in the following block of code:

```
public void drawGameState()
{
    if(moveType == COLUMN)
    {
```

```
    drawBoard();
    System.out.println("Type 'q' to quit program");
    System.out.println(SYMBOL[turn] + "'s move...");
    System.out.print("Enter column number ->> ");
  }
  else
     System.out.print("Enter row number ->> ");
}
```

Notice that we only draw the board if the player is entering the column value to make a move, as this is the first of two entries per move, so we only need to refresh the board at the beginning of the two required inputs: the column and the row moves.

After the game state has been written out to the console, we then initialize a `BufferedReader`, as we did in the previous console input example, so we are able to take input in from the user for retrieving the given column or row value. We create our `BufferedReader` object with the following line of code.

```
BufferedReader reader =
    new BufferedReader(
        new InputStreamReader(System.in));
```

Next, start the main game loop, which will execute until our program is terminated. Once in this loop, we attempt to get input from the user by reading a line from the console. This is accomplished with the following code segment.

```
do
{
    try
    {
        // wait for input from player
        inputLine = reader.readLine();
```

Once we have the input string, extract the first character from it with the following code segment:

```
if(inputLine.length() == 1)
    inputChar = inputLine.charAt(0);
else
    inputChar = (char)-1;
```

Note that we also check if the text input from the user was of length 1, hence one single character, as our input mechanism works with single characters. If it was not 1, set the input character to −1, which will represent an invalid character later on when we analyze this input value. Otherwise, assign the character to our `inputChar` variable.

Now that we have the character, pass it to the `handleInput` method with the following line of code:

```
handleInput(inputChar);
```

Let's look at how this method deals with the input now. Switch the character and check if it was either q, 0, 1, or 2 (or some other character). If the letter q was entered, we know that the user wishes to terminate the game, so we set the `programRunning` variable to `false`, which is used as the condition for termination for the main game loop.

If the user entered `0`, `1`, or `2`, first get the integer value of the character that was entered with the following line of code:

```
moveCoords[moveType] = Integer.valueOf(String.valueOf
        (key)).intValue();
```

As you can see, we set the given `moveCoords` array element to the integer value of the character entered, using the `moveType` variable to determine whether this number relates to the column or row (0 and 1, respectively, in the `moveCoords` array). As we get the column from the user first and then the row, we need to make a check to see if the input type is the second coordinate (i.e., the row), meaning that the complete move has been entered. If it has, we can then make the move by calling the aptly named method `makeMove` and then set the `moveType` back to column. We will look at the all-important `makeMove` method in a moment. If the move entered was the first input (column), simply set the next input type to row. Note that if the input was not valid (i.e., it did not match any of the cases), the switch will jump to the `default` statement, which prints an error message to the screen and resets the `moveType` variable to be the column to restart the move. This can be seen in the following code:

```
default:
    // invalid input to game
    System.out.println("ERROR: Invalid entry, this input has no
        function");
    moveType = COLUMN;
```

Now that we know how the input is handled, let's look at what happens when we call the `makeMove` method.

First check if the board at the select position is empty. This is done with the following `if` statement:

```
if(board[moveCoords[COLUMN]][moveCoords[ROW]] == ' ')
{
```

If the space on the board is free, set the position of the board to the player's symbol and increment the `moveCounter`, which records the number of moves that have been made in the current game. Here are the two lines of code we use to do this:

```
board[moveCoords[COLUMN]][moveCoords[ROW]] = SYMBOL[turn];
moveCounter++;
```

Next check if the player has won the game by calling our `checkForWin` method. We will look at this method in a moment. If the player has won, draw the board by calling the `drawBoard` method to show the victorious board and then display a line of text informing the player that he/she has won. After this, call the `initializeGame` method to set up the application for the next game. This can be seen in the following block of code:

```
if(checkForWin() == true)
{
```

```
    //  player has won
    drawBoard();
    System.out.println("Congratulations, " + SYMBOL[turn]
            + "'s win the game");

    //  start new game
    initializeGame();

}
```

If the player has not won, we need to check if there are still moves available on the board to check for a tie. To check for this, simply compare the area of the board (i.e., the width multiplied by the height) with the current `moveCounter`. If the `moveCounter` is equal to the total area of the board, the game is drawn and we need to tell the players and once again initialize a new game. This can be seen in the following block of code:

```
else if(moveCounter == (BOARD_SIZE * BOARD_SIZE))
{
    //  no win and board is full, so the game has been drawn
    System.out.println("Game drawn");
    drawBoard();

    //  start new game
    initializeGame();
}
```

So if the player has not won and the game is not drawn, we simply need to change the current turn to the other player, which is accomplished with the following code:

```
else    //  else continue playing game, change turn
    turn = (turn + 1) % 2;
```

The code `(turn + 1) % 2` simply turns an odd value into "0" and an even value into "1", hence we swap turns either from 0 to 1 or vice versa.

Finally, we need to add an `else` statement for our initial `if` statement, which will catch if the player has tried to place their counter on a board position that is already taken. This is done with the following two lines of code:

```
else
    System.out.println("Illegal move, board position already
        filled");
```

Now the important part of this game is the `checkForWin` method. This method simply needs to check the conditions for a win in the game of tic-tac-toe. The possible wins consist of three horizontal checks, three vertical checks, and two diagonal checks for three matching symbols in a line. This is quite straightforward. For example, look at the code to check for a vertical win:

```
// check vertical win
    Label1:
    for(int i=0; i<BOARD_SIZE; i++)
    {
        for(int j=0; j<BOARD_SIZE; j++)
            if(board[i][j] != symbol)
```

```
         continue Label1;

      // if reached, winning line found
      return true;
   }
```

This code simply iterates across the three column coordinates, each time checking if all three of the row elements are equal to the given symbol. If one symbol does not match the move symbol in the nested loop, we continue the first loop using a `continue label` statement (these were discussed in detail in Chapter 2). The other checks in this method work in the same way.

Writing Data to a File

Let's now look at a working example of how we could easily write a player's name and high score to a file in the same directory as we executed the code. Note that the player's name will be a string value and the score will be an integer.

Code Listing 6-3: Writing data to a file

```java
import java.io.*;

public class SimpleWrite
{
    public SimpleWrite()
    {
        // Hard code the players name and score...
        String playerName = "George";
        int playerScore = 125;

        // Create out file object...
        File theFile = new File("output.txt");


        try
        {
            // Create a data output stream for the file...
            DataOutputStream outputStream = new DataOutputStream(new
                    FileOutputStream(theFile));

            // Write the data to the output stream...

            // ->> the name...
            outputStream.writeUTF(playerName);

            // ->> the score
            outputStream.writeInt(playerScore);

            // Close the output stream...
            outputStream.flush();
            outputStream.close();
        }
        catch(IOException e)
        {
            System.out.println(e);
```

```
        }
    }

    public static void main(String args[])
    {
        SimpleWrite mainApp = new SimpleWrite();
    }
}
```

When we run this console application, we can see that it has written a file called output.txt to the same directory from which the application was run. Here is how the file we write looks when we open it in Notepad:

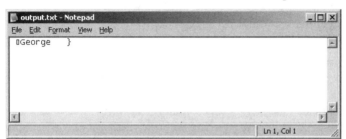

Figure 6-3: How our output file looks

As you can see from the above image, the file we have written is not just plain text but is instead in binary format. Because of this, it makes it much easier to read information back from the file into Java, as we will see in the next example.

For now though, let's look at how the code works to allow us to write the file. Start by creating two variables with information that we wish to write to the file: one a string value and the other just an integer value. This is done with the following two lines of code:

```
String playerName = "George";
int playerScore = 125;
```

Next we need to create a file object, which will create an empty file on the hard drive (or wherever you are trying to create it). In this example, we will create it in the same directory the application was executed from. We have called the file output.txt. (Remember that the file isn't actually a text file, but we have called it this so it is easy to look at in a text editor). To create our file object, use the following line of code:

```
File theFile = new File("output.txt");
```

The path that this file object relates to is the path where your main class is executed.

Now that we have a file object, we can attempt to create a DataOutputStream using the FileOutputStream, to which we pass in our file. A DataOutputStream allows us to output data to wherever we have specified, which in this case is a file. Here is the line of code that we require to do this:

```
try
{
```

```
DataOutputStream outputStream = new DataOutputStream(new
    FileOutputStream(theFile));
```

Note that an `IOException` can be thrown when trying to create the `DataOutputStream`, so we have encapsulated the whole next segment of code in a `try`/`catch` statement to catch the `IOException`.

Next, write the player's name to the output stream. This is done by means of the `writeUTF` method, which writes the string in Unicode format. This can be seen in the following line of code:

```
outputStream.writeUTF(playerName);
```

Once we have our name output to the stream, we then output the player's score by utilizing the `writeInt` method of the output stream. This can be seen in the following code:

```
outputStream.writeInt(playerScore);
```

Note that there are variations of the `write` method for each of the different basic data types, as well as a method simply called `write`, which can be used to output an array of bytes to an output stream. We will look at some of these different methods in more examples later in this chapter.

Once the data is written to the output stream, call the `flush` method of the output stream to ensure that all the data has been written. Then we finally call the `close` method to close our output stream. This can be seen in the following two lines of code:

```
outputStream.flush();
outputStream.close();
```

Reading Data from a File

In this next example, we will use the file that we created in the previous example and attempt to load it in and display the values that were retrieved from the file in the console window. First let's look at the complete code listing for this example console application. Then we will look into how the code works.

Code Listing 6-4: Reading data from a file

```
import java.io.*;

public class SimpleRead
{
    public SimpleRead()
    {
        // Reset players name and score...
        String playerName = "";
        int playerScore = 0;

        // Create our in file object...
        File theFile = new File("output.txt");

        try
        {
            // Create a data input stream for the file...
            DataInputStream inputStream = new DataInputStream(new
```

```
            FileInputStream(theFile));

    // Read the data from the input stream...

    // ->> The name...
    playerName = inputStream.readUTF();

    // ->> The score...
    playerScore = inputStream.readInt();

    // Close the input stream...
    inputStream.close();
}
catch(IOException e)
{
    System.out.println(e);
}

System.out.println("The Players Name was: "+ playerName);
System.out.println("And there score was:  "+ playerScore);
}


public static void main(String args[])
{
    SimpleRead mainApp = new SimpleRead();
}
}
}
```

When we execute this example with the `output.txt` file in the same directory that we are running it from, we can see the following output in the console window.

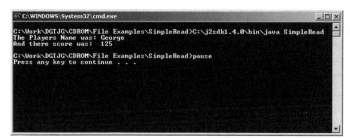

Figure 6-4:
The data
has been
loaded back
in

As you can see from this figure, the data has been loaded back in correctly from the file into our application. Let's now look at the code that we have used to make this work.

First create the two variables in which we are going to eventually store the data that we retrieved from the file. We declare these two variables with the following two lines of code:

```
String playerName = "";
int playerScore = 0;
```

Next create a file object, as we did in the last example, to load in our `output.txt` file. This is accomplished with the following line of code:

```
File theFile = new File("output.txt");
```

Once we have this, attempt to create a `DataInputStream` object by creating a `FileInputStream` with our file object passed into the constructor. As with the `DataOutputStream`, the input stream can also throw an `IOException`, so as with the last example, encase all of the stream manipulation code within a `try/catch` block. Here is the code we use to create our `DataInputStream` object:

```
try
{
    DataInputStream inputStream = new DataInputStream(new
        FileInputStream(theFile));
```

Now that we have an input stream, we need to read the data back in the same order as we wrote it to the file. So the first thing we wish to read from the file is the string containing the player's name. This is done using the `readUTF` method, which reads a string that has been written in Unicode format (i.e., by the `writeUTF` method). This can be seen in the following line of code:

```
playerName = inputStream.readUTF();
```

So now we have the player's name back as a string. Finally, we need to retrieve the player's score, which can be done by simply using the `readInt` method, as the input stream maintains its current position in the file after previous reads. This can be seen in the following line of code:

```
playerScore = inputStream.readInt();
```

Object Serialization

Up until now, we have been looking at quite a low-level way of dealing with writing to and reading from files. In this section you will learn how it is possible to write and read objects to files using serialization, which makes saving and retrieving data far simpler for objects, so we don't need to concern ourselves with saving its data members individually.

Serialization is a method of storing all the instance data (see the note at the end of the chapter about the `transient` keyword to see how to avoid saving certain data) of a class in a single string automatically that can then be sent (for example, via a network or saved to a file). When the data is then read, it is deserialized and returned to its original object form.

The best way to see how this works is to look at a simple example. First we need to create a class to describe the object for storing a player's details. So let's make a class called `PlayerData`, which will store the player's name, score, and username and password for accessing a game. This class can be seen below:

Code Listing 6-5: The `PlayerData` class

```
import java.io.*;

public class PlayerData implements Serializable
{
    public PlayerData(String name, int score, String username,
        String password)
```

```
    {
        this.name = name;
        this.score = score;
        this.username = username;
        this.password = password;
    }

    public String name;
    public int score;
    public String username;
    public String password;
}
```

Let's look at how we have made this class serializable. First we need to import the `java.io.*` package, as it contains the `Serializable` interface, which we need to make this class implement. This can be seen here:

```
public class PlayerData implements Serializable
```

Note that if the class does not implement the `Serializable` interface, it is not possible to use serialization. The great news is that we do not actually have to do anything else to make serialization work; all we need to do is ensure that we abide by the following three rules:

1. The `Serializable` interface must be implemented.
2. The class must be declared as public.
3. If the class extends another class, the class it is extending must contain a default constructor (a constructor with no parameters), and the super class must also handle saving its own objects to the stream if data from the super class is to be serialized also. (The super class would need to implement `Serializable`; otherwise its data would not be recorded but the subclass data would be.)

Now that we have our basic player class, let's look at the main code listing, which will save an instance of this class to a file called `output.txt` and load it back into a new instance of the class and display what was read into the console. Here is the complete code listing for this example:

Code Listing 6-6: Object serialization

```
import java.io.*;

public class SerializationExample
{
    public SerializationExample()
    {
        // Create an instance of our PlayerData class...
        PlayerData playerData = new PlayerData("John", 400,
                "jsmith", "qwerty");

        // Create out file object...
        File theFile = new File("output.txt");

        // Create the file output stream...
        FileOutputStream fileOutputStream = null;
        try
        {
```

Chapter 6

```java
         fileOutputStream = new FileOutputStream(theFile);
}
catch(FileNotFoundException e)
{
   System.out.println(e);
}

// Create the object output stream...
ObjectOutputStream objectOutputStream = null;

try
{
   objectOutputStream = new ObjectOutputStream
         (fileOutputStream);

   // Write the object to the object output stream...
   objectOutputStream.writeObject(playerData);
}
catch(IOException e)
{
   System.out.println(e);
}

// Read the object back into a new instance of our
// 'PlayerData' class
PlayerData newPlayerData = null;

// Create the file input stream...
FileInputStream fileInputStream = null;
try
{
    fileInputStream = new FileInputStream(theFile);
}
catch(FileNotFoundException e)
{
   System.out.println(e);
}

// Create the object input stream...
ObjectInputStream objectInputStream = null;

try
{
   objectInputStream = new ObjectInputStream(fileInputStream);

   // Read the object from the object input stream...
   newPlayerData = (PlayerData) objectInputStream
         .readObject();
}
catch(ClassNotFoundException e)
{
   System.out.println(e);
}
catch(IOException e)
{
   System.out.println(e);
}

// Print what was read in...
System.out.println("The player's name was:
```

```
            "+newPlayerData.name);
   System.out.println("The player's score was:
            "+newPlayerData.score);
   System.out.println("The player's username was:
            "+newPlayerData.username);
   System.out.println("The player's password was:
            "+newPlayerData.password);
   }


   public static void main(String args[])
   {
      SerializationExample mainApp = new SerializationExample();
   }
}
```

When we execute this console application, we will see that the following is visible in the console window:

Figure 6-5: Using serialization

As you can see from this figure, the application has successfully written the data to the file and then read the data back from the file into the application. Let's now look at the main code that we have used to create this.

First, we create a `PlayerData` object called `playerData` with the following line of code.

```
PlayerData playerData = new PlayerData("John", 400,
   "jsmith", "qwerty");
```

We pass the details into the constructor, which are the name, score, username, and password. Now that we have our object, we next create a `File` object so we can specify where we wish our output (and input) file to be in this example. This is accomplished with the following line of code:

```
File theFile = new File("output.txt");
```

Once we have our `File` object, we then need to create a `FileOuputStream`. This is done by passing our `theFile` object into the `FileOutputStream` constructor, as can be seen in the following block of code:

```
FileOutputStream fileOutputStream = null;
try
{
   fileOutputStream = new FileOutputStream(theFile);
```

Chapter 6

```
}
catch(FileNotFoundException e)
{
    System.out.println(e);
}
```

Note that we need to catch the `FileNotFoundException`. Once we have our `fileOutputStream` object, we then use this to create an `ObjectOutputStream`, which is used to write objects to a stream (in this case, our `FileOutputStream`). So to create our `ObjectOutput-Stream`, we pass our `fileOutputStream` into the constructor, as can be seen in the following block of code:

```
// Create the object output stream...
    ObjectOutputStream objectOutputStream = null;

    try
    {
        objectOutputStream = new ObjectOutputStream
            (fileOutputStream);
```

Once our `objectOutputStream` object is created, we can then easily write our `playerData` object to the file with the following line of code:

```
objectOutputStream.writeObject(playerData);
```

Notice how we use the `writeObject` method, which is a member of the `objectOutputStream` class and takes any serializable object as a parameter.

Now that the data is stored in the file, create a new `PlayerData` object called `newPlayerData` and set it to `null`. This is done with the following line of code:

```
PlayerData newPlayerData = null;
```

Next, we need to create a `FileInputStream` that we can use to load the file back in. We create the `FileInputStream` using the same `theFile` object as we did with the `FileOutputStream`. We will be accessing the same file that we just wrote. This is done with the following lines of code:

```
FileInputStream fileInputStream = null;
try
{
    fileInputStream = new FileInputStream(theFile);
}
catch(FileNotFoundException e)
{
    System.out.println(e);
}
```

Again, notice that we need to catch the `FileNotFoundException` exception. Once we have our `fileInputStream` object, we then need to create an `ObjectInputStream`, which can be used to read our `PlayerData` object back in from the file. Here is the code we require to create our `ObjectInputStream`.

```
ObjectInputStream objectInputStream = null;
```

```
try
{
    objectInputStream = new ObjectInputStream(fileInputStream);
```

Notice how we use our `fileInputStream` object in the constructor to create the `ObjectInputStream` so it will use the file as the stream when attempting to read the data.

We now need to read the object back in, which is done by using the `readObject` method of the `objectInputStream` object. Note that we also need to typecast the data that we read in to the correct class type (which in our example is `PlayerData`). This can be seen in the following line of code:

```
newPlayerData = (PlayerData) objectInputStream.readObject();
```

The final part of the reading is to catch both a `ClassNotFound-Exception` exception and an `IOException` exception. We need to catch a `ClassNotFoundException` as a security measure, as we cannot be assured of the type of object being read in, at least Java cannot be assured of us writing correct code for this.

Now that we have read in our player information, all that is left is to simply display it to the console to show that the data has been read back in correctly.

 NOTE: If the class you wish to serialize contains a member that you do not actually wish to save to a file (or send across a network), you can declare the variable as <u>transient</u>. For example, if we had a password stored as a string in a class and we did not wish to serialize it, we would declare it as follows:

```
transient private String password;
```

Summary

In this chapter you learned the basics of using streams and files in your games. In addition, you also created a simple console game, which got some interactivity from the user and gave us a first glance at the inner workings of a game. In the next chapter we will delve into the exciting world of threads.

Chapter 6

Chapter 7

Threads

"The wise man can pick up a grain of sand and envision a whole
universe. But the stupid man will just lie down on some
seaweed and roll around until he's completely draped in it.
Then he'll stand up and say 'Hey, I'm Vine Man.'"

—Jack Handey

Introduction

When programming in Java, you must learn to command and conquer
threads. In Java, threads are important for things such as handling input
and network programming. Before you read any further, you will need to
understand the underlying characteristics of threads, how to use them,
and how to handle them safely with one another.

What Is a Thread?

A *thread* is simply a running process of execution. The simplest way to
explain a thread is to tell you that when an application begins by invoking
the `main` method, the code that is executed is running in a thread. This
thread is started by the Java Virtual Machine and enters the `main` method
to begin flowing through your code. Tracing the path of what we might call
the main thread is relatively simple, as code is executed line by line starting in main; although invoking methods and making loops can complicate
the path of execution, we are still in relative control of the flow of the program. However, I use the term "program" loosely because the main
thread may not be the only thread running in our program. Yes, that is correct; along with our main thread, there can be other threads running at the
same time (although they cannot actually run at the exact same time as
one another, except perhaps on a multiprocessor machine, when they can
take equal processor time slices), which can complicate things immensely
and slow down the code if handled badly. For games programming, you
should use as few threads as possible (using one main thread to handle the
running of the game). In Java we don't quite have that luxury, as some
important aspects of games programming in Java rely on handling multiple

threads. The most important "other thread" is called the Event Dispatch Thread.

The Event Dispatch Thread is what gives a programmer his power. It's an energy field created by all living things. It surrounds us and penetrates us. It binds the galaxy together.

Let me rephrase that a little. The *Event Dispatch Thread* is a thread that handles events in your application. An event in the case of the Event Dispatch Thread could be from the mouse (e.g., mouse pressed), the keyboard (e.g., key pressed), or even a window event (e.g., a window closing event). The basic idea of the Event Dispatch Thread is that it will receive events from other, hidden threads, such as window, mouse, and keyboard events and then dispatch those events to your application, provided you specify that you want to listen for those events. We will look at the Event Dispatch Thread in much more detail in Chapters 9 and 10. For now, it is important to understand how to create and use our own threads before we get caught up in someone else's threads; besides, we haven't mentioned synchronization yet.

Creating a Thread

There are two ways to create a thread. One is by extending the `java`
`.lang.Thread`, and the other is by implementing the `java.lang`
`.Runnable` interface. As the `java.lang` package is included by default, we don't need to define their package path, so from now on we will refer to them as "Thread" and "Runnable." In order to handle code in our thread, we must define a `run` method. The `Runnable` interface defines this very `run` method as follows.

```
public interface Runnable
{
    public void run();
}
```

The thread class itself implements the `Runnable` interface and therefore defines its own version of the `run` method, which does nothing and exits immediately, beautifully placed for us to override with our own implementation. In order to terminate a thread, simply let the `run` method exit. Similarly, as the `main` method is called itself from a thread, that thread will stop shortly after the `main` method has returned. We will discuss stopping threads later in this chapter. First, let's create our first thread.

Extending a Thread

In order to extend a thread, we use the keyword `extends`, as we saw in Chapter 4. We can then override its `run` method and supply our own where we can execute some code. Always remember that the main method is executed in a thread itself. The following example, `Simple-Thread1`, creates a new thread from the main thread and starts its execution.

Chapter 7

Code Listing 7-1: `SimpleThread1.java`

```java
public class SimpleThread1 extends Thread
{
    public void run()
    {
        System.out.println("New thread executing");
    }

    public static void main(String args[])
    {
        SimpleThread1 myThread = new SimpleThread1();
        myThread.start();

        System.out.println("Main's thread executing");
    }
}
```

When you compile and run this example, you could, and I repeat <u>could</u>, get output similar to the following figure.

Figure 7-1

In this code we create a new thread from main and then start it. Notice that we used the `Thread` method `start` to, well, start the thread. This will in turn invoke the `run` method for you. Therefore, you don't need to invoke the `run` method yourself; simply start the thread.

The important thing you need to realize is that the main thread and the new thread are two separate processes and are not executed sequentially. Just because we created and started the new thread from the `main` method does not mean that the new thread will execute first and then return to `main`. If that were the case, we may as well just call `run` as a method. You can view them as almost two separate programs, running alongside one another but under the same program environment.

Now, should you compile this source code again, it is quite likely that you will get output similar to the following figure.

Figure 7-2

As you can see, the text output from inside `main`, in the main thread, is now printed first and the new thread's text printed after. As they are two separate threads, when sections of code inside them are executed is determined by the Java Virtual Machine. However, you can influence the proportion of processor time taken by a thread by setting their priority, as we shall see later.

You may be able to see the main problem with threads, which is handling when they run in concurrence with one another; this is what synchronization is all about, which we will discuss a little later. We can now look at a somewhat more useful way of creating a thread: by implementing the `Runnable` interface.

Using the Runnable Interface

So far we have created a thread by extending the `Thread` class, thus dedicating our own class to being a subclass of `Thread`. As Java does not support multiple inheritance (the ability for a given class to extend more than one other class), it is quite likely that we would not want to make a class just a thread or even go the lengths of typing out a dedicated nested class that extends the `Thread` class. For example, a little later on in this book we will create an applet class that is also used to define the `run` method for a thread to execute. An applet is the Java program that runs embedded in a web browser, defined generally by the `java.awt.Applet` class. The basic creation of an applet entails extending the `java.awt.Applet` class as follows. (Don't worry too much! We will look at applets in detail in the next few chapters.)

```
public class MyClass extends Applet
{

}
```

However, we would not be able to do the following:

```
public class MyClass extends Applet, Thread
{
    // No multiple inheritance!!!
}
```

What we can do is implement the `Runnable` interface, which requires the inclusion of the `run` method in our implementing class. We can then say that an instance of our class is both of type `Applet` and of type `Runnable`. We can then create a new thread, passing a `runnable` object to the constructor. The following example, `SimpleThread2`, illustrates creating a thread with a `runnable` object.

Code Listing 7-2: `SimpleThread2.java`

```
public class SimpleThread2 implements Runnable
{
    public void run()
    {
        System.out.println("New thread executing");
    }

    public static void main(String args[])
    {
        SimpleThread2 runner = new SimpleThread2();
```

```
        Thread myThread = new Thread(runner);
        myThread.start();

        System.out.println("Main's thread executing");
    }
}
```

This code behaves in the same way as the previous example, and running this example will give one of the two previous possible outputs.

 NOTE: You can give a thread a name, which is merely a string value that it stores but makes debugging easier. You can use one of the constructors that supports a name parameter string or the `setName` method that takes a string argument to set the name of a thread. You can also use the `getName` method to retrieve the name of a thread. To find the name of the currently running thread, you would use the following code:

```
String threadName = Thread.currentThread().getName();
```

Stopping a Thread

In order to actually stop a thread, the process is quite simple. All you need to do is simply let the `run` method run out and return. The important thing you need to know is how not to stop a thread, which is using the `stop` method of the `Thread` class. The `stop` method of the `Thread` class is deprecated along with the method `suspend` and also the methods `resume` and `countStackFrames` that were dependent on `suspend` in some manner. As we have said, in order to stop a thread, you can simply let the `run` method finish what it is doing.

```
public void run()
{
    // Implement your code...

    // Just about to return and the thread will then stop soon after
}
```

Note that the thread will not necessarily be declared finished immediately after the `run` method has finished, as the JVM still needs to finish it off in the background, but it should terminate completely soon after.

In most cases when you create a thread of your own, you will be running a continuous task of some sort. A good example of creating your own thread is to listen for network messages coming in. Let's suppose that the network messages block, which means that a line of code waiting to return a message will stop where it is until the message has been received. It would not be ideal to call a blocking method such as this in your main loop thread, as the main loop thread needs to execute continuously without stopping to wait for an incoming network message. So the solution is to have your main loop running in one thread and create another thread to listen for incoming network messages on its own. We will look in detail at creating this for multiplayer games toward the end of this book. In order for the network thread to run again and again, it requires a loop. In order to stop a thread that is looping, we can simply declare a Boolean variable to set to `false` when we want to terminate the thread as follows.

```
// From outside the run method declare variable

boolean running = true;


public void run()
{
    while(running)
    {
        // execute thread code
    }
}


// Somewhere else, effectively terminate the thread

running = false;
```

The way in which we have handled stopping threads in this book is by testing to see if the thread reference we used to start the thread is still equal to a reference of the current thread. It's a little complicated to explain but is really quite simple. Let's just jump into the code this time and have a look. The following example, `StoppingThread`, illustrates the technique we use in this book to handle stopping a thread. Here is the code for `StoppingThread.java`.

Code Listing 7-3: `StoppingThread.java`

```
public class StoppingThread implements Runnable
{
    public void run()
    {
        System.out.println("Thread started");

        Thread thisThread = Thread.currentThread();
        while(loop==thisThread)
        {
            // Implement looped code, e.g. listen for new network
            // messages over and over
        }

        System.out.println("Thread exited");
    }

    public void startThread()
    {
        loop = new Thread(this);
        loop.start();
    }

    public void stopThread()
    {
        loop = null;
    }

    public static void main(String args[])
```

```
    {
        // thread loop started in constructor
        StoppingThread example = new StoppingThread();
        example.startThread();

        // now stop the thread like this
        example.stopThread();
    }

    Thread loop;
}
```

When you compile and run this code, the new thread should be started and stopped similarly to the following figure.

Figure 7-3

The Thread `while` loop is simply controlled by testing if the object refer-enced by the `loop` variable is equal to the currently running `Thread` object referenced by the local variable `thisThread`. We can retrieve a reference to the running thread using the static method `Thread.cur-rentThread()`. This method is used to obtain a reference to the current thread that you are running in. You might say it is to threads what the key-word `this` is to objects. We can then simply terminate the loop, thus leading to the termination of the thread by setting `loop` equal to `null`. Now I should point out that our original way of stopping a thread using a Boolean variable will stop the thread also; we just prefer this way.

Okay, brace yourself. We will now take a look at the important issue of thread synchronization and how to handle it. The following sections of this chapter will be kept quite linear to explain the basic concepts of thread synchronization. We will see plenty of practical synchronization examples in the chapters to follow.

Synchronization

Synchronization is a means of handling the execution of code between multiple threads running at the same time, inevitably making sections of your code secure so that those sections are not executed concurrently (at the same time) in multiple threads, as this can have disastrous effects on what your program computes.

Now, here's a little reminder on why this section is relevant to you from a games-programming-in-Java point of view. In Java the Event Dis-patch Thread runs as a separate process to your main thread of execution. This means that mouse and keyboard event messages, for example, will be posted to event methods for you to then handle appropriately in your game. These methods will be invoked unsynchronized with the main loop, running in the Event Dispatch Thread of execution while the main loop thread continues running on its own. The main loop is basically what controls your game, repeatedly executing, repeatedly handling input, updating the game state, and updating the display of the game each loop cycle. This is similar to our tic-tac-toe game loop in the last chapter but running over and over without pausing for user input each time (we will look at making a main loop from Chapter 9 onward).

Understanding thread synchronization is important because we need to make sure that events coming in from a different thread to our main loop thread are handled in a safe manner, as the threads can lead to executing code that compromises the execution of code in our main loop.

What we are concerned with basically comes down to separate threads sharing the same data and functionality. We can illustrate a very basic example by creating a simple class that handles the getting and setting of a variable. Let's say we had the following simple class:

```
public class GamePlayer
{
    public int getLives()
    {
        return lives;
    }

    public void setLives(int l)
    {
        lives = l;
    }

    private int lives;
}
```

The `GamePlayer` class simply defines the private instance variable `lives` and the instance methods `getLives` and `setLives` in order to manipulate the `lives` variable from outside the object. The `GamePlayer` class has been specially designed in this way for this example.

Now, imagine that two different threads both wanted to execute the following code at relatively the same time:

```
int lives = gamePlayer.getLives();
gamePlayer.setLives(lives - 1);
```

As an example, the main loop thread could process this code, but a network message could be read into the network thread also, requiring you to perform the task of decrementing the player's lives value. The expected result in this case should be that the player loses two lives.

If we say that thread A and thread B are both ready to invoke this method, they may execute the code in the following order:

```
int lives = gamePlayer.getLives();    // thread A
gamePlayer.setLives(lives - 1);       // thread A
int lives = gamePlayer.getLives();    // thread B
gamePlayer.setLives(lives - 1);       // thread B
```

Please note that the two local declarations of the `lives` integer variables in this example have no reference to one another in different threads and should be treated as the separate variables that they are.

With the sequence of execution between the two threads, there are no problems. The lives value of the `gamePlayer` object is retrieved and then set to the retrieved value minus one. Then the same routine is performed by the second thread. Both of the threads have successfully achieved their goals of decrementing the current value of lives by one. If the lives value started at 7, it would now equal 5. However, that doesn't mean that this code is safe and that this would not necessarily be the outcome. The code in each thread could also be executed in the following sequence:

```
int lives = gamePlayer.getLives();    // thread A
int lives = gamePlayer.getLives();    // thread B
gamePlayer.setLives(lives - 1);       // thread A
gamePlayer.setLives(lives - 1);       // thread B
```

If we trace this path of execution and assume that the value of `lives` in the `gamePlayer` object started off at 7, we will get a different outcome. First, both of the threads store the value of the game player's lives into their local `lives` variables of the assumed value 7. Then in thread A, the new value of `lives` is set to its current value minus 1, calculated as 7 – 1 and equaling 6. Then thread B will perform exactly the same calculation (7 – 1 = 6). It will not take one off the new value of `lives`, which is 6, to equal 5 but will take one off the value it originally received, which is 7 and it assumes is still the current value of `lives`. Thus, two executions of this code from two different threads has resulted in just one life being removed. Why? Because the execution of this code is not synchronized.

The keyword `synchronized` is the main way in which we can solve such synchronization issues. The keyword `synchronized` can be used in two distinct ways—to synchronize methods or to synchronize more specific blocks of code. We will begin by looking at synchronized methods.

Synchronized Methods

In order to synchronize a method, you can simply add the keyword `synchronized` to the method declaration. Now let's suppose that we define the two `GamePlayer` class methods we saw earlier as follows. Note that this will not completely solve the problem just yet, but let's see:

```
public class GamePlayer
{
    public synchronized int getLives()
    {
        return lives;
    }

    public synchronized void setLives(int l)
    {
        lives = l;
    }
```

```
    private int lives;
}
```

The methods `getLives` and `setLives` are instance methods of the `GamePlayer` class and are both declared as synchronized. Now let's suppose that we created an instance of the `GamePlayer` class as follows.

```
GamePlayer myPlayer = new GamePlayer();
```

We will keep this explanation fairly abstract to begin with and leave the discussion of the object's monitor until after.

Let's say we have two threads running, thread A and thread B. If thread A enters one of the methods of the `myPlayer` object, thread B cannot execute any one of the two synchronized `myPlayer` methods. When this happens, thread B will pause until thread A releases its hold by exiting the method, whereby thread B can then take its turn.

If, say, one of the two methods is declared as synchronized and the other is not, they are not synchronized with one another. Simply declaring a method alone as being synchronized does not mutually exclude it from other methods of the same object. However, the one synchronized method is synchronized with itself, you might say. A thread executing in this method will prevent any other thread from doing so.

This doesn't solve the problem that two threads could both call `getLives` first and then both make calls to `setLives` thereafter, with the error effects discussed earlier. To solve this, we would probably make a method such as the following:

```
public synchronized void decrementLife()
{
    lives-=1;
}
```

We would probably make the other methods private then for good measure if we needed them at all. Note that all of this seems very messy in general, but the reality is that we can get things synchronized from a higher level at an early stage, as we will see in Chapter 10, "Using the Mouse and Keyboard." So we won't be throwing synchronization statements everywhere like this, but it's essential to understand how things work at the lowest of levels.

Another distinction you need to be aware of is the fact that these methods are only synchronized in the object to which they belong.

Let's say we also declare the following object:

```
GamePlayer mySecondPlayer = new GamePlayer();
```

If thread A is running inside one of the synchronized methods of the `myPlayer` object, thread B cannot access any of the two synchronized methods of the `myPlayer` object, as we know. However, it is still able to access any of the methods of the `mySecondPlayer` object, provided another thread isn't currently running in one of those methods, as they are different objects.

What we have just discussed is a very fixed way of looking at synchronization. All we talked about in terms of synchronized methods was that they were instance methods, and any threads would simply invoke one method and then get the heck out of there to allow another thread a look in. If we are to truly understand synchronized methods and thread synchronization as a whole, we must learn about the concept of a monitor.

Object and Class Monitor

A *monitor* can be seen simply as a lock on an object (or a class, as we will touch on in a moment). With this in mind, when a thread wishes to enter a synchronized method of an object, for example, the thread must check to see if any other thread holds that object's monitor. If the object's monitor is owned by another thread, the thread that required the object's monitor must wait until it is released again. When this object's monitor is free, the thread can then take ownership of it. The thread will release the object's monitor when it exits the original method or code block that originally took ownership of the monitor. A thread can also release its ownership of the object's monitor using the wait methods inherited by all objects from the object class, as we will discuss shortly.

As we saw earlier with the `GamePlayer` object `myPlayer`, the methods were both synchronized with one another because the monitor, or lock, that they used belonged to the `myPlayer` object. If thread A was in `getLives`, thread B could not enter `getLives` or `setLives` because thread A owns that object's monitor, to which both methods were synchronized.

As this is the case, you should now be able to see why the synchronized instance methods of different objects (for example, `myPlayer` and `mySecondPlayer`) are not synchronized with one another; each object has its own monitor. Adding to this fact, you should realize therefore that a thread can own more than one monitor.

Please do not be confused by the term "monitor"; you can simply see it as a lock, almost a Boolean true or false, or better still a reference to a `Thread` object that an object or class stores to indicate who has ownership of it (if indeed the object is owned by any thread at all at a given time, that is).

Synchronized Static Methods

Now, as you might have noticed, in addition to objects having a monitor, a class also has a monitor associated with it. We already know the difference between object methods and class methods. Object methods are instance methods—those that belong to the object—whereas class methods are methods that belong to the class, by declaring them as static. As a class has a monitor itself, we can synchronize static methods of a class by also making them synchronized. We could make the methods of the `Game-Player` class static/class methods and synchronize them as follows. Note that this will also entail that we make the `lives` variable static too.

```
public class GamePlayer
{
    public static synchronized int getLives()
    {
        return lives;
    }

    public static synchronized void setLives(int l)
    {
        lives = l;
    }

    private static int lives;
}
```

If a thread first invokes one of these static methods, it will then have ownership of the class's monitor (not an object monitor), which means that no other threads can enter one of the synchronized static methods of the class until the ownership is released. As objects and classes have their own monitors, synchronization involving different monitors do not affect one another. For example, synchronized static/class methods are not synchronized with synchronized instance methods of that class, as the static methods are synchronized using the monitor of the class and instance methods are synchronized using the monitor of that particular object.

Synchronized Blocks with Objects

A more powerful use of the `synchronization` keyword is to specifically synchronize a block of code by specifying an object on which to synchronize. It is very similar to a synchronized instance method of an object in that the thread takes ownership of that object's monitor. With synchronized instance methods, the thread takes ownership of the object's monitor, but with the synchronized block technique, you can specify the object that you wish to synchronize on (it can be any object you want). Furthermore, synchronized methods are obviously restricted by the fact that the whole method is synchronized, and therefore the entire method, if synched with another method of course, is considered a danger area, whereas only one or two lines of the code in the method could actually cause concurrency errors. Moreover, as we can specify any object on which to synchronize, we can mutually exclude the execution of code in different objects (and classes, providing the objects are declared static).

We can synchronize a specific block of code in a method as follows:

```
public void myMethod
{
    // Code not synchronized here

    synchronized(myObject)
    {
        // Synchronized code here
    }

    // Code not synchronized here
}
```

Chapter 7

In this example, any threads can enter this method and execute any code. They can then take exclusive access to the synchronized block, taking ownership of the monitor of the object argument of the synchronized block statement, if it's available. Please note that the object parameter myObject could be any object you like; it does not need to be the object you are in, but it could be if you want, where you would pass the argument this to it.

As you can see, with this technique, it is possible for a code block in a method of a different object to synchronize on the same object, mutually excluding code in different objects. Now look at this example:

```
public class Alpha
{
    public synchronized void myMethod()
    {

    }
}


public class Beta
{
    public void myMethod()
    {
        synchronized(myAlphaObject)
        {
            // synchronized with myMethod of the Alpha object
            // myAlphaObject
        }
    }
}
```

If we create the Alpha class object myAlphaObject and it is accessible from an object of type Beta, we can synchronize it with the synchronized instance method of myAlphaObject from outside of myAlphaObject.

 NOTE: Synchronizing on a variable reference that is currently equal to null will throw a NullPointerException.

Wait and Notify

It's a good thing that we know how to control exclusive access to areas of our code between multiple threads, but this is not enough. We may also need to control when our threads run and how they can talk to one another. Effectively, the threads can tell each other when to run and pause. This is efficiently performed using the wait and notify methods. If you remember back to Chapter 4, "Multiple Classes," we gave these methods a brief mention. They are instance methods of the object class inherited by all objects. In the most basic terms, a wait method invoked by a thread pauses the execution of that thread until another thread invokes a notify method to wake up the sleeping thread.

When using the `wait` command, you need to make sure that the current thread has ownership of the object's monitor—the object, that is, on which you are invoking the `wait` method. For the `wait` method you also need to `try`/`catch` an `InterruptedException`; we will discuss interrupting threads later on. The following code is a typical illustration of pausing a thread using an object's `wait` method:

```
synchronized(myObject)
{
    try
    {
        myObject.wait();    // Thread A pauses
    }
    catch(InterruptedException e)
    {

    }
}
```

To begin with, thread A synchronizes on the `myObject` object to take ownership of its monitor. We can then call the `wait` method on `myObject`. When we do this, the thread releases its ownership of `myObject`'s monitor and pauses the thread until another thread calls the `notify` or `notifyAll` method of the `myObject` object. When another thread calls the `notify` method, a single waiting thread is awoken and is then a candidate to regain ownership of the object's monitor once it becomes available. When another thread calls `notifyAll`, all threads currently waiting are woken up and become candidates to take ownership of the object's monitor.

 NOTE: There is no guarantee as to which thread, from a list of contenders waiting for ownership of the object's monitor, will be awoken first, although some threads are more likely to be awoken earlier than others. We will look at thread priorities a little later.

The following code illustrates how another thread, thread B, could wake up thread A.

```
// Thread B wakes up thread A
synchronized(myObject)
{
    myObject.notify();
}
```

In this code, we can see that in order to call the `notify` method of an object, the thread must own the object monitor. When thread A called the `wait` method, this released thread A's ownership of `myObject`'s monitor. This allows thread B's synchronized block to be entered, as the monitor was freed by thread A invoking `wait`, provided this was the flow of execution, of course. When `myObject.notify` is invoked, thread B will keep ownership of `myObject`'s monitor until it leaves the synchronized block that encapsulates it. So be aware—calling `notify` does not mean that thread A will immediately start up again.

There are two more versions of the `wait` method that we have not mentioned: `wait(long timeout)` and `wait(long timeout, int nanos)`. The parameter of type `long` represents time in milliseconds (a thousand milliseconds equals one second); `nanos` means nanoseconds (a thousand nanoseconds equals one millisecond).

These methods work in the same way, except they also specify a timeout period for the thread to wait on the object's monitor. The thread will wake if another notifies it, as discussed before, or if the specified timeout period elapses.

 NOTE: The accuracy of timing depends not only on your hardware but also on how your Java Virtual Machine implements getting the time – the resolution of the timer it uses for time-related things like this. We will discuss the importance of timers in Chapter 12.

That is as far as we are going to delve into using `wait` and `notify` for the time being. We will implement some practical examples that involve them later in the book (in Chapter 9 for example). Now that we have covered the difficult elements of threads, we can relax a little and look at some more straightforward stuff where threads are concerned.

Sleeping Threads

Quite similar to the overloaded `wait` methods that take time parameters, a thread object has two sleep methods: `sleep(long timeout)` and `sleep(long timeout, int nanos)`. With these methods, you can pause a thread's execution for a specified amount of time. Note that the `sleep` methods are not concerned with synchronization or monitors or anything like that. We can simply call the `sleep` method encapsulated in a `try/catch` block for an `InterruptedException` (we will look at the intricacies shortly) anywhere in our thread and allow it to pause. The following very simple example shows a simple counter running from 5 to 1, with each countdown taking 1 second (or thereabouts, depending on the resolution of the timer). Here is the code for `Countdown.java`:

Code Listing 7-4: `Countdown.java`

```
public class Countdown
{
    public static void main(String[] args)
    {
        System.out.println("and ready in...\n");

        for(int i=5; i>0; i--)
        {
            System.out.println(i);

            System.out.print((char)7);    // make a bleep sound

            try
            {
                Thread.sleep(1000);       // pause for a second
            }
```

```
        catch(InterruptedException e)
        {
            System.out.println(e);
        }
    }

    System.out.println("\nAction!");
    }
}
```

That's right—I'm not afraid of the fact that `main` is itself a thread. As `main` is running in its own thread like any other, there is no point in us spawning a new thread for this example. When run, the output should be similar to Figure 7-4 and you'll hear some bleep sounds in the countdown.

Figure 7-4

The code for this example is very straightforward. We call the static method `Thread.sleep`, which pauses the current thread that invokes this method by the specified amount of time. You might have noticed the bleeping code in this example, where we can simply print ASCII character number 7, which doesn't actually print anything but should make a system bleep every second for the countdown when you run the code.

 NOTE: If you do not have an internal speaker in your computer, you won't be able to hear anything!

When you send a thread to sleep and "wait" a thread, you are stopping its processor time, allowing other threads to run faster, as they have a higher share of the processor usage. This is important because you might think about making your own special loop to create a time difference, which might work, but as it executes continuously, it takes unnecessary processor time away from other threads that want to run as fast as they can.

There is another important thing to be aware of when calling a thread's `sleep` method. When calling the `sleep` method, the thread does not lose ownership of any monitors that it currently owns. When calling the `sleep` method, the thread does not lose ownership of any monitors that it currently owns. Yes, I said it twice because it's important in the sense that if you are synchronized on an object and then sleep, other threads waiting to execute some fellow synchronized code must wait for the release of that monitor. Hence they will have to wait on a sleep period also. This can be a powerful tool as well as a semantic problem. The important thing to take from this is that you need to analyze exactly what needs to be synchronized and what doesn't and handle your code in that fashion; synchronize to the minimum.

Interrupting a Thread

There is a common misconception about the interrupting of threads, as you plot InterruptedException try/catch blocks everywhere, that you might throw interrupts everywhere thinking, "Oh, I hope an exception doesn't get randomly thrown here from Java or something, fingers crossed." This in fact isn't the case; the interrupts are there as a system for you to utilize when handling your threads. Throughout many examples in this chapter, we have seen the requirement to try/catch InterruptedException exceptions that could be thrown. Interrupting a thread is useful for immediate action when a thread is blocking or to simply give it a status that it can then make a check to during its execution.

There are two main aspects of interrupting a thread that you need to be aware of: interrupting the thread that is in a blocked status or in a non-blocked status.

You should be aware of blocking by now. This simply means, in terms of a thread with a stopped execution, like when we call wait on an object or sleep a thread, it blocks. You'll note that in these circumstances we try/catch an InterruptedException exception. That is how we handle an interrupt when a thread is blocked. In order to interrupt a thread, you can call the interrupt method of a thread object.

```
Thread myThread = new Thread(myRunnableObject);
myThread.start();

// interrupt the thread
myThread.interrupt();
```

When we interrupt a thread that is blocked (e.g., if it's calling sleep or waiting on an object to be notified), the thread will resume and be thrown an InterruptedException, so you can handle the thread being interrupted in the catch block for this exception.

```
try
{
    myThread.sleep();
}
catch(InterruptedException e)
{
    // handle if blocking sleep method is interrupted
}
```

If the thread is in a running status, an interrupted status associated with the thread is set; just see it as a Boolean value, which it probably is. This value can be tested using one of two distinct methods: interrupted and isInterrupted. Both methods will return a Boolean value of the thread's interrupt status, but the interrupt method resets the status to false if it was true, whereas the isInterrupted method merely checks the status without affecting the value. An interesting thing about all this is that a thread can interrupt itself, setting the interrupt status for it to then handle later. The following code snippet will count from 10 to 0 and then stop using thread interrupting:

```
for(int i=10; !Thread.currentThread().interrupted(); i--)
{
    System.out.println(i);

    if(i==0)
        Thread.currentThread().interrupt();
}
```

Many programmers use the thread interrupt system to stop their threads from looping and allow them to exit, instead of the ways we discussed earlier in this chapter. It's basically your own preference.

Daemon Threads

A "demon" is an evil supernatural being that wishes to take over the world and destroy it. A demon doesn't realize that it needs the world for survival. It depends on it. Similarly, somehow, a *daemon* (pronounced like demon) thread is one that depends on other user threads being alive. If a thread is not a daemon thread, it is known as a user thread, meaning it will run on its own independently of other threads, whereas a daemon thread will run but will stop when no more user threads, like main's threads, are running in the application. Basically, the program will exit when the only threads left running are daemon threads, meaning they will then stop too.

You can simply set a thread as a daemon or not by using the setDaemon method of a thread object. Note that this method needs to be called before the thread is started. The following code illustrates a simple example of how a daemon thread relies on its creator. Here is the code for DaemonThread.java:

Code Listing 7-5: DaemonThread.java

```
public class DaemonThread extends Thread
{
    public DaemonThread()
    {
        setDaemon(true);
    }

    public void run()
    {
        while(true)
        {
            System.out.println("How long can we last");
        }
    }

    public static void main(String args[])
    {
        DaemonThread myThread = new DaemonThread();
        myThread.start();
```

```
    }
}
```

When you compile and run this example, you should get multiple lines of the text "How long can we last" until the thread dies, as can be seen in the following screen shot.

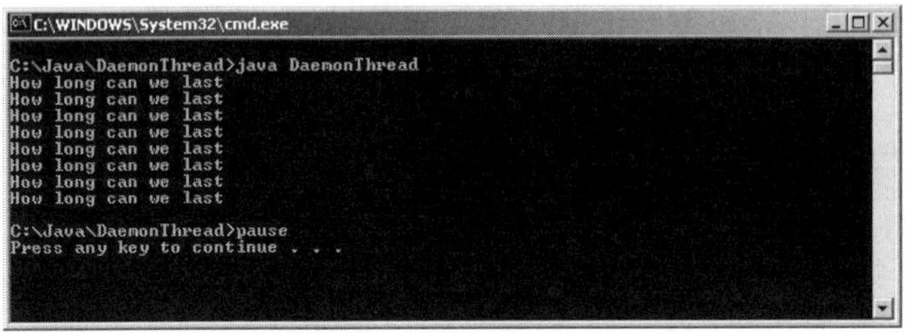

Figure 7-5

In this code, the thread in which `main` is running creates a new thread, which we first set as a daemon before starting it. This means that the daemon thread's existence relies on the main thread staying alive. They're like Romeo and Juliet. When main exits and the user thread it is running in finally dies, the application terminates, as all that is left is a daemon thread. You can use the thread method `isDaemon` to check if a thread is a daemon or not.

The default setting for whether a thread is a daemon or not is determined by the status of the current thread in which the new thread is created. The threads we have created so far have been user threads and not daemon threads by default because the thread they were created from, where main runs, is a user thread. A thread created by a daemon thread will, by default, be a daemon thread.

Thread Priorities

Threads have a priority status associated with them, which determines their importance with other concurrently running threads. By default, a thread has the same priority as its creator. You can set the priority of a thread using the `setPriority` method of a thread object. The scope of a thread's priority ranges from 1 to 10, and 5 is the normal priority that, for example, the main thread runs at. These are defined by the thread constant fields `MIN_PRIORITY`, `NORM_PRIORITY`, and `MAX_PRIORITY`.

A Final Word on Deadlock

Deadlock is the technical term given to the state where you realize you've completely missed some glitch in your multitasking system that allows some threads to get stuck while simultaneously waiting for each other to wake the other up, generally speaking. An example of this could involve threads A and B and objects X and Y. Thread A obtains object X's monitor, and thread B obtains object Y's monitor. Thread A, while owning object

X's monitor, waits for thread B to release its ownership on object Y's monitor. However, thread B, while owning object Y's monitor, then waits for thread A to release its ownership on object X's monitor, resulting in both threads getting stuck. This is an example of deadlock.

Generally speaking, deadlock is something you should always be aware of and take proper precautions to avoid. It's just a matter of properly analyzing the path that your threads can take.

Summary

Although using threads is very complex, it is the task of the programmer to make the management of multiple threads as simple as possible. The easiest way to do this is to run all functionality in one thread. The problem is that functionality can be spawned from different threads, but we can limit this to a safe bare minimum. The main example of this is where mouse and keyboard events are concerned. They are accepted through the Event Dispatch Thread. Instead of handling these events in the event dispatch thread, we can add them to an event pump (basically a list), which can then be polled in the main loop thread and handled there. So there will be no synchronization problems with the functionality in the rest of the main loop. We will implement this feature in Chapter 10, "Using the Mouse and Keyboard."

I must confess, the synchronization elements of this chapter were perhaps among the most difficult things I've ever had to explain (well, that and explaining to my parents how, on a student loan, I managed to gamble £150 (pounds sterling) in one night). It is quite possible that this section went straight over your head. If so, I apologize, but do not worry, as there are many important practical thread synchronization issues that are covered in the rest of this book, which should clear up any misunderstandings you have. We will now take on the visual side of programming games in Java. We must first begin with the very foundation of graphical representations in Java: visual applications and applets.

Chapter 8

Applications and Applets

"Anybody who thinks a little 9,000-line program [Mosaic/Netscape] that's distributed free and can be cloned by anyone is going to affect anything we do at Microsoft has his head screwed on wrong."
—Bill Gates

Introduction

This chapter is all about getting started using applications and applets. Here, we will look at the key elements of applications and applets and the main differences between them. It is important to look at these areas, as they are the foundation for visual programs in the Java Standard Edition.

A Brief Note on Components and Containers

Before we talk about heavyweight and lightweight components, we should mention briefly what components are. A *component* is an object used to represent an area of the screen, which can also be used to handle events. An example of a component is a button, which has a screen presence and can accept mouse events to click the button (or even keyboard events for that matter). A *container* is an extension of a component, whereby it is itself a component, with the ability to contain other components (children). For example, a button component would be placed inside a container, such as an applet. A button is not a container, however, as it cannot contain other components (i.e., you wouldn't add a text field to a button). We will look at components and containers in detail in the next chapter, "Graphics" and in Chapter 13, "Introduction to GUI," where we will make our own hierarchical component container GUI system. For now, we will just make our first applications windows and applets.

Heavyweight and Lightweight Components

A *heavyweight component* is directly associated with a native screen resource and is known as a peer. A *lightweight component*, on the other

197

hand, just "borrows" a screen resource, and hence it has no native resource of its own.

One of the main differences between lightweight and heavyweight components is that heavyweight components must be opaque (i.e., no transparency), implying that they will be rectangular. On the contrary, lightweight components can contain transparency.

With mouse events, a heavyweight component does not pass mouse events to the parent, whereas a lightweight component will.

Finally, and most importantly, if a lightweight component overlaps and is placed above a heavyweight component, the heavyweight component will actually appear above the lightweight component.

Introduction to AWT and Swing

AWT stands for *Abstract Window Toolkit* and is a platform-independent library that greatly simplifies the implementation of user interfaces. The AWT is a peer-based windowing library that contains platform-independent classes that directly associate with native objects on each operating system on which the code is executed.

Swing is a further implementation of AWT that adds a more comprehensive GUI system, but it is still based upon the AWT architecture. The main difference between Swing and AWT is that all the Swing components (except for top-level containers such as JFrame, JDialog, and JApplet) are lightweight components, whereas all of the AWT components are heavyweight.

We say, "except for JFrame, JDialog, and JApplet" because these are known as top-level containers. A *top-level container* is the root of a GUI containment hierarchy; hence, it is the starting point for adding all other containers and components.

As Swing components are completely lightweight, they make better use of resources. Also, the fact they are all written purely in Java and do not rely on the native objects ensures multiplatform consistency, and further, it also allows us to easily integrate look and feel, which we will look at later in this chapter.

In this book, we have chosen to use Swing components as opposed to AWT. However, in Chapter 9 we pay attention to more practical examples of using both AWT and Swing and note their differences.

What Is an Application?

An *application* is a program that can either be a simple console window, which merely outputs text, or it can be a visual windowed program. We have so far been glued to the console window for our applications. In this section, we look at how we can create a windowed application in Java.

A Simple Java Application

To create a windowed application in Swing, you can use an object of type JFrame. We can do this by making our own class extend the JFrame class or contain a JFrame object. The JFrame class is defined in the Swing package, which is imported as javax.swing.*. Note that the equivalent component in the AWT package java.awt.* is simply called Frame. This is consistent with most of the GUI objects (i.e., all the Swing GUI objects are named the same as the AWT versions, except they are prefixed by the letter "J"). Let's now look at two very simple examples of how we can create a 400x300 pixel window with "My Application" in the title bar. They both have the same outcome, but the first extends a JFrame class, whereas the second just has a JFrame as a member of the class. Here are the two code listings.

Code Listing 8-1: Simple application (extending a JFrame)

```java
import javax.swing.*;

public class MyApplication extends JFrame
{
    public MyApplication()
    {
        super("My Application");
        setSize(400, 300);
        setDefaultCloseOperation(EXIT_ON_CLOSE);
        setVisible(true);
    }

    public static void main(String args[])
    {
        MyApplication theApp = new MyApplication();

    }
}
```

Code Listing 8-2: Simple application (JFrame as a member)

```java
import javax.swing.*;

public class MyApplication
{
    public static void main(String args[])
    {
        JFrame appFrame = new JFrame("My Application");
        appFrame.setSize(400, 300);
        appFrame.setDefaultCloseOperation(JFrame.EXIT_ON_CLOSE);
        appFrame.setVisible(true);
    }
}
```

When we execute either of these two example applications, we will see that they create a window that looks like this:

Chapter 8

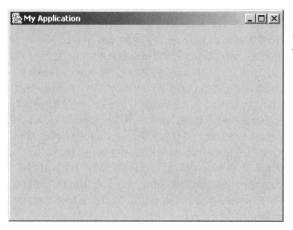

Figure 8-1:
Our basic application
window

Let's now look at the first example, which extends the `JFrame` class in order to create the window. First, we need to include the Swing package, which is accomplished using the following `import` statement:

```
import javax.swing.*;
```

Now we declare our `MyApplication` class to extend the `JFrame` class, which will make it inherit all the members and methods of the `JFrame` class (if you are unsure about inheritance, refer back to Chapter 4). The class declaration can be seen in the following line of code:

```
public class MyApplication extends JFrame
```

Next, we need to declare a `main` method that is the entry point to the application code. All we need to do in this method is instantiate our `MyApplication` class so that the constructor will be called. The complete `main` method can be seen here:

```
public static void main(String args[])
{
    MyApplication theApp = new MyApplication();
}
```

In the constructor of `MyApplication`, we first make a call to the constructor of the super class (i.e., the `JFrame` class that we are extending) and pass a single argument that represents the title of our application. This can be seen here:

```
super("My Application");
```

Note you can also use the method `setTitle` of the `JFrame` to later change the title.

Next, we need to set the size of our application window, which we do by making a call to the `setSize` method, passing the width and the height as parameters, respectively. Note that the `setSize` method is a member of the `JFrame` class. This can be seen in the following line of code:

```
setSize(400, 300);
```

Then we set the default close operation for the application (e.g., what happens when the user clicks the "x" in the top-right corner of the window or presses Alt+F4 in Windows). For this, we specify that we wish the application to `EXIT_ON_CLOSE`. This can be seen in the following line of code:

```
setDefaultCloseOperation(EXIT_ON_CLOSE);
```

We will look at closing windowed applications properly in the next chapter, so do not worry about this section of code in this chapter.

Finally, we make a call to the `setVisible` inherited method. Passing `true` as a parameter informs the `JFrame` heavyweight object to make itself visible. This can be seen in this final line of code:

```
setVisible(true);
```

For the other example code, we do not extend the `JFrame`. Instead, we create a new `JFrame` object in the main method and assign it to our member variable `appFrame`. Note again how we pass the title of our application as the constructor. This can be seen in the following line of code:

```
JFrame appFrame = new JFrame("My Application");
```

Once we have our object instantiated, we can then use the object to call the `setSize`, `setVisible`, and `setDefaultCloseOperation` methods in a similar way to the first example code. This can be seen in the final three lines of code, as well as the default close operation line.

```
appFrame.setSize(400, 300);
appFrame.setVisible(true);
appFrame.setDefaultCloseOperation(JFrame.EXIT_ON_CLOSE);
```

Note here that the `EXIT_ON_CLOSE` definition is a public constant member of the `JFrame` class, and hence we have to specify it as such (i.e., `JFrame.EXIT_ON_CLOSE`). In the previous code listing, we extended the `JFrame`, and hence the `EXIT_ON_CLOSE` variable was therefore a member of our own class as it extended the `JFrame`, inheriting this member.

What Is an Applet?

Along with applications, we can also create applets. An *applet* is a Java program that is executed by the virtual machine within the confines of a web browser. Ever played a game in the web browser and wondered how it works? Well, the most likely culprit is a Java applet.

When we create an applet, we use the `JApplet` class rather than the `JFrame`, and we need to structure the initial code slightly differently. The most important thing to note about the difference between applications and applets is the entry point; there is no `main` method in an applet. Let's look at a simple applet that will extend the `JApplet` class. An important point is that you must run an applet in a browser, as there is no other way to run it (except when developing/testing, you can use AppletViewer, which comes with the SDK). Here is a simple applet example:

A Simple Java Applet

Code Listing 8-3: Simple applet

```java
import javax.swing.*;

public class MyApplet extends JApplet
{
    public void init()
    {
        setSize(400, 300);
    }

    public void start()
    {

    }

    public void stop()
    {

    }

    public void destroy()
    {

    }
}
```

In addition, we can use the following HTML file (which we have called `view.html`) located in the same directory as the .class file to display the applet in the browser.

 NOTE: When developing, it is best to use the AppletViewer utility, which we will look at in the next section.

Code Listing 8-4: `view.html` (used to view the applet)

```html
<HTML>

<HEAD>
 <TITLE>Simple Applet Example</TITLE>
</HEAD>

<BODY>
 <CENTER><B>Simple Applet Example</B>
 <BR>
 <APPLET CODE="MyApplet.class" WIDTH=400 HEIGHT=300></APPLET>
 </CENTER>
</BODY>

</HTML>
```

When we compile the applet code and open the `view.html` file in a web browser, something similar to the following should be visible:

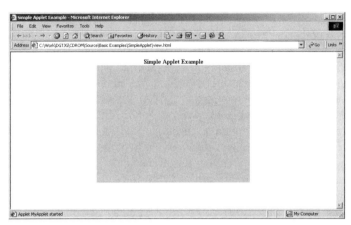

Figure 8-2:
Our basic
applet

If you do not know HTML, you can simply use this template and change the class filename appropriately, along with its width and height settings. For now, all you need to do is enter this into a text file and then save it as an .html file, which you may then load up using a web browser such as Internet Explorer.

Let's now look at the code and see what we have done in more detail.

This time around, we declare our main class so that it extends the `JApplet` class, which is part of the Swing package. This can be seen in the following line of code:

```
public class MyApplet extends JApplet
```

This is where applets differ from applications. For an application, we can create `JFrame` objects in various places, whereas with an applet the Java Virtual Machine is looking to create an instance of an applet class to begin with.

Once we have defined our class to extend the `JApplet`, we can then override the methods important to the running of the applet and provide our own functionality for them. Let's look at each of these methods now and see what their purpose is.

First we have the `init` method. This method is only called once when the applet is first loaded into the browser window and is used to initialize the applet. In our example, we set the size of the applet window in this method to 400x300 pixels. This can be seen in the following block of code:

```
public void init()
{
    setSize(400, 300);
}
```

NOTE: Note that you may not set the size of the applet larger than defined in the HTML file. You can, however, make the applet smaller.

Next, we have the `start` method. This method is always called after the `init` method and can also be called if a browser window is minimized (or hidden) and then maximized again. However, this depends on the browser used, and therefore you should not depend on this happening.

Then we have the `stop` method that again can be called by the browser window if it is minimized or hidden. As with the `start` method, this depends on the browser used when viewing the applet.

Because we cannot depend on these methods being invoked by the browser when it is minimized, we can rely on other means. What we are looking at here from our point of view is the applet's loss of focus. We can handle the loss of focus differently in Java, as we shall see a little later on in the book.

Finally, we have the `destroy` method, which is called when the applet is unloaded from the browser (i.e., the user has closed the browser window), where we can insert any code we need to clean up the program before it exits.

Viewing an Applet with AppletViewer

As well as being able to view the applet in a web browser, included within the Java SDK is a tool called AppletViewer, which allows you to view an applet without a web browser and can be useful for testing purposes, as some browsers have issues with caching applets.

To use AppletViewer, you still need to create the .html file, as we did in the previous example, but instead of opening it in a browser, we pass it as a parameter to the AppletViewer tool. The command line can be seen here (which will work with the previous example):

```
C:\j2sdk1.4.1_01\bin\appletviewer view.html
```

When we run this command from the directory where our applets .class files are located (i.e., where it was compiled), we will see the following:

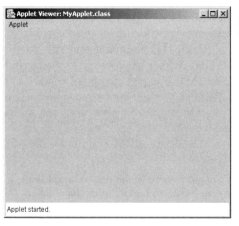

Figure 8-3:
Our applet in AppletViewer

Specifying Program Arguments for Applets in HTML

A useful feature of applets is the ability to pass in parameters directly from HTML code. Let's look at a simple applet that takes in three parameters: a string followed by two numbers. It will then output the string and sum of the two numbers that were passed in. This is useful because it allows you to distribute your class files to other people without giving them the source code, but it allows them to add the applet to their site with some specific elements. For example, a parameter could specify the name of an image that the applet can then load in and display without changing any of the code but simply changing the HTML file under the user's control. Less work for programmers means happier programmers.

The following example shows how we can specify parameters in the HTML file and then read them into our applet. Here is an HTML file and an applet that can read in the HTML parameter data:

Code Listing 8-5: `view.html`

```html
<HTML>

<HEAD>
 <TITLE>Applet Parameter Passing Example</TITLE>
</HEAD>

<BODY>
 <CENTER><B>Applet Parameter Passing Example</B>
 <BR>
 <APPLET CODE="AppletParam.class" WIDTH=400 HEIGHT=300>
 <PARAM NAME="theString" VALUE="Hello World">
 <PARAM NAME="Number1" VALUE=4>
 <PARAM NAME="Number2" VALUE=10>
 </APPLET>
 </CENTER>
</BODY>

</HTML>
```

Code Listing 8-6: `AppletParam.java`

```java
import java.awt.*;
import javax.swing.*;

public class AppletParam extends JApplet
{
    public void init()
    {
        setSize(400, 300);

        // Get and store the parameters...
        theString = getParameter("theString");
        number1 = Integer.parseInt(getParameter("Number1"));
        number2 = Integer.parseInt(getParameter("Number2"));
    }

    public void paint(Graphics g)
    {
        g.drawString("The string value was:  "+theString, 20, 20);
        g.drawString("The first number was:  "+String.valueOf
```

```
            (number1), 20, 40);
    g.drawString("The second number was: "+String.valueOf
        (number2), 20, 60);
    g.drawString("By adding the numbers we get: "+String.valueOf
        ((number1+number2)), 20, 80);
    }

    String theString;
    int number1;
    int number2;
}
```

When we view the applet in the browser using the `view.html` file that we listed above, we should see something similar to the following figure.

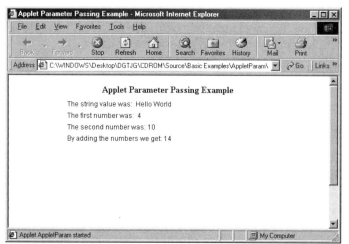

Figure 8-4: Passing parameters to an applet

Now that we have looked at a working example, let's see how it works.

This time we need to include both the AWT and Swing packages using the following two lines of code:

```
import java.awt.*;
import javax.swing.*;
```

We need to include the AWT package because in this example we have used the `Graphics` class to define the `paint` method for this class, as we will look at in a moment.

In the `init` method, we grab the parameters supplied to us by the HTML page and store them in variables ready for drawing. We have defined three variables, as follows, in the main class to store this information:

```
String theString;
int number1;
int number2;
```

In order to get the values, we can use the `getParameter` method of our applet class to retrieve the three parameters, which are called `theString`, `Number1`, and `Number2`. This can be seen in the following few lines of code:

```
theString = getParameter("theString");
        number1 = Integer.parseInt(getParameter("Number1"));
        number2 = Integer.parseInt(getParameter("Number2"));
```

As you can see, we pass the name of the parameter to retrieve as a string to the `getParameter` method, and it then returns the value of the parameter as a string.

Let's take a quick look at the HTML code that we used to pass the parameters in with now.

```
<APPLET CODE="AppletParam.class" WIDTH=400 HEIGHT=300>
<PARAM NAME="theString" VALUE="Hello World">
<PARAM NAME="Number1" VALUE=4>
<PARAM NAME="Number2" VALUE=10>
</APPLET>
```

As can be seen in the above code, specify the parameters within the <APPLET> </APPLET> block using the <PARAM> tag. To specify the parameter, you need to have the NAME and its VALUE. Let's look at the `theString` one now:

```
<PARAM NAME="theString" VALUE="Hello World">
```

So for this parameter, we have specified the name as `theString` and the value as `Hello World`. When we call the `getParameter` method in our applet, passing the string `theString` to it, it will return the string `Hello World`.

Finally, we have created a `paint` method, which is called by the browser every time the applet needs to be refreshed. Do not worry too much about this method now, as it will be explained in detail in Chapter 9. All this method does is output string values to the screen so that we can see the parameters have been passed in correctly.

Applet Security

One very important aspect of Java applets is security. A Java applet, even though it actually downloads and executes automatically on the user's machine, is restricted as to what it can do on the given machine. For example, an applet cannot write to the machine or connect to a network that the applet did not originate from; the applet can only connect to the server that it was downloaded from.

Look at it this way: You open up a web page, and it has an applet. The applet then proceeds, running independently without your knowledge, to delete every file it finds on your computer (not ideal really). Therefore, applets require this security aspect for obvious reasons.

If you really must gain access to the local file system or connect to another server from an applet which is not where the applet was downloaded from, you would require a *signed applet*.

Although creating signed applets is out of the scope of this book, you can find information on it at the following link: http://java.sun.com/products/jdk/1.1/docs/guide/security/.

Chapter 8

Look and Feel

"Look and feel" is a way to make your Java application or applet look like the operating system on which it is being executed, without changing any code. As you can guess, because Java works on most platforms, this is a really useful tool, and it's easy to implement.

As we mentioned earlier in this chapter, it is only possible to use look and feel with Swing. The reason we cannot use it with AWT is that AWT uses heavyweight components, whereas Swing components are actually drawn purely in Java. So it is then possible to change the look (and feel) of the components.

Let's now look at a simple application, which will look and feel like the operating system on which it is being executed.

Code Listing 8-7: Look and feel example

```java
import javax.swing.*;

public class LookandFeel extends JFrame
{
    public LookandFeel()
    {
        super("Look and Feel Example");
        setSize(400, 300);
        setDefaultCloseOperation(EXIT_ON_CLOSE);
        setVisible(true);
    }

    public static void main(String args[])
    {
        try
        {
            UIManager.setLookAndFeel(UIManager.getSystemLookAnd
                FeelClassName());
        }
        catch (Exception e)
        {
            System.out.println(e);
        }

        LookandFeel theApp = new LookandFeel();
    }
}
```

When we run the example, you will see the following window appear on the screen (see Figure 8-5).

This example was run on the Windows platform and therefore uses the Windows-style look and feel. If you compare it to previous windows that we created earlier in this chapter, you can see that the gray color of the windows differs. There are more noticeable differences than this of course, which you will take note of when using different GUI components with different look and feels. We will look at GUI components in more detail in Chapter 13, "Introduction to GUI."

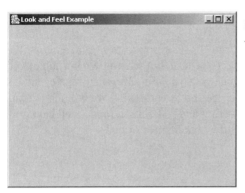

Figure 8-5:
Java look and feel

To change the look and feel, we can simply call the static `setLookAnd-Feel` method of the `UIManager` class. In our example, we pass in a call to the `getSystemLookAndFeelClassName` static method of the `UIManager` class. This can be seen in the following code segment:

```
try
{
    UIManager.setLookAndFeel(UIManager.getSystemLookAnd
        FeelClassName());
}
catch (Exception e)
{
    System.out.println(e);
}
```

This checks to see which operating system you are running the application on and then selects the appropriate look and feel for it.

Alternatively, we can also specify the look and feel directly, but we are not always guaranteed that it will work, as not all implementations of Java have all the look and feels available. Here is a list of the available look and feels we can use:

Look and Feel Class Name	Description
`UIManager.getCrossPlatformLookAndFeelClassName()`	This one is always available, as it is the default.
`UIManager.getSystemLookAndFeelClassName()`	This is the one used in the previous example and will make the application/applet look and feel like the operating system on which it is running.
`"javax.swing.plaf.metal.MetalLookAndFeel"`	If available, this will give the application/applet a metallic look.
`"com.sun.java.swing.plaf.windows.WindowsLookAndFeel"`	If available, this will make the application/applet look like it is running on the Windows platform.
`"com.sun.java.swing.plaf.motif.MotifLookAndFeel"`	If available, this will make the application/applet look like CDE/Motif.
`"javax.swing.plaf.mac.MacLookAndFeel"`	If available, this will make the application/applet look like it is running on the Mac OS.

Summary

In this chapter, we looked at the basics of applications and applets. We now know how to create them and run them, but what now? In the next chapter, we will further this knowledge by delving into the graphics side of Java programming. This is where the fun starts ☺. We will make graphics and a main loop, look at rendering and full-screen mode, and have milk and cookies and do all the fun stuff we've been waiting for.

# Chapter 9

Graphics

"I've seen things you people wouldn't believe. Attack ships on fire
off the shoulder of Orion. I watched c-beams glitter in the dark
near Tanhauser Gate. All those moments will be lost in time,
like tears in rain. Time to die."   —*Blade Runner*

Introduction

Programming graphics is of the utmost importance in games programming. In most circumstances this is the most time-consuming part of your
game loop, and it is essential that it is as efficient as possible. In this chapter you will learn the major aspects of programming 2D graphics in Java.
We will first take a look at creating and loading graphics. Then we will look
at manipulating graphics, beginning with rendering, where you will be
introduced to making a game loop. We will then look at some important
new features to Java 1.4, such as the `BufferStrategy` class and full-
screen exclusive mode. We will also pay particular attention to applications and applets throughout the chapter, showing you the few differences
in getting your games working in terms of graphics.

Template Graphics Windowed Application

To begin with, we will take a look at a basic template windowed application, where we create a window and look at some of the important features
involved in the graphical side of the window. We will begin with the example class `TemplateGraphicsApplication`, building this example up
piece by piece, explaining as we go. Let's start with a template class consisting of the constructor and `paint` method and of course the `main`
method. (Note that the initial base class when run will not create our window and will exit the program straight away.)

```
import java.awt.*;
import javax.swing.*;

public class TemplateGraphicsApplication extends JFrame
{
    public TemplateGraphicsApplication()
```

```
{
    // code to go here
}

public void paint(Graphics g)
{
    // code to go here
}

public static void main(String[] args)
{
}
}
```

The code so far indicates that we have a main class called `Template-GraphicsApplication` that extends the `JFrame` class (we saw about extending the `JFrame` class in the previous chapter) and includes a default constructor and a method called `paint` that takes a parameter object reference of type `Graphics`. The `paint` method that we declare here is the same as the very important `paint` method belonging to the `JFrame` class. Here, we provide our own version of the `paint` method, overriding the one we would have inherited from the `JFrame` class. In order to understand the means by which the `paint` method works, you must first understand about the Event Dispatch Thread that we touched upon briefly in Chapter 7.

Introducing the Event Dispatch Thread

The Event Dispatch Thread is a thread that is part of Java's AWT library and is also known as the AWT thread. Its purpose is to poll the system event queue, listening for events associated with your GUI (graphical user interface), such as the `JFrame` we are currently setting up. Examples of such events are mouse and keyboard events, button click events, and repaint requests. When an event occurs, it is added to an event queue ready for the Event Dispatch Thread to handle. This event is then handled by invoking the appropriate method or methods provided to handle the event.

Going back to our `TemplateGraphicsApplication` class, the `paint` method is invoked whenever a paint refresh request is made for the window and is handled by the Event Dispatch Thread in this way. So when would a repaint be requested on our window? Repaint events can be requested on our window both directly (by the programmer) or indirectly (such as when the user resizes the window at run time or drags another window over our window). In both instances, our window will need to be repainted by a repaint event being queued, which the Event Dispatch Thread will handle, finishing with a call to our `paint` method.

We will look at this in much more depth in the very important "Rendering" section of this chapter a little later. For now, we will continue building our `TemplateGraphicsApplication` class.

Creation and Initialization

There are a whole host of parameters that we may supply in the constructor for our JFrame derivative TemplateGraphicsApplication. The following method calls are a few of the most common that we are interested in at this early stage. We can set up the constructor as follows.

```
public TemplateGraphicsApplication()
{
    super("Template Graphics Application");
    setDefaultCloseOperation(EXIT_ON_CLOSE);
    setResizable(false);
    getContentPane().setLayout(null);

    setBounds(0, 0, 400, 400);
}
```

Part of what we have added we have already seen in the previous chapter. The call to the super class constructor simply allows us to define the window title that will be displayed in its top border. We need to specify the default close operation because a window when closed, by default, is merely hidden (we will look at this in a moment). We also set our window so that it is not resizable because, in most cases, if you create a 2D game, it is more than likely you are working to a fixed pixel resolution, as 2D scaling can be expensive as well as cause unexpected distortion in your graphics.

Disabling the Layout Manager

In Java all component containers have a default layout manager. A *layout manager* is an object that is used to handle the layout of components added to a container; for example, it can be used to calculate the positions and dimensions of a number of buttons that you add to a container automatically and position them in a desired pattern, with little work on your part once they are set up. We discussed components and containers in the last chapter, but just to remind you, speaking in terms of our current example, the content pane of the JFrame is a container that can hold other components, which themselves can be containers, building up what is effectively a containment hierarchy.

For example, adding a JPanel object to the content pane of the JFrame means that the content pane of the JFrame would contain a JPanel, and in turn the JPanel could contain, say, a button object and so on. We will look at the JPanel a little later in this chapter when we look at adding components. We disable the layout manager because a layout manager is used to control the position of your components in the container to which the layout manager belongs. This means that the layout manager will handle repositioning your components when, say, your window is resized. It is very useful for GUI-based applications with coordinated buttons but not really for games where, in simple terms, you want to have complete control over where you draw everything. Note that in many examples in this chapter, we may not set the layout manager to null and leave it as the default one. The layout manager is only important when adding components to containers and not when drawing your own graphics, so it is quite irrelevant for this section. But we thought we'd mention it all the same.

Pixel Coordinates

Before we look into some important issues relating to sizing a window, it is important to understand the system of defining pixel coordinates in Java. Take a look at the following figure.

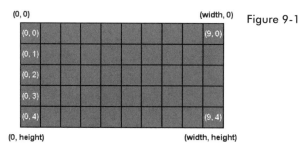

Figure 9-1

This diagram shows a set of pixels of resolution 10x5. This means that the grid is 10 pixels in width and 5 pixels in height. The coordinate system is relative to the top-left corner of a given rectangular area. This is the standard coordinate system for any rectangular screen or off-screen graphics in Java, such as a window or a button or an off-screen image defined by a location (x, y) and a dimension (width, height). The location represents the position of the graphic relative to its parent or, to be more precise, the current translation position of the Graphics object to which it is drawing (translations will be explained a little later in the chapter). There are three basic classes for representing rectangular regions throughout the Java2D API: Point, Dimension, and Rectangle, which are all members of the java.awt package. We will use these classes throughout this chapter and in further chapters.

This brings us to the last line of code added to the constructor of the TemplateGraphicsApplication example: setBounds. This method simply defines the size of our window, with four integer values for the x, y, width, and height, respectively. Alternatively, we could also have passed a reference to a Rectangle object to set the bounds, as follows:

```
JFrame myFrame = new JFrame();

myFrame.setBounds(new Rectangle(0, 0, 400, 400));
```

We can retrieve the size of the window as follows:

```
Rectangle bounds = myFrame.getBounds();
```

You may also set the location and size of the window separately using the methods setLocation and setSize, passing in Point and

Dimension objects respectively. You will get used to all of these methods as you progress through the examples and can easily look up these methods in the Java SDK.

Sizing with the Window Border

When you create a component that contains a border, such as a window, the size of the component that you define includes the border as part of its size. This means that if, for example, you set the size of your JFrame object to the size 400x400, like we have so far in the Template-GraphicsApplication class, the window (including its borders) would make up this size. This means that the displayable area between the borders is not 400x400 but a dimension that is 400x400 minus the total border dimensions. Furthermore, the top-left of the coordinate system (0, 0) lies at the very top of the window, and the displayable area inside the window's border is at the position of the left border width and the top border height. You may only want to define the overall size and be done with it, but it is important that you know the internal display area too. It is also important that you can define this, as you need to know the resolution of the screen area you are drawing to. You would not want the window including its border to be 400x400 pixels in dimension but the internal display area to be 400x400 and the window's border spaced around it. What we want to do is find out the size of the window's borders and resize the window to the desired size, plus the border size. We can do this using the method getInsets of the frame object, which returns an object of type Insets from which we can retrieve this information. However, we can only retrieve this information once the JFrame is visible because the size of the border is dependent on the platform on which you are running. The following example is the completion of our Template-GraphicsApplication class fit with a window resized to our needs and some test graphics added to the paint method. Here is the code for TemplateGraphicsApplication.java.

Code Listing 9-1: TemplateGraphicsApplication.java

```
import javax.swing.*;
import java.awt.*;

public class TemplateGraphicsApplication extends JFrame
{
    public TemplateGraphicsApplication()
    {
        super("Template Graphics Application");
        setDefaultCloseOperation(EXIT_ON_CLOSE);
        setResizable(false);
        getContentPane().setLayout(null);

        setVisible(true);

        Insets insets = getInsets();
        DISPLAY_X = insets.left;
```

```
        DISPLAY_Y = insets.top;
        resizeToInternalSize(DISPLAY_WIDTH, DISPLAY_HEIGHT);
    }


    public void resizeToInternalSize(int internalWidth, int
        internalHeight)
    {
        Insets insets = getInsets();
        final int newWidth = internalWidth + insets.left +
            insets.right;
        final int newHeight = internalHeight + insets.top +
            insets.bottom;

        Runnable resize = new Runnable()
        {
            public void run()
            {
                setSize(newWidth, newHeight);
            }
        };

        if(!SwingUtilities.isEventDispatchThread())
        {
            try
            {
                SwingUtilities.invokeAndWait(resize);
            }
            catch(Exception e) {}
        }
        else
            resize.run();

        validate();
    }


    public void paint(Graphics g)
    {
        Graphics2D g2D = (Graphics2D)g;
        g2D.translate(DISPLAY_X, DISPLAY_Y);

        g2D.setColor(Color.blue);
        g2D.fillRect(0, 0, DISPLAY_WIDTH, DISPLAY_HEIGHT);

        g2D.setColor(Color.white);
        g2D.fillRect(DISPLAY_WIDTH/4, DISPLAY_HEIGHT/4,
            DISPLAY_WIDTH/2, DISPLAY_HEIGHT/2);
    }

    public static void main(String[] args)
    {
        new TemplateGraphicsApplication();
    }

    private final int DISPLAY_X; // value assigned in constructor
    private final int DISPLAY_Y; // value assigned in constructor
    private static final int DISPLAY_WIDTH = 400;
    private static final int DISPLAY_HEIGHT = 400;
}
```

When you compile and run this example, you should get output similar to the following figure.

Figure 9-2

In order to get the border size from the `Insets` object using the `getInsets` method of our `JFrame`, we must make the window frame visible. We can do this by calling the method `setVisible(true)`. However, changing the state of a Swing component outside the Event Dispatch Thread is unsafe when the component is realized. A component is said to be realized when it is in a visible state, such as when we call `setVisible` on our `JFrame` object or add a component to a container that is realized. From then on, calling methods to change the state of the component must be called in a synchronized manner with the Event Dispatch Thread. Otherwise, they are unsafe with code executing in the Event Dispatch Thread. There are exceptions to this rule, such as the `setText` method of the `JTextComponent` and the `repaint` method that we will see later in this chapter. But generally, changes to Swing objects need to be executed in the Event Dispatch Thread. So, in order to change the size of our window, first set the window visible (realize it) and then update our `DISPLAY_X` and `DISPLAY_Y` values as follows in the constructor for `TemplateGraphicsApplication`:

```
Insets insets = getInsets();
DISPLAY_X = insets.left;
DISPLAY_Y = insets.top;
```

We store the left and top inset values of the window's border in the variables `DISPLAY_X` and `DISPLAY_Y` to be used in the `paint` method. In this method we can translate the top corner of the graphics object to these coordinates so that the top corner that we are drawing from is the top corner of the displayable area inside the window, not the very top corner of the window itself. We will see how this can be resolved automatically using components shortly, but note that this is the method we will be sticking with in general for handling windowed applications. Note also that we set the display coordinates before resizing the window so that once this is done, the window will refresh its appearance on screen with the correct coordinates after it resizes itself.

After we have set the window to visible and saved the top corner internal coordinates of the window, we next need to actually resize the window so that the internal area is of the required size. We do this by calling the method `resizeToInternalSize`, passing in the required internal width and height. Let's run through this method step by step and see how it works.

```
public void resizeToInternalSize(int internalWidth, int
        internalHeight)
{
        Insets insets = getInsets();
```

First we need to get the insets of the window's border. Note that the correct inset data can only be retrieved if the window is realized, as discussed earlier.

```
        final int newWidth = internalWidth + insets.left +
            insets.right;
        final int newHeight = internalHeight + insets.top +
            insets.bottom;
```

Next we need to calculate the new overall size of the window, including its borders. This is simply calculated as the desired internal size plus the size of the borders in their respective dimensions. Note also that these values must be declared as final, as they are local variables that will be accessed from the following inner class:

```
        Runnable resize = new Runnable()
        {
            public void run()
            {
                setSize(newWidth, newHeight);
            }
        };
```

As we saw in Chapter 4, we can define object members on the fly, but we can also define interface objects in a similar way. As you can see with the runnable object, we simply need to define the methods of the `Runnable` interface, which in this case consists of the method `run`. By holding a reference to the runnable object, it, in a way, gives a reference to a method, a segment of execution that we can call later using the reference. More importantly in this case, we need a runnable object in order to execute code in the Event Dispatch Thread.

```
        if(!SwingUtilities.isEventDispatchThread())
        {
            try
            {
                SwingUtilities.invokeAndWait(resize);
            }
            catch(Exception e) {}
        }
        else
            resize.run();
```

```
        validate();
    }
```

To begin with, check to see if we are already running in the Event Dispatch Thread. If so, then execute the code safely in the Event Dispatch Thread using the static method `invokeAndWait` of the `SwingUtilities` class. This method will wait until the Event Dispatch Thread gets around to executing this code. Alternatively, there is the method `invokeLater` that doesn't wait and exits the method straight away, leaving it up to the Event Dispatch Thread to execute the code when it's ready, which you should note should be quite soon after. For this implementation, we want to wait until the window is the right size before progressing. If we are running in the Event Dispatch Thread, we can simply invoke the `run` method to resize the window then and there. At the end, make a call to the `validate` method that will lay out subcomponents of the window. This is important for things such as resetting the size of the content pane after the window has been resized, which needs to be correctly sized for things like mouse handling, as we shall see later in the book. Also, the `validate` method is one of those methods that is thread-safe for calling outside of the Event Dispatch Thread, so we can call it just from the main thread.

Note that calling the state changing method before the window is visible (realized) is fine, so if you wanted to just define the size of the overall window using `setSize`, that would be perfectly safe to call before calling `setVisible` on the window.

It's not fair to go into any more detail on this matter now, as we have hardly looked at areas of the Event Dispatch Thread, such as repainting and using event listeners (see Chapter 10). We will return to this discussion in Chapter 13, "Introduction to GUI."

Let's See That in an Applet

The applet conversion of the `TemplateGraphicsApplication` is quite clear-cut. The applet still has a displayable area that you are able to draw to via its `paint` method, but we do not need to bother with any resizing, as the applet does not contain any borders to worry about. We are left with a rectangular canvas to which we can draw and add functionality embedded in a web page, just like a picture. Here is the code for `TemplateGraphicsApplet.java`. (In the previous chapter we discussed how to get applets running in the browser and using AppletViewer.)

Code Listing 9-2: `TemplateGraphicsApplet.java`

```java
import javax.swing.*;
import java.awt.*;

public class TemplateGraphicsApplet extends JApplet
{
    public void init()
    {
```

```
        getContentPane().setLayout(null);
        setSize(DISPLAY_WIDTH, DISPLAY_HEIGHT);
    }

    public void paint(Graphics g)
    {
        Graphics2D g2D = (Graphics2D)g;

        g2D.setColor(Color.blue);
        g2D.fill(getBounds());

        g2D.setColor(Color.white);
        g2D.fillRect(getWidth()/4, getHeight()/4, getWidth()/2,
            getHeight()/2);
    }

    private static final int DISPLAY_WIDTH = 400;
    private static final int DISPLAY_HEIGHT = 400;
}
```

Here is a screen shot of our applet running in Java's AppletViewer program.

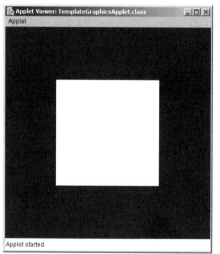

Figure 9-3

We outlined how to get an applet running in AppletViewer (and a web browser) in the previous chapter, so refer to that chapter if you have any problems running your applets.

AWT Notice 1

Some developers prefer to use the AWT components instead of the newer Swing components. One particular reason is that earlier releases of the JRE (Java Runtime Environment) used the earlier AWT components before Swing was introduced. This is especially the case for applet games accessed from the Internet, whereby typically you as a developer (and show-off) want to reach as many people across the web as possible, all running on different machines with different versions of Java. Using Java 1.1 obviously gives you a much wider audience than using 1.4 at the moment, but that's no good. The way forward is to use the most up-to-date version of Java, especially 1.4 with full screen mode, which is cool.

It may sound like a cop-out to dismiss AWT and just use Swing, but it is not. We will try to highlight differences when it comes to using AWT and Swing, beginning with a briefing on the subject and a look at how we would implement our current template graphics application and applet using only AWT classes. It is quite possible that you want to make an applet game in an earlier version of Java so that your friends can play it. For example, say they only have the Java 1.2 JRE installed on their machine and cannot update Java for whatever reason; we will pay particular attention to methods used in earlier versions of Java (for example, image loading, which has changed so much from earlier versions to the one-line command it is today supplied by the new-to-1.4 `javax.imageio` package's `ImageIO` class, as we shall see later in the chapter).

As we noted from the previous chapter, AWT components are based in the `java.awt` package, whereas Swing components are based in the `javax.swing` package. The most obvious programming difference between AWT and Swing components is that Swing components are named the same as their AWT counterparts but with the letter J in front of them. For example, the `Button` class represents a button in AWT, whereas `JButton` represents a Swing button. (For an introduction to AWT and Swing, you may wish to return to the previous chapter.) If we want to alter the `TemplateGraphicsApplication` class to AWT instead of Swing, we would need to make the following distinct changes to the code.

First you need to change the class definition so that you extend a `Frame` and not a `JFrame`. Then we call `setLayout(null)` on the AWT `Frame` object itself, as the content pane is a feature new to Swing and is not part of the way AWT works. We will see more about the content pane in a moment. The changes we need to make so far are as follows:

```
import javax.swing.*;
import java.awt.*;

public class TemplateGraphicsApplication extends Frame
{
    public TemplateGraphicsApplication()
    {
        super("Template Graphics App");
        setDefaultCloseOperation(EXIT_ON_CLOSE);
        setResizable(false);
        setLayout(null);

        // The rest of the code as before
```

The only thing remaining is to remove the Swing `JFrame` method `set-DefaultCloseOperation(EXIT_ON_CLOSE)`.

Closing a Window

The setDefaultCloseOperation method was introduced to Swing as an easy way of specifying a default operation on a frame when the user attempts to close it. Other available constants for this method are DO_NOTHING_ON_CLOSE, HIDE_ON_CLOSE, and DISPOSE_ON_CLOSE. The difference between EXIT_ON_CLOSE and DISPOSE_ON_CLOSE is that EXIT_ON_CLOSE will call the System.exit method, which will terminate your entire program, whereas DISPOSE_ON_CLOSE will hide and then dispose of your frame only; any other independent parts of your program will remain active.

By default, the AWT Frame will do nothing when the user attempts to close the window, whereas a Swing JFrame will hide itself. We know how to change this for the JFrame, but for the AWT Frame we can use a WindowAdapter, as follows.

```
import java.awt.*;
import java.awt.event.*;

public class TemplateGraphicsApplication extends Frame
{
    public TemplateGraphicsApplication()
    {
        super("Template Graphics App");
        setResizable(false);
        setLayout(null);

        addWindowListener(new WindowAdapter() {
            public void windowClosing(WindowEvent e) {
                System.exit(0); }
                });

        // The rest of the code as before
```

First you will notice that we no longer need to include the package javax.swing and have also included the package java.awt.event. The package java.awt.event contains classes used for handling events, such as the window closing, as we have used above. This code may look a little strange, but we will discuss in detail using listeners and their adapter classes in the next chapter when we discuss the mouse and keyboard. After you have read the next chapter, it is advised that you look back upon this code; you should then be able to understand it fully. For now, however, we must move on.

NOTE: Adding a window listener can be used with a Swing JFrame also. If both this method and a default close operation are specified, the listener method windowClosing will first be invoked followed by the default close operation.

Adding Components

To refresh your memory a little, a component is an object used to represent a displayable rectangular area in pixels on screen and can also be used to handle events, such as the mouse and keyboard. For example, our `Frame` is a component; a button or a text field is also a component. A component is defined by the class `java.awt.Component` to which all other components are derived. For example, the `java.awt.Button` class is derived from `Component`. Below a component is the `java.awt.Container` class. Basically, any class that extends this class can "contain" a list of other components, which themselves can be containers (for example, the `java.awt.Panel` class, which is a simple container for storing other components). The `java.awt.Button` class on the other hand directly extends `java.awt.Component` and not `java.awt.Container` because a button can be displayed and receive events, like being clicked by the mouse, but it cannot itself contain other components. The button is therefore said to be an atomic or indivisible component.

We can overcome one problem we have at the moment with our current `TemplateGraphicsApplication` automatically by using a component to represent the displayable screen area of our `Frame`. The component can be added to the frame where drawing can be performed onto that, instead of directly painting in the `paint` method. This means that we can perform our drawing relative to the component, which is added to the displayable area inside the frame where we will not need to handle the top-left border offset pixels when we are drawing (i.e., using the `translate` method we saw before).

We can alter our `TemplateGraphicsApplication` as follows so that it uses a `JPanel` component for drawing. A `JPanel` is a simple Swing container class that we will draw our graphics onto.

```
import javax.swing.*;
import java.awt.*;

public class TemplateGraphicsApplication extends JFrame
{
    public TemplateGraphicsApplication()
    {
        super("Template Graphics Application");
        setDefaultCloseOperation(EXIT_ON_CLOSE);
        setResizable(false);
        getContentPane().setLayout(null);
        getContentPane().add(new DisplayArea(new Rectangle(0, 0,
            DISPLAY_WIDTH, DISPLAY_HEIGHT)));

        setVisible(true);

        resizeToInternalSize(DISPLAY_WIDTH, DISPLAY_HEIGHT);
    }

    public void resizeToInternalSize(int internalWidth, int
        internalHeight)
```

```java
    {
        Insets insets = getInsets();
        final int newWidth = internalWidth + insets.left +
            insets.right;
        final int newHeight = internalHeight + insets.top +
            insets.bottom;

        Runnable resize = new Runnable()
        {
            public void run()
            {
                setSize(newWidth, newHeight);
            }
        };

        if(!SwingUtilities.isEventDispatchThread())
        {
            try
            {
                SwingUtilities.invokeAndWait(resize);
            }
            catch(Exception e) {}
        }
        else
            resize.run();

        validate();
    }


    public class DisplayArea extends JPanel
    {
        public DisplayArea(Rectangle bounds)
        {
            setLayout(null);
            setBounds(bounds);
            setOpaque(false);
        }

        public void paintComponent(Graphics g)
        {
            Graphics2D g2D = (Graphics2D)g;

            g2D.setColor(Color.blue);
            g2D.fill(getBounds());

            g2D.setColor(Color.white);
            g2D.fillRect(getWidth()/4, getHeight()/4, getWidth()/2,
                getHeight()/2);
        }
    }

    public static void main(String[] args)
    {
        new TemplateGraphicsApplication();
    }

    private static final int DISPLAY_WIDTH = 400;
    private static final int DISPLAY_HEIGHT = 400;
}
```

The nested class `DisplayArea` extends `JPanel` where we provide our own overridden painting method `paintComponent` similar to overriding the `paint` method for the top-level frame and applet earlier. In the frames constructor, we add a new instance of our display area to the content pane of the frame. When this is done, we no longer need to worry about the border positions when drawing in the `paintComponent` method, as the component is added at the origin of the viewable display area of the frame. One thing to note about the `JPanel` is that it is opaque by default. This means that it will draw a background rectangle in its given bounds before invoking the `paintComponent` method. Because we are drawing the full displayable area, we do not need to do this so we call `setOpaque-(false)`; this is advantageous if you want to show parts drawn by the underlying parent component. Now that we are using components, the `validate` method is important for resizing the subcomponents of the window. Try leaving the call to `validate` out, and you'll see the non-resized internal `DisplayArea` component instead.

AWT Notice 2

Note that when using Swing components, you should override the method `paintComponent`, but when using AWT components, you should override their `paint` method instead. The AWT alternative to `JPanel` is simply `Panel`. When adding an AWT component, you must add it directly to the top-level container. Swing components must be added to the content pane of the top-level container. Note that the content pane of a Swing top-level container, such as `JFrame` or `JApplet`, is a `JPanel` itself. Also, if you are adding only one component, such as our `JPanel` derivative `DisplayArea`, instead of adding this to the content pane, you can use `setContentPane(myDisplayArea)`, cutting out the middleman as it were. This is a Swing feature.

 NOTE: It is important to understand about components and containers because this technique is used a lot in Java and can be very advantageous in many respects. For example, you may split your screen area up into different components and then add mouse listeners to the individual areas of the screen, making handling mouse events easy, relative to that area of the screen. However, if you are making a serious game, we recommend that you stick to one drawing area (i.e., the paint method of the frame or applet) and perform your drawing all at once. If you use multiple components to represent sections of your screen, they cannot overlap, and drawing routines are completely separate, as each of the components will have its own paint method for drawing to its given rectangular screen area. This would be a problem, say, if you had a component representing the main game display and another component for an inventory of weapons.

What if you wanted to have your graphics overlap from the main game screen to another component, such as an inventory? Perhaps some sparks will fly off or something or maybe an inventory item will be dragged onto the main game screen from the inventory. There are a whole host of reasons you would want to do this; however, this would be virtually impossible with separate drawing methods for each component or at least a nightmare to code. For the drawing example applications that follow, we will add a component for displaying our graphics for convenience but will stick to the top-level paint methods for the passive rendering examples in the "Rendering" section later in the chapter.

Graphics and Graphics2D Overview

The Graphics class provides many methods for manipulating a graphics device, be it a screen or off-screen image. The Graphics2D class is a subclass of the Graphics class and contains even more useful methods for manipulating 2D graphics, such as primitive shape rendering and affine transformations. Most of your image creation should take place before you enter the game but for maximum efficiency stored as off-screen sprites and then drawn in the game as a memory copy routine with as little overhead as possible. We will see about creating off-screen images a little later. In the previous examples in this chapter, we have seen the Graphics object passed as a parameter to the methods paint and paintComponent. This is our context for drawing to the component screen. There we can explicitly cast the object to a reference of type Graphics2D, as the true type of the object is not Graphics but a subclass of Graphics.

```
Graphics2D g2D = (Graphics2D)g;
```

This means that we can now take advantage of the extra methods in the Graphics2D class on our object. The parameter will always remain of type Graphics to maintain backward compatibility (code compiled in previous versions of Java running on a more up-to-date Java Virtual Machine will still need to run, so newer versions of Java need to contain the same structures of older versions).

Graphics Class Basics

The Graphics and Graphics2D classes provide us with standard primitive graphics routines that we can use to draw graphics. Here are some of the most commonly used methods available in the Graphics class.

setColor(Color col)

A Graphics object has a current color state associated with it. When a primitive routine, such as the fillRect method, is invoked, similar to when we used this combination in the paint methods earlier, the rectangle specified is filled with the current color associated with the Graphics object. You can create colors using the java.awt.Color class. Here are a few examples of creating Color objects.

The Color class includes common static colors represented by an RGBA (red, green, blue, alpha) integer value, where the alpha value is opaque. The alpha value determines the transparency of the color with respect to what is behind. We can set the color state of the graphics object to blue as follows:

```
g.setColor(Color.blue);
```

There are various constructors of the `Color` class for creating your own color objects. An example of this is specifying the RGB value of the color by red, green, and blue values as integer parameters in the range 0 to 255, where (0, 0, 0) is black and (255, 255, 255) is white, or as floating-point parameters in the range 0.0 to 1.0, where (0.0, 0.0, 0.0) is black and (1.0, 1.0, 1.0) is white.

```
Color col = new Color(255, 0, 0);       // red
Color col = new Color(1.0, 0.0, 0.0);   // red also
```

dispose()

The `dispose` method should be called when you are finished with a `Graphics` object. This method disposes of the object and releases any system resources it is using. You should call this method when you have finished with any `Graphics` objects you have created manually. Therefore, you do not need to call this method in component paint methods, such as the `paint` method we used earlier, as this is handled for you where it is passed a `Graphics` object that is automatically disposed internally. The `finalize` method of a `Graphics` object performs the dispose task, but the garbage collector is not likely to call the `finalize` method right away, so it's best to do this manually as soon as you are finished with the `Graphics` object. Note that we will look at the garbage collector in Chapter 12, "Game Programming Techniques."

So in short, if you are manually creating a `Graphics` object, as we shall see later, and are not being sent one through a `paint` method, it's best to call `dispose` after it. We will see about using `Graphics` objects in examples later in this chapter, and you will get the hang of this as we work through various examples.

drawLine(int x1, int y1, int x2, int y2)

This method simply draws a straight line from the points (x1, y1) to (x2, y2) in the current color state of the `Graphics` object. Note that clipping is handled for you when drawing to an image using drawing methods in the `Graphics` class.

drawRect(int x, int y, int width, int height) and fillRect(int x, int y, int width, int height)

These methods draw the outline of and fill a rectangular area specified by their parameters, respectively. Note that if you have an area with location (0, 0) and dimension (10, 10), then `drawRect` will add a boundary filling pixels at (0, 0) to (10, 10), whereas `fillRect` will fill all pixels in between, including the area (0, 0) to (9, 9). So if you want to draw a pixel border around your component, you would call:

```
Graphics.drawRect(0, 0, getWidth()-1, getHeight()-1)
```

…whereas if you wanted to fill the area, you would simply call:

```
Graphics.fillRect(0, 0, getWidth(), getHeight()).
```

Chapter 9

drawString(String s, int x, int y)

This method draws a string at the specified location. The drawing of the text depends on the font associated with the `Graphics` object. Similar to having a current color, the `Graphics` object has a current font that you may alter accordingly. We will see about using fonts a little later in the chapter.

These methods are probably the most common and will undoubtedly become common knowledge to you as you get used to rendering graphics in Java.

Drawing Shapes

The Java2D API provides a base interface `java.awt.Shape` that all geometric shape classes implement. The package `java.awt.geom` contains many useful shape classes, such as `Ellipse2D` (which is used for drawing circles too). The classes implementing the Shape interface can then be passed to Graphics2D methods, such as `draw(Shape)` and `fill(Shape)`. The following example shows a few simple shapes being drawn in the `paintComponent` method. The shape in the middle should be quite familiar to most of you, and if not, then shame on you. Here is the code for `DrawingShapes.java`.

Code Listing 9-3: DrawingShapes.java

```java
import javax.swing.*;
import java.awt.*;
import java.awt.geom.*;

public class DrawingShapes extends JFrame
{
    public DrawingShapes()
    {
        super("Drawing Shapes Demo");
        setDefaultCloseOperation(EXIT_ON_CLOSE);
        setResizable(false);
        getContentPane().setLayout(null);
        getContentPane().add(new DisplayArea(new Rectangle(0, 0,
            DISPLAY_WIDTH, DISPLAY_HEIGHT)));

        setVisible(true);

        resizeToInternalSize(DISPLAY_WIDTH, DISPLAY_HEIGHT);
    }


    public void resizeToInternalSize(int internalWidth, int
        internalHeight)
    {
        Insets insets = getInsets();
        final int newWidth = internalWidth + insets.left +
            insets.right;
        final int newHeight = internalHeight + insets.top +
            insets.bottom;
```

```
    Runnable resize = new Runnable()
    {
        public void run()
        {
            setSize(newWidth, newHeight);
        }
    };

    if(!SwingUtilities.isEventDispatchThread())
    {
        try
        {
            SwingUtilities.invokeAndWait(resize);
        }
        catch(Exception e) {}
    }
    else
        resize.run();

    validate();
}


public class DisplayArea extends JPanel
{
    public DisplayArea(Rectangle bounds)
    {
        setLayout(null);
        setBounds(bounds);
        setOpaque(false);
    }

    public void paintComponent(Graphics g)
    {
        Graphics2D g2D = (Graphics2D)g;

        g2D.setColor(Color.black);
        g2D.fillRect(0, 0, getWidth(), getHeight());

        for(int i=0; i<shapeList.length; i++)
        {
            g2D.setColor(colorList[i]);
            g2D.fill(shapeList[i]);
        }
    }
}


public static void main(String[] args)
{
    new DrawingShapes();
}

private static Shape[] shapeList = {
    new Rectangle(10, 10, 100, 100),
    new Ellipse2D.Double(290, 290, 100, 100),
    new Arc2D.Double(150, 150, 100, 100, 45, 270, Arc2D.PIE)
    };

private static Color[] colorList = { Color.red, Color.blue,
```

Chapter 9

```
         Color.yellow };

 private static final int DISPLAY_WIDTH = 400;
 private static final int DISPLAY_HEIGHT = 400;
}
```

When you run this example, you should get output similar to the following figure.

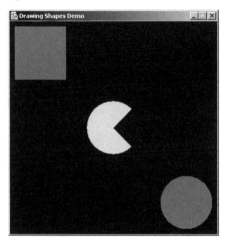

Figure 9-4

A further advantage of shape classes is clipping. *Clipping* is the ability to exclude an area from the drawing process or, alternatively, specify the boundary to which your drawing must be contained. For example, we could have specified in the last example a clipping area of the top-left quarter of the (400x400) displayable area defined by a rectangle at (0, 0) and dimension (200, 200). The effect on our drawing would be that we would see the red square completely, the yellow shape partially, and the blue circle not at all, where any drawing outside of the clipping area is not performed. This is most beneficial when you are unsure of the scope of area that your drawing routine will cover but are sure of the bounding area you want the drawing to be kept within. The Graphics object allows you to set the clipping area to any class, implementing the Shape interface and using most notably the method setClip(Shape) of the Graphics class.

Affined Transformations

Affined transformations allow us to alter the way that we draw geometry, be it by translating, rotating, scaling, or shearing. *Translating* simply entails moving along the x or y axis; this means that you may translate the origin of your Graphics object from the default (0, 0) location to, say, (30, 30) and then draw a shape there. But all things are relative to one another, so the current location of your shape would then need to be set to (0, 0) to draw at position (30, 30) on the Graphics object. *Rotating* means angular rotations about the current origin of the Graphics object.

Scaling is the ability to shrink or enlarge the geometry that you are drawing. *Shearing* allows you to distort your geometry over a given axis. Note that the source geometry is never affected by the transformations, but the way in which the geometry is drawn to the `Graphics` object is.

In Java the `Graphics` object contains a transformation state through the `AffineTransform` class. This state can be manipulated to change the way your drawing is performed. There is a lot of math behind the affined transformations, but luckily in Java we are given simple methods such as `translate` and `rotate` to pass parameters to. The following example `AffinedTransformer.java` draws a square shape spiraling out from the center of the display window. Let's take a look at the code:

Code Listing 9-4: `AffinedTransformer.java`

```java
import javax.swing.*;
import java.awt.*;

public class AffinedTransformer extends JFrame
{
    public AffinedTransformer()
    {
        super("Affined Transformation Demo");
        setDefaultCloseOperation(EXIT_ON_CLOSE);
        setResizable(false);
        getContentPane().setLayout(null);
        getContentPane().add(new DisplayArea(new Rectangle(0, 0,
                DISPLAY_WIDTH, DISPLAY_HEIGHT)));

        setVisible(true);

        resizeToInternalSize(DISPLAY_WIDTH, DISPLAY_HEIGHT);
    }


    public void resizeToInternalSize(int internalWidth, int
            internalHeight)
    {
        Insets insets = getInsets();
        final int newWidth = internalWidth + insets.left +
                insets.right;
        final int newHeight = internalHeight + insets.top +
                insets.bottom;

        Runnable resize = new Runnable()
        {
            public void run()
            {
                setSize(newWidth, newHeight);
            }
        };

        if(!SwingUtilities.isEventDispatchThread())
        {
            try
            {
                SwingUtilities.invokeAndWait(resize);
            }
```

Chapter 9

```
                catch(Exception e) {}
        }
        else
            resize.run();

        validate();
    }


    public class DisplayArea extends JPanel
    {
        public DisplayArea(Rectangle bounds)
        {
            setLayout(null);
            setBounds(bounds);
            setOpaque(false);
        }

        public void paintComponent(Graphics g)
        {
            Graphics2D g2D = (Graphics2D)g;

            g2D.setColor(Color.blue);
            g2D.fillRect(0, 0, getWidth(), getHeight());

            g2D.translate(getWidth()/2, getHeight()/2);

            for(int i=0; i<120; i++)
            {
                g2D.setColor(new Color((float)i/120.0f, 0.0f, 0.0f));
                g2D.rotate(Math.toRadians(12));
                g2D.translate(i, 0);
                g2D.scale(1.01, 1.01);
                g2D.fillRect(-SQUARE_SIZE/2, -SQUARE_SIZE/2,
                        SQUARE_SIZE, SQUARE_SIZE);
                g2D.setColor(Color.white);
                g2D.drawRect(-SQUARE_SIZE/2, -SQUARE_SIZE/2,
                        SQUARE_SIZE, SQUARE_SIZE);
                g2D.translate(-i, 0);
            }
        }
    }


    public static void main(String[] args)
    {
        new AffinedTransformer();
    }

    private static final int SQUARE_SIZE = 10;
    private static final int DISPLAY_WIDTH = 400;
    private static final int DISPLAY_HEIGHT = 400;
}
```

When you compile and run this example, your output should be similar to
the following figure.

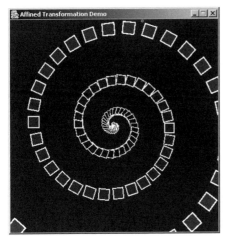

Figure 9-5

The important code is performed inside the method `paintComponent`. First we translate the origin of the `Graphics` object to its center:

```
g2D.translate(getWidth()/2, getHeight()/2);
```

We then perform 120 iterations of drawing the square shape:

```
for(int i=0; i<120; i++)
{
    g2D.setColor(new Color((float)i/120.0f, 0.0f, 0.0f));
    g2D.rotate(Math.toRadians(12));
    g2D.translate(i, 0);
    g2D.scale(1.01, 1.01);
    g2D.fillRect(-SQUARE_SIZE/2, -SQUARE_SIZE/2, SQUARE_SIZE,
            SQUARE_SIZE);
    g2D.setColor(Color.white);
    g2D.drawRect(-SQUARE_SIZE/2, -SQUARE_SIZE/2, SQUARE_SIZE,
            SQUARE_SIZE);
    g2D.translate(-i, 0);
}
```

For each iteration, rotate 12 degrees, translate, scale the scene, and then perform the drawing. Note that the order of the translations and rotations are important, and if we swapped them around, we would get a completely different output. We then translate back to the origin ready for performing this routine again. By continually incrementing our rotation and translation from the origin, we get the effect of a spiralling square shape. We also scale the scene by 1.01 on each axis per iteration. Scaling to 1.0 will not scale the image at all, whereas scaling to 2.0 would draw our shape at double its normal size. Note that scaling to 2.0 twice would therefore draw our shape four times as big as its usual size. For the purpose of this example, we have scaled to a mere 1.01, so the image gets a little bit larger through each of its 120 drawing iterations. You can retrieve the Affine-Transform instance of a `Graphics` object using the method `getTransform` if you want to delve deeper into the functionality of this class. You may also create your own AffineTransform instance and then use the

Chapter 9

method `setTransform(AffineTransform)` of the `Graphics` object too.

Please note that this code is distinctly bad because we are rendering the same image as a series of calculations every time the window refreshes itself, which can be when another window is moved over it, for example. Ideally, we would render this to an off-screen image and then render that in the painting method instead, as we shall see shortly in the "Off-screen Images" section.

Fonts

The class `java.awt.Font` is used to represent a font in Java. Again, as with colors, the `Graphics` object has a current `font` object associated with it, which can be set using the method `setFont(Font)`. We should take a look at creating a `font` object using the `Font` class to begin with.

The main constructor to use for creating your ideal font is as follows:

```
Font(String name, int style, int size);
```

The name of the `Font` object is a `String` representation of the font (for example, `Arial`, `Courier New`, `Times New Roman`, etc.). We will see about getting the available fonts at the end of this section. The style can be one of the following: `Font.PLAIN`, `Font.BOLD`, `Font.ITALIC`, or (`Font.BOLD | Font.ITALIC`). The bold and italic constant ID values are 1 and 2, respectively, and the value for both is the bitwise OR value of 3, so we can simply OR these constants in this fashion. The size is simply the size of the font in standard point sizes (think Word).

Font Objects Are Immutable

Recall in Chapter 3, "Arrays and Strings," that we noted the main difference between `String` objects and `StringBuffer` objects is that `String` objects are immutable. This means that the data of this object cannot be changed; in order to have a `String` object with different data, you need to create a different object altogether. Similarly, `Font` objects are immutable; you cannot change the data of the `Font` object, such as its size or style, but you need to create a new object instead. There are some useful methods of a `Font` object that return new versions of a given `Font` object, with the specific changes (most notably the `deriveFont` methods).

However, creating objects can be very expensive to Java, especially when continually creating objects in the main loop. We will have a detailed discussion on this in Chapter 12, "Game Programming Techniques," along with a discussion on the garbage collector.

Another object that we can note that is immutable is a `Color` object. You may be wondering why all of these objects are immutable. Well, it's quite simple. They are immutable because they need to be safe when used by AWT or Swing components internally for rendering by Java, hence it would be unsafe to alter their contents during this process.

Understanding the Fonts Coordinates

When a `string` value is drawn in a given font using the `drawString-(String text, int x, int y)` method, the position of the string value is drawn starting at the x and y position specified, with x equaling the leftmost part of the first character in the `String` and y equaling the baseline of the font. To understand the coordinate system for fonts, take a look at the following figure.

 Figure 9-6

Using the `drawString` method, your text will sit on the baseline as if you were writing on lined paper (writing without a keyboard, that is—if you can imagine such a silly concept). The ascent is the pixel distance from the top of the font to the baseline, and the descent is the pixel distance from the bottom of the font to the baseline.

In the following example, we will create a small, medium, and large font type and create a useful function for drawing text in a specified location relative to a given point, working irrespective of the current `Graphics` object's font type, style, or size. Let's first take a look at the code for the example `UsingFonts.java`, and then we'll discuss how it all works.

Code Listing 9-5: UsingFonts.java

```java
import javax.swing.*;
import java.awt.*;

public class UsingFonts extends JFrame
{
    public UsingFonts()
    {
        super("Using Fonts");
        setDefaultCloseOperation(EXIT_ON_CLOSE);
        setResizable(false);
        getContentPane().setLayout(null);
        getContentPane().add(new FontArea(new Rectangle(0, 0,
            DISPLAY_WIDTH, DISPLAY_HEIGHT)));

        smallFont = new Font("Courier New", Font.BOLD, 12);
        mediumFont = new Font("Times New Roman", Font.PLAIN, 24);
        largeFont = new Font("Verdana", Font.BOLD+Font.ITALIC, 36);

        setVisible(true);

        resizeToInternalSize(DISPLAY_WIDTH, DISPLAY_HEIGHT);
    }


    public void resizeToInternalSize(int internalWidth, int
        internalHeight)
    {
        Insets insets = getInsets();
```

```
    final int newWidth = internalWidth + insets.left +
        insets.right;
    final int newHeight = internalHeight + insets.top +
        insets.bottom;

    Runnable resize = new Runnable()
    {
        public void run()
        {
            setSize(newWidth, newHeight);
        }
    };

    if(!SwingUtilities.isEventDispatchThread())
    {
        try
        {
            SwingUtilities.invokeAndWait(resize);
        }
        catch(Exception e) {}
    }
    else
        resize.run();

    validate();
}

public class FontArea extends JPanel
{
    public FontArea(Rectangle bounds)
    {
        setLayout(null);
        setBounds(bounds);
        setOpaque(false);
    }

    public void paintComponent(Graphics g)
    {
        Graphics2D g2D = (Graphics2D)g;

        g2D.setColor(Color.black);
        g2D.fill(getBounds());

        g2D.setColor(Color.cyan);
        g2D.setFont(smallFont);
        drawFromPoint("This is the standard coding font from top
            left (0, 0)", 0, 0, -1, -1, g);

        g2D.setColor(Color.red);
        g2D.setFont(mediumFont);
        drawFromPoint(" text from bottom right ("+getWidth()+",
            "+getHeight()+")", getWidth(), getHeight(), 1, 1, g);

        g2D.setColor(Color.green);
        g2D.setFont(largeFont);
        drawFromPoint("text in the middle", getWidth()/2,
            getHeight()/2, 0, 0, g);
    }
}
```

```
public static void drawFromPoint(String text, int x, int y, int
        relativeToX, int relativeToY, Graphics g)
{
    int widthOffset;
    int heightOffset;

    FontMetrics fm = g.getFontMetrics();

    if(relativeToX < 0)
        widthOffset = 0;    // left point x
    else if(relativeToX==0)
        widthOffset = -(fm.stringWidth(text)/2); // from middle x
    else        // relativeToX > 0
        widthOffset = -fm.stringWidth(text);      // from right x

    if(relativeToY < 0)
        heightOffset = fm.getAscent();    // from top y
    else if(relativeToY==0)
        heightOffset = (fm.getHeight()/2)-fm.getDescent();
        // from middle y
    else // relativeToY > 0
        heightOffset = -fm.getDescent(); // from bottom y

    x+=widthOffset;
    y+=heightOffset;

    g.drawString(text, x, y);
}

public static void main(String[] args)
{
    new UsingFonts();
}

private Font smallFont;
private Font mediumFont;
private Font largeFont;

private static final int DISPLAY_WIDTH = 400;
private static final int DISPLAY_HEIGHT = 400;
```

Chapter 9

When you compile and run this example, your output should be similar to the figure at the top of the following page (Figure 9-7).

The class java.awt.FontMetrics is used to hold information about a font on a given screen. This allows us to get information such as the font ascent and descent, as we discussed in an earlier figure. These values can be retrieved from the Graphics object that you are drawing to using the method getFontMetrics, as we do in the method drawFromPoint. This method is used to draw a given string value relative to a specified point. The first parameter is simply the string value to be drawn. The next two parameters are the coordinates of a point from which you wish to draw. Now, the next two parameters are the important ones. They define how the text will be displayed relative to the given point. For example, the first line of text that we draw is positioned relative to position (0, 0) of the displayable FontArea component. The

Figure 9-7

relative position is defined by the values for x and y, as −1 and −1, respectively. The parameter `relativeToX`, when less than 0 (e.g., −1), tells the method that you want to draw the string from the leftmost position of the specified x position, which `drawString` does by default anyway. The parameter `relativeToY`, when less than 0 (e.g., −1), basically tells the method that you want to draw the string directly under the specified y position. We can find this new y position by adding the ascent distance of the font to the specified y position. If you look back at the font figure we discussed earlier, you will see that by moving the font text down from its default baseline y position by the ascent distance, the font text will be moved under the baseline. Thus, you have specified the y position below which your text will be displayed. Specifying the relative values 0 and 0 for x and y will display your text centered to the specified position, and specifying the relative values 1 and 1 for x and y, respectively, will display your text from the bottom-right of the specified location. Of course, you can mix these values (for example, relative values 1 and −1 for x and y, respectively, will display your text from top-right relative to the specified x and y position). By passing the `Graphics` object to the method `drawFromPoint`, we do not need to worry about the font type or color or passing in the font metrics, as this is all stored in the state of the `Graphics` object that we can set before we call this method. (*Groovy and cool.*)

Getting the Available Fonts

A list of available fonts and their text description, which is used as the identification of the font type when creating new `Font` objects, can be retrieved as an array of `strings` as follows.

```
GraphicsEnvironment ge = GraphicsEnvironment.getLocal
        GraphicsEnvironment();
String[] availableFonts = ge.getAvailableFontFamilyNames();

for(int i=0; i<availableFonts.length; i++)
```

```
{
    System.out.println(availableFonts[i]);
}
```

The class `java.awt.GraphicsEnvironment` is used to store a list of `GraphicsDevice` objects, which we will discuss later, and also a list of fonts available to your program.

Note that the static method `createFont` can be used to load your own fonts into a `Font` object. The only supported type is currently TrueType fonts (.ttf), which is the most commonly used font type anyway. Loading a font is done simply by creating an InputStream to read in the font file and passing this as the second parameter to the `createFont` method (the first parameter being the constant `Font.TRUETYPE _FONT`). This is actually a better method when using fonts, as by doing this you are guaranteed that the font you require is going to be available as you supply the file and load it in yourself.

Off-Screen Images

So far we have looked at various primitive graphics routines available to the `Graphics` and `Graphics2D` classes. The main problem with these routines is that many of them involve added functionality that is unnecessary if the output remains constant. Take for example the Affined-Transformer example that we made earlier of the square shape spiraling out from the center. Every time that application receives a repaint message, the paintComponent is called and the drawing routine is performed again, always with the same output. Creating the display once requires a lot of processing, working out rotations and scaling over 120 iterations, and this is done each time the window display needs to be updated. What you want to do is create an off-screen image, a buffer of image data, and perform your drawing to that, just once. You are then left with an off-screen image, prerendered and ready for drawing without the need to run through various drawing routines again and again. In Java, it is possible to create your own off-screen images and load in images from specific image files. To begin with, we shall look at creating your own off-screen images before looking at loading in images of your own.

The Image Class

The `Image` class is a super class of all images in Java. You might say that the `Image` class is to all other Image classes what the `Object` class is to all classes. The `Image` class is abstract and is used as a template for referencing images collectively. The fact that the `Image` class is abstract means that it cannot be instantiated; you cannot create objects of this type explicitly. Furthermore, the `Image` class does not provide any access to the image data, but the `BufferedImage` class does (we will discuss the `BufferedImage` class shortly). The easiest way to obtain your own off-screen image is through either a component or the local graphics configuration. For example, suppose we created an instance of a JFrame, myFrame; we could then create an image of a specified size as follows:

```
JFrame myFrame = new JFrame();
Image offScreenImage = myFrame.createImage(100, 100);
```

The JFrame inherits the method `createImage` from `java.awt.Component`. However, in order to create an image in this way, the component (in this case the JFrame) must be displayable. The most efficient way to create an image is through the graphics configuration of the graphics device on which the program is running. The graphics device represents a screen or printer, of which the graphics environment (that we touched on in the "Fonts" section earlier) can contain multiple numbers. Each graphics device in turn may have one or more graphics configurations associated with it. In Java, the classes `java.awt.GraphicsEnvironment`, `java.awt.GraphicsDevice`, and `java.awt.GraphicsConfiguration` are used for storing and retrieving this information. We can then create an off-screen image from the graphics configuration as follows:

```
GraphicsEnvironment ge = GraphicsEnvironment.getLocalGraphics
        Environment();
GraphicsDevice gd = ge.getDefaultScreenDevice();
GraphicsConfiguration gc = gd.getDefaultConfiguration();

Image offScreenImage = gc.createCompatibleImage(100, 100);
```

More importantly, however, by creating a compatible image, you create an image as close as possible to the graphics configuration in terms of its format, with a data layout and color model compatible with the graphics configuration it is drawing to. This can have a large speed impact when rendering images to, for example, the window running under this graphics configuration, cutting down on any pixel color mapping calculations required during the drawing process.

 NOTE: You may also retain the graphics configuration from the component, such as our JFrame, using the method `component.getGraphicsConfiguration`, and create the compatible image from here. Note also that if the component has not been assigned a specific graphics configuration and has not been added to another component container, then `component.getGraphicsConfiguration` will return null. If the component has been added to a containment hierarchy, the graphics configuration associated with the top-level container (e.g., Frame, JFrame, JApplet, etc.) will be returned instead.

Drawing to an Off-Screen Image

Once an off-screen image has been created, you may then create a graphics context for drawing to the image, as follows:

```
Graphics g = offScreenImage.getGraphics();
```

Once we have done this we are then free to draw to the off-screen image using all of the capabilities of the `Graphics` object. Don't forget you can also cast the returned object to `Graphics2D` for the extra functionality it comes with. A while back we mentioned calling the `dispose` method on any `Graphics` objects created explicitly; we shall see this in the following example.

In the following applet example, `OffScreenSprite.java`, we create an off-screen image, drawing a yellow, pie-sliced little fella to it. We then draw the image multiple times across the screen, having only rendered the image once, stored as a sprite. Here is the code for `Off-ScreenSprite.java`.

Code Listing 9-6: `OffScreenSprite.java`

```java
import javax.swing.*;
import java.awt.*;
import java.awt.geom.*;

public class OffScreenSprite extends JApplet
{
    public void init()
    {
        getContentPane().setLayout(null);
        setSize(DISPLAY_WIDTH, DISPLAY_HEIGHT);

        sprite = createSprite(40, 40);
        drawCoolSprite(sprite);
    }


    public Image createSprite(int width, int height)
    {
        return getGraphicsConfiguration().createCompatibleImage
            (width, height);
    }


    public void drawCoolSprite(Image offScreenImage)
    {
        // create shape to be drawn
        Arc2D.Double coolShape = new Arc2D.Double(0, 0,
            offScreenImage.getWidth(null),
            offScreenImage.getHeight(null), 45, 270, Arc2D.PIE);

        // get graphics context for drawing
        Graphics2D g2D = (Graphics2D)offScreenImage.getGraphics();

        // draw to off-screen image
        g2D.setColor(Color.yellow);
        g2D.fill(coolShape);
        g2D.dispose();
    }


    public void paint(Graphics g)
    {
        Graphics2D g2D = (Graphics2D)g;

        g2D.setColor(Color.blue);
        g2D.fillRect(0, 0, getWidth(), getHeight());
```

```
        for(int i=0; i<getWidth(); i+=sprite.getWidth(null))
            for(int j=0; j<getHeight(); j+=sprite.getHeight(null))
            {
                if(i!=j)
                    g2D.drawImage(sprite, i, j, null);
            }
    }

    private Image sprite;

    private static final int DISPLAY_WIDTH = 400;
    private static final int DISPLAY_HEIGHT = 400;
}
```

When you compile and run this example applet, you should get output similar to the following figure.

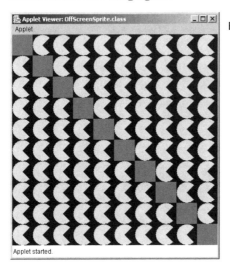

Figure 9-8

The code in this example should be quite simple to follow. First we create the off-screen image and then perform our drawing to the image. Then in the paint method, use the drawImage() method to draw multiple copies of the sprite. The drawImage() method draws the sprite image as a bitmap rather than performing different draw operations, such as draw-Arc(). Similarly, we could have actually created a single 400x400 pixel off-screen image (buffer) and rendered all of these little guys to it first; therefore, we would only have to draw a single larger image in our paint method instead of multiple copies of the smaller image.

The drawImage Method

The version of drawImage that we used in the previous example is defined as follows:

```
drawImage(Image i,
        int x, int y,
        ImageObserver observer)
```

The first parameter is the image itself, which can be of type `Image` or any subclass of `Image`, such as `BufferedImage`, which we will look at shortly. The next two integer parameters are the destination x and y positions at which the image will be drawn. The final parameter is an object that implements the `ImageObserver` interface. Most notably, the `Component` class implements this interface. Before the advances in loading images from files into Java (which we will discuss later) came about, images loaded from files were requested and obtained through the method `imageUpdate` of an object implementing the `ImageObserver` interface. When drawing the image using the method `drawImage`, an `ImageObserver` was passed to tell the method the current state of the image or how much of the image was loaded that could then be drawn. This is no use to us though; we want to load in images at the beginning completely and then use them. Java now provides us with functionality to do such a thing using the `java.awt.MediaTracker` class and the newer `javax.imageio.ImageIO` class introduced in J2SE 1.4. We will discuss image loading using these classes a little later. We no longer require the use of an `ImageObserver` when drawing images, as we will assure ourselves that our loaded-in images are ready for drawing. With off-screen images, such as the one we created earlier, this does not apply, so we can simply set this parameter to null when using the `drawImage` method.

Another version of `drawImage` allows you to specify the destination rectangle (position and size) to which the image should be drawn. This is defined as follows:

```
drawImage(Image i,
         int x, int y, int width, int height,
         ImageObserver observer)
```

This method will scale the specified `Image` object to the destination, meaning that the image will be made to fit into the specified rectangular area (x, y, width, height), squashed or stretched. Note that scaling can be quite costly in a 2D game. If you have a sprite that is scaled all the time when drawn using `drawImage`, it would be much better to create a new off-screen image of the scaled size once and then draw the scaled version and its complete size so that no more scaling needs to be done. Such an image could be resized as follows:

```
public static Image scaleSpriteToSize(Image sourceImage, int width,
       int height, Component c, int transparency)
{
       Image destImage = c.getGraphicsConfiguration().create
               CompatibleImage(width, height, transparency);

       Graphics g = destImage.getGraphics();
       g.drawImage(sourceImage, 0, 0, width, height, null);
       g.dispose();
       return destImage;
}
```

Note that this method is structured for reuse, as it is static and takes a component parameter to create the image from and also a transparency type for the image (we will look at transparency in a moment). The `createSprite` method could also be made in this way and would make a good addition to a sprite library, but that is up to you.

This method can be added to the previous example, `OffScreen-Sprite.java`, and the following line of code may be added at the end of the `init` method of `OffScreenSprite` as follows:

```
public void init()
{
    getContentPane().setLayout(null);
    setSize(DISPLAY_WIDTH, DISPLAY_HEIGHT);

    sprite = createSprite(40, 40);
    drawCoolSprite(sprite);

    // now create a new sprite of size (20, 20) with the specified
    // sprite image scaled onto it and make sprite now reference
    // the new image

    sprite = scaleSpriteToSize(sprite, 20, 20, this,
            Transparency.OPAQUE);
}
```

When these additions and alterations are made to the `OffScreen-Sprite` example, you should get output similar to the following figure of a new sprite that is a scaled version of the original sprite image.

Figure 9-9

A highly useful version of the `drawImage` method allows you to specify the source and destination rectangular areas for drawing an image. This basically means that you can specify a rectangular area of the image that you wish to draw (the source) and then specify the rectangular area on the image (the destination) you wish to draw the source image area to. An example of where this is useful is when you have an image that contains many animation frames, and you only want to draw one of the frames stored in a section of the image. We will look at animation sheets in Chapter 12. The `drawImage` method in question is as follows:

```
drawImage(Image i,
        int destX1, int destY1, int destX2, int destY2,
        int srcX1, int srcY1, int srcX2, int srcY2,
        ImageObserver observer)
```

One thing to note about this method is that the rectangular areas for the source and destination images are not defined by a location and size but two locations to specify the boundary for the rectangle. It is formed in this way because this method will not only scale but can be used for drawing the image data flipped. For example, you could draw an image flipped about the y axis by specifying the first source x position (`srcX1`) as the right boundary position of the rectangular area and the second source x position (`srcX2`) as the left boundary position of the rectangular area, instead of the default left-to-right coordination. Note, however, that we have found this to be slow even if no scaling is involved. So again, this would be another case of drawing the flipped image to another off-screen image and using that instead.

Returning to the example `OffScreenSprite` that we created earlier, the reason we did not draw the image when the counter variables `i` and `j` were equal was to illustrate one important fact about the sprite that we have just created: it is not transparent, or more specifically, the underlying background is shown. When we create the sprite, it is created as opaque (not see-through) with a default black background. Then when we draw our arc shape to the sprite, it is drawn on top of the black rectangular background. Thereafter, we draw the sprite multiple times, and as you can see the true, blue background shows through where we do not draw the sprite at all. Where we do draw the sprite, we fill the entire rectangular area that is the sprite's size. Ideally for this shape, we do not want its own background to be drawn; we want this to be completely transparent so we can draw the sprite data alone to a specific background.

Creating Transparency for a Sprite

Transparency in computing is in essence the art of drawing pixels from a source to a destination in a way that the source pixel appears to a certain transparency level over the top of the destination pixel. In the most common circumstance, the source pixel will appear to be transparent, whereby the original underlying destination pixel appears underneath it to some degree. To do this, it's all about calculating the new color of a given pixel with respect to the current pixel (the destination pixel) and the drawn pixel (the source pixel). The most straightforward color model for pixel data with transparency is an integer with RGBA components. These elements represent the red, green, blue, and alpha components of a pixel. For example, we can define `Color` objects with alpha components as follows.

```
Color fullyTransparent = new Color(1.0f, 0.0f, 0.0f, 0.0f);
Color semiTransparent = new Color(1.0f, 0.0f, 0.0f, 0.5f);
Color fullyOpaque = new Color(1.0f, 0.0f, 0,0f, 1.0f);
```

These three `Color` objects are all totally red with no green or blue contributions, but they have different alpha components ranging from 0.0 (fully transparent) to 1.0 (totally opaque). The value of the alpha component is multiplied by the color components to modify the color contribution of each pixel.

A little earlier we created the static method `scaleSpriteToSize` that included the creation of a new image with a transparency type set to opaque through an integer flag in the `java.awt.Transparency` interface. The `Transparency` interface contains the following three most common transparency states:

- `Transparency.OPAQUE`—This indicates that the image data will contain pixels that are completely opaque with an alpha component of value 1.0, meaning there is no transparency at all.

- `Transparency.BITMASK`—This indicates that the image data will contain pixels that are either completely opaque with an alpha component of value 1.0 or completely transparent with an alpha component of value 0.0. This is suitable in most cases for sprite images.

- `Transparency.TRANSLUCENT`—This indicates that the image data will contain pixels that can each have their own alpha components in the range 0.0 to 1.0. An image that contains an alpha value for each pixel is said to have an alpha channel.

In terms of the problems we had in the example `OffScreen-Sprite.java` where the background pixels of the off-screen image were also drawn, we can create the image of type `Transparency.BITMASK` to clear the original background. To do this, we can simply change the method `createSprite` so that it creates an image that supports the specified transparency format.

The following code, `TransparentSprite.java`, is an example of how we would do this by adapting the code of the previous example.

Code Listing 9-7: `TransparentSprite.java`

```java
import javax.swing.*;
import java.awt.*;
import java.awt.geom.*;

public class TransparentSprite extends JApplet
{
    public void init()
    {
        getContentPane().setLayout(null);
        setSize(DISPLAY_WIDTH, DISPLAY_HEIGHT);

        sprite = createSprite(40, 40);
        drawCoolSprite(sprite);
    }
```

```
public Image createSprite(int width, int height)
{
    // this time specify the transparency type of the image data

    return getGraphicsConfiguration().createCompatibleImage
        (width, height, Transparency.BITMASK);
}


public void drawCoolSprite(Image offScreenImage)
{
    // create shape to be drawn
    Arc2D.Double coolShape = new Arc2D.Double(0, 0,
        offScreenImage.getWidth(null),
        offScreenImage.getHeight(null), 45, 270, Arc2D.PIE);

    // get graphics context for drawing
    Graphics2D g2D = (Graphics2D)offScreenImage.getGraphics();

    // draw to off-screen image
    g2D.setColor(Color.yellow);
    g2D.fill(coolShape);
    g2D.dispose();
}


public void paint(Graphics g)
{
    Graphics2D g2D = (Graphics2D)g;

    g2D.setColor(Color.blue);
    g2D.fillRect(0, 0, getWidth(), getHeight());

    for(int i=0; i<getWidth(); i+=sprite.getWidth(null))
        for(int j=0; j<getHeight(); j+=sprite.getHeight(null))
        {
            if(i!=j)
                g2D.drawImage(sprite, i, j, null);
        }
}

private Image sprite;

private static final int DISPLAY_WIDTH = 400;
private static final int DISPLAY_HEIGHT = 400;
}
```

When you compile and run this code, the output should now show the blue
background behind the off-screen image's shape and not be filled by the
bounds of each of the images drawn, as shown in the figure at the top of
the following page (Figure 9-10).

The simplest way to perform this task is through the AlphaComposite object of a Graphics2D object. The AlphaComposite class
allows you to set rules for how a source image, for example, would be
drawn onto a destination image, taking into account the alpha components
of each image. The most common alpha composite rule is the source-over
rule, which indicates that the source pixels will be drawn over the destination pixels. There are many other rules, such as the source rule, which

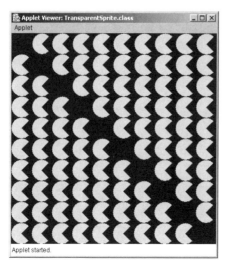

Figure 9-10

means that source pixels replace the destination pixels, and the destination-over rule, which is the opposite of the source rule where the destination pixels are drawn over the source pixels. The `Graphics2D` object contains a current `AlphaComposite` state and can be set using the following method:

```
myGraphics2D.setComposite(AlphaComposite.SrcOver);
```

An `AlphaComposite` object cannot be created explicitly. We can use existing static `AlphaComposite` objects of the `AlphaComposite` class, such as the `SrcOver` fields we have just seen. We can also create an `AlphaComposite` object through the static methods `AlphaComposite.getInstance(int rule)` and `AlphaComposite.getInstance(int rule, float alpha)`. There are static fields for each of the rules supported by the `AlphaComposite` class, such as `SRC_OVER`, `DST_OVER`, `CLEAR`, etc. When we specify the alpha parameter of the `getInstance` method, this alpha value is first multiplied by the alpha of the source image before composition with the destination takes effect.

In the following example, `BlendingTest.java`, we draw a sprite about the screen interpolating the alpha composite value from left (fully transparent) to right (fully opaque). We also add a few shapes in the background to illustrate the effect.

Code Listing 9-8: `BlendingTest.java`

```java
import javax.swing.*;
import java.awt.*;
import java.awt.geom.*;

public class BlendingTest extends JApplet
{
    public void init()
    {
        getContentPane().setLayout(null);
```

```
    setSize(DISPLAY_WIDTH, DISPLAY_HEIGHT);

    sprite = createSprite(40, 40);
    drawCoolSprite(sprite);
}

public Image createSprite(int width, int height)
{
    return getGraphicsConfiguration().createCompatibleImage
        (width, height, Transparency.BITMASK);
}


public void drawCoolSprite(Image offScreenImage)
{
    // create shape to be drawn
    Arc2D.Double coolShape = new Arc2D.Double(0, 0,
        offScreenImage.getWidth(null),
        offScreenImage.getHeight(null), 45, 270, Arc2D.PIE);

    // get graphics context for drawing
    Graphics2D g2D = (Graphics2D)offScreenImage.getGraphics();

    // draw to off-screen image
    g2D.setColor(Color.yellow);
    g2D.fill(coolShape);
    g2D.dispose();
}


public void paint(Graphics g)
{
    Graphics2D g2D = (Graphics2D)g;

    g2D.setColor(Color.blue);
    g2D.fillRect(0, 0, getWidth(), getHeight());

    g2D.setColor(Color.black);
    g2D.fill(rect);

    g2D.setColor(Color.red);
    g2D.fill(circle);

    for(int i=0; i<getWidth(); i+=sprite.getWidth(null))
        for(int j=0; j<getHeight(); j+=sprite.getHeight(null))
        {
            float alpha = (float)i / getWidth();

            g2D.setComposite(AlphaComposite.getInstance
                (AlphaComposite.SRC_OVER, alpha));
            g2D.drawImage(sprite, i, j, null);
        }
}

private Image sprite;

private Rectangle rect = new Rectangle(0, 0, DISPLAY_WIDTH/2,
        DISPLAY_HEIGHT/2);
private Ellipse2D.Double circle = new Ellipse2D.Double
        (DISPLAY_WIDTH/2, DISPLAY_HEIGHT/2, DISPLAY_WIDTH/2,
```

Chapter 9

```
                DISPLAY_HEIGHT/2);

    private static final int DISPLAY_WIDTH = 400;
    private static final int DISPLAY_HEIGHT = 400;
}
```

When you compile and run this example, you should get output similar to the following figure.

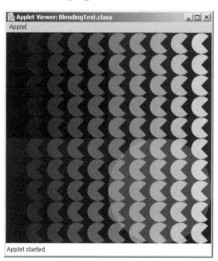

Figure 9-11

The key to this method is in the alpha interpolation code. The term "interpolate" is used a lot in computer graphics and computer games development in general. In its simplest term, interpolation means to calculate a number of steps within a start and end range. For example, you may want to span the movement of an image over 200 pixels within 10 frames of animation. You would interpolate the movement so that the image moved 20 pixels per frame, calculated simply by total distance (200) divided by frames (10). The position of the image at frame X would then be the pixels per frame (20) multiplied by frame X. The color interpolation code works in this way, working out the ratio of the position that the sprite is drawn along the x-axis and the width of the applet.

Note that the highest calculated value of alpha in this example is given as 360/400, equaling 0.9. If we wanted the range of alpha to be 0.0 to 1.0, where the rightmost sprites' alpha value was 1.0, we could replace the value of getWidth(), which is equal to 400 in this example, with 360.

Clearing the Sprite Background

In the last two examples, when creating the sprite images, the pixels were initialized with alpha components of 0.0 (completely transparent) by default. There may well come a time when you need to clear an existing image so that the alpha values of its pixels are all set to 0.0 once again, or even a subsection of it. The following method will therefore come in handy when you wish to clear an image that supports transparency so that none of the pixels in the image make a contribution, making the image completely transparent.

```
public static void clearSprite(Image image)
{
    Graphics2D g2D = (Graphics2D)image.getGraphics();

    g2D.setComposite(AlphaComposite.getInstance
        (AlphaComposite.CLEAR, 0.0f));
    g2D.fillRect(0, 0, image.getWidth(null), image.getHeight(null));
    g2D.dispose();
}
```

This method could easily be adapted to take parameters specifying a rectangular area on the image that you wish to clear if you do not wish to clear the entire image. Furthermore, you could specify a clipping shape and just clear the area within the bounds of the shape (we looked at shapes earlier in this chapter when we discussed clipping issues).

The BufferedImage Class

The BufferedImage class is a direct subclass of the Image class that provides access to a buffer containing the image data itself. Most if not all of the images we have created so far in this section have been of type BufferedImage, which we have been merely casting to the image base class java.awt.image. The BufferedImage class belongs to the java.awt.image package and includes a ColorModel object and a Raster object to define its pixel data. The color model defines the format to which the pixels are stored, and the raster stores the values for those pixels. Examples of color models available in the BufferedImage class, as static flags, are TYPE_INT_RGB and TYPE_INT_ARGB, to name a couple. The BufferedImage class contains useful methods for getting and setting the values of its pixels at the high level. The following example, RandomImage.java, creates a BufferedImage of TYPE_INT_ARGB and randomizes all of the pixels that it contains before drawing it to the applet. Here is the code for RandomImage.java:

Code Listing 9-9: RandomImage.java

```
import javax.swing.*;
import java.awt.*;
import java.awt.geom.*;
import java.awt.image.*;
import java.util.*;

public class RandomImage extends JApplet
{
    public void init()
    {
        getContentPane().setLayout(null);
        setSize(DISPLAY_WIDTH, DISPLAY_HEIGHT);

        randomImage = createRandomBufferedImage(DISPLAY_WIDTH,
            DISPLAY_HEIGHT);
    }
```

```
public BufferedImage createRandomBufferedImage(int width, int
    height)
{
    BufferedImage bImage = new BufferedImage(width, height,
        BufferedImage.TYPE_INT_ARGB);

    Graphics2D g2D = (Graphics2D)bImage.getGraphics();


    Random rand = new Random();

    for(int i=0; i<bImage.getWidth(); i++)
        for(int j=0; j<bImage.getHeight(); j++)
            bImage.setRGB(i, j, rand.nextInt());


    return bImage;
}


public void paint(Graphics g)
{
    Graphics2D g2D = (Graphics2D)g;

    g2D.setColor(Color.black);
    g2D.fillRect(0, 0, getWidth(), getHeight());

    g2D.setColor(Color.yellow);
    g2D.fill(coolShape);

    g2D.drawImage(randomImage, 0, 0, null);
}

private BufferedImage randomImage;

private Arc2D.Double coolShape = new Arc2D.Double(0, 0,
    DISPLAY_WIDTH, DISPLAY_HEIGHT, 45, 270, Arc2D.PIE);

private static final int DISPLAY_WIDTH = 400;
private static final int DISPLAY_HEIGHT = 400;
}
```

When you compile and run this example, you should get output reasonably similar to Figure 9-12.

The first thing to note about this example is that we have imported the package `java.awt.image` where the `BufferedImage` belongs. In this example we can explicitly create a `BufferedImage` of the specified width, height, and image type. The image type is of the type `TYPE_INT_ARGB` for each pixel. When we create the image, we can therefore take any random integer value, which means that the red, green, blue, and alpha values that the integer is comprised of will all be random too in essence. This gives the effect that when the random image is drawn, it shows elements of the underlying background, as its alpha values are random too, and the image is translucent, which therefore means that each of the pixels has its own alpha component associated with it.

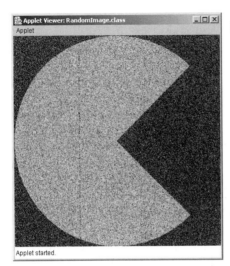

Figure 9-12

There is a lot more to the `BufferedImage` class than we have touched on here, such as manipulating the raster of the buffered image, which is beyond the scope of this book.

There is also the `VolatileImage` class, which is new to J2SE 1.4 and allows images to be stored in hardware, where they are fittingly hardware accelerated. We will look at the `VolatileImage` class in the "Rendering" section a little later in this chapter and discuss its features there.

Loading Images

Loading images into your Java programs has gone through quite some changes in the lifetime of Java. We touched on this earlier when looking at the `drawImage` method and its `ImageObserver` parameter, which we in turn ignored. The `java.awt.MediaTracker` class was introduced as an easy means of loading an image and waiting until the image had completely loaded. Before this, programmers were forced to write their own methods using an `ImageObserver`. However, using the `MediaTracker` class still meant writing a code routine to load in the images; though this was relatively easy, it could have been easier still. Enter `ImageIO`. With the release of J2SE 1.4, the introduction of the `javax.imageio.ImageIO` class means that it is even easier to load images into your Java programs, cutting the implementation required on your part down to just one simple line of code. In the next few sections we will look at using the `MediaTracker` class and then the `ImageIO` class for loading images. First we will take a look at the types of image files supported in the J2SE.

Supported Image Formats

The following is a list of the supported image file formats that can be loaded into your Java programs through the J2SE 1.4 API.

- GIF—The GIF format (Graphics Interchange Format) allows the storage of up to 256 different colors. You should take note that these colors are selected from a palette of 16 million different colors, but there can only be 256 that contribute to the final image. This is not as bad as it seems; if you have many different types of images and you are storing them as type GIF, it is best that they are added to their own individual image files, as each file contains its own 256-color palette in the GIF file format. A GIF image can also contain a transparent layer of one single color that can be set normally in any decent paint package in which the graphic is created. This is on par with the bitmask transparency that we saw earlier. When a GIF image file is loaded into your Java program with transparency built in, the image will be created in this style, so you can just load it in and use it right away. Because of the limitations on colors, the size of GIF images is kept small, making it suitable for downloading from the web (e.g., in an applet).

- JPEG—The JPEG format (Joint Photographic Experts Group) is designed in a way so that it is best for storing photographic images, but it also relies on compression techniques to cut down on the memory size of the image at the price of possible loss of quality from the original image (this is known as a "lossy" format). The JPEG format can contain millions of different colors, however, which is useful for storing photographic images in more detail than GIF images. The JPEG format does not support transparency, making it less useful for holding sprite data that contains transparent areas. Both the GIF and JPEG image formats are supported across most platforms.

- PNG—The PNG format (Portable Network Graphics) allows the storage of images in a lossless form. The PNG format is suitable for storing image data that will not be affected when compressed. The PNG format can also include an alpha channel so individual pixels may have their own alpha components. The cost of using the PNG format is that the image files are likely to use up more memory, taking longer to download for applets, though this all depends on how the PNG image is created and the format to which its data is stored.

Loading Images with the MediaTracker Class

We will first take a look at how to load in images using the media tracker in both applications and applets. A `MediaTracker` object is used to hold references to image objects that have been created but may not have been loaded completely. The job of the media tracker is to wait for an image or a group of images to be fully loaded. The following application example, `TrackerImageLoadingApplication.java`, loads in the Wordware Publishing logo and then displays it. Note that the image used in this example is available in the source code section of the companion CD. You can easily supply your own image for testing in this example also.

Code Listing 9-10: `TrackerImageLoadingApplication.java`

```java
import javax.swing.*;
import java.awt.*;
import java.awt.image.*;

public class TrackerImageLoadingApplication extends JFrame
{
    public TrackerImageLoadingApplication()
    {
        super("Tracker Image Loading Application Demo");
        setDefaultCloseOperation(EXIT_ON_CLOSE);
        setResizable(false);
        getContentPane().setLayout(null);

        // get image
        logo = getToolkit().getImage("wordwarelogo.gif");

        MediaTracker mediaTracker = new MediaTracker(this);

        // add the image to the media tracker
        mediaTracker.addImage(logo, 0);

        // wait for any added images with id = 0 to be loaded
        try
        {
            mediaTracker.waitForID(0);
        }
        catch(InterruptedException e)
        {
            System.out.println(e);
        }

        if(mediaTracker.isErrorAny())
            System.out.println("Errors encountered loading image");


        getContentPane().add(new ImageDisplayArea(new Rectangle(0, 0,
            DISPLAY_WIDTH, DISPLAY_HEIGHT)));

        setVisible(true);

        resizeToInternalSize(DISPLAY_WIDTH, DISPLAY_HEIGHT);
    }


    public void resizeToInternalSize(int internalWidth, int
        internalHeight)
    {
        Insets insets = getInsets();
        final int newWidth = internalWidth + insets.left +
            insets.right;
        final int newHeight = internalHeight + insets.top +
            insets.bottom;

        Runnable resize = new Runnable()
        {
            public void run()
            {
                setSize(newWidth, newHeight);
```

```
                }
            };

            if(!SwingUtilities.isEventDispatchThread())
            {
                try
                {
                    SwingUtilities.invokeAndWait(resize);
                }
                catch(Exception e) {}
            }
            else
                resize.run();

            validate();
        }

        public class ImageDisplayArea extends JPanel
        {
            public ImageDisplayArea(Rectangle bounds)
            {
                setLayout(null);
                setBounds(bounds);
                setOpaque(false);
            }

            public void paintComponent(Graphics g)
            {
                g.drawImage(logo,
                            0, 0, getWidth(), getHeight(),
                            0, 0, logo.getWidth(null),
                            logo.getHeight(null), null);
            }
        }

        public static void main(String[] args)
        {
            new TrackerImageLoadingApplication();
        }

        private Image logo;

        private static final int DISPLAY_WIDTH = 400;
        private static final int DISPLAY_HEIGHT = 400;
}
```

When we compiled and ran this example with our image, we got the output shown in Figure 9-13.

The process of obtaining an image through an application with a MediaTracker object is quite straightforward. To begin with, we need to obtain a reference to an Image object from a specific file. We can do this in an application through the java.awt.Toolkit instance obtained through the getToolkit method of the JFrame object. Once we've done this, the image object can then be added to the media tracker. When we do this in this example, we also specify an ID value of 0 for the image. This ID value is associated with the image and can then be used for tracking the image. When we call the method waitForID(0), it tells the

Figure 9-13

media tracker to wait for any images that have been added to it with the ID of 0. Multiple images can be added with the same ID for waiting for groups of images. If you wish to wait for all images added to the `Media-Tracker` class, you can simply call the method `waitForAll` of the `MediaTracker` class instead of `waitForID`.

The code for loading images into an applet is the same in terms of using the media tracker, but this time we do not use the Toolkit to get our image. The following example, `TrackerImageLoadingApplet.java`, is very similar to the previous example, but this time in an applet to illustrate how to load images into your applets from the web.

Code Listing 9-11: `TrackerImageLoadingApplet.java`

```java
import javax.swing.*;
import java.awt.*;
import java.net.*;

public class TrackerImageLoadingApplet extends JApplet
{
    public void init()
    {
        getContentPane().setLayout(null);
        setSize(DISPLAY_WIDTH, DISPLAY_HEIGHT);

        // get image

        try
        {
            logo = getImage(new URL(getCodeBase(),
                "wordwarelogo.gif"));
        }
        catch(MalformedURLException e)
        {
            System.out.println(e);
        }

        MediaTracker mediaTracker = new MediaTracker(this);
```

```
        // add the image to the media tracker
        mediaTracker.addImage(logo, 0);


        // wait for any added images with id = 0 to be loaded
        try
        {
            mediaTracker.waitForID(0);
        }
        catch(InterruptedException e)
        {
            System.out.println(e);
        }

        if(mediaTracker.isErrorAny())
            System.out.println("Errors encountered loading image");
    }

    public void paint(Graphics g)
    {
        g.drawImage(logo,
                    0, 0, getWidth(), getHeight(),
                    0, 0, logo.getWidth(null), logo.getHeight(null),
                    null);
    }

    private Image logo;

    private static final int DISPLAY_WIDTH = 400;
    private static final int DISPLAY_HEIGHT = 400;
}
```

This time, instead of using the `java.awt.Toolkit` classes' method
`getImage`, we use the `getImage` method belonging to the `Applet`
class of which `JApplet` is a subclass. A `java.net.URL` object is used
as a reference to a resource, such as a file or directory. A URL can take
many different forms, but in this example we use it to reference our image
file. The method `getCodeBase` of the `Applet` class is used to return
the URL where the applet is loaded. This, along with the filename, which
is added relative to the URL that `getCodeBase` returned, gives us a new
URL pointing to a file that is assumed to be located in the same directory
as the applet's class file. You can also find out which file the applet is running in, such as `index.html` using the `Applet` class's method
`getDocumentBase`.

Loading Images with the ImageIO Class

The `ImageIO` class belongs to the package `java.imageio`, which is
new to J2SE 1.4 and allows images to be loaded into Java programs
using just one simple line of code, where the image is loaded then and
there, nice and simple. The method also returns the image of type
`BufferedImage`. The following example, `ImageIOLoading-`
`Application.java`, is a copy of the previous example
`TrackerImageLoadingApplication`, but this time it uses the
`ImageIO` class to load an image.

Code Listing 9-12: `ImageIOLoadingApplication.java`

```java
import javax.swing.*;
import java.awt.*;
import java.awt.image.*;
import javax.imageio.*;
import java.io.*;

public class ImageIOLoadingApplication extends JFrame
{
    public ImageIOLoadingApplication()
    {
        super("ImageIO Loading Application Demo");
        setDefaultCloseOperation(EXIT_ON_CLOSE);
        setResizable(false);
        getContentPane().setLayout(null);

        // load image using ImageIO
        try
        {
            logo = ImageIO.read(new File("wordwarelogo.gif"));
        }
        catch(IOException e)
        {
            System.out.println(e);
        }

        getContentPane().add(new ImageDisplayArea(new Rectangle(0, 0,
            DISPLAY_WIDTH, DISPLAY_HEIGHT)));

        setVisible(true);

        resizeToInternalSize(DISPLAY_WIDTH, DISPLAY_HEIGHT);
    }


    public void resizeToInternalSize(int internalWidth, int
        internalHeight)
    {
        Insets insets = getInsets();
        final int newWidth = internalWidth + insets.left +
            insets.right;
        final int newHeight = internalHeight + insets.top +
            insets.bottom;

        Runnable resize = new Runnable()
        {
            public void run()
            {
                setSize(newWidth, newHeight);
            }
        };

        if(!SwingUtilities.isEventDispatchThread())
        {
            try
            {
                SwingUtilities.invokeAndWait(resize);
            }
            catch(Exception e) {}
```

```
        }
    else
        resize.run();

    validate();
}


public class ImageDisplayArea extends JPanel
{
    public ImageDisplayArea(Rectangle bounds)
    {
        setLayout(null);
        setBounds(bounds);
        setOpaque(false);
    }

    public void paintComponent(Graphics g)
    {
        g.drawImage(logo,
            0, 0, getWidth(), getHeight(),
            0, 0, logo.getWidth(null), logo.getHeight(null),
            null);
    }
}

public static void main(String[] args)
{
    new ImageIOLoadingApplication();
}

private BufferedImage logo;

private static final int DISPLAY_WIDTH = 400;
private static final int DISPLAY_HEIGHT = 400;
}
```

As you can see, the replacement code for loading in an image is a lot smaller than using the MediaTracker class for loading images in a blocking fashion (that is, waiting until the image is loaded before continuing). Also note that the type of image returned from the read method of ImageIO is BufferedImage.

Now because it is better for performance to create a compatible image through the current graphics configuration, which we discussed earlier in this chapter, the following method may be useful to convert loaded-in images to a more compatible image for rendering:

```
public static Image convertToCompatibleImage(BufferedImage bImage,
        Component c)
{
    int width = bImage.getWidth();
    int height = bImage.getHeight();
    int transparencyType = bImage.getColorModel().getTransparency();

    Image newImage = c.getGraphicsConfiguration().create
        CompatibleImage(width, height, transparencyType);

    Graphics g = newImage.getGraphics();
```

```
    g.drawImage(bImage, 0, 0, null);
    g.dispose();

    return newImage;
}
```

This method takes a `BufferedImage` to convert and a `Component` from which to get the graphics configuration that you are running on. From here, we can create a new compatible image of the same width, height, and transparency setting of the passed `BufferedImage` object. We then draw the `BufferedImage` image data to the new compatible image, returning a reference to it, of type `Image`, at the end.

We will now look at rendering in Java, a most important topic, where we can actually get things moving (forgive the pun).

Rendering

The technique of rendering graphics in Java has gone through some very important changes in J2SE 1.4, with the ability to use full-screen exclusive mode and hardware acceleration. By rendering graphics, we refer to continuously updating the display of your game within the game loop. In this section, we will begin with a basic rendering loop and progress through various techniques for making your rendering as efficient as possible, ending up in full-screen exclusive mode. Of course, we will also cover applet rendering as well.

First of all, we should take a look at two classes that we are going to use throughout this section to illustrate different rendering techniques: the `HotSpot` and `Animator` classes.

The `HotSpot` class is used to create and store a colored circle image and also provides a `render` function for the circle image to be drawn onto the `Graphics` object passed to it. Here is the code for `HotSpot.java`.

```java
import java.awt.*;
import java.awt.geom.*;
import java.awt.image.*;

public class HotSpot
{
    public HotSpot(Point pos, int diameter, Color col)
    {
        bounds = new Rectangle(pos.x, pos.y, diameter, diameter);
        image = new BufferedImage(diameter, diameter,
            BufferedImage.TYPE_INT_ARGB);

        Graphics2D g2D = (Graphics2D)image.getGraphics();
        Ellipse2D.Double circle = new Ellipse2D.Double(0, 0,
            diameter, diameter);
        g2D.setColor(col);
        g2D.fill(circle);

        g2D.dispose();
    }

    public void render(Graphics g)
```

```
        {
            g.drawImage(image, bounds.x, bounds.y, null);
        }

    public Rectangle bounds;
    private BufferedImage image;
}
```

The `Animator` class is used to control the movement of a `HotSpot` object around a given rectangular area and also provides a `render` function for drawing this information. Here is the code for `Animator.java`.

```
import java.awt.*;
import java.util.*;

public class Animator
{
    public Animator(Rectangle bounds)
    {
        this.bounds = bounds;

        createHotSpot();
    }


    public void createHotSpot()
    {
        Random rand = new Random();

        int diameter = 100+rand.nextInt(200);
        Color col = new Color(rand.nextInt(Integer.MAX_VALUE));

        hotSpot = new HotSpot(new Point(0,
            (bounds.height-diameter)/2), diameter, col);
        moveDir.setLocation(3, 3);
    }


    public void animate()
    {
        if(hotSpot != null)
        {
            if(moveDir.x>0)
            {
                hotSpot.bounds.x+=moveDir.x;
                if(hotSpot.bounds.x+hotSpot.bounds.width >=
                    bounds.width)
                {
                    hotSpot.bounds.x = (2*bounds.width)-
                    hotSpot.bounds.x-(2*hotSpot.bounds.width);
                    moveDir.x = -moveDir.x;
                }
            }
            else if(moveDir.x<0)
            {
                hotSpot.bounds.x+=moveDir.x;
                if(hotSpot.bounds.x <= 0)
                {
                    hotSpot.bounds.x = Math.abs(hotSpot.bounds.x);
                    moveDir.x = -moveDir.x;
```

```
            }
        }

        if(moveDir.y>0)
        {
            hotSpot.bounds.y+=moveDir.y;
            if(hotSpot.bounds.y+hotSpot.bounds.height >=
                bounds.height)
            {
                hotSpot.bounds.y = (2*bounds.height)-
                hotSpot.bounds.y-(2*hotSpot.bounds.height);
                moveDir.y = -moveDir.y;
            }
        }
        else if(moveDir.y<0)
        {
            hotSpot.bounds.y+=moveDir.y;
            if(hotSpot.bounds.y <= 0)
            {
                hotSpot.bounds.y = Math.abs(hotSpot.bounds.y);
                moveDir.y = -moveDir.y;
            }
        }
    }
}

public void render(Graphics g)
{
    g.translate(bounds.x, bounds.y);

    g.setColor(Color.blue);
    g.fillRect(0, 0, bounds.width, bounds.height);

    if(hotSpot!=null)
        hotSpot.render(g);

    g.translate(-bounds.x, -bounds.y);
}

public HotSpot hotSpot;
public Point moveDir = new Point();
public Rectangle bounds;
}
```

It is important to note the significance of the two main functions in the
Animator class: animate and render. The animate method represents the logical side of the code, whereas the render method
represents the drawing side of the code. Calling these in a main loop over
and over again will give us a continuously updating display of a circle moving around the screen and bouncing off the walls.

The Main Game Loop

In order for your game to run repeatedly on its own, there must be a main game loop. There are various ways that a main game loop can be implemented, but the most general of main game loops will behave in the following way:

```
while(gameRunning)
{
    Handle input
    Do game logic
    Update display
}
```

Handling input could be anything from a mouse press to a network message to a fellow online player (likely via the game server). The game logic will typically handle character movements, collision detection, AI, or anything that needs to run independently in the game. Updating the display is self-explanatory. Java uses separate threads for many aspects of what was just explained, such as mouse input from the (separate to your main loop thread) Event Dispatch Thread or when using passive rendering, which is also handled by the Event Dispatch Thread, or creating your own listener thread for listening to incoming network messages, as we shall see in the network chapters toward the end of this book. This can become a problem when you have a main loop running and handling game logic that is out of synch with events coming in from other threads. In this chapter and many other chapters, we will show appropriate ways to get all of these events handled completely in synch with the main loop, starting with passive rendering.

Passive Rendering

If you recall back to the beginning of this chapter when we discussed the Event Dispatch Thread and regurgitate your knowledge gained from reading Chapter 7, "Threads," we talked about how the `paint` method was invoked by the Event Dispatch Thread when an update was requested. It is recommended at this stage that you return to the "Introducing the Event Dispatch Thread" section of this chapter if you do not recall this thoroughly.

The default way to repaint a component is through a call to the method `repaint` on the component you wish to be redrawn (e.g., your main frame). However, this will not automatically repaint your component (though it should occur not long after) but will send a request to the Event Dispatch Thread to repaint your component. This technique is known as *passive rendering*, where you basically render the display passively as opposed to rendering actively then and there. The problem with passive rendering is that repaint requests are unreliable, and unwanted ones can come in from the Event Dispatch Thread; we want to render when we want, synchronized in the main loop. Also, there is the problem that in some cases we would want to time the actual drawing to measure performance. That is very difficult if not impossible with the passive rendering.

The end goal of this section of the chapter is to turn the passive rendering `repaint` command into what is effectively an active rendering main loop. First of all, we should just concentrate on creating a rendering main loop using the previously mentioned `Animator` and `HotSpot` classes that can be instantly plugged into almost all of the following rendering examples in this section.

The main class for the following application example is called `PassiveRendering` and must be compiled along with the `Animator` and `HotSpot` classes shown earlier. We will first take a look at the `PassiveRendering` class and then discuss how it works; there is a lot to note about this example alone.

Code Listing 9-13: `PassiveRendering.java`

```java
import java.awt.*;
import java.awt.image.*;
import javax.swing.*;
import java.awt.event.*;

class PassiveRendering extends JFrame implements Runnable
{
    public PassiveRendering()
    {
        setTitle("Very Passively Rendering Example");
        getContentPane().setLayout(null);
        setResizable(false);

        addWindowListener(new WindowAdapter() {
            public void windowClosing(WindowEvent e) {
            exitProgram();
                }
            });

        animator = new Animator(new Rectangle(0, 0, DISPLAY_WIDTH,
            DISPLAY_HEIGHT));

        backBuffer = new BufferedImage(DISPLAY_WIDTH, DISPLAY_HEIGHT,
            BufferedImage.TYPE_INT_RGB);
        bbGraphics = (Graphics2D)backBuffer.getGraphics();

        setVisible(true);

        Insets insets = getInsets();
        DISPLAY_X = insets.left;
        DISPLAY_Y = insets.top;
        resizeToInternalSize(DISPLAY_WIDTH, DISPLAY_HEIGHT);
    }

    public void resizeToInternalSize(int internalWidth, int
        internalHeight)
    {
        Insets insets = getInsets();
        final int newWidth = internalWidth + insets.left +
            insets.right;
        final int newHeight = internalHeight + insets.top +
            insets.bottom;
```

```
    Runnable resize = new Runnable()
    {
        public void run()
        {
            setSize(newWidth, newHeight);
        }
    };

    if(!SwingUtilities.isEventDispatchThread())
    {
        try
        {
            SwingUtilities.invokeAndWait(resize);
        }
        catch(Exception e) {}
    }
    else
        resize.run();

    validate();
}


public void run()
{
    long startTime, waitTime, elapsedTime;
    // 1000/25 Frames Per Second = 40 millisecond delay
    int delayTime = 1000/25;

    Thread thisThread = Thread.currentThread();
    while(loop==thisThread)
    {
        startTime = System.currentTimeMillis();

        // move circle
        animator.animate();

        // request repaint
        repaint();

        // handle frame rate
        elapsedTime = System.currentTimeMillis() - startTime;
        waitTime = Math.max(delayTime - elapsedTime, 5);

        try
        {
            Thread.sleep(waitTime);
        }
        catch(InterruptedException e) {}

        mainLoopCounter++;
    }

    System.out.println("Program Exited");

    dispose();
    System.exit(0);
}
```

```java
public void renderCounterInfo(Graphics g)
{
    g.setColor(Color.yellow);
    g.drawString("Main Loop cycles: "+mainLoopCounter, 20, 20);
    g.drawString("Repaint count: "+repaintCounter, 20, 40);
    g.drawString("Difference: "+(mainLoopCounter-repaintCounter),
        20, 60);
}


public void paint(Graphics g)
{
    Graphics2D g2D = (Graphics2D)g;
    g2D.translate(DISPLAY_X, DISPLAY_Y);

    if(isDoubleBuffered)
    {
        animator.render(bbGraphics);
        renderCounterInfo(bbGraphics);
        g2D.drawImage(backBuffer, 0, 0, null);
    }
    else
    {
        animator.render(g2D);
        renderCounterInfo(g2D);
    }

    repaintCounter++;
}

public void update(Graphics g)
{
    paint(g);
}

public void exitProgram()
{
    loop = null;
}

public static void main(String args[])
{
    PassiveRendering app = new PassiveRendering();

    app.loop = new Thread(app);
    app.loop.start();
}

private int mainLoopCounter = 0;
private int repaintCounter = 0;

private Animator animator;
private Thread loop;
private BufferedImage backBuffer;
private Graphics2D bbGraphics;

private final int DISPLAY_X;    // value assigned in constructor
private final int DISPLAY_Y;    // value assigned in constructor
private static final int DISPLAY_WIDTH = 400;
```

Chapter 9

```
    private static final int DISPLAY_HEIGHT = 400;

    private boolean isDoubleBuffered = true;
}
```

When you run this example, along with the `Animator` and `HotSpot` classes shown at the start of the "Rendering" section, you should get output of a circle bouncing around the screen, similar to the following figure.

Figure 9-14

Introducing the Main Loop

To begin with, we create a new thread to handle the main loop. We do this by declaring that the main class implements the `Runnable` interface. This means that our main class, which extends `JFrame`, may also be treated as a thread in the respect that it defines a `run` method. Our code begins in `main` as follows:

```
public static void main(String args[])
{
    PassiveRendering app = new PassiveRendering();

    app.loop = new Thread(app);
    app.loop.start();
}
```

Here we create the main frame app and display it. We then create our main loop thread and start it. The call to `start` commences the thread's execution, invoking the `run` method supplied by the object that we passed to the thread's constructor, `app`, which is of type `Runnable` so it defines a `run` method to call.

 NOTE: It would be perfectly fine to actually program your main loop from the `main` method (e.g., call a main loop method from there and run your main loop code from the main thread, as it is a running thread just like the one we created anyway). The reason we create a new thread is because we need to for applets in this way anyway, so it keeps things consistent when we switch between applets and applications. Just to note, going straight into a main loop from (or in) `main` would be fine also (of course, the main loop termination condition would be different, where we would just use a Boolean flag instead).

The `PassiveRendering` constructor, as well as setting up the frame, also creates an `Animator` object and creates a back buffer. (We will discuss the back buffer in a moment.) Now let's run through the main loop one bit at a time and look at how it works.

```
public void run()
{
    long startTime, waitTime, elapsedTime;

    // 1000/25 Frames Per Second = 40 millisecond delay
    int delayTime = 1000/25;
```

Here we declare the variables `startTime`, `waitTime`, and `elapsedTime`. We will discuss these as we work our way through this `run` method. `delayTime` defines the delay in the main loop per frame/cycle in milliseconds. This is taken by dividing the number of frames that you want to display per second by 1000 milliseconds (1 second). We look at some important facts about handling the frame rate in Java a little later in Chapter 12, "Game Programming Techniques."

```
    Thread thisThread = Thread.currentThread();

    while(loop==thisThread)
    {
```

Here we define the termination condition for our main loop thread. This technique for stopping a thread was discussed in detail in Chapter 7 along with other useful techniques.

```
        startTime = System.currentTimeMillis();
```

Here we get the current time from the method `System.current-TimeMillis`. We are not actually interested in the time but a numeric counter to compare with a later time in order to synchronize our frame rate. Handling the frame rate efficiently is discussed in Chapter 12. However, we will show a simple method later in this example.

```
        // move circle
        animator.animate();
```

A call to the `animate` method of our `Animator` object will handle moving the position of the `circle` object by its given pixel speed. This call represents where game logic would be handled in the main loop.

```
        // request repaint
        repaint();
```

Calling the method `repaint` will send out a request to update the display of our frame, resulting in the `paint` method being invoked. We will discuss this properly in a moment also.

```
        // handle frame rate
        elapsedTime = System.currentTimeMillis() - startTime;
        waitTime = Math.max(delayTime - elapsedTime, 5);
```

```
        try
        {
            Thread.sleep(waitTime);
        }
        catch(InterruptedException e) {}
```

Handling the frame rate is important to ensure that your loop runs as smoothly as possible at the required speed. Again, later we will learn that in Java this isn't entirely the case. In this code we first calculate the elapsed time in milliseconds by subtracting the time at which the frame started (which we recorded then in the variable startTime) from the current time. The elapsed time is also generally known as the delta time. We then find out how long we should wait by subtracting the elapsed time (the time it has taken the frame to execute) from the required delay time of 40 milliseconds (1000/40 = 25 frames per second). We then call the sleep method, which will cause this thread to sleep for the calculated duration.

However, we also need to give other threads a chance to execute. This is important in a multithreaded language like Java. Starving other threads such as the Event Dispatch Thread, Garbage Collection, etc., can have disastrous results on your game. For this, we detect if the time to sleep is less than 5 milliseconds and sleep for this time instead. We will discuss handling your game when the frame rate goes slower than expected a little later in the book.

```
            mainLoopCounter++;
        }
```

Here is the end of our main loop where we increment the variable mainLoopCounter, which is storing the number of iterations that the loop has performed. This is recorded to illustrate problems with passive rendering, which we shall discuss in a moment.

```
        System.out.println("Program Exited");

        dispose();
        System.exit(0);
    }
```

The main loop is terminated by setting loop to null in the exitProgram method. This method is invoked when the user closes the window, causing the windowClosing method to be invoked by the Event Dispatch Thread. We will look at event listeners in the next chapter, so do not worry too much about them for now. The method System.exit(0) will terminate the program completely. A non-zero parameter indicates the program terminated because of a problem, so here we pass 0 as we exit safely.

Reducing Flickering

Overriding the Update Method

When a repaint is requested on an AWT Frame or a Swing JFrame, or an Applet or JApplet for that matter, it is invoked through a call to the update method, which in turn calls `paint` directly. (Note that in some instances, `paint` will be called directly, without a call to `update`). By default, `update` will first clear the background region itself in the background color of the component in question, which in this instance is our `JFrame`. The background color of a component can be set using the method `setBackground(Color)`. However, we do not want to draw the background in this way, as in most circumstances we will be drawing our own background, perhaps as an image. So what we want to do is simply override the `update` method and make a call to `paint` ourselves, without painting a component-sized rectangle first. This is the first step in reducing screen flicker with passive rendering.

Double Buffering

Double buffering is the standard way to prevent flicker and achieve smooth animations. A buffer in this context is simply an area of memory to and from which data is written. Double buffering simply entails using two buffers. When using double buffering for drawing, we are able to draw to one buffer while the other is being drawn to the screen. When using just one buffer, there is the problem that you could be drawing to the buffer that is also being drawn to the screen concurrently or has already had a portion of its data drawn to the screen. The result is that you will see a partial drawing of the original buffer image and then whatever your drawing code has just written to the buffer at the same time. This will cause flicker, made obvious by the change in display, as with our circle object moving its position every frame, or any game updating its screen display. In this example, you can set the Boolean variable `isDoubleBuffered` to `false` to see what the rendering looks like without double buffering. In Java, the standard means of double buffering is to create an off-screen image the size of the displayable area. We do this in our example in the constructor of the `PassiveRendering` frame with the following lines of code:

```
backBuffer = new BufferedImage(DISPLAY_WIDTH, DISPLAY_HEIGHT,
    BufferedImage.TYPE_INT_RGB);
bbGraphics = (Graphics2D)backBuffer.getGraphics();
```

We discussed creating images earlier in this chapter. The `backBuffer` variable is declared as a member of the main class of type `Buffered-Image`. Here we can also create and store the `Graphics` object of this buffer for rendering to later using the method `getGraphics` of the image. Now we can take a look at the `paint` method where this drawing takes place:

```
public void paint(Graphics g)
{
    Graphics2D g2D = (Graphics2D)g;
    g2D.translate(DISPLAY_X, DISPLAY_Y);

    if(isDoubleBuffered)
    {
        animator.render(bbGraphics);
```

```
        renderCounterInfo(bbGraphics);
        g2D.drawImage(backBuffer, 0, 0, null);
```

If the variable `isDoubleBuffered` is true, we draw first to the off-screen image `backBuffer` and then draw this image to the displayable component drawn to the screen.

```
    }
    else
    {
        animator.render(g2D);
        renderCounterInfo(g2D);
```

However, if the variable `isDoubleBuffered` is set to false, we simply draw our graphics straight to the displayable component without double buffering it first.

```
    }

    repaintCounter++;
}
```

When the painting is done, we increment the variable `repaint-Counter`. We will discuss this in a moment.

Synchronized Drawing with the Main Loop

The main problem with passive rendering is that you have two threads running at the same time, the main loop thread and the Event Dispatch Thread calling your `paint` method. The problem with having these two threads running at the same time (in principle, anyway) is the same problem you have with any threads running alongside one another: synchronization. In terms of the `paint` method being called while the main loop is running, you have no real control over the time at which the `paint` method is called in conjunction with the main loop. The fact that the `paint` method should be called very soon after the repaint request should not be taken for granted. Besides this fact, further repaint requests can also be posted that are unnecessary when you are updating the display with your own calls to repaint many times per second. In the previous example, `PassiveRendering`, we recorded the number of times the main loop executed in the variable `mainLoopCounter` and the number of times the `paint` method was invoked in the variable `repaint-Counter`, drawing these values to the window area every time `paint` was invoked. As you can see in Figure 9-14, the number of paint iterations (431) exceeds the number of main loop iterations (368) by 63. This was mainly due to the fact that another window was dragged over our window repetitively to emphasize the point.

The real problem with two threads like these lies in handling objects in general. Suppose you hold a reference to an object, like a HotSpot from the `HotSpot` class we defined earlier. Part of the way through the main loop you decide that you want to remove this object; you remove it, setting your reference to null, but your `paint` method then interrupts and tries to draw the object with your reference now referring to null. You may add a check in the `paint` code to see if the reference is not equal to null before drawing, which would decrease the likelihood of such an error occurring but would still not remove the possibility completely. In the next chapter, we will look at this in much more detail when handling mouse and keyboard events, which are received similarly to the Event Dispatch Thread, so do not worry overly about this problem for now if you do not fully understand it.

The easiest method of synchronizing the main loop with the `paint` code is simply to do your drawing in the main loop. We can achieve this by calling the method `getGraphics` on our main component, the `JFrame` itself, and draw to it within the main loop. The following example, `ActiveRendering`, is an example of this technique for rendering and again uses the classes `Animator` and `HotSpot`, defined at the beginning of the "Rendering" section. You will need to use them in order to compile and run this code.

Code Listing 9-14: `ActiveRendering.java`

```java
import java.awt.*;
import java.awt.image.*;
import javax.swing.*;
import java.awt.event.*;

public class ActiveRendering extends JFrame implements Runnable
{
    public ActiveRendering()
    {
        setTitle("Active Rendering Application");
        getContentPane().setLayout(null);
        setResizable(false);
        setIgnoreRepaint(true);

        addWindowListener(new WindowAdapter() {
            public void windowClosing(WindowEvent e) {
                exitProgram();
            }
            });

        animator = new Animator(new Rectangle(0, 0, DISPLAY_WIDTH,
            DISPLAY_HEIGHT));

        backBuffer = new BufferedImage(DISPLAY_WIDTH, DISPLAY_HEIGHT,
            BufferedImage.TYPE_INT_RGB);
        bbGraphics = (Graphics2D) backBuffer.getGraphics();

        setVisible(true);

        Insets insets = getInsets();
        DISPLAY_X = insets.left;
        DISPLAY_Y = insets.top;
        resizeToInternalSize(DISPLAY_WIDTH, DISPLAY_HEIGHT);
    }


    public void resizeToInternalSize(int internalWidth, int
        internalHeight)
```

```
{
    Insets insets = getInsets();
    final int newWidth = internalWidth + insets.left +
        insets.right;
    final int newHeight = internalHeight + insets.top +
        insets.bottom;

    Runnable resize = new Runnable()
    {
        public void run()
        {
            setSize(newWidth, newHeight);
        }
    };

    if(!SwingUtilities.isEventDispatchThread())
    {
        try
        {
            SwingUtilities.invokeAndWait(resize);
        }
        catch(Exception e) {}
    }
    else
        resize.run();

    validate();
}

public void run()
{
    long startTime, waitTime, elapsedTime;
    // 1000/25 Frames Per Second = 40 millisecond delay
    int delayTime = 1000/25;

    Thread thisThread = Thread.currentThread();
    while(loop==thisThread)
    {
        startTime = System.currentTimeMillis();

        animator.animate();

        // render to back buffer now
        render(bbGraphics);

        // render back buffer image to screen
        Graphics g = getGraphics();
        g.drawImage(backBuffer, DISPLAY_X, DISPLAY_Y, null);
        g.dispose();


        //  handle frame rate
        elapsedTime = System.currentTimeMillis() - startTime;
        waitTime = Math.max(delayTime - elapsedTime, 5);

      try
      {
          Thread.sleep(waitTime);
      }
      catch(InterruptedException e) {}
```

```
        mainLoopCounter++;
    }

    System.out.println("Program Exited");

    dispose();
    System.exit(0);
}


public void renderCounterInfo(Graphics g)
{
    g.setColor(Color.yellow);
    g.drawString("Main Loop cycles: "+mainLoopCounter, 20, 20);
    g.drawString("Repaint count: "+repaintCounter, 20, 40);
    g.drawString("Difference: "+(mainLoopCounter-repaintCounter),
        20, 60);
}


public void render(Graphics g)
{
    animator.render(g);
    renderCounterInfo(g);

    repaintCounter++;
}

public void exitProgram()
{
    loop = null;
}

public static void main(String args[])
{
    ActiveRendering app = new ActiveRendering();

    app.loop = new Thread(app);
    app.loop.start();
}

private int mainLoopCounter = 0;
private int repaintCounter = 0;

private Animator animator;
private Thread loop;
private BufferedImage backBuffer;
private Graphics2D bbGraphics;

private final int DISPLAY_X; // value assigned in constructor
private final int DISPLAY_Y; // value assigned in constructor
private static final int DISPLAY_WIDTH = 400;
private static final int DISPLAY_HEIGHT = 400;
}
```

Chapter 9

When you compile and run this code, you should get output similar to Figure 9-14, but this time the main loop counter and the paint counter values should be equal.

The first, quite irrelevant difference between this example and the PassiveRendering example is that we have taken out the Boolean isDoubleBuffered option for double buffering just to neaten up the code a little. The first thing to note about this example is that we have moved the painting code from the paint method to our own method called render, which is not an inherited method but simply our own method for rendering. Furthermore, we have removed the methods paint and update and included the call setIgnoreRepaint(true) in the constructor of our application, which will prevent them from being invoked from the Event Dispatch Thread. So Event Dispatch Thread paint messages will be ignored and will not interfere with our rendering process. All that is left is for us to render actively in the main loop. We do this by passing the back buffer's Graphics object to the render method. We then draw the back buffer image to the screen at the specified top-left coordinates, which is neater than translating to the coordinates first. The painting is now performed in the main loop under our control.

Let's See That in an Applet

The conversion of the code for ActiveRendering into an applet is relatively straightforward, and the technique remains the same. Here is the code for the example ActiveRenderingApplet.java, which requires the Animator and HotSpot classes, too.

Code Listing 9-15: ActiveRenderingApplet.java

```java
import java.awt.*;
import java.awt.image.*;
import javax.swing.*;
import java.awt.event.*;

public class ActiveRenderingApplet extends JApplet implements
    Runnable
{
    public void init()
    {
        getContentPane().setLayout(null);
        setSize(DISPLAY_WIDTH, DISPLAY_HEIGHT);
        setIgnoreRepaint(true);

        animator = new Animator(new Rectangle(0, 0, DISPLAY_WIDTH,
            DISPLAY_HEIGHT));

        backBuffer = new BufferedImage(DISPLAY_WIDTH, DISPLAY_HEIGHT,
            BufferedImage.TYPE_INT_RGB);
        bbGraphics = (Graphics2D) backBuffer.getGraphics();
    }

    public void start()
    {
        loop = new Thread(this);
        loop.start();
    }

    public void stop()
```

```
{
    loop = null;
}

public void run()
{
    long startTime, waitTime, elapsedTime;
    // 1000/25 Frames Per Second = 40 millisecond delay
    int delayTime = 1000/25;

    Thread thisThread = Thread.currentThread();
    while(loop==thisThread)
    {
        startTime = System.currentTimeMillis();

        animator.animate();

        // render to back buffer now
        render(bbGraphics);

        // render back buffer image to screen
        Graphics g = getGraphics();
        g.drawImage(backBuffer, 0, 0, null);
        g.dispose();

        // handle frame rate
        elapsedTime = System.currentTimeMillis() - startTime;
        waitTime = Math.max(delayTime - elapsedTime, 5);

      try
      {
          Thread.sleep(waitTime);
      }
      catch(InterruptedException e) {}

      mainLoopCounter++;
    }
}


public void renderCounterInfo(Graphics g)
{
    g.setColor(Color.yellow);
    g.drawString("Main Loop cycles: "+mainLoopCounter, 20, 20);
    g.drawString("Repaint count: "+repaintCounter, 20, 40);
    g.drawString("Difference: "+(mainLoopCounter-repaintCounter),
        20, 60);
}


public void render(Graphics g)
{
    animator.render(bbGraphics);
    renderCounterInfo(bbGraphics);

    repaintCounter++;
}


private int mainLoopCounter = 0;
```

```
    private int repaintCounter = 0;

    private Animator animator;
    private Thread loop;
    private BufferedImage backBuffer;
    private Graphics2D bbGraphics;

    private static final int DISPLAY_WIDTH = 400;
    private static final int DISPLAY_HEIGHT = 400;
}
```

Much of the code in this example should be relatively familiar to you, as we discussed applets in the early stages of this chapter and the new rendering code is almost the same as the rendering code for the application made earlier. You should note that there is no `main` method in the applet. Instead, the `JApplet` object is created through the JVM and the browser, whereby the `init` method is first invoked. Initialization code, such as image loading, should be provided here. Then the `start` method of the applet is invoked where we create and start the main loop thread.

Synchronized Painting Using Threads

The aim of this example is to illustrate how thread manipulation can be used to synchronize repaint calls with the main loop. Although this technique is not essential to us because we have already discussed a suitable means of synchronizing the main loop with painting earlier, this example should act as a good lesson in understanding threads, which are a major part of the Java language.

In order to synchronize `paint` method calls with the main loop by calling the `repaint` method, we can use the `wait` and `notify` methods of a given object. This will allow us to request a repaint (using the `repaint` method of our component) and then pause the main loop thread immediately after the request until the `paint` method has not only been invoked but has performed its painting routine. We also take action to prevent extra, unwanted paint requests from being performed in the `paint` method in the following example, `ActivelyPassiveRendering-Repaints`. This example again uses the classes `Animator` and `HotSpot`, defined at the beginning of the "Rendering" section, so you will need to use them to compile and run this code.

Code Listing 9-16: `ActivelyPassiveRenderingRepaints.java`

```java
import java.awt.*;
import java.awt.image.*;
import javax.swing.*;
import java.awt.event.*;

class ActivelyPassiveRenderingRepaints extends JFrame implements
    Runnable
{
    public ActivelyPassiveRenderingRepaints()
    {
        setTitle("Actively Passive Rendering Application");
        getContentPane().setLayout(null);
```

```
        setResizable(false);

        addWindowListener(new WindowAdapter() {
                public void windowClosing(WindowEvent e) {
                exitProgram();
                    }
                        });
                    animator = new Animator(new Rectangle(0, 0,
                        DISPLAY_WIDTH, DISPLAY_HEIGHT));

        backBuffer = new BufferedImage(DISPLAY_WIDTH, DISPLAY_HEIGHT,
            BufferedImage.TYPE_INT_RGB);
        bbGraphics = (Graphics2D) backBuffer.getGraphics();

        setVisible(true);

        Insets insets = getInsets();
        DISPLAY_X = insets.left;
        DISPLAY_Y = insets.top;
        resizeToInternalSize(DISPLAY_WIDTH, DISPLAY_HEIGHT);
}


public void resizeToInternalSize(int internalWidth, int
    internalHeight)
{
        Insets insets = getInsets();
        final int newWidth = internalWidth + insets.left +
            insets.right;
        final int newHeight = internalHeight + insets.top +
            insets.bottom;

        Runnable resize = new Runnable()
        {
            public void run()
            {
                setSize(newWidth, newHeight);
            }
        };

        if(!SwingUtilities.isEventDispatchThread())
        {
            try
            {
                SwingUtilities.invokeAndWait(resize);
            }
            catch(Exception e) {}
        }
        else
            resize.run();

        validate();
}

public void run()
{
        long startTime, waitTime, elapsedTime;
        // 1000/25 Frames Per Second = 40 millisecond delay
        int delayTime = 1000/25;
```

```
        Thread thisThread = Thread.currentThread();
        while(loop==thisThread)
        {
            startTime = System.currentTimeMillis();

            animator.animate();

            rendered = false;
            repaint();
            waitForPaint();

            //  handle frame rate
            elapsedTime = System.currentTimeMillis() - startTime;
            waitTime = Math.max(delayTime - elapsedTime, 5);

          try
          {
              Thread.sleep(waitTime);
          }
          catch(InterruptedException e) {}

          mainLoopCounter++;
        }

        System.out.println("Program Exited");

        dispose();
        System.exit(0);
    }


    public void renderCounterInfo(Graphics g)
    {
        g.setColor(Color.yellow);
        g.drawString("Main Loop cycles: "+mainLoopCounter, 20, 20);
        g.drawString("Repaint count: "+repaintCounter, 20, 40);
        g.drawString("Difference: "+(mainLoopCounter-repaintCounter),
            20, 60);
    }


    public void paint(Graphics g)
    {
        if(!rendered)
        {
            // render to the back buffer
            animator.render(bbGraphics);
            renderCounterInfo(bbGraphics);

            // render back buffer to screen
            g.drawImage(backBuffer, DISPLAY_X, DISPLAY_Y, null);

            synchronized(this)
            {
                rendered = true;
                notify();
            }

            repaintCounter++;
        }
```

```
    }

    public void update(Graphics g)
    {
        paint(g);
    }

    public void waitForPaint()
    {
        synchronized(this)
        {
            while(!rendered)
            {
                try
                {
                    wait();
                }
                catch(InterruptedException e) {}
            }
        }
    }

    public void exitProgram()
    {
        loop = null;
    }

    public static void main(String args[])
    {
        ActivelyPassiveRenderingRepaints app = new
            ActivelyPassiveRenderingRepaints();

        app.loop = new Thread(app);
        app.loop.start();
    }

    private int mainLoopCounter = 0;
    private int repaintCounter = 0;

    private boolean rendered = true;
    private Animator animator;
    private Thread loop;
    private BufferedImage backBuffer;
    private Graphics2D bbGraphics;

    private final int DISPLAY_X;        // value assigned in constructor
    private final int DISPLAY_Y;        // value assigned in constructor
    private static final int DISPLAY_WIDTH = 400;
    private static final int DISPLAY_HEIGHT = 400;
}
```

When you compile and run this code, the main loop counter and the paint counter values should again be equal, whereby this time a call is made to repaint in the main loop, which then waits for the paint method to be invoked successfully before continuing.

So how does it work? To begin with, let's look at the new paint request code in the main loop thread:

```
rendered = false;
repaint();
waitForPaint();
```

The `boolean` variable `rendered` is set to `false` to indicate to both the `paint` method and the `waitForPaint` method that the paint job still needs to be performed. This is also used to prevent unwanted paints from being performed, as we shall see in a moment in the new paint method. The basic concept of this paint request code is to, as the method suggests, wait for painting to be performed before continuing. Let's now take a closer look at the `paint` method and the `waitForPaint` method and discuss the possible paths that each could take and understand how all will lead to a successful wait routine. First, here is the `paint` method:

```
public void paint(Graphics g)
{
    if(!rendered)
    {
```

We will only perform our paint routine if the `rendered` variable is set to `false`, so this will prevent unwanted paint requests from continuing into the painting code, namely unwanted invocations from the Event Dispatch Thread.

```
        // render to the back buffer
        animator.render(bbGraphics);
        renderCounterInfo(bbGraphics);

        // render back buffer to screen
        g.drawImage(backBuffer, DISPLAY_X, DISPLAY_Y, null);

        synchronized(this)
        {
            rendered = true;
            notify();
        }
```

Here we synchronize on the frame object (`this`) and then set the variable `rendered` to `true` and notify our main loop thread. The main loop thread is waiting on this object's monitor so that it can awake and continue out of the `waitForPaint` method and continue on with the main loop from which it was called. We'll look at the `waitForPaint` method and then go into more detail on this in a moment.

```
        repaintCounter++;
    }
}


public void waitForPaint()
{
    synchronized(this)
    {
        while(!rendered)
        {
            try
            {
                wait();
```

```
        }
        catch(InterruptedException e) {}
    }
  }
}
```

The method `waitForPaint` is called from the main loop thread immediately after the call to repaint. As we do not know if `waitForPaint` will be called from the main loop thread before the `paint` method is called from the Event Dispatch Thread, we have two possible code paths to account for in order to successfully wait for the paint job to be performed:

■ Path 1—We set `rendered` to `false` and called `repaint`. The `paint` method is invoked before the `waitForPaint` method and reaches the `synchronized(this)` code block inside the `paint` method before `waitForPaint` synchronizes the object with its own `synchronized(this)` code block. This means that while `paint` is in its `synchronized(this)` code block, `waitForPaint` will not enter its own `synchronized(this)` code block. Then in the `paint` method we set `rendered` to `true`, call `notify` and exit the synch-block, allowing `waitForPaint` to now enter its own synch-block. When the method `waitForPaint` enters its synch-block, it finds that `rendered` is true and never performs the `while(!rendered)` routine. It swiftly exits from the method, returning to the main loop having successfully waited until the `paint` method was complete. This is the easy path.

■ Path 2—The more complicated scenario is where the synch-block in `waitForPaint` is entered before the synch-block in the `paint` method is reached (i.e., the paint routine is incomplete). Now the synch-block in `waitForPaint` will be entered. You will find that `rendered` is still equal to false because it cannot yet be set to true, as the synch-block in the `paint` method cannot currently be entered. We then call the `wait` method in `waitForPaint`. The `wait` method will stop until another thread calls the `notify` or `notify-All` method on the current object. Remember when we looked at the `Object` class in Chapter 4? These methods belong to it and are therefore inherited by all objects, hence any object can be used for synchronization in this way. The `wait` method also causes the current thread (the main loop thread in this case) to release any ownership on synchronizing this object, allowing the `synchronized-(this)` block in the `paint` method to now be entered, as the main loop thread currently waits to be re-awoken. When this happens the variable `rendered` is then set to `true` and the `notify` method is invoked. The call to `notify` awakens a thread that is currently waiting on the object in question, notably our call to wait in the `wait-ForPaint` method. The `wait` method is then passed and the `while` loop exits as the variable `rendered` is now equal to true. Once again, we are synchronized and the main loop can continue knowing the paint job has completed successfully.

Chapter 9

Hopefully this has not been too draining to understand; you should also understand threads a little better too.

Using a VolatileImage Back Buffer

The `VolatileImage` class provides a means of storing your image directly in the hardware memory of the graphics card (as opposed to system memory like `BufferedImage`), whereby the image will become hardware accelerated. The non-accelerated images, such as `Buffered-Image`, need to be copied over to the screen from system memory for drawing together with any color depth and scaling operations required per frame. With hardware acceleration, the image is stored in VRAM, accelerated video memory, whereby the graphics card can take on specialized graphics operations, performing routines faster and rendering more efficiently to the screen. Note that if the system that you are running on does not support accelerated video memory, your image will be stored in system memory just like `BufferedImage`.

The problem with `VolatileImage` is that it is volatile, whereby its contents can be lost by being overwritten in video memory by another application. This can occur by such an action as changing the display mode in your operating system or a window taking over full-screen exclusive mode. For this irregularity, the `VolatileImage` class allows us to test the image to see if the contents have been lost, giving us the chance to restore the image soon after. The following example, `VolatileImage-Rendering`, is an example of rendering to a `VolatileImage` back buffer in an applet. So go and get the `Animator` and `HotSpot` classes and take a look at the following code.

Code Listing 9-17: `VolatileImageRendering.java`

```
import java.awt.*;
import java.awt.image.*;
import javax.swing.*;
import java.awt.event.*;

public class VolatileImageRendering extends JApplet implements
    Runnable
{
    public void init()
    {
        getContentPane().setLayout(null);
        setSize(DISPLAY_WIDTH, DISPLAY_HEIGHT);
        setIgnoreRepaint(true);

        animator = new Animator(new Rectangle(0, 0, DISPLAY_WIDTH,
            DISPLAY_HEIGHT));

        createVolatileImageBackBuffer();
    }


    public void     createVolatileImageBackBuffer()
    {
        volatileImageBackBuffer = getGraphicsConfiguration().create
```

```
            CompatibleVolatileImage(DISPLAY_WIDTH, DISPLAY_HEIGHT);
    vibbGraphics = (Graphics2D)
        volatileImageBackBuffer.getGraphics();
}

public void start()
{
    loop = new Thread(this);
    loop.start();
}

public void stop()
{
    loop = null;
}

public void run()
{
    long startTime, waitTime, elapsedTime;
    // 1000/25 Frames Per Second = 40 millisecond delay
    int delayTime = 1000/25;

    Thread thisThread = Thread.currentThread();
    while(loop==thisThread)
    {
        startTime = System.currentTimeMillis();

        animator.animate();

        // render to back buffer
        render(vibbGraphics);

        // render back buffer to screen

        Graphics g = getGraphics();
        g.drawImage(volatileImageBackBuffer, 0, 0, null);
        g.dispose();

        // handle frame rate
        elapsedTime = System.currentTimeMillis() - startTime;
        waitTime = Math.max(delayTime - elapsedTime, 5);

        try
        {
            Thread.sleep(waitTime);
        }
        catch(InterruptedException e) {}
    }
}


public void render(Graphics g)
{
    do
    {
        int state = volatileImageBackBuffer.validate
            (getGraphicsConfiguration());
        if(state==VolatileImage.IMAGE_INCOMPATIBLE)
            createVolatileImageBackBuffer();
            // create a new image
```

```
            // render to volatileImage back buffer
            animator.render(g);

        } while(volatileImageBackBuffer.contentsLost());
    }

    private Animator animator;
    private Thread loop;
    private VolatileImage volatileImageBackBuffer;
    private Graphics2D vibbGraphics;    // volatile image bbGraphics

    private static final int DISPLAY_WIDTH = 400;
    private static final int DISPLAY_HEIGHT = 400;
}
```

We create the `VolatileImage` in the method `createVolatile-ImageBackBuffer`, obtained from the graphics configuration of the screen. This is important because we may be running on a dual monitor display, where each monitor could likely have its own graphics card. The method `createVolatileImageBackBuffer` may also be re-called in the main rendering loop from the `render` method if the contents of `VolatileImage` are found to have been overwritten by our out-of-control operating system.

VolatileImage in its Current State

For the vast majority of 2D games, the sprites used in these games will not always be rectangular and fully opaque but will have transparent pixels. For example, Mario's character does not fill up an entire rectangular area but uses the pixels it takes to shape his body. At the moment, `VolatileImage` does not support transparency, which makes it unusable for non-rectangular filling sprite data. This important feature of `VolatileImage` will hopefully be supported soon though.

Active Rendering and Full-Screen Exclusive Mode

Probably the most important new feature of Java 1.4 for games development is full-screen exclusive mode. This feature enables us to take direct control over the screen, suspending the underlying windowing environment. This means that we can render to the full bounds of the monitor display and not have to worry about any of the window problems that we have encountered so far. Furthermore, when going into full-screen exclusive mode, we may also change the screen resolution and bit depth to any supported by the destination system, instead of being forced to use the current windowed mode configuration. The screen resolution is simply the number of pixels that fill the monitor display in width and height (e.g., 800x600, 1024x768) and the bit depth is the number of bits used for storing the color value for each pixel (e.g., 8-bit—256 colors, 32-bit—roughly 16.8 million colors).

There is much to discuss on this subject, as we shall see in the coming sections, but you can be sure of one thing: in Java it's very easy to venture into full-screen exclusive mode. In a moment, we will create a template full-screen rendering application, which also gives you the option of running in debug/windowed mode instead. But first we will take a look at the all-important `BufferStrategy` class, also a new feature in Java 1.4.

Introducing the BufferStrategy Class

The class `java.awt.image.BufferStrategy` was designed to provide an all-purpose means of actively rendering to a window or canvas.

The buffer strategy will attempt to use the most efficient method for rendering for your given display component. However, this implementation is dependent on the capabilities of the hardware and software on which you are running. If possible, the buffer strategy of choice for rendering is page flipping. If page flipping is not available, it will perform double buffering similar to when we created the off-screen buffers in previous examples. In this case the buffer strategy will take advantage of volatile image capabilities if supported; otherwise it will perform double buffering without accelerated images.

The two main methods of the `BufferStrategy` class that we will use in our main rendering loop are `getDrawGraphics` and `show`. The method `getDrawGraphics` will simply return the `Graphics` object to which we can perform our drawing routines, and the `show` method is called when you are finished and are ready to draw to the screen. Another important point is that rendering, using `BufferStrategy`, can be performed in windowed mode and full-screen exclusive mode, meaning that you may use the same main rendering loop code to be performed in both. We will perform this in the upcoming example, `FullScreenDemo`, in a moment, allowing you to choose whether or not you wish to go into full-screen exclusive mode or stay in windowed mode, using the same rendering loop whatever the choice.

Page Flipping

When using double buffering techniques, we are required to first of all render our scene to an off-screen back buffer, as we did in previous examples in this section, and then copy the back buffer to the destination component's `Graphics` object for drawing to the screen. Using page flipping, the buffers are created in video memory, where we can draw directly to them. They may then be swapped using a video pointer. The video pointer is merely the address in video memory pointing (in this case, to either one of our buffers, making that buffer the primary surface). When we wish to swap the buffers, instead of copying the contents of our back buffer to the primary buffer, we can simply swap the video pointer so that it now points to the new primary surface (previously the back buffer that we have just drawn the latest scene to), leaving us with the old primary surface, which becomes our new back buffer ready to be overwritten with a newer scene, and so on with the swapping. In Java, you can also easily specify the number of buffers that you wish to use for your buffer strategy. This means you can perform chain flipping where two or more back buffers can be used with a primary surface, increasing the smoothness of your rendering at the cost of using more memory.

The FullScreenDemo Example

In this example we will look at all of the basics of moving into full-screen exclusive mode and using the `BufferStrategy` to control our rendering. We will take a look at this example step by step, as it is quite large. Be aware that the complete source code for this example is here, but it has explanations interspersed among the code.

Note also that you will need to grab the `Animator` and `HotSpot` classes to be compiled along with this example.

Code Listing 9-18: `FullScreenDemo.java`

```java
import java.awt.*;
import java.awt.image.*;
import java.awt.event.*;
import javax.swing.*;

class FullScreenDemo extends JFrame implements Runnable, KeyListener
{
```

One small thing to note at this stage is that we implement the `KeyListener` interface in this example class. We implement this interface in order to read keyboard input events into our program (namely the Escape key being pressed) so that we can exit from full-screen mode as the close button on the window will not be available in this instance. We will go into depth about keyboard and mouse events in the next chapter, so do not concern yourself with this too much for the time being.

```java
public FullScreenDemo(GraphicsDevice graphicsDevice)
{
    super(graphicsDevice.getDefaultConfiguration());
    this.graphicsDevice = graphicsDevice;
    getContentPane().setLayout(null);
    setIgnoreRepaint(true);
    setResizable(false);

    animator = new Animator(new Rectangle(0, 0, DISPLAY_WIDTH,
        DISPLAY_HEIGHT));

    addWindowListener(new WindowAdapter()
    {
        public void windowClosing(WindowEvent e)
        {
            exitProgram();
        }
    });

    addKeyListener(this);
}
```

In the call to the constructor in the method `main`, we pass a `GraphicsDevice` object of the local graphics environment. We can then pass this to the super class (`JFrame`) constructor also and store our own reference to it to be used later for actually moving into full-screen mode. We also make a call to `setIgnoreRepaint` here, which will tell the Event Dispatch Thread to ignore any painting requests coming in from the operating system so we can actively render on our own, as we did in previous active rendering examples. We also add a window listener for when a window-closing event comes in from the user action. Note that even though in full-screen mode we will not have a close button on the window (the x button), the user can still use shortcut keys, such as Alt+F4 in Windows, to close the window. So even in full-screen mode, this will dispatch a window-closing window event.

The following method, `setMode`, is used to eventually display our `JFrame` in a given display mode. The parameter passed is 0 for full-screen or 1 for windowed mode.

```
public void setMode(int mode)
{
    if(mode==FULLSCREEN_MODE)
        if(!graphicsDevice.isFullScreenSupported())
        {
            mode = WINDOWED_MODE;
            System.out.println("Sorry, fullscreen mode not
                supported, continuing in windowed mode");
        }
```

Here we can make a check to the method `isFullScreenSupported` of the `GraphicsDevice` object. If full-screen mode is not supported, we will carry on in windowed mode.

```
    this.mode = mode;

    try
    {
        if(mode==FULLSCREEN_MODE)
        {
            setUndecorated(true);
```

The call to the method `setUndecorated` allows us to remove the windowed decorations from around our `JFrame` object when going into full-screen mode. An earlier hack of pretending to be in full-screen mode before it became available in Java was to create a screen size window and turn off the decorations; now we can do it properly.

```
        graphicsDevice.setFullScreenWindow(this);
```

To go into full-screen, all we need to do is simply make a call to the method `setFullScreenWindow` of the `GraphicsDevice` object passing a reference to our `JFrame` object (`this`), and there we go.

Once in full-screen mode, we can change the display mode (that is, the resolution, bit depth, and monitor refresh rate of the screen) using the class `java.awt.DisplayMode`. We can first check to see if we are able to change the display mode and then attempt our change.

```
        if(graphicsDevice.isDisplayChangeSupported())
        {
            DisplayMode dm = new DisplayMode(DISPLAY_WIDTH,
                DISPLAY_HEIGHT, 16,
                DisplayMode.REFRESH_RATE_UNKNOWN);
```

```
                    if(isDisplayModeAvailable(dm))
                    graphicsDevice.setDisplayMode(dm);
```

The method `isDisplayModeAvailable` checks through a list of available modes to see if any of them match up to the one that we desire. This method is implemented further in this example.

```
                else
                {
                    System.out.println("Display mode not
                        available: "+
                        dm.getWidth()+":"+
                        dm.getHeight()+":"+
                        dm.getBitDepth());

                    System.exit(0);
                }
            }
            else
            {
                System.out.println("Display change not
                    supported");
                System.exit(0);
            }
        }
        else // WINDOWED_MODE
        {
```

If we are moving into normal windowed mode, we can reproduce the window setup code that we have used in earlier windowed examples in this section.

```
            setTitle("Windowed Mode");

            setVisible(true);

            Insets insets = getInsets();
            DISPLAY_X = insets.left;
            DISPLAY_Y = insets.top;
            resizeToInternalSize(DISPLAY_WIDTH, DISPLAY_HEIGHT);
        }
```

At this point, we have set up and displayed our `JFrame`, be it in full-screen mode or windowed mode. All that remains is for us to create the `BufferStrategy` for rendering to our displayable area. We can perform this by calling the method `createBufferStrategy` of the `JFrame` component, simply passing to it the number of buffers that we are going to use. We then get the buffer strategy and store a reference to it in the variable `strategy` to be used for rendering later on.

```
        createBufferStrategy(3);
        strategy = getBufferStrategy();
    }
    catch(Exception e)
    {
        graphicsDevice.setFullScreenWindow(null);
        e.printStackTrace();
    }
```

We can also make a test to see if page flipping is being used, as follows:

```
if(!strategy.getCapabilities().isPageFlipping())
        System.out.println("Page flipping is not available in
            this mode");
```

While writing this book using the initial release of J2SE 1.4, we experienced a problem with using full-screen mode and rendering `Buffer-Strategy`, where it appeared that the `BufferStrategy` created was not immediately ready for rendering, possibly due to a slight delay in the changing of the display mode. For this purpose, we have included the method `waitForReadyStrategy`, implemented later on in this example, which is designed to continue to catch exceptions until the `Buffer-Strategy` is ready for drawing. It is a bit of a hack, but it does work. Alternatively, we were forced to continually restart our application until it worked, which was annoying.

```
        waitForReadyStrategy();
    }
```

Here is simply the window resizing method that we have been using throughout this chapter for running in windowed mode:

```
public void resizeToInternalSize(int internalWidth, int
    internalHeight)
{
    Insets insets = getInsets();
    final int newWidth = internalWidth + insets.left +
        insets.right;
    final int newHeight = internalHeight + insets.top +
        insets.bottom;

    Runnable resize = new Runnable()
    {
        public void run()
        {
            setSize(newWidth, newHeight);
        }
    };

    if(!SwingUtilities.isEventDispatchThread())
    {
        try
        {
            SwingUtilities.invokeAndWait(resize);
        }
        catch(Exception e) {}
    }
    else
        resize.run();

    validate();
}
```

Next is a simple method used in the initialization stage of going into full-screen mode.

```
public boolean isDisplayModeAvailable(DisplayMode dm)
{
    DisplayMode[] availableModes =
        graphicsDevice.getDisplayModes();
```

Chapter 9

```
for(int i=0; i<availableModes.length; i++)
{
    if(dm.getWidth()==availableModes[i].getWidth() &&
        dm.getHeight()==availableModes[i].getHeight() &&
        dm.getBitDepth()==availableModes[i].getBitDepth())
        return true;
}

return false;
}
```

This simple method obtains a list of available display modes using the method `graphicsDevice.getAvailableDisplayModes` and then searches through the available modes, returning `true` if the argument parameter mode is one of those available and `false` otherwise.

```
public void waitForReadyStrategy()
{
    int iterations = 0;

    while(true)
    {
        try
        {
            Thread.sleep(20);
        }
        catch(InterruptedException e) {}

        try
        {
            strategy.getDrawGraphics();
            break;
        }
        catch(IllegalStateException e)
        {
            System.out.println("BufferStrategy not ready yet");
        }

        iterations++;
        if(iterations == 100)
        {
            // (Unlikely event) No use after 2 seconds
            // (100*20ms = 2secs) give up trying
            System.out.println("Exiting Program, unable to use
                BufferStrategy");
            System.exit(0);
        }
    }
}
```

As you can see, this method is quite straightforward. In it, we simply attempt to retrieve the `Graphics` object from our buffer strategy, catching an exception if thrown. We give this test a life of two seconds before giving up and exiting out of the program. Note that we have never experienced such an exception with one single sleep of 20 milliseconds alone (though we have without a sleep), so exiting unsuccessfully should be very unlikely with this method.

```
public void start()
{
    loop = new Thread(this);
    loop.start();
}
```

The `start` method is called after the display has been set up to begin the main loop rendering process. Once the thread "loop" is created and started, the `run` method is called.

```
public void run()
{
    long startTime, waitTime, elapsedTime;
    // 1000/25 Frames Per Second = 40 millisecond delay
    int delayTime = 1000/25;

    Thread thisThread = Thread.currentThread();
    while(loop==thisThread)
    {
        startTime = System.currentTimeMillis();
```

We call the method `animator.animate`, as we have in many of the previous examples, to perform the movement of the `HotSpot` around the screen.

```
        animator.animate();
```

We are now ready to draw our scene by retrieving the `Graphics` object to draw to from `strategy.getDrawGraphics`. We can then draw to this and finally make a call to `strategy.show` when finished.

```
        Graphics g = strategy.getDrawGraphics();

        if(!strategy.contentsLost())
        {
            g.translate(DISPLAY_X, DISPLAY_Y);

            animator.render(g);

            g.dispose();
            strategy.show();
        }

            //  handle frame rate
            elapsedTime = System.currentTimeMillis() - startTime;
            waitTime = Math.max(delayTime - elapsedTime, 5);

        try
        {
            Thread.sleep(waitTime);
        }
        catch(InterruptedException e) {}
    }

System.out.println("Program Exited");

    dispose();
    System.exit(0);
}
```

```
public void exitProgram()
{
    loop = null;
}
```

The `main` method performs all of the calls required to get this example up and running. In this method we also create our option pane for choosing whether to go into full-screen or windowed mode, but do not worry too much about this aspect of the code for now; we will look at graphical user interface objects (GUI) in Chapter 13.

```
public static void main(String args[])
{
    GraphicsEnvironment ge =
        GraphicsEnvironment.getLocalGraphicsEnvironment();

    FullScreenDemo testFrame = new
        FullScreenDemo(ge.getDefaultScreenDevice());

    Object[] options = {"FullScreen Mode", "Windowed Mode"};

    int choice = JOptionPane.showOptionDialog(null,
                "Select Display Mode:",
                "FullScreenDemo Option Pane",
                JOptionPane.DEFAULT_OPTION,
                JOptionPane.QUESTION_MESSAGE,
                null,
                options,
                options[0]);

    if(choice!=JOptionPane.CLOSED_OPTION)
    {
        // choice will be either 0 or 1 corresponding to our mode
        // flags FULLSCREEN_MODE = 0, WINDOWED_MODE = 1

        testFrame.setMode(choice);
        testFrame.start();
    }
    else
        System.exit(0);
}
```

When running in full-screen mode, we no longer have a close button to click, so for this purpose we have added a key listener so that when the user presses the Escape key, the program will exit successfully. We will look at key events in the next chapter.

```
public void keyPressed(KeyEvent e)
{
    if(e.getKeyCode() == KeyEvent.VK_ESCAPE)
        exitProgram();
}


public void keyReleased(KeyEvent e) {}
public void keyTyped(KeyEvent e) {}
```

```
    private Thread loop;
    private GraphicsDevice graphicsDevice;
    private Animator animator;

    // not final - may need to adjust these coordinates to adapt to
    // windowed border
    private int DISPLAY_X = 0;
    private int DISPLAY_Y = 0;

    private final int DISPLAY_WIDTH = 800;
    private final int DISPLAY_HEIGHT = 600;

    private BufferStrategy strategy;

    private static final int FULLSCREEN_MODE = 0;
    private static final int WINDOWED_MODE = 1;

    private int mode;
}
```

When you compile and run this example, you should first of all be queried by an option dialog asking whether you wish to go into full-screen or windowed mode.

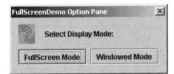

Figure 9-15

Hopefully, the example should venture into the desired display mode. Here is a screen shot of this example moving into windowed mode, rendering the circle about the screen using the buffer strategy:

Figure 9-16

This example should provide you with a good template to work from when developing games of your own. The windowed mode is especially useful for debugging purposes, logging run-time stats in the console window.

Summary

It's safe to say that the Java language is heading in a positive direction for games development with the new features in J2SE 1.4 discussed in this chapter. Let's hope it becomes a force to be reckoned with in the future. The true advantage of Java is its platform independence; as Java becomes more powerful for games development, we may see game companies turning to Java as the development language of choice, with the end goal that development could be a one-time event, running immediately on any system with an up-to-date Java Virtual Machine, even consoles. But this we shall leave blowing in the wind. In the next chapter we will look at reading mouse and keyboard events in Java, paying particular attention to integration into the main loop and thread safety issues along the way.

# Chapter 10

Using the Mouse and Keyboard

"Now press any key; where's the 'any' key?"

—Homer Simpson

Introduction

The ability to read input into a program is a major step in the process of creating Java games. In this chapter we first of all use some simple examples to show how keyboard and mouse events are read into an applet and application, respectively, and then we look at some more advanced techniques for reading the input. In the previous chapter we learned how to display graphics, which together with the subject of this chapter gives us the ability to make real-time games.

Using Listeners

A *listener* in Java is an object that is used to handle events. In effect, it is implemented to listen for events and then tell the program the required information about that event, which you may then handle. For example, if the player moves the mouse, a listener will alert the program that the mouse has been moved and give details of its position, relative to the component currently occupying that area of the screen.

The most commonly used event listeners are shown below and are found in the package `java.awt.event`.

ActionListener	FocusListener	KeyListener
MouseListener	MouseMotionListener	WindowListener

In this chapter we will concentrate on the `KeyListener`, `Mouse-Listener`, and `MouseMotionListener` interfaces (we will look at the `FocusListener` toward the end of this chapter also). The following tables show details of the abstract methods defined in these three listeners and the events that invoke them.

KeyListener

`void keyPressed(KeyEvent e)`	A key is pressed down (these events will continue to occur when the user holds the key down but with a key delay).
`void keyReleased(KeyEvent e)`	A key is released.
`void keyTyped(KeyEvent e)`	A key is pressed and then released (note that this event is only posted for keys that are deemed to be type-able, such as alpha characters and numbers and not keys such as F1, Ctrl, and Alt, for example).

MouseListener

`void mouseClicked(MouseEvent e)`	A mouse button is pressed and then released on a component.
`void mouseEntered(MouseEvent e)`	Mouse enters a component area.
`void mouseExited(MouseEvent e)`	Mouse exits a component area.
`void mousePressed(MouseEvent e)`	A mouse button is pressed on a component.
`void mouseReleased(MouseEvent e)`	A mouse button is released on a component.

MouseMotionListener

`void mouseDragged(MouseEvent e)`	A mouse button is held down on a component, and then the mouse is moved.
`void mouseMoved(MouseEvent e)`	Mouse is moved on a component and no buttons are down.

For convenience, `javax.swing.event.MouseInputListener` implements all of the methods included in the `MouseListener` and `MouseMotionListener` interfaces together.

Information about an event is stored in an event object, which is passed as a parameter to a listener method when it is invoked. This is shown in the previous tables, with the class `KeyEvent` for events associated with the keyboard and the class `MouseEvent` for events associated with the mouse.

Reading Keyboard Input

In this example we learn how to recognize keyboard events and relative information associated with them. The following example, `Simple-Keyboard.java`, is an applet program that displays information about keyboard events.

```
import java.awt.*;
import javax.swing.*;
import java.awt.event.*;

public class SimpleKeyboard extends JApplet implements KeyListener
{
    public void init()
```

```
{
    getContentPane().setLayout(null);
    setSize(250,200);
    addKeyListener(this);
}

public void start()
{
    lastKeyEvent = null;
    requestFocus();
}

public void paint(Graphics g)
{
    g.setColor(Color.black);
    g.fillRect(0,0,250,200);
    g.setColor(Color.white);
    g.drawString("Example: Simple Keyboard",50,20);
    g.drawString("Press a key",90,165);

    if(lastKeyEvent!=null)
    {
        g.drawString("Key description:",30,65);
        g.drawString(lastKeyEvent.getKeyText(lastKeyEvent
            .getKeyCode()),120,65);

        g.drawString("Key character:",30,80);
        g.drawString(String.valueOf(lastKeyEvent
            .getKeyChar()),120,80);

        g.drawString("Key code:",30,95);
        g.drawString(String.valueOf(lastKeyEvent
            .getKeyCode()),120,95);

        g.drawString("Is an Action key:",30,110);
        g.drawString(String.valueOf(lastKeyEvent
            .isActionKey()),120,110);

        g.drawString("Modifier keys:",30,125);
        g.drawString(lastKeyEvent.getKeyModifiersText
            (lastKeyEvent.getModifiers()),120,125);
    }
}

public void keyPressed(KeyEvent e)
{
    lastKeyEvent = e;
    repaint();
}

    // The methods keyReleased(..) and KeyTyped(..) inherited
    // from KeyListener interface
    // must be defined, but we can ignore them if we choose
public void keyReleased(KeyEvent e)
{
    // ignore
}

public void keyTyped(KeyEvent e)
{
```

Chapter 10

```
    // ignore
  }

  private KeyEvent lastKeyEvent;
}
```

Now run the example and hold down the Shift key at the same time as the r key on the keyboard. When this is done, the output should look the same as the following screen shot. (Note that you may need to click on the applet with the mouse to gain the keyboard focus when running in a web browser if the focus is lost to another aspect of the browser—e.g., the address bar.) Notice that the key character is an uppercase R. This is because the Caps Lock is turned off on the keyboard, and holding down Shift turns lowercase to uppercase, and vice versa.

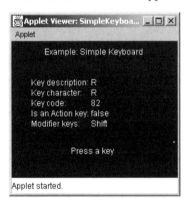

Figure 10-1

The `SimpleKeyboard` class implements the interface `KeyListener`, which means that it must provide functionality for the three methods declared in the `KeyListener` interface: `keyPressed`, `keyReleased`, and `keyTyped`. The `KeyListener` interface can be implemented by any classes that you want; we did not need to choose the main applet class but could have made a separate class for handling the key events just as easily. But it is common sense to handle the key events in the object concerned. Use the identifier `lastKeyEvent` to reference the newly received keyboard events, which are then accessed in the `paint` method. When we retrieve new key events, we also call the `repaint` method for the applet so that it can refresh itself. This is a quick-fix way to update the display. We'll look into handling events in a proper graphics processing main loop a little later.

We add the key listener to listen to our main class instance in the `init` method, which is called when the applet is loaded with the following line of code:

```
addKeyListener(this);
```

This adds a key listener object to our main applet object (a key listener object being an object that implements the `KeyListener` interface and therefore provides functionality for the event handling methods). In this line of code, we declare that our main applet component itself will be used as the key listener and will therefore handle the events itself. Once this line of code is added, the event thread, invoking the appropriate listener method, such as `keyPressed`, will report any key events that occur while the main applet has focus.

However, the Event Dispatch Thread is another thread separate from the main loop thread. This means trouble, as when an event occurs, it will interrupt your main loop and invoke one of the event handling methods. We will discuss why this is a problem in more detail and will make an all-effective callback routine to handle this problem a little later, integrating received events with the main loop thread. For now, however, we will concentrate on retrieving relevant information from these events.

In the `paint` method in the previous example, we get hold of the `KeyEvent lastKeyEvent`, and display five attributes associated with that event. The first attribute is a text description of the key that has been pressed, returned from the method `getKeyText` (e.g., HOME, DELETE, C, etc.). This method requires one parameter, which is the key code of the key that has been pressed. The next attribute is the character associated with the key pressed, returned from the method `getKeyChar`. The third attribute is the key code of the key pressed, returned from the method `getKeyCode`. The `KeyEvent` class contains a large list of static key codes using plain text identifiers beginning with VK_ (virtual key) and then the string description of the key pressed. For example, we could add the following `switch` statement to identify key presses for the keys E, t, Escape, and Home in the `keyPressed` method.

```java
public void keyPressed(KeyEvent e)
{
    lastKeyEvent = e;
    repaint();

    switch(e.getKeyCode())
    {
        case KeyEvent.VK_E:
            // handle event of (uppercase) key 'E' being pressed
            break;
        case KeyEvent.VK_T:
            // handle event of (lowercase) key 't' being pressed
            break;
        case KeyEvent.VK_ESCAPE:
            // handle event of ESCAPE key being pressed
            break;
        case KeyEvent.VK_HOME:
            // handle event of HOME key being pressed
            break;
        default:
            // Do nothing or inform user about invalid key
            break;
    }
}
```

In this code snippet we are also looking for an uppercase E and a lowercase t. The key codes are not case sensitive. Therefore, in order to determine if the key pressed was uppercase or lowercase, we need to use the method discussed earlier, `getKeyChar`, which will return the character value of type `char` with case sensitivity.

```
case KeyEvent.VK_T:
    if(e.getKeyChar() == 't')
        System.out.println("Lowercase t was pressed);
break;
```

Note that in this example (as you know, the key pressed was the t key anyway), you could just as easily use the static method `Character.isLowerCase(e.getKeyChar())` to check the case, which returns a Boolean result.

The fourth attribute in the `paint` method in the previous example is a Boolean value, true or false, retrieved from the method `isActionKey`. Examples of action keys are F1-F12, Insert, Left, Right, etc. The fifth and final attribute associated with the key event is the modifier key or keys, such as Alt or Ctrl+Shift. This string value is returned from the method `getKeyModifiersText`, which takes one integer parameter: the modifier's flag for the event. The modifier's flag is retrieved as a return value of `getModifiers`, a method inherited by `KeyEvent` from its super class `InputEvent`. The modifier value simply holds bitwise information about the event. We will need these modifiers in order to obtain information about which mouse button was pressed a little later in the chapter.

There is no distinct difference in using the key and mouse listeners in an applet or in an application. In an application, we would have added the key listener to the main `JFrame`, and our main `JFrame` would also have implemented the `KeyListener` interface if we chose for it to. To keep our mutual application and applet approach, we will use an application for the upcoming mouse example.

Adapter Classes

The adapter classes implement the corresponding listener interfaces and define empty methods for you, thus the adapter class can be extended instead and only the methods required need to be overridden. The adapter classes that we are interested in are `KeyAdapter` (implements `KeyListener`), `MouseAdapter` (implements `MouseListener`), and `MouseMotionAdapter` (implements `MouseMotionListener`). These adapter classes are found in the package `java.awt.event`. If you prefer to combine the two mouse listener classes using `MouseInputListener` mentioned earlier, it has an associated adapter class: `javax.swing.event.MouseInputAdapter`. The adapter classes are used for added convenience; for example, for the `SimpleKeyboard` example, we could have added a nested class called `MyKeyListener` that extended the `KeyAdapter` class instead of implementing the `KeyListener` interface as follows:

```
public class MyKeyListener extends KeyAdapter
{
    public void keyPressed(KeyEvent e)
```

```
        {
            lastKeyEvent = e;
            repaint();
        }
}
```

`MyKeyListener` extends the `KeyAdapter` class, which implements empty `KeyListener` methods, so we only need to override the ones that we require. You could then add a key listener to the main applet in the `init` method of `SimpleKeyboard`, as follows:

```
addKeyListener(new MyKeyListener());
```

With this method, the main applet class would no longer need to implement the `KeyListener` interface and define the three methods itself.

However, do not let this added convenience put you off using the interface listeners. The advantage of using interfaces over extending classes is that you can have a class that implements, say, the `KeyListener` and the `MouseListener` or as many as you need, whereas you could not have a class that extended both the `KeyAdapter` and `MouseAdapter`, as Java does not support multiple inheritance.

 TIP: When using the adapter classes, remember to name the overridden methods correctly. Otherwise, you will not override them at all; you will simply be declaring a new method. This generally occurs when starting the method name with a capital letter (e.g., `KeyPressed` instead of `keyPressed`). Another reason it is better to use the interfaces is because the debugger will look for these methods and alert you if one is missing (or incorrectly spelled as the case may be).

However, arguably the neatest way to add a key listener is by defining a class "on the fly." We saw this in the previous chapter with the `WindowListener`, where we handled the closing of a window. With this method, you can simply do the following in the `init` method, for example.

```
addKeyListener(new KeyAdapter()
{
    public void keyPressed(KeyEvent e)
    {
        lastKeyEvent = e;
        repaint();
    }
});
```

Here we define our method for a new instance of `KeyAdapter`, as we define it. Though this method might seem quite unconventional to you if you're new to it, it's perfectly feasible and should grow on you.

Reading Mouse Input

The mouse is probably the most important input device for PC games, especially for real-time games where reaction times are important. With Java, mouse events are easy to detect using the same methods already used to detect keyboard events earlier. The example `SimpleMouse` is a

Chapter 10

simple application program similar to the ones we created at the beginning of Chapter 9. This example implements all of the important mouse events that can occur in your program, such as the position of the mouse and button clicking information. The example shows mouse event information and also allows you to move a square shape about the window by clicking the left mouse button. The structure of this example is a little different from the `SimpleKeyboard` example. For starters, this example is an application, whereas `SimpleKeyboard` was an applet. In this example, we also create our own custom drawing class `MouseMat`, adding this to the main `JFrame` object's content pane. We also add the mouse listener to the `MouseMat` component instead of the main frame to illustrate how a listener can be applied to any component. This example contains two source files: `SimpleMouse.java` and `MouseMat.java`. Here is the source code for the classes `SimpleMouse` and `MouseMat`.

Code Listing 10-1: `SimpleMouse.java`

```java
import java.awt.*;
import javax.swing.*;

public class SimpleMouse extends JFrame
{
    public SimpleMouse()
    {
        super("Simple Mouse Example");
        getContentPane().setLayout(null);
        setDefaultCloseOperation(EXIT_ON_CLOSE);
        setResizable(false);

        MouseMat mouseMat = new MouseMat(new Rectangle(10, 10,
            380, 380));
        getContentPane().add(mouseMat);

        showToInternalSize(DISPLAY_WIDTH, DISPLAY_HEIGHT);
        validate();
    }


    public Insets showToInternalSize(int internalWidth, int
        internalHeight)
    {
        setVisible(true);
        Insets insets = getInsets();

        final int newWidth = internalWidth + insets.left +
            insets.right;
        final int newHeight = internalHeight + insets.top +
            insets.bottom;
        try
        {
            EventQueue.invokeAndWait(new Runnable()
            {
                public void run()
                {
                    setSize(newWidth, newHeight);
                }
            });
```

```
        }
        catch(Exception e)
        {
            System.out.println(e);
        }

        return insets;
    }


    public static void main(String[] args)
    {
        new SimpleMouse();
    }

    private static final int DISPLAY_WIDTH = 400;
    private static final int DISPLAY_HEIGHT = 400;
}
```

`SimpleMouse` is a basic class extending the `JFrame` class to create a windowed application. Here we create a window with an internal graphics component of resolution 400x400. We then create a `MouseMat` object with the following line of code:

```
MouseMat mouseMat = new MouseMat(new Rectangle(10, 10, 380, 380));
```

The `Rectangle` object parameter to the `MouseMat` constructor defines the location and size of the `MouseMat` component. The reason we create the `MouseMat` of this size and not at (`0, 0, 400, 400`) is to illustrate how the mouse listener works relative to the component to which it is added. You will understand this fact when you run the example code, and we will touch on this a little later. Before we go any further, let's take a look at the code for `MouseMat.java`. The code for this class is quite bulky but is designed to illustrate all of the important features of the `MouseEvent` object received.

```
import java.awt.*;
import javax.swing.*;
import java.awt.event.*;

public class MouseMat extends JComponent implements MouseListener,
    MouseMotionListener
{
    public MouseMat(Rectangle bounds)
    {
        setBounds(bounds);
        setLayout(null);
        rect = new Rectangle(getWidth()/4, getHeight()/4,
            getWidth()/2, getHeight()/2);

        addMouseListener(this);
        addMouseMotionListener(this);
    }

    public void paintComponent(Graphics g)
    {
        Graphics2D g2D = (Graphics2D)g;
        g2D.setColor(Color.cyan);
```

Chapter 10

```
      g2D.fillRect(0, 0, getWidth(), getHeight());
      if(mouseOver) g2D.setColor(Color.red);
      else g2D.setColor(Color.blue);
      g2D.fill(rect);
      g2D.setColor(Color.black);
      g2D.drawString("You can't lose me!!!!!",rect.x+40,rect.y+100);
      g2D.drawString("Example: Simple Mouse",120,20);


      g2D.drawString("Last recorded mouse position:
         ("+mousePoint.x+","+mousePoint.y+")",80,300);
      g2D.drawString("Last click count: "+clickCount,80,315);

      String lmStr = "Last mouse press event: ";
      if(lastMouseEvent!=null)
      {
         switch(lastMouseEvent.getID())
         {
            case MouseEvent.MOUSE_PRESSED:
               lmStr+="Mouse Pressed";
               break;
            case MouseEvent.MOUSE_RELEASED:
               lmStr+="Mouse Released";
               break;
            case MouseEvent.MOUSE_CLICKED:
               lmStr+="Mouse Clicked";
               break;
         }
      }
      g2D.drawString(lmStr,80,330);

      String lmmStr = "Last mouse motion event: ";
      if(lastMouseMotionEvent!=null)
      {
         switch(lastMouseMotionEvent.getID())
         {
            case MouseEvent.MOUSE_MOVED:
               lmmStr+="Mouse Moved";
               break;
            case MouseEvent.MOUSE_DRAGGED:
               lmmStr+="Mouse Dragged";
               break;
         }
      }
      g2D.drawString(lmmStr,80,345);
   }

   public void mousePressed(MouseEvent e)
   {
      if((e.getModifiers() & MouseEvent.BUTTON1_MASK)!=0)
      {
         rect.setLocation(e.getX()-(rect.width/2),e.getY()-
            (rect.height/2));
         lastMouseEvent = e;
         repaint();
      }
   }

   public void mouseReleased(MouseEvent e)
   {
```

```
      if((e.getModifiers() & MouseEvent.BUTTON1_MASK)!=0)
      {
         lastMouseEvent = e;
         repaint();
      }
   }

   public void mouseClicked(MouseEvent e)
   {
      if((e.getModifiers() & MouseEvent.BUTTON1_MASK)!=0)
      {
         clickCount = e.getClickCount();
         lastMouseEvent = e;
         repaint();
      }
   }

   public void mouseEntered(MouseEvent e)
   {
      mouseOver = true;
      repaint();
   }

   public void mouseExited(MouseEvent e)
   {
      mouseOver = false;
      repaint();
   }


   public void mouseMoved(MouseEvent e)
   {
      mousePoint.setLocation(e.getX(), e.getY());
      lastMouseMotionEvent = e;
      repaint();
   }

   public void mouseDragged(MouseEvent e)
   {
      mousePoint.setLocation(e.getX(), e.getY());
      lastMouseMotionEvent = e;
      repaint();
   }

   private int clickCount;
   private Rectangle rect;
   private Point mousePoint = new Point(0, 0);
   private MouseEvent lastMouseEvent;
   private MouseEvent lastMouseMotionEvent;
   private boolean mouseOver;
}
```

When you compile and run this example, your output should be similar to the following figure. This screen shot is an illustration of when the mouse is not currently over the component, resulting in the square shape being colored blue. The mouse was clicked near the top-left corner of the component area, moving the square shape centered to that position.

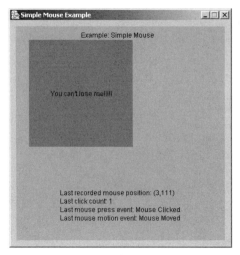

Figure 10-2

In the `SimpleKeyboard` example, the key listener is added to the main applet object. In this example, the mouse and mouse motion listeners are added to the `MouseMat` component itself. This is implemented in the constructor of `MouseMat` with the following code:

```
addMouseListener(this);
addMouseMotionListener(this);
```

As you can see, the `MouseMat` class implements the listener interfaces `MouseListener` and `MouseMotionListener` and therefore implements their respective methods.

We use the `MouseMat` class as a canvas for displaying mouse event information. It contains a constructor, a paint method, and the mouse listener methods. The constructor first of all uses the method `setBounds` to set its x and y position (and also its width and height) relative to its parent `SimpleMouse`.

The size of the component `MouseMat` is 380x380 pixels starting at position (`10, 10`), to illustrate how the mouse listeners have been added to the `MouseMat` component and not to the main frame `SimpleMouse`. When you run this example, you will see a 10-pixel gray border around the light blue `MouseMat` component. Try moving the mouse over this gray area, and you will see that mouse events are not registered by your program, as we are not "listening" to that area; we are listening to the `MouseMat` component area defined by the light blue area in the window. Note that mouse drag events continue to register with your program when the mouse is dragged out of the component area.

The `MouseMat` class contains the `rect` variable, which stores the location and size for the shape that you can move around the screen by pressing the left mouse button somewhere on the `MouseMat` component. The rectangle's coordinates are changed when the `listener` method `mousePressed` is invoked. Here we retrieve the mouse coordinates relative to the `MouseMat` component from the `MouseEvent e` parameter (passed to `mousePressed`) with the methods `getX` and `getY`. Alternatively, the method `getPoint` returns a `Point` object with the coordinates.

In each of the three mouse button-related methods, `mousePressed`, `mouseReleased`, and `mouseClicked`, we check to make sure that the button causing the event was the left mouse button with the following code:

```
if((e.getModifiers() & MouseEvent.BUTTON1_MASK)!=0)
{
    // Event caused by left button/button 1
}
```

If you want actions from any of the mouse buttons to affect the program, simply remove the `if` statement and its brackets, as the methods are invoked regardless of the type of button causing the event. We perform a bitwise operation on the event modifier's value with the left button mask value `BUTTON1_MASK` to test if the left mouse button caused the event. The field `BUTTON3_MASK` is the mask for the right mouse button and the field `BUTTON2_MASK` is the mask for the middle mouse button.

We use the methods `mouseEntered` and `mouseExited` to determine when the `MouseMat` component has lost the mouse focus, hence the mouse is no longer pointing at the component. When this occurs, we alter the Boolean variable `mouseOver` accordingly, which is then used to determine the color of the moveable shape.

The position of the mouse is updated when either of the mouse motion events, `mouseMoved` or `mouseDragged`, is invoked. This is because only one of these events is invoked for a particular mouse motion event and not both (e.g., when the mouse is dragged, the `mouseMoved` method is not invoked, just the `mouseDragged` method).

The mouse-clicking count of the left mouse button is stored in the integer variable `clickCount` in the class `MouseMat` object, set using the method `setClickCount`. The click count is the amount of consecutive mouse clicks on the mouse button and is assigned its value when the method `mouseClicked` is invoked in the mouse listener in `MouseMat`. Notice that the click count is not updated when the mouse is dragged; a click count increments when the mouse is clicked within a small time frame from the occurrence of the last mouse click and without the mouse moving in that time.

Also in the paint method is the use of the method `getID`. This is used because we have an instance of `MouseEvent` from which we need to extract the type of event. The return value of `getID` can be compared with one of the static members in `MouseEvent` (e.g., `MOUSE_PRESSED`, `MOUSE_DRAGGED`, etc.).

If you were to add a number of components and provide one mouse listener for them all, you would need some way to determine on which component the event occurred. You can check this using the `getSource` method of the `MouseEvent` event object passed to your listener method as follows:

Chapter 10

```
public void mousePressed(MouseEvent e)
{
    if(e.getSource() == myMouseMat)
    {
    }
}
```

We will now look at integrating mouse events with the main game loop.

Integrating Mouse Events with the Main Loop

The first two examples in this chapter have been kept relatively simple to get you familiar with the use of event listeners. They are event-driven programs, where an event occurs and then we update the state of the program accordingly. This is why they are simple (with respect to application programmers, that is), because there is no main game loop handling logic and updating the display on its own periodically. Instead, an event occurs causing an event method to be invoked, which then in turn handles the event and calls a `repaint` method, updating the display with the new event information. This method is fine when your program is only altered by a user-caused event but not for real-time gaming. The main problem lies in the fact that these events are registered in a separate thread from your main loop thread (the Event Dispatch Thread), interrupting it at random times—whenever an event occurs. This can become a problem when you create another thread (in our case, the main loop thread of execution, like we created in Chapter 9). The problem arises that we cannot predict when the event will occur in terms of where we are in the main loop, similar to problems we discussed with passive rendering in the main loop in Chapter 9.

For example, we could have an object in our game, say a `Monster` object, that moves about in the game. This movement code could be executed in the main loop, as follows:

```
while(mainLoopRunning)
{
    if(myMonster!=null)
        myMonster.move();

    // Update display
}
```

We may then have a mouse listener method that can lead to the possibility of killing the monster and removing the object completely, as follows:

```
public void mousePressed(MouseEvent e)
{
    if(monsterKilledFromEvent())
    {
        myMonster = null;
    }
}
```

Our program could crash, caused by a `NullPointerException` exception, however unlikely. It is still possible though.

- First check in the main loop to see if(myMonster!=null). This check is returned true, as myMonster currently references a Monster object.
- The event listener thread then interrupts the main loop thread, and we press the mouse button, causing an input that kills the monster. We handle the killing of the monster by setting the reference myMonster to null.
- The main loop thread then continues execution, already passing the check to see if(myMonster!=null), which has already been validated, and then attempts to access the move method of myMonster, which now equals null. This would then cause a NullPointerException exception to be thrown.

We can handle thread synchronization problems such as this in a number of ways, like controlling when code in separate threads executes relative to another.

One way we could handle this problem is by using the keyword synchronized with an object to protect the threads from performing their code at dangerous times relative to one another. We could do this, as follows, in both our main loop and the keyPressed event method:

```
while(mainLoopRunning)
{
    synchronized(myMonster)
    {
        if(myMonster!=null)
            myMonster.move();
    }

    // Update display
}


public void mousePressed(MouseEvent e)
{
    if(monsterKilledFromEvent)
    {
        synchronized(myMonster)
        {
            myMonster = null;
        }
    }
}
```

The synchronized(myMonster) code block acts as a lock for the code in its thread. If we enter the synchronized code block in the main loop, we cannot enter the synchronized block in the mousePressed method at the same time. One thread must wait until the other is no longer executing in the synchronized block, which is controlled using the myMonster object as the lock; hence they are synchronized with one another. This means that our NullPointerException exception can no longer occur. For a detailed explanation on thread synchronization issues, please refer back to Chapter 7, "Threads."

Creating the MouseProcessor

The problem with just using the `synchronized` keyword is that we still cannot control exactly when we are handling events in our game in terms of where our main loop is located, and as a game grows bigger, more and more synchronization problems will arise. The last thing you want to do is throw the `synchronized` keyword everywhere, as this can affect the speed of execution heavily if handled poorly. Keeping your main loop and event interrupts synchronized in this way can make your code more complex than it needs to be. The most convenient solution is to handle any events that could cause problems with the main loop in the main loop itself. Ideally, our main game loop will be structured like this:

```
while(mainLoopRunning)
{
    // Handle input
    // Do game logic
    // Update display
    // Handle Frame Rate
}
```

This will involve storing a list of input events coming in from the listener thread and then emptying the events stored in this list in the main loop thread. We can perform this effectively by creating a class called `Mouse-Processor` and an interface called `MouseProcessable`. Let's take a look at some source code.

Code Listing 10-2: `MouseProcessable`

```
import java.awt.event.*;

public interface MouseProcessable
{
    public void handleMouseEvent(MouseEvent e);
}
```

This is a simple interface defining the method `handleMouseEvent`, taking one `MouseEvent` parameter. An object of a class that implements this interface will then provide an implementation of this method for handling events gathered by the mouse processor.

Code Listing 10-3: `MouseProcessor`

```
import java.awt.event.*;
import java.util.*;

public class MouseProcessor
{
    public MouseProcessor(MouseProcessable handler)
    {
        mouseEventList = new LinkedList();
        mouseMotionEventList = new LinkedList();

        this.handler = handler;
    }

    public void addMouseEvent(MouseEvent event)
```

```
{
    synchronized(mouseEventList)
    {
        mouseEventList.add(event);
    }
}


public void addMouseMotionEvent(MouseEvent event)
{
    synchronized(mouseMotionEventList)
    {
        mouseMotionEventList.add(event);
    }
}


public void processMouseEventList()
{
    MouseEvent event;

    while(mouseEventList.size() > 0)
    {
        synchronized(mouseEventList)
        {
            event = (MouseEvent) mouseEventList.removeFirst();
        }

        handler.handleMouseEvent(event);
    }
}

public void processMouseMotionEventList()
{
    MouseEvent event;

    while(mouseMotionEventList.size() > 0)
    {
        synchronized(mouseMotionEventList)
        {
            event = (MouseEvent) mouseMotionEventList
                .removeFirst();
        }

        handler.handleMouseEvent(event);
    }
}
```

There are two basic implementations in the MouseProcessor class. One is adding an event to one of its LinkedList list objects, be it the mouseEventList or the mouseMotionEventList. The other is handling the contents of these lists with the methods processMouse-EventList and processMouseMotionEventList. The functionality of the MouseProcessor revolves around mouse events coming in from the listener thread, with those events being added to their respective lists. Then, in the main loop thread, we can repeatedly make calls to the methods processMouseEventList and `processMouseMotionEventList` and handle any mouse events that occur, where we can see exactly when these events are being handled completely in synch with our game logic and rendering code. The beauty of the `MouseProcessor` is using the `MouseProcessable` interface. This interface defines the one method, `handleMouseEvent(MouseEvent e)`, which acts as a callback method to handle the mouse events in the main loop thread. The constructor of the `MouseProcessor` requires a `MouseProcessable` object as a parameter, which will be stored internally and used as the object to handle the mouse events. We will implement this completely in an example shortly.

Adding Events to the MouseProcessor

The methods `addMouseEvent` and `addMouseMotionEvent` simply add `MouseEvent` objects as they are retrieved. Before we add the data to the lists, we need to synchronize adding events to those lists with those lists being processed (emptied) in the `processMouseEventList` and `processMouseMotionEventList` methods, respectively, which will be executed in the main loop thread. Here we can use the list object itself for synchronization, and therefore we also need to do this in the process methods.

Processing Events in the MouseProcessor

The methods `processMouseEventList` and `processMouse-MotionEventList` are designed for invocation in the main loop, which will run through the given list containing recorded mouse events and handle them accordingly. The mouse events are removed from their list first in, first out (FIFO) as a queue, handled each time by calling the `handleMouseEvent` method of the `MouseProcessable` object originally passed when the `MouseProcessor` was constructed.

 NOTE: If you were merely listening for mouse motion events to track the latest position of the mouse, a mouse motion event list would not be required. Instead, you could just have one `MouseEvent` reference variable, simply holding a reference to the most recently received mouse motion event instead.

The MouseProcessor in Action

The following example, `AdvancedMouse`, is a demo applet of a circle object moving about the screen and bouncing off each of the four boundary walls. In this example we use the main loop code that we learned in Chapter 9, but this time we remove and recreate new `HotSpot` objects at the press of a mouse button, handling this removal/recreation code securely in the main loop using the `MouseProcessor`. This example uses five source files, two of which are the aforementioned `MouseProcessor` class and `MouseProcessable` interface. The other three classes that make up this example are `AdvancedMouse` (main class), `Animator`, and `HotSpot`. The `Animator` and `HotSpot` classes were used in the previous chapter as a means of quickly assembling an animation of a circle about the screen, so we could concentrate on the theory. The source code for these two classes is discussed in the previous chapter and must be used in order to compile this example. Before we go any further, let's take a look at the source code for AdvancedMouse.java.

Code Listing 10-4: AdvancedMouse.java

```java
import java.awt.*;
import java.awt.image.*;
import javax.swing.*;
import java.awt.event.*;

public class AdvancedMouse extends JApplet
        implements Runnable, MouseProcessable, MouseListener
{
    public void init()
    {
        getContentPane().setLayout(null);
        setSize(DISPLAY_WIDTH, DISPLAY_HEIGHT);
        setIgnoreRepaint(true);

        animator = new Animator(new Rectangle(0, 0, DISPLAY_WIDTH,
            DISPLAY_HEIGHT));

        backBuffer = new BufferedImage(DISPLAY_WIDTH, DISPLAY_HEIGHT,
            BufferedImage.TYPE_INT_RGB);
        bbGraphics = (Graphics2D)backBuffer.getGraphics();

        addMouseListener(this);
        mouseProcessor = new MouseProcessor(this);
    }

    public void start()
    {
        loop = new Thread(this);
        loop.start();
    }

    public void stop()
    {
        loop = null;
    }

    public void run()
    {
        long startTime, waitTime, elapsedTime;
        // 1000/25 Frames Per Second = 40 millisecond delay
        int delayTime = 1000/25;

        Thread thisThread = Thread.currentThread();
        while(loop==thisThread)
        {
            startTime = System.currentTimeMillis();

            // handle mouse events in main loop
            mouseProcessor.processMouseEventList();
            mouseProcessor.processMouseMotionEventList(); // not used
```

```java
            // handle logic
            animator.animate();

            // render to back buffer
            render(bbGraphics);

            // render to screen
            Graphics g = getGraphics();
            g.drawImage(backBuffer, 0, 0, null);
            g.dispose();

            // handle frame rate
            elapsedTime = System.currentTimeMillis() - startTime;
            waitTime = Math.max(delayTime - elapsedTime, 5);

            try
            {
                Thread.sleep(waitTime);
            }
            catch(InterruptedException e) {}
        }
    }

    public void render(Graphics g)
    {
        animator.render(g);
    }

    public void mousePressed(MouseEvent e)
    {
        System.out.println("Mouse Pressed");

        mouseProcessor.addMouseEvent(e);
    }

    // not used
    public void mouseReleased(MouseEvent e) {}
    public void mouseClicked(MouseEvent e)  {}
    public void mouseEntered(MouseEvent e)  {}
    public void mouseExited(MouseEvent e)   {}


    public void handleMouseEvent(MouseEvent e)
    {
        if(e.getID()==MouseEvent.MOUSE_PRESSED)
        {
            System.out.println("Mouse Press Handled");

            if(animator.hotSpot==null)
                animator.createHotSpot();
            else
                animator.hotSpot = null;
        }
    }

    private Animator animator;
    private Thread loop;
    private BufferedImage backBuffer;
    private Graphics2D bbGraphics;
    private MouseProcessor mouseProcessor;
```

```
    private static final int DISPLAY_WIDTH = 400;
    private static final int DISPLAY_HEIGHT = 400;
}
```

The vast majority of the main class `AdvancedMouse` should already be familiar to you, as we have already looked at creating a similar main game loop in the previous chapter. The main class `AdvancedMouse` implements both the `MouseListener` and the `MouseProcessable` interfaces. This means that this class provides methods for receiving the information on the mouse event from the Event Dispatch Thread, notably through the `mousePressed` method in this example, and provides the method `handleMouseEvent` for handling those events in the main loop thread through a call to the method `processMouseEventList` of the `MouseProcessor` object. It all begins in the `mousePressed` method, where we add a mouse press event to the mouse event list in the mouse processor.

```
public void mousePressed(MouseEvent e)
{
    System.out.println("Mouse Pressed");

    mouseProcessor.addMouseEvent(e);
}
```

Here we simply pass the `MouseEvent` object to the `addMouseEvent` method of the `mouseProcessor` object. The main class `Advanced-Mouse` itself implements the `MouseProcessable` interface and is used to handle the mouse event through its method `handleMouseEvent`. This was defined in the `init` method of `AdvancedMouse` with the following line of code:

```
mouseProcessor = new MouseProcessor(this);
```

Here we tell the `mouseProcessor` object that we want `Advanced-Mouse` to handle the mouse events.

When the `MouseProcessor` method `processMouseEventList` is next invoked in the main loop, any events in the queue will be processed one at a time in the order they were read.

```
mouseProcessor.processMouseEventList();
```

A call to this method means that each object stored in the mouse event list of the mouse processor will then be handled and removed from the list until the list is empty. Hence the list is checked and emptied at every cycle of the main loop.

```
public void processMouseEventList()
{
    MouseEvent event;

    while(mouseEventList.size() > 0)
    {
        synchronized(mouseEventList)
        {
            event = (MouseEvent) mouseEventList.removeFirst();
        }
```

```
        handler.handleMouseEvent(event);
    }
}
```

The handler object, of type `MouseProcessable`, that we originally passed in the constructor, is then used where its `handleMouseEvent` method is called. The handler object in this example is the instance of the main class `AdvancedMouse`.

```
public void handleMouseEvent(MouseEvent e)
    {
        if(e.getID()==MouseEvent.MOUSE_PRESSED)
        {
            System.out.println("Mouse Press Handled");

            if(animator.hotSpot==null)
                animator.createHotSpot();
            else
                animator.hotSpot = null;
        }
    }
```

In this example, we handle the event if it is a mouse pressed event, which is not exactly necessary because we only add events of this type to the `mouseProcessor` list anyway, but I have left this in to illustrate differentiating between different types of mouse events being handled.

When you compile and run the `AdvancedMouse` example, you should get output similar to Figure 10-3. In this screen shot, we have clicked on the applet four times. As you can see in the console window, the text "Mouse Pressed" is followed by "Mouse Press Handled." The first text output is printed when the event is first received. The second text output indicates when the event is handled safely in the main loop thread.

A good thing to take a look at in this example is to set the variable `delayTime` in the `run` method of `AdvancedMouse` to a longer period of time than just a few milliseconds—try 1000 milliseconds (1 second) for example. When you do this, run the applet and click on the applet with the mouse quickly a number of times. You should see that your mouse events are accepted first and added to the mouse processor, and then all of these mouse events are processed when the next main loop cycle comes around again, showing the effect of adding and handling the events in the main loop more obviously.

In this example we do not actually listen for any mouse motion events (moving or dragging), but we have left this in to illustrate how you would call this. We now have our mouse events completely synchronized with the main loop thread. When a mouse button is pressed and processed in the main loop, we remove the reference to the current `HotSpot` object and then create a new `HotSpot` with which to replace it (with a further mouse button press). Synchronization problems highlighted earlier in this section no longer apply, as the event handling code is executed in synch with the rest of the code in the main loop.

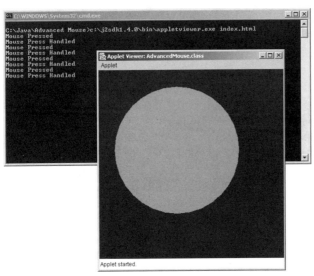

Figure 10-3

If you want to see an example of our code failing because we have failed to synchronize the mouse event handling with a part of the main loop code, try the following:

■ In the `animate` method of the `Animator` class, just after the check to see if the hotspot reference is not equal to null, add a `Thread.sleep(1000)` call. You will need to try/catch an `InterruptedException` exception for this.)

■ In the `mousePressed` method of the `AdvancedMouse` class, replace all of the code with an immediate call to the `handle-MouseEvent` method, passing the mouse event to it as a parameter.

■ Compile and run the applet and continue to click on the applet. After a few lucky clicks, you should get an unlucky one that throws a `NullPointerException` exception. The `Thread.sleep(1000)` call is placed immediately after the `(hotSpot!=null)` check to increase the likeliness that a mouse event will be handled at this stage, where we still believe that `hotSpot!=null`. This scenario was explained at the start of this section.

Handling Repetitive Key Input

When talking about repetitive key input, we refer to the event of holding down a key and moving an object while the key is held down. Then when the key is released, the object will stop moving. Omitting the synchronization problems highlighted in the last section for the time being, you may be thinking of handling repetitive key input as follows:

```
public void keyPressed(KeyEvent e)
{
    switch(e.getKeyCode())
    {
        case KeyEvent.VK_LEFT:
```

```
            player1.moveLeft();
            break;
      case KeyEvent.VK_RIGHT:
            player1.moveRight();
            break;
   }
}
```

In order to understand why this is a problem, you need to understand how key events are read into your program. Imagine when using Microsoft Word, the text editor has focus and you hold down the letter s on the keyboard. What happens? Well, an initial s will be displayed followed by a sufficient pause. This pause is designed to allow for time to let go of the key if repetitive input is not wanted. If this pause is passed and the s key is still held down, then s key press events will be dispatched one at a time with an even shorter delay between them. When you hold a key down, an initial key event is passed to the `keyPressed` method, and then, if the key is still down after a short delay, more key pressed events are passed, separated by shorter intervals. This is not suitable for continuously moving objects at a constant rate; if you use this method to move your objects, their movement will not be fluid, but they will move at the pace of the key pressed events, with pauses in between.

You need to record the state of your keys. If the key has been pressed, that is, read by an event received in the `keyPressed` method, store the fact that the key is currently held down in a variable (Boolean is suitable). When the key is no longer down, that is, read by an event received in the `keyReleased` method, store in your state variable that the key has been released. In your main loop, you can move your object if the state variable says that the key is currently being held down. Simple.

In the following example, `AdvancedKeyboard`, we handle repetitive key input to move a circle around the screen. Here we also create a `KeyProcessor` and its associated `KeyProcessable` interface. Although it is not essential in this example that our key events are synchronized with the main loop, we have added a `KeyProcessor` class into this example anyway. You may find situations such as these where events do not need to be handled in synch with the main loop, but for some, as we have seen earlier in this chapter, it is essential.

The `AdvancedKeyboard` example contains three classes to go with the `KeyProcessor` and `KeyProcessable` interfaces. They are `AdvancedKeyboard` (main class), `Animator`, and `HotSpot`. The `HotSpot` class used is exactly the same as the one we defined in Chapter 9, so you will need to get the source code for it from there. The `Animator` class we are using in this example is implemented a little differently from the one we have been using so far. In this `Animator` class, we handle key events and move the `hotSpot` object about the applet, depending on the state of the cursor keys Up, Down, Left, and Right. Let's take a look at the code for the remaining four source files (`KeyProcessable`, `KeyProcessor`, `Animator`, and `AdvancedKeyboard`) for this example (to be compiled with the `HotSpot` class).

Code Listing 10-5: `KeyProcessable`

```java
import java.awt.event.*;

public interface KeyProcessable
{
    public void handleKeyEvent(KeyEvent e);
}
```

Code Listing 10-6: `KeyProcessor`

```java
import java.awt.event.*;
import java.util.*;

public class KeyProcessor
{
    public KeyProcessor(KeyProcessable handler)
    {
        keyEventList = new LinkedList();
        this.handler = handler;
    }

    public void addEvent(KeyEvent event)
    {
        synchronized(keyEventList)
        {
            keyEventList.add(event);
        }
    }

    public void processKeyEventList()
    {
        KeyEvent event;

        while(keyEventList.size()>0)
        {
            synchronized(keyEventList)
            {
                event = (KeyEvent)keyEventList.removeFirst();
            }
            handler.handleKeyEvent(event);
        }
    }

    private LinkedList keyEventList;
    private KeyProcessable handler;
}
```

The `KeyProcessor` class is implemented in exactly the same way as the `MouseProcessor` class in the previous section of this chapter, though this time we only require one event list for key events alone, whereas the `MouseProcessor` class provided separate lists for mouse events and mouse motion events. However, in this example, we will use it a little differently, by applying the animator object to handle key events, as we shall see.

Code Listing 10-7: `Animator`

```java
import java.awt.*;
import java.util.*;
```

Chapter 10

```java
import java.awt.event.*;

public class Animator implements KeyProcessable
{
    public Animator(Rectangle bounds)
    {
        this.bounds = bounds;
        keyState = new boolean[256];

        createHotSpot();

        speedX = 4;
        speedY = 4;
    }


    public void createHotSpot()
    {
        Random rand = new Random();

        int diameter = 100+rand.nextInt(200);
        Color col = new Color(rand.nextInt(Integer.MAX_VALUE));

        int xPos = (bounds.width-diameter)/2; // center x
        int yPos = (bounds.height-diameter)/2; // center y

        hotSpot = new HotSpot(new Point(xPos, yPos), diameter, col);
    }


    public void animate()
    {
        if(keyState[KeyEvent.VK_LEFT] &&
            !keyState[KeyEvent.VK_RIGHT])
            moveLeft();
        else if(keyState[KeyEvent.VK_RIGHT] &&
            !keyState[KeyEvent.VK_LEFT])
            moveRight();

        if(keyState[KeyEvent.VK_UP] && !keyState[KeyEvent.VK_DOWN])
            moveUp();
        else if(keyState[KeyEvent.VK_DOWN] &&
            !keyState[KeyEvent.VK_UP])
            moveDown();
    }


    public void moveLeft()
    {
        hotSpot.bounds.x-=speedX;
        if(hotSpot.bounds.x<0)
            hotSpot.bounds.x = 0;
    }

    public void moveRight()
    {
        hotSpot.bounds.x+=speedX;
        if(hotSpot.bounds.x+hotSpot.bounds.width > bounds.width)
            hotSpot.bounds.x = bounds.width-hotSpot.bounds.width;
```

```
    }

    public void moveUp()
    {
        hotSpot.bounds.y-=speedY;
        if(hotSpot.bounds.y<0)
            hotSpot.bounds.y = 0;
    }

    public void moveDown()
    {
        hotSpot.bounds.y+=speedY;
        if(hotSpot.bounds.y+hotSpot.bounds.height > bounds.height)
            hotSpot.bounds.y = bounds.height-hotSpot.bounds.height;
    }

    public void render(Graphics g)
    {
        g.translate(bounds.x, bounds.y);

        g.setColor(Color.blue);
        g.fillRect(0, 0, bounds.width, bounds.height);

        hotSpot.render(g);

        g.translate(-bounds.x, -bounds.y);
    }

    public void handleKeyEvent(KeyEvent e)
    {
        switch(e.getID())
        {
            case KeyEvent.KEY_PRESSED:
                keyState[e.getKeyCode()] = true;
                break;
            case KeyEvent.KEY_RELEASED:
                keyState[e.getKeyCode()] = false;
                break;
        }
    }

    public int speedX;
    public int speedY;

    public HotSpot hotSpot;
    public Rectangle bounds;

    public boolean[] keyState;
}
```

This `Animator` class is similar to the one created for the Advanced-
Mouse example in that it is used as a canvas for rendering our display and
also contains a `HotSpot` object. However, this `Animator` class has an
array of type `boolean` and length `256` called `keyState`. This array is
used to store the current state of all of the keys on the keyboard. The key

codes of the keys read in map to values in the range from 0 to 255, which means we are able to set them straight into an array using this value and then test these states using the virtual key codes, such as `KeyEvent.VK _LEFT` for example.

The method `handleKeyEvent` in this class is invoked via the `processKeyEventList` method of the `keyProcessor` object in the main loop thread. When this is invoked, we simply update the state of our keys based on the type of key event received (key pressed or key released). The `animate` method of this class is called in the main loop thread repeatedly in `AdvancedKeyboard` (as we shall see in moment) where the `HotSpot` object is moved accordingly, based on the state set in the `keyState` array for the respective direction keys. This gives us a fluid repetitive movement (well, at least as fluid as the main loop runs, of course). We will discuss important truths about timing and animation in Chapter 12, "Game Programming Techniques." Here is the code for `AdvancedKeyboard.java`.

Code Listing 10-8: `AdvancedKeyboard.java`

```
import java.awt.*;
import java.awt.image.*;
import javax.swing.*;
import java.awt.event.*;


public class AdvancedKeyboard extends JApplet
                    implements Runnable, KeyListener
{
    public void init()
    {
        getContentPane().setLayout(null);
        setSize(DISPLAY_WIDTH, DISPLAY_HEIGHT);
        setIgnoreRepaint(true);

        animator = new Animator(new Rectangle(0, 0, DISPLAY_WIDTH,
            DISPLAY_HEIGHT));

        backBuffer = new BufferedImage(DISPLAY_WIDTH, DISPLAY_HEIGHT,
            BufferedImage.TYPE_INT_RGB);
        bbGraphics = (Graphics2D)backBuffer.getGraphics();

        addKeyListener(this);
        keyProcessor = new KeyProcessor(animator);
    }

    public void start()
    {
        requestFocus();
        loop = new Thread(this);
        loop.start();
    }

    public void stop()
    {
        loop = null;
    }
```

```
public void run()
{
    long startTime, waitTime, elapsedTime;
    // 1000/25 Frames Per Second = 40 millisecond delay
    int delayTime = 1000/25;

    Thread thisThread = Thread.currentThread();
    while(loop==thisThread)
    {
        startTime = System.currentTimeMillis();

        // handle mouse events in main loop
        keyProcessor.processKeyEventList();

        // handle logic
        animator.animate();

        // render to back buffer
        render(bbGraphics);

        // render to screen
        Graphics g = getGraphics();
        g.drawImage(backBuffer, 0, 0, null);
        g.dispose();

        // handle frame rate
        elapsedTime = System.currentTimeMillis() - startTime;
        waitTime = Math.max(delayTime - elapsedTime, 5);

        try
        {
            Thread.sleep(waitTime);
        }
        catch(InterruptedException e) {}
    }
}

public void render(Graphics g)
{
    animator.render(g);
}

public void keyPressed(KeyEvent e)
{
    keyProcessor.addEvent(e);
}

public void keyReleased(KeyEvent e)
{
    keyProcessor.addEvent(e);
}

public void keyTyped(KeyEvent e)  {}


private Animator animator;
private Thread loop;
private BufferedImage backBuffer;
private Graphics2D bbGraphics;
```

Chapter 10

```
    private KeyProcessor keyProcessor;

    private static final int DISPLAY_WIDTH = 400;
    private static final int DISPLAY_HEIGHT = 400;
}
```

When you run the example, you should get output similar to the following figure, which is a circle object that can be moved smoothly about the viewing area.

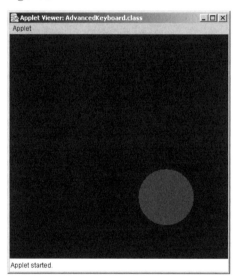

Figure 10-4

This time we implement and add the key listener to AdvancedKeyboard itself. This illustrates the complete reusability of the KeyProcessor, as we use this class to receive key event information, but tell the keyProcessor object to handle the key events using the animator object, since the animator object implements KeyProcessable. This can be seen in the constructor of the AdvancedKeyboard class, where we pass a reference to the Animator instance when creating the keyProcessor object. This means that when we make a call to the keyProcessor.processKeyEventList method in the main loop thread, the events are processed in the handleKeyEvents method implemented in the animator object.

An All-Purpose Event Queue

What we have so far is a number of event lists, with each list containing a certain type of event (e.g., a list for key events, a list for mouse events, etc.). When these events are handled in the main loop thread, the lists are processed individually (i.e., we may first process all of the key events that were added to the key event list within the last main loop cycle and then process all of the mouse events). With this system, the order of events can get mixed up (say, if two key events come in, perhaps key pressed followed by key released, and a mouse press event in between them within one main loop cycle). With separate event lists, the two key events will be processed first and then finally the mouse event, when in reality that wasn't their order. However, it's important to note that your main loop will probably run at a superior rate to the possibilities of the user, creating a mixture of events in this fashion, all generated within the same main loop cycle. But synchronization issues, however small, can arise if the code can find a way through the cracks. For this, we propose an all-around event processor that takes in all events in which you are interested, as and when they are received, and handles them in that order from the main loop.

The class java.awt.AWTEvent is the root class of all AWT events, such as MouseEvent, KeyEvent, and FocusEvent (which we'll look at later), so for the all-around event processor we can cast all events to this type for handling. The following two source listings show the code for an event processor that works just like the MouseProcessor and KeyProcessor we made earlier in this chapter. Here is the code for the interface EventProcessable and the class EventProcessor.

Code Listing 10-9: EventProcessable

```
import java.awt.*;

public interface EventProcessable
{
    public void handleEvent(AWTEvent e);
}
```

Code Listing 10-10: EventProcessor

```
import java.awt.*;
import java.util.*;

public class EventProcessor
{
    public EventProcessor(EventProcessable handler)
    {
        eventList = new LinkedList();
        this.handler = handler;
    }

    public void addEvent(AWTEvent event)
    {
        synchronized(eventList)
        {
            eventList.add(event);
        }
    }

    public void processEventList()
    {
        AWTEvent event;

        while(eventList.size() > 0)
        {
            synchronized(eventList)
```

```
        {
            event = (AWTEvent) eventList.removeFirst();
        }

        handler.handleEvent(event);
    }
}

private LinkedList eventList;
private EventProcessable handler;
}
```

Using the same techniques that we learned in the earlier examples, the
`handleEvent` method when set up properly could then be defined as follows, provided, for this example, that we have added a mouse listener and
a key listener for the process.

```
public void handleEvent(AWTEvent e)
    {
        switch(e.getID())
        {
            case KeyEvent.KEY_PRESSED:
                System.out.println("Key Pressed");
                break;
            case KeyEvent.KEY_RELEASED:
                System.out.println("Key Released");
                break;
            case MouseEvent.MOUSE_PRESSED:
                System.out.println("Mouse Pressed");
                break;
        }
    }
```

So with this system, we deal with events in the order that Java sends
them in our main loop. We will now implement this new system and look
at handling the loss and gain of focus along the way.

Losing Focus

In order for a component to deal with keyboard events, it must have focus.
A good example of focus is filling in forms using a web browser. Imagine
that you're filling out a form that requires your name in one text field and
your e-mail address in the next; you click on the Name text field and the
cursor (that flashy line thing where the text outputs goes) appears, and
you have given the text field focus. By then pressing the Tab key, you
would probably transfer the keyboard focus to the E-mail text field. In Java
a component can have the focus, such as a window or applet or a button or
text field component. We are interested simply in the focus of the main
component, the applet or the window for applications. For this, we can
attach a focus listener, defined by the interface `java.awt.event.Fo-
cusListener` (or if you prefer using an adapter class instead—
`java.awt.event.FocusAdapter`). Again, these work in the same
way as key and mouse listeners.

It is important to handle whether the focus is lost for a number of reasons. In the most basic sense, you might want to alert the player that the focus has been lost; this is most notable in an applet where the focus can be transferred quite easily from your applet to other elements of the browser, such as the address bar or another window altogether. When the focus is lost, you may also want to pause the game and need to handle special cases along the way. One notable case is a problem that can occur with the key states in the previous `AdvancedKeyboard` example. Let's say that you hold down the left key, causing the `HotSpot` object to move to the left. You then click away from the applet (for example, to elsewhere in the browser), causing the applet to lose focus. Then you let go of the key. Because the applet no longer has focus, the key released event for the left key will not be sent to your applet when you let go of it. This means that the `HotSpot` object will continue to move leftward because no `keyReleased` method has come in to tell it to do otherwise—to reset our `keyState` flag value. So the main loop continues to move the `HotSpot` because it still has the key state for the left key as being held down. You can try this out by running the previous example, `AdvancedKeyboard`, and performing the aforementioned routine yourself. You should see the `HotSpot` continue moving in the given direction even when you release the given key.

The following example is a fix of the previous `AdvancedKeyboard` example, this time using the event processor system and handling the loss of the keyboard focus. For this example, we use five source files. To begin with, you need to grab the `HotSpot` class again and get the source for `EventProcessor` and `EventProcessable` from which we defined the source code earlier. All that is left for us to create is a slightly different `Animator` class and the main class `EventAndFocusHandling`.

To begin with, let's take a look at the new `Animator` class. This time, the `Animator` will not handle key events itself straight from an event list but will provide some methods to be called from the main class `EventAndFocusHandling`, which will itself handle all events from the event processor pump. Here is the code for the new `Animator` class:

Code Listing 10-11: `Animator.java`

```java
import java.awt.*;
import java.util.*;
import java.awt.event.*;

public class Animator
{
    public Animator(Rectangle bounds)
    {
        this.bounds = bounds;
        keyState = new boolean[256];

        createHotSpot();

        speedX = 4;
        speedY = 4;
```

```
    }


    public void createHotSpot()
    {
        Random rand = new Random();

        int diameter = 100+rand.nextInt(200);
        Color col = new Color(rand.nextInt(Integer.MAX_VALUE));

        int xPos = (bounds.width-diameter)/2;   // center x
        int yPos = (bounds.height-diameter)/2;  // center y

        hotSpot = new HotSpot(new Point(xPos, yPos), diameter, col);
    }


    public void animate()
    {
        if(keyState[KeyEvent.VK_LEFT] &&
            !keyState[KeyEvent.VK_RIGHT])
            moveLeft();
        else if(keyState[KeyEvent.VK_RIGHT] &&
            !keyState[KeyEvent.VK_LEFT])
            moveRight();

        if(keyState[KeyEvent.VK_UP] && !keyState[KeyEvent.VK_DOWN])
            moveUp();
        else if(keyState[KeyEvent.VK_DOWN] &&
            !keyState[KeyEvent.VK_UP])
            moveDown();
    }


    public void moveLeft()
    {
        hotSpot.bounds.x-=speedX;
        if(hotSpot.bounds.x<0)
            hotSpot.bounds.x = 0;
    }


    public void moveRight()
    {
        hotSpot.bounds.x+=speedX;
        if(hotSpot.bounds.x+hotSpot.bounds.width > bounds.width)
            hotSpot.bounds.x = bounds.width-hotSpot.bounds.width;
    }


    public void moveUp()
    {
        hotSpot.bounds.y-=speedY;
        if(hotSpot.bounds.y<0)
            hotSpot.bounds.y = 0;
    }


    public void moveDown()
    {
```

```
        hotSpot.bounds.y+=speedY;
        if(hotSpot.bounds.y+hotSpot.bounds.height > bounds.height)
            hotSpot.bounds.y = bounds.height-hotSpot.bounds.height;
    }


    public void render(Graphics g)
    {
        g.translate(bounds.x, bounds.y);

        g.setColor(Color.blue);
        g.fillRect(0, 0, bounds.width, bounds.height);

        hotSpot.render(g);

        g.translate(-bounds.x, -bounds.y);
    }


    public void handleKeyPressed(KeyEvent e)
    {
        keyState[((KeyEvent)e).getKeyCode()] = true;
    }

    public void handleKeyReleased(KeyEvent e)
    {
        keyState[((KeyEvent)e).getKeyCode()] = false;
    }

    public void resetAllKeyStates()
    {
        Arrays.fill(keyState, false);
    }


    public int speedX;
    public int speedY;

    public HotSpot hotSpot;
    public Rectangle bounds;

    public boolean[] keyState;
}
```

This time, as you can see, the `Animator` class no longer handles events straight from an event list processor but defines the methods `handleKeyPressed`, `handleKeyReleased`, and `resetAllKeyStates` instead to handle input. The idea is that events will be fed to the `Animator` object from an all-purpose event pump handled in the main class `EventAndFocusHandling`, as we will now see. Here is the source code for the main class `EventAndFocusHandling`.

Code Listing 10-12: `EventAndFocusHandling.java`

```java
import java.awt.*;
import java.awt.image.*;
import javax.swing.*;
import java.awt.event.*;
```

```java
public class EventAndFocusHandling extends JApplet
                    implements Runnable, KeyListener,
                    MouseListener, FocusListener, EventProcessable
{
    public void init()
    {
        getContentPane().setLayout(null);
        setSize(DISPLAY_WIDTH, DISPLAY_HEIGHT);
        setIgnoreRepaint(true);

        animator = new Animator(new Rectangle(0, 0, DISPLAY_WIDTH,
            DISPLAY_HEIGHT));

        backBuffer = new BufferedImage(DISPLAY_WIDTH, DISPLAY_HEIGHT,
            BufferedImage.TYPE_INT_RGB);
        bbGraphics = (Graphics2D)backBuffer.getGraphics();

        eventProcessor = new EventProcessor(this);

        addKeyListener(this);
        addMouseListener(this);
        addFocusListener(this);
    }

    public void start()
    {
        isFocused = isFocusOwner();
        loop = new Thread(this);
        loop.start();
    }

    public void stop()
    {
        loop = null;
    }

    public void run()
    {
        long startTime, waitTime, elapsedTime;
        // 1000/25 Frames Per Second = 40 millisecond delay
        int delayTime = 1000/25;

        Thread thisThread = Thread.currentThread();
        while(loop==thisThread)
        {
            startTime = System.currentTimeMillis();

            // handle any events listened for, in main loop
            eventProcessor.processEventList();

            // handle logic
            animator.animate();

            // render to back buffer
            render(bbGraphics);

            // render to screen
            Graphics g = getGraphics();
            g.drawImage(backBuffer, 0, 0, null);
```

```
        g.dispose();

        // handle frame rate
        elapsedTime = System.currentTimeMillis() - startTime;
        waitTime = Math.max(delayTime - elapsedTime, 5);

        try
        {
            Thread.sleep(waitTime);
        }
        catch(InterruptedException e) {}
    }
}

public void render(Graphics g)
{
    if(isFocused)
        animator.render(g);
    else
        renderPauseScreen(g);
}


public void renderPauseScreen(Graphics g)
{
    g.setColor(Color.black);
    g.fillRect(0, 0, DISPLAY_WIDTH, DISPLAY_HEIGHT);
    g.setColor(Color.white);
    g.drawString("Game Paused: Click mouse on applet to
        continue", 60, 200);
}

public void handleFocusLost()
{
    isFocused = false;
    animator.resetAllKeyStates();
}

public void handleFocusGained()
{
    isFocused = true;
}


public void handleEvent(AWTEvent e)
{
    switch(e.getID())
    {
        case KeyEvent.KEY_PRESSED:
            System.out.println("Key Pressed");
            animator.handleKeyPressed((KeyEvent)e);
            break;
        case KeyEvent.KEY_RELEASED:
            System.out.println("Key Released");
            animator.handleKeyReleased((KeyEvent)e);
            break;
        case MouseEvent.MOUSE_PRESSED:
            System.out.println("Mouse Pressed");
            break;
        case FocusEvent.FOCUS_LOST:
```

```
                        System.out.println("Focus Lost");
                        handleFocusLost();
                        break;
                    case FocusEvent.FOCUS_GAINED:
                        System.out.println("Focus Gained");
                        handleFocusGained();
                        break;
            }
        }


    public void keyPressed(KeyEvent e) { eventProcessor
        .addEvent(e); }
    public void keyReleased(KeyEvent e) { eventProcessor
        .addEvent(e); }
    public void keyTyped(KeyEvent e)   {}       // not used

    public void focusGained(FocusEvent e) { eventProcessor
        .addEvent(e); }
    public void focusLost(FocusEvent e) { eventProcessor
        .addEvent(e); }

    public void mousePressed(MouseEvent e) { eventProcessor
        .addEvent(e); }
    public void mouseReleased(MouseEvent e) {} // not used
    public void mouseClicked(MouseEvent e) {}   // not used
    public void mouseEntered(MouseEvent e) {}  // not used
    public void mouseExited(MouseEvent e) {}    // not used


    private Animator animator;
    private Thread loop;
    private BufferedImage backBuffer;
    private Graphics2D bbGraphics;
    private EventProcessor eventProcessor;

    private boolean isFocused;

    private static final int DISPLAY_WIDTH = 400;
    private static final int DISPLAY_HEIGHT = 400;
}
```

To begin with, we first create the event processor and add the action listeners to the applet, with the following code added to the `init` method of the applet:

```
eventProcessor = new EventProcessor(this);

addKeyListener(this);
addMouseListener(this);
addFocusListener(this);
```

Notice also that our main class implements all of the associated listener interfaces and the `EventProcessable` interface, so this class will provide methods for both receiving and processing event messages.

The next thing to be aware of is in the `start` method of this class, where we have the following code:

```
isFocused = isFocusOwner();
```

We use the variable `isFocused` to hold the current state of focus—if we have the focus or not. In the `start` method, this is initialized from the applet component method `isFocusOwner`. Originally, we used the method `requestFocus` to ask for the focus, but this method cannot be trusted to transfer the focus to our applet component as it behaves differently on different platforms (where its action is said to be platform-dependent). So with this, we just set the focus to the current state so we know for certain if we have the focus or not, and then rely on focus listeners from there. If the applet is not focused to begin with, the user will be alerted of this fact as we show them a different screen (telling them to click on the applet to get focus back to the HotSpot screen). Many applets will start up with an introduction screen that requires the user to click on the applet to begin, which is really a hidden way of getting them to give the applet the focus.

The next thing to look at is the event listener methods and how they are implemented; take the following lines of code that can be found in the main applet class:

```java
public void keyPressed(KeyEvent e) { eventProcessor.addEvent(e); }

public void focusGained(FocusEvent e) { eventProcessor.addEvent(e); }
```

This is where our events come in from the Event Dispatch Thread, and we simply add them to the new "all-purpose" event processor. We could make the `EventProcessor` implement all of the event listeners itself and just add events straight into the event list itself, but that's only if we want all events of a given type (e.g., all mouse events, all mouse motion events, all key events, etc.) to be added and not just a selection of types. For example, here we only add key pressed and key released events but don't bother with key typed events, so we can select what needs to be processed ourselves, but there would be no harm in adding such functionality to the `EventProcessor` class also.

When the events are processed in the main loop, each event is handled in the `handleEvent` method defined by the `EventProcessable` interface that the main applet implements, adding itself to the `EventProcessor` object, `eventProcessor`, when it was creating in the applet's `init` method. Here is the `handleEvent` method:

```java
public void handleEvent(AWTEvent e)
    {
        switch(e.getID())
        {
            case KeyEvent.KEY_PRESSED:
                System.out.println("Key Pressed");
                animator.handleKeyPressed((KeyEvent)e);
                break;
            case KeyEvent.KEY_RELEASED:
                System.out.println("Key Released");
                animator.handleKeyReleased((KeyEvent)e);
                break;
            case MouseEvent.MOUSE_PRESSED:
                System.out.println("Mouse Pressed");
```

Chapter 10

```
                        break;
                case FocusEvent.FOCUS_LOST:
                    System.out.println("Focus Lost");
                    handleFocusLost();
                    break;
                case FocusEvent.FOCUS_GAINED:
                    System.out.println("Focus Gained");
                    handleFocusGained();
                    break;
        }
    }
```

As you can see, the key handling methods of the `animator` object are called appropriately. The methods `handleFocusLost` and `handle-FocusGained` are called when their respective focus events are sent to us. The method `handleFocusGained` simply sets the `isFocused` variable to `true`. However, we also need to handle the `keyStates` array of the `animator` object for the `handleFocusLost` method, as well as set the `isFocused` variable to `false`.

```
public void handleFocusLost()
{
    isFocused = false;
    animator.resetAllKeyStates();
}
```

This method, as seen in the `Animator` class, sets all elements of the `keyStates` array to `false`, so now we don't have the problem of the `HotSpot` object moving along its given vector when the applet loses focus and the key is released.

Changes for an Application

On the companion CD in the source directory for this chapter, we have also included the previous code in an application with one change that you need to be aware of. Apart from the obvious differences between applications and applets that we have looked at in previous chapters, there is the issue of the position of mouse events in a windowed application. When a mouse or mouse motion listener is added to the main `JFrame` object, the position of the mouse is registered in reference to the very top corner of the window, where the top leftmost pixel of its border appears and not at the top leftmost position of the displayable area. One way to handle this in our application would be to translate the mouse event's x and y position back by the left and top border insets before adding the event to the event processor, as follows:

```
public void mousePressed(MouseEvent e)
{
    e.translatePoint(-DISPLAY_X, -DISPLAY_Y);
    eventProcessor.addEvent(e);
}
```

This is going by our coding standard so far in this book of saving the border insets (left and top) to the variables `DISPLAY_X` and `DISPLAY_Y`, respectively, for a real-time rendering application.

We could also, however, simply add the mouse listeners to the content pane of the main `JFrame` instead of the `JFrame` itself.

```
// In JFrame constructor
getContentPane().addMouseListener(this);
```

This code is added to the extra example on the companion CD and gives us mouse events with coordinates relative to the displayable area within the window's borders.

 NOTE: When we close an application, we do this using the `WindowEvent` passed to the `windowClosing` method of a window listener. When this method is invoked, it is also not synchronized with the main loop thread, as it comes from the Event Dispatch Thread. However, in our examples, this doesn't really matter, as all we do is set the thread variable loop to `null`, which in turn causes the main game loop and program to terminate. You could quite easily add the `WindowEvent` to the event processor and handle it there if closing the window included some extra code that needed to be synchronized with the main loop. We can do this, as a `WindowEvent` is also derived from `AWTEvent`, like the other events such as `MouseEvent` and `KeyEvent`. You can also test the event's ID for handling against the static variable `WindowEvent.WINDOW_CLOSING`.

Where's My Tab Key?

Because the Tab key is used to transfer focus from one component to another, it is consumed by components interested in handling such a process and is therefore not passed on as a key event for us to then handle. We can stop this by calling the following method on our `JFrame` or `JApplet` objects, however, which will then allow Tab key events to reach us.

```
setFocusTraversalKeysEnabled(false);
```

Summary

In this chapter we have not only looked at how to use the mouse and keyboard at a basic level but have attacked the integration of their respective events within the main loop thread. This chapter not only should have allowed you to understand how mouse and keyboard events are read and used but also should have pushed your understanding of threads and synchronization up a notch or two. Now that we know how to display graphics and handle real-time input, and more importantly know how to handle these features in a main loop thread, we can now create a game framework to base our games upon, which we will look into in Chapter 12, "Game Programming Techniques." For now, however, we will take a look at implementing sound in Java.

Chapter 10

Using Sound and Music

"I don't know anything about music. In my line you don't have to."
—Elvis Presley

Introduction

Although sound in games has not reached the standards or importance of sound in film, sound still remains an element that should at least be included in every game. In this chapter, you will learn how to add both sound effects and MIDI music to your games in Java (for both applications and applets).

Supported Sound Formats

There are three supported sound formats in Java to date, as well as the MIDI music format, which we will discuss later in the chapter. The available sound formats can be seen in the following table:

File Extension	Description
.wav	This is the most common file format for Windows-based computers, although the Apple Mac also supports it.
.au (or .snd)	This format tends to be used mainly on Sun workstations and also on the Internet; however, it is only really useful for speech samples.
.aif	The AIFF (Audio Interchange File Format) is most commonly used on the Apple Mac.

Applet Simple Sound Example

Let's first look at the simplest example of how we can load a sound file into a Java applet and play it. After we have shown a similar example for a Java application, we will then take a look into the Java Sound API, which gives us much more control over our sounds and access to MIDI also. Here is the code for our example applet:

339

Code Listing 11-1: Loading and playing a sound in an applet

```java
import javax.swing.*;
import java.applet.*;
import java.net.*;


public class SimpleSoundApplet extends JApplet
{
    public void init()
    {
        // Attempt to load our 'siren.wav' file...
        try
        {
            theSound = getAudioClip(new URL(getDocumentBase(),
                "siren.wav"));
        }
        catch(MalformedURLException e)
        {
            System.out.println(e);
        }

        // Play the audio clip...
        theSound.play();
    }

    private AudioClip theSound;
}
```

To execute this example, we also need to create the following HTML file
in the directory in which we compile the applet in order to load it into the
web browser. Here is the listing for the HTML file that we require:

Code Listing 11-2: HTML for viewing the applet

```html
<html>
 <title>Simple Applet Sound</title>

 <body bgcolor="#FFFFFF">

  <p align="center">
   <b>
    Simple Sound Example
   </b>
  </p>

  <p align="center">
   <applet code="SimpleSoundApplet.class" width="100"
     height="100"></applet>
  </p>
</html>
```

When we view the HTML page that we have created, it will load our
applet and play the wav file siren.wav, which we specified in the code
(note that this file can be found on the companion CD-ROM). Note also
that when the sound is played, you will recognize it as the most annoying
sound ever made. When the applet loads, it will appear as a simple gray
square, as we have not declared anything to appear on it; all we have done
is play the sound. Here is how it looks in the web browser:

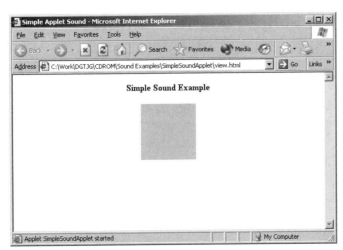

Figure 11-1:
Simple applet
sound
example

Let's now take a look at the code and see how it works. First we attempt to load our sound file using the following segment of code:

```
try
{
    theSound = getAudioClip(new URL(getDocumentBase(), "siren.wav"));
}
catch(MalformedURLException e)
{
    System.out.println(e);
}
```

As you can see, we call the `getAudioClip` method, which is a member of the `JApplet` class inherited from `java.applet.Applet`. The `getAudioClip` method takes a URL object as a parameter, which we create using the `getDocumentBase` method as the first parameter and then the actual filename of our audio clip as the second parameter. Note that we can use any of the three supported file types here. Note also that we need to catch a `MalformedURLException`, which catches an invalid URL (e.g., the file did not exist or could not be found).

Once our audio clip is loaded, we can then play it by calling its `play` method. This can be seen in the following line of code:

```
theSound.play();
```

Note also that the `AudioClip` class declares methods called `stop` and `loop`. The `stop` method simply stops the audio clip playback, and the `loop` method can be called instead of the `play` method to indefinitely loop the audio clip.

Chapter 11

Application Simple Sound Example

In this example, we will load and play the same sound, as we did in the previous example, but this time we are going to create an application instead of an applet. Let's look at the entire example source code now.

Code Listing 11-3: Loading and playing a sound in an application

```java
import java.applet.*;
import java.io.*;
import java.net.*;

public class SimpleSoundApplication
{
    public static void main(String args[])
    {
        File soundFile = new File("siren.wav");

        AudioClip theSound = null;
        try
        {
            theSound = Applet.newAudioClip(soundFile.toURL());
        }
        catch(MalformedURLException e)
        {
            System.out.println(e);
        }

        // Play the audio clip...
        theSound.play();
    }
}
```

When we execute the application, a console window will appear and the siren.wav sound sample will be played. Let's now look at how the code works.

First we load in the file by creating a new File object, passing the name of our wav file (siren.wav) into the constructor. This can be seen here:

```java
File soundFile = new File("siren.wav");
```

Next, we need to create an AudioClip object by passing a URL object into the constructor. As you know, we currently have a File object representing our sound, so we need to first convert this into a URL by calling the conveniently named toURL method of the File object. This can be seen here:

```java
AudioClip theSound = null;
try
{
    theSound = Applet.newAudioClip(soundFile.toURL());
}
catch(MalformedURLException e)
{
    System.out.println(e);
}
```

As you can see, we use the `newAudioClip` static method of the `Applet` class, which allows us to pass in a URL for the location of the sound. Using our file object, calling its `toURL` method, we create a new `Audio-Clip` object called `theSound`.

Once it is loaded, we then simply call the `play` method, as we did in the applet example. Note that we are still using the `AudioClip` class to store our sound, so the `loop` and `stop` methods are also available to us.

Using the Java Sound API

Playing Sampled Sound

The Java Sound API, introduced in the Java 1.3 release, gives us more control over our sound. As well as play sound samples as we did in the previous example, the Sound API also allows us to record audio, stream audio, and play MIDI music. Before we look at these useful features, let's first look at an example of using the Sound API (rather than the old method) to play a wav file in an application, as we did in the previous simple example.

Code Listing 11-4: Playing samples in the Java Sound API

```
import java.awt.event.*;
import javax.swing.*;
import java.io.*;
import javax.sound.sampled.*;      // Import the Sound API

public class SoundAPIApplication extends JFrame implements
    ActionListener
{
    public SoundAPIApplication()
    {
        super("Sound API Example");
        setDefaultCloseOperation(EXIT_ON_CLOSE);
        getContentPane().setLayout(null);
        setResizable(false);
        setBounds(0, 0, 306, 100);

        // Get the current directory...
        File soundFile = new File("siren.wav");

        // Attempt to load the sound file...
        try
        {
            AudioInputStream source = AudioSystem
                .getAudioInputStream(soundFile);
            DataLine.Info clipInfo = new DataLine.Info(Clip.class,
                source.getFormat());

            if(AudioSystem.isLineSupported(clipInfo))
            {
                theSound = (Clip) AudioSystem.getLine(clipInfo);
                theSound.open(source);
            }
            else
            {
```

```
                JOptionPane.showMessageDialog(null, "The Clip was not
                    supported", "Error", JOptionPane.ERROR_MESSAGE);
        }
    }
    catch(UnsupportedAudioFileException e)
    {
        System.out.println(e);
    }
    catch(LineUnavailableException e)
    {
        System.out.println(e);
    }
    catch(IOException e)
    {
        System.out.println(e);
    }

    // Set up the GUI...
    playButton = new JButton("Play");
    playButton.setBounds(0, 0, 100, 74);
    playButton.addActionListener(this);
    getContentPane().add(playButton);

    loopButton = new JButton("Loop");
    loopButton.setBounds(100, 0, 100, 74);
    loopButton.addActionListener(this);
    getContentPane().add(loopButton);

    stopButton = new JButton("Stop");
    stopButton.setBounds(200, 0, 100, 74);
    stopButton.addActionListener(this);
    getContentPane().add(stopButton);

    setVisible(true);
}

public void actionPerformed(ActionEvent e)
{
    if(e.getSource() == playButton)
    {
        if(theSound.isActive())
        {
            theSound.stop();
        }
        theSound.setFramePosition(0);
        theSound.loop(0);
    }
    else if(e.getSource() == loopButton)
    {
        if(theSound.isActive())
        {
            theSound.stop();
        }
        theSound.setFramePosition(0);
        theSound.loop(Clip.LOOP_CONTINUOUSLY);
    }
    else if(e.getSource() == stopButton)
    {
        theSound.stop();
        theSound.setFramePosition(0);
```

```
        }
    }

    public static void main(String args[])
    {
        SoundAPIApplication simpleSoundApplication = new
            SoundAPIApplication();
    }

    private Clip theSound;

    // GUI
    private JButton playButton;
    private JButton loopButton;
    private JButton stopButton;
}
```

In this example, we have added some GUI to allow us to control the sound from the application. Here is how the application looks when we compile and execute it:

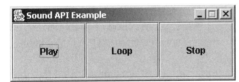

Figure 11-2:
Playing sampled sound example

When the Play button is pressed, the application checks to see if the sound is playing. If it is, it stops the sound, resets its position back to the start, and starts it playing again. The Loop button does the same, except it plays the sample on a loop indefinitely. Finally, the Stop button just stops the sample outright.

Let's now look at the code for this example in detail and see how it differs from the old method of adding sound in Java.

First we include the Sound API package with the following line of code:

```
import javax.sound.sampled.*;
```

Note that this package contains everything we need for sampled sounds (such as wav files). As we will see later, we require another package for playing MIDI music.

Next, we create a `File` object called `soundFile`, which holds the complete path to the sound sample we wish to load (which in this case is in the same directory as the code and is called `siren.wav`). Here is the line of code we require to do this:

```
File soundFile = new File("siren.wav");
```

Once we have the complete path to our file, we then have to enter a `try/catch` block, as the Sound API code will throw various exceptions that we need to catch if thrown. Once in our `try` block, we can then attempt to get an `AudioInputStream` by calling the `getAudio-InputStream` static method of the `AudioSystem` class. Note that we pass the complete file path `soundFile` into the method's constructor. This can be seen in the following code segment:

```
try
{
    AudioInputStream source = AudioSystem
        .getAudioInputStream(soundFile);
```

Once we have our `AudioInputStream` created, we then create an `Info` object, which is a subclass of the `DataLine` class. We create this object by creating an instance of the `Info` subclass, passing the class described by the `Info` object, as well as the audio format of the file we have loaded (note that this is retrieved by the `getSource` method of the `AudioInputStream` class). This can be seen in the following line of code:

```
DataLine.Info clipInfo = new DataLine.Info(Clip.class,
    source.getFormat());
```

Next we need to check if the audio format (line) is supported by the operating system. This is accomplished by checking if the line is supported, which is implemented with the following line of code:

```
if(AudioSystem.isLineSupported(clipInfo))
```

Note that `isLineSupported` is a static method of the `AudioSystem` class and that we pass in our `clipInfo` variable, which is of type `DataLine.Info`.

So, if the audio format is supported, then we can get a `Clip` object from the line and then open our `source`. We can then use the clip to manipulate our audio sample. This is done with the following two lines of code:

```
theSound = (Clip) AudioSystem.getLine(clipInfo);
theSound.open(source);
```

Note that if the audio line was not supported, we simply display an error dialog to the user with the following line of code:

```
JOptionPane.showMessageDialog(null, "The Clip was not supported",
    "Error", JOptionPane.ERROR_MESSAGE);
```

The final part of our loading is to catch the three possible exceptions that can be thrown. They are `UnsupportedAudioFileException`, `LineUnavailableException`, and `IOException`.

Next, we add three GUI buttons to allow us to manipulate the sound from within the application. Note that the application implements the `ActionListener` interface, so we can handle the user clicking on the buttons (we will see more on the GUI in Chapter 13). Here is the code we use to add our buttons to the application:

```
playButton = new JButton("Play");
playButton.setBounds(0, 0, 100, 74);
playButton.addActionListener(this);
getContentPane().add(playButton);

loopButton = new JButton("Loop");
loopButton.setBounds(100, 0, 100, 74);
loopButton.addActionListener(this);
getContentPane().add(loopButton);
```

```
stopButton = new JButton("Stop");
stopButton.setBounds(200, 0, 100, 74);
stopButton.addActionListener(this);
getContentPane().add(stopButton);
```

Let's now look at the code that we have added within the `actionPer-formed` method for the Play, Loop, and Stop buttons.

- Play Button

```
if(theSound.isActive())
{
    theSound.stop();
}
theSound.setFramePosition(0);
theSound.loop(0);
```

For the Play button, we first check if our sound is active and if so, we stop the sound from playing by calling the `stop` method. Then we set the position of the sound to the start by calling `setFramePosition` with 0 as the argument, which represents the start of the sample. Then we finally call the `loop` method with 0 as the argument, meaning it will only play the sound once.

- Loop Button

```
if(theSound.isActive())
{
    theSound.stop();
}
theSound.setFramePosition(0);
theSound.loop(Clip.LOOP_CONTINUOUSLY);
```

For the Loop button, we again check if our sound is active and if so, we stop the sample from playing. Then we set the position of the sample back to the start by calling the `setFramePosition` method. Finally, we call the loop, but this time we specify the constant `Clip.LOOP_CONTIN-UOUSLY`, which does what it says—makes the sample play in a loop indefinitely.

- Stop Button

```
theSound.stop();
theSound.setFramePosition(0);
```

For the Stop button, we simply stop the sample from playing and reset the sample's position back to the start by calling the `setFramePosition` method.

Streaming Audio

One major problem with playing sampled audio is the size of the file that you are trying to play. If, for example, you have a 100 MB wav file (in our previous examples), it would load the entire 100 MB file into RAM and then begin playing, which as you can guess is not ideal.

In this section, we will learn a better way to handle larger audio data by only reading and playing sections of the file at one time, rather than loading the whole file into memory. This is a technique known as *streaming*.

Let's now look at an example similar to the previous example, except this time we will use streaming audio.

Code Listing 11-5: Streaming audio

```
import java.awt.event.*;
import javax.swing.*;
import java.io.*;
import javax.sound.sampled.*;      // Import the Sound API


public class StreamingSoundExample extends JFrame implements
    ActionListener, Runnable
{
    public StreamingSoundExample()
    {
        super("Streaming Example");
        setDefaultCloseOperation(EXIT_ON_CLOSE);
        getContentPane().setLayout(null);
        setResizable(false);
        setBounds(0, 0, 209, 97);

        // Get the current directory...
        File soundFile = new File("ambience.wav");

        // Attempt to load the sound file...
        try
        {
            audioInputStream = AudioSystem.getAudioInputStream
                (soundFile);

            if(audioInputStream.markSupported())
            {
                audioInputStream.mark(Integer.MAX_VALUE);
            }

            AudioFormat format = audioInputStream.getFormat();
            DataLine.Info audioInputStreamInfo = new
                DataLine.Info(SourceDataLine.class, format);

            if(AudioSystem.isLineSupported(audioInputStreamInfo))
            {
                sourceDataLine = (SourceDataLine)
                    AudioSystem.getLine(audioInputStreamInfo);
                bufferSize = (int) (format.getFrameSize()*format
                    .getFrameRate()/2.0f);
                System.out.println("Set Buffer Size to: " +
                    bufferSize);
                sourceDataLine.open(format, bufferSize);
                soundData = new byte[bufferSize];
            }

        }
        catch(UnsupportedAudioFileException e)
        {
            System.out.println(e);
```

```
    }
    catch(LineUnavailableException e)
    {
        System.out.println(e);
    }
    catch(IOException e)
    {
        System.out.println(e);
    }

    // Set up the GUI...
    playButton = new JButton("Play");
    playButton.setBounds(0, 0, 100, 70);
    playButton.addActionListener(this);
    getContentPane().add(playButton);


    stopButton = new JButton("Stop");
    stopButton.setBounds(100, 0, 100, 70);
    stopButton.addActionListener(this);
    getContentPane().add(stopButton);

    setVisible(true);
}

public void actionPerformed(ActionEvent e)
{
    if(e.getSource() == playButton)
    {
        startStreaming();
    }
    else if(e.getSource() == stopButton)
    {
        stopStreaming();
    }
}


public void startStreaming()
{
    if(sourceDataLine == null)
    {
        JOptionPane.showMessageDialog(null, "The line is not
            available", "ERROR", JOptionPane.ERROR_MESSAGE);
        return;
    }
    thread = new Thread(this);
    sampleStreaming = true;
    thread.start();
}


public void stopStreaming()
{
    sampleStreaming = false;
}


public void run()
```

```
{
    sourceDataLine.start();
    int readBytes = 0;
    try
    {
        while(sampleStreaming)
        {
            readBytes = audioInputStream.read(soundData, 0,
                soundData.length);

            if(readBytes == -1)
            {
                if(audioInputStream.markSupported())
                    audioInputStream.reset();
                sourceDataLine.drain();
                sampleStreaming = false;
                break;
            }
            sourceDataLine.write(soundData, 0, readBytes);
        }
    }
    catch(IOException e)
    {
        System.err.println(e);
    }
    sourceDataLine.stop();
}

public static void main(String args[])
{
    StreamingSoundExample simpleSoundApplication = new
        StreamingSoundExample();
}

private int bufferSize;
private byte soundData[];
AudioInputStream audioInputStream;
SourceDataLine      sourceDataLine;
Thread thread;

// GUI
private JButton playButton;
private JButton stopButton;
boolean sampleStreaming = false;
}
```

When we execute the streaming audio example, we can see that it looks like the following figure:

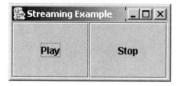

Figure 11-3:
Streaming audio example

As well as the application window, you will also notice that in the console window we have output the buffer size that was allocated by the application to allow it to stream the sound correctly.

Let's now look at the code to see how we implemented the streaming audio.

First we create a `File` object based upon the current directory and the name of the wav file we wish to read. This can be seen in the following line of code:

```
File soundFile = new File("ambience.wav");
```

After we have created our `File` object, we then pass it as an argument to the static `getAudioInputStream` method of the `AudioSystem` class to obtain a reference to an `AudioInputStream` object, which we store in a variable called `audioInputStream`. This can be seen in the following line of code:

```
audioInputStream = AudioSystem.getAudioInputStream(soundFile);
```

Next, we do something special to allow us to reset the audio file back to the start. This is called *marking* the stream and is done with the following segment of code:

```
if(audioInputStream.markSupported())
{
    audioInputStream.mark(Integer.MAX_VALUE);
}
```

Notice how we check first if marking is supported, and if so, we set the mark to the maximum possible value of an integer. This is to ensure that our mark is valid for as long as possible.

Next, we need to get the audio format, so we call the `getFormat` method of our `audioInputStream` and store it in a local variable called `format`. This can be seen in the following line of code:

```
AudioFormat format = audioInputStream.getFormat();
```

Once we have the audio format, we can then create a `DataLine.Info` object based upon the format information. This can be seen in the following line of code:

```
DataLine.Info audioInputStreamInfo = new
    DataLine.Info(SourceDataLine.class, format);
```

Next, we check that our audio format is supported by using the following code:

```
if(AudioSystem.isLineSupported(audioInputStreamInfo))
```

If it is, we then create an object from the `SourceDataLine` class called `sourceDataLine` by calling the static `getLine` method of the `AudioSystem` class and passing our `DataLine.Info` subclass object `audioInputStreamInfo` into the method. This can be seen in the following line of code:

```
sourceDataLine = (SourceDataLine)
    AudioSystem.getLine(audioInputStreamInfo);
```

Now we need to define a size for the audio buffer (i.e., how much data we wish to load into RAM at one time). By allocating too little data, you will find that the sound stutters as it runs out of buffer to play. If you allocate too much buffer, it defeats the whole point of streaming the data, as it will be clogging up the system resources. So for our buffer size, we have chosen to read in enough data to store half a second of audio data. We work this out by dividing the frame rate of the audio format by two and multiplying the result by the frame size of the audio format. This can be seen in the following line of code:

```
bufferSize = (int) (format.getFrameSize()
    *format.getFrameRate()/2.0f);
```

Now that we have the buffer size, we open our `sourceDataLine` by calling the `open` method, passing in the audio format `format` and the size of the buffer that we wish to have, which in this case is our variable `bufferSize`. This can be seen in the following line of code:

```
sourceDataLine.open(format, bufferSize);
```

Next we need to allocate an array of bytes, which will actually hold the sound data and act as our buffer. This is allocated as follows:

```
soundData = new byte[bufferSize];
```

The final part of our initialization is simply to add our Play button to the application with the following code segment:

```
playButton = new JButton("Play");
playButton.setBounds(0, 0, 100, 70);
playButton.addActionListener(this);
getContentPane().add(playButton);
```

Now that we have our initialization complete, let's look at the `start-Streaming` method that we have defined in our main class.

First we check that our `sourceDataLine` object is valid, and if not we display a message box to the user informing them of this and cancel the streaming by returning out of the method. This can be seen in the following code segment:

```
if(sourceDataLine == null)
{
    JOptionPane.showMessageDialog(null, "The line is not available",
        "ERROR", JOptionPane.ERROR_MESSAGE);
    return;
}
```

If our `sourceDataLine` is valid, we proceed by creating a thread whose execution is handled by our main class (i.e., we define the `run` method in our main class). Then we set the class member `sampleStreaming` to `true` so our thread continues execution when we start it in our final line. This can be seen in the code segment that follows.

```
thread = new Thread(this);
sampleStreaming = true;
thread.start();
```

Let's now take a look at the `run` method that we have implemented to handle the execution of the thread. The first thing we do in `our` run method is start our `sourceDataLine` by calling the `start` method. This can be seen in the following line of code:

```
sourceDataLine.start();
```

Next we declare a local variable called `readBytes`, which will record how many bytes of data that we have read from our `audioInput-Stream`. We then enter a `while` loop, which continues while our `sampleStreaming` variable is true.

So in our `while` loop, we first attempt to read from our `audio-InputStream` to fill up the buffer that we created in our initialization (which we called `soundData`). Here is the line of code we use to read the sound data into the buffer. (Note also that the `read` method we use to read in the data returns the amount of data that has been read, which we store in the `readBytes` variable.)

```
readBytes = audioInputStream.read(soundData, 0, soundData.length);
```

After we have read the sound data into our `soundData` buffer, check if there was data to read by comparing `readBytes` to –1. If there was no data read, check if marking is supported and if so, call the `reset` method to reset our audio stream. Then call the `drain` method of our `sourceDataLine` object, which plays the remaining data in the buffer. Finally we set our `sampleStreaming` variable to `false`. This can be seen in the following block of code:

```
if(readBytes == -1)
{
    if(audioInputStream.markSupported())
        audioInputStream.reset();
    sourceDataLine.drain();
    sampleStreaming = false;
    break;
}
```

However, if there was data read in, we simply call the `write` method of our `sourceDataLine` class, passing in our `soundData` buffer as an argument of what to be written. This can be seen in the following line of code:

```
sourceDataLine.write(soundData, 0, readBytes);
```

Finally, after the `sampleStreaming` variable has been set to `false` and the `while` loop has been terminated, call the `stop` method of our `sourceDataLine`.

```
sourceDataLine.stop();
```

Now let's take a final look at the `stopStreaming` method. All we do here is set the value of our `sampleStreaming` variable to `false` so that the thread is informed that the user wishes to stop the stream from playing. This method can be seen in the block of code that follows.

```
public void stopStreaming()
{
```

```
        sampleStreaming = false;
    }
```

Playing MIDI Music

The word "MIDI" is an acronym for Musical Instrument Digital Interface. A MIDI music file has the file extension .mid and does not actually contain any sampled sound. Instead, it contains a list of commands that are used to recreate music from instruments that are available in the computer's MIDI synthesizer.

Let's get back to the point, however, and look at how we can play MIDI music in Java by looking at the following example application:

Code Listing 11-6: Playing MIDI music with the Java Sound API

```java
import javax.swing.*;
import java.io.*;
import java.awt.event.*;
import javax.sound.midi.*;


public class MIDIExample extends JFrame implements ActionListener
{
    public MIDIExample()
    {
        super("MIDI Example");
        setDefaultCloseOperation(EXIT_ON_CLOSE);
        getContentPane().setLayout(null);
        setResizable(false);
        setSize(200, 200);

        // Set up the MIDI
        try
        {
            theSequencer = MidiSystem.getSequencer();
            theSequencer.open();
        }
        catch(MidiUnavailableException e)
        {
            JOptionPane.showMessageDialog(null, "There was no
                available sequencer.", "ERROR",
                JOptionPane.ERROR_MESSAGE);
            System.exit(1);
        }

        File theMidiFile = new File("music.mid");
        try
        {
            theSequence = MidiSystem.getSequence(theMidiFile);
            theSequencer.setSequence(theSequence);
        }
        catch(InvalidMidiDataException e)
        {
            JOptionPane.showMessageDialog(null, "The MIDI file was
                not valid.", "ERROR", JOptionPane.ERROR_MESSAGE);
            System.exit(1);
        }
        catch(IOException e)
        {
```

```
                    JOptionPane.showMessageDialog(null, "The file did not
                        exist.", "ERROR", JOptionPane.ERROR_MESSAGE);
                    System.exit(1);
        }

        // Create the button...
        playButton = new JButton("Play");
        playButton.setBounds(45, 30, 100, 100);
        playButton.addActionListener(this);
        getContentPane().add(playButton);

        setVisible(true);
    }

    public void actionPerformed(ActionEvent e)
    {
        if(e.getSource() == playButton)
        {
            if(playButton.getText().compareTo("Play") == 0)
            {
                playButton.setText("Stop");
                theSequencer.start();
            }
            else
            {
                playButton.setText("Play");
                theSequencer.stop();
                theSequencer.setTickPosition(0);
            }
        }
    }

    public static void main(String[] args)
    {
        MIDIExample theApp = new MIDIExample();
    }

    private JButton playButton;

    private Sequencer theSequencer;
    private Sequence  theSequence;
}
```

When we execute the MIDI example, it will look like the following figure.

Figure 11-4:
MIDI example

When the application starts, it first loads a file called music.mid from the current directory into a MIDI sequence. When the Play button is pressed, the sequence is instructed to be played and the button changes to a Stop button. When the Stop button is pressed, the sequence is told to stop playing and its position is set back to the beginning.

Let's now look at the code that makes this work. The first thing we must do is include the MIDI package, which is `javax.sound.midi.*`.

Then we attempt to get the MIDI sequencer by using the static member of the `MidiSystem` class, which is defined within the MIDI package. Once we have the sequencer, we then attempt to open it by calling the `open` method of the `Sequencer` class. This is accomplished with the following code segment:

```
try
{
    theSequencer = MidiSystem.getSequencer();
    theSequencer.open();
}
catch(MidiUnavailableException e)
{
    JOptionPane.showMessageDialog(null, "There was no available
        sequencer.", "ERROR", JOptionPane.ERROR_MESSAGE);
    System.exit(1);
}
```

Note that it can throw the `MidiUnavailableException`, which is thrown if a MIDI sequencer is not available to use. If this is the case, show the user a dialog stating this and then exit the application.

Now that we have the sequencer, we need to get our MIDI sequence, which the sequencer will play. First though, create a `File` object called `theMidiFile` by passing the name of our MIDI file into the `File` constructor. This can be seen in the following line of code.

```
File theMidiFile = new File("music.mid");
```

Once we have the `File` object, we can then attempt to get the sequence from it and set the sequence in our sequencer. This is done with the following block of code:

```
try
{
    theSequence = MidiSystem.getSequence(theMidiFile);
    theSequencer.setSequence(theSequence);
}
catch(InvalidMidiDataException e)
{
    JOptionPane.showMessageDialog(null, "The MIDI file was not
        valid.", "ERROR", JOptionPane.ERROR_MESSAGE);
    System.exit(1);
}
catch(IOException e)
{
    JOptionPane.showMessageDialog(null, "The file did not exist.",
        "ERROR", JOptionPane.ERROR_MESSAGE);
    System.exit(1);
}
```

First we attempt to get the MIDI sequence by calling the static `get-Sequence` method of the `MidiSystem` class, passing our `File` object into the constructor. Once we have the sequence, we call the `set-Sequence` method of our `theSequencer` object, passing our sequence in as the argument of the constructor. Note that we need to catch both an `InvalidMidiDataException` and an `IOException`, which can be seen in the previous code segment.

At this point, our sequencer is now set up and ready to play, so we can create our button to allow us to play it with the following few lines of code:

```
playButton = new JButton("Play");
playButton.setBounds(45, 30, 100, 100);
playButton.addActionListener(this);
getContentPane().add(playButton);
```

Now that we have everything set up, let's look at the `actionPerformed` method. We are going to make it so that when the Play button is pressed, the text will change to Stop. When Stop is pressed, it will change back to Play, etc. So when Play is pressed, we start the MIDI sequencer, `theSequencer`, by calling its `start` method with the following line of code:

```
theSequencer.start();
```

This will start the MIDI file playing. When the Stop button is then pressed, we need to call the `stop` method and then also the `setTickPosition` method with 0 as a parameter to set the MIDI file back to the start again. This can be seen in the following two lines of code:

```
theSequencer.stop();
theSequencer.setTickPosition(0);
```

Creating a Sound Manager

In the previous examples we have simply looked at how to play single sound effects (i.e., one at a time). As you can guess, it would be a very rare case in a game that you would ever just have a single sound effect; most have hundreds of different sounds, with many being played at the same time.

The solution to this is to create a class to manage your sound effects easily, so that is what we are going to do in this section.

In Java, there are 64 channels through which sound can be played simultaneously. However, 32 of these channels are reserved for MIDI playback, leaving us with 32 usable channels for our sound effects. So we need to create a class that will handle the loading and playback of sound effects by managing the sound channels for us.

We will call this class `SoundManager`, and we need to implement the `LineListener` interface, as we need to react to events happening with the sound channels (lines). This class definition can be seen here:

```
public class SoundManager implements LineListener
```

Note we have also declared the following members of the class:

```
private Clip channelArray[];
private int channelSoundIdRef[];
```

Chapter 11

```
private Vector soundByteData;
public static final int AUTO_ASSIGN_CHANNEL = -1;
```

`channelArray` holds an array of the 32 channels, which are known as *clips* in Java. The second array, called `channelSoundIdRef`, holds the numbers of the sounds that are playing in the related channels. The third is a vector to hold the actual byte data of each of the sound effects that are loaded into the manager. Finally, we have a definition called `AUTO_ASSIGN_CHANNEL`, which we will see the use for soon.

So now that we know the members, we need to initialize these members in the constructor to the default values. This can be seen in the following block of code:

```
public SoundManager()
{
    // Initialize the vector to hold the sound data...
    soundByteData = new Vector();
    channelSoundIdRef = new int[32];
    channelArray = new Clip[32];

    for(int i=0; i<32; i++)
    {
        channelSoundIdRef[i] = -1;
    }
}
```

So here we create a vector for `soundByteData` and also allocate storage for an array of 32 integer values to the `channelSoundIdRef` array. In addition, we allocate storage for 32 clip objects to the `channelArray`. Finally, we initialize all the elements of the `channelSoundIdRef` to be −1, as there are no sounds playing in any of the channels when the sound manager is created.

Next, we need functionality within the class so that we can load sound files into it. This is going to be achieved by means of an `addSound` method. Let's look at how we create this now.

Take a string parameter into the method, which will denote the relative or absolute path and filename of the sound file that is to be loaded. Then create a `File` object by passing the string parameter into the `File` class constructor. This can be seen here:

```
public int addSound(String filepath)
{
    File soundFile = new File(filepath);
```

Once we have the `soundFile` object, we can then check if the sound that is trying to be loaded exists by calling the `isFile` method of the `sound-File` object.

```
if(!soundFile.isFile())
{
    System.out.println("Sound File '"+filepath+"' does not exist!");
    System.exit(1);
}
```

Next, we need to allocate an array of bytes, which will be used to store the sound data within memory (accessing the file every time we wish to play the file would be sinful!). Do this by calling the `length` method of our `soundFile` object to find out the size of the file in bytes, which is returned as a long, so a simple cast to an `int` is also required. This can be seen in the following line of code:

```
byte[] tempArray = new byte[(int)soundFile.length()];
```

Then attempt to read in the file by means of a `DataInputStream`, which is created by passing in a `FileInputStream` object that is created by passing in the `soundFile` object. The `read` method is then called on the stream with the `tempArray` empty array of bytes passed into it, so the bytes in the file will be read into the `tempArray` object. The stream is then closed with the `close` method. Note also that we enclose this within a `try/catch` block, as it is possible that an `IOException` could be thrown. This can be seen here:

```
try
{
    DataInputStream inputStream = new DataInputStream(new
        FileInputStream(soundFile));
    inputStream.read(tempArray);
    inputStream.close();
}
catch(IOException e)
{
    System.out.println(e);
    System.out.println("There was a problem reading the
        sound file: "+filepath);
    System.exit(1);
}
```

Next, place the reference to the array of bytes that we have read into the vector that we created in the constructor called `soundByteData`. This call can be seen here:

```
soundByteData.add(tempArray);
```

Finally, return the position in which the sound was added into the vector. This can be used later to reference the sound within the manager (i.e., to play it). This final line of the method can be seen here:

```
return soundByteData.size()-1;
```

Okay, so we can now load the sound data into memory. Next we need functionality to actually play the sounds, so we will create a method called `play` to do just that.

The `play` method will take three parameters, the first being the ID of the sound to be played (remember the `addSound` method returned the sound's ID). The second will be a Boolean value to state whether the sound should be looped or not, and the final parameter specifies on which channel (0-31) the sound should be played. This is declared as follows:

```
public void play(int soundId, boolean loop, int channelId)
```

If you remember, we made a definition called AUTO_ASSIGN_CHANNEL that can be used instead of a channel ID, which will tell the method to automatically assign a free channel to the sound.

First ensure that the channel is a valid number (either 0-31 or –1—the AUTO_ASSIGN_CHANNEL value). This can be accomplished with the following simple if statement.

```
if(channelId < -1 || channelId >= 32)
{
    System.out.println("Channel ID was out of range");
    return;
}
```

Next, we need to ensure that the soundId that has been specified is contained within the range of the soundByteData vector, so we can check this with the following if statement:

```
// Check the soundId is valid...
        if(soundId < 0 || soundId >= soundByteData.size())
        {
            System.out.println("Sound ID was out of range");
            return;
        }
```

Now that we know the parameters are valid, we then need to either assign the sound to a channel or find a suitable channel, depending on the channelId parameter.

First, however, create a temporary integer called validChannelId, which will be used regardless of whether the channel is auto assigned or not to hold the final channel to be used. Initially, this will be set to –1, as in no channel has been found.

So if a channel must be assigned automatically, we need to loop through the array of channels (channelArray) to find a channel that is not currently being used (either it will be null or not open). If we find one, simply assign it to the validChannelId variable, then break out of the loop. This can be seen in the following block of code:

```
for(int i=0; i<32; i++)
{
    if(channelArray[i] == null || !channelArray[i].isOpen())
    {
        // this one will do...
        validChannelId = i;
        break;
    }
}
```

Next, check if a valid channel could be found and if not, return from the method without doing anything else. This can be seen here:

```
if(validChannelId == -1)
{
    System.out.println("Could not find a suitable channel");
    return;
}
```

Alternatively, if a channel ID has been specified, we need to first stop the channel if it is currently playing, which is handled by the stopChannel method that we will implement soon. Then once we have ensured the channel has stopped, assign that channel ID to the `validChannelId` variable. This can be seen in the following two lines of code:

```
stopChannel(channelId);
validChannelId = channelId;
```

Next, once we have a valid channel, we need to try and obtain an `Audio-InputStream`, using the sound data from within the correct element of the `soundByteData` vector (specified by the `soundId` parameter that was passed into the method).

```
try
{
    AudioInputStream audioInputStream = AudioSystem
        .getAudioInputStream(new ByteArrayInputStream((byte[])
        soundByteData.get(soundId)));
```

After we have our input stream, we need to get the format of the audio from it so we can then in turn get a line that is capable of playing that audio format. Obtaining the format can be seen in the following line of code:

```
AudioFormat audioFormat = audioInputStream.getFormat();
```

Once we have the format, we can then set up the line with the following line of code (as we did in the previous examples).

```
DataLine.Info dataLineInfo = new
    DataLine.Info(Clip.class,
    audioInputStream.getFormat(),
    ((int)audioInputStream.getFrameLength() *
    audioFormat.getFrameSize()));
```

We then get a line by calling the static `getLine` method to play the sound and store the assigned clip (channel) into the correct position in the `channelArray` array (denoted by the `validChannelId` variable). This can be seen here:

```
channelArray[validChannelId] = (Clip)
    AudioSystem.getLine(dataLineInfo);
```

Next, we need to add a `LineListener` to the channel to handle the stopping of the audio, which we will look at the implementation for soon. The code to add the `LineListener` can be seen here:

```
channelArray[validChannelId].addLineListener(this);
```

Then, open the stream and note the sound ID that is playing in the channel in the `channelSoundIdRef` array. This can be seen here:

```
channelArray[validChannelId].open(audioInputStream);
channelSoundIdRef [validChannelId] = soundId;
```

We then check if the sound is to be played once or looped indefinitely and react accordingly to it. This can be seen in this block of code:

```
if(loop == true)
    channelArray[validChannelId].loop(Clip.LOOP_CONTINUOUSLY);
else
    channelArray[validChannelId].loop(1);
```

Chapter 11

Note that we have been within a `try` block since we attempted to obtain the `AudioInputStream`, so we need to catch any possible exceptions that could have been thrown. The exception handling code can be seen here:

```
catch(Exception e)
{
    System.out.println(e);
    if(channelArray[validChannelId] != null)
    {
        if(channelArray[validChannelId].isOpen())
        {
            channelArray[validChannelId].close();
        }
        channelArray[validChannelId] = null;
        channelSoundIdRef[validChannelId] = -1;
    }
}
```

All we are doing here is cleaning the channel if something goes wrong by closing it if it is open and then setting it to `null` and the `channel-SoundIdRef` back to -1, meaning there is no sound (ID) playing in that channel.

So far, we can add sounds and play them. Now let's look at stopping them!

For this, we will implement two methods—the first for stopping a sound and the second for stopping a channel directly. The first will take a single integer parameter, which will denote the ID of the sound that needs to be stopped. Of course, it is possible that more than one occurrence of the same sound may be playing, so in this method we will just stop the first occurrence of the sound. The complete method can be seen here:

```
public void stop(int soundId)
{
    // find the first occurrence of the sound and stop it...
    for(int i=0; i<32; i++)
    {
        if(channelSoundIdRef[i] == soundId)
        {
            // reset the channel...
            System.out.println("Stopping Channel "+i);
            channelArray[i].stop();
            break;
        }
    }
}
```

As you can see, we loop through the `channelSoundIdRef` trying to find the requested `soundId`, and if we find it, we then stop the associated channel and break out of the method. Simple!

The second method is called `stopChannel` and allows a channel to be stopped directly by passing in a channel ID (0-31). The complete definition of this method can be seen here:

```
public void stopChannel(int channelId)
{
```

```
    if(isChannelPlaying(channelId))
    {
        channelArray[channelId].stop();
        // note the 'update' method closes the channel properly
    }
}
```

So basically, all we do here is take in the channel ID as an integer parameter and check if it is playing by calling the isChannelPlaying method (which we will create next), passing in the channel ID. If it is playing, we simply call the stop method of the channel.

 NOTE: Each time the stop method is called, it will trigger an event in the LineListener, which we will look at soon.

In the previous method, we called the method isChannelPlaying, so let's define that now. All we want this method to do is return a Boolean denoting whether the specified channel is playing or not. We can tell if it is playing if the channel is not null and is open so we can declare the method as follows.

```
public boolean isChannelPlaying(int channelId)
{
    return (channelArray[channelId] != null &&
        channelArray[channelId].isOpen());
}
```

It may also be useful if we had a method that could tell us if a sound was playing or not, so let's make a method that can do just that. This method will be called isSoundPlaying and will take a sound ID (integer) as a parameter. All this method needs to do is loop through the channel-SoundIdRef array and see if it can match any of the values within the array to the sound ID that was passed into the method. The complete definition for this method can be seen here:

```
public boolean isSoundPlaying(int soundId)
{
    // check to see if any occurrence of the sound is playing...
    for(int i=0; i<32; i++)
    {
        if(channelSoundIdRef[i] == soundId)
        {
            return true;
        }
    }
    return false;
}
```

Next, because we implemented the LineListener in this class, we need to implement the update method that is called every time a LineEvent occurs. However, we are only interested in when a line's stop method is called, which generates a LineEvent.Type.STOP event. So the first thing we need to do is define our method and check for this event, which is done with the following few lines of code:

```
public void update(LineEvent e)
{
```

Chapter 11

```
// handles samples stopping...
if(e.getType() == LineEvent.Type.STOP)
{
```

If we get a `stop` event, we basically have to update our member information to reflect it, so we first need to cycle through our list of channels to
find out which one triggered the event. We can do this by comparing the
elements of the `channelArray` to the `getLine` method of the `Line-`
`Event` object e that was passed into the `update` method. Once we find
the line, we can then set the reference to `null` and also update the correct element in the `channelSoundIdRef` array to say there is no sound
playing in that channel. This can be seen in the following block of code:

```
for(int i=0; i<32; i++)
{
    if(channelArray[i] == e.getLine())
    {
        // reset the channel...
        System.out.println("Closing Channel "+i);
        channelArray[i] = null;
        channelSoundIdRef[i] = -1;
    }
}
```

Finally, all we need to do in this method is close the line (channel), which
we do by calling the `close` method that can be seen in the following line
of code:

```
e.getLine().close();
```

The last method we are going to implement in our sound manager is one
to allow us to stop all the channels playing. To do this, all we need to do is
cycle through the 32 channels, calling the `stopChannel` method for each
one. This can be seen in this final block of code:

```
public void stopAllChannels()
{
    // stop active channels...
    for(int i=0; i<32; i++)
        stopChannel(i);
}
```

Before we move on, let's look at the complete code listing for the sound
manager.

Code Listing 11-7: The sound manager

```
import java.util.*;
import java.io.*;
import javax.sound.sampled.*;     // Import the Sound API

public class SoundManager implements LineListener
{
    public SoundManager()
    {
        // Initialize the vector to hold the sound data...
        soundByteData = new Vector();
        channelSoundIdRef = new int[32];
        channelArray = new Clip[32];
```

```
        for(int i=0; i<32; i++)
        {
            channelSoundIdRef[i] = -1;
        }
    }

    public int addSound(String filepath)
    {
        File soundFile = new File(filepath);

        if(!soundFile.isFile())
        {
            System.out.println("Sound File '"+filepath+"' does not
                exist!");
            System.exit(1);
        }

        byte[] tempArray = new byte[(int)soundFile.length()];

        try
        {
            DataInputStream inputStream = new DataInputStream(new
                FileInputStream(soundFile));
            inputStream.read(tempArray);
            inputStream.close();
        }
        catch(IOException e)
        {
            System.out.println(e);
            System.out.println("There was a problem reading the
                sound file: "+filepath);
            System.exit(1);
        }

        // Add it to the vector...
        soundByteData.add(tempArray);

        // return its position in the vector...
        return soundByteData.size()-1;
    }

    public void play(int soundId, boolean loop, int channelId)
    {
        // Check the channelId is valid...
        if(channelId < -1 || channelId >= 32)
        {
            System.out.println("Channel ID was out of range");
            return;
        }

        // Check the soundId is valid...
        if(soundId < 0 || soundId >= soundByteData.size())
        {
            System.out.println("Sound ID was out of range");
            return;
        }

        int validChannelId = -1;
        if(channelId == AUTO_ASSIGN_CHANNEL)
        {
```

```
        // we need to find a suitable channel...

        // first find a free channel...

        for(int i=0; i<32; i++)
        {
            if(channelArray[i] == null ||
                !channelArray[i].isOpen())
            {
                // this one will do...
                validChannelId = i;
                break;
            }
        }

        if(validChannelId == -1)
        {
            System.out.println("Could not find a suitable
                channel");
            return;
        }
    }
    else
    {
        // we need to ensure the selected channel is stopped...
        stopChannel(channelId);

        // set the valid channel id...
        validChannelId = channelId;
    }

    System.out.println("Allocating Channel "+validChannelId);

    try
    {
        AudioInputStream audioInputStream =
            AudioSystem.getAudioInputStream(new
            ByteArrayInputStream((byte[])
            soundByteData.get(soundId)));

        // retrieve the audio format...
        AudioFormat audioFormat = audioInputStream.getFormat();

        // set the line up
        DataLine.Info dataLineInfo = new
            DataLine.Info(Clip.class,
            audioInputStream.getFormat(),
            ((int)audioInputStream.getFrameLength() *
            audioFormat.getFrameSize())));

        // assign a clip (channel) for the sample
        channelArray[validChannelId] = (Clip)
            AudioSystem.getLine(dataLineInfo);

        channelArray[validChannelId].addLineListener(this);

        channelArray[validChannelId].open(audioInputStream);
        channelSoundIdRef[validChannelId] = soundId;

        // play the clip (or loop it)
```

```
            if(loop == true)
                channelArray[validChannelId].loop
                    (Clip.LOOP_CONTINUOUSLY);
            else
                channelArray[validChannelId].loop(1);


    }
    catch(Exception e)
    {

        System.out.println(e);
        if(channelArray[validChannelId] != null)
        {
            if(channelArray[validChannelId].isOpen())
            {
                channelArray[validChannelId].close();
            }

            channelArray[validChannelId] = null;
            channelSoundIdRef[validChannelId] = -1;
        }
    }
}

public void stop(int soundId)
{
    // find the first occurrence of the sound and stop it...
    for(int i=0; i<32; i++)
    {
        if(channelSoundIdRef[i] == soundId)
        {
            // reset the channel...
            System.out.println("Stopping Channel "+i);
            channelArray[i].stop();
            break;
        }
    }
}

public void stopChannel(int channelId)
{
    if(isChannelPlaying(channelId))
    {
        channelArray[channelId].stop();
        // note the 'update' method closes the channel properly
    }
}

public boolean isChannelPlaying(int channelId)
{
    return (channelArray[channelId] != null &&
        channelArray[channelId].isOpen());
}

public boolean isSoundPlaying(int soundId)
{
    // check to see if any occurence of the sound is playing...
    for(int i=0; i<32; i++)
    {
        if(channelSoundIdRef[i] == soundId)
```

Chapter 11

```
        {
            return true;
        }
    }
    return false;
}

public void update(LineEvent e)
{
    // handles samples stopping...
    if(e.getType() == LineEvent.Type.STOP)
    {
        // find the channel this line relates to...
        for(int i=0; i<32; i++)
        {
            if(channelArray[i] == e.getLine())
            {
                // reset the channel...
                System.out.println("Closing Channel "+i);
                channelArray[i] = null;
                channelSoundIdRef[i] = -1;
            }
        }

        // close the line...
        e.getLine().close();
    }
}

public void stopAllChannels()
{
    // stop active channels...
    for(int i=0; i<32; i++)
        stopChannel(i);
}

private Clip channelArray[];
private int channelSoundIdRef[];
private Vector soundByteData;
public static final int AUTO_ASSIGN_CHANNEL = -1;
}
```

So there you have it—a cool sound manager that will allow you to play up to 32 sounds simultaneously!

Using the Sound Manager

Now that we've made the sound manager, let's see it in action by looking at a simple application that implements it (note also that we will be using it again later when we create the game framework in Chapter 12). Let's first look at the complete code listing for the application and the expected output (although sadly this book doesn't have built-in speakers).

Code Listing 11-8: Sound manager example application

```
import java.awt.*;
import java.awt.event.*;
import javax.swing.*;
```

```
public class SoundManagerExample extends JFrame implements
    ActionListener
{
    public SoundManagerExample()
    {
        super("Sound Manager Example");
        setDefaultCloseOperation(EXIT_ON_CLOSE);
        getContentPane().setLayout(null);
        setResizable(false);
        setBounds(0, 0, 430, 75);

        // Initialize the Sound Manager...
        soundManager = new SoundManager();

        soundId = new int[4];

        soundId[DEEPBASS_SOUND] = soundManager.addSound
            ("DeepBass.wav");
        System.out.println("DEEPBASS_SOUND is now defined as
            "+soundId[DEEPBASS_SOUND]);

        soundId[DISCO_SOUND] = soundManager.addSound("Disco.wav");
        System.out.println("DISCO_SOUND is now defined as
            "+soundId[DISCO_SOUND]);

        soundId[SLOWDRUM_SOUND] = soundManager
            .addSound("SlowDrum.wav");
        System.out.println("SLOWDRUM_SOUND is now defined as
            "+soundId[SLOWDRUM_SOUND]);

        soundId[BOOM_SOUND] = soundManager.addSound("Boom.wav");
        System.out.println("BOOM_SOUND is now defined as
            "+soundId[BOOM_SOUND]);

        toggleSoundButton = new JButton[soundId.length];

        // Setup the GUI...
        for(int i=0; i<soundId.length; i++)
        {
            toggleSoundButton[i] = new JButton("Sound "+i+" Off");
            toggleSoundButton[i].setBounds(5+(i*105), 5, 100, 40);
            toggleSoundButton[i].setBackground(Color.red);
            toggleSoundButton[i].addActionListener(this);
            getContentPane().add(toggleSoundButton[i]);
        }

        setVisible(true);
    }

    public void actionPerformed(ActionEvent e)
    {
        for(int i=0; i<soundId.length; i++)
        {
            if(e.getSource() == toggleSoundButton[i])
            {
                if(soundManager.isSoundPlaying(soundId[i]))
                {
                    soundManager.stop(soundId[i]);
                    toggleSoundButton[i].setText("Sound "+i+" Off");
```

Chapter 11

```
                        toggleSoundButton[i].setBackground(Color.red);
            }
            else
            {
                soundManager.play(soundId[i], true,
                    SoundManager.AUTO_ASSIGN_CHANNEL);
                toggleSoundButton[i].setText("Sound "+i+" On");
                toggleSoundButton[i].setBackground(Color.green);
            }

            return;
        }
    }
}

public static void main(String args[])
{
    SoundManagerExample soundManagerExample = new
        SoundManagerExample();
}

public static SoundManager soundManager;

// GUI
public JButton[] toggleSoundButton;

public int[] soundId;

// Sound Definitions...
public static final int DEEPBASS_SOUND   = 0;
public static final int DISCO_SOUND      = 1;
public static final int SLOWDRUM_SOUND   = 2;
public static final int BOOM_SOUND       = 3;
}
```

When we run this application, it should look like the following figure.

Note first though that you'll need to copy the following sound files off the companion CD into your code directory:

- DeepBass.wav
- Disco.wav
- SlowDrum.wav
- Boom.wav

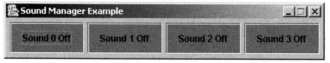

Figure 11-5:
Sound man-
ager example

Let's have a look at the relevant parts of the application. First create an instance of the sound manager by calling its constructor in the usual way. This can be seen here:

```
soundManager = new SoundManager();
```

Next, allocate an array of four integers to hold the IDs of the sounds that we are about to load. This can be seen here:

```
soundId = new int[4];
```

Then load four sounds into the sound manager by calling the `addSound` method, and store the ID of each sound in the appropriate position in the `soundId` array. The code to load one of the sounds can be seen here:

```
soundId[DEEPBASS_SOUND] = soundManager.addSound("DeepBass.wav");
    System.out.println("DEEPBASS_SOUND is now defined as
        "+soundId[DEEPBASS_SOUND]);
```

Notice also how we have created the following definitions to allow more readable access to the array of sound IDs.

```
public static final int DEEPBASS_SOUND    = 0;
public static final int DISCO_SOUND       = 1;
public static final int SLOWDRUM_SOUND    = 2;
public static final int BOOM_SOUND        = 3;
```

Hence we can get the ID for the DEEPBASE_SOUND by accessing element 0 of the `soundId` array.

After we have loaded the sounds, we check if the associated sound is playing on the relevant button click by calling the `isSoundPlaying` method and passing in the ID of the sound. If it is playing, we stop it, and if it isn't, we play it.

To stop the sound, we simply invoke the `stop` method of the `soundManager` object, passing in the relevant sound ID, which can be seen in the following line of code:

```
soundManager.stop(soundId[i]);
```

Again, to play the sound, just call the `play` method of the sound manager, passing in the sound ID and specifying whether it should be looped or not. In this example, we use the auto channel allocation feature by specifying `SoundManager.AUTO_ASSIGN_CHANNEL` as the third parameter instead of a specific channel number. This can be seen in this final line of code:

```
soundManager.play(soundId[i], true,
    SoundManager.AUTO_ASSIGN_CHANNEL);
```

Summary

In this chapter, you learned the key aspects of playing sound and music in Java. Also, you created a reusable `SoundManager` class, which we will see working in a game environment in the next chapter when we develop a reusable game framework and look at some important game programming techniques.

Chapter 11

Game Programming Techniques

"Any intelligent fool can make things bigger, more complex, and
more violent. It takes a touch of genius—and a lot of courage—
to move in the opposite direction."   —Albert Einstein

Introduction

This chapter covers a variety of important topics for creating games in
Java. In this chapter, we will create a reusable framework for a game and
look at how we can use animation and tiles within our games. We will also
cover topics such as using timers and creating objects—two key issues
with Java right now—and discuss measures to overcome these hurdles.

Animation

If the imagery for a given object in a game was always the same, it would
lack visual appeal. Furthermore, moving objects would not look as if they
were moving in a realistic manner. The key to 2D animation is in alternat-
ing between animation frames, where one frame represents a game sprite
in a given position at a given time. It's similar to the way in which film is
recorded, as simply a consecutive series of images. In a programming
sense, you need to create your own animation frames in a straightforward
manner and then build the animation code to support its structure.

Animation with One-Dimensional Image Sheets

First, we will look at a basic linear animation set consisting of images of
numbers from 0 to 9. The following image shows this animation set:

0 1 2 3 4 5 6 7 8 9 Figure 12-1

The dimension of this entire image is 320x32 pixels with ten frames. One
number fills one frame of the animation sheet. Thus, each frame of the
animation set is 32x32 pixels in size. The red squares represent the

top-left corner of each frame, which we will discuss in more detail in a moment. The important part of making animation sheets is the order of the frames. In this animation sheet, the numbers are in order, so we can access their position in the animation sheet in a linear fashion. But how do we handle drawing the frames?

We need an index for the animation sheet or a current state within the sheet that acts as a description of what should be drawn. We have used the numbers from 0 to 9 here on purpose to illustrate the index state because they are the values that you can use as the index values to store the current frame. Let's say that we have a counter variable that cycles in the main loop repeatedly from 0 to 9 (just an integer value), and we want to display this number as a bitmapped image using this one-dimensional animation sheet and drawing the correct frame relating to the counter value. We need to work out the top-left (x0, y0) and bottom-right (x1, y1) coordinates of the frame that we want to draw, which will use the Graphics object method drawImage that we saw in Chapter 9 for drawing a section of an image. So, if we say the current number of the counter variable is 4, we can work out these coordinates as follows, based on what we know about the dimensions of the animation sheet and its frames.

```
static final int FRAME_WIDTH = 32;
static final int FRAME_HEIGHT = 32;

int counter = 4; // our counter variable

// Source image coordinates for the frame
int srcX0 = counter*FRAME_WIDTH;
int srcY0 = 0;
int srcX1 = srcX0+FRAME_WIDTH;
int srcY1 = FRAME_HEIGHT;

// Destination coordinates to draw to
int dstX0 = 50;
int dstY0 = 50;
int dstX1 = dstX0+FRAME_WIDTH;
int dstY1 = dstY0+FRAME_HEIGHT;

// render the single frame

Graphics g = // a graphics object to draw onto
g.drawImage(numberSheet,
    dstX0, dstY0, dstX1, dstY1,
    srcX0, srcY0, srcX1, srcY1,
    null);
```

This code illustrates how we can get the image coordinates for the frame that is represented by the counter variable, which in the code example is equal to 4. We begin by calculating the source coordinates; these are the coordinates on the actual image. We are looking at finding the position of that red square shown on the number sheet image earlier. This can be retrieved as simply the counter variable's value multiplied by the width of a single frame. So for the counter value 4, this would be 4x32, equaling pixel coordinate 128 on the tile sheet for the left position of the tile. The right coordinate is simply the left (128) plus the width of one frame, and the y coordinates are merely 0 to the height of one frame, as this animation sheet is one-dimensional. (We'll look at two-dimensional animation sheets in the next section.)

Let's create an example that loads in the animation sheet of numbers and then get it to cycle the value of a variable per loop and display the variable's value as a frame of the image, animating it based on a given state. The following example, AnimatedNumbers.java, is an applet program; the animation sheet is available on the companion CD.

Code Listing 12-1: AnimatedNumbers.java

```java
import java.awt.*;
import java.awt.image.*;
import javax.swing.*;
import java.awt.event.*;

public class AnimatedNumbers extends JApplet implements Runnable
{
    public void init()
    {
        getContentPane().setLayout(null);
        setSize(DISPLAY_WIDTH, DISPLAY_HEIGHT);
        setIgnoreRepaint(true);

        backBuffer = new BufferedImage(DISPLAY_WIDTH, DISPLAY_HEIGHT,
            BufferedImage.TYPE_INT_RGB);
        bbGraphics = (Graphics2D) backBuffer.getGraphics();

        // load in animation image sheet
        numberSheet = getImage(getCodeBase(), "numbersheet.gif");

        MediaTracker m = new MediaTracker(this);
        m.addImage(numberSheet, 0);

        try
        {
            m.waitForID(0);
        }
        catch(InterruptedException e)
        {
            System.out.println(e);
        }
    }

    public void start()
    {
        loop = new Thread(this);
        loop.start();
    }

    public void stop()
    {
        loop = null;
    }

    public void run()
    {
```

```java
        long startTime, waitTime, elapsedTime;
        //    1000/25 Frames Per Second = 40 millisecond delay
        int delayTime = 1000/25;

        Thread thisThread = Thread.currentThread();
        while(loop==thisThread)
        {
            startTime = System.currentTimeMillis();

            changeState();

            // render to back buffer now
            render(bbGraphics);

            // render back buffer image to screen
            Graphics g = getGraphics();
            g.drawImage(backBuffer, 0, 0, null);
            g.dispose();

            // handle frame rate
            elapsedTime = System.currentTimeMillis() - startTime;
            waitTime = Math.max(delayTime - elapsedTime, 5);

            try
            {
                Thread.sleep(waitTime);
            }
            catch(InterruptedException e) {}
        }
    }

    public void changeState()
    {
        if(counter<9) counter++;
        else counter = 0;
    }


    public void render(Graphics g)
    {
        g.clearRect(0, 0, DISPLAY_WIDTH, DISPLAY_HEIGHT);

        int srcX0 = counter*FRAME_WIDTH;
        int srcY0 = 0;
        int srcX1 = srcX0+FRAME_WIDTH;
        int srcY1 = FRAME_HEIGHT;

        // start pos to center in applet
        int dstX0 = (DISPLAY_WIDTH-FRAME_WIDTH)/2;
        int dstY0 = (DISPLAY_HEIGHT-FRAME_HEIGHT)/2;
        int dstX1 = dstX0+FRAME_WIDTH;
        int dstY1 = dstY0+FRAME_HEIGHT;

        g.drawImage(numberSheet,
                    dstX0, dstY0, dstX1, dstY1,
                    srcX0, srcY0, srcX1, srcY1,
                    null);
    }
```

```
    private Image numberSheet;
    private int counter = 0; // our counter variable

    private static final int FRAME_WIDTH = 32;
    private static final int FRAME_HEIGHT = 32;

    private Thread loop;
    private BufferedImage backBuffer;
    private Graphics2D bbGraphics;

    private static final int DISPLAY_WIDTH = 400;
    private static final int DISPLAY_HEIGHT = 400;
}
```

When you compile and run the applet, you should get the counter value animating in the center of the applet as a frame of animation similar to Figure 12-2. Note that you might want to slow down the frame rate a bit in this example, but for the sake of the next example, we have left it as is.

The previous code is all very well, but it doesn't help if we have numbers with more than one digit. We will make two changes to the previous code to allow us to render numbers with multiple digits; this is going slightly off-track of animation in general, but we'll return with two-dimensional animations in a moment.

So, first you need to alter the `changeState` method so that it resets to zero when it is at a larger, multi-digit value, such as 999, instead of its current value of 9.

Figure 12-2

Next we need to rewrite the `render` method so that it handles drawing each digit in the variable `counter`. We will position the number in the center of the screen. Here is the code for a `render` method that will draw the entire number centered in the middle of the applet:

```
public void render(Graphics g)
{
    g.clearRect(0, 0, DISPLAY_WIDTH, DISPLAY_HEIGHT);

    // calculate length of the counter in characters,
    // i.e. 945 = 3 digit characters

    int digitLength;
    int scope = 10;

    for(digitLength=1; scope<=counter; digitLength++)
        scope*=10;

    // the x left:right coordinates on the animation sheet
    int srcX0;      // calculated later
```

```
    int srcX1;      // calculated later

    // top left start position for centering in applet
    int dstX = (DISPLAY_WIDTH-(digitLength*FRAME_WIDTH))/2;
    int dstY = (DISPLAY_HEIGHT-FRAME_HEIGHT)/2;

    int base;
    int digit;

    for(int i=digitLength; i>0; i--)
    {
        base = (int)Math.pow(10, i);
        digit = (counter % base) / (base / 10);

        srcX0 = digit*FRAME_WIDTH;
        srcX1 = srcX0+FRAME_WIDTH;

        g.drawImage(numberSheet,
                dstX, dstY, dstX+FRAME_WIDTH, dstY+FRAME_HEIGHT,
                srcX0, 0, srcX1, FRAME_HEIGHT,
                null);

        dstX+=FRAME_WIDTH;
    }
}
```

When you make these two changes to the previous example, you can see that it will draw multiple-digit numbers in the applet as follows:

Figure 12-3

Let's decode our main rendering loop in the case of the number shown (240) and see how this works:

```
for(int i=digitLength; i>0; i--)
{
```

We are going to iterate from the total number of digits to 1, so the variable i will iterate from 3 to 1 for the number 240.

```
    base = (int)Math.pow(10, i);
    digit = (counter % base) / (base / 10);
```

In order to actually retrieve the digit that we are interested in, we need to perform some special code. First calculate the value of base in order to work out the current number. When we want to find the number 2, `base` will be assigned the value 10^3 (10x10x10 = 1000). Then perform `counter % base`. This will give us the number from its current position to the right side, in character terms. Thus, 240 % 1000 gives us 240, which isn't so relevant. But for the next digit in the next loop cycle, it is, as it will perform 240 % 100, which will give us the value 40. In the next loop cycle, it will perform 240 % 10, giving us the value 0. When we get the values 240, 40, and 0 for the respective iterations of this loop, we then divide the values by `(base / 10)`, giving us the values 240 / 100 = 2, 40 / 10 = 4, and 0 / 1 = 0. So there we have it; we have retrieved the values 2, 4, and 0, stored in the variable `digit`, and we can then go on to render it.

Note that it would also be possible to make the number into a string object and get the character value using the `charAt` method and then change it back into an integer (or subtract the numeric value of the character 0 from your retrieved character). This would be more expensive and mean creating many string objects per loop. This is the reason that we retrieved the number of digits to begin with by cycling through powers of ten instead of converting to a string object and then calling its `length` method. We will look at the problem of creating objects a little later in this chapter in greater detail. Note you could get around this by using a `StringBuffer` to prevent further object creation also, but this would only be convenient if the value wasn't changed very often, as it involves consistent number-to-string conversions.

```
srcX0 = digit*FRAME_WIDTH;
srcX1 = srcX0+FRAME_WIDTH;

g.drawImage(numberSheet,
dstX, dstY, dstX+FRAME_WIDTH, dstY+FRAME_HEIGHT,
srcX0, 0, srcX1, FRAME_HEIGHT,
          null);
```

This is the basic rendering code that we saw in the last example—this time rendering the value of the digit variable.

```
dstX+=FRAME_WIDTH;
```

All that is left is to move the on-screen (destination) position where the next loop cycle will render the next frame.

```
} // end of method
```

Note that you could also cycle through the digits from right to left, taking the modulus of the number to get the rightmost digit. Then after rendering, divide the current number by 10 in each loop, basically shifting the digits rightward each time. This would obviously mean changing the screen position to draw each frame, also.

One thing that many games do, however, is fill a number to a specific, fixed amount of digits. If the actual number of digits in the current number is less than that fixed value, the number will be filled to this value, adding appropriate zeros onto the left-hand side of the number when drawn. For example, if the fixed amount of digits is 4, the number "72" would appear on screen as the number "0072." The great thing about our code is that all

Chapter 12

you need to do instead of calculating the length of digits is store the value in the variable `digitLength`. You can just set the `digitLength` to whatever you want it to be, and the algorithm for finding the current digit will find zeros for invalid character places on the right with its calculations. The following figure illustrates how it would look if you merely set the `digitLength` variable to 5, irrespective of the real number of digits, with the current value equal to 466.

Another consideration for this technique would be incorporating a negative (–) character into the animation sheet and adding a check to see if the value was less than 0. If so, you would render the minus frame first and move the destination x position along by the width of one frame before entering the render loop. For this, the negative character would be best placed on the end of the animation sheet so that it doesn't mess up the rendering code, or the rendering code could be changed appropriately.

Figure 12-4

With these techniques, you can now create bitmapped fonts of your own. In these previous examples, we have basically created just this but only supporting ten different frames consisting of the numbers 0 to 9. But this could easily be extended to incorporate a larger set, such as a full ASCII set or perhaps the ASCII range of 32 to 128, which contains the most important characters in the set. Creating a bitmapped character set as opposed to using `drawString` is faster because a bitmapped font is an equal copy (provided you don't scale it), whereas drawing from a TrueType font can be slow because it requires calculations to work out its form, based on its TrueType description when it is drawn. Also, monotype fonts actually look more structured, as they are characters with fixed widths and heights. So the strings WWWWW and LLLLL would span the same width in frames, whereas TrueType font characters are positioned next to each other after a short space following the edge of the last character. With monotype fonts you can be dedicated to a fixed area of the screen to contain that textual data as a bitmapped font.

We will now look at animation with two-dimensional image sheets and the coolest little example on the planet, `StickWalker`.

Animation with Two-Dimensional Image Sheets

The use of one-dimensional animation sheets has its limitations in circumstances where your primary frames will also have an animation state, making two-dimensional animation sheets a more realistic structure to build your animation code. For example, with the numbered animation sheets, we might also want to change the color of each of the numbers through a second animation counter. Adding an extra dimension onto the animation sheet will allow us to do this in a way that will be easy to handle in code. The following image is an illustration of a structure supporting different colored states for each number in the original one-dimensional animation sheet. (Note that the rows are, from the top, black, blue, green, and red.)

Figure 12-5

As you can see, the x-axis of the new two-dimensional animation sheet is concerned with storing the actual data value (i.e., the numbers 0 to 9), whereas the y-axis is concerned with the color of that value. From this frame set, we want to be able to draw a given number in a selected color. For this we can use two indices: one for the number (x position) and one for the color (y position). The following code is an illustration of how we could draw the red number 7 using two index variables to control the value of the current frame.

```
static final int FRAME_WIDTH = 32;
static final int FRAME_HEIGHT = 32;

int value = 7; // the number we want to draw
int color = 3; // the row index for the color

// Obtain the coordinates in the image of the current frame
// based on the value and color variables

int srcX0 = value*FRAME_WIDTH;
int srcY0 = color*FRAME_HEIGHT;
int srcX1 = srcX0+FRAME_WIDTH;
int srcY1 = srcY0+FRAME_HEIGHT;

// Destination coordinates to draw to
int dstX0 = 50;
int dstY0 = 50;
int dstX1 = dstX0+FRAME_WIDTH;
int dstY1 = dstY0+FRAME_HEIGHT;

// render the single frame

Graphics g = // a graphics object to draw onto
g.drawImage(coloredNumberSheet,
    dstX0, dstY0, dstX1, dstY1,
    srcX0, srcY0, srcX1, srcY1,
    null);
```

A more practical example of using two-dimensional animation sheets is for game character animations. Typically, a 2D character will have various directions of movements, having a different pose in each direction. For example, a character looking downward will look different than when it is facing upward. These are the direction characteristics of the character's graphical representation. However, for each of the directional poses, the character may also need a walk cycle so that it looks like it is walking when it is moved in a given direction. This is the perfect setup for a two-dimensional animation sheet, as we saw with the colored numbers. In the following example, we are going to make a character walk continuously from the left edge to the right edge of the screen, while animating the walk cycle and changing the direction appropriately. The following image is the animation set that will be loaded into the program. Note that the background of the character's animation sheet image is set to transparent in the .gif file that is available on the companion CD-ROM.

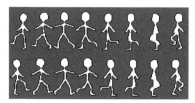

Figure 12-6

The idea for this example is that an animation counter cycles through the x coordinate of the frame constantly and does not interfere with the directional counter that we also use. The following example, StickWalker, shows this character walking between the left and right edges of the screen. Each frame in this animation sheet is 32x64 pixels in size.

Note that a background image is also drawn in this example. (The background image is also available on the companion CD.) Here is the code for the applet program StickWalker.java.

Code Listing 12-2: StickWalker.java

```
import java.awt.*;
import java.awt.image.*;
import javax.swing.*;
import java.awt.event.*;

public class StickWalker extends JApplet implements Runnable
{
    public void init()
    {
        getContentPane().setLayout(null);
        setSize(DISPLAY_WIDTH, DISPLAY_HEIGHT);
        setIgnoreRepaint(true);

        backBuffer = new BufferedImage(DISPLAY_WIDTH, DISPLAY_HEIGHT,
            BufferedImage.TYPE_INT_RGB);
        bbGraphics = (Graphics2D) backBuffer.getGraphics();

        // load in animation image sheet
        characterSheet = getImage(getCodeBase(),
            "stickmansheet.gif");
        backgroundImage = getImage(getCodeBase(), "backdrop.gif");

        MediaTracker m = new MediaTracker(this);
        m.addImage(characterSheet, 0);
        m.addImage(backgroundImage, 0);
```

```
    try
    {
        m.waitForID(0);
    }
    catch(InterruptedException e)
    {
        System.out.println(e);
    }

    // assign start walk animation, direction and position
    walkAnim = 0;
    walkDir = 0;
    xPos = 200;
    yPos = 184;

    // work frame limits on the fly
    MAX_WALK_ANIMATIONS = characterSheet.getWidth(null)
        / FRAME_WIDTH;
    MAX_WALK_DIRECTIONS = characterSheet.getHeight(null)
        / FRAME_HEIGHT;
}

public void start()
{
    loop = new Thread(this);
    loop.start();
}

public void stop()
{
    loop = null;
}

public void run()
{
    long startTime, waitTime, elapsedTime;
    // 1000/25 Frames Per Second = 40 millisecond delay
    int delayTime = 1000/25;

    Thread thisThread = Thread.currentThread();
    while(loop==thisThread)
    {
        startTime = System.currentTimeMillis();

        walk();

        // render to back buffer now
        render(bbGraphics);

        // render back buffer image to screen
        Graphics g = getGraphics();
        g.drawImage(backBuffer, 0, 0, null);
        g.dispose();

        //  handle frame rate
        elapsedTime = System.currentTimeMillis() - startTime;
        waitTime = Math.max(delayTime - elapsedTime, 5);

        try
```

```
                {
                    Thread.sleep(waitTime);
                }
                catch(InterruptedException e) {}
        }
    }


    public void walk()
    {
        // handle animations
        walkAnim++;
        if(walkAnim >= MAX_WALK_ANIMATIONS)
            walkAnim = 0;

        // move character position and handle direction changing
        switch(walkDir)
        {
            case 0: // left
                xPos-=4;
                if(xPos<0)
                {
                    xPos = 0;
                    walkDir = 1;
                }
                break;

            case 1: // right
                xPos+=4;
                if(xPos+FRAME_WIDTH>DISPLAY_WIDTH)
                {
                    xPos = DISPLAY_WIDTH-FRAME_WIDTH;
                    walkDir = 0;
                }
                break;
        }
    }


    public void render(Graphics g)
    {
        g.drawImage(backgroundImage, 0, 0, null);

        // render current frame to current screen position

        int srcX0 = walkAnim*FRAME_WIDTH;
        int srcY0 = walkDir*FRAME_HEIGHT;
        int srcX1 = srcX0+FRAME_WIDTH;
        int srcY1 = srcY0+FRAME_HEIGHT;

        g.drawImage(characterSheet,
                    xPos, yPos, xPos+FRAME_WIDTH, yPos+FRAME_HEIGHT,
                    srcX0, srcY0, srcX1, srcY1,
                    null);
    }


    private Image characterSheet;
    private int xPos;
    private int yPos;
```

```
    private int walkAnim;
    private int walkDir;

    private int MAX_WALK_ANIMATIONS;
    private int MAX_WALK_DIRECTIONS;

    private static final int FRAME_WIDTH = 32;
    private static final int FRAME_HEIGHT = 64;

    private Image backgroundImage;

    private Thread loop;
    private BufferedImage backBuffer;
    private Graphics2D bbGraphics;

    private static final int DISPLAY_WIDTH = 400;
    private static final int DISPLAY_HEIGHT = 400;
}
```

When you compile and run, you will hopefully get an animated character walking across the screen in a very artistic fashion (who says programmers aren't artistic? :)).

Figure 12-7

The walk direction is controlled using the variable `walkDir`. The value of this variable is 0 for left and 1 for right. The animation state of the character's walk movement is controlled using the variable `walkAnim`, which cycles continuously (once per main loop cycle) from 0 to 7 (as there are eight walk animations for a given direction). In the `walk` method, we first handle the walk animation state and then the walk movement and possible direction change. The code in this area is quite self-explanatory. One thing to note about this example is the way in which we store the maximum number of frames for the animation and walk (x and y) frames of the animation sheet, with the following code:

```
MAX_WALK_ANIMATIONS = characterSheet.getWidth(null) / FRAME_WIDTH;
MAX_WALK_DIRECTIONS = characterSheet.getHeight(null) / FRAME_HEIGHT;
```

Once the character sheet has been loaded in completely using the media tracker, we can then work out the number of frames, which for the animation sheet used was eight across and two down, at run time. We do this by simply dividing the width of the image by the width of one frame and the same for the height of the image and the height of one frame. This sort of code makes a program more reusable and is very good programming practice. If the image is later changed by the artist, perhaps to contain 16 walk animations instead of eight in our example, the code will not need changing, as the variable `MAX_WALK_ANIMATIONS` is calculated based on the image loaded in, and this variable is used in the `walk` method when we change the variable `walkAnim` also. We would obviously need to make some specific code changes if the direction rows of the image changed, however. For example, if the artist added two extra rows for up and down movements to the animation sheet, we would need to support these directions by adding movement code for them, but the variable `MAX_WALK_DIRECTIONS` would still be set to its correct value.

Note that in the previous code, the methods `getWidth` and `getHeight` of the image `characterSheet` were both passed the parameter `null`. The parameter type is `ImageObserver`, and this is used for watching the loading progress of an image, which we are not concerned with, as we have used the `MediaTracker` class to load our images completely before continuing. The `ImageObserver` was discussed back in Chapter 9, "Graphics."

Mapping One Dimension to Two

As we mentioned at the beginning, there needs to be an efficient mix between the artwork and the programming, where you can build the most efficient code to support the animation sheet in question. Having the frames ordered linearly is the most basic and effective way to achieve this. However, it might be more practical that this not be the case from an artist's point of view (although programmers might disagree) or perhaps the format of an animation sheet must be the way it is for a certain reason. One case could be that instead of having a large linear sequence in one dimension, such as the ASCII character set of length 256 characters, the animation sheet could be made two-dimensional using 16x16 frames to make up the full 256, instead of just 256 frames in one row. The best structure would be for the characters to span from left to right, move down a row and start at the beginning again, move left to right, and so on, so that character number 16 appeared in the frame directly below character 0.

We would now need to find the x and y indices for a given ASCII character value's integer form, such as the character (capital) A, which is really the number 65, based on the structure (16x16 frames) of the animation sheet. We can do this simply with the following code:

```
// number of frame in sheet across and down
int TOTAL_FRAMES_X = 16;
int TOTAL_FRAMES_Y = 16;

char myChar = 'A';
int value = myChar; // equals 65, just to simplify this example


int frameXIndex = value % TOTAL_FRAMES_X;
int frameYIndex = value / TOTAL_FRAMES_X;
```

Yes, this is right; both use the `TOTAL_FRAMES_X` value. If we imagine that we want to access the character with value 17, just think about where its frame would be positioned on the animation sheet. Frame 16 would be the frame at the first column and the second row, underneath frame 0, as the first row of frames span from 0 to 15. So frame 17 would be at the second column and second row, giving the indices of (1, 1), as the first row and first column are indices (0, 0). Using this algorithm, we can calculate these indices from `(value = 17) % (TOTAL_FRAMES_X = 16)`, giving us 1 for the x indices, and `(value = 17) / (TOTAL_FRAMES_X = 16)`, giving us 1 also for the y indices. If value was 15, these indices would work out as (15, 0). For the bottom-right corner and value 255, these indices would work out as (15, 15)

Alternatively, there could come a time where you have two indices and want a one-dimensional value for those indices. For example, what if we wanted to know which character is at the frame with indices (1, 4) in the animation sheet? We could do this with the following formula:

```
// number of frame in sheet across and down
int TOTAL_FRAMES_X = 16;
int TOTAL_FRAMES_Y = 16;

// 2 Dimensional frame indices
int xIndex = 1;
int yIndex = 4;

char myChar = xIndex + (yIndex*TOTAL_FRAMES_X);
```

The character in the 16x16 frame animation sheet in this case would be the character with ASCII value 1+(4*16), which is 65—the capital letter A.

More commonly, this is the technique used to find the position in an image raster based on the screen's x, y position. An example of an image raster is an array of elements, with each element storing the pixel data (e.g., its color, its alpha component) on the image. As this array is a one-dimensional array, with the first element representing the pixel at the top-left corner of the image and the last element representing the pixel at the bottom-right corner of the image, you need some way to set the pixel at position x, y. Using this technique, you can work out the position in the raster to which the x and y coordinates refer. You can obtain the raster of a `BufferedImage` object in Java and go into lower-level pixel manipulation yourself, but this is not covered in this book.

Timing in Java

In the animations example in this chapter, all of the animation frames were changed in sequence with the running of the main loop. That is, the animations were updated based on the timing of the main loop. In those examples, we were aiming at around 25 frames per second. This means that the program's display will refresh itself with a new display 25 times every second, at least in principle. In Java, this is not exactly the case, at least not to a respectable accuracy, as we will look at shortly. But in general, animation and the updating of the game world should be handled independently from the frame rate, based on the real time that has elapsed. For our `StickWalker` example, the program running on a fast enough computer will run at around 25 frames per second (ignoring the low timer accuracy issue for the moment). However, a slower computer that cannot keep up with the expected frame rate will run with the animation updating at a slower rate. Not only this, however, but the character will not walk as fast across the screen. Both of these occur because the animation and movement code is executed per frame, in timing with the speed of the frame rate. A frame rate could lag on a faster computer also if other programs are taking up processor slices. Ideally, the change in the game world, which can consist of updating player positions, animation, AI elements etc., should be performed based on real time instead of the frame rate, as we mentioned before. It's true that this might not be required at all if you are just interested in making a little applet game and are not too bothered that the game actually runs a little slower if a particular computer cannot keep up (perhaps your game will run very efficiently or have little to do, decreasing this likelihood with the speed of computers today). But this is an important topic for professional gaming, especially for multiplayer online games, where computers of any speed are your players, everyone is moving about in everyone else's programs, and they will need to be moving at the same rate in real time. This is generally known as updating the game world in real time.

The problem in Java is that the available time getters (such as the method `currentTimeMillis` that we have been using for frame rate synching so far in this book) are not accurate enough at the moment for us to be able to do this to a tolerable level, generally ranging in accuracy from about 10 milliseconds on most platforms. The resolution of the time read is different from platform to platform and with no means of querying the accuracy. In terms of the accuracy being, say, 10 milliseconds, this means that if we calculate the elapsed time in one main loop cycle as lasting 20 milliseconds, the real elapsed time might actually be 15 milliseconds but the timer was not accurate enough to give us the correct time. Note that the timer value will usually be a great big number that is useful when compared to an older great big number, hence working out the time that elapsed. A basic scenario for updating the world, based on the real elapsed time per main loop cycle, would be to say that your character moves 4 pixels in 30 milliseconds, with the expected frame rate being 30 milliseconds. If the real time recorded for the time it took to execute one frame was 30 milliseconds, the character will move 4 pixels. If the recorded elapsed time was 60 milliseconds, the character will move 8 pixels. This is a very basic example, and we can use very basic math to work this algorithm, as we will see shortly

Typically for Windows games, for example, the high-resolution timer has accuracy in the microseconds (even to one millisecond is generally accurate enough) with the opportunity to find out the frequency of the timer that is available, which we will look at a little later. Note that the accuracy of a timer used inevitably depends on the hardware of the computer, but most modern computers will be amply sufficed.

High-resolution timing is also important for things like benchmark test-ing parts of your code to see how fast the code runs. This is especially useful for executing small segments of code thousands of times and seeing how long all of it took for comparing the speed of different algorithms. When the time frame between two comparative sections of code might be negligible, the higher the resolution of the timer, the more accurate the results will be. Oh, and it's essential if you want to simulate real-time physics also.

Using a Native High-Resolution Timer in Windows

In this section, we look at using a native high-resolution timer for the Window's platform using JNI (Java Native Interface) and C code. This is quite an advanced area, but we will narrow the code down to a high-reso-lution time-getting method in Java to get the current time and discuss how it would be used to update the world. We will also show you the full pro-cess of gaining the native high-resolution timer but cannot go into detail about JNI and the C/C++ programming language in this book. We apolo-gize to any users who are not on the Windows platform, as the actual code here can only be used on that platform. The theory is still there, and gain-ing a high-resolution timer for your platform will be done using the same techniques (i.e., through the JNI).

About the JNI

JNI stands for Java Native Interface and is a requirement if you need to use platform-specific code not available in pure Java. The term "pure Java" or "100% Java" is the general term for code that is all Java and will exe-cute on a Java Virtual Machine independent of the platform on which it is running. When using the JNI to allow your program to make use of plat-form-specific code, your program will be incompatible with platforms other than the one to which your code relates. The code is therefore known as native code. For the high-resolution timer example, we will use Windows (Win32 API) methods to gain the high-resolution time, which means that the program will only run on Windows machines, losing the platform independence of a program coded in "Pure Java." This is an obvi-ous disadvantage to using native code, but if we need this functionality to make games, this is more important in the long run. Creating many native high-resolution timer implementations, one for each of the target operat-ing systems on which your game is going to run, is better than trying to handle poor-resolution timing. Hopefully, high-resolution timer support will be available using pure Java in the future, but for now, we can use native methods.

Creating a Java Timer

In this book we cannot assume that you know anything about C/C++ code, so the idea here is to make this as painless as possible; we just want to get the time in Java by calling a simple `getTime` method. As an over-view to how this all works, we begin by creating a .dll file containing

Windows high-resolution timer code. DLL stands for Dynamic Link Library, and it is the library structure that we can access from Java through the JNI. However, the C/C++ code that is added to the DLL needs to be converted through the JNI to make it compatible with Java. If the following "native" section is a complete mystery to you, or you are not too interested in how to create the .dll file for yourself, do not worry, as the .dll file you will need for running the high-resolution timer example is available on the companion CD. Eventually, all we will need once the .dll file is creating is that file and our Java code, which will load in its functionality at run time. To begin with, we need to define the Java code in order to outline the basis for using the native code. The structure of the Java side will revolve around the `BaseClock` class. This class is as follows:

```
public abstract class BaseClock
{
    public abstract long getTime();
    public abstract int getDefaultUnit();
    public abstract void stampTime();
    public abstract long getElapsedTime();
    public abstract long getElapsedTime(int unit);

    public long stampTime;

    public static final int UNIT_SECONDS = 1;           //     10^0
    public static final int UNIT_MILLIS = 1000;         //     10^3
    public static final int UNIT_MICROS = 1000000;      //     10^6
    public static final int UNIT_NANOS = 1000000000;    //     10^9
}
```

The `BaseClock` class is simply a template super class for two more distinct classes, `StandardClock` and `NativeWinClock`, that both extend the `BaseClock`. The method `getTime` will return the current counter time of the clock (e.g., the `StandardClock` implementation will return the `System.currentTimeMillis` value). The `getDefaultUnit` method will return the default unit in which the clock's time is returned (e.g., the `StandardClock` time value is in milliseconds, where the `NativeWinClock` will return its default counter value in seconds). This method is needed so that you know which format the time retrieved is in. However, these two abstract methods are supplied more for completion because the class defines some more specific abstract methods for measuring what we want—the elapsed time.

The `stampTime` method saves the current counter time in a variable within the class. The `getElapsedTime` methods return the time difference between the current time and the value stored in the save time method. The idea is simply to stamp the time, which is like starting a stopwatch, and then get the elapsed time, which is like stopping the stopwatch (except in reality we are pulling the time distance out of the watch rather than stopping it altogether). The default `getElapsedTime` method will return the time in milliseconds for both the `Standard-Clock` and `NativeWinClock` subclasses of `BaseClock`. The `get-ElapsedTime(int unit)` method returns the elapsed time in the given unit. So by passing UNIT_MICROS into this method, we can get the elapsed time in microseconds; whether the timer class instance used can deliver this value to an accurate level will vary between the two classes in question (i.e., the StandardClock should not, but the NativeWin-Clock should be pretty accurate).

The StandardClock simply uses System.currentTimeMillis to retrieve its counter value, which is of course in milliseconds and designed to provide a clock in the event that a high-resolution timer is not available. The code for StandardClock is as follows:

```java
public class StandardClock extends BaseClock
{
    public long getTime()
    {
        return System.currentTimeMillis();
    }

    public int getDefaultUnit()
    {
        return UNIT_MILLIS;
    }

    public void stampTime()
    {
        stampTime = System.currentTimeMillis();
    }

    public long getElapsedTime()
    {
        return System.currentTimeMillis() - stampTime;
    }

    public long getElapsedTime(int unit)
    {
        return ((System.currentTimeMillis() - stampTime) * unit)
            / UNIT_MILLIS;
    }
}
```

Because the default time unit for the time retrieved is in milliseconds, we need to divide the elapsed time specified by the unit parameter back by 1000; we are working in a format where a second is "1", whereas by default in this class, a second is in the format of 1000 milliseconds.

The NativeWinClock works quite differently than the Standard-Clock implementation. We have to do a little more work ourselves, even when we get the native counter values. The native calls give us a counter value and a frequency value. The counter value is a large number, which changes through time but means nothing to us without the frequency. The frequency gives us the number of counts per second of the high-resolution counter. This value cannot change during run time, so we only need to retrieve it once during initialization.

Therefore, we can obtain a counter value in seconds by dividing the counter value retrieved by the frequency. Note this does not mean that we are limited to seconds; we can simply multiply the initial counter by 1000, for example, before dividing by the frequency to get the counter value in milliseconds. Here is the code for the `NativeWinClock` class:

```java
public class NativeWinClock extends BaseClock
{
    public NativeWinClock()
    {
        frequency = getFrequency();
    }

    public long getTime()
    {
        return getCounter() / frequency;
    }

    public int getDefaultUnit()
    {
        return UNIT_SECONDS;
    }

    public void stampTime()
    {
        stampTime = getCounter();
    }

    public long getElapsedTime()
    {
        return ((getCounter() - stampTime) * UNIT_MILLIS)
            / frequency;
    }

    public long getElapsedTime(int unit)
    {
        return ((getCounter() - stampTime) * unit) / frequency;
    }

    public static boolean isAvailable()
    {
        return available;
    }

    private native long getFrequency();
    private native long getCounter();

    private long frequency;
    private static boolean available;

    static
    {
        try
        {
            System.loadLibrary("WinClock");
            available = true;
        }
        catch(UnsatisfiedLinkError e1) {}
        catch(SecurityException e2)    {}
    }
}
```

In the constructor, we retrieve the frequency for the high-resolution timer and store it in the variable `frequency`. This only needs to be done once, as the frequency does not change from here on, as we mentioned before. When we return the elapsed time, we can convert the time into an understandable format by working out the elapsed time in the counter's default format first and then divide this elapsed counter value by the frequency. Note that the default `getElapsedTime` method returns the time in milliseconds to conform to the `StandardClock` class's return format.

The native methods that require native functionality are the methods `getFrequency` and `getCounter`, defined in the `NativeWinClock` class as follows:

```
private native long getFrequency();
private native long getCounter();
```

As you can see, all we need to do is include the keyword `native` in the method declaration and not include a code body for the methods, similar to abstract methods, which in a way they are. In the `static` block seen at the bottom of `NativeWinClock`, we actually load the native methods from the .dll file that we are to create. Note that this file is available for use on the companion CD if you are unable to make your own from the next section. If the native library could not be loaded, the variable `available` will remain its default value of `false`. This can be used to test the high-resolution timers availability in your program. The static block will be invoked when the class is loaded, so this will be determined before the `main` method is entered.

Creating WinClock.dll

In order to create the DLL, we first need to generate a C++ header file, which will contain function prototypes for the native methods for which we can then define the implementations in our C++ source file. Creating the header file, which has a .h file extension, is very simple. All you need to do is run the `javah.exe` utility with the class file that defines the native methods in the command line, as follows:

```
javah -jni NativeWinClock
```

Note that the `javah.exe` utility can be found in the bin directory of the Java SDK installation directory (where `javac.exe` and `java.exe` are found) and the `NativeWinClock` parameter refers to the `Native-WinClock.class` file and not its `.java` source file (hence you need to compile the `.java` file first). Once this is done, a new `NativeWin-Clock.h` file should have been created. This file will look similar to the following:

```
/* DO NOT EDIT THIS FILE - it is machine generated */
#include <jni.h>
/* Header for class NativeWinClock */

#ifndef _Included_NativeWinClock
#define _Included_NativeWinClock
#ifdef __cplusplus
```

```
extern "C" {
#endif
/* Inaccessible static: available */
/*
 * Class:     NativeWinClock
 * Method:    getFrequency
 * Signature: ()J
 */
JNIEXPORT jlong JNICALL Java_NativeWinClock_getFrequency
  (JNIEnv *, jobject);

/*
 * Class:     NativeWinClock
 * Method:    getCounter
 * Signature: ()J
 */
JNIEXPORT jlong JNICALL Java_NativeWinClock_getCounter
  (JNIEnv *, jobject);

#ifdef __cplusplus
}
#endif
#endif
```

Then the actual C code implementation for obtaining the high-resolution time is as follows. This code was entered into the file `WinClock.cpp`, also available on the companion CD.

```
#include <windows.h>
#include "NativeWinClock.h"

JNIEXPORT jlong JNICALL Java_NativeWinClock_getFrequency
    (JNIEnv *, jobject)
{
    LARGE_INTEGER freq;
    QueryPerformanceFrequency(&freq);
    return freq.QuadPart;
}

JNIEXPORT jlong JNICALL Java_NativeWinClock_getCounter
    (JNIEnv *, jobject)
{
    LARGE_INTEGER counter;
    QueryPerformanceCounter(&counter);
    return counter.QuadPart;
}
```

To compile the code into a DLL, you will also need important JNI header files, which can be found in the include and include\win32 directories of the Java SDK installation directory. Once this is done, the C++ file, along with the `NativeWinClock.h` header file and the JNI header files, can be compiled into the DLL using a compiler such as Microsoft Visual C++.

Sadly, we cannot go into more detail about the use of JNI or C/C++, as it is beyond of the scope of the book, but at least we have the compiled DLL and a high-resolution timer.

Using the High-Resolution Timer

When updating the game world based upon real time, we need to determine important parameters based on time. In previous examples where objects have moved about the screen, the movement has been defined in pixels per frame (e.g., the object might have been moving to the left at a rate of 4 pixels each frame—main loop cycle). If the object is going to move in real time, the movement must be defined in pixels over time. So, we can say that an object will move at a rate of 160 pixels per second along the x-axis. This means that if the frame rate is running at 25 frames per second, the object would move 160 / (1000 / 25) = 4 pixels every frame. Of course, the updating of the game world is now running independently of the frame rate, so this is just an observational comparison. We can put this into practice in an example to see the numerical movement of an object using the high-resolution timer. Note that for those of you who cannot use the Windows high-resolution timer, this example will still run, using the StandardClock if the native one is not available, and is still worth a look. Here is the code for the class HiresTimeExample, which must be compiled along with the BaseClock, StandardClock, and NativeWinClock classes. The DLL (if used) can be placed in the same folder as the class files.

Code Listing 12-3: HiresTimeExample

```
public class HiresTimeExample
{
    public static void main(String[] args)
    {
        BaseClock clock = null;

        if(NativeWinClock.isAvailable())
        {
            System.out.println("Using native clock");
            clock = new NativeWinClock();
        }
        else
        {
            System.out.println("Using standard clock");
            clock = new StandardClock();
        }

        // movement vector defined in pixels per microsecond
        // 160 and 240 represent pixels per second
        double xPixelsPerMicrosecond = (double)160
            / BaseClock.UNIT_MICROS;
        double yPixelsPerMicrosecond = (double)240
            / BaseClock.UNIT_MICROS;

        // current position to update with movement
        double posX = 0;
        double posY = 0;

        long elapsedTime;

        int counter = 0;
```

```
    int secondsCounter = 0;

    clock.stampTime();

    while(secondsCounter<10)       // if not passed 10 seconds
    {
        // get elasped time
        elapsedTime = clock.getElapsedTime
            (BaseClock.UNIT_MICROS);

        // stamp clock
        clock.stampTime();

        // increase counter
        counter+=elapsedTime;

        // update world
        posX += (xPixelsPerMicrosecond * elapsedTime);
        posY += (yPixelsPerMicrosecond * elapsedTime);

        if(counter >= BaseClock.UNIT_MICROS)
        // if 1 second elapsed
        {
            System.out.println("Counter = "+counter);
            counter -= BaseClock.UNIT_MICROS;
            System.out.println("Pos = "+posX+", "+posY);
            secondsCounter++;
        }


        try
        {
            Thread.sleep(5);
        }
        catch(Exception e) {}
    }
}
}
```

To begin with, we create the clock we are going to use for timing using the NativeWinClock if available; otherwise we use the StandardClock, which simply uses System.currentTimeMillis. The variables xPixelsPerMicrosecond and yPixelsPerMicrosecond define the amount of pixels an object should travel in one microsecond about the x- and y-axis, respectively, as a basis for real-time movement. Note that there are a thousand milliseconds in a second and a thousand microseconds in a millisecond. The variables xPos and yPos simply store the current position of an object. The reason we have the movement vector values stored in pixels per microsecond is because we are using microseconds as the base for the high-resolution time. Therefore, the object can then be moved by the recorded elapsed time multiplied by the respective x and y movement values, as seen in the code. The code terminates execution after ten seconds. Now take a look at the screen shot of an expected outcome when using the native high-resolution timer:

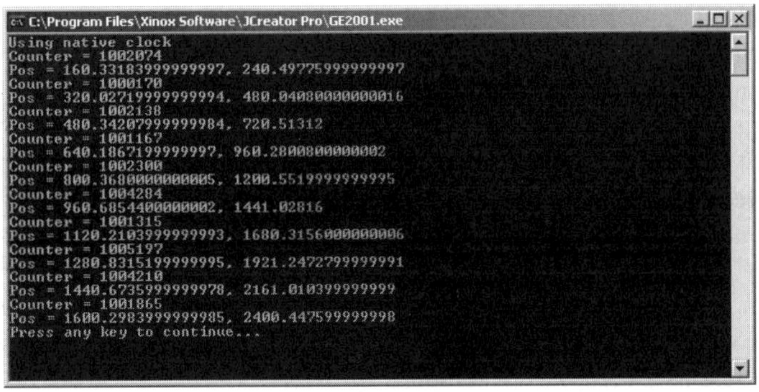

Figure 12-8

The position of the object is printed to the screen at one-second intervals for a total of ten seconds. Notice that the object's current position is not very accurate at each interval. Should the position after one second not be almost exactly (160, 240) and not (160.33, 240.5) approximately? After all, we are using the high-resolution timer. Well, it is not actually the high-resolution time that is the problem but the `Thread.sleep` command. By calling the `sleep` command, the thread will sleep for that duration, or at least roughly that duration, as the sleep is not high resolution. Therefore, during this sleep we cannot test to see if the "one-second lapse" has passed accurately enough. Ideally, we would just remove the `sleep` command altogether and poll at full speed, checking over and over until the time had elapsed. This is how we may implement a frame rate limiter, by polling the main loop and only updating the game world and rendering when the counter has passed, say, 40 milliseconds. As the main loop is polling without a sleep, the time elapsed check is picked up almost right away. The problem is that Java is a multithreaded language, with (most notably) the garbage collector and the Event Dispatch Thread also needing processor time to run alongside the main loop. So the main loop simply cannot just take over and with "brute force" run forever; the sleep is needed.

It is important to note that the position of our imaginary object is being updated at great accuracy with the high-resolution timer in the previous example, so that is nothing to worry about.

Garbage Collection and Creating Objects

In many other programming languages, a programmer will specifically allocate memory in the loading stage of the game before the actual game bit begins. During the actual game (by this we mean the fast rendering, fast action part as opposed to the game menu area), the process of allocating new memory will be kept as minimal as possible; preferably, all memory will be allocated before the main game starts, as memory allocation is time consuming. An example of memory allocation would be when loading in an image; memory is allocated for the data of the image (e.g., its pixels), and then the image data is loaded into this memory. When memory is finished with (for example, that image is no longer required), the programmer will specifically deallocate the memory, usually after the level of the game is complete, and move onto the next level stage.

In Java, we are most concerned with creating objects. When an object is created, new memory for the object is allocated and the object is controlled under the watchful eye of the garbage collector. The *garbage collector* is a mechanism used for handling objects created in your program environment. Therefore, it is not specifically up to you, the programmer, to deallocate the memory of any objects you create. Let's take the following method as a very basic example:

```
public void myMethod()
{
    Object myObject = new Object();
}
```

When the object is created, its lifetime is controlled internally. Basically, the garbage collector watches for when the object loses its scope, and when it is no longer accessible from any references in your program, the object is lost. What needs to happen then is that the object's memory needs to be deallocated and eventually the object is destroyed once and for all since the object is of no further use once the method exits. However, the object would have further use if you assigned another variable with scope outside of this method to reference that object, which means it would not be garbage collected, as something else would still reference it in your program.

Objects can be created from anywhere in your program. Sometimes you won't even be aware of it (for example, when you specify a string literal, like "This is a string literal," this is really a `String` object like any other that you might have created using a string class constructor). Objects can also be created from methods of classes and objects in the standard Java packages, such as the `getBounds` method of a `Component` object (or a derived class of `Component`). Take the following code using the `Component` object `myComponent` as an example.

```
int x = myComponent.getBounds().x;
int y = myComponent.getBounds().y;
```

Each call to the component method `getBounds` is actually creating a new `Rectangle` object. So in this code, we have created two new `Rectangle` objects, when all we needed was two integer variables. The objects created will be up for garbage collection right away, as we no longer hold a reference to the newly created objects after each line of code (provided the `getBounds` method doesn't hold on to the new objects created internally).

There are two immediate problems with creating objects consistently in the main loop. The first is that when many objects are garbage collected, it means that the garbage collector needs to do more work. As the garbage collector is running in a thread itself, the more it runs, the less processor share we have for the game logic and rendering, etc. The effect of this is that noticeable pauses can occur in the game's rendering, which basically means pauses in the main loop's execution as the garbage collector takes an increased gulp of the processor time. A new addition to J2SDK 1.4.1 is the command-line flag `-XX:+UseConcMarkSweepGC` that turns on concurrent garbage collection, whereby it uses more processor time in order to reduce garbage collection pause times. This command-line flag can be added when running your program as follows:

```
java -XX:+UseConcMarkSweepGC MyMainClass
```

The other problem is more severe and can come in the event that you create many objects in the main loop and don't allow the garbage collector to collect and remove these objects appropriately. The result is that you run out of memory and an `OutOfMemoryError` error is thrown. This is the reason why we always sleep in the main loop for at least 5 milliseconds—so that we do not starve other threads, such as the Garbage Collector.

Object Pooling

As creating and garbage collecting objects can be a serious bottleneck in the main loop, it is obviously best to do this as little as possible. However, a lot of the data structures that we need will be dynamic and require adapting through creating more objects or removing the ones you have, as opposed to just creating a set number of objects and using them. But that's the key right there; instead of creating, using, and removing (where the objects will be garbage collected), we can create and use without letting go of our objects. For this, we can create what is known as an *object pool*. The idea is that a set number of objects are created and added to the pool. These objects are now available to be used in your main game, grabbed from the object pool. Once the object has finished its use, it can then be returned to the object pool, ready for reuse later on, perhaps when a new object is needed, instead of it being garbage collected and newer objects being created when they are needed again. The emphasis is on object reuse.

The following code is a basic illustration of how an object pool might be implemented:

```
public class ObjectPool
{
    public ObjectPool(int size)
    {
        list = new Object[size];
    }

    public void dump(Object o)
    {
        if(currentObject<list.length)
            list[currentObject++] = o;
        else
            System.out.println("List is full");
    }
```

```
public Object grab()
{
    if(currentObject > 0)
    {
        Object newObject = list[--currentObject];
        list[currentObject] = null;
        return newObject;
    }
    else
    {
        System.out.println("List is empty");
        return null;
    }
}


private Object list[];
private int currentObject;
}
```

When creating the ObjectPool, we define the size of the list in which to store objects. The format for the list is simply an array. The list would then need to be filled with an initial set of objects, which may be added using the dump method. Then when an object is required, it can be returned through a call to the grab method and removed from the object pool. When the object is finished in the main game, the object can then be passed back to the object pool using the dump method once again. Of course, you will need to specifically handle when a new object is required and when it is no longer needed in your code.

When an object is obtained from the pool, its data may also need to be reinitialized. An initialization method can be defined to mimic what the constructor would usually do. The variable currentObject is used to handle the current index position in the pool of available objects, with the next available object stored at index currentObject - 1. Note that an object pool is only suitable for objects of the same type (or same base type, perhaps) but not for mixed types of objects. So if you wanted to store both Alien objects, and MagicStar objects for example, which are imagined to be completely different types of objects, you would need an object pool for each. Note that for new objects needed occasionally rather than every loop cycle, it is probably more beneficial to create the objects as usual than to go through the motions of using an object pool.

Notice that in this code we have print statements indicating if the list is full or empty. Both of these instances should not occur if you have added the maximum possible number of objects that you expect to use into the pool, but this may not be something that is easily estimated in your game. If this is the case, the list may be resized in the event of underestimating the amount of objects required. In the ObjectPool class to support this, a dynamic list object, such as java.util.LinkedList, would be more suitable for the object pool implementation.

There are other, more simplistic means of avoiding removing and recreating new objects in general. Suppose you have a list of "baddies." When one of the baddies is killed, it needs to be removed from the game. Instead of removing the baddie from the list (which would be expensive when removing an object from an ArrayList/Vector), and even dumping it back in an object pool, an `isAlive` or `isActive` state could simply be set in the object. This indicates to accessing elements of the game loop, such as rendering and collision detection, that they can ignore that element in the list, as the baddie is labeled dead. The downside to this is that unnecessary accessing and checking is performed continuously in the list. If you had a list of 100 baddies and only two were still alive, it would be a large waste to check through the entire list searching for live baddies.

 NOTE: The use of the `finalize` method should be avoided because it can prolong the object's lifetime when it is ready to be garbage collected. When it gets to the final stage, removal, if the `finalize` method has been overridden, the object's destruction is delayed as the object's finalize method needs to be queued for invocation. Although the `finalize` method is convenient, in general you should know at what stage in your code you are finished with an object and should provide the cleanup functionality for it yourself at that point.

The final note is on creating many small objects. The more objects that are created, the more work the JVM has to do to look after the larger group of objects. This involves checking to see if the objects are still visible (i.e., if any more references exist to that object, and if not, the object needs be garbage collected). This is something to be aware of, as in many circumstances a collection of objects could actually be defined in fewer objects. For example, a list of simple screen elements in your game might only be defined by individual x and y coordinates but share the same rendering code. Instead of creating an object for each of these screen elements, encapsulating the x and y coordinates, and rendering code into a class structure, the elements might be better handled as a group. Say you had 100 of these elements, which would mean using 100 objects; you could store each of the x and y values in arrays. An array is itself an object, but this would mean having two large objects in the place of 100 small ones. The rendering code could be adapted to pick these values out of the array for drawing. Of course, this system is not suitable for all types of grouped, similar objects and would become more complex the larger the number of attributes involved.

Collision Detection

In games programming, collision detection is an important topic, as it is a key factor to most games. By *collision detection*, we mean checking whether two "objects" in your game are intersecting (overlapping each other). It would, in fact, be possible to write an entire book on collision detection, and if you search for this topic on the Internet, you will find hundreds of articles and a variety of techniques that can be used.

In the following sections, however, we are going to focus on two simple methods of performing collision detection in a game—bounding circle and bounding box collision detection—which give us good approximations of whether two objects have collided, regardless of the actual form of the object (i.e., the object (game character, etc.) does not necessarily need to be square or round; we just approximate to either a box or a circle for the collision testing). So let's start by looking at how we can do bounding circle collision detection.

Bounding Circle

The more common name for this method of collision detection is actually "bounding sphere," but since we are in 2D, circle is more appropriate, as a sphere is a 3D object. This form of collision detection is relatively simple. All we need to do is get the distance between the two center points of the circles that we are testing and then compare this to the sum of the two circles' radii (half the diameter).

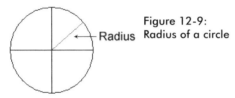

Figure 12-9:
Radius of a circle

If the distance between the center points is less than the sum of the two radii, the circles will be intersecting; otherwise, they will not be overlapping each other.

To work out the distance between the two circles, we can use the Pythagorean theorem (urg, I know we all hate math, but don't worry, this is simple). Let's first look at the following diagram of a right-angled triangle (one corner at a 90 degree angle) with its three sides denoted as A, B, and C.

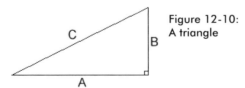

Figure 12-10:
A triangle

Using the Pythagorean theorem, we can work out the length of side C by squaring the lengths of sides A and B and taking the square root of the sum. This can be seen in the following formula:

$$C = \sqrt{A^2 + B^2}$$

So that's fine for a triangle, but it still doesn't give us the distance between two circles... or does it?

Take a look at the following diagram:

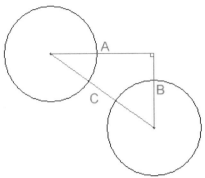

Figure 12-11:
The magic of Pythagoras

As you can see, if you think about the distance between the two center points as being the C line of the triangle, we can construct a right-angled triangle from this to create our A and B lines. We can also work out the length of the lines A and B by finding the absolute (positive) values of:

Length A = x2 – x1

Length B = y2 – y1

...where (x1, y1) and (x2, y2) are the two center points of the circles. Then we can simply apply the length of A and B to the formula that we saw before to obtain the length of C, which is the distance between the circles.

Now that we have looked at the basic theory behind bounding circle collision detection, let's look at a working applet example where we have two circles, one of which we can move with the arrow keys and change the radius with the Page Up and Page Down keys. When the circles intersect, their colors will change to red. Here is the complete source code listing for this example.

Listing 12-4: Bounding circle example

Circle.java

```java
import java.awt.*;
import java.awt.geom.*;

public class Circle
{
    public Circle(int x, int y, int radius)
    {
        this.x = x;
        this.y = y;
        this.radius = radius;
    }


    public void render(Graphics g)
    {
        int diameter = radius*2;
        g.fillOval(x-radius, y-radius, diameter, diameter);
    }
```

```java
    public boolean intersects(Circle otherCircle)
    {
        int xDiff = (x-otherCircle.x);
        int yDiff = (y-otherCircle.y);
        int distance = xDiff*xDiff + yDiff*yDiff;

        int totalRadius = (radius + otherCircle.radius);

        return (distance < (totalRadius*totalRadius));
    }

    public int x, y, radius;
}
```

BoundingCircleIntersection.java

```java
import java.awt.*;
import java.awt.image.*;
import java.awt.event.*;
import javax.swing.*;


public class BoundingCircleIntersection extends JApplet
    implements Runnable, KeyListener
{
    public void init()
    {
        getContentPane().setLayout(null);
        setSize(DISPLAY_WIDTH, DISPLAY_HEIGHT);
        setIgnoreRepaint(true);
        addKeyListener(this);

        backBuffer = new BufferedImage(DISPLAY_WIDTH, DISPLAY_HEIGHT,
            BufferedImage.TYPE_INT_RGB);
        bbGraphics = (Graphics2D) backBuffer.getGraphics();

        // create two circles...
        circle1 = new Circle(DISPLAY_WIDTH/2, DISPLAY_HEIGHT/2, 30);
        circle2 = new Circle(100, 100, 15);
    }

    public void start()
    {
        loop = new Thread(this);
        loop.start();
    }

    public void stop()
    {
        loop = null;
    }

    public void run()
    {
        long startTime, waitTime, elapsedTime;
        // 1000/25 Frames Per Second = 40 millisecond delay
        int delayTime = 1000/25;

        Thread thisThread = Thread.currentThread();
        while(loop==thisThread)
```

```
    {
        startTime = System.currentTimeMillis();

        // render to back buffer now
        render(bbGraphics);

        // render back buffer image to screen
        Graphics g = getGraphics();
        g.drawImage(backBuffer, 0, 0, null);
        g.dispose();

        // handle frame rate
        elapsedTime = System.currentTimeMillis() - startTime;
        waitTime = Math.max(delayTime - elapsedTime, 5);

        try
        {
            Thread.sleep(waitTime);
        }
        catch(InterruptedException e) {}
    }
}

public void render(Graphics g)
{
    g.clearRect(0, 0, DISPLAY_WIDTH, DISPLAY_HEIGHT);

    if(circle1.intersects(circle2)) // change the color to red...
        g.setColor(Color.red);
    else
        g.setColor(Color.green);

    circle1.render(g);
    circle2.render(g);
}


public void keyTyped(KeyEvent e) { }
public void keyReleased(KeyEvent e) { }

public void keyPressed(KeyEvent e)
{
    switch(e.getKeyCode())
    {
        case KeyEvent.VK_LEFT:
            circle2.x--;
            break;

        case KeyEvent.VK_RIGHT:
            circle2.x++;
            break;

        case KeyEvent.VK_UP:
            circle2.y--;
            break;

        case KeyEvent.VK_DOWN:
            circle2.y++;
            break;
```

```
           case KeyEvent.VK_PAGE_UP:
               if(circle2.radius < 50)
                   circle2.radius++;
               break;

           case KeyEvent.VK_PAGE_DOWN:
               if(circle2.radius > 2)
                   circle2.radius--;
               break;
       }
   }

   private Thread loop;
   private BufferedImage backBuffer;
   private Graphics2D bbGraphics;

   private static final int DISPLAY_WIDTH = 400;
   private static final int DISPLAY_HEIGHT = 400;

   private Circle circle1, circle2;

}
```

Here is a screen shot of the applet in action:

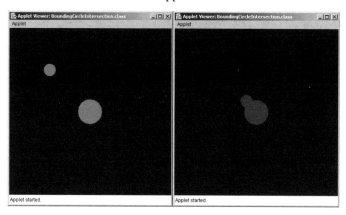

Figure 12-12:
Before and
after
intersection

Remember that you may need to click on the applet to gain the key focus. Also note that we have just implemented a `KeyListener` to get the input, rather than using our main loop synchronized `EventProcessor` to keep the example code to a minimum.

Let's first look at the `Circle` class, as this is where the actual intersection code is. First, however, declare the constructor to take in three parameters: the x, y positions and the radius. The constructor then simply sets the member variables to be equal to these values. Nothing complicated there.

Next, we have the `render` method, which will be called from the main loop to render this circle to the screen. All this method actually does is call the `fillOval` method of the `Graphics` object g. Notice how we first deduct the radius of the circle from the x, y coordinates before we pass them into the method; this is simply so that our coordinates represent the center and not the top left. The `render` method can be seen here:

```
public void render(Graphics g)
{
    int diameter = radius*2;
    g.fillOval(x-radius, y-radius, diameter, diameter);
}
```

Now comes the good bit—the `intersects` method. This method will take another `Circle` object as a parameter, so we can easily compare "this" circle to another one and return either true or false, depending on whether it intersects.

In the `intersects` method, we first need to get the lengths of the A and B lines that we spoke of before (the horizontal and vertical sides of the triangle). So we do this simply by taking away the circle's x and y positions from the other circle's x, y positions. This can be seen here:

```
int xDiff = (x-otherCircle.x);
int yDiff = (y-otherCircle.y);
```

Note that we do not have to worry about these values being absolute (positive), as in the next step we will be squaring the values that will always make them positive.

```
int distance = xDiff*xDiff + yDiff*yDiff;
```

Here we are using a slightly modified version of the Pythagorean theorem, in that we have omitted the square root altogether, as we don't really require it (we'll see why in a minute). So now we have the distance between the two center points of the two circles that we are testing; we can proceed by getting the value of the sum of the two radii. This can be seen in the next line of code:

```
int totalRadius = (radius + otherCircle.radius);
```

Then we perform the actual test by returning the result of testing, whether the `distance` was less than the `totalRadius` squared. We square the total radius to simply balance the two sides of the `if` statement—if you remember before, we omitted the square root from where we found the distance, so the distance we have is actually the distance squared. To compensate for this, we simply square the total radius. Note that although finding the square root is very easy, as there is a static method called `Math.sqrt(double)`, it is very expensive to execute. For this situation, we don't actually require it. The line of code that performs the test can be seen here:

```
return (distance < (totalRadius*totalRadius));
```

The `Circle` class and our intersection test are now covered. Let's have a quick look at the key points in the main class `BoundingCircleInter-section`. Note that we have used the `ActiveRenderingApplet` example from Chapter 9 as a base for this example.

Chapter 12

First we declare two `Circle` objects, `circle1` and `circle2`, as members to the main class. Then we initialize them in the constructor with the following two lines of code:

```
circle1 = new Circle(DISPLAY_WIDTH/2, DISPLAY_HEIGHT/2, 30);
circle2 = new Circle(100, 100, 15);
```

Then, in the `render` method, we call the `intersects` method of `circle1`, passing the `circle2` object in as a parameter. This will then return true or false (i.e., whether they intersect or not). If they do intersect, we set the color to red so both circles will be drawn in red; otherwise, we set it to green. This can be seen here:

```
if(circle1.intersects(circle2)) // change the color to red...
    g.setColor(Color.red);
else
    g.setColor(Color.green);
```

After this, we can simply render the circles to the screen by calling their render methods, as can be seen in the following two lines of code:

```
circle1.render(g);
circle2.render(g);
```

The final relevant part of the main class is the `keyPressed` method where we handle adjusting the position of the `circle2` object using the arrow keys and also allow the user to adjust the radius of `circle2`, making it larger and smaller, by means of the Page Up and Page Down keys.

Bounding Box

As we mentioned before, the second collision detection technique that we are going to look at is bounding box collisions, where we test if the rectangular bounds of our object intersect with another object's rectangular bounds.

The best and easiest way to implement this is to actually test if the bounding boxes do not intersect, as we will see in the code to follow.

Let's first look at an example applet, which shows bounding box collisions in action. Then we will look at the underlying theory. Here is the complete code listing for the bounding box example:

Listing 12-5: Bounding box example

Box.java

```
import java.awt.*;

public class Box
{
    public Box(int x, int y, int w, int h)
    {
        this.x = x;
        this.y = y;
        this.w = w;
        this.h = h;
    }
```

```
public void render(Graphics g)
{
    g.fillRect(x, y, w, h);
}


public boolean intersects(Box otherBox)
{
    return !(otherBox.x >= x+w || otherBox.x+otherBox.w <= x ||
        otherBox.y >= y+h || otherBox.y+otherBox.h <= y);
}

public int x, y, w, h;
}
```

BoundingBoxIntersection.java

```
import java.awt.*;
import java.awt.image.*;
import java.awt.event.*;
import javax.swing.*;


public class BoundingBoxIntersection extends JApplet implements
    Runnable, KeyListener
{
    public void init()
    {
        getContentPane().setLayout(null);
        setSize(DISPLAY_WIDTH, DISPLAY_HEIGHT);
        setIgnoreRepaint(true);
        addKeyListener(this);

        backBuffer = new BufferedImage(DISPLAY_WIDTH, DISPLAY_HEIGHT,
            BufferedImage.TYPE_INT_RGB);
        bbGraphics = (Graphics2D) backBuffer.getGraphics();

        // create two boxes...
        box1 = new Box(DISPLAY_WIDTH/2 - 50, DISPLAY_HEIGHT/2 - 25,
            100, 50);
        box2 = new Box(100, 100, 50, 50);
    }

    public void start()
    {
        loop = new Thread(this);
        loop.start();
    }

    public void stop()
    {
        loop = null;
    }

    public void run()
    {
        long startTime, waitTime, elapsedTime;
        // 1000/25 Frames Per Second = 40 millisecond delay
        int delayTime = 1000/25;

        Thread thisThread = Thread.currentThread();
```

```
        while(loop==thisThread)
        {
            startTime = System.currentTimeMillis();

            // render to back buffer now
            render(bbGraphics);

            // render back buffer image to screen
            Graphics g = getGraphics();
            g.drawImage(backBuffer, 0, 0, null);
            g.dispose();

            //  handle frame rate
            elapsedTime = System.currentTimeMillis() - startTime;
            waitTime = Math.max(delayTime - elapsedTime, 5);

            try
            {
                Thread.sleep(waitTime);
            }
            catch(InterruptedException e) {}
        }
    }


    public void render(Graphics g)
    {
        g.clearRect(0, 0, DISPLAY_WIDTH, DISPLAY_HEIGHT);

        if(box1.intersects(box2)) // change the color to red...
            g.setColor(Color.red);
        else
            g.setColor(Color.green);

        box1.render(g);
        box2.render(g);
    }


    public void keyTyped(KeyEvent e) { }
    public void keyReleased(KeyEvent e) { }

    public void keyPressed(KeyEvent e)
    {
        switch(e.getKeyCode())
        {
            case KeyEvent.VK_LEFT:
                box2.x--;
                break;

            case KeyEvent.VK_RIGHT:
                box2.x++;
                break;

            case KeyEvent.VK_UP:
                box2.y--;
                break;

            case KeyEvent.VK_DOWN:
                box2.y++;
```

```
                    break;
        }
    }

    private Thread loop;
    private BufferedImage backBuffer;
    private Graphics2D bbGraphics;

    private static final int DISPLAY_WIDTH = 400;
    private static final int DISPLAY_HEIGHT = 400;

    private Box box1, box2;
}
```

The following figure is a screen shot of this example in action:

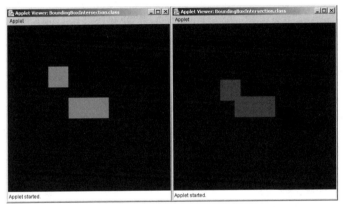

Figure 12-13: Before and after intersection

So let's look at the Box class. First, we have the constructor that takes in four parameters—the x, y locations, the width, and the height of the box. It then assigns the parameters to an instance member of the class, in the same way as we did with the Circle class in the previous example.

Next, we have defined a render method that draws the rectangle to the Graphics object g which is passed into the render method, using the fillRect method of the Graphics object. The render method can be seen here.

```
public void render(Graphics g)
{
    g.fillRect(x, y, w, h);
}
```

Finally, we have our intersects method, which takes a Box object as a parameter so we can compare this Box object to the Box object that was passed in. The check for the intersection is accomplished in a single line of code that can be seen inside the intersects method here:

```
public boolean intersects(Box otherBox)
{
    return !(otherBox.x >= x+w || otherBox.x+otherBox.w <= x ||
        otherBox.y >= y+h || otherBox.y+otherBox.h <= y);
}
```

Here we are actually checking if the box passed in does not intersect with this box, and then we swap the result (i.e., false to true and true to false) so that true will represent the boxes intersecting.

The first check here is if the box passed in, otherBox's x position, is to the right of this box's x position plus this box's width. We are checking if the leftmost side of the otherBox is to the right of the rightmost side of this box. If it is, it will not be intersecting and true is generated (which will then be returned as false due to the ! part of the code).

This process is then repeated for the other three sides of the boxes. If you are still not sure, study the line of code and try to figure out what is happening—it does make sense!

Let's now look at the key parts of the main class BoundingBox-Intersection that we use to display the boxes. We define two boxes in the class called box1 and box2. In the constructor we initialize them with the following two lines of code:

```
box1 = new Box(DISPLAY_WIDTH/2 - 50, DISPLAY_HEIGHT/2 - 25, 100, 50);
box2 = new Box(100, 100, 50, 50);
```

In the render method, we do the same move as in the previous bounding circle example—we call the intersects method of box1, passing in box2 as an argument (as we want to test if box2 intersects box1). If it does intersect, we color both boxes red; otherwise, we set the color to green. The code for this can be seen here:

```
if(box1.intersects(box2)) // change the color to red...
    g.setColor(Color.red);
else
    g.setColor(Color.green);
```

Once we have set the color appropriately, we can call the render methods of both the boxes, passing in the Graphics object g, which will be used to render them. This can be seen here:

```
box1.render(g);
box2.render(g);
```

Finally we have the keyPressed method, as with the bounding circle example, to move box2 around the screen with the cursor keys so we can test the intersections.

Note that the java.awt.Rectangle class contains an inter-sects method built in, which takes another Rectangle if you choose to define your box regions as instances of this class.

Creating a Game Framework

The aim of this section is to create a screen management system for your games, so you can create distinct screens within your game that have their own logic and rendering code, as well as methods that will perform the necessary loading and unloading of the screens.

The game framework is a cocktail of three different examples from the book, with some extra bits here and there to make them all work nicely together. We use the rendering techniques from the `FullScreenDemo` example in Chapter 9, the input system from the `EventAndFocus-Handling` example in Chapter 10, and finally the Sound Manager from Chapter 11.

Let's start with looking at how we are going to define a screen within our game framework. Here is the complete source listing for our `TemplateScreen` class.

Code Listing 12-6: `TemplateScreen.java`

```java
import java.awt.*;
import java.awt.event.*;

public abstract class TemplateScreen
{
    public abstract void render(Graphics g);

    public void process()
    {

    }

    public void handleEvent(AWTEvent e)
    {

    }

    public void load()
    {

    }

    public void unload()
    {

    }

    public Rectangle bounds = new Rectangle(0, 0 ,
        Globals.DISPLAY_WIDTH, Globals.DISPLAY_HEIGHT);
}
```

As you can see, our `TemplateScreen` class is abstract, so to use it we need to extend it and implement the `render` method, which all the screens in the framework must implement.

Along with the `render` method, we also have the option of overriding four other methods in the `TemplateScreen`: the `handleEvent` method that will be passed events from the event processor when the screen is active, the `load` method that will be called once each time the screen is loaded (i.e., made the current screen), the `unload` method that will be called once just before another screen is loaded to replace this one as the current screen, and finally the `process` method that will handle any game logic relevant to this screen.

Note also that we store the bounds of the screen in a `Rectangle` object. Notice also that we access two static members called

DISPLAY_WIDTH and DISPLAY_HEIGHT from a class called Globals. Let's look at this class now.

Code Listing 12-7: Globals.java

```
public class Globals
{
    public static GameFramework framework;

    public static Keyboard keyboard;
    public static Mouse mouse;

    public static TemplateScreen currentScreen;
    public static TemplateScreen previousScreen;

    public static SampleScreen sampleScreen;

    public static int DISPLAY_WIDTH = 800;
    public static int DISPLAY_HEIGHT = 600;
    public static String WINDOW_TITLE = "Game Framework";

    public static SoundManager soundManager;
}
```

In the Globals class, we have a reference to our main GameFramework object, which we have called framework (don't worry, we will look at the main GameFramework class soon). Then we have references to a Keyboard object and a Mouse object, which will be used to access the keyboard and mouse states from within the screens. Then we have two references to our abstract TemplateScreen class that we just saw. The first one, currentScreen, contains a reference to the current screen that should be handling the logic for the game and the rendering to the screen. In addition, we have the previousScreen reference, which we will use when we look at handling focus lost and gained in the framework.

Next, we have a SampleScreen object, which is going to be a class that extends the TemplateScreen class and will be a sample screen for the game framework, as you need at least one screen to see it working.

Then we define the width and height of the application as the integer variables DISPLAY_WIDTH and DISPLAY_HEIGHT. Remember here that if you wish to use the full-screen mode as well as windowed mode, you need to define the width and height of the screen as a valid screen resolution (such as 640x480, 800x600, 1024x768, etc.). After this we then have a String object called WINDOW_TITLE, which is used to define the title for our application (although this is only relevant in windowed mode).

Finally, we have a reference in here to a SoundManager object, so we can use the sound manager through the scope of the game framework (i.e., in all the screens we define).

Let's now have a quick look at the SampleScreen class (screen) that we have created by extending our TemplateScreen class. Here is the complete code listing:

Code Listing 12-8: `SampleScreen.java`

```
import java.awt.*;
import java.awt.event.*;

public class SampleScreen extends TemplateScreen
{
    public SampleScreen()
    {
        // setup the screen here...
    }

    public void process()
    {
        // place screen logic code here...
    }

    public void render(Graphics g)
    {
        // rendering code goes here...
        g.setColor(Color.white);
        g.fillRect(0, 0, bounds.width, bounds.height);

        g.setColor(Color.black);
        g.drawString("Sample Screen", 10, 15);
    }

    public void handleEvent(AWTEvent e)
    {
        // handle events here...
    }

    public void load()
    {
        // put screen loading code here...
    }

    public void unload()
    {
        // put screen unloading code here...
    }
}
```

In the constructor of our screen classes, we can put all the initialization code that is performed once at the initial loading of the game. Then, for things that should happen when the screen is set as the current screen, we can use the `load` method (which if you remember is inherited from the `TemplateScreen` class), just as we use the `unload` method if the screen used to be the current screen and now it is not.

Other than that, we have implemented the `render` method, which if you remember is declared as abstract in the `TemplateScreen` class. In it we have simply cleared the screen to white and displayed the text "Sample Screen" at the top-left corner of the screen.

Next, we have created a `Keyboard` class to handle the states of the keys within the framework. The complete `Keyboard` class can be seen here:

Code Listing 12-9: `Keyboard.java`

```
public class Keyboard
{
    public Keyboard()
    {
        keyState = new boolean[256];
    }

    public void resetAllStates()
    {
        for(int i=0; i<keyState.length; i++)
            keyState[i] = false;
    }

    public boolean keyState[];
}
```

As you can see, this class is very simple. All it has is a Boolean array of size 256, which will be used to store the state of the keys on the keyboard, as we have seen before in Chapter 10. Note we have also created a method here that will reset the state of all the keys called resetAll-States, which we will use when we handle the loss of focus within the framework.

As well as the Keyboard class, we have also declared a Mouse class to handle the current position and states of the mouse buttons:

Code Listing 12-10: `Mouse.java`

```
public class Mouse
{
    public Mouse()
    {
        button = new boolean[3];
    }

    public void resetAllStates()
    {
        for(int i=0; i<button.length; i++)
            button[i] = false;
    }

    public int x, y;
    public boolean button[];

    public static final int LEFT_BUTTON = 0;
    public static final int RIGHT_BUTTON = 1;
    public static final int MIDDLE_BUTTON = 2;
}
```

Note in this class how we have also defined three static final integer values, which represent the three buttons on the mouse and can be used as indices for the button array, which will contain the states of the three mouse buttons (i.e., whether they are up or down).

Now that we have seen all the new supporting classes for this example, you will also need to grab the EventProcessor.java and Event-Processable.java source files from Chapter 10 and also the SoundManager.java source file from Chapter 11.

Let's now look at our main class GameFramework.java, which is the core of our framework. The complete source listing for it can be seen here:

Code Listing 12-11: GameFramework.java

```java
import java.awt.*;
import java.awt.image.*;
import java.awt.event.*;
import javax.swing.*;

public class GameFramework extends JFrame implements Runnable,
                                                     KeyListener,
                                                     MouseListener,
                                                     MouseMotionListener,
                                                     FocusListener,
                                                     EventProcessable
{
    public GameFramework(GraphicsDevice graphicsDevice)
    {
        super(graphicsDevice.getDefaultConfiguration());
        this.graphicsDevice = graphicsDevice;

        getContentPane().setLayout(null);
        setIgnoreRepaint(true);
        setResizable(false);

        addWindowListener(new WindowAdapter()
                        {
                            public void windowClosing(WindowEvent e)
                            {
                                exitProgram();
                            }
                        });

        addKeyListener(this);
        getContentPane().addMouseListener(this);
        getContentPane().addMouseMotionListener(this);
        addFocusListener(this);

        eventProcessor = new EventProcessor(this);

        Globals.framework = this;

        // set up the sound manager...
        Globals.soundManager = new SoundManager();

        // set up mouse and keyboard
        Globals.keyboard = new Keyboard();
        Globals.mouse = new Mouse();
    }


    public void setMode(int mode)
    {
        if(mode==FULLSCREEN_MODE)
            if(!graphicsDevice.isFullScreenSupported())
            {
                mode = WINDOWED_MODE;
                System.out.println("Sorry, fullscreen mode not
```

```
                            supported, continuing in windowed mode");
        }

    this.mode = mode;

    try
    {
        if(mode==FULLSCREEN_MODE)
        {
            setUndecorated(true);
            graphicsDevice.setFullScreenWindow(this);

            if(graphicsDevice.isDisplayChangeSupported())
            {
                DisplayMode dm = new DisplayMode(Globals
                    .DISPLAY_WIDTH, Globals.DISPLAY_HEIGHT, 16,
                    DisplayMode.REFRESH_RATE_UNKNOWN);
                if(isDisplayModeAvailable(dm))
                    graphicsDevice.setDisplayMode(dm);
                else
                {
                    System.out.println("Display mode not
                        available: "+
                                        dm.getWidth()+":"+
                                        dm.getHeight()+":"+
                                        dm.getBitDepth());

                    System.exit(0);
                }
            }
            else
            {
                System.out.println("Display change not
                    supported");
                System.exit(0);
            }
        }
        else // WINDOWED_MODE
        {
            setTitle("Windowed Mode");

            setVisible(true);

            Insets insets = getInsets();
            DISPLAY_X = insets.left;
            DISPLAY_Y = insets.top;
            resizeToInternalSize(Globals.DISPLAY_WIDTH,
                Globals.DISPLAY_HEIGHT);
        }

        createBufferStrategy(3);
        strategy = getBufferStrategy();
    }
    catch(Exception e)
    {
        graphicsDevice.setFullScreenWindow(null);
        e.printStackTrace();
    }

    if(!strategy.getCapabilities().isPageFlipping())
```

```
            System.out.println("Page flipping is not available in
                this mode");

        waitForReadyStrategy();
    }


public void resizeToInternalSize(int internalWidth, int
    internalHeight)
{
    Insets insets = getInsets();
    final int newWidth - internalWidth + insets.left +
        insets.right;
    final int newHeight = internalHeight + insets.top +
        insets.bottom;

    Runnable resize = new Runnable()
    {
        public void run()
        {
            setSize(newWidth, newHeight);
        }
    };

    if(!SwingUtilities.isEventDispatchThread())
    {
        try
        {
            SwingUtilities.invokeAndWait(resize);
        }
        catch(Exception e) {}
    }
    else
        resize.run();

    validate();
}

public boolean isDisplayModeAvailable(DisplayMode dm)
{
    DisplayMode[] availableModes = graphicsDevice
        .getDisplayModes();

    for(int i=0; i<availableModes.length; i++)
    {
        if(dm.getWidth()==availableModes[i].getWidth() &&
            dm.getHeight()==availableModes[i].getHeight() &&
            dm.getBitDepth()==availableModes[i].getBitDepth())
            return true;
    }

    return false;
}


public void waitForReadyStrategy()
{
    int iterations = 0;

    while(true)
```

```
        {
            try
            {
                Thread.sleep(20);
            }
            catch(InterruptedException e) {}

            try
            {
                strategy.getDrawGraphics();
                break;
            }
            catch(IllegalStateException e)
            {
                System.out.println("BufferStrategy not ready yet");
            }

            iterations++;
            if(iterations == 100)
            {
                // (Unlikely event) No use after 2 seconds (100*20ms
                //  = 2secs) give up trying
                System.out.println("Exiting Program, unable to use
                    BufferStrategy");
                System.exit(0);
            }
        }
    }


    public void start()
    {
        loop = new Thread(this);
        loop.start();
    }


    public void run()
    {
        long startTime, waitTime, elapsedTime;
        // 1000/25 Frames Per Second = 40 millisecond delay
        int delayTime = 1000/25;

        Thread thisThread = Thread.currentThread();
        while(loop==thisThread)
        {
            startTime = System.currentTimeMillis();

            eventProcessor.processEventList();

            Globals.currentScreen.process();

            Graphics g = strategy.getDrawGraphics();

            if(!strategy.contentsLost())
            {
                g.translate(DISPLAY_X, DISPLAY_Y);

                Globals.currentScreen.render(g);
```

```
                g.dispose();
                strategy.show();
        }

        // handle frame rate
        elapsedTime = System.currentTimeMillis() - startTime;
        waitTime = Math.max(delayTime - elapsedTime, 5);

        try
        {
            Thread.sleep(waitTime);
        }
        catch(InterruptedException e) {}
    }

    System.out.println("Program Exited");

    dispose();
    System.exit(0);
}


public void exitProgram()
{
    loop = null;
}


public void initGame()
{
    // create your screens...
    Globals.sampleScreen = new SampleScreen();

    // load any sounds into the sound manager...

    // set the current (starting) screen...
    Globals.currentScreen = Globals.previousScreen =
        Globals.sampleScreen;
    Globals.currentScreen.load();
}


public boolean handleGlobalEvent(AWTEvent e)
{
    // handle global events...
    switch(e.getID())
    {
        case KeyEvent.KEY_PRESSED:
            KeyEvent keyEvent = (KeyEvent) e;
            Globals.keyboard.keyState[keyEvent.getKeyCode()]
                = true;

            switch(keyEvent.getKeyCode())
            {
                case KeyEvent.VK_ESCAPE:
                    exitProgram();
                    return true;
            }
            break;
```

```
case KeyEvent.KEY_RELEASED:
    Globals.keyboard.keyState[((KeyEvent)e).getKeyCode()]
        = false;
    break;

case MouseEvent.MOUSE_MOVED:
case MouseEvent.MOUSE_DRAGGED:
{
    MouseEvent mouseEvent = (MouseEvent) e;
    Globals.mouse.x = mouseEvent.getX();
    Globals.mouse.y = mouseEvent.getY();
    break;
}

case MouseEvent.MOUSE_PRESSED:
    switch(((MouseEvent)e).getButton())
    {
        case MouseEvent.BUTTON1:
            Globals.mouse.button[Mouse.LEFT_BUTTON]
                = true;
            break;
        case MouseEvent.BUTTON2:
            Globals.mouse.button[Mouse.MIDDLE_BUTTON]
                = true;
            break;
        case MouseEvent.BUTTON3:
            Globals.mouse.button[Mouse.RIGHT_BUTTON]
                = true;
            break;
    }
    break;

case MouseEvent.MOUSE_RELEASED:
    switch(((MouseEvent)e).getButton())
    {
        case MouseEvent.BUTTON1:
            Globals.mouse.button[Mouse.LEFT_BUTTON]
                = false;
            break;
        case MouseEvent.BUTTON2:
            Globals.mouse.button[Mouse.MIDDLE_BUTTON]
                = false;
            break;
        case MouseEvent.BUTTON3:
            Globals.mouse.button[Mouse.RIGHT_BUTTON]
                = false;
            break;
    }
    break;

case FocusEvent.FOCUS_LOST:
    // reset key states...
    Globals.keyboard.resetAllStates();

    // reset mouse button states...
    Globals.mouse.resetAllStates();
    break;

case FocusEvent.FOCUS_GAINED:
    break;
```

```
    }

    return false;
}


public void handleEvent(AWTEvent e)
{
    if(!handleGlobalEvent(e))
        Globals.currentScreen.handleEvent(e);
}


public void setCurrentScreen(TemplateScreen screen)
{
    // unload the current screen...
    Globals.currentScreen.unload();

    // set this screen to the previous screen...
    Globals.previousScreen = Globals.currentScreen;

    // assign the new screen...
    Globals.currentScreen = screen;

    // load it...
    Globals.currentScreen.load();
}


// key listener methods
public void keyPressed(KeyEvent e)
    { eventProcessor.addEvent(e); }
public void keyReleased(KeyEvent e)
    { eventProcessor.addEvent(e); }
public void keyTyped(KeyEvent e)            {} // not used

// mouse listener methods
public void mousePressed(MouseEvent e)
    { eventProcessor.addEvent(e); }
public void mouseReleased(MouseEvent e)
    { eventProcessor.addEvent(e); }
public void mouseClicked(MouseEvent e)   {} // not used
public void mouseEntered(MouseEvent e)   {} // not used
public void mouseExited(MouseEvent e)    {} // not used

// mouse motion listener methods
public void mouseMoved(MouseEvent e)
    { eventProcessor.addEvent(e); }
public void mouseDragged(MouseEvent e)
    { eventProcessor.addEvent(e); }

// focus listener methods
public void focusGained(FocusEvent e)
    { eventProcessor.addEvent(e); }
public void focusLost(FocusEvent e)
    { eventProcessor.addEvent(e); }


public static void main(String args[])
{
```

```
GraphicsEnvironment ge = GraphicsEnvironment
    .getLocalGraphicsEnvironment();

GameFramework mainAppFrame = new GameFramework
    (ge.getDefaultScreenDevice());


Object[] options = {"FullScreen Mode", "Windowed Mode"};


int choice = JOptionPane.showOptionDialog(null,
                            "Select Display Mode:",
                            "Display Mode",
                            JOptionPane.DEFAULT_OPTION,
                            JOptionPane.QUESTION_MESSAGE,
                            null,
                            options,
                            options[0]);


if(choice!=JOptionPane.CLOSED_OPTION)
{
    // choice will be either 0 or 1 corresponding to our mode
    // flags, FULLSCREEN_MODE = 0, WINDOWED_MODE = 1

    // initialize and start the game...
    mainAppFrame.initGame();
    mainAppFrame.setMode(choice);
    mainAppFrame.start();
}
else
    System.exit(0);
}


private Thread loop;
private GraphicsDevice graphicsDevice;

// not final - application may need to adjust these coordinates
// to adapt to windowed border
private int DISPLAY_X = 0;
private int DISPLAY_Y = 0;

private BufferStrategy strategy;

private static final int FULLSCREEN_MODE = 0;
private static final int WINDOWED_MODE = 1;
private int mode;

private EventProcessor eventProcessor;
}
```

Since we are using the `FullScreenDemo` example from Chapter 9 as a
base for this class, there is no point re-explaining all the code, so we are
just going to look at what we have added into the example to make it work
as a framework.

The only new member that we have added to the class is a reference to
an `EventProcessor` object called `eventProcessor`, which will be

used to synchronize all the events that occur with the main loop in our framework.

Starting in our `main` method, the first new part is creating an instance of our `GameFramework` class. So let's look at the additions to the constructor now.

In the constructor, we have added four listeners so that we receive mouse, keyboard, and focus events into our main class via the defined methods in each listener.

```
addKeyListener(this);
getContentPane().addMouseListener(this);
getContentPane().addMouseMotionListener(this);
addFocusListener(this);
```

Next we create a new instance of the `EventProcessor` class, passing in a reference to this object so that the event processor will know that our main class will be handling the events. This can be seen here:

```
eventProcessor = new EventProcessor(this);
```

Then we store a reference to our `GameFramework` object, `this`, in the `Globals.framework` object so we can reference our main class from within the screens (note that our main class will contain the method for changing the current screen, so we need access to this object to call this method).

Then we create an instance of our `soundManager` class, again storing the reference in a static `SoundManager` reference in the `Globals` class, so it can be used easily from anywhere in the framework. This can be seen here:

```
Globals.soundManager = new SoundManager();
```

Finally, in the constructor, we create instances of the `Keyboard` and `Mouse` classes that we looked at earlier and once again store them as static references in the `Globals` class.

```
Globals.keyboard = new Keyboard();
Globals.mouse = new Mouse();
```

So now back to the `main` method. For the next new part, before we set the mode (i.e., windowed or full screen) and start the main loop running, we have added a call to an `initGame` method, which can be seen in full here:

```
public void initGame()
{
    // create your screens...
    Globals.sampleScreen = new SampleScreen();

    // load any sounds into the sound manager...

    // set the current (starting) screen...
    Globals.currentScreen = Globals.previousScreen
        = Globals.sampleScreen;
        Globals.currentScreen.load();
}
```

The first thing we do in the `initGame` method is create instances of all the screens contained within our game. In this first demo of the framework, we have only one screen called `SampleScreen`, so we create an instance of it and store a reference to it in the `Globals` class. Then we load any sounds into the sound manager that we will require during the game, and finally we set the starting screen that the framework should initially display once it is initialized. This is done by assigning the reference to our `SampleScreen` to the `Globals.currentScreen` and `Globals.previousScreen` variables. Then lastly we call the `load` method of the current screen. Note here that loading and unloading is handled automatically after we have set our first screen, as we have defined a method called `setCurrentScreen`, which we will look at shortly.

Before we move on any further, however, let's take a look at how events are handled within the framework.

As you know, we are using the `EventProcessor` that we developed in Chapter 10 for the game framework, so when events come in from the listeners, such as the `MouseListener` and the `KeyboardListener`, we add the events to the `eventProcessor` object by calling the `addEvent` method.

In our main loop, we call the `processEventList` method, which will in turn call the `handleEvent` method in our main class for each event waiting to be processed.

So in our main class, we have defined the `handleEvent` method as follows:

```
public void handleEvent(AWTEvent e)
{
    if(!handleGlobalEvent(e))
        Globals.currentScreen.handleEvent(e);
}
```

This first passes the event to another method that we have defined called `handleGlobalEvent` (that we will look at in a minute), which handles events that are not related to any specific screen. Then this method will return true or false, depending on whether the event was dealt with in the method or not. If the event was not dealt with, we pass the event onto the current active screen (referenced by the `Globals.currentScreen` reference) by calling the `handleEvent` method of that screen, passing in the `AWTEvent`. If you remember, the `TemplateScreen` class defined the `handleEvent` method so all screens we derive from this class will also have a `handleEvent` method.

As we mentioned a moment ago, the `handleGlobalEvent` method will deal with any events that are to be handled globally within the framework, so let's look at the different cases that we have defined for possible global events now.

The first global event that we deal with is if a key is pressed on the keyboard. The case for this event can be seen here:

```
case KeyEvent.KEY_PRESSED:
    KeyEvent keyEvent = (KeyEvent) e;
```

```
        Globals.keyboard.keyState[keyEvent.getKeyCode()] = true;

    switch(keyEvent.getKeyCode())
    {
        case KeyEvent.VK_ESCAPE:
            exitProgram();
            return true;
    }
    break;
```

First, we cast the `AWTEvent` object to be a `KeyEvent` and then update the relative key state in the `keyState` array in the static object `keyboard` in the `Globals` class. So, in this case, if the key has been pressed, we update the state of the key with `true`.

Note that this does not consume the event, as we just want to record the state of the keys so that all screens have access to the current state. Then we create a `switch` statement, which looks at the key code. We then create a special case for the Esc key; if it is pressed, it will exit the program. Note also here that we return `true` from the method, indicating that this event has been dealt with globally and does not need to be passed onto the current screen for processing.

The next main case that we have created is for a `KEY_RELEASED` event. When this event occurs, all we want to do is update the relative key in the global `keyState` array, stating that it is now in the up state. This is done by simply setting the correct value in the array to `false`. This complete `KEY_RELEASED` case can be seen here:

```
case KeyEvent.KEY_RELEASED:
    Globals.keyboard.keyState[((KeyEvent)e).getKeyCode()] = false;
    break;
```

Next on the list is to handle the `MOUSE_MOVED` and `MOUSE_DRAGGED` events; we want to update the x, y position of the mouse in the static `mouse` object that we refer to in the `Globals` class. The complete case for this can be seen here:

```
case MouseEvent.MOUSE_MOVED:
case MouseEvent.MOUSE_DRAGGED:
{
    MouseEvent mouseEvent = (MouseEvent) e;
    Globals.mouse.x = mouseEvent.getX();
    Globals.mouse.y = mouseEvent.getY();
    break;
}
```

After this, we then have a case for the mouse being pressed, `MOUSE_PRESSED`, which updates the current state of the mouse buttons in the `mouse` object. This can be seen here:

```
case MouseEvent.MOUSE_PRESSED:
    switch(((MouseEvent)e).getButton())
    {
        case MouseEvent.BUTTON1:
            Globals.mouse.button[Mouse.LEFT_BUTTON] = true;
        break;
        case MouseEvent.BUTTON2:
            Globals.mouse.button[Mouse.MIDDLE_BUTTON] = true;
```

Chapter 12

```
            break;
        case MouseEvent.BUTTON3:
                Globals.mouse.button[Mouse.RIGHT_BUTTON] = true;
            break;
    }
    break;
```

Then we have virtually the same case again, except this time we handle the mouse buttons being released (and update the state of the `button` array with the `mouse` object to show this). The `MOUSE_RELEASED` case can be seen here:

```
case MouseEvent.MOUSE_RELEASED:
    switch(((MouseEvent)e).getButton())
    {
        case MouseEvent.BUTTON1:
                Globals.mouse.button[Mouse.LEFT_BUTTON] = false;
            break;
        case MouseEvent.BUTTON2:
                Globals.mouse.button[Mouse.MIDDLE_BUTTON] = false;
            break;
        case MouseEvent.BUTTON3:
                Globals.mouse.button[Mouse.RIGHT_BUTTON] = false;
            break;
    }
    break;
```

The next events that we handle globally are `FOCUS_LOST` and `FOCUS_GAINED`. When the focus is lost, we want to reset the `keyState` array in the `keyboard` object and the `button` state array in the `mouse` object. We can do this really easily by using the helper methods that we made earlier called `resetAllStates`, which are defined in both the `Mouse` and `Keyboard` classes. In this example, we have not implemented any handling for the gain of focus; however, in the next section, "A Framework Demo," we will see this being used to display a different screen. Here are the two cases that we have added for focus lost and gained:

```
case FocusEvent.FOCUS_LOST:
    // reset key states...
    Globals.keyboard.resetAllStates();

    // reset mouse button states...
    Globals.mouse.resetAllStates();
    break;

case FocusEvent.FOCUS_GAINED:
    break;
```

Therefore, after the events are handled in the main loop by the call to the `processEventList` method, we then call the `process` method of the `Globals.currentScreen` reference so that any logic specific to the current screen that is visible will be dealt with. Again, remember that our `TemplateScreen` class defines the `process` method, so when we create a screen by extending the `TemplateScreen`, it ensures the existence of this method (which of course we can override to put in our own logic code for the screen).

After the logic code has been dealt with, we then translate the graphics object to the correct position and call the `render` method of `Globals.currentScreen`, which again, if you remember, is defined as abstract in the `TemplateScreen` class. Therefore, any screens that we derive from it <u>must</u> implement their own `render` method.

The only part that we haven't looked at in the framework yet is the way that screens are changed, so let's take a look at the `setCurrentScreen` method that we have defined in the `GameFramework` class now.

```
public void setCurrentScreen(TemplateScreen screen)
{
    // unload the current screen...
    Globals.currentScreen.unload();

    // set this screen to the previous screen...
    Globals.previousScreen = Globals.currentScreen;

    // assign the new screen...
    Globals.currentScreen = screen;

    // load it...
    Globals.currentScreen.load();
}
```

This is very simple really; all we do is pass in a screen that we wish to make active (note it is passed in as a `TemplateScreen`, but since all our screens in the framework must be derived from this class, it is ideal). Then, the `unload` method of the current screen will be called, and the `Globals.previousScreen` reference will be set to refer to the `Globals.currentScreen` reference. Then we simply assign the screen to which we wish to change to the `Globals.currentScreen` reference. Finally, we call the `load` method of our new current screen.

If you now compile the framework, run it, and select windowed mode, you should see something similar to the following on the screen:

Figure 12-14: The Game framework (showing Sample Screen)

A Framework Demo

Now that we have looked at how the framework works, let's create a simple demo that contains three different screens, each of which does something different. The first screen will show the StickWalker animation that we created in the animation section of this chapter, the second will show a hot spot that we can move around with the cursor keys (just like in Chapter 9), and the third screen will let you draw a rectangle with the mouse. In addition, we will create another screen that will be displayed if the application loses focus.

Let's now look at the changes in the code for each of the three screens (changes from the original examples that you have seen previously, except the third screen, which is new code).

■ **Demo Screen 1: Stick Walker**—Here is the complete code listing for our first screen, DemoScreen1.java.

Code Listing 12-12: DemoScreen1.java

```java
import java.awt.*;
import java.awt.event.*;
import javax.imageio.*;
import java.io.*;

public class DemoScreen1 extends TemplateScreen
{
    public DemoScreen1()
    {
        // setup the screen here...
        try
        {
            characterSheet = ImageIO.read(new File
                ("stickmansheet.gif"));
            backgroundImage = ImageIO.read(new File("backdrop.gif"));
        }
        catch(IOException e)
        {
            System.out.println(e);
        }

        // assign start walk animation, direction and position
        walkAnim = 0;
        walkDir = 0;
        xPos = 200;
        yPos = 386;

        // work frame limits on the fly
        MAX_WALK_ANIMATIONS = characterSheet.getWidth(null)
            / FRAME_WIDTH;
        MAX_WALK_DIRECTIONS = characterSheet.getHeight(null)
            / FRAME_HEIGHT;
    }

    public void process()
    {
        // place screen logic code here...

        // handle animations
```

```
        walkAnim++;
        if(walkAnim >= MAX_WALK_ANIMATIONS)
            walkAnim = 0;

        // move character position and handle direction changing
        switch(walkDir)
        {
            case 0: // left
                xPos-=4;
                if(xPos<0)
                {
                    xPos = 0;
                    walkDir = 1;
                }
                break;

            case 1: // right
                xPos+=4;
                if(xPos+FRAME_WIDTH>bounds.width)
                {
                    xPos = bounds.width-FRAME_WIDTH;
                    walkDir = 0;
                }
                break;
        }
    }

    public void render(Graphics g)
    {
        // rendering code goes here...
        g.drawImage(backgroundImage, 0, 0, null);

        // render current frame to current screen position

        int srcX0 = walkAnim*FRAME_WIDTH;
        int srcY0 = walkDir*FRAME_HEIGHT;
        int srcX1 = srcX0+FRAME_WIDTH;
        int srcY1 = srcY0+FRAME_HEIGHT;

        g.drawImage(characterSheet,
                    xPos, yPos, xPos+FRAME_WIDTH, yPos+FRAME_HEIGHT,
                    srcX0, srcY0, srcX1, srcY1,
                    null);

        g.setColor(Color.black);
        g.drawString("Stick Walker Screen", 10, 15);
    }

    public void handleEvent(AWTEvent e)
    {
        // handle events here...
    }

    private Image characterSheet;
    private int xPos;
    private int yPos;
    private int walkAnim;
    private int walkDir;

    private int MAX_WALK_ANIMATIONS;
```

```
        private int MAX_WALK_DIRECTIONS;

        private static final int FRAME_WIDTH = 32;
        private static final int FRAME_HEIGHT = 64;

        private Image backgroundImage;
    }
```

All we have really done here is use `ImageIO` instead of the media tracker to load in our two tile sheets in the constructor. Then we have placed the code to handle the animation and movement of the StickWalker in the `process` method, which if you remember from the framework will be called every cycle of the main loop while the screen is currently being displayed. Finally, we placed the code to render the StickWalker into the `render` method, which again is called every cycle of the main loop.

- **Demo Screen 2: Circle Moving Screen**—Here is the complete code listing for our second screen, `DemoScreen2.java`.

Code Listing 12-13: `DemoScreen2.java`

```
import java.awt.*;
import java.awt.event.*;

public class DemoScreen2 extends TemplateScreen
{
    public DemoScreen2()
    {
        animator = new Animator(bounds);
    }

    public void process()
    {
        // place screen logic code here...
        animator.animate();
    }

    public void render(Graphics g)
    {
        // clear the background...
        g.setColor(Color.black);
        g.fillRect(0, 0, bounds.width, bounds.height);

        // draw the movable hotspot...
        animator.render(g);

        // draw the screen title...
        g.setColor(Color.green);
        g.drawString("Circle Moving Screen", 10, 15);

    }

    public void handleEvent(AWTEvent e)
    {
        // handle events here...
    }

    Animator animator;
}
```

The code required for this screen is much less, as we are using the HotSpot class from Chapter 9 and a slightly modified version of the Animator class, also from Chapter 9.

In the actual screen, we create an instance of the Animator class in the constructor by passing the bounds of the screen into the constructor. Then in the process method, we call the animate method of our animator object, which handles the key input that we will see shortly. Then in the render method, we simply call the render method of the animator object, passing in the Graphics object g that was passed to the screen's render method.

So, for handling input in the Animator class, we now use the Globals.keyboard.keyState array to determine the states of the relevant keys. Here is the complete animate method:

```
public void animate()
{
    if(Globals.keyboard.keyState[KeyEvent.VK_LEFT]
        && !Globals.keyboard.keyState[KeyEvent.VK_RIGHT])
            moveLeft();
    else if(Globals.keyboard.keyState[KeyEvent.VK_RIGHT]
        && !Globals.keyboard.keyState[KeyEvent.VK_LEFT])
            moveRight();

    if(Globals.keyboard.keyState[KeyEvent.VK_UP]
        && !Globals.keyboard.keyState[KeyEvent.VK_DOWN])
            moveUp();
    else if(Globals.keyboard.keyState[KeyEvent.VK_DOWN]
        && !Globals.keyboard.keyState[KeyEvent.VK_UP])
            moveDown();
    }
```

As you can see, it is very similar to before, but instead of holding a local reference to the array of key states, we are accessing the array defined in the Globals.keyboard object, which is updated by the framework.

The only other part of the Animator class that we have changed is the constructor, which now takes a Rectangle object as a parameter to define the area in which the hot spot can move around. The complete constructor method can be seen here:

```
public Animator(Rectangle bounds)
{
    this.bounds = bounds;

    createHotSpot();

    speedX = 4;
    speedY = 4;
}
```

- **Demo Screen 3: Mouse Example Screen**—Here is the complete code listing for our third screen, DemoScreen3.java.

Code Listing 12-14: DemoScreen3.java

```
import java.awt.*;
import java.awt.event.*;
```

```java
public class DemoScreen3 extends TemplateScreen
{
    public void process()
    {
        // place screen logic code here...

        // start dragging
        if(Globals.mouse.button[Mouse.LEFT_BUTTON] && dragStartX
            == -1 && dragStartY == -1)
        {
            dragStartX = Globals.mouse.x;
            dragStartY = Globals.mouse.y;
        }

        if(Globals.mouse.button[Mouse.RIGHT_BUTTON])
        {
            dragStartX = dragStartY = -1;
        }
    }

    public void render(Graphics g)
    {
        // rendering code goes here...
        g.setColor(Color.white);
        g.fillRect(0, 0, bounds.width, bounds.height);

        g.setColor(Color.black);

        // draw the dragged rectangle...
        if(dragStartX != -1 && dragStartY != -1)
        {
            int x, y, w, h;

            if(dragStartX < Globals.mouse.x)
            {
                x = dragStartX;
                w = Globals.mouse.x - dragStartX;
            }
            else
            {
                x = Globals.mouse.x;
                w = dragStartX - Globals.mouse.x;
            }

            if(dragStartY < Globals.mouse.y)
            {
                y = dragStartY;
                h = Globals.mouse.y - dragStartY;
            }
            else
            {
                y = Globals.mouse.y;
                h = dragStartY - Globals.mouse.y;
            }

            g.drawRect(x, y, w, h);
        }
```

```
        // draw the mouse positions...
        g.drawString("Mouse Example Screen", 10, 15);
        g.drawString("Mouse X: "+Globals.mouse.x+"   Mouse Y:
            "+Globals.mouse.y, 10, 35);

        // and the button states...
        g.drawString("Left Button: "+Globals.mouse.button
            [Mouse.LEFT_BUTTON], 10, 55);
        g.drawString("Middle Button: "+Globals.mouse.button
            [Mouse.MIDDLE_BUTTON], 10, 75);
        g.drawString("Right Button: "+Globals.mouse.button
            [Mouse.RIGHT_BUTTON], 10, 95);
    }

    public void handleEvent(AWTEvent e)
    {
        // handle events here...
    }

    public void load()
    {
        dragStartX = dragStartY = -1;
    }


    int dragStartX, dragStartY;
}
```

In the third screen, `DemoScreen3`, we want to be able to start drawing a "dragging" rectangle with the mouse and then cancel with the right mouse button. The first thing to notice in this screen is that we have over-ridden the `load` method so that the starting x, y position of the dragged rectangle is reset every time the screen is loaded.

Then, in the `process` method, we first check to see if the starting point of the rectangle has not been defined. If so, we check if the left mouse button is currently down. If it is, we then assign the `dragStartX` and `dragStartY` values to be equal to the current mouse x, y position (retrievable from the `mouse` object in the `Globals` class).

Then, also in the `process` method, we check if the right mouse button is pressed down. If it is, we simply reset the start x, y position for the dragging so the rectangle is no longer drawn (as the `render` method will only draw the rectangle if the `dragStartX` and `dragStartY` variables do not equal –1).

In the `render` method, we first check if the `dragStartX` and `dragStartY` variables do not equal –1, and if they do not, we find out which values should be used for the starting position of the rectangle, as passing a negative width or height into the `g.drawRect` method will simply not draw it.

■ **The Pause Screen**—In addition to our three main screens, we are going to define a `PauseScreen`, which will be displayed when the application loses focus. Here is the complete source listing for the pause screen:

Chapter 12

Code Listing 12-15: PauseScreen.java

```java
import java.awt.*;
import java.awt.event.*;

public class PauseScreen extends TemplateScreen
{
    public PauseScreen()
    {
        // set up the screen here...
    }

    public void process()
    {
        // place screen logic code here...

    }

    public void render(Graphics g)
    {
        // rendering code goes here...
        g.setColor(Color.red);
        g.fillRect(0, 0, bounds.width, bounds.height);

        g.setColor(Color.black);
        g.drawString("[ LOST FOCUS ]", 370, 300);
    }

    public void handleEvent(AWTEvent e)
    {
        // handle events here...
    }
}
```

All we have actually implemented in here is the `render` method, where we first fill the screen red and then draw [LOST FOCUS] in the middle of the screen in black.

Integrating the Screens into the Framework

Now that we have seen the four screens, we are going to look at the modifications to the `GameFramework` class to allow for the screens to work correctly.

Rather than regurgitating the entire code for the `GameFramework` class, it is probably best to look at the changes to the code. We will first start off with the minor change to the `Globals` class, where we have removed the reference to the `SampleScreen` class and replaced it with the following four references:

```java
public static DemoScreen1 demoScreen1;
public static DemoScreen2 demoScreen2;
public static DemoScreen3 demoScreen3;
public static PauseScreen pauseScreen;
```

Next, back in the `GameFramework` class, we have created an instance of each of our screens, which will then be stored in these references that we have just added to the `Globals` class. These are to be placed in the `initGame` method in place of where we created our `SampleScreen` object.

```
// create your screens...
Globals.demoScreen1 = new DemoScreen1();
Globals.demoScreen2 = new DemoScreen2();
Globals.demoScreen3 = new DemoScreen3();
Globals.pauseScreen = new PauseScreen();
```

Next, once the screen instances are created, we assign the current and previous screen references in the `Globals` class to be `Globals.demo-Screen1` and then we call the `load` method of the `Globals.cur-rentScreen` method. This can be seen here:

```
Globals.currentScreen = Globals.previousScreen = Globals.demoScreen1;
Globals.currentScreen.load();
```

The next change is in the `handleGlobalEvent` method, when we add an extra three keys to handle where we originally just had the handling for the Esc key. The new case for the `KEY_PRESSED` event should now look as follows:

```
case KeyEvent.KEY_PRESSED:
    KeyEvent keyEvent = (KeyEvent) e;
    Globals.keyboard.keyState[keyEvent.getKeyCode()] = true;

    switch(keyEvent.getKeyCode())
    {
        case KeyEvent.VK_ESCAPE:
            exitProgram();
            return true;

        case KeyEvent.VK_1:
            setCurrentScreen(Globals.demoScreen1);
            return true;

        case KeyEvent.VK_2:
            setCurrentScreen(Globals.demoScreen2);
            return true;

        case KeyEvent.VK_3:
            setCurrentScreen(Globals.demoScreen3);
            return true;
    }
    break;
```

Notice that the three extra keys that we now handle here are 1, 2, and 3, which enable us to change the screens. Also note that we have placed these in the `handleGlobalEvent` method so that the screen can be set from any other screen (just as we can exit the program from any screen with the Esc key). We could of course not handle the events here but handle them in each screen, making it so that you could only get to screen 2 from screen 1 and only get to screen 3 from screen 2, etc.

The final change that we have made to the framework is for the `FOCUS_GAINED` and `FOCUS_LOST` events, again in the `handleGlo-balEvent` method. The new cases for both these events can be seen here:

```
case FocusEvent.FOCUS_LOST:
            setCurrentScreen(Globals.pauseScreen);

    // reset key states...
    Globals.keyboard.resetAllStates();

    // reset mouse button states...
    Globals.mouse.resetAllStates();
    break;

case FocusEvent.FOCUS_GAINED:
        if(Globals.previousScreen != null)
            setCurrentScreen(Globals.previousScreen);
    break;
```

So for the FOCUS_LOST event, we have simply added a call to the set-CurrentScreen method, passing in a reference to the PauseScreen object stored in the Globals class. Then we reset the key and mouse states, as we did in the previous example. For the FOCUS_GAINED event, we first ensure that the previousScreen reference in the Globals class is not null, as it may not have been initialized before we receive our first FOCUS_GAINED event when the application initially gains focus. Then, if it does contain a valid reference, we call the setCurrent-Screen method, passing in the Globals.previousScreen reference so the screen will return to the same screen as it was before it was changed to the pause screen when the FOCUS_LOST event occurred.

That is all there is to it. Try it out by compiling it all and running it, using the 1, 2, and 3 keys to switch between the different screens.

Here is how the four different screens look when you run the framework demo:

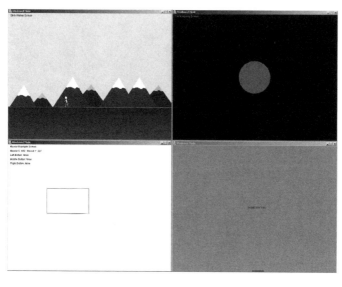

Figure 12-15: The four screens in the framework demo

Tile Scroller Example

Possibly the most essential structure for most two-dimensional games is a tiled engine. The levels of almost every two-dimensional platform game will be made up of many screen tiles, all put together as a 2D grid like the structure of the two-dimensional animation sheets that we saw at the beginning of this chapter. If you recall games such as Super Mario Bros. and Bomberman, you will see that the sections of the screen are divided into tiled regions. There are many important advantages to using a level that is tile based, as the level is in a fixed structure. Collision detection is simple to handle in a tiled structure, and large maps can be created from very few graphics. Since we do not need a graphic the size of our map, we can build the map from individual tiles, where each tile can be reused elsewhere in the map.

Now that we have a good solid game framework in place, we are going to use it to create a simple, yet robust tile engine. The aim of this engine is to handle the following key features:

- Support for any map size
- Support for any number of different tiles (i.e., tile images)
- Support for any tile size (i.e., any width and any height)
- Ability to scroll the map (if it is larger than the viewable area) at any speed
- Support for the tile engine to work in any application size (any viewable screen area), although full screen must be a valid resolution (i.e., 640x480, 800x600, etc.)

So where do we start then? Well, since we are using the framework that we created in the previous section, there would be no point in regurgitating the code in the book, so we will just look at the game screen that will easily "plug in" to the game framework with a mere few lines of code. So let's now look at the complete code listing of the tile engine and then see a sample screen shot of how it will look when we run it.

Listing 12-16: Tile Scroller example (works with the framework)

```java
import java.awt.*;
import java.awt.event.*;
import java.awt.image.*;
import javax.imageio.*;
import java.io.*;
import java.util.*;

public class MainScreen extends TemplateScreen
{
    public MainScreen()
    {
        // set max map viewable screen size
        VIEW_LIMIT_X = Math.min(bounds.width, MAP_PIXEL_WIDTH);
        VIEW_LIMIT_Y = Math.min(bounds.height, MAP_PIXEL_HEIGHT);
```

```
    // load the tiles...
    try
    {
        tileSheet = ImageIO.read(new File("tilesheet.jpg"));
    }
    catch(IOException e)
    {
        System.out.println(e);
    }

    // place the walls around the edge...

    // horizontal walls
    for(int i=0; i<MAP_WIDTH; i++)
    {
        mapArray[i][0] = WALL_TILE;
        mapArray[i][MAP_HEIGHT-1] = WALL_TILE;
    }

    // vertical walls
    for(int i=0; i<MAP_HEIGHT; i++)
    {
        mapArray[0][i] = WALL_TILE;
        mapArray[MAP_WIDTH-1][i] = WALL_TILE;
    }

    // fill in middle with grass tiles...
    for(int i=1; i<MAP_WIDTH-1; i++)
        for(int j=1; j<MAP_HEIGHT-1; j++)
            mapArray[i][j] = GRASS_TILE;

    int numTrees = Math.min(MAX_TREES, (MAP_WIDTH-2)
        * (MAP_HEIGHT-2));

    // place random trees in grass area...
    Random r = new Random();
    int x, y;
    for(int i=0; i<numTrees; i++)
    {
        x = r.nextInt(MAP_WIDTH-2)+1;
        y = r.nextInt(MAP_HEIGHT-2)+1;

        // make sure we set the full amount of trees
        if(mapArray[x][y] != TREE_TILE)
            mapArray[x][y] = TREE_TILE;
        else
            i--;
    }

    // set the default scroll position...
    setScrollX(0);
    setScrollY(0);
}

public void process()
{
    // handle scroll key states...

    // vertical scrolling
    if(Globals.keyboard.keyState[KeyEvent.VK_LEFT]
```

```java
            && !Globals.keyboard.keyState[KeyEvent.VK_RIGHT])
    {
        setScrollX(scrollPosX - scrollSpeed);
    }
    else if(Globals.keyboard.keyState[KeyEvent.VK_RIGHT]
        && !Globals.keyboard.keyState[KeyEvent.VK_LEFT])
    {
        setScrollX(scrollPosX + scrollSpeed);
    }

    // horizontal scrolling
    if(Globals.keyboard.keyState[KeyEvent.VK_UP]
        && !Globals.keyboard.keyState[KeyEvent.VK_DOWN])
    {
        setScrollY(scrollPosY - scrollSpeed);
    }
    else if(Globals.keyboard.keyState[KeyEvent.VK_DOWN]
        && !Globals.keyboard.keyState[KeyEvent.VK_UP])
    {
        setScrollY(scrollPosY + scrollSpeed);
    }
}

public void setScrollX(int x)
{
    scrollPosX = x;
    scrollPosX = Math.max(scrollPosX, 0);
    scrollPosX = Math.min(scrollPosX, MAP_PIXEL_WIDTH
        - VIEW_LIMIT_X);

    tileOffsetX = scrollPosX % TILE_WIDTH;
    startTileX = scrollPosX / TILE_WIDTH;
}

public void setScrollY(int y)
{
    scrollPosY = y;
    scrollPosY = Math.max(scrollPosY, 0);
    scrollPosY = Math.min(scrollPosY, MAP_PIXEL_HEIGHT
        - VIEW_LIMIT_Y);

    tileOffsetY = scrollPosY % TILE_HEIGHT;
    startTileY = scrollPosY / TILE_HEIGHT;
}


public void render(Graphics g)
{
    // rendering code goes here...
    g.setColor(Color.black);
    g.fillRect(0, 0, bounds.width, bounds.height);

    int srcX;
    int tileX = startTileX;
    int tileY;
    for(int x=-tileOffsetX; x<VIEW_LIMIT_X; x+=TILE_WIDTH)
    {
        tileY = startTileY;
```

```
            for(int y=-tileOffsetY; y<VIEW_LIMIT_Y; y+=TILE_HEIGHT)
            {
                srcX = mapArray[tileX][tileY]*TILE_WIDTH;

                g.drawImage(tileSheet, x, y, x+TILE_WIDTH,
                    y+TILE_HEIGHT,
                    srcX, 0, srcX+TILE_WIDTH, TILE_HEIGHT, null);
                tileY++;
            }
            tileX++;
        }

        g.setColor(Color.yellow);
        g.drawString("Tile Scroller Demo", 10, 15);
        g.drawString("Scroll Speed: "+scrollSpeed, 10, 30);
    }

    public void handleEvent(AWTEvent e)
    {
        // handle specific non-flagging key events
        if(e.getID() == KeyEvent.KEY_PRESSED)
        {
            KeyEvent keyEvent = (KeyEvent) e;
            if((keyEvent.getKeyCode() == KeyEvent.VK_PAGE_DOWN)
                && (scrollSpeed > MIN_SCROLL_SPEED))
                scrollSpeed--;
            else if((keyEvent.getKeyCode() == KeyEvent.VK_PAGE_UP)
                && (scrollSpeed < MAX_SCROLL_SPEED))
                scrollSpeed++;
        }
    }

    // array to store the tile id's...
    int mapArray[][] = new int[MAP_WIDTH][MAP_HEIGHT];

    // map and tile sizes
    static final int MAP_WIDTH = 50;
    static final int MAP_HEIGHT = 50;

    static final int TILE_WIDTH = 32;
    static final int TILE_HEIGHT = 32;

    static final int MAP_PIXEL_WIDTH = TILE_WIDTH * MAP_WIDTH;
    static final int MAP_PIXEL_HEIGHT = TILE_HEIGHT * MAP_HEIGHT;

    int VIEW_LIMIT_X;    // set in the constructor...
    int VIEW_LIMIT_Y;    // set in the constructor...

    // scroll position of the map...
    int scrollPosX = 0;
    int scrollPosY = 0;

    int scrollSpeed = 10;
    static final int MIN_SCROLL_SPEED = 1;
    static final int MAX_SCROLL_SPEED = 50;

    // keyboard flag states
    boolean keyState[] = new boolean[256];

    // tile definitions...
```

```
    static final int GRASS_TILE = 0;
    static final int WALL_TILE = 1;
    static final int TREE_TILE = 2;
    static final int MAX_TILES  = 3;


    // Tile sheet to store the tiles...
    Image tileSheet;

    static final int MAX_TREES = 150;

    int tileOffsetX;
    int tileOffsetY;

    int startTileX;
    int startTileY;
}
```

As we are using the framework, when we run the tile scroller demo, we will first be given the option of full-screen or windowed mode. The following figure is a screen shot of it in windowed mode, but for the best results, you should run it yourself.

Remember that you will need to create an instance of the screen in the gameInit method of the framework and store a reference to the screen in the Globals class.

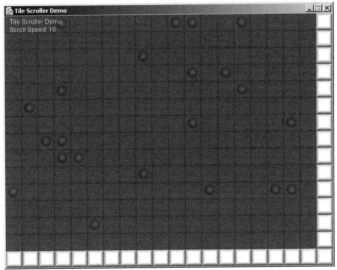

Figure 12-16: The Tile Scroller

Now that we have seen the tile scroller in action, let's delve into the inner workings of the code to see what makes it what it is. First, let's look over the member variables that we have defined and find out what each of them are for (although most are pretty self-explanatory).

```
int mapArray[][] = new int[MAP_WIDTH][MAP_HEIGHT];
```

First we have the mapArray two-dimensional array, which will hold integer values that will relate to the tile. So this array will directly map to our map coordinates (i.e., if we accessed array position 0, 0, we could find out what tile "type" was at the top-left position of the map). Note that we have declared the array using the variables MAP_WIDTH and MAP_HEIGHT which are defined as follows:

```
static final int MAP_WIDTH = 50;
static final int MAP_HEIGHT = 50;
```

These two variables simply specify how many tiles across and down are used to make up the complete map. Next we declare the width and height in pixels of each individual tile in the map. This can be seen here:

```
static final int TILE_WIDTH = 32;
static final int TILE_HEIGHT = 32;
```

Note that by changing these values, the engine will adapt accordingly and work with any specified tile sizes (just ensure that the images that you supply for the tiles are the same dimensions).

So now that we have the size of the map in tiles and the size of each tile, we can work out the actual width and height of the map in pixels by simply multiplying the width of the tiles by the width in tiles of the map and the same for the height. Store the results in the variables called MAP_PIXEL_WIDTH and MAP_PIXEL_HEIGHT. This can be seen here:

```
static final int MAP_PIXEL_WIDTH = TILE_WIDTH * MAP_WIDTH;
static final int MAP_PIXEL_HEIGHT = TILE_HEIGHT * MAP_HEIGHT;
```

Then we declare two variables to hold the maximum extents of the map that can be seen on the screen, which were at one time called VIEW_LIMIT_X and VIEW_LIMIT_Y. However, these will be assigned in the constructor.

Next up we have the actual pixel scroll position (x, y) that we are currently looking at on the map. If we can't physically view the entire map within the screen size, we need to note the position on the map that we are actually looking at, so we store this in scrollPosX and scroll-PosY. We'll see these values get used later in this example when we get to moving around and rendering the map to the screen.

Because we want to create a robust tile engine, it would be nice to be able to change the speed in pixels at which the map scrolls, so we need to store the current scroll speed and also the minimum and maximum limits. This can be seen here:

```
int scrollSpeed = 10;
static final int MIN_SCROLL_SPEED = 1;
static final int MAX_SCROLL_SPEED = 50;
```

Then we have our tile definitions, which are simply integer values that will be used within our engine to reference different types of tiles in an easy-to-read manner. These definitions can be seen here:

```
static final int GRASS_TILE = 0;
static final int WALL_TILE = 1;
static final int TREE_TILE = 2;
static final int MAX_TILES = 3;
```

Once we have defined our tile types, we need storage for the tile sheet, which will represent our tiles, so we create an `Image` reference for this. This can be seen in the following line of code:

```
Image tileSheet;
```

Next we have an integer value to determine the maximum number of trees that are to be placed on the map called MAX_TREES. Then finally, we have declared variables to store the current offset and start tiles of the map (don't worry about these for now). The next logical step is to look at the constructor for the screen where we set everything up. First we assign the VIEW_LIMIT_X and VIEW_LIMIT_Y variables to be the maximum value of either the bounds of the screen or the pixel width of the map.

```
VIEW_LIMIT_X = Math.min(bounds.width, MAP_PIXEL_WIDTH);
VIEW_LIMIT_Y = Math.min(bounds.height, MAP_PIXEL_HEIGHT);
```

Why? This is really just to handle if our map is smaller than the dimensions of the screen. We will see these values being used later when we perform the scrolling.

Next we load in the tile sheet, which is available on the companion CD-ROM and called `tilesheet.gif`. The image loading code can be seen here:

```
try
{
    tileSheet = ImageIO.read(new File("tilesheet.jpg"));
}
catch(IOException e)
{
    System.out.println(e);
}
```

Next, we place walls around the edge of the map by simply setting the appropriate values of the two-dimensional `mapArray` array to be WALL_TILE. This can be seen in the following segment of code:

```
for(int i=0; i<MAP_WIDTH; i++)
{
    mapArray[i][0] = WALL_TILE;
    mapArray[i][MAP_HEIGHT-1] = WALL_TILE;
}

for(int i=0; i<MAP_HEIGHT; i++)
{
    mapArray[0][i] = WALL_TILE;
    mapArray[MAP_WIDTH-1][i] = WALL_TILE;
}
```

Now that we have the walls, the rest of the map does not have any tiles set, so then we can fill in the rest of the map with grass tiles using the following code:

```
for(int i=1; i<MAP_WIDTH-1; i++)
    for(int j=1; j<MAP_HEIGHT-1; j++)
        mapArray[i][j] = GRASS_TILE;
```

Then finally, we place trees randomly across the map to the limit of MAX_TREES or the area of grass, whichever is least, and then we set the starting scroll position to the top-left corner (0, 0). We'll look at the methods setScrollX and setScrollY shortly.

So now that we have our map set up, let's look at the code to scroll it. All we do here is check if one of the arrow keys is down and then adjust the scroll position (either x or y, depending on the arrow key) by the current scroll speed (defined as scrollSpeed). The magic, however, actually happens within the setScrollX and setScrollY methods, so let's have a look at these now.

```
public void setScrollX(int x)
{
    scrollPosX = x;
    scrollPosX = Math.max(scrollPosX, 0);
    scrollPosX = Math.min(scrollPosX, MAP_PIXEL_WIDTH
        - VIEW_LIMIT_X);

    tileOffsetX = scrollPosX % TILE_WIDTH;
    startTileX = scrollPosX / TILE_WIDTH;
}
```

To set a new x scroll position, first assign the new value to our member variable scrollPosX. Then check if the scroll position is greater than zero by assigning it to be the maximum value of itself or zero. Then check if it is within the right edge of the map. Do this by picking the minimum value of itself and the MAP_PIXEL_WIDTH minus the VIEW_LIMIT_X. If you think about it, you will only be able to scroll far enough right to display the whole map, so this takes what you can actually see on the screen (VIEW_LIMIT_X) into account.

Once the new scrollPosX value is checked for validity, we can then assign our tileOffsetX and startTileX values ready for the rendering process. The tileOffsetX is how many pixels the tile at the left of the screen is "off" the screen by. startTileX is simply the starting horizontal tile that the renderer should begin drawing.

We work out the offset by taking the remainder of the current scroll position divided by the tile width. If the tiles are 32 pixels wide and the current scroll position is 40, we could work out that the leftmost tile should be drawn 8 pixels to the left of the visible area, making it appear as if the map had scrolled by 40 pixels.

As for the start tile, a simple division does it, giving us the leftmost tile from that current scroll position (this discards the remainder since we are using integer values, not floating-point). Going back to our previous example, the starting tile would be "1", as tile "0" would not be visible and only (32 – 8) = 24 pixels of tile "1" would be visible.

If you take a quick look back at the code for setScrollY, you'll notice the code is pretty much the same with the x's replaced with y's, so nothing exciting there.

Finally, we need to look at the actual rendering part, which is not that complex now that we have seen how the map scrolls.

First we set the current `tileX` position to be the `startTileX` position, which we set in our `setScrollX` method. Therefore, this will be the leftmost tile that is drawn (from the `mapArray`).

Next we perform the rendering with two `for` loops to fill the screen with tiles at the current scroll position in the map. Let's have a look at the conditions for this loop now:

```
for(int x=-tileOffsetX; x<VIEW_LIMIT_X; x+=TILE_WIDTH)
```

We start by setting the x position to the negative value of the `tileOffsetX`, which if we remember from before is simply how many pixels of the leftmost tile cannot be seen due to the scrolling. The termination condition for the loop is that we go past the `VIEW_LIMIT_X`, meaning we do not draw outside the right-hand side of the screen. Finally, we move along by the width of a tile, so we are ready to place the next one.

Once inside the first `for` loop, set the current `tileY` to be equal to `startTileY`, which we assigned the `setScrollY` method. Note that because this is placed here, after every cycle through the first `for` loop, the `tileY` variable will be reset to the start. Thus, we will draw the tiles from top to bottom and then move along a column and repeat the process. Let's look at the second `for` loop now.

```
for(int y=-tileOffsetY; y<VIEW_LIMIT_Y; y+=TILE_HEIGHT)
```

As you can see, this is the same as the first `for` loop, except it is in respect to y this time. Within these two `for` loops are the two magical lines of code that draw our map. This can be seen here:

```
srcX = mapArray[tileX][tileY]*TILE_WIDTH;

g.drawImage(tileSheet, x, y, x+TILE_WIDTH, y+TILE_HEIGHT,
        srcX, 0, srcX+TILE_WIDTH, TILE_HEIGHT, null);
```

This draws the tile referenced by the ID contained within the location in the `mapArray`. Notice how we use the `tileX` and `tileY` values to retrieve the correct tile type from the map and then multiply this value by the `TILE_WIDTH` to find the correct source x position in the tile sheet (this is the same technique that we saw in the animation section earlier in this chapter). Then specify the x and y as the position we draw (as this takes into account our x and y tile offsets).

After this, simply increment the `tileY` variable, and then outside the inner `for` loop, increment the `tileX` variable. Here is the complete `render` method for you to refer to:

```
public void render(Graphics g)
{
    // rendering code goes here...
    g.setColor(Color.black);
    g.fillRect(0, 0, bounds.width, bounds.height);

    int srcX;
    int tileX = startTileX;
    int tileY;
    for(int x=-tileOffsetX; x<Globals.DISPLAY_WIDTH;
        x+=TILE_WIDTH)
```

```
        {
            tileY = startTileY;
            for(int y=-tileOffsetY; y<Globals.DISPLAY_HEIGHT;
                y+=TILE_HEIGHT)
            {
                srcX = mapArray[tileX][tileY]*TILE_WIDTH;

                g.drawImage(tileSheet, x, y, x+TILE_WIDTH,
                    y+TILE_HEIGHT,
                    srcX, 0, srcX+TILE_WIDTH, TILE_HEIGHT, null);
                tileY++;
            }
            tileX++;
        }

        g.setColor(Color.yellow);
        g.drawString("Tile Scroller Demo", 10, 15);
        g.drawString("Scroll Speed: "+scrollSpeed, 10, 30);
    }
```

And that's it! Look over the code again and make sure you understand what's happening before moving on to the next example, as we are going to be building upon this simple, yet robust tile engine.

Just before we move on though, let's see how robust this baby is! If you grab the oddtilesheet.gif image off the CD-ROM, it will give you the same three tiles in a sheet. However, each tile in the sheet is 32x64 pixels, giving us a rectangular tile rather than a square one. To use these new tiles in the engine, all we need to do is change the TILE_HEIGHT variable to 64 and change the part in the constructor that loads the image. We will get something that looks like the following figure when we run it.

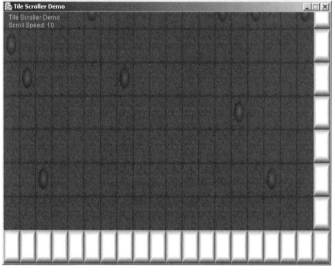

Figure 12-17: The Tile Scroller with 32x64 pixel tiles instead of 32x32 pixel tiles

As you can see, it looks awful, as all we have done is stretch the original images in a paint package. But the actual tile engine works perfectly for any sized tiles.

Tile Walker Example

Now that we have a scrollable tile engine, the aim for this section is to get a character walking about on the tiles. However, to make it a little cooler, we are going to make it so that a character of any size can walk about on tiles of any size, and all the collision detection will work without any code changes, apart from some static definitions such as the tile width and height. The character will also be able to move at any speed.

As with the Tile Scroller example, we will be using the framework, so all we will be looking at here is the code for the pluggable screen, which will be the core of our tile walker. So, let's look at the complete source code for this example before we look at it in detail and see how it all works:

Code Listing 12-17: Tile Walker example (works with the framework)

```java
import java.awt.*;
import java.awt.event.*;
import java.awt.image.*;
import javax.imageio.*;
import java.io.*;
import java.util.*;

public class MainScreen extends TemplateScreen
{
    public MainScreen()
    {
        try
        {
            // load the tiles sheet
            tileSheet = ImageIO.read(new File("tilesheet.gif"));

            // load the player direction image (8 directions)
            playerSheet = ImageIO.read(new File("playersheet.gif"));
        }
        catch(IOException e)
        {
            System.out.println(e);
        }

        // place the walls around the edge...

        // horizontal walls
        for(int i=0; i<MAP_WIDTH; i++)
        {
            mapArray[i][0] = WALL_TILE;
            mapArray[i][MAP_HEIGHT-1] = WALL_TILE;
        }

        // vertical walls
        for(int i=0; i<MAP_HEIGHT; i++)
        {
            mapArray[0][i] = WALL_TILE;
            mapArray[MAP_WIDTH-1][i] = WALL_TILE;
        }

        // fill in middle with grass tiles...
```

```
        for(int i=1; i<MAP_WIDTH-1; i++)
            for(int j=1; j<MAP_HEIGHT-1; j++)
                mapArray[i][j] = GRASS_TILE;


    int numTrees = Math.min(MAX_TREES, (MAP_WIDTH-2)
        * (MAP_HEIGHT-2));

    // place random trees in grass area...
    Random r = new Random();
    int x, y;
    for(int i=0; i<numTrees; i++)
    {
        x = r.nextInt(MAP_WIDTH-2)+1;
        y = r.nextInt(MAP_HEIGHT-2)+1;

        // make sure we set 150 trees
        if(mapArray[x][y] != TREE_TILE)
            mapArray[x][y] = TREE_TILE;
        else
            i--;
    }

    // set max map viewable screen size
    VIEW_LIMIT_X = Math.min(bounds.width, MAP_PIXEL_WIDTH);
    VIEW_LIMIT_Y = Math.min(bounds.height, MAP_PIXEL_HEIGHT);

    // set the default scroll position...
    setScrollX(0);
    setScrollY(0);

    // set the players starting position...
    playerWorldX = 3 * TILE_WIDTH;
    playerWorldY = 3 * TILE_HEIGHT;

    updatePlayerScreenPosition();
}


public boolean isClearTile(int x, int y)
{
    return mapArray[x][y]==GRASS_TILE;
}

public boolean isValidRow(int x1, int x2, int row)
{
    for(int i=x1; i<=x2; i++)
        if(!isClearTile(i, row))
            return false;

    return true;
}

public boolean isValidColumn(int y1, int y2, int column)
{
    for(int j=y1; j<=y2; j++)
        if(!isClearTile(column, j))
            return false;

    return true;
```

```java
    }

public boolean moveLeft()
{
    int newPosX = playerWorldX-1;

    // check out of map bounds
    if(newPosX < 0)
        return false;

    // check for blocked tiles
    int leftColumn = newPosX / TILE_WIDTH;
    int topTile = playerWorldY / TILE_HEIGHT;
    int bottomTile = (playerWorldY+PLAYER_HEIGHT-1)
        / TILE_HEIGHT;

    if(isValidColumn(topTile, bottomTile, leftColumn))
    {
        playerWorldX--;
        return true;
    }
    else
        return false;
}

public boolean moveRight()
{
    int newPosX = playerWorldX+1;

    // check out of map bounds
    if(newPosX+PLAYER_WIDTH > MAP_PIXEL_WIDTH)
        return false;

    // check for blocked tiles
    int rightColumn = (newPosX+PLAYER_WIDTH-1) / TILE_WIDTH;
    int topTile = playerWorldY / TILE_HEIGHT;
    int bottomTile = (playerWorldY+PLAYER_HEIGHT-1)
        / TILE_HEIGHT;

    if(isValidColumn(topTile, bottomTile, rightColumn))
    {
        playerWorldX++;
        return true;
    }
    else
        return false;
}


public boolean moveUp()
{
    int newPosY = playerWorldY-1;

    // check out of bounds
    if(newPosY < 0)
        return false;

    // check for blocked tiles
    int topRow = newPosY / TILE_HEIGHT;
```

```
        int leftTile = playerWorldX / TILE_WIDTH;
        int rightTile = (playerWorldX+PLAYER_WIDTH-1) / TILE_WIDTH;

        if(isValidRow(leftTile, rightTile, topRow))
        {
            playerWorldY--;
            return true;
        }
        else
            return false;
    }

    public boolean moveDown()
    {
        int newPosY = playerWorldY+1;

        // check out of bounds
        if(newPosY+PLAYER_HEIGHT > MAP_PIXEL_HEIGHT)
            return false;

        // check for blocked tiles
        int bottomRow = (newPosY+PLAYER_HEIGHT-1) / TILE_HEIGHT;
        int leftTile = playerWorldX / TILE_WIDTH;
        int rightTile = (playerWorldX+PLAYER_WIDTH-1) / TILE_WIDTH;

        if(isValidRow(leftTile, rightTile, bottomRow))
        {
            playerWorldY++;
            return true;
        }
        else
            return false;
    }



    public void updateScrollPosition()
    {
        int newPlayerScreenX = playerWorldX - scrollPosX;
        if(newPlayerScreenX < SCROLL_THRESHOLD) // check left
        {
            setScrollX(scrollPosX - (SCROLL_THRESHOLD
                - newPlayerScreenX));
        }
        else if(newPlayerScreenX > VIEW_LIMIT_X - SCROLL_THRESHOLD
            - PLAYER_WIDTH) // check right
        {
            setScrollX(scrollPosX + (newPlayerScreenX - (VIEW_LIMIT_X
                - SCROLL_THRESHOLD - PLAYER_WIDTH)));
        }

        int newPlayerScreenY = playerWorldY - scrollPosY;
        if(newPlayerScreenY < SCROLL_THRESHOLD) // check top
        {
            setScrollY(scrollPosY - (SCROLL_THRESHOLD
                - newPlayerScreenY));
        }
        else if(newPlayerScreenY > VIEW_LIMIT_Y - SCROLL_THRESHOLD
            - PLAYER_HEIGHT) // check bottom
        {
```

```
            setScrollY(scrollPosY + (newPlayerScreenY - (VIEW_LIMIT_Y
                - SCROLL_THRESHOLD - PLAYER_HEIGHT)));
    }
}

public void setScrollX(int x)
{
    scrollPosX = x;
    scrollPosX = Math.max(scrollPosX, 0);
    scrollPosX = Math.min(scrollPosX, MAP_PIXEL_WIDTH
        - VIEW_LIMIT_X);

    tileOffsetX = scrollPosX % TILE_WIDTH;
    startTileX = scrollPosX / TILE_WIDTH;
}

public void setScrollY(int y)
{
    scrollPosY = y;
    scrollPosY = Math.max(scrollPosY, 0);
    scrollPosY = Math.min(scrollPosY, MAP_PIXEL_HEIGHT
        - VIEW_LIMIT_Y);

    tileOffsetY = scrollPosY % TILE_HEIGHT;
    startTileY = scrollPosY / TILE_HEIGHT;
}


public void updatePlayerScreenPosition()
{
    playerScreenX = playerWorldX - scrollPosX;
    playerScreenY = playerWorldY - scrollPosY;
}


public void movePlayer()
{
    int playerVectorX = (Globals.keyboard.keyState
        [KeyEvent.VK_LEFT]?-1:0) + (Globals.keyboard.keyState
        [KeyEvent.VK_RIGHT]?1:0);
    int playerVectorY = (Globals.keyboard.keyState
        [KeyEvent.VK_UP]?-1:0) + (Globals.keyboard.keyState
        [KeyEvent.VK_DOWN]?1:0);

    if(playerVectorX==0 && playerVectorY==0)
        return;

    // update player direction frame
    if(playerVectorY<0) playerDir = 1+playerVectorX;
    else if(playerVectorY>0) playerDir = 4+playerVectorX;
    else if(playerVectorX<0) playerDir = 6;
    else if(playerVectorX>0) playerDir = 7;

    boolean blockedMoveX = true;
    boolean blockedMoveY = true;

    for(int i=0; i<playerSpeed; i++)
    {
        if(playerVectorX<0)
            blockedMoveX = !moveLeft();
```

Chapter 12

```
            else if(playerVectorX>0)
                blockedMoveX = !moveRight();

            if(playerVectorY<0)
                blockedMoveY = !moveUp();
            else if(playerVectorY>0)
                blockedMoveY = !moveDown();

            if(blockedMoveX && blockedMoveY) // if can't move further
                break;
        }

        updateScrollPosition();
        updatePlayerScreenPosition();
    }


    public void process()
    {
        movePlayer();
    }

    public void render(Graphics g)
    {
        // rendering code goes here...
        int srcX;
        int tileX = startTileX;
        int tileY;
        for(int x=-tileOffsetX; x<VIEW_LIMIT_X; x+=TILE_WIDTH)
        {
            tileY = startTileY;
            for(int y=-tileOffsetY; y<VIEW_LIMIT_Y; y+=TILE_HEIGHT)
            {
                srcX = mapArray[tileX][tileY]*TILE_WIDTH;

                g.drawImage(tileSheet, x, y, x+TILE_WIDTH,
                        y+TILE_HEIGHT,
                        srcX, 0, srcX+TILE_WIDTH, TILE_HEIGHT, null);
                tileY++;
            }
            tileX++;
        }

        // draw the player (above the tiles)
        srcX = playerDir*PLAYER_WIDTH;

        g.drawImage(playerSheet, playerScreenX, playerScreenY,
            playerScreenX+PLAYER_WIDTH, playerScreenY+PLAYER_HEIGHT,
            srcX, 0, srcX+PLAYER_WIDTH, PLAYER_HEIGHT, null);

        // draw players bounding box
        g.setColor(Color.yellow);
        g.drawRect(playerScreenX, playerScreenY, PLAYER_WIDTH-1,
            PLAYER_HEIGHT-1);

        g.drawString("Tile Walker Demo", 10, 15);
        g.drawString("Player Speed: "+playerSpeed, 10, 30);
    }

public void handleEvent(AWTEvent e)
```

```
{
    switch(e.getID())
    {
        case KeyEvent.KEY_PRESSED:
        {
            KeyEvent keyEvent = (KeyEvent) e;
            int key = keyEvent.getKeyCode();

            // handle key events here...
            if(key == KeyEvent.VK_PAGE_UP)
            {
                if(playerSpeed < MAX_MOVE_SPEED)
                {
                    playerSpeed++;
                }
            }
            else if(key == KeyEvent.VK_PAGE_DOWN)
            {
                if(playerSpeed > MIN_MOVE_SPEED)
                {
                    playerSpeed--;
                }
            }
            break;
        }
    }
}

// player variables
Image playerSheet;

int playerWorldX;
int playerWorldY;

int playerScreenX;
int playerScreenY;

int playerDir;
int playerSpeed = 8;

static final int PLAYER_WIDTH = 32;
static final int PLAYER_HEIGHT = 32;

static final int MIN_MOVE_SPEED = 1;
static final int MAX_MOVE_SPEED = 50;


// tile variables
Image tileSheet;

int tileOffsetX;
int tileOffsetY;

int startTileX;
int startTileY;

static final int TILE_WIDTH = 32;
static final int TILE_HEIGHT = 32;

static final int GRASS_TILE = 0;
```

```
static final int WALL_TILE = 1;
static final int TREE_TILE = 2;


// map variables
static final int MAP_WIDTH = 50;
static final int MAP_HEIGHT = 50;

static final int MAP_PIXEL_WIDTH = TILE_WIDTH * MAP_WIDTH;
static final int MAP_PIXEL_HEIGHT = TILE_HEIGHT * MAP_HEIGHT;

int mapArray[][] = new int[MAP_WIDTH][MAP_HEIGHT];

final int VIEW_LIMIT_X;      // set in the constructor...
final int VIEW_LIMIT_Y;      // set in the constructor...

int scrollPosX = 0;
int scrollPosY = 0;
static final int SCROLL_THRESHOLD = 4 * TILE_WIDTH;

static final int MAX_TREES = 150;
}
```

When we execute this code with the game framework, we should be able to see something similar to the following:

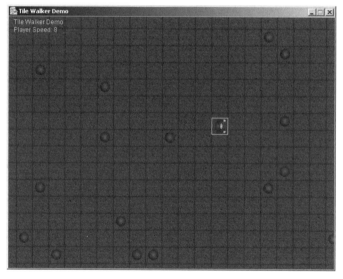

Figure 12-18: The Tile Walker

Let's first look at what extra definitions we have added to our tile engine to incorporate the player into it. First, we have added a new image called playerSheet, which will hold the player character tile sheet that contains the character facing eight different directions. The playerSheet image that we are going to load (called playersheet.gif on the companion CD-ROM) can be seen here:

Figure 12-19:
The player's
tile sheet

Note here that the order of the images is not random, but we will see why they are in this order when we look at the movement code later in this section.

Next we have declared two integer variables to hold the actual world position where the player is located. This is simply an x, y coordinate in pixels of the actual position on the map (not the screen). The declaration for these two variables can be seen here:

```
int playerWorldX;
int playerWorldY;
```

As the world position of the player is not the same as the screen position, we also are going to create two screen coordinate variables to store the current screen x, y position of the player, which will be worked out from the player's world coordinates when we make any movements. The declaration for these two variables can be seen here:

```
int playerScreenX;
int playerScreenY;
```

Next we have two variables to record the current direction of the player (which will relate to the `playerSheet` graphic to get the correct image direction) and also the current movement speed of the player in pixels. These two can be seen here:

```
int playerDir;
int playerSpeed = 8;
```

Finally, we have four new final static variables, which define the width and height of the player (remember that we are coding this so it will work for any size of player) and also the minimum and maximum movement speeds (as we will also be able to change this). These four static variables can be seen here:

```
static final int PLAYER_WIDTH = 32;
static final int PLAYER_HEIGHT = 32;

static final int MIN_MOVE_SPEED = 1;
static final int MAX_MOVE_SPEED = 50;
```

Now that we have looked at the additional member variables that we have added to our engine, let's look at what we have changed and added into the constructor. First off, we have added an extra line of code into the image loading part so we can load our player tile sheet, which we saw earlier in our `playerSheet` image. The complete image loading section can be seen here:

```
try
{
    // load the tiles sheet
    tileSheet = ImageIO.read(new File("tilesheet.gif"));
```

```
    // load the player direction image (8 directions)
    playerSheet = ImageIO.read(new File("playersheet.gif"));
}
catch(IOException e)
{
    System.out.println(e);
}
```

The next change is that we have added two lines of code to specify the player's initial world position (i.e., the x, y coordinate, in pixels, where the player is located in our virtual world). Initially, we are going to place the player on tile (3, 3), which is the fourth down from the top and the fourth across from the left, remembering the tile at the very top left is denoted by (0, 0). If you remember also that our world x, y positions are in pixels, you will realize that we also need to multiply the tiles on which we wish the player to start by the `TILE_WIDTH` and `TILE_HEIGHT` variables. This can be seen here:

```
playerWorldX = 3 * TILE_WIDTH;
playerWorldY = 3 * TILE_HEIGHT;
```

So now that we have the player placed at the correct position in our world coordinates, we need to get the actual screen position of the player (as this may be different from the world coordinates if the map has been scrolled in any direction). We have created a method called `update-PlayerScreenPosition()`, which will do this for us. Let's look at this method now:

```
public void updatePlayerScreenPosition()
{
    playerScreenX = playerWorldX - scrollPosX;
    playerScreenY = playerWorldY - scrollPosY;
}
```

As you can see, this method only deducts the current scroll positions from both the x and y coordinates, giving us the screen position of the player, relative to the current scrolled position of the map.

Next we are going to look at moving the player. We handle this in the `process` method, which, as we know from developing the framework, is called every frame before the `render` method is called. In the `process` method, we simply make a call to a method called `movePlayer()`. Let's look at this method step by step now.

In the `movePlayer` method, we first check the key states for the cursor keys. For the left and right keys, if the left key is pressed, it will return –1; otherwise it will return 0. If the right key is pressed, it will return 1; otherwise it will return 0. So if we add these two results together, we will obtain one of the following results.

Left Key		Right Key	Result
Not Pressed (0)	+	Not Pressed (0)	0
Pressed (–1)	+	Not Pressed (0)	–1
Not Pressed (0)	+	Pressed (1)	1
Pressed (–1)	+	Pressed (1)	0

So as you can see from the table, if the left key is down but the right is not, we will get a value of –1. If the right is down but the left is not, we will get the value 1. If they are either both up or both down, we will get the result 0. The line of code that does this for us can be seen here:

```
int playerVectorX = (Globals.keyboard.keyState
    [KeyEvent.VK_LEFT]?-1:0) + (Globals.keyboard.keyState
    [KeyEvent.VK_RIGHT]?1:0);
```

Notice how we store this result in a variable called `playerVectorX`. This variable will now hold which x direction the player should move—to the right (1), to the left (–1), or not at all (0).

We use this exact technique again for the up and down keys to find out the movement required in the y direction. The line of code that does this can be seen here:

```
int playerVectorY = (Globals.keyboard.keyState
    [KeyEvent.VK_UP]?-1:0) + (Globals.keyboard.keyState
    [KeyEvent.VK_DOWN]?1:0);
```

Next we have a special case for checking to see if both the `player-VectorX` variable and the `playerVectorY` variable are equal to 0. If this is the case, either all the keys are in a released state or all the keys are being held down (see the previous table). If this is so, the player will not be moving this frame and we can return from this method. This `if` statement can be seen here:

```
if(playerVectorX==0 && playerVectorY==0)
    return;
```

Now we are going to assign the correct value to the `playerDir` variable (declared as a member of our class), which is used to reference the correct image within the `playerSheet` to basically make the player face the direction that he or she is moving. Let's first look at this section of code, and then we will look into it in more detail, as it is not obvious at first glance.

```
if(playerVectorY<0) playerDir = 1+playerVectorX;
else if(playerVectorY>0) playerDir = 4+playerVectorX;
else if(playerVectorX<0) playerDir = 6;
else if(playerVectorX>0) playerDir = 7;
```

The first line of the four lines of code checks to see if the `playerVectorY` is less than 0 (i.e., the player is going to be moving in an upward direction). So if we look at the following player sheet image:

Figure 12-20

...we can see that tile 1 refers to the player image facing upward (remembering that the first tile is 0). So we set the base tile to 1 and proceed by adding the `playerVectorX`, which will be –1 if we are also moving left as well as up; this will then access tile 0 when we add it to the initial value 1, which is an image of the player moving diagonally up to the left. If the player is not moving in the x direction, we will add 0 to the initial 1 value, meaning it will use tile 1, which is the player facing upward. Finally, if the player is also moving right (i.e., the `playerVectorX` value is 1), we will get 1+1, meaning that we will then be referencing tile 2, which is the player facing diagonally up to the right.

This process is then repeated if the `playerVectorY` is positive (i.e., the player is moving downward). For this we use the initial value of 4 to add `playerVectorX`, so the span of the tiles in the tile sheet would be as follows:

Figure 12-21

The final two lines of code in this are used to handle the cases where the player is just simply going left or right (i.e., `playerVectorX` is negative or positive), and we set these values directly as 6 and 7, which reference the last two tiles in the sheet, respectively.

Another approach to this would have been to use a 3x3 tile sheet to represent the player as follows:

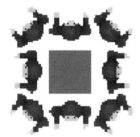

Figure 12-22:
Another approach to
the player's tile sheet

By using this style of sheet, our `playerVectorX` and `playerVectorY` values would have mapped to the `playerSheet` easier. However, we have the disadvantage of the blank tile in the middle.

Anyway, next we declare two variables to determine whether a player can move in the x and y directions, respectively. These two declarations can be seen here:

```
boolean blockedMoveX = true;
boolean blockedMoveY = true;
```

Notice how we set the initial values to `true`; this is because if the player is not moving in either of the directions, we will assume the player is blocked, as we will not need to perform any calculations anyway.

Next we create a `for` loop, which starts at 0 and loops until the player's speed is reached (defined as `playerSpeed`). This can be seen here:

```
for(int i=0; i<playerSpeed; i++)
{
    ...
}
```

So what we are really saying here is that for each pixel that the player is going to move, we want to check for any collisions.

Within the `for` loop, we are only going to need to check for x and y movements if the player is actually moving in that direction. This can be seen for the movement along the x-axis as follows:

```
if(playerVectorX<0)
    blockMoveX = !moveLeft();
else if(playerVectorX>0)
    blockMoveX = !moveRight();
```

This first checks if the `playerVectorX` is less than 0 (i.e., the player is moving left) and then if the player cannot move left (we will look at the `moveLeft` method in a moment; for now, note that it returns `true` if the player can move left and `false` if it cannot). Therefore, if the player is moving left and `moveLeft` returns `false`, `blockedMoveX` will then be equal to `true`, meaning the player cannot move in the x direction. The other part of this statement is just the same, except we are checking the right direction.

Let's have a look at the `moveLeft` method to see how it works. Here is a listing of the complete `moveLeft` method:

```
public boolean moveLeft()
{
    int newPosX = playerWorldX-1;

    // check out of map bounds
    if(newPosX < 0)
        return false;

    // check for blocked tiles
    int leftColumn = newPosX / TILE_WIDTH;
    int topTile = playerWorldY / TILE_HEIGHT;
    int bottomTile = (playerWorldY+PLAYER_HEIGHT-1) / TILE_HEIGHT;

    if(isValidColumn(topTile, bottomTile, leftColumn))
    {
        playerWorldX--;
        return true;
    }
    else
        return false;
}
```

First we work out the player's new world position, `newPosX`, which will be the current world position `playerWorldX` minus one (as we are moving left one pixel).

Next we check that this is still within the bounds of the map—in this case checking that `newPosX` is greater than 0, as the leftmost border of the world has an x coordinate of 0.

Then we can perform a check for blocked tiles. For moving left, we first work out on which "column" of tiles the player will be moving (i.e., basically just the new tile x position that can be worked out by dividing the `newPosX` world position by the width of the tile's `TILE_WIDTH`). We then store this value in the `leftColumn` variable.

Now, if you have a look at the following diagram of the player moving left, you should see an instant problem:

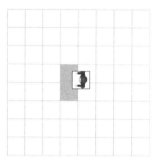

Figure 12-23:
Tile collisions

We in fact need to check two tiles. What we can do to check this is first find the tile that the top-left pixel is over, using the following line of code:

```
int topTile = playerWorldY / TILE_HEIGHT;
```

Then we can find out the bottom tile that the player is covering using this next line of code:

```
int bottomTile = (playerWorldY+PLAYER_HEIGHT-1) / TILE_HEIGHT;
```

Note that these are only the y positions; however, remember we also worked out the column that it was going to cover. We use these two new values, as well as the column, by passing them into another method now called `isValidColumn`, which we will look at now.

The `isValidColumn` method is really simple and, in fact, adds a lot to our engine, as it allows us to have any size of player with respect to testing collisions. This method loops from the top tile that was passed in, down every tile in the column, until it reaches the bottom tile, testing each tile to see if it is clear. In the previous example, it would test the tiles as follows:

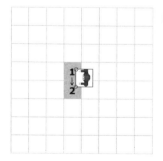

Figure 12-24

If you can imagine having a larger player, however, the testing would look as follows:

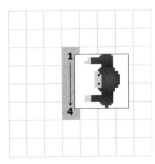

Figure 12-25

So let's actually have a look at the `isValidColumn` method. Here it is in full:

```
public boolean isValidColumn(int y1, int y2, int column)
{
    for(int j=y1; j<=y2; j++)
        if(!isClearTile(column, j))
            return false;

    return true;
}
```

So for each row in the column, starting at y1, we simply call the `is-ClearTile` method, which returns `true` or `false` depending on whether the tile at the position passed in is either clear or blocked. If any of the tiles are not clear, during the `for` loop the method returns `false`; otherwise, we return `true`, meaning the column was valid and the player can make the move successfully. Let's have a quick look at the `isClear-Tile` method now.

```
public boolean isClearTile(int x, int y)
{
    return mapArray[x][y]==GRASS_TILE;
}
```

As you can see, all we are doing is looking at the `mapArray` as the specified tile position to check if the tile is a `GRASS_TILE`, which in our map is the only tile you can walk on. Of course, if you have more tiles that you could move about on (such as sand tiles or gravel tiles), you could adapt this method accordingly.

That's all there is to checking the horizonal movement. If you have a quick look over the vertical movement, it is exactly the same idea, except we are checking the rows instead of the columns.

If we now go back to where we were in the `movePlayer` method, we can see that the next part checks the y movement (which as we mentioned a minute ago is pretty much the same as the x movement). Then we have a simple check that finds out if either of the x and y movements is blocked. If it is, we break out of the `for` loop. This can be seen here:

```
if(blockedMoveX && blockedMoveY) // if can't move further
    break;
```

Next, after the `for` loop, we need to update the scroll position of the map based upon the player's new world position. Basically, this method will allow us to scroll the map when the player goes within a certain distance of one of the edges of the application window. Let's first have a look at the complete method here:

```
public void updateScrollPosition()
{
    int newPlayerScreenX = playerWorldX - scrollPosX;
    if(newPlayerScreenX < SCROLL_THRESHOLD) // check left
    {
        setScrollX(scrollPosX - (SCROLL_THRESHOLD
            - newPlayerScreenX));
    }
    else if(newPlayerScreenX > VIEW_LIMIT_X - SCROLL_THRESHOLD
        - PLAYER_WIDTH) // check right
    {
        setScrollX(scrollPosX + (newPlayerScreenX - (VIEW_LIMIT_X
            - SCROLL_THRESHOLD - PLAYER_WIDTH)));
    }

    int newPlayerScreenY = playerWorldY - scrollPosY;
    if(newPlayerScreenY < SCROLL_THRESHOLD) // check top
    {
        setScrollY(scrollPosY - (SCROLL_THRESHOLD
            - newPlayerScreenY));
    }
    else if(newPlayerScreenY > VIEW_LIMIT_Y - SCROLL_THRESHOLD
        - PLAYER_HEIGHT) // check bottom
    {
        setScrollY(scrollPosY + (newPlayerScreenY - (VIEW_LIMIT_Y
            - SCROLL_THRESHOLD - PLAYER_HEIGHT)));
    }
}
```

First we work out what the player's new x position on the screen will be by subtracting the current x scroll position from the player's new world position, `playerWorldX`. Then we check the left-hand side of the screen and see if the player's new x screen position is less than the SCROLL_ THRESHOLD, which we have defined at the bottom of the class to be 4*TILE_WIDTH, meaning that if the player goes within four tiles of any edge on the screen, it will start to scroll. If the player is within the threshold of the left-hand side, we simply call the `setScrollX` method that we created in the previous example to be the current scroll position `scrollPosX` minus the SCROLL_THRESHOLD, less the player's new screen position. Note that the variables `newPlayerScreenX` and `newPlayerScreenY` are local variables and used to work out where the player has moved, simply for adapting the scrolling to the movement. The player's real new screen position is worked out after this method is called, after the scroll position has been worked out properly.

We then simply repeat this process for the right-hand side and also the top and bottom of the screen.

The final part of the `movePlayer` method makes a call to the method `updatePlayerScreenPosition`, which updates the player's real screen position based on the player's world map position and the newly updated scroll position, as we just discussed.

Now that we have looked at player movement, let's take a look in the `render` method and see how the player is actually drawn to the screen.

This is actually very simple to do now that we have performed all of the working out in the `movePlayer` method. First we get the source x position in the `playerSheet`, which we can work out from the `playerDir` variable that we set in the `movePlayer` method. This can be seen here:

```
srcX = playerDir*PLAYER_WIDTH;
```

Then we just call the `drawImage` method of the `Graphics` object g, using the player's `playerScreenX` and `playerScreenY` variables to denote the position at which to draw the player. This can be seen here:

```
g.drawImage(playerSheet, playerScreenX, playerScreenY,
        playerScreenX+PLAYER_WIDTH, playerScreenY+PLAYER_HEIGHT,
        srcX, 0, srcX+PLAYER_WIDTH, PLAYER_HEIGHT, null);
```

And that's it! Let's do a few experiments now with our tile engine to see how it will easily adapt to different player and screen sizes.

Changing the Player Size

Okay, so what if our player has a big brother? Let's see how our engine handles a character that is three times the size of our original player, making each of our player images 96x96 pixels. You can either resize the `playersheet.gif` image yourself to try this or you can use the supplied one on the companion CD-ROM called `bigplayersheet.gif` (remember to change the filename of the image loaded in the constructor appropriately). As well as the image, the only other thing to change is the `PLAYER_WIDTH` and `PLAYER_HEIGHT` variables to 96 and reduce the tree count to 10 (i.e., set `MAX_TREES` to 10) as he is a big boy.

With these changes, if you compile the code, you should get something that looks similar to the following:

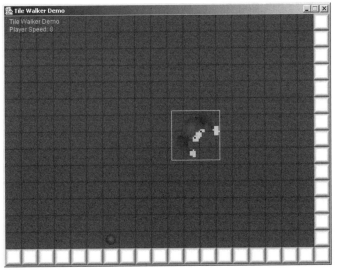

Figure 12-26: The red man's big brother Bungle

Move him about a bit...see how the collisions work perfectly? It's great isn't it? Go on, admit it.

Changing the Application Size

Although this would have worked in the Tile Scroller example as well, we just thought it would be nice to show it here. First, put the player back to the original size and put the tree count back to 150 (although you don't have to if you don't want to!). Then simply change both the DISPLAY_ WIDTH and DISPLAY_HEIGHT to 200 (note that we won't be able to use the full-screen mode, as it is not a supported full-screen resolution). Then just change the SCROLL_THRESHOLD to 1*TILE_WIDTH (or just set it to be TILE_WIDTH) so the map will scroll if the player is within one tile of the edge of the screen.

When we run the Tile Walker with these few changes, it should look as follows.

Figure 12-27:
A mini Tile Walker application

Changing the Map Size

Our final little experiment will be to change the map to a smaller size than the viewable area, so there will be no scrolling involved. All we need to do is change the MAP_WIDTH and MAP_HEIGHT variables to 10 instead of 50. Also, we need to reduce the number of trees, so change MAX_TREES to be 3 instead of 150.

When you make these changes, you will see a screen shot similar to Figure 12-28 on the following page when you run the Tile Walker application.

So, as you can see from these three little experiments, the tile engine can easily adapt to changes. Of course, there are many, many more features that you could implement into this tile engine, but we will leave the research and implementation of these features to you. However, you have got a good base to start from now!

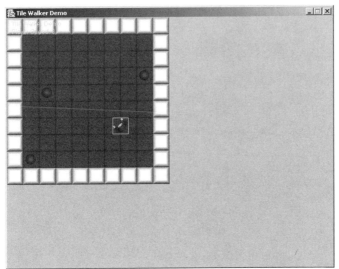

Figure 12-28:
A small
10x10 tile
map

Summary

In this chapter, we looked at many of the essential aspects of creating games in general: animation, timing, object creation, collision detection, a game framework, and a 2D tile engine. Of course, there are many, many more topics that could be covered here, ranging from pixel-perfect collision detection to interpolated movement using Bresenhams line algorithm, which dedicated game theory books cover in detail. For highly technical game theory, we would recommend having a look over the *Game Programming Gems* series of books published by Charles River Media, although be warned that they are quite technical. In the next chapter we will look at using GUI in your games.

Introduction to GUI

"The cow was outstanding in her field."   —Unknown

Introduction

In this chapter we will look at what Java has to offer with its built-in GUI packages AWT and Swing and how we can use them, abuse them, and then disown them. We will also learn to create our own GUI system to get around the frailties of the Java GUI system.

GUI is sometimes overlooked in game development, but every game really requires a GUI system. As you may know already, GUI is an acronym for graphical user interface and is the general name for all the widgets, such as buttons and scroll bars, that are commonly found in a windowed environment.

Java's GUI system is very well designed and easy to use, which makes it an excellent choice for creating game tools such as map editors and the like. But when it comes to games programming, we require complete control over everything and because of the way Java is structured, using the Java GUI does not allow us complete control, which we will discuss through the course of this chapter.

First though, let's look at how we can implement a couple of the Swing GUI components (check back to Chapter 8, "Applications and Applets," to find out more about Swing).

Using Buttons

Every Swing component (not including the top-level containers, such as `JApplet` and `JFrame`) extends the `JComponent` class, which means that `JComponent` is the base class for all Swing components. The `JComponent` class contains methods that are relevant to all GUI objects.

Also, the Swing architecture is a hierarchical system that uses containers and components. A *container* is simply a component that can contain other components, and if we look at how the `JComponent` is derived, we can see that it itself is in fact a container.

- `java.lang.Object`
    - `java.awt.Component`
        - `java.awt.Container`
            - `javax.swing.JComponent`

As you can see, Swing objects are based upon the AWT (Abstract Window Toolkit) classes, which was Swing's predecessor.

To add GUI components, we can simply call the `add` method of the top-level container's content pane once we have actually created the objects by calling the constructor method and set up the positions, etc. (for example, in an application, the top-level container is the `JFrame`, whereas in an applet it is `JApplet`).

The `JButton` is one of the most useful objects in the Swing package, but it is not a direct subclass of the `JComponent` class. In fact, it is a subclass of the `AbstractButton` class, which is a more generic representation of a button that is then extended to create the `JButton` class. Note that the `AbstractButton` class first extends the `JComponent` class though.

The `JButton` component allows us to perform an action if the user clicks on it by implementing an `ActionListener`. Basically, this works by making our class handle events that are sent via the Event Dispatch Thread, informing us that the button has been clicked. When we implement the `ActionListener`, we override a method called `action-Performed`, which is called every time an `ActionEvent` is dispatched via a component that has a listener associated with it. Which button was clicked can then be determined by the `ActionEvent` parameter, which is passed into the `actionPerformed` method. Let's take a look at an example now to try and make this clearer. In the example, we will create three buttons, each of which will update a `JLabel` (another simple GUI component that can be used to easily output static text), informing you as to which button was pressed last.

Code Listing 13-1: Using the `JButton` object

```
import java.awt.*;
import java.awt.event.*;
import javax.swing.*;

public class JButtonExample extends JFrame implements ActionListener
<>
    public JButtonExample()
    <>
        super("JButton Example");
        setBounds(0, 0, 300, 300);
        getContentPane().setLayout(null);
        setResizable(false);
        setDefaultCloseOperation(EXIT_ON_CLOSE);

        // Create the label...
        label = new JLabel("No button pressed");
        label.setLocation(10, 10);
        label.setSize(label.getPreferredSize());
```

```
        // Create the three buttons...
        button1 = new JButton("Button 1");
        button1.setLocation(10, 40);
        button1.setSize(button1.getPreferredSize());

        button2 = new JButton("Button 2");
        button2.setBounds(10, 80, 270, 40);

        button3 = new JButton("Button 3");
        button3.setBounds(60, 140, 160, 100);
        button3.setBackground(new Color(255, 0, 0));
        button3.setForeground(new Color(0, 255, 0));

        // Add the action listeners
        button1.addActionListener(this);
        button2.addActionListener(this);
        button3.addActionListener(this);

        // Add the objects to the content pane...
        getContentPane().add(label);
        getContentPane().add(button1);
        getContentPane().add(button2);
        getContentPane().add(button3);

        setVisible(true);
    <>

    public void actionPerformed(ActionEvent e)
    <>
        if(e.getSource() == button1)
        <>
            label.setText("Button 1 was pressed last");
            label.setSize(label.getPreferredSize());
        <>
        else if(e.getSource() == button2)
        <>
            label.setText("Button 2 was pressed last");
            label.setSize(label.getPreferredSize());
        <>
        else if(e.getSource() == button3)
        <>
            label.setText("Button 3 was pressed last");
            label.setSize(label.getPreferredSize());
        <>
    <>

    public static void main(String[] args)
    <>
        JButtonExample mainApp = new JButtonExample();
    <>

    JLabel label;
    JButton button1;
    JButton button2;
    JButton button3;
<>
```

When we execute the JButton example code, we can see that it looks like the following:

Figure 13-1:
The JButton Example application

As you can see from this figure, our application shows the three buttons that we added. When we press each of the buttons, they update the JLabel above the buttons to show which button was pressed last. Let's look now at the code that we used to create the buttons.

First we create a JLabel object, which is simply a component that can be used to display a string of text. We are going to use this to display which button was pressed last by the user. We create the JLabel using the following code segment:

```
label = new JLabel("No button pressed");
label.setLocation(10, 10);
label.setSize(label.getPreferredSize());
```

Note how we set the default text to be displayed in the label by passing a string to the constructor. Also notice how we call the setLocation method to set the x, y position of the label relative to its container and also the setSize method, to which we pass in the preferred size (which is obtained by calling the getPreferredSize method of the JLabel object).

To create Button 1 we simply specify the text to appear on the button by passing it to the JButton constructor and then set its location and size appropriately. This can be seen in the following segment of code:

```
button1 = new JButton("Button 1");
button1.setLocation(10, 40);
button1.setSize(button1.getPreferredSize());
```

For our second button, we use the setBounds method instead of the setLocation and setSize methods to simply specify the dimensions of the button. This can be seen in the following line of code:

```
button2.setBounds(10, 80, 270, 40);
```

In this case, the top-left corner of the button will be positioned at 10, 80, and it will be 270 pixels wide and 40 pixels high.

For our final button, we again call the setBounds method, but this time we also set the background color of the button to red and the text color (foreground color) to green. This is achieved with the following two lines of code:

```
button3.setBackground(new Color(255, 0, 0));
button3.setForeground(new Color(0, 255, 0));
```

Once we have all of our buttons created, we next add action listeners to each of the buttons using the `addActionListener` method, which is defined in the `AbstractButton` super class. In this particular case, the listener is our class itself (as it implements the `ActionListener` interface). Therefore, it is passed as a parameter to the `addAction-Listener` method. The action listener works in the same way as mouse and keyboard listeners that we used in Chapter 10. The action listener handles the user clicking on the button and allows us to execute code when this happens. Here is our complete `actionPerformed` method:

```
public void actionPerformed(ActionEvent e)
<>
    if(e.getSource() == button1)
    <>
        label.setText("Button 1 was pressed last");
        label.setSize(label.getPreferredSize());
    <>
    else if(e.getSource() == button2)
    <>
        label.setText("Button 2 was pressed last");
        label.setSize(label.getPreferredSize());
    <>
    else if(e.getSource() == button3)
    <>
        label.setText("Button 3 was pressed last");
        label.setSize(label.getPreferredSize());
    <>
<>
```

Notice how we use the `getSource` method of the `ActionEvent` object, which is passed to the `actionPerformed` method to determine which button the user clicked. So in this example, to test if the `button1` object was clicked, we use the following segment of code:

```
if(e.getSource() == button1)
<>
    // code to be executed when the button is clicked goes here
<>
```

 NOTE: You can, of course, as we saw in Chapter 10, add action listeners on the fly as follows:

```
button3.addActionListener(new ActionListener(
<>
    public void actionPerformed(ActionEvent e)
    <>
        System.out.println("Button 3 pressed!");
    <>
<>);
```

Using Text Fields

The JTextField allows us to get input from the user by creating a rectangular area in which the user can enter text. Let's look at how we create a JTextField in an example application now:

Code Listing 13-2: Using the JTextField

```
import java.awt.*;
import java.awt.event.*;
import javax.swing.*;

public class JTextFieldExample extends JFrame
    implements ActionListener
<>
    public JTextFieldExample()
    <>
        super("JTextField Example");
        setBounds(0, 0, 450, 125);
        getContentPane().setLayout(null);
        setResizable(false);
        setDefaultCloseOperation(EXIT_ON_CLOSE);

        // Create the text field...
        textfield = new JTextField(20);
        textfield.setLocation(120, 10);
        textfield.setSize(textfield.getPreferredSize());

        // Create the labels...
        label = new JLabel("Enter your name:");
        label.setLocation(10, 10);
        label.setSize(label.getPreferredSize());

        nameLabel = new JLabel("The name you entered was: ");
        nameLabel.setLocation(10, 60);
        nameLabel.setSize(nameLabel.getPreferredSize());

        // Create the button...
        button = new JButton("Update");
        button.setLocation(350, 10);
        button.setSize(button.getPreferredSize());

        // Add the action listeners
        button.addActionListener(this);

        // Add the objects to the content pane...
        getContentPane().add(textfield);
        getContentPane().add(label);
        getContentPane().add(nameLabel);
        getContentPane().add(button);

        setVisible(true);
    <>

    public void actionPerformed(ActionEvent e)
    <>
        if(e.getSource() == button)
        <>
            nameLabel.setText("The name you entered was: "
```

```
            + textfield.getText());
        nameLabel.setSize(nameLabel.getPreferredSize());
    <>
<>


public static void main(String[] args)
<>
    JTextFieldExample mainApp = new JTextFieldExample();
<>


JLabel label;
JLabel nameLabel;
JButton button;
JTextField textfield;
<>
```

When you run the example program, you can see that we have created a text field, which allows user input. When we click the Update button, the label below the text field is updated to show what the user has entered (this is an example of how we can get what the user has input into the text field). Here are two screen shots displaying before and after the button was clicked:

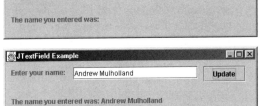

Figure 13-2:
The JTextField Example application

Figure 13-3:
The label below the JTextField is updated to show the name the user entered into the JTextField.

Let's now look at the code we used to create and manipulate the JText-Field. First we create the JTextField by specifying how many characters you expect the field to be able to hold (visually, that is, for sizing purposes) in the constructor (note that the text field will scroll if the user enters more characters than can be displayed. Then we specify the size and location of the JTextField (note that in this example we use the setSize and setLocation methods, but we could equally use the setBounds method, as we have seen with the JButton example.) Here is the code segment we use to create the JTextField:

```
textfield = new JTextField(20);
textfield.setLocation(120, 10);
textfield.setSize(textfield.getPreferredSize());
```

Once we have created it, we simply add it to the content pane, as we have with the other objects. This can be seen in the following line of code:

```
getContentPane().add(textfield);
```

Finally, we can see in the `actionPerformed` method that when the button is clicked, we call the `getText` method of the `JTextField`, which simply returns a string that is the text the user has entered. This can be seen in the following line of code where we are updating the `nameLabel` to represent what the user has entered in our example.

```
nameLabel.setText("The name you entered was: "
    + textfield.getText());
```

Here we start to see one of the problems with using the Swing GUI system when we are looking from a games point of view. The `JTextField` grabs the focus of the keyboard input, and hence the game no longer would have control of the user input until the `JTextField` releases it.

 NOTE: In the last example, if we added an action listener to the `textfield` object and then handled an action event for this object in the `actionPerformed` method as we did for the Update button, this would update the label when the user presses Return after entering text into the text field.

GUI Extra Section

As well as the aforementioned GUI objects, `JButton` and `JTextField`, there are many other great components that can be used easily. In a bid to save the trees, however, we are only going to list the most useful ones here, and as a bonus, we have included a chapter on the companion CD that will give an example of each GUI object and explain how each works. This chapter can be found in the Bonus Chapter folder on the CD-ROM.

Here is a complete list of the Swing components covered in this bonus chapter.

Component	What it is/does
JLabel	Used to display static text
JButton	Seen in the previous example and used to create buttons
JTextField	Again seen previously. Used to take keyboard input from the user
JPasswordField	Same as a `JTextField`, but the visible input is replaced by asterisks (*)
JTextArea	A component to display (or input) a large volume of text
JComboBox	Used to give a drop-down menu of a defined list of options
JCheckBox	Used for Boolean options (i.e., if some feature should be enabled or disabled)
JRadioButton	Used to create a list of selectable options in which only a single option can be picked
JProgressBar	A bar used to show progress to the user
JList	Used to display a list of data
JTable	Used to contain tabulated data. We will also see this being used in Chapter 16.

Component	What it is/does
JTree	Used to display hierarchical information, such as the directory structure
JEditorPane	Can be used to contain HTML pages, as you will see in the bonus chapter example on the companion CD.
JOptionPane	Used to create message boxes that pop up to display simple information to the user. We have seen some of these already, such as in Chapter 9 when choosing whether to go into full-screen or windowed mode.
JMenu	Used to create a menu at the top of your application
Tool Tips	Those little pop-up thingies that tell you what a button does

Setting Images for Buttons

Although text buttons allow us to show a string of text to inform the user of the function of the button, it is more likely in a game context that we will require the button to be a set of images that represent the up, over, and down states of the button. This is very easy to implement using Swing, as we will see in the following example.

Code Listing 13-3: Using the JButton object

```java
import java.awt.*;
import java.awt.event.*;
import javax.swing.*;


public class ImageButtonExample extends JFrame implements
    ActionListener
<>
    public ImageButtonExample()
    <>
        super("Image Button Example");
        setBounds(0, 0, 300, 300);
        getContentPane().setLayout(null);
        setResizable(false);
        setDefaultCloseOperation(EXIT_ON_CLOSE);

        // Create the label...
        label = new JLabel("No button pressed");
        label.setLocation(10, 10);
        label.setSize(label.getPreferredSize());

        // Create the three buttons...
        button1 = new JButton(new ImageIcon("button1_up.gif"));
        button1.setPressedIcon(new ImageIcon("button1_down.gif"));
        button1.setRolloverIcon(new ImageIcon("button1_over.gif"));
        button1.setFocusPainted(false);
        button1.setContentAreaFilled(false);
        button1.setBorderPainted(false);
        button1.setMargin(new Insets(0, 0, 0, 0));
        button1.setLocation(10, 40);
        button1.setSize(button1.getPreferredSize());

        button2 = new JButton(new ImageIcon("button2_up.gif"));
        button2.setPressedIcon(new ImageIcon("button2_down.gif"));
```

```
        button2.setRolloverIcon(new ImageIcon("button2_over.gif"));
        button2.setFocusPainted(false);
        button2.setContentAreaFilled(false);
        button2.setBorderPainted(false);
        button2.setMargin(new Insets(0, 0, 0, 0));
        button2.setLocation(150, 150);
        button2.setSize(button1.getPreferredSize());

        // Add the action listeners
        button1.addActionListener(this);
        button2.addActionListener(this);

        // Add the objects to the content pane...
        getContentPane().add(label);
        getContentPane().add(button1);
        getContentPane().add(button2);

        setVisible(true);
    <>

    public void actionPerformed(ActionEvent e)
    <>
        if(e.getSource() == button1)
        <>
            label.setText("Button 1 was pressed last");
            label.setSize(label.getPreferredSize());
        <>
        else if(e.getSource() == button2)
        <>
            label.setText("Button 2 was pressed last");
            label.setSize(label.getPreferredSize());
        <>
    <>

    public static void main(String[] args)
    <>
        ImageButtonExample mainApp = new ImageButtonExample();
    <>

    JLabel label;
    JButton button1;
    JButton button2;
<>
```

When we execute this code with the appropriate image files, which can be found in the example directory on the companion CD-ROM, the application shown here will be visible.

As you can see from this figure, we have loaded images in to represent the buttons. The code is very similar to the previous example, as all we have really changed is the way that we create the JButton objects. Let's look at the code that we have used to create Button 1.

Figure 13-4: The Image Button Example application

First, we call the constructor specifying the up image of the button instead of the text we wish the button to display. The image is loaded by creating an instance of the `ImageIcon` class, specifying the filename of the image into its constructor. This can be seen in the following line of code:

```
button1 = new JButton(new ImageIcon("button1_up.gif"));
```

Once our `button` object is created, we then want to set another two images so that the button will change when both the mouse is over the button and when the button is pressed. This is accomplished by calling `setRolloverIcon` and `setPressedIcon` respectively. These functions again take an `ImageIcon` object as the parameter, which is created by means of the `ImageIcon` constructor. This handles loading in the image for you. Here are the two lines of code that accomplish this:

```
button1.setPressedIcon(new ImageIcon("button1_down.gif"));
button1.setRolloverIcon(new ImageIcon("button1_over.gif"));
```

Note that it is also possible to specify a disabled-button image by calling the `setDisabledIcon` method in the same way we did for the over and pressed images.

Next we need to remove the decorations that Java adds to the button by default, such as the border, focus rectangle (when the button is highlighted), and gray background. This is achieved by calling the following three methods:

```
button1.setFocusPainted(false);
button1.setContentAreaFilled(false);
button1.setBorderPainted(false);
```

Finally, we call the `setMargin` method to remove the preset margin that Java assigns to the button by specifying the insets to zero. This can be seen in the following line of code:

```
button1.setMargin(new Insets(0, 0, 0, 0));
```

Then we do exactly the same for the second button, except we specify a different location for it to be displayed. Note also that the rest of the example code is the same as the previous example, the exception being that we are only using two buttons instead of three.

Extending the GUI

In the previous three examples, you can see that you have had very little control over the actual drawing of the components; they just magically appeared on the screen once you performed the correct setup for them, and it's all very high level.

It is possible to extend the GUI and provide your own functionality for certain aspects of them, such as rendering. For example, we could extend a `JButton` and provide our own painting code, as follows:

```
public class MyButton extends JButton
<>
```

```
public void paintComponent(Graphics g)
<>
    // custom paint here
<>
<>
```

Note that for Swing components derived from `JComponent`, not top-level Swing containers, you would override the `paintComponent` method, whereas with AWT components you would override the `paint` method.

However, even using this method we still feel that we don't have complete control over the GUI, especially if the GUI is involved in the real-time running of the game, such as in a role-playing game or real-time strategy game where GUI is an important part of the in-game functionality and not just used for the outer-game menu system. For example, in the last example we defined buttons that were actually shaped as circles, whereas the collision detection of the mouse press with the buttons involved bounding rectangle tests (i.e., the bounds of the button). It is quite possible that we may be able to override a method to provide our own mouse detection code somewhere in the depths of Swing, but quite frankly we would highly recommend creating your own GUI system.

A Recap on the Event Dispatch Thread

Before we go any further, we should recap the Event Dispatch Thread a little. As you know, the Event Dispatch Thread processes events from repaints to mouse events to action events, as we have seen in this chapter. Whenever a method is invoked as a result of one of these events, such as `actionPerformed`, `mousePressed`, `paint`, `keyReleased`, or `windowClosing`, all of which we have seen in previous chapters of the book, they are all running in the Event Dispatch Thread. As we mentioned in Chapter 9, you are able to run your own code from another thread using the `SwingUtilities` static methods `invokeAndWait` and `invokeLater`.

Creating Your Own GUI System

In our opinion, it is better to write your own GUI system to ensure that you have full control over it. C/C++ programmers using DirectX or OpenGL would have to write their own anyway, so writing your own in Java is no different.

A quick note before we start, however. The greatest advantage of creating your own GUI system is that it gives you control of all aspects of it. So we are really saying is this is how we would implement the base of a GUI system, but you may have an equally valid alternative that would suit your purposes better (i.e., using Java's AWT or Swing GUI). But really in our opinion, ours is a pretty solid foundation to work from and build upon.

As we mentioned before, all GUI components in Swing extend the `JComponent` class, which contains all the base methods that are relevant to all GUI components, such as setting the bounds and the background color, etc. This is a really good system, so we should start by looking at creating a base component class for our GUI system.

We'll call this base component class GUIComponent. Let's first look at the complete class definition, and then we'll go over the purpose of each of the methods.

Code Listing 13-4: The GUIComponent class

```java
import java.awt.*;
import java.awt.event.*;

public class GUIComponent
<>
    public GUIComponent()
    <>
        visible = true;
        bgColor = Color.black;
    <>

    public boolean withinBounds(int x, int y)
    <>
        if(x >= this.x && x < this.x+this.w && y >= this.y && y
            < this.y+this.h)
            return true;
        else
            return false;
    <>


    public GUIComponent getComponentAt(int x, int y)
    <>
        if(visible && x >= this.x && x < this.x+this.w && y
            >= this.y && y < this.y+this.h)
            return this;
        else
            return null;
    <>

    public void handleMouse(MouseEvent e)
    <>

    <>

    public void render(Graphics g)
    <>
        if(visible)
        <>
            g.setColor(bgColor);
            g.fillRect(x, y, w, h);
        <>
    <>

    public void setLocation(int x, int y)
    <>
        this.x = x;
        this.y = y;
    <>
```

```
public void setSize(int w, int h)
<>
    this.w = w;
    this.h = h;
<>

public void setBounds(int x, int y, int w, int h)
<>
    this.x = x;
    this.y = y;
    this.w = w;
    this.h = h;
<>

public void setBackground(Color c)
<>
    bgColor = c;
<>

public void setVisible(boolean v)
<>
    visible = v;
<>

public void notifyMouseClicked(MouseEvent e, GUIComponent c)
<>

<>

public void notifyMousePressed(MouseEvent e, GUIComponent c)
<>

<>

public void notifyMouseReleased(MouseEvent e, GUIComponent c)
<>

<>

public void notifyMouseDragged(MouseEvent e, GUIComponent c)
<>

<>

public void notifyMouseMoved(MouseEvent e, GUIComponent c)
<>

<>

Color bgColor;
int x, y, w, h;
boolean visible;
<>
```

Let's look at each of the methods in our base GUIComponent class now,
starting with the constructor.

```
public GUIComponent()
<>
    visible = true;
```

```
    bgColor = Color.black;
<>
```

All we do in the constructor is set the defaults for the component (i.e., we want it to be visible and have the standard background color of black).

Next we create a method called `withinBounds`, which simply tests if the x, y coordinates passed into the method are within the boundaries of the component or not. If the specified point was within the boundaries, we return `true`; otherwise, we return `false`. This can be seen here:

```
public boolean withinBounds(int x, int y)
<>
    if(x >= this.x && x < this.x+this.w && y >= this.y && y
        < this.y+this.h)
        return true;
    else
        return false;
<>
```

Now we create a very similar method called `getComponentAt`, which again takes an x, y coordinate and tests if the point is within the bounds. This time, however, it takes into account whether or not the component is visible and either returns the object if it was within the bounds and visible or null if it was not. This method is used when we implement the mouse handling into the GUI for testing which component the mouse is over. It can be seen in full here:

```
public GUIComponent getComponentAt(int x, int y)
<>
    if(visible && x >= this.x && x < this.x+this.w && y
        >= this.y && y < this.y+this.h)
        return this;
    else
        return null;
<>
```

Next on the list to create is the `handleMouse` method, which does not have any functionality. The method is simply there for us to override if the component that is extending the `GUIComponent` class requires mouse interaction. We will see later in this section how it is used to handle the mouse input for a button style component.

After the `handleMouse` method, we implement a basic `render` method, which will be used to render the component to the supplied `Graphics` object (passed in as g). Again, it is expected that this method will be overridden by a subclass to correctly render the particular GUI component that is overriding it. However, all the default `render` method does is render a filled rectangle (using the component's background color) to the supplied `Graphics` object. The complete definition for the `render` method can be seen here:

```
public void render(Graphics g)
<>
    if(visible)
    <>
        g.setColor(bgColor);
        g.fillRect(x, y, w, h);
```

```
<>
<>
```

Next we have five setter methods that simply allow us to set the bounds of the component (i.e., the position, width, and height), the background color, and finally whether the component is visible or not.

Then we declare another five methods to handle notifications. These are used when we override the GUIComponent class to handle any events that should occur when the mouse performs an action that's not in the bounds of the component. But the component still needs to react to this event (we'll see a good example of these methods when we look at how to create a button later in this example).

That's all there is to the base class. Now comes the clever stuff! What we want to be able to do within the GUI system is have many GUI components on the screen at once and position them within containers so they are relevant to the containers rather than the actual screen. A good example of this is a movable window; when you move a window, all the components inside a window move relative to the parent window, giving the effect that they are contained within the window.

In addition though, it would be useful if we could place containers within containers, as this would allow us to create a completely hierarchical GUI system. See Figure 13-5 for a visual representation of this.

So now let's look at how we can create a container can be used to contain the components and also other containers. Our idea for this is that once all components are added together, we can simply call the render method for what would be our own top-level container, which will proceed to render all component children added to it. We'll look at the complete class definition of GUIContainer first. Then we'll look at the methods in more detail.

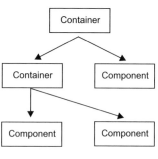

Figure 13-5

Code Listing 13-5: The GUIContainer class

```
import java.awt.*;
import java.awt.event.*;
import java.util.*;

public class GUIContainer extends GUIComponent
<>
    public GUIContainer()
    <>
        componentList = new ArrayList();
    <>


    public GUIComponent getComponentAt(int x, int y)
    <>
        if(withinBounds(x, y))
```

```
{
        x -= this.x;
        y -= this.y;
        for(int i=componentList.size()-1; i>=0; i--)
        {
            GUIComponent tempComponent = (GUIComponent)
                componentList.get(i);
            tempComponent = tempComponent.getComponentAt(x, y);
            if(tempComponent != null)
                return tempComponent;
        }

        if(visible)
            return this; // i.e., it was not one of the children
        else
            return null;
    }
    else
        return null;
}


public void render(Graphics g)
{
    super.render(g);

    g.translate(x, y);

    for(int i=0; i<componentList.size(); i++)
    {
        GUIComponent tempComponent = (GUIComponent)
            componentList.get(i);
        tempComponent.render(g);
    }

    g.translate(-x, -y);
}

public void add(GUIComponent c)
{
    componentList.add(c);
}

public void remove(GUIComponent c)
{
    componentList.remove(c);
}

ArrayList componentList;
}
```

The first thing you will probably notice is that we first extend the GUI-Component class, as the container is itself a component but with the ability to contain children (e.g., as containers are components too, a container can contain other containers). For this, it will require some very clever but altogether quite straightforward code.

Keeping in mind that we have all the functionality of the GUICompo-nent class, we first define a member called componentList, which is simply an ArrayList that will hold a list of all the references to this container's children (other containers and components). As we mentioned before, we want to be able to add components (and containers) to the container and also have the facility to remove them. To do this, all we need is two simple methods, `add` and `remove`, which add `GUIComponent` objects to and remove them from the ArrayList `componentList`. Note that because this `GUIContainer` class extends the `GUIComponent` class, we can cast up easily to a `GUIComponent` so we can add a `GUIContainer` reference into the `componentList` via the same `add` and `remove` methods and any object derived from the `GUIComponent` class, such as the GUIButton that we will make a little later.

For rendering the container, we first need to call the super class's `render` method (i.e., call the `render` method of the `GUIComponent` class), which will simply render a filled rectangle of where the container is (note also that we can make the container invisible by calling the `setVisible` method with a false parameter, meaning its background will not be drawn). Earlier, we said that components (and containers) within a container should be relative to the actual container, so to do this we simply translate the graphics to the x, y position of this container by calling the `translate` method of the `Graphics` object. After this, we then cycle through the list of children (`componentList`) and for each one we call its `render` method.

You should now start to see the nifty idea behind this. If the reference in the `componentList` is a `GUIComponent`, it will render the component; however, if the reference is a container, thanks to polymorphism, it will call the `render` method of the container that overrides the `render` method of the `GUIComponent`, which will then in turn render its own children, too (which could also contain more containers), running through the entire hierarchy rendering everything. So we get this great recursive system, which will handle all of our rendering perfectly and in a very neat way. Note also that after we finish rendering the children, we translate the `Graphics` object back to the original position because if we didn't, we could adversely affect any rendering that was performed after the translation. Here is the listing for the `render` method.

```
public void render(Graphics g)
<>
    super.render(g);

    g.translate(x, y);

    for(int i=0; i<componentList.size(); i++)
    <>
        GUIComponent tempComponent = (GUIComponent)
            componentList.get(i);
        tempComponent.render(g);
    <>

    g.translate(-x, -y);
<>
```

Now let's look at the final method in the `GUIContainer` class, which is the `getComponentAt` method (another little stunner!). Recall that in the `GUIComponent` class, this method checked if the mouse was within the bounds of the component and if it was visible; if so, it returned a reference to itself. So for the container, we are overriding this method and first checking if the mouse is within the bounds of the container. If it is within the bounds, we then adjust the coordinates that we passed in to make them suitable for testing the container's children (remember that all the component's coordinates are relative to the container, so we need to deduct the x, y coordinates of the container to make the passed-in coordinates relative to it).

After this, we then cycle through the list of components backward. Why, you say? Well, we want to get the topmost component that the specified coordinates are within the bounds of. We need to perform this task backward because the list of components is drawn from start to finish in the list order, so the topmost component is at the end of the list, which would be the first to check collisions.

For each component in the list, we call the `getComponentAt` method and store a reference to the returned object (which will either be a `GUIComponent` or a null value). Remember that the list `componentList` can contain both `GUIContainer` objects and `GUIComponent` objects, as discussed on the previous page. But again, thanks to the wonder that is polymorphism, this works to our advantage. If the object we refer to, which we are currently calling the `getComponentAt` method on in the list, is a `GUIContainer`, it will then call the overridden method (i.e., this one) and check all its children (which again could contain more containers). So after we get the `tempComponent` object returned from the `getComponentAt` method, we then check to see if it was a valid `GUIComponent` reference (i.e., not null), and if so, we return it (which works nicely with the recursion, as it will just filter back through to the top). Finally, if none of the children return any valid references, we resort to returning a reference to the container if it is a visible one, as we have already checked that the coordinates are in this container's bounds. Otherwise, we simply return `null`. The complete listing for this method can be seen here:

```
public GUIComponent getComponentAt(int x, int y)
<>
    if(withinBounds(x, y))
    <>
        x -= this.x;
        y -= this.y;
        for(int i=componentList.size()-1; i>=0; i--)
        <>
            GUIComponent tempComponent = (GUIComponent)
                componentList.get(i);
            tempComponent = tempComponent.getComponentAt(x, y);
            if(tempComponent != null)
                return tempComponent;
        <>
```

```
        if(visible)
            return this;    // i.e. it was not one of the children
        else
            return null;
    <>
    else
        return null;
<>
```

We just have one part missing from the base of our GUI system now. We need to create a top-level container (think `JFrame`, `JApplet`) to control the mouse events through the GUI system. So we have aptly named this final part of the base GUI system the `GUISystem` class. Here is the complete listing for the `GUISystem` class:

Code Listing 13-6: The `GUISystem` class

```
import java.awt.*;
import java.awt.event.*;
import java.util.*;

public class GUISystem extends GUIContainer
<>
    public void handleMouse(MouseEvent e)
    <>
        GUIComponent c = getComponentAt(e.getX(), e.getY());

        if(c != null && c != this)
            c.handleMouse(e);

        // determine the mouse event type...
        // notify events lost to last active component

        switch(e.getID())
        <>
            case MouseEvent.MOUSE_MOVED:
                if(lastMouseOver != null && lastMouseOver != c)
                    lastMouseOver.notifyMouseMoved(e, c);

                lastMouseOver = c;
                break;

            case MouseEvent.MOUSE_RELEASED:
                if(lastMouseOver != null && lastMouseOver != c)
                    lastMouseOver.notifyMouseReleased(e, c);

                lastMouseOver = c;
                break;
        <>
    <>

    GUIComponent lastMouseOver;
<>
```

As you can see, we extend our `GUIContainer` class since we want our `GUISystem` class to be the container that will hold all other containers and components and will also be the controller for mouse input events. So all we have overridden here is the `handleMouse` method, which was defined originally in the GUIComponent class. For this method, we pass in any mouse events that occur (which are contained within a Mouse-Event object, created by the MouseListener and MouseMotion-Listener interfaces that we looked at in Chapter 10).

So when a mouse event is passed in, we first find out which component the mouse is on top of by calling the getComponentAt method, passing in the x, y position of the mouse that can be retrieved from the Mouse-Event object by calling the getX and getY methods. We then store the reference that was returned from this method in a temporary reference to a GUIComponent called c. This can be seen in the following line of code:

```
GUIComponent c = getComponentAt(e.getX(), e.getY());
```

Then, if the component that is returned is valid, we simply call the handleMouse method of the component, passing in the MouseEvent object. As we mentioned before, each custom GUI component you create will override the standard handleMouse method declared in the GUI-Component class. So in effect, your component's handleMouse method will be called, and you can then add code to handle the mouse event yourself.

However, in addition, if you recall, we also defined five notify methods for mouse events within the GUIComponent object. This again is because a component may need to react if the mouse performed an action that was not on the component but the component needs to be notified of this event. So we first switch the type of event that the MouseEvent relates to and then call the appropriate notify method. In this GUISystem class we only deal with the MOUSE_MOVED and MOUSE_RELEASED events, but you can add the rest if you need them.

In each of these events, we check if the current object the mouse is over is not the same as the last object. We also check that the last object is not null. Then we simply call the appropriate notify method, again passing in the MouseEvent object. After this, we set the lastMouseOver component to refer to the temporary GUIComponent that we are dealing with at the moment (i.e., c). The switch statement for this can be seen here:

```
switch(e.getID())
<>
    case MouseEvent.MOUSE_MOVED:
        if(lastMouseOver != null && lastMouseOver != c)
            lastMouseOver.notifyMouseMoved(e, c);

        lastMouseOver = c;
        break;

    case MouseEvent.MOUSE_RELEASED:
        if(lastMouseOver != null && lastMouseOver != c)
            lastMouseOver.notifyMouseReleased(e, c);

        lastMouseOver = c;
        break;
<>
```

That is our base to the GUI system. We can now extend our GUI by creating custom components. Let's look at how we can create a push button by extending the `GUIComponent` class. We'll call this new class `GUIButton` and have a look at the complete definition now:

Code Listing 13-7: The `GUIButton` class

```
import java.awt.*;
import java.awt.event.*;
import java.awt.image.*;

public class GUIButton extends GUIComponent
<>
    public GUIButton(Image up, Image down)
    <>
        upImage = up;
        downImage = down;
        currentState = BUTTON_NORMAL;
    <>

    public GUIButton(Image up, Image down, Image over)
    <>
        this(up, down);
        overImage = over;
    <>

    public void setButtonListener(GUIButtonListener l)
    <>
        listener = l;
    <>

    public void handleMouse(MouseEvent e)
    <>
        switch(e.getID())
        <>
            case MouseEvent.MOUSE_PRESSED:
                currentState = BUTTON_PRESSED;
                break;

            case MouseEvent.MOUSE_RELEASED:
                if(currentState == BUTTON_PRESSED)
                    onClick();
                currentState = BUTTON_NORMAL;
                break;

            case MouseEvent.MOUSE_MOVED:
                currentState = BUTTON_MOUSE_OVER;
                break;
        <>
    <>


    public void render(Graphics g)
    <>
        if(visible)
        <>
            switch(currentState)
            <>
                case BUTTON_NORMAL:
```

```
                        g.drawImage(upImage, x, y, null);
                        break;

                case BUTTON_PRESSED:
                        g.drawImage(downImage, x, y, null);
                        break;

                case BUTTON_MOUSE_OVER:
                        if(overImage != null)
                                g.drawImage(overImage, x, y, null);
                        else
                                g.drawImage(upImage, x, y, null);
                        break;
                <>
            <>
    <>


    public void notifyMouseMoved(MouseEvent e, GUIComponent c)
    <>
        currentState = BUTTON_NORMAL;
    <>

    public void notifyMouseReleased(MouseEvent e, GUIComponent c)
    <>
        currentState = BUTTON_NORMAL;
    <>

    public void onClick()
    <>
        if(listener != null)
        <>
            listener.buttonClicked(this);
        <>
    <>

    int currentState;

    public static final int BUTTON_MOUSE_OVER  = 0;
    public static final int BUTTON_NORMAL      = 1;
    public static final int BUTTON_PRESSED     = 2;

    Image upImage;
    Image downImage;
    Image overImage;

    GUIButtonListener listener;
<>
```

We first define the three states that the button can have—up, mouse over, and down—as final integer values and also an integer that holds the current state of the button, which can be seen here:

```
int currentState;

public static final int BUTTON_MOUSE_OVER  = 0;
public static final int BUTTON_NORMAL      = 1;
public static final int BUTTON_PRESSED     = 2;
```

Then we create references to the three possible images that the button requires—the up, down, and over images. This can be seen here:

```
Image upImage;
Image downImage;
Image overImage;
```

Once we have the image references, we then create a reference to a GUIButtonListener interface, which looks as follows and should be placed in a file called GUIButtonListener.java.

```
public interface GUIButtonListener
<>
    public void buttonClicked(GUIButton b);
<>
```

We'll see the use for this listener soon. However, let's now look at the methods in the GUIButton class. Note that we first create the class by extending the GUIComponent class, giving us the functionality of a standard GUI component and also allowing us to use our button with the GUI system (i.e., we will be able to add it to containers, etc.).

First, we define two constructors, one that takes two images (the up and down image) and another that calls the first constructor and then sets an over image for the button. Additionally, the constructors set the currentState of the button to BUTTON_NORMAL, which means that it does not have the mouse over it and is not currently pressed.

Once we have our constructors in place, we then create a simple setter method called setButtonListener, which will take an object that implements the GUIButtonListener interface handle the event of the button being clicked (note this method will be optional, as there will be two ways to handle a button click, which we will see in the example program later in this chapter).

Next we want to override the handleMouse method defined in the GUIComponent class (which has no functionality in it) and replace it with code to handle how the button should react to mouse events. All we need to do here is find out what the event was and set the button state accordingly. This can be seen here:

```
public void handleMouse(MouseEvent e)
<>
    switch(e.getID())
    <>
        case MouseEvent.MOUSE_PRESSED:
            currentState = BUTTON_PRESSED;
            break;

        case MouseEvent.MOUSE_RELEASED:
            if(currentState == BUTTON_PRESSED)
                onClick();
            currentState = BUTTON_NORMAL;
            break;

        case MouseEvent.MOUSE_MOVED:
            currentState = BUTTON_MOUSE_OVER;
            break;
```

```
<>
    <>
```

Note the only special case here is when the mouse button is released over the button (and the button is currently in a pressed state). When this happens, we want to trigger the `onClick` method, which we will look at now.

Because we have no idea of the purpose of a generic button, we need to allow the user to define the actions to be performed when the button is clicked, so we have given two options for this with our system. The first is to override the `onClick` method, which can be done on the fly, as you will see in the example application soon. The second is to make your class implement a `GUIButtonListener` (which we defined earlier) and then set your class to be the listener for the button. If you have not overridden the `onClick` method, it first checks to see that the listener is a valid reference (not null) and then calls the abstract `buttonClicked` method, which is declared in the `GUIButtonListener` interface, passing in the current object as a parameter so the class that is listening can determine which button was clicked (in the same way as you would use the `get-Source` method with standard listeners in Java, such as mouse and keyboard listeners). The definition for the `onClick` method can be seen here:

```
public void onClick()
<>
    if(listener != null)
    <>
        listener.buttonClicked(this);
    <>
<>
```

While we are still on the subject of input and the mouse, let's mention the notify methods that we have also overridden from the `GUIComponent` class. If the mouse has moved or has been released outside the bounds of the button, we want to reset its state back to normal. This functionality is controlled by the `GUISystem` object itself.

Finally, we have the `render` method, which again overrides the `render` method in the `GUIComponent` class and handles the actual drawing of the button. In this method, we first check if the button is visible; if so, we have a `switch` statement to determine the state of the button and then draw the appropriate image by calling the `drawImage` method of the `Graphics` object, which is passed into the `render` method. The complete definition for the `render` method can be seen here:

```
public void render(Graphics g)
<>
    if(visible)
    <>
        switch(currentState)
        <>
            case BUTTON_NORMAL:
                g.drawImage(upImage, x, y, null);
                break;
```

```
        case BUTTON_PRESSED:
            g.drawImage(downImage, x, y, null);
            break;

        case BUTTON_MOUSE_OVER:
            if(overImage != null)
            g.drawImage(overImage, x, y, null);
            else
                g.drawImage(upImage, x, y, null);
            break;
    <>
  <>
<>
```

Using Our New GUI System

Now that we have created the foundation for the GUI and a custom button component, let's look at an example application that implements this GUI system. Let's first look at the complete code listing, and then we will focus on the key parts where the GUI is implemented.

Code Listing 13-8: Using the custom GUI system

```
import java.awt.*;
import java.awt.image.*;
import javax.swing.*;
import java.awt.event.*;
import java.io.*;
import javax.imageio.*;


public class ExampleApp extends JFrame implements Runnable,
                                                  MouseListener,
                                                  MouseMotionListener,
                                                  GUIButtonListener
<>
    public ExampleApp()
    <>
        setTitle("Custom GUI System");
        getContentPane().setLayout(null);
        setResizable(false);
        setIgnoreRepaint(true);

        addWindowListener(new WindowAdapter()
                    <>
                        public void windowClosing(WindowEvent e)
                        <>
                            exitProgram();
                        <>
                    <>);

        backBuffer = new BufferedImage(DISPLAY_WIDTH, DISPLAY_HEIGHT,
            BufferedImage.TYPE_INT_RGB);
        bbGraphics = (Graphics2D)backBuffer.getGraphics();

        // add the mouse listeners
        getContentPane().addMouseListener(this);
        getContentPane().addMouseMotionListener(this);
```

```
                    // initialize the GUI system...
                    guiSystem = new GUISystem();
                    guiSystem.setBounds(0, 0, DISPLAY_WIDTH, DISPLAY_HEIGHT);

                    GUIContainer gc = new GUIContainer();
                    gc.setBounds(10, 10, 150, 250);
                    gc.setBackground(Color.red);

                    GUIContainer gc2 = new GUIContainer();
                    gc2.setBounds(250, 10, 150, 200);
                    gc2.setBackground(Color.yellow);

                    // load the button images...
                    BufferedImage up = null;
                    BufferedImage down = null;
                    BufferedImage over = null;
                    try
                    <>
                        up = ImageIO.read(new File("up.jpg"));
                        down = ImageIO.read(new File("down.jpg"));
                        over = ImageIO.read(new File("over.jpg"));
                    <>
                    catch(IOException e)
                    <>
                        System.out.println(e);
                    <>

                    globalButton1 = new GUIButton(up, down, over);
                    globalButton1.setLocation(21, 10);
                    globalButton1.setSize(103, 38);
                    globalButton1.setButtonListener(this);
                    gc.add(globalButton1);


                    GUIButton button2 = new GUIButton(up, down, over)
                        <>
                            public void onClick()
                            <>
                                System.out.println("Button 2 was clicked!");
                                globalButton1.visible = !globalButton1.visible;
                            <>
                        <>;

                    button2.setLocation(21, 110);
                    button2.setSize(103, 38);
                    gc.add(button2);

                    globalButton2 = new GUIButton(up, down, over);
                    globalButton2.setLocation(400, 300);
                    globalButton2.setSize(103, 38);
                    globalButton2.setButtonListener(this);

                    guiSystem.add(globalButton2);
                    guiSystem.add(gc);
                    guiSystem.add(gc2);

                    setVisible(true);

                    Insets insets = getInsets();
                    DISPLAY_X = insets.left;
```

```
        DISPLAY_Y = insets.top;
        resizeToInternalSize(DISPLAY_WIDTH, DISPLAY_HEIGHT);
    <>


    public void resizeToInternalSize(int internalWidth, int
        internalHeight)
    <>
        Insets insets = getInsets();
        final int newWidth = internalWidth + insets.left
            + insets.right;
        final int newHeight = internalHeight + insets.top
            + insets.bottom;

        Runnable resize = new Runnable()
        <>
            public void run()
            <>
                setSize(newWidth, newHeight);
                validate();
            <>
        <>;

        if(!SwingUtilities.isEventDispatchThread())
        <>
            try
            <>
                SwingUtilities.invokeAndWait(resize);
            <>
            catch(Exception e) <><>
        <>
        else
            resize.run();
    <>


    public void run()
    <>
        Thread thisThread = Thread.currentThread();
        while(loop==thisThread)
        <>
            render(bbGraphics);

            Graphics g = getGraphics();
            g.drawImage(backBuffer, DISPLAY_X, DISPLAY_Y, null);
            g.dispose();

            try
            <>
                Thread.sleep(20);
            <>
            catch(InterruptedException e) <>/*  ignore */<>
        <>

        System.out.println("Program Exited");

        dispose();
        System.exit(0);
    <>
```

```
public void render(Graphics g)
<>
    g.clearRect(0, 0, DISPLAY_WIDTH, DISPLAY_HEIGHT);
    guiSystem.render(g);
<>


public void exitProgram()
<>
    loop = null;
<>

// mouse handling...
public void mouseDragged(MouseEvent e)
    <> guiSystem.handleMouse(e); <>
public void mouseMoved(MouseEvent e)
    <> guiSystem.handleMouse(e); <>
public void mouseClicked(MouseEvent e)
    <> guiSystem.handleMouse(e); <>
public void mousePressed(MouseEvent e)
    <> guiSystem.handleMouse(e); <>
public void mouseReleased(MouseEvent e)
    <> guiSystem.handleMouse(e); <>
public void mouseEntered(MouseEvent e)
    <> guiSystem.handleMouse(e); <>
public void mouseExited(MouseEvent e)
    <> guiSystem.handleMouse(e); <>
// end of mouse handling

public void buttonClicked(GUIButton source)
<>
    if(source == globalButton1)
    <>
        System.out.println("The globalButton 1 was clicked");
    <>
    else if(source == globalButton2)
    <>
        System.out.println("The globalButton 2 was clicked");
    <>
<>


public static void main(String args[])
<>
    ExampleApp app = new ExampleApp();

    app.loop = new Thread(app);
    app.loop.start();
<>

private Thread loop;
private BufferedImage backBuffer;
private Graphics2D bbGraphics;

private final int DISPLAY_X; // value assigned in constructor
private final int DISPLAY_Y; // value assigned in constructor
private static final int DISPLAY_WIDTH = 640;
private static final int DISPLAY_HEIGHT = 480;
```

```
    private GUIButton globalButton1;
    private GUIButton globalButton2;
    private GUISystem guiSystem;
<>
```

Here is a screen shot of it in action:

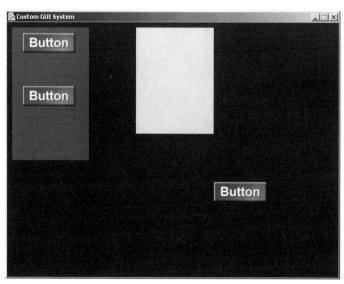

Figure 13-6:
Custom GUI
example

If you want to play with the example, try holding the mouse down over a button, moving the mouse around, and then releasing it back on the originally pressed down button (cool eh?).

First we define our GUISystem and two GUIButtons as members of our main class using the following code:

```
private GUIButton globalButton1;
private GUIButton globalButton2;
private GUISystem guiSystem;
```

Also note that our main class implements the GUIButtonListener interface so we have to declare the buttonClicked method in the class, which we will look at soon.

The first important thing to do is actually create our GUISystem object, so we just call the default constructor and set the width and height (bounds) to the same as our application window, which can be seen in the following line of code:

```
guiSystem = new GUISystem();
guiSystem.setBounds(0, 0, DISPLAY_WIDTH, DISPLAY_HEIGHT);
```

Next, create two GUIContainers and set the first to red and the second to yellow, just so we can determine which is which when we run the example. This can be seen here:

```
GUIContainer gc = new GUIContainer();
gc.setBounds(10, 10, 150, 250);
gc.setBackground(Color.red);
```

```
GUIContainer gc2 = new GUIContainer();
gc2.setBounds(250, 10, 150, 200);
gc2.setBackground(Color.yellow);
```

We then load in three JPEG images to represent the three possible states of the buttons (up, over, and down). This is done simply by using `Image-IO`, which we learned about in Chapter 9. The code to load the images can be seen here:

```
BufferedImage up = null;
BufferedImage down = null;
BufferedImage over = null;
try
<>
    up = ImageIO.read(new File("up.jpg"));
    down = ImageIO.read(new File("down.jpg"));
    over = ImageIO.read(new File("over.jpg"));
<>
catch(IOException e)
<>
    System.out.println(e);
<>
```

Once we have the images loaded in, we can then create our first button (called `globalButton1`) by calling the constructor with the three images as parameters.

```
globalButton1 = new GUIButton(up, down, over);
```

Then, as the `GUIButton` extends the `GUIComponent` class, we can call the `setLocation` and `setSize` methods to position it (remembering the position will be relative to the container that we place it inside). This can be seen here:

```
globalButton1.setLocation(21, 10);
globalButton1.setSize(103, 38);
```

For this button, it will be placed 21 pixels from the left of the container and 10 pixels down from the top of the container.

Next we call the `setButtonListener` method to state that this class will implement the `buttonClicked` method (declared in the `GUIButtonListener` interface) and hence handle any events that should occur when the `globalButton1` is clicked. This can be seen here:

```
globalButton1.setButtonListener(this);
```

Finally, we call the `add` method of the first (red) container, passing our `globalButton1` object as a parameter. Hence, our button will then become a child of this container. This can be seen here:

```
gc.add(globalButton1);
```

We then add another button called `button2` to the same container in a different location; however, we implement the handling code for the clicking of this button slightly differently. Instead of using the `setButton-Listener` method, as we did with the last button, this time we override the `GUIButton` `onClick` method on the fly when we create the instance of the GUIButton object, placing the click-handling code directly inside the onClick method. This can be seen here:

```
GUIButton button2 = new GUIButton(up, down, over)
        <>
            public void onClick()
            <>
                System.out.println("Button 2 was clicked!");
                globalButton1.visible = !globalButton1.visible;
            <>
        <>;
```

When button2 is clicked, it will toggle the visibility of globalButton1. Neat, eh?

We then set the location and size for button2 and add it to the first container, as we did with the previous button.

Next we declare another button called globalButton2 and set the listener to be this class also, so we will have to handle two different buttons in the same class. Also, instead of adding this new button into one of the two containers, we add it directly to our GUISystem object guiSystem, as it is a container (the top-level container). After this, we then add the two containers and that's all there is to the setup part.

For rendering the GUI, all we need to do is place a call to the GUISystem render method in our main game loop, passing in the Graphics object that we wish to use to render it.

```
guiSystem.render(g);
```

As you know from before, the GUISystem class needs to also handle the mouse events for the GUI, so we need to pass this information into our guiSystem object every time an event occurs. To do this, we simply implement the MouseListener and MouseMotionListener interfaces into our main class, and then for each of the methods that we have to declare, we call the handleMouse method of the guiSystem object, passing in the MouseEvent object. Note, however, that these mouse events are not synchronized with the main loop, and hence they are not synchronized with the GUI system, which is being rendered from the main loop. This is easy to change, however, if you require it to be synchronized by using the Event Processor that we discussed in detail in Chapter 10.

Remember also that we need to add the MouseListener and MouseMotionListener to the content pane (not the JFrame), as this gives us mouse coordinates relative to the internal area inside the window's borders, which is seen in the following two lines of code:

```
getContentPane().addMouseListener(this);
getContentPane().addMouseMotionListener(this);
```

Finally, let's look at how we deal with the GUIButtonListener method buttonClicked, which we have to implement. As you know, when a button is clicked and it has an associated listener, it will pass itself as a parameter to the listener's buttonClicked method in the form of a GUIComponent, so we can use this to test which button the click has come from by simply comparing the references for equality. The entire `buttonClicked` method can be seen here for reference:

```
public void buttonClicked(GUIButton source)
<>
    if(source == globalButton1)
        <>
            System.out.println("The globalButton 1 was clicked");
        <>
    else if(source == globalButton2)
        <>
            System.out.println("The globalButton 2 was clicked");
        <>
<>
```

In the previous chapter, we defined a screen system with the base class `TemplateScreen`, which was used to handle many screens from the game framework from one `currentScreen` reference. In reality, the `GUISystem` we have just developed is an advanced version of the screen system defined in the previous chapter, incorporating a solid component-container hierarchy. This could be used even for the structure of your actual game screens by overriding the render methods and supplying your in-game rendering code yourself, all being called through the original top-level `GUISystem` object when added to it.

Summary

In this chapter, you learned how to use some basic Swing components, and we built the foundation for a powerful hierarchical custom GUI system. While it's fresh in your mind, now would be a good time to start trying to add extra components to the custom GUI system. In no time, you will have your own powerful GUI library, which will serve you far better for games programming than Swing. Plus you have full control over how it works, and you will also understand how all your components work!

Chapter 14

Introduction to Databases

"No matter how much the hardware team improves things,
the software team will waste it."

—Unknown

Introduction

In this chapter, you will learn how a database can be utilized within a Java game. Also, we will explain the need to understand and use databases in the creation of games in Java. Finally, we will give you an overview of SQL (Structured Query Language), which is the language used to interact with databases.

What Is a Database?

A *database* is simply an organized collection of information. It allows many different types of data to be stored and retrieved in a highly efficient manner. Information within a database is organized into tables. A *table* is simply a collection of fields, which can each have their own unique data type. For example, you could have a single table in your database that contains a player's name, age, and e-mail address. Once you have tables defined in your database, you can then add records into the tables. A *record* is a single entry in a table that contains data for each of the fields specified in the table.

There are many different types of databases, but the one we are most interested in is the relational database. A *relational database* is a database that contains tables of information that relate to each other in some way or another, and the information in the tables can be accessed and organized in many ways. This is usually accomplished by means of unique identification

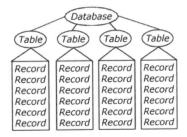

Figure 14-1: A visual interpretation of a database

503

numbers, although this identification can be done with any data type, but the most effective way is to do it with number types. Therefore, each record that is added to a table in a relational database will be automatically assigned a unique number if the field is numeric and if a sequence and a trigger is defined to the table to do that. There are database packages that can do this almost automatically by defining that the field is an identity field. This unique field will differentiate it from all other entries in the same table (but not entries in other tables). This allows us to optimize the data within the database as we can simply make a field in a table an integer (or any data type—actually, sometimes there are situations where varchar (string) fields are better reference fields than integer).

A good example of where a relational database could be used is in a simple chat applet. The user's information could be stored in a table called userinfo, which would contain the login name, password, and e-mail address. Also, each record (of user information) would be assigned a unique identification number automatically by the database, so there would always be one field in the userinfo table (the unique number field) that could identify a single record from all the rest. Now our database would contain a single table that held user information. What would we do, though, if we wanted users to have a contacts list into which they could add their associates to the chat system? We could have a separate table that would be named using the user's login name (for example, if the user was called "bobby," the table would be named "bobby_contacts") for each user. Each of these tables for the users would contain duplicate records of their contacts' information for all the users that they have added to their contacts list. Here is how our tables would look in the database if Bobby had added two other users called "Sandra" and "Jenny" to his contact list.

As you can see, this would be a very inefficient method of storing the contact information, as the same information would be replicated many times and the database could have hundreds of tables in it (i.e., one for each user), which would be inefficient from a data access and storage point of view.

'userinfo' Table

Login Name	Password	Email Address
Bobby	qwerty	bobby@email.net
Sandra	letmein	sandra@email.net
Jenny	jen123	jenny@email.net
John	john999	john@email.net

'Bobby_contact' Table

Login Name	Password	Email Address
Sandra	letmein	sandra@email.net
Jenny	jen123	jenny@email.net

'Sandra_contact' Table

Login Name	Password	Email Address

'Jenny_contact' Table

Login Name	Password	Email Address

'John_contact' Table

Login Name	Password	Email Address

Figure 14-2: Visualization of an inefficient method for storing user contact information

The ideal way to deal with this problem would be to use the features of the relational database. That is, use the unique number field that has been assigned to each user automatically by the database. Instead of creating an individual table for each user, all we need to do is create a single table for use by all the users, which "pairs" up users with other users that have been added to their contact list. We will call this new table relate_contacts_to_users. This kind of table is often referred to as a *link table*. The table will contain two integer fields to store two users' unique numbers and also its own uniquely assigned number to conform to being a relational database. So when a user adds a friend to his or her contact list, the applet will add an entry into this new table by adding the user's unique number into the first field and then the friend's unique number in the second field. This constitutes a complete record in the new table. Therefore, we can add many friends to a single user with the expense of only three integer values, rather than duplicating the many strings and integers that represent users' details. Here is how our database would look if Bobby had added Sandra and Jenny as contacts using this more efficient method:

'userinfo' Table			
Unique ID	Login Name	Password	Email Address
1	Bobby	qwerty	bobby@email.net
2	Sandra	letmein	sandra@email.net
3	Jenny	jen123	jenny@email.net
4	John	john999	john@email.net

Figure 14-3: Visualization of an efficient method for storing user contact information

'relate_contacts_to_users' Table		
Unique ID	User Id	Contact Id
1	1	2
2	1	3

Therefore, using this better method, if we then wished to add Bobby and John as contacts for Jenny, all we would need to do is add two extra records into the relate_contacts_to_users table to relate the unique ID numbers of Bobby and John to Jenny's unique ID. Here is how our relate_contacts_to_users table would look after we add this information into it:

'relate_contacts_to_users' Table		
Unique ID	User Id	Contact Id
1	1	2
2	1	3
3	3	1
4	3	4

Figure 14-4: How the relate_contacts_to_user table looks after the addition of Jenny's contacts

This technique has many applications when it comes to storing data in an optimal way and can also lead to accessing data faster. Also, it removes the limitation of predefined fields, as players can have as many friends as they want due to each new friend simply being added as a record to the relational table.

Now that we have the basic idea of what a database is in our minds, let's look at why we would use one in the creation of a game in Java.

Why Do I Need To Know about Databases?

You would be forgiven for thinking that databases are only useful in business software and similar applications, but in reality, they can be used as an excellent form of data storage for Java games on a server.

The only other real option that we have other than databases is using files on the server to store the data, but the access would be much slower and files can become corrupt much more easily. In contrast to that though, the simplest type of database is a flat file database, which constitutes the use of normal text files to structure a relational database. This is commonly done with the use of CSV (comma-separated values) to represent the fields of data within the tables and separate files to represent the actual tables of the database. This is how a sample table of information would look in CSV format:

```
Ian,Smith,24,ian.smith@email.net
Jenny,Wethersby,19,jenny@email.net
Harry,Ashby,43,h.ashby@email.net
Rachel,Henderson,32,r.henderson@email.net
Lucy,Jones,18,jones@email.net
```

This would represent a table that held a user's first name, surname, age, and e-mail address and would be contained in a single flat file.

Although we have little interest in flat file databases, they can be useful for storing backups of data. For example, you could export a database into CSV and write it to a CD-ROM every day to ensure that you have a safe backup. CSV is very easy to import into a database, and we will see this in the next chapter on using a real database package.

Database Packages

There are many database packages on the market now; some are free, and some require commercial licenses. In this book, we will focus on MySQL, which is free for non-commercial use. So basically, if you make money from the direct application of a MySQL database, you have to share the fruits of your success, which in our opinion is fair. Of course, this all depends on terms and conditions (you can find information regarding this at http://www.mysql.com).

So what are the differences between database packages then? Some are faster and some have extensions and additional script languages, but on the whole, they are very similar to one another. The main reasoning for this is that they all use the same language to access and input data, the Structured Query Language (SQL).

On the whole, it does not really matter which database package you select to start off with because, as you will see later, it is easy to use most of the popular database packages by simply changing the package that you are using within your Java code. However, different database packages can have different syntax requirements, so it's not always that easy.

Introduction to SQL

SQL is an acronym for Structured Query Language and is the standard language for interaction with databases. SQL is both an ISO (International Organization for Standardization) and ANSI (American National Standards Institute) standard, but many database packages contain proprietary extensions that are not part of the standard. As a matter of fact, there are not many database servers that would have 100% support of the SQL standard.

Let's first look at some simple interactions that we can perform using the SQL language. Let's say, for example, that we had a table called user_table, which held information on players in a Java game. The information is a unique identification number followed by the player's username, password, and e-mail address. Here is a graphical representation of the table in the database with some sample data in it:

'user_table' Table			
Unique ID	Username	Password	Email
1	harry	har123	harry@email.net
2	george	geo321	george@email.net
3	lucy	luc462	lucy@email.net
4	paul	pau196	paul@email.net

Figure 14-5:
user_table containing some sample data

Assuming all the data had been previously entered into the database and we wanted to get the password of the player who had the username of george, we would use the following SQL statement to retrieve his password:

```
SELECT password FROM user_table WHERE username = 'george';
```

As you can see from the previous statement, the great thing about SQL is its similarities to the English language. By that I mean it is very easy to read and understand what the statement is trying to do. In this example, we are "SELECT"ing, which means retrieving, the password field "FROM" the user_table "WHERE" the username is equal to the string "george." When this query is executed, the database would then return the password (which is geo321) from the user with the username george.

So what would happen if there were two users with the username george? Well, the database would return a *recordset* (there is the possibility of getting an actual array to the programming language, but it must first be retrieved row-by-row from the database via the `recordset` object) containing the passwords for the records that it found. Unless you specifically want users to have the same usernames, the best way around this would be to check for duplicate usernames when you are inputting the users' data into your game or defining the username as a primary key. We will find out how to do this in the next chapter, along with many more useful tips and features of SQL.

Let's look at another simple example for listing all the high scores from a game in a descending order (i.e., start by getting the highest score, then the next highest, etc.). Let's assume our user_table also had a field called highscore that recorded the players' high score in a game. The default ordering is in ascending order; therefore the database would retrieve the lowest score first if we selected all the high scores from the database. The solution to this is to use the `DESC` keyword, which tells the database to order the results in descending order (i.e., highest first). Here is the SQL statement that we would require to do this:

```
SELECT username,highscore FROM user_table ORDER BY highscore DESC;
```

 NOTE: If you are defining an ordering field, it must be defined also in the select field section. You cannot sort your resultset with a field that is not included in the result.

This previous statement would retrieve the username and high score from the user_table ordered by the highscore field in descending order. Note how we can retrieve more than one field in a single statement, separating fields you wish to retrieve with commas. We can also use a *, which is known as a wildcard and simply tells the database to return all the fields from the table rather than a defined number of fields, like in the first example where we just retrieved the password field. Don't worry too much about this at the moment, as we will cover this in depth in the next chapter where everything will become clear.

Let's now look at one final example of the more powerful features of SQL and databases. This is the use of regular expressions. A *regular expression* in simple terms is a way to express to SQL a specific pattern of text to look for in the fields in a table. We touched on regular expressions earlier in Chapter 3; regular expressions are supported in the J2SDK 1.4 also. Although, note that the regular expressions used in SQL are not compatible with the ones used in Java.

Here is an example statement that would retrieve all the usernames from the user_table that begin with the letter G:

```
SELECT username FROM user_table WHERE username LIKE 'G%';
```

Notice that all we are really doing differently here is using the `LIKE` keyword instead of the equals sign. Also, the % acts as a wildcard when using the `LIKE` keyword. Therefore, the statement will select (retrieve) any usernames that start with G, as the names that start with G will fit the regular expression `'G%'`. If we wished to select any names that just contained the letter G anywhere in the string, we would use the following statement:

```
SELECT username FROM user_table WHERE username LIKE "%G%";
```

As you can see, all we have changed is the regular expression by adding another wildcard (%) before the G, allowing zero or more different characters both before and after the G when the database is searching.

Summary

In this chapter we have learned what a database is and why you would want to use one. Also, you were introduced to the basic concepts of the SQL language. In the next chapter, we will learn about SQL in much more depth, as we will install MySQL and create some real databases to experiment with using the MySQL package. It is always much easier to learn if you get hands-on experience, so let's move on to the next chapter.

Chapter 14

Chapter 15

Using SQL with MySQL

"Stimpy hated procedural programming. He liked programs to form
one unbroken wedge of source, with a minimum of annotation.
All variable names had to be prefixed with 'THE', as in
'THE_ITEM_COUNT', 'THE_VAT_TOTAL'. The programming (all
done under DOS) had to take place in a 40-column window. Minimum tab size for any indentation was 10 characters. John often
wondered what planet Stimpy was from."   —Unknown

Introduction

In our experience, many books cover the use of databases, and many
cover how to access databases from various programming languages. The
problem is it tends to be one or the other. The aim of this chapter is to
familiarize you with how to use the database application MySQL, which is
available free for nonprofit use. Of course, it is possible for other database
applications (such as Access, Oracle, etc.) to be used in Java, but MySQL
is relatively easy to install and access. It is also becoming one of the most
popular in the development community.

In this chapter, we will cover how to install and use MySQL so that in
the following chapter we can use it in conjunction with JDBC (Java Database Connectivity) to allow storing and retrieving game-related data in our
Java applets/applications.

What Is MySQL?

MySQL is an open-source relational database management system. Its
purpose is to store and allow easy and relatively fast access to data. The
speed depends on various aspects (such as network speed and server
load) and using a database is not always (although almost always) the fast-
est solution.

Installing MySQL

Installing MySQL is relatively painless. First, you need the installation program for MySQL, which is available on the companion CD. You can also download the latest version from http://www.mysql.com.

 NOTE: If you choose to install MySQL in a different folder than the default (C:\MYSQL) or you wish to start MySQL on NT/Win2000 as a service, you need to create a file named MY.CNF in the root of your C:\ drive with the following information in it (or append the following information to either \Windows\my.ini or \winnt\my.ini, depending on your OS):

```
[mysqld]
basedir=E:/installation-path/
datadir=E:/data-path/
```

After you have installed MySQL, the directory will contain the my-example.cnf file. You can use this as a template to create your own my.cnf file.

Once you start the installation, it will first ask you which type of setup you would prefer: typical, compact, or custom installation. Here we will select the Typical option, as it will install all the components that we require in order to work with MySQL.

After selecting Typical, press the Next button and the installation process will be automatically completed.

Now that we have MySQL installed, we will first browse the directory so we can see what it has installed for us. If we open the directory to which you installed MySQL (typically c:\mysql), we can see the following directory structure:

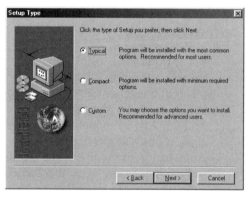

Figure 15-1:
Select the typical install option.

Figure 15-2:
The MySQL directory structure

All we really have use for here (with respect to Java) is the bin directory, which contains the MySQL server and client executables, and the docs directories, which contain the HTML version of the MySQL manual.

 NOTE: An Adobe PDF version of the MySQL manual has also been supplied on the companion CD-ROM. We find this easier to read, but you will also require the free program Adobe Acrobat Reader to view this manual, which is available to download at http://www.adobe.com/products/acrobat/readermain.html.

Let's now take a look in the bin directory and see what is of use to us there. The contents can be seen in the following image:

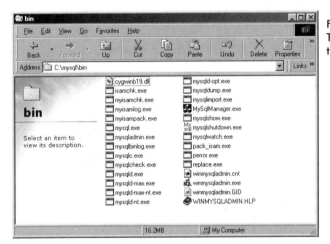

Figure 15-3:
The contents of
the bin directory

As you can see, there are many executables in this directory; some are daemons (i.e., the MySQL server), and some are console-based clients to access the MySQL server with.

 NOTE: A daemon is simply a program or process that sits idly in the background until it is invoked to perform its task.

`mysqld.exe` is the best server to use when developing software. The others are used more to adjust speed and support extra features. Here are each of the different server versions and their uses:

- `mysqld`—Compiled with full debugging and automatic memory allocation checking, symbolic links, and InnoDB and BDB tables
- `mysqld-opt`—Optimized binary with no support for transactional tables
- `mysqld-nt`—Optimized binary for NT with support for named pipes. You can run this version on Win98, but in this case no named pipes are created and you must have TCP/IP installed.
- `mysqld-max`—Optimized binary with support for symbolic links and InnoDB and BDB tables

■ `mysqld-max-nt`—Like `mysqld-max`, but compiled with support for named pipes

If you do not fully understand the meaning of the different versions, simply stick to using `mysqld.exe`, as you probably will not require the others.

The executable `mysql.exe` is a console-based client, which is used to interact with the MySQL server by means of the SQL language of which we had a brief overview in the previous chapter. We will cover SQL in much greater depth in this chapter; however, we are going to put this to the side for now, as it is not relevant to the current situation.

So if we try and run the console client (`mysql.exe`) now, the following screen will appear for a couple of seconds and then disappear:

Figure 15-4: A blank window?!

Why? The reason the window appears and promptly disappears is because there is currently no MySQL server to connect to (i.e., there is no MySQL daemon running for the client to interact with).

So the obvious thing to do now is run a MySQL server so we can access it via the client. The executable we want for this is called `mysqld.exe`. There might be cases when the debug version of MySQL is better (information about errors, etc.). But in general, one version is as good as the other for running the MySQL server in the background. If you now execute this, a black window will appear for a very short period of time and disappear. You can check that the MySQL server is running by hitting **Ctrl**, **Alt**, and **Delete** at the same time to bring up the list of tasks that are currently running in Windows. This can be seen in Figure 15-5.

NOTE: In Windows NT and Windows 2000, Ctrl+Alt+Del produces a different window than in Windows 98. Windows XP also has a different view.

Windows NT and Windows 2000 have a slightly different approach when starting the MySQL server. This can be seen in the following "Starting the MySQL Server Automatically" section.

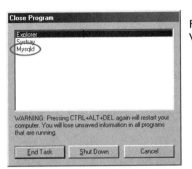

Figure 15-5:
Viewing the current running tasks

Note that you may have more on this list if you are running other programs. Also, the Mysqld daemon may not be at the bottom of the list.

Now, if we try to run the MySQL console client (mysql.exe), we can see that it will connect to the MySQL server and display a welcome message and then await input. This can be seen in the following figure.

Figure 15-6:
The MySQL
console client

Now we are able to connect to the MySQL server from the MySQL console client. One problem is that every time we restart Windows, the MySQL server will not be restarted, meaning we would have to manually go to the directory and run the mysqld-opt.exe every time we start Windows. This can be solved by adding the MySQL server as a service that is started every time Windows is loaded up. See the following section for how to do this.

Starting the MySQL Server Automatically

NOTE for Windows NT/2000/XP Users: There is a much easier way to install MySQL as a service in NT/2000. Execute the following command in the command prompt:

```
C:\mysql\bin> mysqld-max-nt --install
```

This command will remove the service:

```
C:\mysql\bin> mysqld-max-nt --remove
```

This will only work on Windows NT/2000 and XP, and mysql will be registered as a service. mysqld-max-nt can be replaced to be other executables, as listed before. There is more information about NT issues in the MySQL documentation in the MySQL Manual, "Starting MySQL on Windows NT or Windows 2000," on the CD-ROM, which can also be accessed online at http://www.mysql.com.

To get the server to start automatically, we need to edit the Windows registry so that it will load the server as a service when Windows starts. Let's go through this step by step.

NOTE: If you do not want to touch your Windows registry manually, we have supplied a file called mysql.reg on the CD-ROM, which, when executed, will add the data into the registry for you, so the server will start automatically. However, we recommend that you still read this section, as it will enable you to understand how it works.

First we need to load up the Registry Editor, so click on the **Start** button and then select **Run....** A dialog will appear awaiting input; enter **regedit** into it and click **OK**.

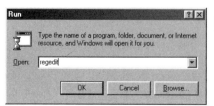

Figure 15-7:
The Run dialog

Once you click OK, the Registry Editor application will be visible.

CAUTION: Be careful when using the Registry Editor. Do not change anything you do not understand as you can damage your system.

On the left-hand side of the Registry Editor is a tree view of all the possible sections that can be changed. First expand the HKEY_LOCAL_MACHINE branch, and then expand the Software branch. This can be seen in the following figure.

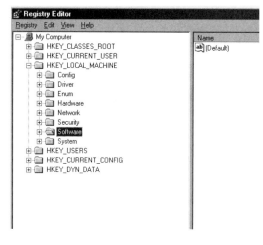

Figure 15-8:
The Registry Editor

In the Software branch, find Microsoft and expand it. In this branch you will find Windows. Expand the Windows branch and then finally expand the CurrentVersion branch. Once you have expanded these branches, you should be able to find a folder called RunServices. Click on this folder, and the contents of the right pane should change. The following figure is a screen shot of what you should now be looking at (note that it may differ slightly due to different computer configurations, etc.):

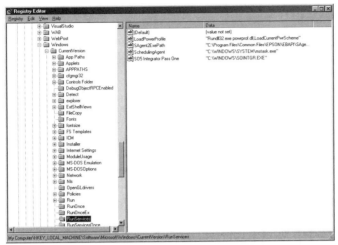

Figure 15-9:
The
RunServices
folder (key)

Next we need to right-click on the right pane and select **New** followed by
String Value from the pop-up menu. This can be seen in the following
figure.

Figure 15-10:
Pop-up menu

Once this is done, a new entry will appear below the current list in the
right pane. Now you can enter a name if you wish, but this is optional. The
important part is to double-click the new entry that was added to the list.
When you do this, the following dialog will appear:

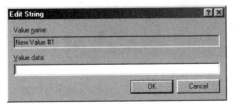

Figure 15-11:
The Edit String dialog box

In the Value data box, you need to enter the name of the MySQL server
executable, including the full path. So, if you installed it to the default
directory (recommended), you would enter the following in the box:

```
C:\mysql\bin\mysqld-opt.exe
```

Once entered, click the **OK** button and then simply close the Registry
Editor. Now each time you restart Windows, the MySQL server will start
automatically.

Note that if you do not wish MySQL to start automatically at a later
date, you can remove this by highlighting the new entry that you just
added on the right pane and pressing the **Delete** key.

SQL Statements

Now that we have the MySQL server running, it is time to load up the MySQL console client. This is done the same way that we loaded it before (i.e., run the `mysql.exe` executable that is located in the c:\mysql\bin\ directory).

In SQL, there are two types of statements that we can execute. These are DDL (Data Definition Language) and DML (Data Manipulation Language). DDL is used to affect the structure of the database (i.e., add databases, add tables, etc.), whereas DML is used to add and modify data in an existing database and also retrieve information.

First we will look at the DDL language, as we require a database to work with before we can manipulate any data within it.

Data Definition Language

Creating and Dropping Databases

First, let's see what databases already exist in the MySQL server. We can view this information by using the SHOW command. Enter the following (except the `mysql>` part) into the MySQL console client, followed by a return:

```
mysql> SHOW DATABASES;
```

The following should be visible in the console display:

```
C:\mysql\bin\mysql.exe                                    _ |□| x|
Welcome to the MySQL monitor.  Commands end with ; or \g.
Your MySQL connection id is 3 to server version: 3.23.47-nt

Type 'help;' or '\h' for help. Type '\c' to clear the buffer.

mysql> SHOW DATABASES;
+----------+
| Database |
+----------+
| mysql    |
| test     |
+----------+
2 rows in set (0.01 sec)

mysql> _
```

Figure 15-12: Viewing existing databases

As you can see, there are two databases already created in the MySQL server. The mysql database contains administration information for the MySQL server and should not be modified. The other database, test, is exactly what it sounds like: a test for the MySQL server. The test database does not contain anything, and it can be removed safely if required.

Creating a Database

So how do we add our own database in the MySQL server? To do this, we use the CREATE command. Let's say we wish to create a database called mydata; we would use the following syntax.

 NOTE: The following table lists the length and character restrictions that are imposed on the names of databases, tables, columns, and aliases.

Identifier	Max Length	Valid Characters
Database	64	All valid directory name characters except "." and "/".
Table	64	All valid directory name characters except "." and "/".
Column	64	All are valid.
Alias	15	All are valid.

```
mysql> CREATE DATABASE mydata;
```

Notice that the semicolon is added after every command in the SQL language. When we press Return after entering this command, the console informs us that the query was okay. This is shown below.

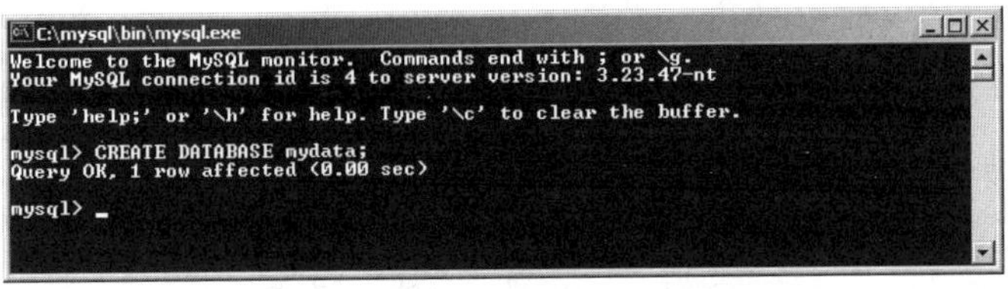

Figure 15-13: Creating a database

Now that we have created the database, we can ensure it is on the server by again using the SHOW command, as follows:

```
mysql> SHOW DATABASES;
```

When we press Return with this command, we can see our database has been added to the list (note that the list is in alphabetical order, not the order in which the databases were created), as seen in the following figure:

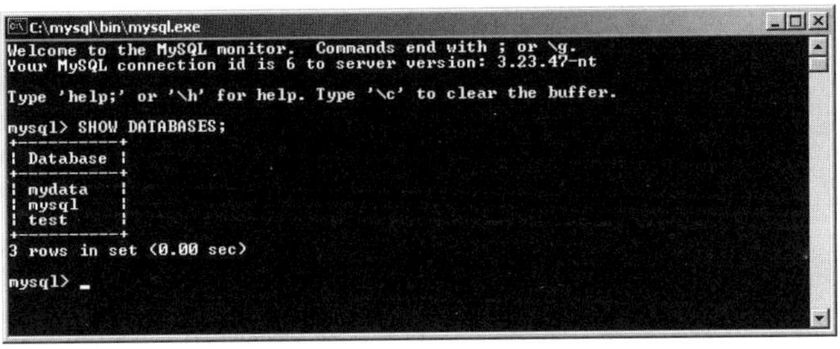

Figure 15-14: The mydata database has been added to the list.

Dropping a Database

Now we will remove the database from the server. Note that when we do this, all data (if any) will be lost. To remove a database, we "drop" it from the server by using the DROP command. So to drop our new mydata database, we would use the following command:

```
mysql> DROP DATABASE mydata;
```

When we execute this command by pressing Return, the query will be reported as okay. This can be seen in the following figure:

Chapter 15

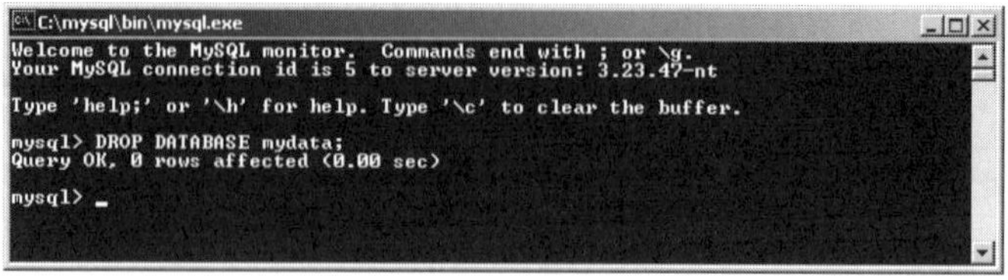

Figure 15-15: Dropping a database

Now, if we again list the databases using the `SHOW` command:

```
mysql> SHOW DATABASES;
```

...we can see that our mydata database is no longer visible on the list. This can be seen in the following figure.

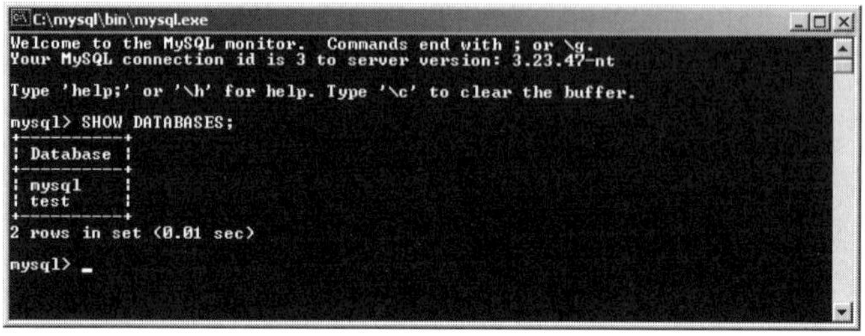

Figure 15-16: Database listing after the DROP command

Column (Field) Types in MySQL

Before we discuss the creation of tables within databases, now is a good time to mention the different column types that we can have in tables.

Each column in a table must be assigned a type, which represents the type of information that field is going to hold. Here is a complete list of available types you can use:

Type	Description
TINYINT	A very small integer. Signed range is –128 to 127. Unsigned range is 0 to 255.
SMALLINT	A small integer. Signed range is –32768 to 32767. Unsigned range is 0 to 65535.
MEDIUMINT	A medium sized integer. Signed range is –8388608 to 8388607. Unsigned range is 0 to 16777215.
INT	A normal sized integer. Signed range is –2147483648 to 2147483647. Unsigned range is 0 to 4294967295.
BIGINT	A large sized integer. Signed range is –9223372036854775808 to 9223372036854775807. Unsigned range is 0 to 18446744073709551615.
FLOAT	A small, single-precision floating-point number that cannot be unsigned. Signed range is –3.402823466E+38 to –1.755494351E–38, 0, and 1.755494351E–38 to 3.402823466E+38.
DOUBLE	A double-precision floating-point number that cannot be unsigned. Signed range is –1.7976931348632157E+308 to –2.2250738585072014E–308, 0, and 2.2250738585072014E–308 to 1.7976931348632157E+308.

Type	Description
DECIMAL	An unpacked floating-point number that cannot be unsigned. Works like a "char" column in that the number is stored as a string (i.e., each number uses one character in the string).
DATE	A date. Range is 1000-01-01 to 9999-12-31 and is in the format YYYY-MM-DD.
TIME	A time. Range is –838:59:59 to 838:59:59 and is in the format HH:MM:SS.
DATETIME	A combination of date and time. Range is 1000-01-01 00:00:00 to 9999-12-31 21:59:59 and is in the format YYYY-MM-DD HH:MM:SS.
YEAR[(2|4)]	A year in 2- or 4-digit format (default is 4). Range is 1901 to 2155 and also 0000.
TIMESTAMP	A timestamp. Range is 1970-01-01 00:00:00 to sometime in the year 2037 in the format YYYYMMDDHHMMSS.
CHAR(length)	A fixed-length string that is always right-padded with spaces to the specified length when stored. The range is 1 to 255 characters depending on the "length" specified.
VARCHAR	A variable-length string.
TINYBLOB/ TINYTEXT	A tiny binary object. Maximum length of 255 characters. *See NOTE below table.
BLOB/TEXT	A binary object. Maximum length of 65535 characters. *See NOTE below table.
MEDIUMBLOB/ MEDIUMTEXT	A medium binary object. Maximum length of 16777215 characters. *See NOTE below table.
LONGBLOB/ LONGTEXT	A large binary object. Maximum length of 4294967295 characters. *See NOTE below table.
ENUM('val1', 'val2'...)	An enumeration. A list of string values of which only one can be selected. Maximum of 65535 distinct values.
SET('val1', 'val2'...)	A set. A string object that can have zero or more values, each of which must be chosen from the list (i.e., 'val1', 'val2', etc.). Maximum of 64 characters.

 NOTE: The only difference between the BLOB and TEXT types is that for sorting and comparisons, a BLOB is case-sensitive, whereas the TEXT type is not case-sensitive.

Creating, Modifying, and Dropping Tables

Creating Tables

Now that we know the possible types for the columns in our tables, let's look at how we actually go about creating a table.

Let's say that we wish to create a table to hold some user details within a database. In fact, we will be using a similar table later in the book.

We want to store the user's title, first name, surname, age, e-mail address, and the date the user was added to the database. So we will require the following columns in our table:

```
Title
Firstname
Surname
Age
```

Chapter 15

```
EmailAddress
DateAdded
```

Before we get into how to actually add it, let's first think how we are going to store the information—or more to the point, what types we require for each of the columns.

For the title, first name, and surname, we can use the TEXT type, as it contains plenty of characters to allow for all possibilities.

NOTE: VARCHAR can work faster and is maybe a better choice if the string length can be restricted to less than 255 characters.

For age, an unsigned TINYINT would be an obvious choice, as ages are numerical and no one has ever been known to live past 255. For e-mail address, we can again use a TEXT type, as it will give us substantial storage space for the address. Finally, for the date that the user was added to the table, we can use a TIMESTAMP.

NOTE: With Java, it is possible to use an INT data type and store System.currentTimeMillis() / 1000 as the value. This value can later be fetched from the database. Then multiply it by 1000 and convert it to the DATE type (i.e., date = new Date(value);). This is useful when doing localization and/or conversion between different databases

The TIMESTAMP also has a great property in that the time and date can be retrieved automatically into the database. This is discussed later in the chapter.

Now that we know which types we want for our columns, we need to create a database to add the table into. This goes back to what we learned in the previous section. Let's create a database called myinfo with the following command:

```
mysql> CREATE DATABASE myinfo;
```

When we execute this command, the console should report that the query was okay. We can now check that our database has been created with the following command:

```
mysql> SHOW DATABASES;
```

When we execute this, the following should be visible in the console.

![MySQL console screenshot showing the SHOW DATABASES command output]

Figure 15-17: The myinfo database is now visible in the console after using the SHOW DATABASES command.

Now we need to tell MySQL that we wish to perform actions on the myinfo database. This is accomplished by using the USE command:

```
mysql> USE myinfo;
```

NOTE: Without USE, all tables in the myinfo database should be referred to as myinfo.mytable, which is of course quite inconvenient.

After executing this command, any DDL (Data Definition Language) and DML (Data Manipulation Language) statements that are executed will affect the database in use, which in this case is our myinfo database.

Now that we have our database set up and ready to accept commands, we can create our table (which we will name userinfo) with the following statement:

```
mysql> CREATE TABLE userinfo (
    -> id INT auto_increment,
    -> title TEXT,
    -> firstname TEXT,
    -> surname TEXT,
    -> age TINYINT,
    -> email TEXT,
    -> dateadded TIMESTAMP,
    -> PRIMARY KEY(id));
```

 NOTE: auto_increment is not a standard SQL option. MSSQL (Microsoft SQL) has a similar option and so does Postgre, but Oracle does not have a way to do this as a create table option. It must be done with sequences and triggers.

Let's break this up a little so we can see what is happening. First we declare that we wish to create a table by entering CREATE TABLE. Next we specify the name that we wish to call the table; in this case, the name is userinfo. Then we use parentheses to contain all of the columns that we require in our table and simply list all of the column names and types that we require. Note how we have added an extra field named id. This makes it easier to handle data in a relational way, as we will discuss later in this chapter. Finally, note the addition of the primary key as the last parameter. This is used to determine how the table is optimized within the database. Again, we will discuss the use of keys later in this chapter.

We can now check that our table was created successfully by executing the following command:

```
mysql> SHOW TABLES;
```

When this is executed, the following output should be visible in the console.

```
C:\mysql\bin\mysql.exe
Welcome to the MySQL monitor.  Commands end with ; or \g.
Your MySQL connection id is 9 to server version: 3.23.47-nt

Type 'help;' or '\h' for help. Type '\c' to clear the buffer.

mysql> USE myinfo;
Database changed
mysql>
mysql> SHOW TABLES;
+------------------+
| Tables_in_myinfo |
+------------------+
| userinfo         |
+------------------+
1 row in set (0.00 sec)

mysql> _
```

Figure 15-18: Here the userinfo table can be seen as part of our database.

Chapter 15

Note you can also view the columns in a table by using the following command:

```
mysql> DESCRIBE userinfo;
```

When you execute this command, the console will display all the details for each of the columns in the userinfo table. This can be seen in the following screen shot of the console:

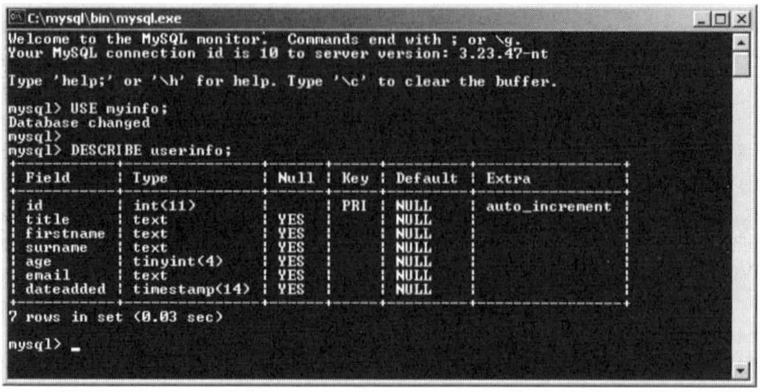

Figure 15-19: Describing the userinfo table

This information can be useful for both ensuring the table was created as you envisioned and to recap the columns a table contains at a later date.

Modifying Tables

So now that we know how to create a table, let's look at how we go about modifying it. Modifying a table can range from simply changing the type of one of the columns to adding a completely new column (or removing an existing column).

Let's first look at how we change the name of an existing column. In our userinfo table, we have a column called firstname, but let's now change this to read forename, a synonym for a person's first name.

To make this change, we need to use the following syntax:

```
mysql> ALTER TABLE userinfo CHANGE firstname forename TEXT;
```

TIP: It is always highly recommended to design the database before creating it because there may be problems modifying/altering database tables or structure after there is data inserted in the tables.

Note we also must supply the data type for the column as well as its old and new names. Here is how this should look in the MySQL console client:

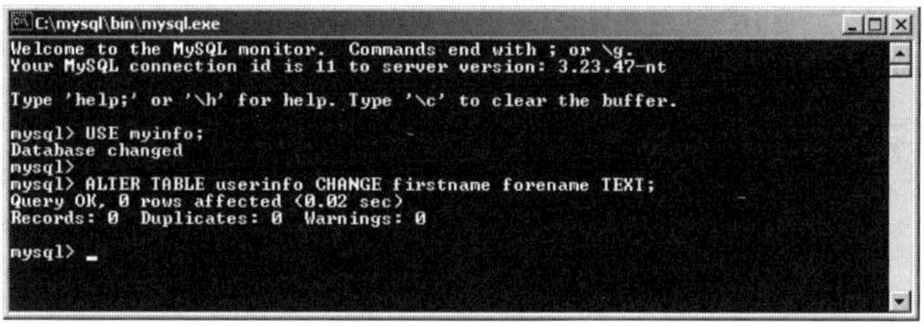

Figure 15-20: Modifying a column name

If we describe the userinfo table with the following command:

```
mysql> DESCRIBE userinfo;
```

...we can see that the column firstname has been renamed to forename. Here is how it looks in the console:

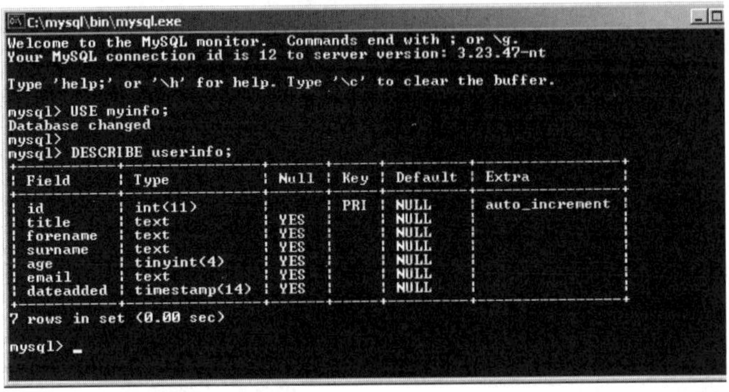

Figure 15-21: Description of the updated userinfo table

We can also change the data types of columns in tables. Let's say that we want to change the age column from a TINYINT to an INT. We would use the following command:

```
mysql> ALTER TABLE userinfo MODIFY age INT;
```

After executing this command, if we describe the table, we can see the type has changed to INT. This can be seen in the following figure:

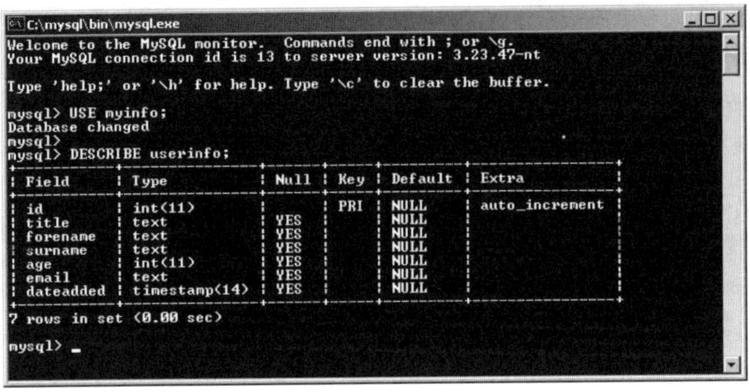

Figure 15-22: Now the age column is of type INT rather than TINYINT.

Finally, it is good to know how to remove fields from a table (for example, if they are no longer required). Let's now say that we no longer require the e-mail field in our userinfo table. What we want to do is "drop" the field from our table, just as we did earlier in the chapter when we dropped the database. Here is the syntax for removing the e-mail field.

```
mysql> ALTER TABLE userinfo DROP email;
```

Here is how this looks in the MySQL console:

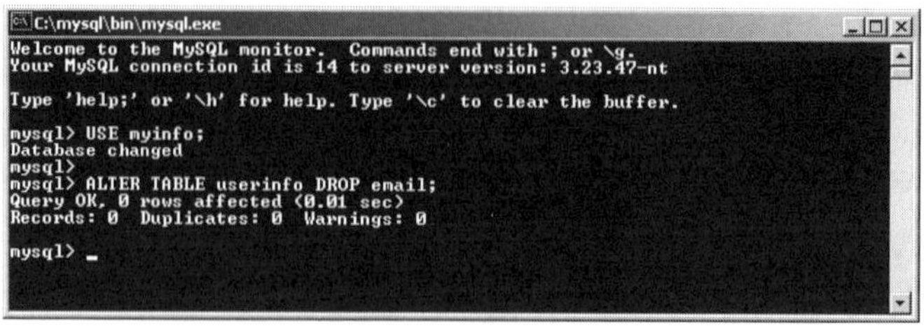

Figure 15-23: Dropping a field from a table

Once this command is executed, we describe the table with the following command:

```
mysql> DESCRIBE userinfo;
```

We can see in the following figure that the e-mail field has been removed (or in other words, dropped) from our userinfo table.

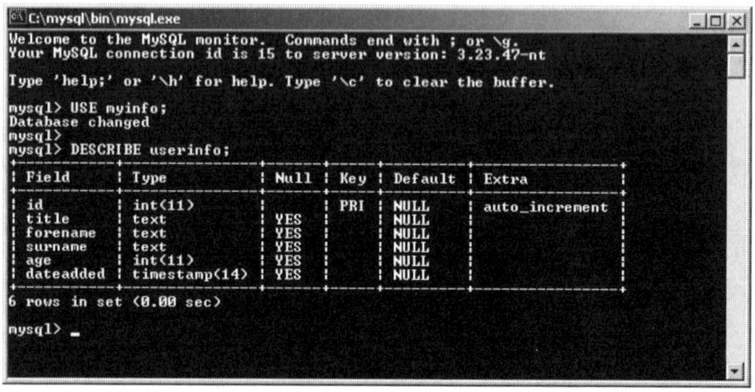

Figure 15-24: As you can see, the e-mail field has now been removed.

Dropping (Removing) Tables

Removing tables from a database is very simple, but without careful use it can have disastrous effects. The main thing to note is that when dropping a table, you also lose all the data contained within the table. Therefore, it is always wise to back up a database before executing any DROP commands. We will look into how to back up a database later in this chapter.

Let's now look at how we drop the userinfo table from our myinfo database. To do this, we need to execute the following command in the MySQL console client.

NOTE: You cannot drop the table if there are actual relations to other tables that could break the integrity of the database. If relations are not "real," tables can be removed without errors, but the integrity is then compromised. If the administrator is not careful, the database can be permanently corrupted.

```
mysql> DROP TABLE userinfo;
```

Once this command is executed, we can check that the table has been removed by listing what tables are currently in our myinfo database by executing the following command:

```
mysql> SHOW TABLES;
```

As you can see from Figure 15-25, the table no longer exists in the database.

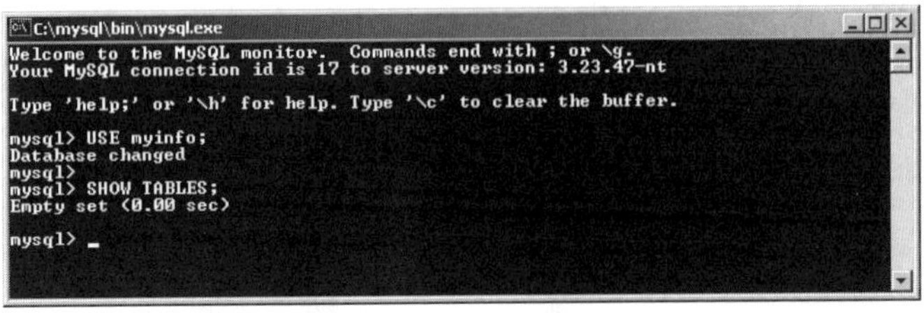

Figure 15-25: After dropping the userinfo table, we have an empty database.

Data Manipulation Language (DML)

Now that we have covered the use of Data Definition Language, we will look at how to add, modify, and remove data from tables in the database using Data Manipulation Language. Without this knowledge, we would not really have any use for a database; it would simply be a static entity with no purpose.

Let's first create a database and table to work with in this section, using the DDL we learned in the previous section. Our database will be called dmlexample, so let's create that now with the following statement:

```
mysql> CREATE DATABASE dmlexample;
```

Once created, we need to specify that we wish to use the new database by executing this statement:

```
mysql> USE dmlexample;
```

The console should now inform us that the database has changed; this can be seen in the following figure:

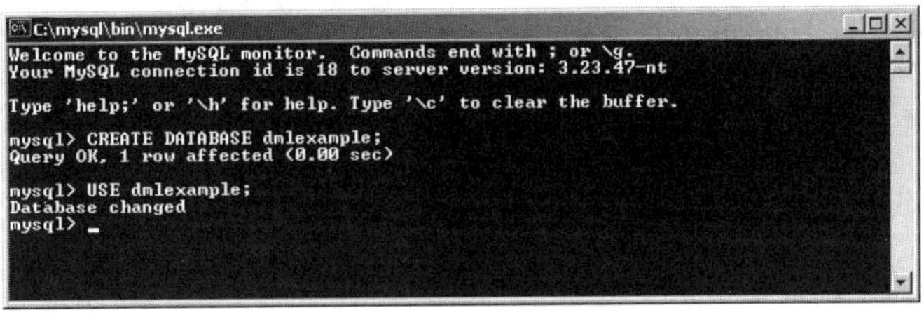

Figure 15-26: Creating the dmlexample database

Now that we have our database set up, let's create a table to experiment with called sampletable. This table will contain the following fields: username, password, age, e-mail, and the date the entry was created.

This is accomplished using the knowledge that we gained in the section, "Data Definition Language." We can then create our table with the following DDL statement:

```
mysql> CREATE TABLE sampletable (
    -> username TEXT,
    -> password TEXT,
    -> age INT,
    -> email TEXT,
    -> datecreated TIMESTAMP);
```

Here is how this should look in the MySQL console client:

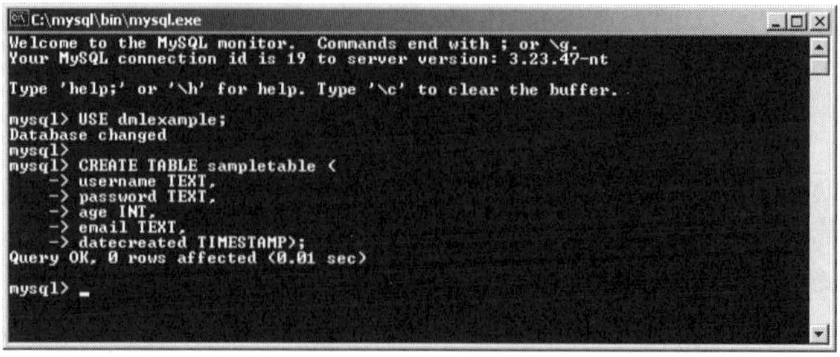

Figure 15-27:
Creating our
sample table

Inserting Data

Now that we have our table created, let's look at how we go about adding rows (records) of information into it. To add rows into the table, we need to use the INSERT command. Here is how we would add a single row to our sampletable.

```
mysql> INSERT INTO sampletable VALUES ('andrew', 'qwerty', 20,
    'andrew@dreamcircle.co.uk', NULL);
```

Figure 15-28 shows how this looks when we enter it into the MySQL console. Notice how the feedback from the console tells us that one row has been affected. Hence, we have added one row to our sampletable table.

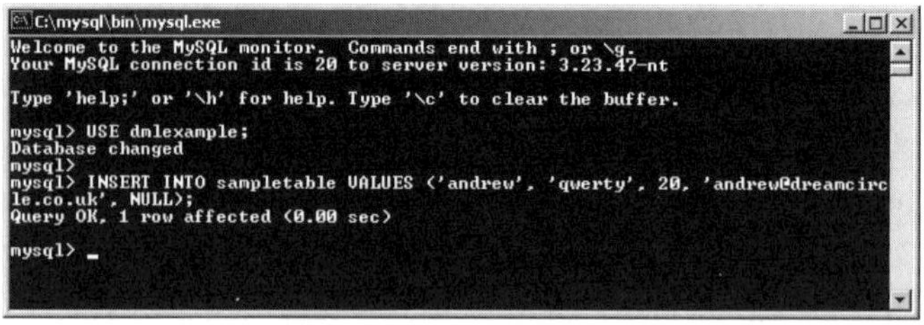

Figure 15-28:
Inserting a
single row of
data

We can then use a command called SELECT to view the data in the table. We will go into more detail about this command later in this section, as it is very important, but for now we will just use it blindly. Let's see what data is in our dmlexample table:

```
mysql> SELECT * FROM sampletable;
```

When we execute this statement, the following will be visible in the MySQL console:

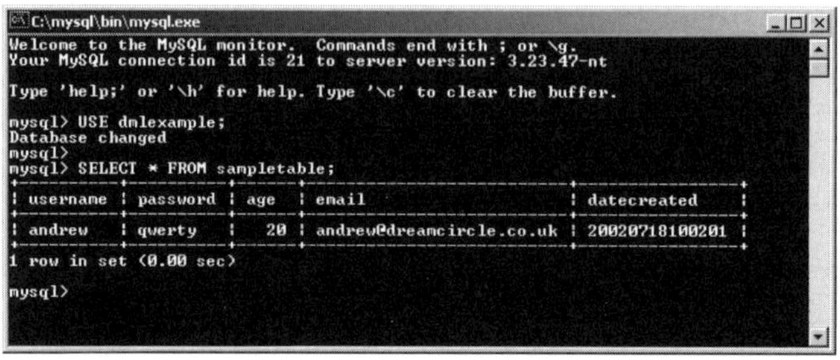

Figure 15-29:
Viewing the
new row in
the table

NOTE: Notice how the datecreated field reflects the time and date when we added the row into the table. This is because we specified NULL when we added the row, and doing this will make a TIMESTAMP field grab the current date and time from the system by default.

It is also possible to add several rows of data in a single command. Let's try this now by adding another three rows to our table in a single `INSERT` command. This is done as follows:

```
mysql> INSERT INTO sampletable VALUES
    -> ('glenn', 'gimboid', 21, 'glenn@chopsewage.com', NULL),
    -> ('jim', 'letmein', 23, 'jim@email.net', NULL),
    -> ('wes', 'opensesame', 31, 'wes@email.net', NULL);
```

When we execute this command, the following can be seen in the MySQL console client:

Figure 15-30: Inserting multiple rows in a single statement

As you can see, this time the feedback from the console suggests that three rows have been affected; hence, we have added three rows to our table. We can verify this by again using the `SELECT` command:

```
mysql> SELECT * FROM sampletable;
```

When this is executed, you will now see that the table contains four rows (or records, if you like) of information. Here is a screen shot of the MySQL console after the `SELECT` statement has been executed:

Figure 15-31: Now we have four rows in the table.

Modifying Data

Now that we know how to add data to a table, let's look at how we go about modifying existing table data.

To modify data in a table, we require the use of the UPDATE command. First let's try to change all the passwords in all the rows in the table to "changeme." This can be accomplished with the following statement:

```
mysql> UPDATE sampletable SET password = 'changeme';
```

 CAUTION: The UPDATE command (as well as all of the SQL commands) is quite powerful. With reckless use you can destroy a lot of data with a simple mistake. Almost every query should have at least one where condition.

When we execute this statement, the console will inform us that four rows have been affected, as we have changed the password for every row in that table.

Now we can see the effect on the table by using the SELECT command, as follows:

```
myql> SELECT * FROM sampletable;
```

Here is a screen shot of this command being executed in the console:

```
C:\mysql\bin\mysql.exe
Welcome to the MySQL monitor.  Commands end with ; or \g.
Your MySQL connection id is 30 to server version: 3.23.47-nt

Type 'help;' or '\h' for help. Type '\c' to clear the buffer.

mysql> USE dmlexample;
Database changed
mysql> SELECT * FROM sampletable;
+----------+----------+-----+------------------------+----------------+
| username | password | age | email                  | datecreated    |
+----------+----------+-----+------------------------+----------------+
| andrew   | changeme |  20 | andrew@dreamcircle.co.uk | 20020718110234 |
| glenn    | changeme |  21 | glenn@chopsevage.com   | 20020718110234 |
| jim      | changeme |  23 | jim@email.net          | 20020718110234 |
| wes      | changeme |  31 | wes@email.net          | 20020718110234 |
+----------+----------+-----+------------------------+----------------+
4 rows in set (0.01 sec)

mysql>
```

Figure 15-32: The password field has been updated in all of the rows.

An obvious question now is, what if I only want to update a single row? Let's say that we wish to change Glenn's password from changeme back to gimboid. We would use the following statement to do this:

```
mysql> UPDATE sampletable SET password = 'gimboid' WHERE
    username = 'glenn';
```

When we execute this command in the console, it informs us that one row has been affected. This is because it will only update the password field if the username field is equal to glenn. If we use the SELECT command on the table now, we can see that only Glenn's password has changed. The following screen shot of the console reflects this:

Figure 15-33:
Updating
only a single
row

We can also apply this technique to enable us to update only certain fields. For example, we could change all the passwords of the people who are age 30 or younger. Here is the command we would require to do this:

```
mysql> UPDATE sampletable SET password = 'young' WHERE age <= 30;
```

When we execute this command, it will inform us that three rows have been affected, as three of the four records in our table have an age equal to or less than 30. If we then use the SELECT command, we can see the following output in the console:

Figure 15-34:
Conditional
updates

TIP: A useful idea is to update a timestamp field with NULL. This will retrieve the latest time from the system that the database is running on (i.e., a practical use would be to note the last time a player logged in).

Removing (Deleting) Data

Removing data from a table is done in a very similar way to updating data. First we will look at how to delete a single row of data. Let's now delete glenn from the database using the following statement:

```
mysql> DELETE FROM sampletable WHERE username = 'glenn';
```

When we execute this command, the MySQL console client will inform us that one row was affected (i.e., deleted). If we now use the SELECT command on the table, the following can be seen in the console:

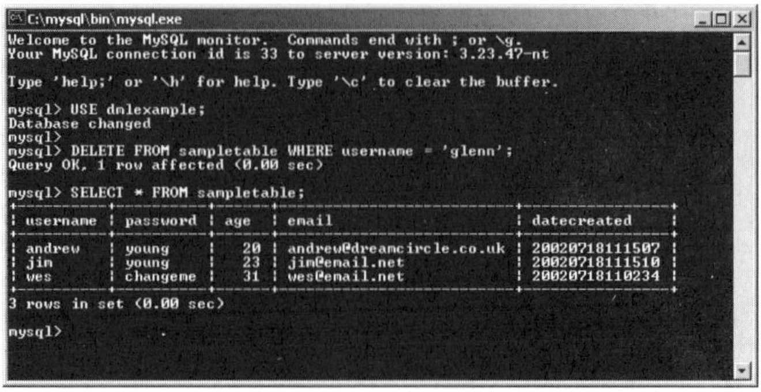

Figure 15-35: Deleting a single row

Again, as with the UPDATE statements, we can specify conditions to allow us to delete, for example, everyone with an age less than 30. Let's do this now with the following statement:

```
mysql> DELETE FROM sampletable WHERE age < 30;
```

When we execute this statement, the client will inform us that two rows have been affected, or in this case, deleted. If we now use the SELECT command on our table, we will see that only one row is left in the table:

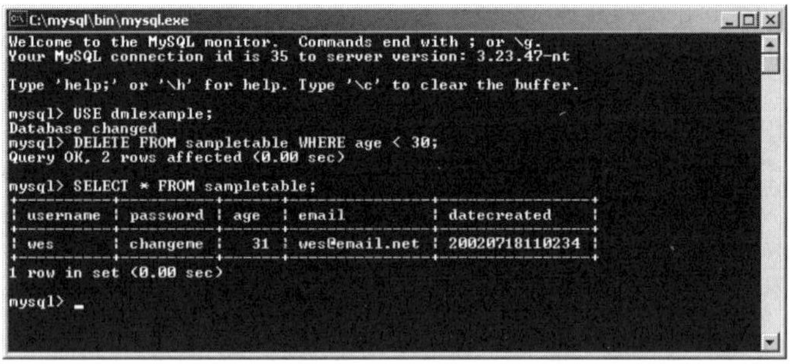

Figure 15-36: Conditional deleting

Finally, it is also possible to delete all the rows from a table in a single statement. All we need to do is not specify any condition, as we did when we updated all the password fields to changeme. Here is the statement to delete all the rows in a table (i.e., empty the table).

```
mysql> DELETE FROM sampletable;
```

After executing this, if we select all the information in the table using the SELECT command, the following will be shown in the console:

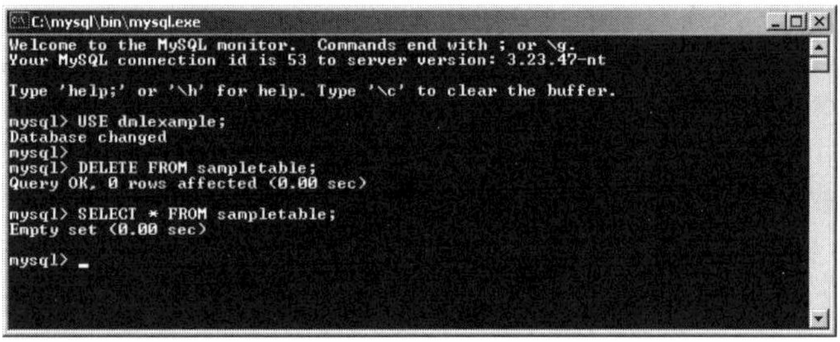

Figure 15-37: Deleting all the data from a table

As you can see, the table now contains no information.

Using SELECT Statements

Until now, we have simply used the following command to show all the data in our sampletable table:

```
mysql> SELECT * FROM sampletable;
```

This is actually fetching all the fields from the sampletable table and returning them. The * is a wildcard, which means basically it represents anything (or in this case, any field).

Before we go into the SELECT statement further, let's first add some data to experiment with into our sampletable table. Use the following statement to insert some data:

```
mysql> INSERT INTO sampletable VALUES
    -> ('andrew', 'qwerty', 20, 'andrew@dreamcircle.co.uk', NULL),
    -> ('andrew', 'letmein', 27, 'andrew@email.net', NULL),
    -> ('george', 'paper', 19, 'george@email.net', NULL),
    -> ('jenny', 'jen999', 27, 'jen@email.net', NULL),
    -> ('sandra', 'sdra2', 27, 'sandra@email.net', NULL);
```

Here is a screen shot of how this should look when we enter it into the console and execute it:

Figure 15-38: Inserting our new data into the sample-table table

Now that we have added our data into the table, if we use the SELECT statement with the wildcard (*), as we were doing before, it will retrieve and display all of the information from the table into the console. Let's try this now with the following statement.

```
mysql> SELECT * FROM sampletable;
```

Here is a screen shot of the output from the console:

Figure 15-39: Using the wildcard with a SELECT statement

As you can see, the statement has retrieved all of the information from the table (i.e., all of the rows and all of the columns contained in each of the rows).

Let's say that all we want to retrieve is the password field. To get all of the passwords from the sampletable table, we would use the following statement:

```
mysql> SELECT password FROM sampletable;
```

When we execute this statement, we can expect the following output from the console:

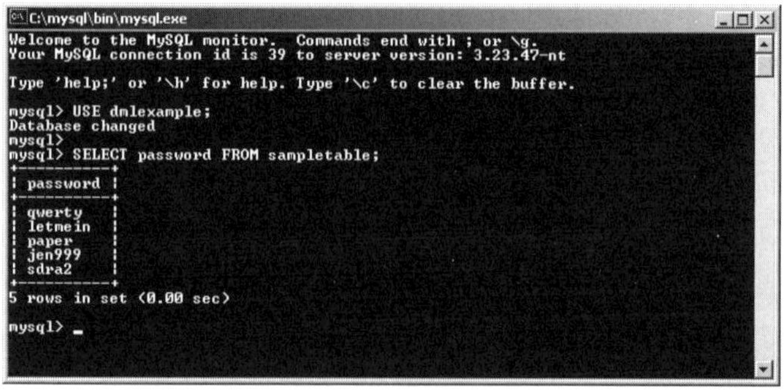

Figure 15-40: Retrieving only a single column

Notice how we simply replace the wildcard (*) with the column we wish to retrieve. We can also retrieve multiple columns by using a comma to delimit them. Let's try to select both the username column and password column only. Here is the statement we require for this:

```
mysql> SELECT username, password FROM sampletable;
```

When we execute this statement, we can see in the console that only the username and password fields have been selected from the table. Here is a screen shot of the console that shows this:

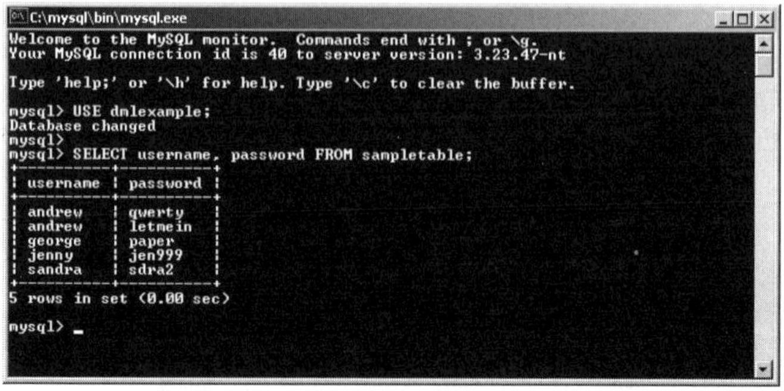

Figure 15-41: Retrieving multiple columns

Now that we know how to retrieve individual fields from the tables, how do we retrieve a single row? We can easily apply a condition to a SELECT statement, just as we did when we were updating the table and deleting from the table. Using a conditional SELECT statement, let's only display Jenny's information from the database. Here is the statement we require for this:

```
mysql> SELECT * FROM sampletable WHERE username = 'jenny';
```

When we execute this statement, only Jenny's details will be displayed in the MySQL client console. This can be seen in the following figure:

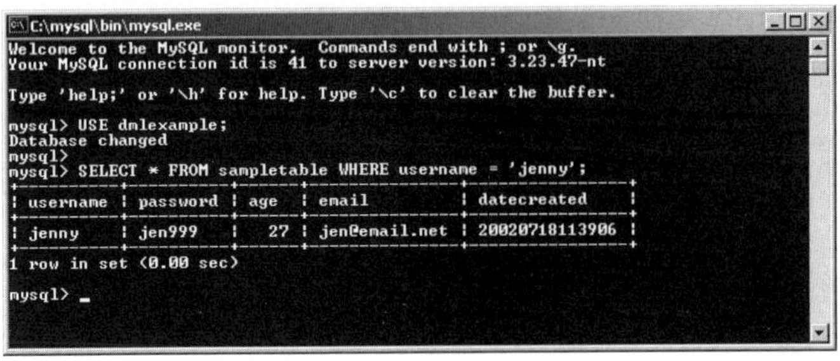

Figure 15-42: Selecting a single row

We can also incorporate the idea of selecting specified fields. A practical example of this would be to find the password that relates to a username. Here is how we would get the password that belonged to George:

```
mysql> SELECT password FROM sampletable WHERE username = 'george';
```

When we execute this statement, we can see that only a single field is displayed, which happens to be George's password. This can be seen in Figure 15-43.

NOTE: When we specify specific fields, as in this example, we are not limited to the fields that we are selecting for use in the WHERE clause.

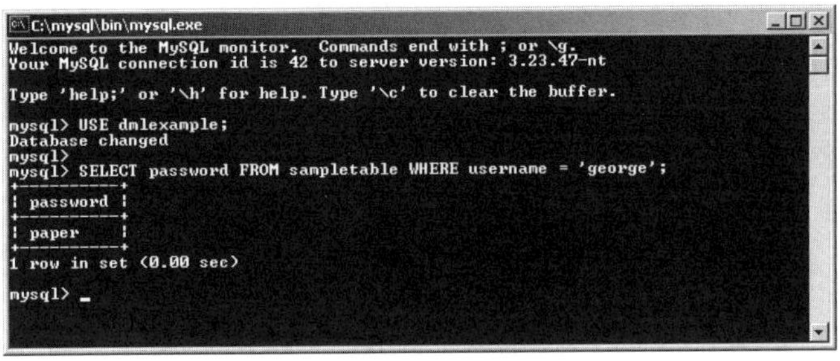

Figure 15-43: Selecting a single row with specified columns

In our sample data, there are two rows with the username andrew. If we try to use a conditional statement to get the password for andrew, we will in fact get two passwords, one for each andrew entry in the database. Let's try this now just for proof. Here is the statement that we need:

```
mysql> SELECT password FROM sampletable WHERE username = 'andrew';
```

When we execute this statement, we can see that we have two passwords showing in the console. The result is shown in the following figure:

Chapter 15

Figure 15-44:
The two-
password
problem!

 NOTE: Duplicates can be removed from the result by using the
DISTINCT **option. For example:** SELECT DISTINCT username FROM
sampletable.

Later in this chapter, we will discuss a way around this problem with the
use of relational databases and keys, but let's not go into that just yet.

Instead let's have a look at how the LIKE command can help us find
the information that we require. Using LIKE is ideal for finding strings in
databases, especially if you only have a part of the complete string (i.e., for
a search engine). For example, let's say that we wish to find someone in
the database whose name starts with the letter j. To accomplish this, we
would require the following statement:

```
mysql> SELECT * FROM sampletable WHERE username LIKE 'j%';
```

When we execute this statement, we can expect the following output from
the MySQL console:

Figure 15-45:
Using LIKE
with a
SELECT state-
ment

Notice here how jenny was retrieved, as her username was the only one
to start with a j. The % represents a wildcard when used with LIKE, so if
we used the following statement instead:

```
mysql> SELECT * FROM sampletable WHERE username LIKE '%j%';
```

...the letter j could appear anywhere in the string. Also, note that you can
have more than a single character:

```
mysql> SELECT * FROM sampletable WHERE username LIKE '%nny';
```

This would retrieve all of the people who have names that end with the
text "nny." Finally, if we used the following statement:

```
select * from sampletable where username like '%nny%a';
```

...it would retrieve all rows containing "nny" in their names, but the name would have to end with "a".

Relational Databases

Up until now, we have been looking mainly at how to create database structures and do simple data manipulation within them. However, there are many useful ideas and theories that make databases even more useful to us. For a definition of a relational database, please see the previous chapter.

Let's now look at what sort of structure we would want for a relational database. Think of a database that related the players in a game to one another (for example, to determine who was a friend of each player and who was an enemy of each player).

First let's create a table to store the data for each of the players. Notice the addition of a primary key, which allows you to rely on the fact that all rows have a unique field that can be used as a reference. Note also that every row of data in the primary key must be unique to one another. Here is the statement required to create our database (called gamedata) and our playerdata table.

```
mysql> CREATE DATABASE gamedata;

mysql> USE gamedata;

mysql> CREATE TABLE playerdata (
    -> username CHAR(255) UNIQUE NOT NULL,
    -> password CHAR(255),
    -> age INT,
    -> datecreated TIMESTAMP,
    -> PRIMARY KEY(username));
```

Notice here how we set the username column to `UNIQUE` and also `NOT NULL`. In simple terms, this means that it must contain a value, and that value must not be the same as any other username in any other record in the table. Note also that we have set the primary key of the table to be the username field, as we will be mainly searching on this field, which you will see in a moment.

In addition to this information, we also need some way to store friends and enemies. This is done by means of a *link table*. A link table is really just a normal database table, but its main purpose is to relate data in some way or another to conserve space and optimize the way the database accesses the information.

Let's create two link tables, one for relating friends and one for relating enemies to each other. Following are the statements that are required to accomplish this.

NOTE: If link tables are used, the optimized way is to store INT values there and have an ID field with auto_increment in the playerdata table as a primary key. It is not as readable when you perform a SELECT, but it is faster from within your applications. When updating a player's name, it does not break the integrity of the database. Also, link tables are often structures to be used only when there are n amount of relations from one row to other rows. If there is always only one relation (one friend or enemy), a direct link should be used.

```
mysql> CREATE TABLE relatefriends (
    -> player CHAR(255),
    -> friend CHAR(255));
```

Also:

```
mysql> CREATE TABLE relateenemies (
    -> player CHAR(255),
    -> enemy CHAR(255));
```

If we now show the tables in the database with the following command:

```
mysql> SHOW TABLES;
```

...we can see from the following figure that our database now contains three different tables—our playerdata table and the two link tables.

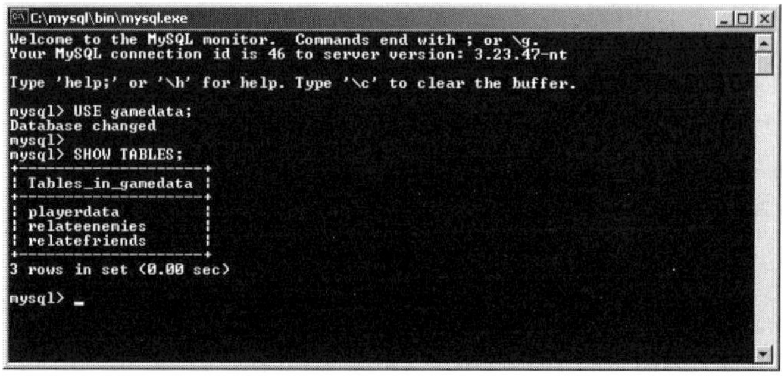

Figure 15-46: Our three tables in the gamedata database

Let's now add a sample of data to the player data table, so we can experiment with the link tables and understand the logic of how to use them effectively. Here is the statement required to add our sample data to the playerdata table:

```
mysql> INSERT INTO playerdata VALUES
    -> ('Andrew', 'qwerty', 20, NULL),
    -> ('Henry', 'letmein', 34, NULL),
    -> ('Sandra', 'dra33', 19, NULL),
    -> ('John', 'j12d', 23, NULL),
    -> ('Jenny', 'jen123', 34, NULL);
```

If we select all the information from the playerdata table now using the following command:

```
mysql> SELECT * FROM playerdata
```

...we can see from the following figure that all of our data is now in the playerdata table.

Figure 15-47:
Our data in
the
playerdata
table

Now that we have some sample data, let's try to create some relations
between the players in the database. First add to the relatefriends link
table the fact that Henry is friends with Sandra. Here is the statement
required to add this to the link table:

```
mysql> INSERT INTO relatefriends VALUES
    -> ('Henry', 'Sandra');
```

If we now show all of the data from the relatefriends link table, the following will be visible in the MySQL console:

Figure 15-48:
Our data in
the relate-
friends table

Let's now add some more sample data into both the relatefriends and
relateenemies link tables and see how we can manipulate the data. The
two statements required to add in the sample data are below:

> **NOTE:** To prevent being a friend and enemy at the same time, one
> relation table could be used. Just add a field "enemy" flag, and if it is set,
> it means that they are enemies; otherwise they are friends.

```
mysql> INSERT INTO relatefriends VALUES
    -> ('Andrew', 'Henry'),
    -> ('Andrew', 'John'),
    -> ('Andrew', 'Jenny'),
    -> ('Sandra', 'Jenny');
```

And also:

```
mysql> INSERT INTO relateenemies VALUES
    -> ('Andrew', 'Sandra'),
    -> ('Henry', 'Jenny'),
    -> ('Henry', 'John');
```

Now that we have all of our sample data, let's see if we can find out who Andrew is friends with by using the following statement:

```
mysql> SELECT friend FROM relatefriends WHERE player = 'Andrew';
```

When we execute this statement, the console displays a list of all the players that Andrew is friends with. Here is a screen shot of the expected console output:

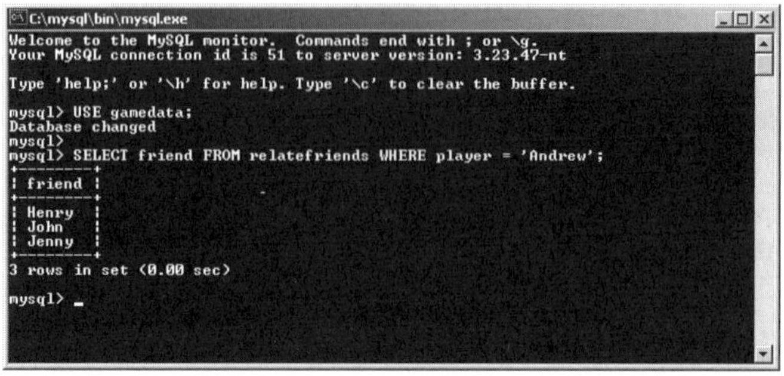

Figure 15-49:
Finding out a
player's
friend list

When we start implementing databases in Java in the next chapter, we will use this data to find out more information about each of Andrew's friends.

Again, we can do exactly the same with the relateenemies link table. For example, we could find out all of Henry's enemies with the following statement:

```
mysql> SELECT enemy FROM relateenemies WHERE player = 'Henry'
```

When we execute this statement, the following console output can be expected.

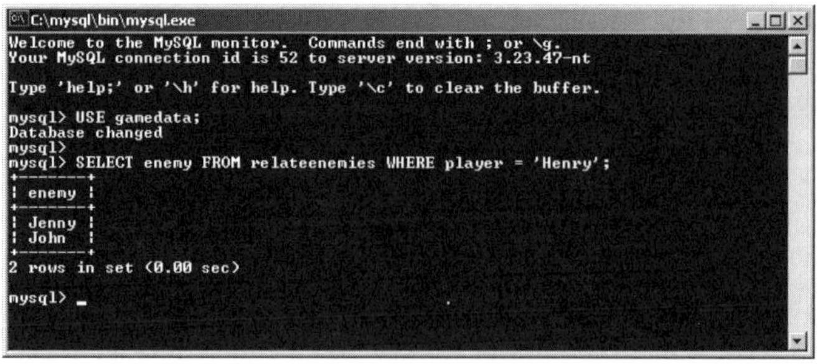

Figure 15-50:
Finding out a
player's
enemy list

With this data, if we then wanted to find out more information about Henry's enemy that has the username of Jenny, we would use the following statement:

```
mysql> SELECT * FROM playerdata WHERE username = 'Jenny';
```

Here is a screen shot of our expected console output:

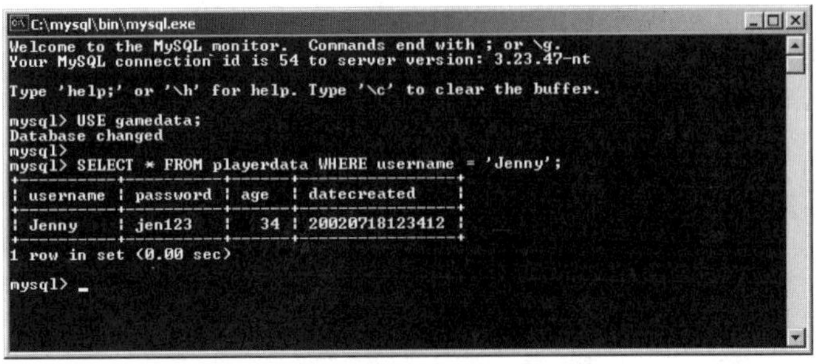

Figure 15-51:
Finding more
data about
an enemy

This may seem a rather pointless exercise at the moment, but rest assured that it has many uses, as you will find out in the next chapter, "Using the JDBC."

Joining Tables

When accessing information within database tables, we may sometimes need to look at data from two or more different tables, as we saw in the previous example. There is another useful way to access relational data, using a technique called *joining*. When we say "joining," we mean that we compare actual fields by their names in different tables, rather than the actual data within them (although when the statement is executed the actual data is compared).

For an example of how we can use joining, let's look back to the previous example. Let's say that we wanted to retrieve a detailed listing of Henry's enemies and not just their names; in the previous example, we would first execute this statement:

```
SELECT enemy FROM relateenemies WHERE player = 'Henry'
```

Then, for each name on the retrieved list, we would call the following SQL statement:

```
SELECT * FROM playerdata WHERE username = '????';

(where ???? represents each name on the list in turn)
```

With the joining technique, however, this can be done in a single SQL statement, meaning less code. It will also execute faster (rather than using two statements). Here is the join statement we would require to do this:

```
mysql> SELECT * FROM playerdata, relateenemies WHERE
    playerdata.username = relateenemies.enemy AND
    relateenemies.player = 'Henry';
```

When we execute this statement, we can expect the following output in the MySQL console window:

Figure 15-52:
Using a join
statement

So first we are selecting all the data from both the playerdata and relate-enemies tables and then placing a condition upon the joining of the tables, so that data will only be selected where the username field in the player-data table is equal to the enemy field in the relateenemies table. If we just left it with the single condition, it would return the full results from both tables for each enemy in the relateenemies table. So our second condition limits the results to only show Henry's enemies by comparing the player field in the relateenemies table to the string Henry. Useful, eh?

Data Import Methods

Importing from a Text File

To create a text file that contains several records to be added to our playerdata table, simply denote each column with a tab and each row by a new line. Here is a screen shot of five lines of data to be added to the database in Windows Notepad:

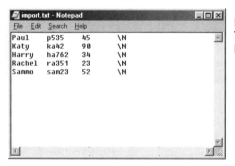

Figure 15-53:
The data to import in Windows
Notepad

Note how we use \N to specify a field that contains NULL and an extra tab is required after each row of data to signify the end of that row. We have saved this file in the MySQL bin directory (i.e., c:\mysql\bin) with the filename import.txt.

Now go to the MySQL console client and type the following:

```
mysql> LOAD DATA LOCAL INFILE 'import.txt' INTO TABLE playerdata;
```

The console will inform us that five rows have been affected or, in this case added to our database. This can be seen in the following screen shot of the console:

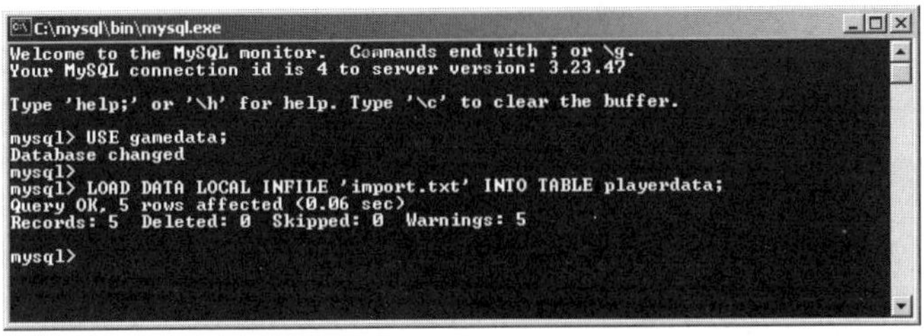

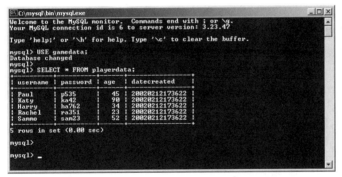

Figure 15-54: Importing data from a text file

If we now select all the information from the playerdata table, we can see that our five rows of data have been imported correctly into the database. Here is a screen shot of the client that shows our imported data in the table:

Figure 15-55: The imported data in our playerdata table

Importing from a Native Source

Another method available to use for importing data is using the Microsoft Excel spreadsheet program or any other application that can export data as tab-delimited data.

For this example, however, we will use Microsoft Excel. Let's enter another five rows of data that we wish to add to our playerdata table in Excel. Once this is done, it should look similar to the figure below:

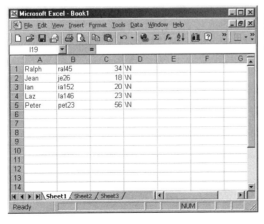

Figure 15-56: Entering the data in Microsoft Excel

Once our data is entered, we need to save the data in a format that MySQL can understand. In this case, we will use tab-delimited values and save them in a text file called excel.txt in the MySQL bin directory.

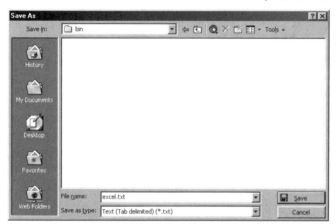

Figure 15-57:
Saving as a
tab-delimited
text file

Now the process is the same as importing a text file, as we did in the last section. In fact, if you open up the text file in Windows Notepad, you will see that the file format is identical to what we created in the previous section. Here is a screen shot of how the file looks when we open it in Notepad:

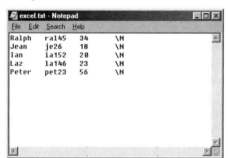

Figure 15-58:
The excel.txt file in Notepad

Backing Up and Restoring Data

Let's now look at how we can export and import a database in MySQL. This is a relatively simple process, but it is extremely important for backing up data.

Backing Up a Database to a File

When we back up a database from MySQL, it is written to a text file and is simply a list of the SQL statements that are required to recreate the database.

Let's now try to export the gamedata database that we created in the previous section to a text file called gamedata.txt. First we need to open up a command line by first clicking **Run** under the Start button in Windows. When the Run dialog appears, type in **command** and press the **OK** button.

> **NOTE:** On Windows 2000/XP, instead of typing **command**, you need to type **cmd**.

A command-line window will now appear. Next, you need to go to the bin directory of MySQL using the following command:

```
cd C:\mysql\bin
```

Note that you may have to change the above line if you modified the default MySQL installation directory. Here is a screen shot of how this should look:

```
C:\WINNT\System32\cmd.exe                           _ □ ×
Microsoft Windows 2000 [Version 5.00.2195]
(C) Copyright 1985-2000 Microsoft Corp.

C:\>cd c:\mysql\bin

C:\mysql\bin>_
```

Figure 15-59: The command-line window (MS-DOS)

Now that we are in the correct directory, we will use a utility called mysqldump, which exports a specified database to a file of our choice. Here is how we would export our gamedata database to a text file called gamedata.txt:

```
mysqldump gamedata > gamedata.txt
```

If we now open up the text file (which is located in the mysql/bin/ directory), we can see that it contains many SQL statements and comments added by the mysqldump utility. Here is a listing of our exported database text file:

```
# MySQL dump 8.16
#@code =
# Host: localhost     Database: gamedata
#--------------------------------------------------------
# Server version    3.23.47

#
# Table structure for table 'playerdata'
#

CREATE TABLE playerdata (
  username char(255) NOT NULL default '',
  password char(255) default NULL,
  age int(11) default NULL,
  datecreated timestamp(14) NOT NULL,
  PRIMARY KEY (username),
  UNIQUE KEY username (username)
) TYPE=MyISAM;

#
# Dumping data for table 'playerdata'
#
```

```
INSERT INTO playerdata VALUES ('Andrew','qwerty',20,20020209203741);
INSERT INTO playerdata VALUES ('Henry','letmein',34,20020209203741);
INSERT INTO playerdata VALUES ('Sandra','dra33',19,20020209203741);
INSERT INTO playerdata VALUES ('John','j12d',23,20020209203741);
INSERT INTO playerdata VALUES ('Jenny','jen123',34,20020209203741);


#
# Table structure for table 'relateenemies'
#

CREATE TABLE relateenemies (
  player char(255) default NULL,
  enemy char(255) default NULL
) TYPE=MyISAM;


#
# Dumping data for table 'relateenemies'
#

INSERT INTO relateenemies VALUES ('Andrew','Sandra');
INSERT INTO relateenemies VALUES ('Henry','Jenny');
INSERT INTO relateenemies VALUES ('Henry','John');


#
# Table structure for table 'relatefriends'
#

CREATE TABLE relatefriends (
  player char(255) default NULL,
  friend char(255) default NULL
) TYPE=MyISAM;


#
# Dumping data for table 'relatefriends'
#

INSERT INTO relatefriends VALUES ('Henry','Sandra');
INSERT INTO relatefriends VALUES ('Andrew','Henry');
INSERT INTO relatefriends VALUES ('Andrew','John');
INSERT INTO relatefriends VALUES ('Andrew','Jenny');
INSERT INTO relatefriends VALUES ('Sandra','Jenny');
```

Restoring a Backed Up Database

Now that we can back up a database, let's look at how we would go about restoring it. First let's drop our gamedata database from MySQL using the following statement:

```
mysql> DROP DATABASE gamedata;
```

Now that we have removed our gamedata database, we need to create a new, empty database in which to import our data. Do this now with the following statement:

```
mysql> CREATE DATABASE newgamedata;
```

Next, we need to open up a command-line window again (by using the Run dialog and entering `command`). Now change to the mysql\bin\ directory, as we did previously when we exported the data, and then type in the following command to import the data from our gamedata.txt text file into our newgamedata database:

```
mysql newgamedata < gamedata.txt
```

Here is a screen shot of the command-line window:

Figure 15-60: Importing a text file into MySQL

Summary

In this chapter, you learned more about the SQL language and how to use it practically with the database application MySQL. In the next chapter, we will cover how to connect to a MySQL database from a Java application using the JDBC (Java Database Connectivity) library.

Chapter 15

Chapter 16

Using the JDBC

"Imagine if every Thursday your shoes exploded if you tied
them the usual way. This happens to us all the time with
computers, and nobody thinks of complaining." —Jeff Raskin

Introduction

In this chapter, we show you how to utilize a database from within a Java
application by means of the Java Database Connectivity library (JDBC).
This is a very powerful tool, especially when used in conjunction with a
server application for handling the back end of a multiplayer network
game over the Internet (or, at the most basic of levels, a high-score table).

What Is the JDBC?

The idea behind the JDBC was to create a library that allowed the execution of SQL statements from Java without directly worrying about the
database package that was going to be used with it (e.g., MySQL, as we
have chosen to use in this book). When using the JDBC, simply specify a
driver for the required database and it takes care of the rest.

Note that the JDBC only defines an interface for how to access the
database. However, because different database systems do not conform to
the same standard, some of the JDBC's functions may not be available. For
example, some database packages do not support prepared statements;
therefore, when using such packages, the prepared statement functionality
will not be available in the JDBC. Note also that the SQL language may
not be the same for all databases due to proprietary extensions.

Getting the MySQL Driver for the JDBC

A JDBC driver that allows connection to a MySQL database from the
JDBC is available at: http://mmmysql.sourceforge.net/.

Note that the driver available at the time of publication is on the companion CD with the filename mm.mysql-2.0.11-you-must-unjar-me.jar.

Creating a Connection to a Database

Now that we have had a brief introduction to the JDBC, we can look at how to establish a connection from a console application to a MySQL database. Let's first create a database called firsttest in MySQL using the MySQL console client (for more information on this, please look at the previous chapter). Here is the SQL statement that we require to create an empty database:

```
mysql> CREATE DATABASE firsttest;
```

Now we need to extract the JDBC driver to the directory that our source code is going to be stored in (in my case, this will be c:\java\jdbcex1). Let's now extract the JDBC driver to our source directory. First, copy the jar file to the source directory, and then load up the command prompt window. Enter the following command and press **Return**.

```
C:\java\jdbcex1>jar xvf mm.mysql-2.0.11-you-must-unjar-me.jar
```

Next we need to "cut" all of the files and directories out of the mm.mysql-2.0.11 directory that it created and simply paste them into the source directory (i.e., c:\java\jdbcex1). When this is done, we can then delete the mm.mysql-2.0.11 directory, as it will be empty, and also the original file that we extracted (i.e., mm.mysql-2.0.11-you-must-unjar-me.jar). Figure 16-1 is a screen shot of how our directory should now be structured:

Figure 16-1:
Our source directory
structure

Now let's create a simple Java console application that will connect to and then disconnect from the database. First we'll look at and compile the complete source for the console application and then we will discuss in detail why each part of the code is there.

Code Listing 16-1: Connecting to a database

```
import java.sql.*;

public class DatabaseExample1
```

```
{
    public static void main(String[] args)
    {
        try
        {
            Class.forName("org.gjt.mm.mysql.Driver");
        }
        catch(ClassNotFoundException e)
        {
            System.out.println(e);
        }

        try
        {
            Connection conn;

            System.out.println("Attempting to connect...\n");

            conn = DriverManager.getConnection(
            "jdbc:mysql://localhost/firsttest?user=root&password=");

            System.out.println("Connected\n");

            System.out.println("Attempting to disconnect...\n");

            conn.close();

            System.out.println("Disconnected\n");
        }
        catch(SQLException e)
        {
            System.out.println(e);
        }
    }
}
```

When we execute the code with the MySQL server also running, the following console output can be seen from the application:

Figure 16-2:
JDBC Example 1

Chapter 16

In our `main` method, the first code that we have added is to ensure that the MySQL driver is available and initialized. This is accomplished by calling the static `forName` method of the `Class` class, which can be seen in the following block of code.

```
try
{
    Class.forName("org.gjt.mm.mysql.Driver");
}
catch(ClassNotFoundException e)
{
```

```
         System.out.println(e);
     }
```

Note that if the driver class cannot be found, a `ClassNotFound-Exception` exception is thrown. After we have checked that the driver class is initialized, we can then create a `Connection` object, which handles our connection to the database. Here is the line of code that we used in our example to declare our `Connection` object:

```
     Connection conn;
```

Once we have declared our `Connection` object, we then attempt to establish a connection to the database with the following chunk of code:

```
         conn = DriverManager.getConnection(
         "jdbc:mysql://localhost/firsttest?user=root&password=");
```

We use the static method `getConnection` of the `DriverManager` class (which is part of the JDBC) to obtain the connection to the database. Note that we can replace `firsttest` with the name of any database to which we wish to connect, and we can also specify a username and password if they are required to gain access to the database.

After our connection is complete, we then terminate the connection to the database with the following statement:

```
     conn.close();
```

Also note that we encapsulate all of our database code within a `try/catch` statement, as the JDBC can throw an `SQL` exception if anything goes wrong.

 NOTE: All connections should be closed after use, as there is a limited amount of simultaneous connections, and if you forget to close connections, the database runs out of them quite quickly. However, note that a connection is closed when a `Connection` object is garbage collected (when no more references to it exist), and certain fatal errors will also cause the connection to close.

Inserting Data into a Table

Now that we have discovered how to create a connection to a database from Java, let's look at how we can add data into a table in MySQL directly from a Java application. Before we go any further, let's add a table to our firsttest database in MySQL using the following SQL statement in the MySQL console client. Remember, you need to also execute the `USE firsttest` statement so that MySQL knows which database you want to work with. Here is the SQL statement that we require for this:

```
mysql> CREATE TABLE playerdata (
    -> forename TEXT,
    -> surname TEXT,
    -> email TEXT);
```

This table will be able to hold a forename, surname, and an email address. Let's create a simple Java console application that will insert a single row of data into this table. Here is the complete code listing that we require to do this:

Code Listing 16-2: Inserting data into a table from Java

```java
import java.sql.*;

public class DatabaseExample2
{
    public static void main(String[] args)
    {
        try
        {
            Class.forName("org.gjt.mm.mysql.Driver");
        }
        catch(ClassNotFoundException e)
        {
            System.out.println(e);
        }

        try
        {
            Connection conn;

            System.out.println("Attempting to connect...\n");

            conn = DriverManager.getConnection("jdbc:mysql://
                localhost/firsttest?user=root&password=");

            System.out.println("Connected\n");

            System.out.println("Inserting 1 row of data...\n");

            Statement myStatement = conn.createStatement();

            myStatement.executeUpdate("INSERT INTO playerdata VALUES
                ('Andrew', 'Mulholland', 'andrew@dreamcircle.co.uk')");

            System.out.println("Attempting to disconnect...\n");

            conn.close();

            System.out.println("Disconnected\n");
        }
        catch(SQLException e)
        {
            System.out.println(e);
        }
    }
}
```

When we compile and execute this code, it will insert one row of data into our playerdata table in our firsttest database. If we go to the MySQL console client and select all the data in the table using this statement:

```
mysql> SELECT * FROM playerdata;
```

...we can see that the data has been entered successfully. Figure 16-3 is a screen shot of the MySQL console showing the data entered from Java:

Chapter 16

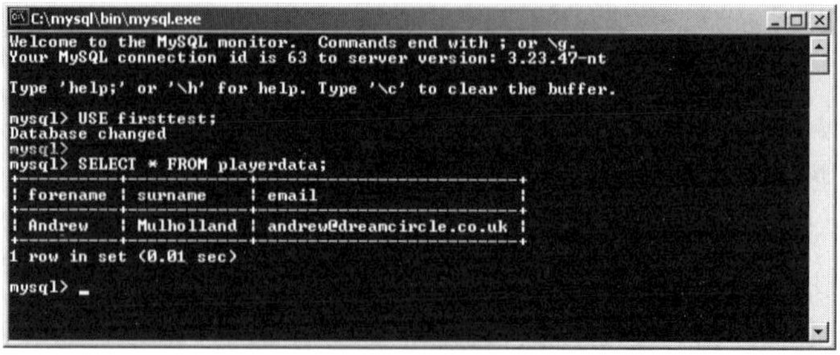

Figure 16-3: This shows the data in MySQL, which has been inserted from our Java console application.

All we have added to this code since the first example is the following two lines:

```
Statement myStatement = conn.createStatement();

myStatement.executeUpdate("INSERT INTO playerdata VALUES ('Andrew',
    'Mulholland', 'andrew@dreamcircle.co.uk')");
```

The first line of code creates a `Statement` object from our database connection, which is an object used to handle sending SQL statements to the database. The second simply executes the statement that we specify. Note that for this, we are using the `executeUpdate` method to execute the statement. This is the method that we use to alter data in tables, whereas we will see in the next section that we use the `executeQuery` method to retrieve data from tables.

> **NOTE:** It is possible to use the `execute ("String statement")` method to execute an SQL statement, which returns a Boolean value of `true` if a resultset was returned from the database (e.g., if we performed a `SELECT` statement) or `false` if the number of rows that were affected was returned (e.g., if we executed an `UPDATE` statement) or when no result is returned.
>
> `executeQuery()` returns a `ResultSet` object containing the result data that we will see in the next example.
>
> `executeUpdate()` returns an integer value telling the user how many rows were affected by the SQL statement.

Retrieving Data from a Table

Now that we can insert data into a table, let's look at how we can retrieve data back from tables into Java. First, let's add some more sample data into our playerdata table, which we created in the previous section. We will do this directly from the MySQL console client with the following SQL statement:

```
mysql> INSERT INTO playerdata VALUES
    -> ('John', 'Jenkings', 'jsmith@email.net'),
    -> ('Rachel', 'Peterson', 'rpeterson@email.net'),
    -> ('Peter', 'Thompson', 'pthompson@email.net'),
    -> ('Katy', 'McKenzie', 'kmckenzie@email.net');
```

Now we have five rows total in the database. Let's look at a sample program that will allow us to read these five rows from the database and display them into the console.

Code Listing 16-3: Retrieving data from a table into Java

```java
import java.sql.*;

public class DatabaseExample3
{
    public static void main(String[] args)
    {
        try
        {
            Class.forName("org.gjt.mm.mysql.Driver");
        }
        catch(ClassNotFoundException e)
        {
            System.out.println(e);
        }

        try
        {
            Connection conn;

            System.out.println("Attempting to connect...\n");

            conn = DriverManager.getConnection("jdbc:mysql://
                localhost/firsttest?user=root&password=");

            System.out.println("Connected\n");

            System.out.println("Attempting to retrieve table
                data...\n");

            Statement myStatement = conn.createStatement();

            ResultSet myResultSet = myStatement.executeQuery("SELECT
                * FROM playerdata");

            while(myResultSet.next())
            {
                System.out.print(myResultSet.getString
                    ("forename")+"\t\t");
                System.out.print(myResultSet.getString
                    ("surname")+"\t");
                System.out.print(myResultSet.getString
                    ("email")+"\n");
            }

            System.out.println("\nAttempting to disconnect...\n");

            conn.close();

            System.out.println("Disconnected\n");
        }
        catch(SQLException e)
        {
            System.out.println(e);
        }
    }
}
```

Chapter 16

When we execute this code, it produces the following output:

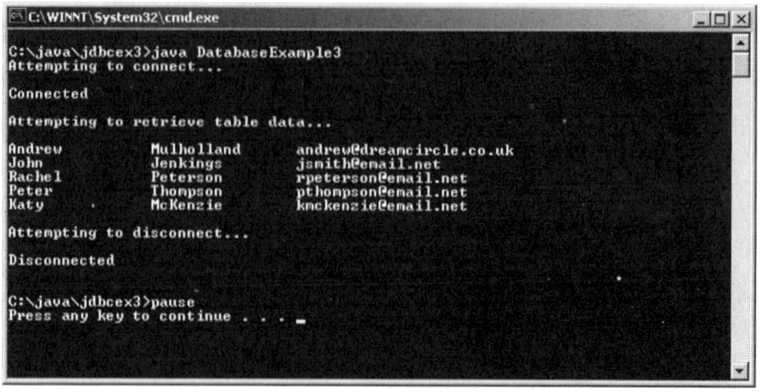

Figure 16-4: This screen shot shows the output from code listing 16-3.

Let's look at what we have changed and added to the code to retrieve the data from MySQL. First, we have used the `executeQuery` method instead of the `executeUpdate` method. This can be seen in the following code fragment:

```
ResultSet myResultSet = myStatement.executeQuery("SELECT
    * FROM playerdata");
```

Notice how the method returns a `ResultSet` object, which is part of the JDBC. The `ResultSet` object stores a pointer to the first row of information that was retrieved from the database. The other code that we have added is the `while` loop to enable us to traverse through the data from the `ResultSet`. This can be seen in the following code segment:

```
while(myResultSet.next())
{
    System.out.print(myResultSet.getString
        ("forename")+"\t\t");
    System.out.print(myResultSet.getString
        ("surname")+"\t");
    System.out.print(myResultSet.getString
        ("email")+"\n");
}
```

Basically, while we have more "rows" in our result set, we cycle through the `while` loop. Then, for each of the rows in the resultset, we use the `getString` method to access the data relating to the fields of the database.

In other words, `ResultSet` is like an iterator. The `ResultSet`, however, does not actually contain any data. When you call the `next()` method, it fetches one row at a time from the database server. That is because if the result (from the SQL query) is very large, we do not want to transfer all of the data to the application at once. `ResultSet` could be traversed in backward also, but that is not supported in all of the JDBC implementations.

A Sample Windowed Database Application

Now let's look at how we can use both inserting and retrieving data in a real windowed application. What we are going to create is a simple application that lists the top five high scores and allows users to input their name and the score they attained. First let's create a skeleton application that we can expand upon. Here is the basic code that we require to create an application frame:

Code Listing 16-4: The skeleton application frame

```
import javax.swing.*;

public class Highscore extends JFrame
{
    public Highscore()
    {
        super("Highscore Example");
        setBounds(0, 0, 300, 300);
        setDefaultCloseOperation(EXIT_ON_CLOSE);
        setResizable(false);
        getContentPane().setLayout(null);

        // We will add our GUI objects here...

        setVisible(true);
    }

    public static void main(String[] args)
    {
        Highscore mainApp = new Highscore();
    }
}
```

When we execute this code, we will see that it creates a simple application frame, which can be seen in the following figure.

Figure 16-5:
Our skeleton application

Next we need to add some GUI objects to allow the user to view the top five high scores in a list and also some input boxes to allow the user to enter his or her name and score and add the data to the database.

Let's now add a GUI table to contain the high-score list, two labels, two input boxes, and a button to allow a user to add a score. The GUI code is going to be added to the constructor of our application, and the full source so far can be seen in the following code listing. The new code is marked by comments in the code.

Code Listing 16-5: The skeleton application frame with GUI objects

```java
import java.awt.*;
import javax.swing.*;
import javax.swing.table.*;

public class Highscore extends JFrame
{
    public Highscore()
    {
        super("Highscore Example");
        setBounds(0, 0, 300, 300);
        setDefaultCloseOperation(EXIT_ON_CLOSE);
        setResizable(false);
        getContentPane().setLayout(null);

        // NEW ->
        scoreTable = new JTable(5, 2);
        scoreTable.setEnabled(false);
        scoreTable.setBounds(20, 20, 250, 80);

        nameLabel = new JLabel("Enter Your Name:");
        nameLabel.setLocation(10, 140);
        nameLabel.setSize(nameLabel.getPreferredSize());

        scoreLabel = new JLabel("Enter Your Score:");
        scoreLabel.setLocation(10, 170);
        scoreLabel.setSize(scoreLabel.getPreferredSize());

        nameField = new JTextField();
        nameField.setBounds(120, 140, 140, 20);

        scoreField = new JTextField();
        scoreField.setBounds(120, 170, 140, 20);

        submitButton = new JButton("Submit your Score!");
        submitButton.setBounds(20, 220, 250, 30);

        Container content = getContentPane();

        content.add(scoreTable);
        content.add(nameLabel);
        content.add(scoreLabel);
        content.add(nameField);
        content.add(scoreField);
        content.add(submitButton);
        // <- NEW

        setVisible(true);
    }

    public static void main(String[] args)
    {
        Highscore mainApp = new Highscore();
    }
```

```
    // NEW ->
    JTable        scoreTable;     // List box to hold the high scores
    JLabel        nameLabel;      // Label for the player's name
    JLabel        scoreLabel;     // Label for the player's score
    JTextField    nameField;      // Field for inputting player's name
    JTextField    scoreField;     // Field for inputting player's score
    JButton       submitButton;   // Button for submitting a score
    // <- NEW
}
```

When we then execute this code, we can see that our five GUI objects are
now visible in the application frame.

Figure 16-6:
Our skeleton application with GUI objects
in place

If you are unsure about how to use the GUI in Java, please see Chapter 13,
which explains the Java GUI in detail, and the bonus GUI chapter available
on the companion CD-ROM.

Okay, so now that we have our basic application, let's create a database
in which we can then store the players' scores. Once we have the database
ready, we can then add code to the application to allow it to interact with
the database.

Now open up the MySQL console client and execute the following set
of statements:

```
mysql> CREATE DATABASE highscore;

mysql> USE highscore;

mysql> CREATE TABLE scoredata (
    -> name TEXT,
    -> score INT);
```

Execute the DESCRIBE command in the MySQL console to ensure that
our table has been created as we planned. Here is the statement that we
require to do this:

```
mysql> DESCRIBE scoredata;
```

TIP: If you have an artistic slant, it may be that you are slightly lazier
than your average programmer. If so, you may want to use the shortened
keyword DESC to describe your tables.

The following figure is a screen shot of the expected output from the
MySQL console:

Chapter 16

Figure 16-7:
Our
scoredata
table in our
highscore
database

Let's go back to Java and add a method to our `Highscore` class that will
retrieve the top five high scores from the database and insert them into
our `JTable` object. To allow the table to be filled with data, we need to
create a `TableHandler` class to control how the data is added into the
table. Let's look at the complete code listing for this class, and then we
will break it down to see how it works.

Code Listing 16-6: The `TableHandler` class

```java
import java.sql.*;
import javax.swing.table.*;
import java.util.*;

class TableHandler extends AbstractTableModel
{
    public void updateTable()
    {
        try
        {
            Connection conn;

            conn = DriverManager.getConnection("jdbc:mysql://
                localhost/highscore?user=root&password=");

            Statement myStatement = conn.createStatement();

            ResultSet rs = myStatement.executeQuery("SELECT * FROM
                scoredata ORDER BY score DESC LIMIT "+MAX_ROWS);

                int row = 0;
            while(rs.next())
            {
                list[row][0] = rs.getString("name");
                list[row][1] = rs.getString("score");
                row++;
            }

            conn.close();

            // Tell the table there is new data so it can update
            // itself...
            fireTableDataChanged();
        }
        catch(SQLException e)
        {
            System.out.println(e);
```

```
        }
    }

    public int getColumnCount()
    {
        return MAX_COLUMNS;
    }

    public int getRowCount()
    {
        return MAX_ROWS;
    }

    public Object getValueAt(int row, int column)
    {
        return list[row][column];
    }

    String[][] list = new String[MAX_ROWS][MAX_COLUMNS];

    static final int MAX_ROWS = 5;
    static final int MAX_COLUMNS = 2;
}
```

The `TableHandler` class extends the `AbstractTableModel` class that allows it to specify the data added to a table. The first method that we have implemented, `updateTable`, is not actually part of the `AbstractTableModel` class, but it does access methods from it (which are implemented below the `updateTable` method).

The `updateTable` method first creates a connection to the database and then executes the following SQL query:

```
SELECT * FROM scoredata ORDER BY score DESC LIMIT 5
```

This selects all of the data from the scoredata table in descending order using the score field to order it. Note that ordering is done <u>after</u> the filter (*) and where options. Note that the "`LIMIT 5`" on the end of the statement means that the database will only return the first five results it finds matching our query.

Next we cycle through the `ResultSet` and add each of the results to a two-dimensional string array used to store the row and column information for the table. Here is the code fragment that does this for us:

```
    int row = 0;
while(rs.next())
{
    list[row][0] = rs.getString("name");
    list[row][1] = rs.getString("score");
    row++;
}
```

Finally, we call a method that is part of the `AbstractTableModel` called `fireTableDataChanged` so that the table knows that its data has been changed and it refreshes itself.

This leads us nicely into the `getValueAt` method that we have implemented in this class. This method is used by the table to read in the values for each of the rows and columns in our actual `JTable`. Note that all this function does is return string values from our two-dimensional string array `list` (which we filled with values from the database in the `updateTable` method). Hence, we can define our own table values in this method for the table to call internally to retrieve the table data.

The other two methods are used to tell the table the number of rows and columns it currently contains. Hence, if we stored row data in a linked list, we could return the size of the list in the `getRowCount` method and then handle obtaining the row data in the `getValueAt` method accordingly.

Now we need to integrate the `TableHandler` class into our main `Highscore` class. Here is the complete source listing for the `Highscore` class with the `TableHandler` implemented. We have also made it so that you can click the button to add your score into the database.

Code Listing 16-7: The final Highscore class

```
import java.awt.*;
import java.awt.event.*;    // NEW
import javax.swing.*;
import java.sql.*;

public class Highscore extends JFrame implements ActionListener
// NEW
{
    public Highscore()
    {
        super("Highscore Example");
        setBounds(0, 0, 300, 300);
        setDefaultCloseOperation(EXIT_ON_CLOSE);
        setResizable(false);
        getContentPane().setLayout(null);

        // NEW ->
        tableHandler = new TableHandler();
        tableHandler.updateTable();
        // <- NEW

        scoreTable = new JTable(tableHandler); // new constructor
        scoreTable.setBounds(20, 20, 250, 80);
        scoreTable.setEnabled(false);

        nameLabel = new JLabel("Enter Your Name:");
        nameLabel.setLocation(10, 140);
        nameLabel.setSize(nameLabel.getPreferredSize());

        scoreLabel = new JLabel("Enter Your Score:");
        scoreLabel.setLocation(10, 170);
        scoreLabel.setSize(scoreLabel.getPreferredSize());

        nameField = new JTextField();
        nameField.setBounds(120, 140, 140, 20);

        scoreField = new JTextField();
        scoreField.setBounds(120, 170, 140, 20);

        submitButton = new JButton("Submit your Score!");
```

```
    submitButton.setBounds(20, 220, 250, 30);

    submitButton.addActionListener(this);   // NEW

    Container content = getContentPane();

    content.add(scoreTable);
    content.add(nameLabel);
    content.add(scoreLabel);
    content.add(nameField);
    content.add(scoreField);
    content.add(submitButton);

    setVisible(true);
}

// NEW ->
public void actionPerformed(ActionEvent e)
{
    if(e.getSource() == submitButton)
    {
        // Check the fields contain values
        String name = nameField.getText();
        String score = scoreField.getText();

        if(name.length()>0 && score.length()>0)
        {
            // Insert the score into the database
            try
            {
                Connection conn;

                conn = DriverManager.getConnection(
                    "jdbc:mysql://localhost/highscore?
                    user=root&password=");

                Statement myStatement = conn.createStatement();

                myStatement.executeUpdate("INSERT INTO scoredata
                    VALUES ('"+name+"',"+score+")");

                conn.close();
            }
            catch(SQLException ex)
            {
                System.out.println(ex);
            }

            // Finally, refresh the highscore table and blank
            // the fields
            tableHandler.updateTable();
        }
    }
}
// <- NEW


public static void main(String[] args)
{
    // NEW ->
```

```
        try
        {
            Class.forName("org.gjt.mm.mysql.Driver");
        }
        catch(ClassNotFoundException e)
        {
            System.out.println(e);
        }
        // <- NEW

        Highscore mainApp = new Highscore();
    }

    JTable          scoreTable;     // List box to hold the high scores
    JLabel          nameLabel;      // Label for the player's name
    JLabel          scoreLabel;     // Label for the player's score
    JTextField      nameField;      // Field for inputting player's name
    JTextField      scoreField;     // Field for inputting player's score
    JButton         submitButton;   // Button for submitting a score

    // NEW ->
    TableHandler tableHandler;
    // <- NEW
}
```

When we compile and execute the complete application, we can see that when we enter scores and submit them, the five highest scores are shown. The following figure is a screen shot with some sample scores in

Figure 16-8:
The final Highscore application

it.

We first added a call to the static Class.forName method, which (as we saw before) initializes the MySQL driver class that is used by the JDBC.

Let's have a look now at how we integrated the TableHandler. First we created a TableHandler object and assigned it as the "model" for the table by passing it as a parameter to the JTable constructor. This was accomplished with the following code segment:

```
// NEW ->
        tableHandler = new TableHandler();
        tableHandler.updateTable();
        // <- NEW

        scoreTable = new JTable(tableHandler); // new constructor
```

Notice how we also call the `updateTable` method of the `Table-Handler` here. This will update our `JTable` object with the data from the database when we start our application. We also call this function again when the user presses the button to submit their scores.

We have attached an `ActionListener` to the submit button, so that any time the button is clicked it will invoke the `actionPerformed` method. When the button is clicked, the application checks to ensure that there is data in both the text fields, and then it inserts the score into the database using the following code:

```
myStatement.executeUpdate("INSERT INTO scoredata VALUES
    ('"+name+"',"+score+")");
```

Note that after the data has been inserted, the `updateTable` function is called so the scores are relisted in the correct order again, taking into account the new score that has just been added into the database.

Accessing Database Metadata from a ResultSet

Now that we are able to insert data into and retrieve data from database tables, we can look at how we can actually get structural information about the database, which is referred to as *metadata*. Here is a simple program that will read all of the tables from the database and display the names of all of the columns in each of those tables.

Code Listing 16-8: Accessing database metadata

```
import java.sql.*;

public class MetaExample1
{
    public static void main(String[] args)
    {
        try
        {
            Class.forName("org.gjt.mm.mysql.Driver");
        }
        catch(ClassNotFoundException e)
        {
            System.out.println(e);
        }

        try
        {
            Connection conn;

            System.out.println("Attempting to connect...\n");

            conn = DriverManager.getConnection("jdbc:mysql:
                //localhost/firsttest?user=root&password=");

            System.out.println("Connected\n");

            System.out.println("Getting Database Meta Data...\n");

            DatabaseMetaData metadata = conn.getMetaData();
```

```
        String[] validTypes = {"TABLE"};
        ResultSet theTables = metadata.getTables(null, null,
            null, validTypes);

        while(theTables.next())
        {
            String tableName = theTables.getString("TABLE_NAME");
            System.out.println("Table Found: "+tableName);

            // Now get the columns in that table
            ResultSet theColumns = metadata.getColumns(null,
                null, tableName, null);

            while(theColumns.next())
            {
                String columnName = theColumns.getString
                    ("COLUMN_NAME");
                System.out.println("\tColumn Found:
                    "+columnName);
            }
            System.out.print("\n");
        }

        System.out.println("\nAttempting to disconnect...\n");

        conn.close();

        System.out.println("Disconnected\n");
    }
    catch(SQLException e)
    {
        System.out.println(e);
    }
}
}
```

When we execute this console application, we can see that it will list all of the tables (of which there is only one) and columns in the table. In this example we are using the firsttest database that we created earlier in this chapter. Here is the output that we can expect in the console:

Figure 16-9: Output from our metadata example, using the firsttest database

Let's now look at how this is achieved. We connect to the database, as we have done in previous examples, but instead of using a query, we use the `Connection` object to retrieve the metadata from the database. The line of code used to do this is as follows:

```
DatabaseMetaData metadata = conn.getMetaData();
```

Once we have the metadata stored in a `DatabaseMetaData` object, we can then obtain a `ResultSet` containing information about our tables with the following code segment:

```
String[] validTypes = {"TABLE"};
ResultSet theTables = metadata.getTables(null, null, null,
    validTypes);
```

Once we have our `ResultSet`, we can use the normal method of cycling through rows with a `while` loop. Notice, though, how we actually get the names of the tables:

```
String tableName = theTables.getString("TABLE_NAME");
```

Prepared Statements

Finally, let's look at prepared statements and how we can use them in our applications. A *prepared statement* is basically a way to create an SQL statement that contains placeholders for data. So, a statement can be used like a method to which you pass parameters. This is a good method to use when you will be using the same statement many times with different data, and it is typically quicker to execute as well. Let's look at a sample console application that implements a prepared statement. Note that we will be using the highscore database for this application. Here is the complete source code listing:

Code Listing 16-9: Using prepared statements

```
import java.sql.*;

public class PreparedStatementExample
{
    public static void main(String[] args)
    {
        try
        {
            Class.forName("org.gjt.mm.mysql.Driver");
        }
        catch(ClassNotFoundException e)
        {
            System.out.println(e);
        }

        try
        {
            Connection conn;

            System.out.println("Attempting to connect...\n");

            conn = DriverManager.getConnection("jdbc:mysql:
                //localhost/highscore?user=root&password=");

            System.out.println("Connected\n");

            // Create our prepared statement
            String ourStatement = "INSERT INTO scoredata VALUES
```

```
            (?, ?)";

        PreparedStatement addNewScore = conn.prepareStatement
            (ourStatement);

        // Now insert three rows of data using the prepared
        // statement...
        addNewScore.setString(1, "George");
        // set the name placeholder to 'George'
        addNewScore.setInt(2, 1000);
        // set the score placeholder to 1000
        addNewScore.executeUpdate();

        addNewScore.setString(1, "Sandra");
        // set the name placeholder to 'Sandra'
        addNewScore.setInt(2, 500);
        // set the score placeholder to 500
        addNewScore.executeUpdate();

        addNewScore.setString(1, "Billy");
        // set the name placeholder to 'Billy'
        addNewScore.setInt(2, 200);
        // set the score placeholder to 200
        addNewScore.executeUpdate();

        System.out.println("\nAttempting to disconnect...\n");

        conn.close();

        System.out.println("Disconnected\n");
    }
    catch(SQLException e)
    {
        System.out.println(e);
    }
}
}
```

When this console application is executed, it will insert three rows of data into the scoredata table in our highscore database. The following figure is a screen shot of the data contained in our scoredata table after the application has been executed:

Figure 16-10: The prepared statement has inserted three rows into our database.

Now look at what we have changed in the code to allow us to use prepared statements. First, we created the prepared statement by creating a string with the following line of code:

```
String ourStatement = "INSERT INTO scoredata VALUES (?, ?)";
```

Notice how we use the ? to define placeholders for unknown values. Note also that you can have as many placeholders as you require for your statement. So in this statement, we have defined the actual values that we are inserting into the scoredata table as unknowns.

Next we need to actually create a PreparedStatement object using the Connection object. This is accomplished with the following line of code:

```
PreparedStatement addNewScore = conn.prepareStatement(ourStatement);
```

So now that we have a PreparedStatement object, we can specify the unknowns and then execute it to insert the data into the database. We specify the unknown values using the following two lines of code in our example program:

```
addNewScore.setString(1, "George");
// set the name placeholder to 'George'
addNewScore.setInt(2, 1000);
// set the score placeholder to 1000
```

Notice that the first parameter of the setString/setInt method specified which placeholder (?) that you are referring to, and the first placeholder is 1 and not 0. In this code segment, the first line will set the first placeholder to the value "George," and the second line will set the second placeholder to the integer value 1000.

Finally, once we have set our placeholder values, we can then execute the prepared statement using the following line of code:

```
addNewScore.executeUpdate();
```

This process can then be repeated as many times as you wish, using the same PreparedStatement.

Summary

In this chapter, you discovered how to interact with MySQL databases directly from a Java application using the powerful JDBC package. Using a back-end database to store game data is extremely efficient and secure, and it is highly recommended for data storage in online multiplayer games. But how can we go about writing the multiplayer code itself? In the next chapter, we will move on to greener pastures and look at network programming in Java.

Chapter 16

Introduction to Networking

> "In all large corporations, there is a pervasive fear that someone,
> somewhere is having fun with a computer on company time.
> Networks help alleviate that fear." —John C. Dvorak

Introduction

In this chapter, you will learn how to create games that can be played by multiple players over a local network or the Internet. Adding this extra feature to games can add much to their life expectancy, as the best opponents are always other human players. First you will learn the basic theory behind networking, and then we will look at some simple networking examples and connecting multiple clients to a server with the game that we call "I'm a circle" at the end of this chapter.

Fundamentals of Networking

Protocols

One of the first things that you must consider with networking is that you may be communicating with native operating systems. For example, if you have your server on a computer with the Linux operating system installed, you would want clients using, say, Windows and Macs to also be able to access your server. To accomplish this, the operating systems all need to use the same *data transmission language.* This is achieved by using *protocols.*

A protocol is simply a standard of how data should be transferred across a network. Although there are many different protocols, we will focus on TCP/IP, which is the most common protocol on the Internet. The name of the protocol is in fact a little misleading, however, in that there are actually two different protocols available under TCP/IP. These are TCP, which stands for Transmission Control Protocol, and UDP, which stands for User Datagram Protocol. Let's now look at the differences between these two protocols.

TCP: Transmission Control Protocol

When using the TCP protocol in networking, you are first required to create a connection to another computer. This may seem obvious, but not all protocols require a connection, as we will see in the next section with the UDP protocol. Once a connection is established, you can then use incoming and outgoing streams to send and receive data over the network. The main advantage of using the TCP protocol is that it guarantees delivery of your data (in the correct order) and handles duplicate packets. TCP also has congestion control and flow control mechanisms, which are useful when streaming lots of data.

When sending data with TCP, there are many things that are done to the data before it is sent. First, TCP adds extra headers to the data and may split it up into many different packets, etc. All this is important if the data must be optimized as small as possible. It is quite a waste if a game sends one-byte data packets with TCP. In addition, if too large an amount of data is put into one package, it can be inefficient.

 NOTE: A packet is simply a unit of data that is sent over a network.

UDP: User Datagram Protocol

UDP can be described as a connectionless protocol, as you do not actually create a connection to the remote computer. With UDP, you simply specify where the information is going to go, and you never know if it gets there or not. This makes UDP an unreliable protocol, as it can easily lose packets and create duplicates. This sounds terrible, doesn't it? The advantage of UDP over TCP is that it can be much more efficient. For example, the TCP protocol has flow control built into it, which limits the initial bandwidth of the network connection to alleviate network congestion, whereas UDP has no such thing, meaning we get full available bandwidth. In addition, we can handle lost packets by adding our own simple notification message to determine if it has sent correctly or not. However, adding too much error checking can make UDP not any better than TCP for efficiency.

IP Addresses

An *IP address* is a way that you can identify computers on a network (or the Internet). If you have Internet access via a modem or cable (or on a local area network), you can find your IP address by going to the command prompt in Windows and typing:

```
ipconfig
```

When you do this, you will see something similar to the following figure. (Note that you may see two IP addresses if you are also connected to a local area network.)

```
C:\WINNT\System32\cmd.exe                                        _ □ ×
Microsoft Windows 2000 [Version 5.00.2195]
(C) Copyright 1985-2000 Microsoft Corp. '

C:\>ipconfig

Windows 2000 IP Configuration

Ethernet adapter Local Area Connection:

        Connection-specific DNS Suffix  . :
        IP Address. . . . . . . . . . . . : 192.168.0.113
        Subnet Mask . . . . . . . . . . . : 255.255.255.0
        Default Gateway . . . . . . . . . : 192.168.0.1

C:\>
```

Figure 17-1:
Finding out
your IP
address

If you have a dial-up connection to the Internet, it is likely that you will be assigned a new IP address dynamically each time you connect to the Internet. However, if you are lucky enough to have a cable connection, you will be assigned a static IP address.

So we now know how to find out IP addresses; let's see what they actually are. Currently, IP addresses consist of a 32-bit number, which is broken down into four bytes in the form x.x.x.x, where "x" is a single byte. Looking at the previous image, the IP address is 192.168.0.133. Note that the way IP addresses are being represented is being revised. The current 32-bit system is known as IPv4, but the new system will represent IP addresses by means of a 128-bit number, which will be called IPv6. More information on this new standard can be found at the following web site: http://www.ipv6.org/.

Ports

We now know computers can be distinguished from each other over a network via IP addresses, but what if there are several server applications running on a single computer? How do you determine the server for which the network message is intended? The answer to this is *ports*. A port isn't actually a physical thing but is simply a 16-bit value. The operating system keeps track of which ports are in use and which are not. The first 1 to 1023 ports are reserved by the system for common services (such as FTP, which runs on port 21). This leaves ports 1024 to 65535 free for us to use in our applications. Note that there is no such thing as port 0.

> **NOTE:**   There is a body known as IANA (Internet Assigned Numbers Authority), which records well-known used ports. For more information on this, see the following web page: http://www.iana.org/.

Sockets

As IP addresses and ports are used to uniquely identify machines and servers, a *socket* is used to establish connections and send data between machines. The best way to think of a socket is as a pipe through which data can flow between two machines on a network. There are two major types of sockets that we are interested in: stream sockets and datagram sockets.

Chapter 17

Stream and Datagram Sockets

A *stream socket* is used with the TCP protocol, and as you know from before, TCP requires a connection to the remote machine before data can be sent. When a connection is established, we use a stream socket to obtain either an output or input stream (or both) for the connection so we can easily send and receive data via the streams.

A *datagram socket* is different in that it does not have any streams associated with it. It works by sending packets of information that also contain information regarding where the packet came from. By using this method, it is then possible to reply to the message by using the information that was contained in the packet regarding where it came from.

Networking Applets

In this chapter we will focus on networking applications; however, the same code techniques can also be applied to applets. The important issue with applets is security. When creating a networked applet, it is only possible to connect to the computer that the applet was executed from (i.e., the web server). However, this is no problem as long as your game server is running on the same machine as the web server. Note that it is possible to get around this by creating a signed applet, but this process requires an official certificate and is generally a lot of hassle unless you are a big-shot company with money to spend. Signed applets are really beyond the scope of this book.

Example: TCP Echo Server

Now that we have looked at the basic network theory, let's try creating our first server application using the TCP protocol. The aim for this application is to allow a single connection from another application and then send back any strings that are sent to it. First we will look at the complete code listing and output, and then we will go into detail as to how the code works.

Code Listing 17-1: TCP echo server

```
import java.net.*;
import java.io.*;

public class TCPEchoServer
{
    public static void main(String args[])
    {
        int port = 8000;
        ServerSocket serverSocket = null;
        DataInputStream dataInputStream = null;
        DataOutputStream dataOutputStream = null;

        try
        {
```

```
        // open a server socket
        serverSocket = new ServerSocket(port);

        System.out.println("Server created on port "+port);

        System.out.println("Awaiting client connection...");

        // await for a client connection
        Socket clientSocket = serverSocket.accept();

        System.out.println("Client connected from
            "+clientSocket.getInetAddress());

        dataInputStream = new DataInputStream
            (clientSocket.getInputStream());
        dataOutputStream = new DataOutputStream
            (clientSocket.getOutputStream());
    }
    catch(IOException e)
    {
        System.out.println("Problems initializing server: "+e);
        System.exit(1);
    }


    // communicate with the client
    try
    {
        dataOutputStream.writeUTF("Welcome to the TCP Echo
            Server!");
        String input;
        while(true)
        {
            // read data in from client
            input = dataInputStream.readUTF();
            System.out.println("You typed: "+input);

            // write data back to client
            dataOutputStream.writeUTF(input);
        }
    }
    catch(IOException e)
    {
        System.out.println("Client disconnected from server");
    }

    try
    {
        serverSocket.close();
    }
    catch(Exception e) { }
    }
}
```

When we run the console application, it will sit and wait for a connection from a client. This looks like the following:

Figure 17-2:
The TCP
echo server

Let's now look at the code and see how this works.

First we import the `java.net.*` package, which contains all of the network-related code. We also import the `java.io.*` package, which we need for the streams. This can be seen in the following two lines of code:

```
import java.net.*;
import java.io.*;
```

Now we define the default port number as `8000` in a variable called `port` and also create three variables, which we will use to store our `Server-Socket`, as well as `DataInputStream` and `DataOutputStream`, which we will obtain from the connecting client. This can be seen here:

```
ServerSocket serverSocket = null;
DataInputStream dataInputStream = null;
DataOutputStream dataOutputStream = null;
```

Next, we need to actually set up the server on the port that we have defined. To do this, enter a `try/catch` block and create a `Server-Socket` object, which creates a stream socket. To create the `Server-Socket` object, pass the port number into the constructor as follows:

```
ServerSocket serverSocket = new ServerSocket(port);
```

Now that we have our server socket, we need to get it to accept a connection from an incoming client. This is done by calling the `accept` method, which blocks (waits) until a client connects to the server, hence the code does not pass this point until a client connects to the server. When a client does connect, the connecting socket is then returned by our `Server-Socket` object, and we store it in a `Socket` object called `client-Socket`. This can be seen in the following line of code:

```
Socket clientSocket = serverSocket.accept();
```

Once a client has established a connection with our server, we then need to set up streams to handle the incoming and outgoing data. To do this, we call the `getInputStream` and `getOutputStream` methods of the `Socket` class to obtain the streams associated with our `clientSocket` object. We then pass these streams into the constructor for `DataInput-Stream` and `DataOutputStream` objects, respectively. This can be seen in the following two lines of code:

```
dataInputStream = new DataInputStream(clientSocket.getInputStream());
dataOutputStream = new DataOutputStream
   (clientSocket.getOutputStream());
```

Note that we also need to catch a possible `IOException`, which will tell us if the setup of the server has failed. Note that a possible cause of this failing would be if a server were already running on the port that we specified.

Next, we want to send the client a welcome message from our server application so that they know they are connected. To do this, we call the `writeUTF` method of our `dataOutputStream` object to which we pass a `String` object. This can be seen here:

```
dataOutputStream.writeUTF("Welcome to the TCP Echo Server!");
```

After this, we then go into a loop that loops indefinitely and calls the `readUTF` method of the `dataInputStream`, which blocks (waits) for a string to be received from the client. Each time a string is received, it is printed to the server's console window and is then sent straight back to the client via the `writeUTF` method of the `dataOutputStream` object. Note that we also catch a possible `IOException` that will be thrown when the client terminates the connection to the server, which is the normal way for a client to disconnect.

Finally, we need to ensure that the socket is closed after the client disconnects, and we need to catch the possible `IOException` that could be thrown. This can be seen here:

```
try
{
    serverSocket.close();
}
catch(Exception e) { }
```

Example: TCP Echo Client

Now that we know how the server works, we can look at how we can create a simple client in Java that will interact with our TCP echo server. Let's first look at the complete client-side code to connect to our server and the expected output, and then we will look at how it all works.

Code Listing 17-2: TCP echo client

```java
import java.net.*;
import java.io.*;

public class TCPEchoClient
{
    public static class TCPEchoReader extends Thread
    {
        public TCPEchoReader(DataInputStream input)
        {
            dataInputStream = input;
            active = true;
        }

        public void run()
        {
            while(active)
            {
                try
                {
                    String message = dataInputStream.readUTF();
                    System.out.println("Received from server:
                        "+message);
```

Chapter 17

```
                }
            catch(IOException e)
            {
                System.out.println(e);
                active = false;
            }
        }
    }

    public boolean active;
    public DataInputStream dataInputStream;
}


public static void main(String[] args)
{
    String address = "127.0.0.1";
    int port = 8000;

    Socket socket = null;
    DataInputStream dataInputStream = null;
    DataOutputStream dataOutputStream = null;
    BufferedReader keyboardReader = null;

    // Connect to the server...
    try
    {
        socket = new Socket(address, port);

        // Obtain the streams...
        dataInputStream = new DataInputStream
            (socket.getInputStream());
        dataOutputStream = new DataOutputStream
            (socket.getOutputStream());

        keyboardReader = new BufferedReader
            (new InputStreamReader(System.in));
    }
    catch(IOException e)
    {
        System.out.println("Problems initialising: "+e);
        System.exit(1);
    }


    try
    {
        // Start the listening thread...
        TCPEchoReader reader = new TCPEchoReader
            (dataInputStream);
        reader.setDaemon(true);
        reader.start();

        String input;
        while(true)
        {
            // read data in from the keyboard
            input = keyboardReader.readLine();

            // send data to server
```

```
            dataOutputStream.writeUTF(input);
        }
    }
    catch(IOException e)
    {
    }

    try
    {
        socket.close();
    }
    catch(IOException e) { }
}
```

So, if we ensure that we are running our TCP echo server to run this new TCP echo client, we will see that it connects to the server. To see it working, type in a line of text followed by a Return, and the same line of text will be echoed back from the server. The following figure is a screen shot showing this in action:

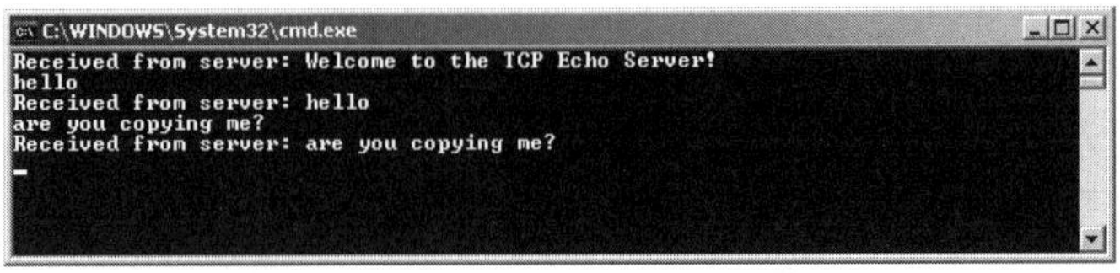

Figure 17-3:
The TCP
echo client

As you can see, all the data that we send to the server is sent back and output to the console window. Let's look at the client code and see how we interact with our server.

First we include the network and I/O package, as we did with the server. Then we declare a nested class called TCPEchoReader, which extends the Thread class. This nested class is used to read in data from the server in a separate thread. To the constructor of the TCPEchoReader, we pass in a DataInputStream object, which will relate to the connected socket and be stored in an instance member called dataInputStream. Then we simply set the Boolean flag active to true, so our thread will execute when started. This can be seen here:

```
public TCPEchoReader(DataInputStream input)
{
    dataInputStream = input;
    active = true;
}
```

Next, we have the run method, which overrides the inherited run method of the Thread class. In this method, we create a loop, which will run while the active flag is true. Then, we simply call the readUTF method of the dataInputStream, which will block until a string message is read in from the server. When this occurs, it will store the String object in our variable called message, which we then output to the console window. The entire run method can be seen here:

Chapter 17

```
public void run()
{
    while(active)
    {
        try
        {
            String message = dataInputStream.readUTF();
            System.out.println("Received from server:
                "+message);
        }
        catch(IOException e)
        {
            System.out.println(e);
            active = false;
        }
    }
}
```

Note also here that we caught a possible `IOException`, which can be thown. If it is thrown, we terminate the loop by setting the `active` flag to `false`.

 NOTE: Generally, if any `IOException` occurs, it means that the socket has been disconnected.

So, let's now look at the entry point of the application, the `main` method. We use the `main` method thread as the thread for writing data to the server. It may have been a better technique to create a new class, like the `TCPEchoReader` class, for writing data to the server; however, we are trying to keep the example as simple as possible.

First, we define the address and port of the server that we wish to connect to using the following two variables: `address` and `port`.

```
String address = "127.0.0.1";
int port = 8000;
```

Then we create four variables to contain references to: a `Socket`, a `DataInputStream`, a `DataOutputStream`, and finally a `Buffered-Reader`. This can be seen here:

```
Socket socket = null;
DataInputStream dataInputStream = null;
DataOutputStream dataOutputStream = null;
BufferedReader keyboardReader = null;
```

Next we create a `socket` by passing in the `address` and `port` of the server to which we wish to connect. The connection is performed when you create the `Socket` object, which is then stored in our `socket` variable. Once we have the `socket`, we can then obtain the `DataIn-putStream` and `DataOutputStream` from it, as we did with the server. Then finally, we create a `BufferedReader` object to read in input from the keyboard. This entire section can be seen here:

```
try
{
    socket = new Socket(address, port);

    // Obtain the streams...
```

```
dataInputStream = new DataInputStream(socket.getInputStream());
dataOutputStream = new DataOutputStream
    (socket.getOutputStream());

keyboardReader = new BufferedReader
    (new InputStreamReader(System.in));
}
catch(IOException e)
{
    System.out.println("Problems initialising: "+e);
    System.exit(1);
}
```

Notice again how we catch the possible `IOException` and exit the program at this stage, as an error at this stage would be fatal (i.e., not being able to establish a connection to the server or not being able to get input from the keyboard).

Next we create an instance of the `TCPEchoReader`, set it as a daemon thread and start it reading for incoming messages. Note that it is a daemon thread, so it will terminate if and when the main thread it is running in terminates. Here is the section of code that does this:

```
TCPEchoReader reader = new TCPEchoReader(dataInputStream);
reader.setDaemon(true);
reader.start();
```

Finally, we create a `while` loop, which loops indefinitely (until the program is closed by the user or an `IOException` occurs). All we do within the loop is read a line from the keyboard by calling the `readLine` method of the `keyboardReader` object that we created, and then we send the string retrieved to the server using the `writeUTF` method of the `dataOutputStream`. The `TCPEchoReader` thread will then handle the message coming back from the server. The input handling can be seen here.

```
String input;
while(true)
{
    // read data in from the keyboard
    input = keyboardReader.readLine();

    // send data to server
    dataOutputStream.writeUTF(input);
}
```

Example: UDP Echo Server/Client

Now that we have seen how to create a TCP client and server, let's find out how to do it with the use of the UDP protocol. As we mentioned before, UDP is a connectionless protocol, meaning that the client will never actually connect to the server but will just send packets of information to the server's IP address and port. Let's first look at the complete source code to the UDP echo server, and then we will take a more in-depth look at the code and see the differences between UDP and TCP from a coding point of view.

Code Listing 17-3: UDP echo server

```java
import java.net.*;
import java.io.*;

public class UDPEchoServer
{
    public static void main(String args[])
    {
        int port = 8000;

        // create the server...
        DatagramSocket serverDatagramSocket = null;
        try
        {
            serverDatagramSocket = new DatagramSocket(port);

            System.out.println("Created UDP Echo Server on port
                "+port);
        }
        catch(IOException e)
        {
            System.out.println(e);
            System.exit(1);
        }

        try
        {
            byte buffer[] = new byte[1024];
            DatagramPacket datagramPacket = new
                DatagramPacket(buffer, buffer.length);

            String input;

            while(true)
            {
                // listen for datagram packets
                serverDatagramSocket.receive(datagramPacket);
                input = new String(datagramPacket.getData(), 0,
                    datagramPacket.getLength());
                System.out.println("Received from server: "+input);

                // send received packet back to the client
                serverDatagramSocket.send(datagramPacket);
            }
        }
        catch(IOException e)
        {
            System.out.println(e);
        }
    }
}
```

When we run the UDP echo server console application, it will look like the following on the screen:

Figure 17-4:
The UDP
echo server

First, in the `main` method, we define a port for the server to be created. In this example, we use port 8000, which is declared as follows:

```
int port = 8000;
```

Next we need to actually create the server, which will work in a similar way to the TCP echo server in that it will continually loop until it receives data, printing the messages it receives and then sending the message back to where it came from. Of course, UDP has no connections, as it is a connectionless protocol; therefore, there are no streams associated with it, so we first need to create a `DatagramSocket` on the specified port, which we can then use later to look for incoming data. Here is how we create the `DatagramSocket`.

```
serverDatagramSocket = new DatagramSocket(port);
```

Notice that all we need to do is pass the port to the constructor of the `DatagramSocket` class. So now we have a datagram socket. At the moment, it is not actually doing anything so we now need to enter an infinite `while` loop, which we can use to wait for incoming data (packets). After we create a buffer to store any incoming data, we declare the infinite `while` loop. We can then create a `DatagramPacket` object, which we can use to store the incoming and outgoing data packets by passing our buffer into the constructor, as well as the length of the buffer (i.e., the array size). This can be seen here:

```
byte buffer[] = new byte[1024];
DatagramPacket datagramPacket = new DatagramPacket(buffer,
    buffer.length);
```

We then call the `receive` method of our `DatagramSocket` object, `serverDatagramSocket`. This method blocks (waits) until a packet is sent to the server and then stores it in the packet, from which we then retrieve the byte data within the packet to create a `String` object (which is our network message). This can be seen here:

```
serverDatagramSocket.receive(datagramPacket);
input = new String(datagramPacket.getData(), 0,
    datagramPacket.getLength());
```

Once we have our received message in the `String` object `input`, we then output the string to the console window, and finally we send the packet back to the sender by passing the packet we received to the `send` method of the `serverDatagramSocket` object. This can be seen here:

```
serverDatagramSocket.send(datagramPacket);
```

The final part of our application is then to simply catch the possible `IOException`, which will not occur when a client application closes, however, as they are never actually connected. This will only occur by other means, such as a network failure where the server is running.

Now that we have created the server code, let's look at the complete source to the UDP echo client:

Code Listing 17-4: UDP echo client

```
import java.net.*;
import java.io.*;

public class UDPEchoClient
{
    public static class UDPEchoReader extends Thread
    {
        public UDPEchoReader(DatagramSocket socket)
        {
            datagramSocket = socket;
            active = true;
        }

        public void run()
        {
            byte[] buffer = new byte[1024];
            DatagramPacket incoming = new DatagramPacket(buffer,
                buffer.length);
            String receivedString;
            while(active)
            {
                try
                {
                    // listen for incoming datagram packet
                    datagramSocket.receive(incoming);

                    // print out received string
                    receivedString = new String(incoming.getData(),
                        0, incoming.getLength());
                    System.out.println("Received from server:
                        "+receivedString);
                }
                catch(IOException e)
                {
                    System.out.println(e);
                    active = false;
                }
            }
        }

        public boolean active;
        public DatagramSocket datagramSocket;
    }

    public static void main(String[] args)
    {
        InetAddress address = null;
        int port = 8000;

        DatagramSocket datagramSocket = null;
        BufferedReader keyboardReader = null;
```

```
        // Create a Datagram Socket...
        try
        {
            address = InetAddress.getByName("127.0.0.1");
            datagramSocket = new DatagramSocket();
            keyboardReader = new BufferedReader(new
                InputStreamReader(System.in));

        }
        catch (IOException e)
        {
            System.out.println(e);
            System.exit(1);
        }


        // Start the listening thread...
        UDPEchoReader reader = new UDPEchoReader(datagramSocket);
        reader.setDaemon(true);
        reader.start();

        System.out.println("Ready to send your messages...");

        try
        {
            String input;
            while (true)
            {
                // read input from the keyboard
                input = keyboardReader.readLine();

                // send datagram packet to the server
                DatagramPacket datagramPacket = new DatagramPacket
                    (input.getBytes(), input.length(), address, port);
                datagramSocket.send(datagramPacket);
            }
        }
        catch(IOException e)
        {
            System.out.println(e);
        }
    }
}
```

When we run the UDP echo client example with the server also running, we can see that each line we enter is sent to the server, which then sends the message back, where it is handled in the reader thread of the client application. The following figure is a screen shot of what we can expect:

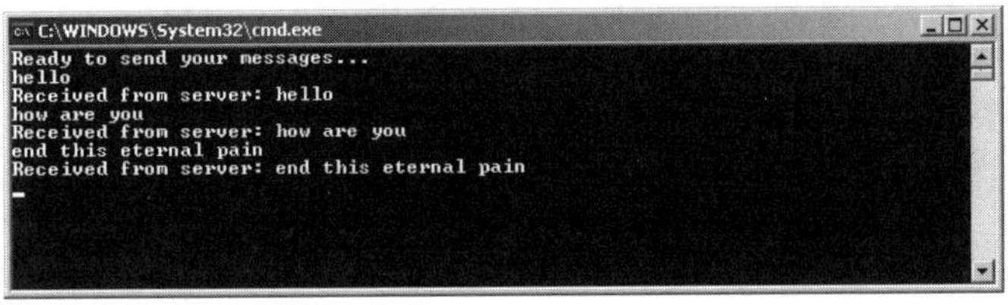

Figure 17-5:
The UDP
echo client

Let's now look at the source code of the client in more detail and see how it works.

To begin with, we start in the `main` method in which we first assign a `port` variable to be 8000 and also set an `address` variable to the IP address 127.0.0.1. Once we have done this, we then create our `DatagramSocket` object `datagramSocket` using the following line of code:

```
datagramSocket = new DatagramSocket();
```

Straight after, we create a `BufferedReader` object called `keyboardReader`, as we did in the TCP echo client to read in the keyboard input.

Next, we need to start a thread to handle incoming data (packets). This is done simply by creating a new thread by creating an instance of a `UDPEchoReader` class (which we will look at in a moment), setting it as a daemon thread, and then calling the `start` method to begin execution of the `run` method. Let's now look at the `UDPEchoReader` class.

In the constructor, we pass in a `DatagramSocket` object, which in this example is the one we created in the `main` method, and we simply assign this to an instance variable called `datagramSocket`. Then we set the flag `active` to `true`, which is the condition for the `while` loop in the `run` method (just like the `TCPEchoReader`).

Next, we declare the `run` method and create a buffer that will be used to store incoming data. This is done with the following line of code:

```
byte[] buffer = new byte[1024];
```

Then, we need to create a `DatagramPacket` (which we have called `incoming`), passing in the buffer and its length (size) to the constructor. This can be seen in the following line of code:

```
DatagramPacket incoming = new DatagramPacket(buffer, buffer.length);
```

After this is done, we then enter a `while` loop (using the `active` flag as a condition) and call the `receive` method of our `datagramSocket` object, which will block (wait) until it receives a packet from a remote source. Note that we need to pass our `incoming DatagramPacket` object into the `receive` method, as when it is received the data will be stored in that object (as well as information regarding where it came from, as we saw with the server). This can be seen in the following code segment:

```
datagramSocket.receive(incoming);
```

Once we have data (a packet) from the server, we need to construct a string from the byte data that is stored within the packet. To do this, we use the `String` class constructor to pass in the data and the length of the data from our packet by calling the `getData` and `getLength` methods. This can be seen in the following line of code:

```
receivedString = new String(incoming.getData(), 0,
    incoming.getLength());
```

Therefore, once we have the data as a string, we then simply output it to the console with the following line of code:

```
System.out.println(receivedString);
```

After this, all we need to do is catch the possible IOException and then end our while loop. This is done with the following block of code:

```
    }
    catch (IOException e)
    {
        System.out.println(e);
        active = false;
    }
}
```

Now that we have seen the run method, let's go back to the main code where we left it (after calling the start method).

We now simply call the readLine method of the keyboardReader object within an infinite while loop.

```
input = keyboardReader.readLine();
```

Then when a line of text is obtained from the keyboard, we just create a new DatagramPacket object called datagramPacket, passing in a byte array of the string data (obtained by calling the getBytes method), the length of the string, the address to send the packet to, and finally the port at that address. This can be seen here:

```
DatagramPacket datagramPacket = new DatagramPacket(input.getBytes(),
    input.length(), address, port);
```

Once we have the packet ready, we then send it using the send method of our datagramSocket object, passing our packet datagramPacket as the parameter. This can be seen in the following line of code:

```
datagramSocket.send(datagramPacket);
```

All we need to do now is end the while loop and catch the possible IOException.

Creating a Network Framework

In this section, we are going to look at how to create a TCP network framework, which will be fully synchronized with the main game loop on the client side and handle multiple clients simultaneously on the server side. The problem with network code is that when you are listening for messages coming in from, say, a server, you call a read method that will block (wait) for a message to come in, so there is no possible way we could have this in our main loop. Hence, we need to create a separate thread to handle the listening of messages. Because the messages are going to be read in on a separate thread, they will not be synchronized with our main game loop (i.e., they could come in at any point, which is the same problem that we had in Chapter 10 with mouse and keyboard events).

So, what is the solution to this? It is exactly the same solution that we had for the mouse and keyboard events—use the event processor that we created earlier to handle the network events. But wait—we don't actually have any network events as such; all we have is an input stream from the socket, which will block until it reads a message on the separate thread.

If you remember back again to the event processor in Chapter 10, it handles a list of `AWTEvent` objects, as `AWTEvent` is the class that all other events, such as `MouseEvents` and `KeyEvents`, are derived. Therefore, what we can do is create our own `NetworkEvent` class, which will extend the `AWTEvent` class, just as the `MouseEvent` class extends the `AWTEvent` class. Then we can use it with the event processor that we created earlier.

Rather than explain all the theory, it's best if we look at a full example of the framework and then at the individual parts that make it all work. So, let's look at the "I'm a circle!" sample network game.

Multiplayer "I'm a circle!" —A Sample Network Game

Before we start, the aim of this example is <u>not</u> to make a cool network game but rather to show you how to create a solid foundation for one. The aim of this example is to have a server that will run in the console window, which clients can connect to and move their position around by clicking where they want to go to with the mouse. In addition, the player's name will be displayed to the right of them (the player will just be represented by a circle).

By the end of this example, you will have a great network framework, which you can easily implement into your own games just as easily as you can now handle input and graphics in your games.

Let's start by looking at the server, as it is the simpler of the two applications that we need (the server and the client). Note we need several source files for both, but we will look at them one at a time (however, all the code will be shown here, just one file at a time). As a reference, the server application consists of the following four .java source files: `SampleServer` (main class), `ClientHandler`, `Player`, and `Protocol`. Let's take a look at the source code.

Creating the Server

Let's start by looking at the complete listing of the `main` class, which we have called `SampleServer`. The complete code listing can be seen here:

Code Listing 17-5: `SampleServer.java`

```java
import java.net.*;
import java.io.*;
import java.util.*;

public class SampleServer implements Runnable
{
    public SampleServer(int port)
    {
        // create the server socket...
```

```
    try
    {
        serverSocket = new ServerSocket(port);
    }
    catch(IOException e)
    {
        System.out.println("-> Could not create Server on port
            "+port);
        System.exit(1);
    }

    System.out.println("-> Server created on port "+port);
}

public void run()
{
    while(true)
    {
        // wait for a client connection...
        try
        {
            System.out.println("-> Waiting for client
                connections...");
            new ClientHandler(serverSocket.accept());
        }
        catch(IOException e)
        {
            System.out.println("-> Error accepting client
                connection: "+e);
        }
    }
}

public static void main(String args[])
{
    // create the server...
    SampleServer server = new SampleServer(9000);
    new Thread(server).start();
}

private ServerSocket serverSocket;
}
```

Starting in the main method, we first create a new instance of our
SampleServer class, passing in 9000, which represents the port on
which we wish to create the server. In the constructor of Sample-
Server, we first attempt to create the server by creating a new
ServerSocket, passing in the port value. The code to do this can be
seen here:

```
try
{
    serverSocket = new ServerSocket(port);
}
catch(IOException e)
{
    System.out.println("-> Could not create Server on port "+port);
    System.exit(1);
}
```

Notice how we catch the IOException in case the server could not be created (a possible cause of this would be a server already running on the specified port). If this occurs, we simply exit the application by calling the System.exit method.

Next we jump back to the main method and create a new thread to run the server on by creating a new Thread object, passing in our sample-Server object that we just created. The run method for the server is then invoked when we create and start the thread.

Execution now goes into the run method, so let's look at this now. This is simple, actually. First, we create an infinite while loop, and then we call the accept method of our serverSocket object that we created in the constructor. Note that this method blocks, so when we call it, it will wait until a client connects to the server; and when this occurs, it will return a Socket object that will contain the two streams associated with the client. The returned Socket object is then passed when constructing a new ClientHandler object. So when we get a client connection, it will create a new ClientHandler object (we will look at this class in a second), passing in the Socket object associated with that client.

Let's now look at the complete source code listing for the Client-Handler class.

Code Listing 17-6: ClientHandler.java

```java
import java.net.*;
import java.io.*;
import java.util.*;
import java.awt.*;

public class ClientHandler implements Protocol
{
    public ClientHandler(Socket socket)
    {
        try
        {
            this.socket = socket;

            DataInputStream in = new DataInputStream
                (socket.getInputStream());
            DataOutputStream out = new DataOutputStream
                (socket.getOutputStream());

            incomingMessageHandler = new IncomingMessageHandler(in);
            outgoingMessageHandler = new OutgoingMessageHandler(out);

            connected = true;

            Random rand = new Random();

            player = new Player(rand.nextInt(640), rand.nextInt(480),
                rand.nextInt(Player.colors.length), uniqueIdCount);
            uniqueIdCount++;


            synchronized(clientList)
            {
```

```java
                        clientList.add(this);
            }

            sendMessage(MSG_INIT_PLAYER+"|"+player.x+"|"+player.y+"|"
                +player.colId+"|"+player.uniqueId);
    }
    catch(IOException e)
    {
        System.out.println("Unable to connect: "+e);
    }
}


public class IncomingMessageHandler implements Runnable
{
    public IncomingMessageHandler(DataInputStream in)
    {
        inStream = in;
        receiver = new Thread(this);
        receiver.start();
    }

    public void run()
    {
        Thread thisThread = Thread.currentThread();
        while(receiver==thisThread)
        {
            try
            {
                String message = inStream.readUTF();
                handleMessage(message);
            }
            catch(IOException e)
            {
                disconnect();
            }
        }
    }

    public void destroy()
    {
        receiver = null;
    }

    Thread receiver;
    private DataInputStream inStream;
}


public class OutgoingMessageHandler implements Runnable
{
    public OutgoingMessageHandler(DataOutputStream out)
    {
        outStream = out;
        messageList = new LinkedList();

        sender = new Thread(this);
        sender.start();
    }
```

```java
    public void addMessage(String message)
    {
        synchronized(messageList)
        {
            messageList.add(message);
            messageList.notify();
        }
    }

    public void run()
    {
        String message;

        Thread thisThread = Thread.currentThread();
        while(sender==thisThread)
        {
            synchronized(messageList)
            {
                if(messageList.isEmpty() && sender!=null)
                {
                    try
                    {
                        messageList.wait();
                    }
                    catch(InterruptedException e) { }
                }
            }

            while(messageList.size()>0)
            {
                synchronized(messageList)
                {
                    message = (String)messageList.removeFirst();
                }

                try
                {
                    outStream.writeUTF(message);
                }
                catch(IOException e)
                {
                    disconnect();
                }
            }
        }
    }

    public void destroy()
    {
        sender = null;

        synchronized(messageList)
        {
            messageList.notify();
            // wake up if stuck in waiting stage
        }
    }

    Thread sender;
    LinkedList messageList;
```

```
    DataOutputStream outStream;
}


public synchronized void disconnect()
{
    if(connected)
    {
        synchronized(clientList)
        {
            clientList.remove(this);
        }

        broadcast(MSG_REMOVE_PLAYER+"|"+player.uniqueId);


        connected = false;

        incomingMessageHandler.destroy();
        outgoingMessageHandler.destroy();

        try
        {
            socket.close();
        }
        catch(Exception e) {}
        socket = null;
    }

    System.out.println("-> Client Disconnected");
}


public static void broadcast(String message)
{
    synchronized(clientList)
    {
        ClientHandler client;
        for(int i=0; i<clientList.size(); i++)
        {
            client = (ClientHandler)clientList.get(i);
            client.sendMessage(message);
        }
    }
}


public void broadcastFromClient(String message)
{
    synchronized(clientList)
    {
        ClientHandler client;

        for(int i=0; i<clientList.size(); i++)
        {
            client = (ClientHandler)clientList.get(i);
            if(client!=this)
                client.sendMessage(message);
        }
    }
```

```
        }

    public void sendMessage(String message)
    {
        outgoingMessageHandler.addMessage(message);
    }


    public void handleMessage(String message)
    {
        StringTokenizer st = new StringTokenizer(message, "|");
        int type = Integer.parseInt(st.nextToken());

        switch(type)
        {
            case MSG_SET_NAME:
            {
                player.name = st.nextToken();
                sendMessage(MSG_SET_NAME+"|"+player.name);
                broadcastFromClient(MSG_ADD_NEW_PLAYER+"|"+player.x+
                    "|"+player.y+"|"+player.colId+"|"+player.uniqueId
                    +"|"+player.name);

                Player p;
                // tell this player about everyone else

                synchronized(clientList)
                {
                    for(int i=0; i<clientList.size(); i++)
                    {
                        p = ((ClientHandler)clientList.get(i))
                            .player;
                        if(player != p)
                        {
                            sendMessage(MSG_ADD_NEW_PLAYER+"|"+p.x
                                +"|"+p.y+"|"+p.colId+"|"+p.uniqueId+
                                "|"+p.name);
                        }
                    }
                }
                break;
            }

            case MSG_MOVE_POSITION:
            {
                player.x = Integer.parseInt(st.nextToken());
                player.y = Integer.parseInt(st.nextToken());

                broadcast(MSG_MOVE_POSITION+"|"+player.uniqueId+"|"
                    +player.x+"|"+player.y);
                break;
            }
        }
    }

    private Socket socket;

    private IncomingMessageHandler incomingMessageHandler;
    private OutgoingMessageHandler outgoingMessageHandler;
```

```
    public boolean connected;

    public static ArrayList clientList = new ArrayList();

    public Player player;
    public static int uniqueIdCount;
}
```

Yes, it is slightly larger but nothing to fear. We'll start by looking at the constructor, which, as you noted a minute ago, is called from the `SampleServer`'s `run` method when a client connects.

First, we store a copy of the `socket` reference, which was passed into the constructor as an instance member of the `ClientHandler` class. This can be seen here:

```
this.socket = socket;
```

Next, we obtain the input and output streams from the `Socket` object by calling the `getInputStream()` and `getOutputStream()` methods and passing them into the constructors of `DataInputStream` and `DataOutputStream` objects, respectively. This can be seen here:

```
DataInputStream in = new DataInputStream(socket.getInputStream());
DataOutputStream out = new DataOutputStream(socket
    .getOutputStream());
```

Next we create `IncomingMessageHandler` and `Outgoing-MessageHandler` objects by passing in the input and output streams, resectively. We will look at these inner classes and their purpose in a moment. Once these are created, we then set a Boolean variable called `connected` to `true`, which simply notes that this client is now connected to the server.

Next we have some specific code for this circle example, which creates a new `Player` object when a client connects and assigns it some random values (such as the screen position and color). In addition, it assigns the client (player) a unique ID value, which can be used to reference the player at a later time. Here is the code we use in the constructor to create the `Player` object.

```
Random rand = new Random();

player = new Player(rand.nextInt(640), rand.nextInt(480),
    rand.nextInt(Player.colors.length), uniqueIdCount);
uniqueIdCount++;
```

The `player` class is a simple data structure for storing data to make each player individual from any other. Each instance of `ClientHandler` will have its own `Player` object, as each `ClientHandler` instance is a client itself. Here is the source code for the `player` class:

Code Listing 17-7: `Player.java`

```
import java.awt.*;

public class Player
{
```

Chapter 17

```
public Player(int x, int y, int colId, int uniqueId)
{
    this.x = x;
    this.y = y;
    this.colId = colId;
    this.uniqueId = uniqueId;
}

public int x, y;
public String name;
public int colId;
public int uniqueId;

public static final Color[] colors = {Color.red, Color.green,
    Color.blue, Color.yellow, Color.magenta};
}
```

Note that we will be reusing this `player` class when we come to creating the client. Once the `Player` object is created in the `ClientHandler` constructor, we then add this new client (`ClientHandler` object) to a `clientList`, which is simply a static `ArrayList` object containing a list of all the `ClientHandler` objects created, hence all of the clients connected to the server. This can be seen here:

```
synchronized(clientList)
{
    clientList.add(this);
}
```

Note how we have synchronized adding to the `clientList` object. This is because we may be performing other operations, such as looping through it or removing other clients, as we do later in the code. So we want to keep all these operations synchronized to avoid any problems. We will see later why we are storing all the clients in a list.

The final part of the constructor is where we send a message to the client, which tells them information that the server has initialized for them (i.e., the x, y position, its color, and the player's unique ID). This is done by means of the `sendMessage` method, which we will look at in a moment. Note how we have used MSG_INIT_PLAYER as the type of message that we are sending. This is simply a static final int value that we have defined in a `Protocol` interface, which this class (`Client-Handler`) implements. Let's look at the `Protocol` interface in full now.

Code Listing 17-8: `Protocol.java`

```
public interface Protocol
{
    public static final int MSG_MOVE_POSITION = 0;
    public static final int MSG_SET_NAME = 1;
    public static final int MSG_INIT_PLAYER = 2;
    public static final int MSG_ADD_NEW_PLAYER = 3;
    public static final int MSG_REMOVE_PLAYER = 4;
}
```

We will see all of these messages getting used as we progress. Also, note how we are sending the data in the message. We are going to be sending strings across the network; however, we are separating the data within the string with the | character. Note that we are sending string values for simplicity purposes. As we will see, when we retrieve a message, we can use a `StringTokenizer` to first get the type of message (the first token converted to an integer value) and then use this to know which tokens the rest of the message contains.

The message that we are going to be sending to the client can be seen here:

```
sendMessage(MSG_INIT_PLAYER+"|"+player.x+"|"+player.y+"|"
    +player.colId+"|"+player.uniqueId);
```

The first token is the message type (which is `MSG_INIT_PLAYER`), and then we send the x position, followed by the y position, the color ID, and finally the unique ID of the player.

Let's have a look at how we are sending these messages. If you remember in the constructor, we created an `outgoingMessage-Handler`, which we will use now to send our messages. In the `sendMessage` method, all we actually do is add the message to the `outgoingMessageHandler`. This can be seen here:

```
public void sendMessage(String message)
{
    outgoingMessageHandler.addMessage(message);
}
```

Now let's look at the constructor of the `OutgoingMessageHandler`, which we called in the constructor of our `ClientHandler` class, passing in the socket's output stream. Here is the complete constructor for the `OutgoingMessageHandler` (note that the `OutgoingMessage-Handler` is a nested class of our `ClientHandler`).

```
public OutgoingMessageHandler(DataOutputStream out)
{
    outStream = out;
    messageList = new LinkedList();

    sender = new Thread(this);
    sender.start();
}
```

All we do here is store a reference to the output stream passed in called `out` in an instance member called `outStream`. Then we create a `LinkedList` called `messageList`, which will store a list of messages that are waiting to be sent. We then create a thread that will be used to actually send the messages and start it.

Next in this class we have defined a method called `addMessage` (which if you remember, we called from the `sendMessage` method in our `ClientHandler`). Here is the complete code for this `addMessage` method:

```
public void addMessage(String message)
{
    synchronized(messageList)
    {
        messageList.add(message);
```

```
        messageList.notify();
    }
}
```

As you can see, this method takes in the message to be sent as a parameter and then adds the message to the `messageList` (which contains a list of outgoing messages waiting to be sent). Then we call the `notify` method, which will wake up the sender thread that we created in the constructor, which goes to sleep when there are no messages to be sent. We synchronize on the `messageList` object here, as we also synchronize on this object when removing messages from the list in the sender thread and when going to sleep in the sender thread.

The next method we have is the actual `run` method, which first goes into a loop and then executes the following block of code:

```
synchronized(messageList)
{
    if(messageList.isEmpty() && sender!=null)
    {
        try
        {
            messageList.wait();
        }
        catch(InterruptedException e) { }
    }
}
```

This code first synchronizes on the `messageList` (so no messages can be added when the execution enters this block of code); if you notice before the actual adding of messages, we also synchronized on the `messageList`. So once we enter this synchronized block, we then check to see if the `messageList` is empty (i.e., there are no messages waiting to be sent) and the thread is still running (i.e., `sender != null`). The `sender!=null` is for disconnection purposes, as `destroy`, which we will see later, defines some code to support exiting from this thread safely in this scenario. If there are no messages to be sent, we can put the thread to sleep by calling the `wait` method, which will also release the monitor on the `messageList` object so messages can be added again. If you remember from before, when a message is added, it calls the `notify` method of the `messageList`, so the thread will be signaled to wake up again from the wait call.

When the thread wakes up, it will then send all the messages that are waiting to be sent. So we create a `while` loop, which ensures there is at least one message to be sent—this can be seen here:

```
while(messageList.size()>0)
{
```

Then we remove the first message from the `messageList` (as new messages are added to the end so this gives us a first in, first out queue). This can be seen here.

```
synchronized(messageList)
{
    message = (String)messageList.removeFirst();
```

```
}
```

Notice also that we have synchronized on the `messageList` object again here, as we do not want any other operation occurring that requires exclusive access while we are removing and obtaining the message from it, hence adding to it.

We then have the message to be sent in a `String` object called `message`. Once we have this, we can then send the message by calling the `writeUTF` method of the `DataOutputStream`, passing in the `String` object to be sent. This can be seen here:

```
try
{
    outStream.writeUTF(message);
}
catch(IOException e)
{
    disconnect();
}
```

Notice here how we also call the `disconnect` method of the `Client-Handler` class if an `IOException` occurred when trying to write to this output stream, as this would signify that a connection to the client no longer existed. We will look at the `disconnect` method soon. However, for now let's look at the final method declared in the `OutgoingMessage-Handler` class, the `destroy` method:

```
public void destroy()
{
    sender = null;

    synchronized(messageList)
    {
        messageList.notify(); // wake up if stuck in waiting stage
    }
}
```

The purpose of this method is to simply stop the thread from running (by setting `sender` to `null`) and wake up the thread if it is sleeping. This method is called from the `disconnect` method in the `ClientHandler` class, which we will look at shortly. Note the order of actions means that we will still terminate the thread's execution if the `run` method is currently executing at the point just before entering the synchronized block where it will go to sleep, as we saw before. With this code, the `run` method is guaranteed to exit, as the sender reference is set to `null`, and then the thread is woken up if it is asleep. In the `run` method, you'll see that it won't go to sleep if `sender` equals `null`. This is all so that we don't notify just before going to sleep at the start of the loop in the `run` method, where we could have gone to sleep after calling `notify`.

As well as the `sendMessage` method, we have also created two other useful methods in the `ClientHandler` class for sending messages; these are `broadcast` and `broadcastFromClient`. The `broadcast` method simply loops through the `clientList` (remember that we add each client which connects to this list), calling the `sendMessage` method

Chapter 17

of each of the clients, so a message is sent to everyone connected to the server. The `broadcast` method can be seen here:

```
public static void broadcast(String message)
{
    synchronized(clientList)
    {
        ClientHandler client;
        for(int i=0; i<clientList.size(); i++)
        {
            client = (ClientHandler)clientList.get(i);
            client.sendMessage(message);
        }
    }
}
```

Notice here that we synchronize on the `clientList` object, so no clients can be added or removed while we are adding our messages to their respective `OutgoingMessageHandler` objects. In case you weren't aware of this fact, each client has its own `OutgoingMessageHandler` and `IncomingMessageHandler`.

The other method, `broadcastFromClient`, is pretty much the same, but it sends to all the clients except the client that the method is being called from. This can be seen here:

```
public void broadcastFromClient(String message)
{
    synchronized(clientList)
    {
        ClientHandler client;
        for(int i=0; i<clientList.size(); i++)
        {
            client = (ClientHandler)clientList.get(i);
            if(client!=this)
                client.sendMessage(message);
        }
    }
}
```

The only difference in this method is that we have the extra `if` check to ensure that the client in the list that we are about to send to does not equal `this` client object. This is useful when we don't need to tell the client who sent the data about an update, as it already knows about this data because it sent it.

Now that we have looked at the sending of messages, let's look at how the `IncomingMessageHandler` class works. This class is actually a lot simpler than the `OutgoingMessageHandler`, as we will see now. Let's first look at the constructor, which is called in the constructor of the `ClientHandler` class, where we pass in a `DataInputStream` object, which was created from the input stream of the socket. All we do in the constructor of the `IncomingMessageHandler` is copy the reference of the input stream passed in as `in` to an instance member called `inStream`. Then we create a thread called `receiver` and start it.

```
public IncomingMessageHandler(DataInputStream in)
{
```

```
        inStream = in;
        receiver = new Thread(this);
        receiver.start();
    }
```

Let's look at the `run` method of this class now. All we do here is start a loop as we normally do and then call the `readUTF` method of the `inStream`, which is the input stream connected to the socket that was passed into the constructor. The `readUTF` method blocks until there is a string ready to be read from the stream; then it reads it in and returns it. We then assign the input `String` object to the `message` reference. Then we pass this message to a method defined in the `ClientHandler` class called `handleMessage`, which we will look at in a moment. Finally, we catch a possible `IOException`, which could occur if the connection is broken either by a client closing or a hardware failure (i.e., someone pulling out a network cable). If this does occur, as with the `Outgoing-MessageHandler`, we simply call the `disconnect` method of the `ClientHandler` class (which again we will look at soon). The complete `run` method can be seen here:

```
public void run()
{
    Thread thisThread = Thread.currentThread();
    while(receiver==thisThread)
    {
        try
        {
            String message = inStream.readUTF();
            handleMessage(message);
        }
        catch(IOException e)
        {
            disconnect();
        }
    }
}
```

Finally, in our `IncomingMessageHandler`, we have a `destroy` method, which simply stops the `receiver` thread from running by setting the `receiver` reference to `null`. We will see this being used in the `disconnect` method. Here is the short but sweet `destroy` method:

```
public void destroy()
{
    receiver = null;
}
```

So when a message is received in the `incomingMessageHandler` thread, it is then passed to the `handleMessage` method of the `ClientHandler` class, which we are going to use to actually determine what the message is and react to it accordingly. So, in the `handle-Message` method, we first determine the type of message that has been received by using the following two lines of code:

```
StringTokenizer st = new StringTokenizer(message, "|");
int type = Integer.parseInt(st.nextToken());
```

The first line creates a `StringTokenizer` object using the message as the string to tokenize and the character | to denote the different tokens. Then we get the first token from the message, which is always going to be the type of message (as defined in the `Protocol` interface that we created earlier in this section). So we can then switch the message type and create a case for each different type of message that a client could receive.

The first message that we are going to make the server handle is when the player sets his or her name. We first need to create a case for this, as follows:

```
switch(type)
{
    case MSG_SET_NAME:
    {
```

Then we obtain the player's name from the next token, which can be seen here:

```
player.name = st.nextToken();
```

Then we send a message back to the player to confirm that the name has been set using the following line of code, which will then update the player's name data in the client:

```
sendMessage(MSG_SET_NAME+"|"+player.name);
```

This may not make much sense now, but it should all come together when you read about how the client works.

We then broadcast the addition of a new player and all his details to everyone (except the current client that the player belongs to), so all the other connected clients can add this player to their programs, as we shall see later in the client. The line of code to do this can be seen here:

```
broadcastFromClient(MSG_ADD_NEW_PLAYER+"|"+player.x+"|"+player.y+"|"
    +player.colId+"|"+player.uniqueId+"|"+player.name);
```

Finally, for this message, we need to send this client a list of all the players that are currently connected to the server, To do this, we need to cycle through our `clientList` and send each of the clients' player details to this client (without sending this player's details to him/herself). This is done with the following block of code:

```
Player p;
// tell this player about everyone else

synchronized(clientList)
{
    for(int i=0; i<clientList.size(); i++)
    {
        p = ((ClientHandler)clientList.get(i)).player;
        if(player != p)
        {
        sendMessage(MSG_ADD_NEW_PLAYER+"|"+p.x+"|"+p.y+"|"
            +p.colId+"|"+p.uniqueId+"|"+p.name);
        }
    }
}
```

All this does is loop through the `clientList`, obtain each of the player's details, and checks that the player p that was obtained is not this client's player `player`. If it isn't, send a `MSG_ADD_NEW_PLAYER` message with all the player details.

So the `MSG_SET_NAME` message is dealt with. Let's now have a look at the other message that the server needs to handle, which is the `MSG_MOVE_POSITION` message that is sent by a client whenever the mouse is clicked within the bounds of the application window, It signifies that the player wants to move the circle to the location that was clicked on.

So again, we need to create a case for this message as follows:

```
case MSG_MOVE_POSITION:
{
```

Once we get the message that a player has moved, we can simply retrieve the x, y position from the message using the next two lines of code:

```
player.x = Integer.parseInt(st.nextToken());
player.y = Integer.parseInt(st.nextToken());
```

Then we just need to broadcast this new position along with the unique ID of the player, so the clients can determine which player has moved. This can be seen in the following line of code. Notice that we also send the updated position to the client that is doing the moving. Most functionality should always be controlled through the server, as inevitably the server is the only one that can be trusted.

```
broadcast(MSG_MOVE_POSITION+"|"+player.uniqueId+"|"+player.x+
    "|"+player.y);
```

That's all the message handling, so now let's take a final look at the `disconnect` method, which we have mentioned a couple of times previously. This method is used to clean up a client that has been disconnected for some reason or another. A client disconnecting can occur from possible `IOException` exceptions being thrown from either the `IncomingMessageHandler` thread or the `OutgoingMessageHandler` thread. With this in mind, we must handle calling the `disconnect` method from both and handle terminating both threads from here on. Note also that the `disconnect` method is synchronized so that it cannot be invoked by the outgoing message and incoming message threads at the same time.

We first check that the client is connected by checking our Boolean flag `connected`, using the following line of code:

```
if(connected)
```

This is so that if one of the outgoing or incoming message threads has handled disconnecting, the other doesn't need to if it tries.

If it is currently connected, remove the client from the `clientList` and then broadcast a message to all the other players informing them that this player has been disconnected. In the client, the player will be removed from the player lists, as we shall see later. (Note that we send the player's unique ID here also, so the client applications can determine which player has left the game.) The code to do this can be seen here:

```
synchronized(clientList)
{
    clientList.remove(this);
}

broadcast(MSG_REMOVE_PLAYER+"|"+player.uniqueId);
```

Again, also note the synchronization with the `clientList`, as we are removing a client from it, which should be mutually exclusive to any other operations on the `clientList ArrayList`.

Next, we set the `connected` flag to `false`, which can be seen here:

```
connected = false;
```

Then we call the `destroy` method of both the `incomingMessage-Handler` and the `outgoingMessageHandler` objects, so both their threads stop. This can be seen here.

```
incomingMessageHandler.destroy();
outgoingMessageHandler.destroy();
```

Then finally we attempt to `close` the socket and set its reference to `null`. That's our complete server. If you now run the code, you should see the following in a console window, which is stunning (we're sure you'll agree):

Figure 17-6: The game server console application

Creating the Client

Now that we have our server ready, let's look at how we can make the client, which we can connect multiple instances of to the server. For this example, we are using the `ActiveRendering` example code from Chapter 9 as a base. You will also need the `EventProcessor` and `EventProcessable` source files from the end of Chapter 10 and the `Protocol.java` and `Player.java` source files we created for the server as we will be reusing them for the client. The remaining four source code files for this example are `SampleClient` (main class), `NetworkHandler`, `NetworkListener`, and `NetworkEvent`. The client application consists of eight source files in total.

Before we actually look at the main parts of the code, there are two foundation classes that we need to see first, which will be used in the core of our client network framework. These classes are the `Network-Listener` and the `NetworkEvent`. If you remember from our brief discussion before, we are going to deal with network events in the same manner as mouse and keyboard events, so we can easily synchronize them with the main loop and process them in order with other events received. To do this, we are going to need to actually create our own

`NetworkEvent` class that extends the `AWTEvent` class, so let's have a look at our definition for the `NetworkEvent` class.

Code Listing 17-9: `NetworkEvent.java`

```java
import java.awt.*;

public class NetworkEvent extends AWTEvent
{
    public NetworkEvent(Object source, int id, String message)
    {
        super(source, id);
        this.message = message;
    }

    public String message;

    public static final int NETWORK_MESSAGE_RECEIVED = 2000;
    public static final int NETWORK_DISCONNECTED = 2001;
}
```

There's nothing really complicated here; we simply extend the `AWTEvent` class and take in the standard source `Object` and `id`, which the `AWTEvent` constructor requires (when we call the super class constructor), and also the network message (which is simply a `String` object). In the constructor, we then call the `super` constructor (i.e., the constructor of the `AWTEvent` class) and we store the reference to the message within an instance member called `message`. Note also that we have two types of events defined in the class called `NETWORK_MESSAGE_RECEIVED` and `NETWORK_DISCONNECTED`, in the same way that we can have `MOUSE_PRESSED` and `MOUSE_RELEASED` events, etc. We can use these static members later for comparison to the event's ID, similarly to how we do with other events when handling the events in the main loop. Note that the reason that we have assigned the event values as 2000 and 2001 is so that they do not conflict with any of the other `AWTEvent` IDs, such as the `MouseEvent` IDs like `MOUSE_PRESSED`, etc.

So that's all there is to our `NetworkEvent`. Let's also have a quick look at the `NetworkListener` interface that we require. Here is the complete listing for it:

Code Listing 17-10: `NetworkListener.java`

```java
public interface NetworkListener
{
    public void networkMessageReceived(NetworkEvent e);
    public void networkDisconnected(NetworkEvent e);
}
```

This is easy really; all we have done here is create two methods that can be overridden to handle the two different types of events in the same way that a `MouseListener` has methods such as `mouseClicked` and `mousePressed`.

Let's now move on by looking at the `NetworkHandler` class. Note that this is quite similar to the `ClientHandler` class that we used for the server. Let's look at the complete code listing now.

Code Listing 17-11: NetworkHandler.java

```java
import java.net.*;
import java.io.*;
import java.util.*;
import java.awt.*;


public class NetworkHandler
{
    public NetworkHandler(String address, int port, NetworkListener
        listener)
    {
        try
        {
            socket = new Socket(address, port);

            this.listener = listener;

            DataInputStream in = new DataInputStream
                (socket.getInputStream());
            DataOutputStream out = new DataOutputStream
                (socket.getOutputStream());

            incomingMessageHandler = new IncomingMessageHandler(in);
            outgoingMessageHandler = new OutgoingMessageHandler(out);

            connected = true;
        }
        catch(IOException e)
        {
            System.out.println("Unable to connect: "+e);
            listener.networkDisconnected(new NetworkEvent
                (this, NetworkEvent.NETWORK_DISCONNECTED, null));
        }
    }


    public class IncomingMessageHandler implements Runnable
    {
        public IncomingMessageHandler(DataInputStream in)
        {
            inStream = in;
            receiver = new Thread(this);
            receiver.start();
        }

        public void run()
        {
            Thread thisThread = Thread.currentThread();
            while(receiver==thisThread)
            {
                try
                {
                    String message = inStream.readUTF();
                    listener.networkMessageReceived(new NetworkEvent
                        (this, NetworkEvent.NETWORK_MESSAGE_RECEIVED,
                        message));
                }
                catch(IOException e)
```

```
                {
                    disconnect();
                }
        }
    }

    public void destroy()
    {
        receiver = null;
    }

    Thread receiver;
    private DataInputStream inStream;
}


public class OutgoingMessageHandler implements Runnable
{
    public OutgoingMessageHandler(DataOutputStream out)
    {
        outStream = out;
        messageList = new LinkedList();

        sender = new Thread(this);
        sender.start();
    }

    public void addMessage(String message)
    {
        synchronized(messageList)
        {
            messageList.add(message);
            messageList.notify();
        }
    }

    public void run()
    {
        String message;

        Thread thisThread = Thread.currentThread();
        while(sender==thisThread)
        {
            synchronized(messageList)
            {
                if(messageList.isEmpty() && sender!=null)
                {
                    try
                    {
                        messageList.wait();
                    }
                    catch(InterruptedException e) { }
                }
            }

            while(messageList.size()>0)
            {
                synchronized(messageList)
                {
                    message = (String)messageList.removeFirst();
```

```
                    }
                try
                {
                    outStream.writeUTF(message);
                }
                catch(IOException e)
                {
                    disconnect();
                }
            }
        }
    }

    public void destroy()
    {
        sender = null;

        synchronized(messageList)
        {
            messageList.notify();
            // wake up if stuck in waiting stage
        }
    }

    Thread sender;
    LinkedList messageList;
    DataOutputStream outStream;
}


public synchronized void disconnect()
{
    if(connected)
    {
        connected = false;
        incomingMessageHandler.destroy();
        outgoingMessageHandler.destroy();

        try
        {
            socket.close();
        }
        catch(Exception e) {}
        socket = null;

        listener.networkDisconnected(new NetworkEvent(this,
            NetworkEvent.NETWORK_DISCONNECTED, null));
    }
}


public void sendMessage(String message)
{
    outgoingMessageHandler.addMessage(message);
}


private Socket socket;
```

```
    private IncomingMessageHandler incomingMessageHandler;
    private OutgoingMessageHandler outgoingMessageHandler;

    private NetworkListener listener;
    public boolean connected;
}
```

Let's look at the differences between this and the `ClientHandler` class that we made for the server. First, for the parameters in the constructor, we will take in a string that represents either the IP address or machine name to which we wish to connect, followed by the port that the server will be running on and a reference to an object that implements the `NetworkListener` interface.

In the constructor, we first attempt to create a `Socket` object by passing in the address and port into the `socket` class constructor. This will establish a connection to the server and can be seen in the following line of code:

```
socket = new Socket(address, port);
```

Next we store a reference to the object that implements the `Network-Listener` interface in an instance member called `listener`, which can be seen here:

```
this.listener = listener;
```

The rest of the constructor is then the same as the server (i.e., creating the incoming and outgoing message handlers). However, note that if we get an `IOException` in the constructor (i.e., the client could not connect to the server), we create a new `NetworkEvent` object and then pass it as a parameter to the `networkDisconnected` method of the listener. This can be seen here:

```
listener.networkDisconnected(new NetworkEvent(this,
    NetworkEvent.NETWORK_DISCONNECTED, null));
```

Another difference between this and the `ClientHandler` of the server is that we don't have `broadcast` and `broadcastFromClient` methods, as messages can only be sent to the server. In addition, instead of having a `handleMessage` method and calling it in the `Incoming-MessageHandler` class, we instead create a new `NetworkEvent` object each time we receive a message and then call the `network-MessageReceived` method of the `Listener` object, passing in the new `NetworkEvent` object with the message in it. This can be seen here:

```
listener.networkMessageReceived(new NetworkEvent(this,
    NetworkEvent.NETWORK_MESSAGE_RECEIVED, message));
```

The final change is that at the end of the `disconnect` method, we call the listener's `networkDisconnected` method, passing a network disconnected event to it. This can be seen here:

```
listener.networkDisconnected(new NetworkEvent(this,
    NetworkEvent.NETWORK_DISCONNECTED, null));
```

Chapter 17

Now let's look at how we implement all of this in the actual application. Here is the complete code listing for the `SampleClient` class, which contains our `main` method.

Code Listing 17-12: `SampleClient.java`

```
import java.awt.*;
import java.awt.image.*;
import javax.swing.*;
import java.awt.event.*;
import java.util.*;

public class SampleClient extends JFrame implements Runnable,
                             EventProcessable,
                             NetworkListener,
                             MouseListener,
                             Protocol
{
    public SampleClient()
    {
        setTitle("Sample Network Client - "+playerName);
        getContentPane().setLayout(null);
        setResizable(false);
        setIgnoreRepaint(true);

        addWindowListener(new WindowAdapter() {
                        public void windowClosing(WindowEvent e) {
                        exitProgram();
                        }
                        });

        backBuffer = new BufferedImage(DISPLAY_WIDTH, DISPLAY_HEIGHT,
            BufferedImage.TYPE_INT_RGB);
        bbGraphics = (Graphics2D) backBuffer.getGraphics();

        playerList = new ArrayList();

        eventProcessor = new EventProcessor(this);
        getContentPane().addMouseListener(this);

        networkHandler = new NetworkHandler("127.0.0.1", 9000, this);

        setVisible(true);

        Insets insets = getInsets();
        DISPLAY_X = insets.left;
        DISPLAY_Y = insets.top;
        resizeToInternalSize(DISPLAY_WIDTH, DISPLAY_HEIGHT);
    }


    public void resizeToInternalSize(int internalWidth, int
        internalHeight)
    {
        Insets insets = getInsets();
        final int newWidth = internalWidth + insets.left
            + insets.right;
        final int newHeight = internalHeight + insets.top
            + insets.bottom;
```

```
    Runnable resize = new Runnable()
    {
        public void run()
        {
            setSize(newWidth, newHeight);
        }
    };

    if(!SwingUtilities.isEventDispatchThread())
    {
        try
        {
            SwingUtilities.invokeAndWait(resize);
        }
        catch(Exception e) {}
    }
    else
        resize.run();

    validate();
}

public void run()
{
    long startTime, waitTime, elapsedTime;
    //    1000/25 Frames Per Second = 40 millisecond delay
    int delayTime = 1000/25;

    Thread thisThread = Thread.currentThread();
    while(loop==thisThread)
    {
        startTime = System.currentTimeMillis();

        // process received events
        eventProcessor.processEventList();

        // render to back buffer now
        render(bbGraphics);

        // render back buffer image to screen
        Graphics g = getGraphics();
        g.drawImage(backBuffer, DISPLAY_X, DISPLAY_Y, null);
        g.dispose();


        //  handle frame rate
        elapsedTime = System.currentTimeMillis() - startTime;
        waitTime = Math.max(delayTime - elapsedTime, 5);

        try
        {
            Thread.sleep(waitTime);
        }
        catch(InterruptedException e) {}
    }

    System.out.println("Program Exited");

    dispose();
    System.exit(0);
```

```
    }

public void render(Graphics g)
{
    g.clearRect(0, 0, DISPLAY_WIDTH, DISPLAY_HEIGHT);

    // render all players...

    Player p;

    for(int i=0; i<playerList.size(); i++)
    {
        p = (Player)playerList.get(i);
        g.setColor(Player.colors[p.colId]);
        g.fillOval(p.x-10, p.y-10, 20, 20);
        g.drawString(p.name, p.x+20, p.y);
    }
}


public void handleEvent(AWTEvent e)
{
    switch(e.getID())
    {
        case MouseEvent.MOUSE_PRESSED:
        {
            System.out.println("Mouse Pressed Event");
            MouseEvent mouseEvent = (MouseEvent)e;
            networkHandler.sendMessage(MSG_MOVE_POSITION+"|"+
                mouseEvent.getX()+"|"+mouseEvent.getY());
            break;
        }

        case NetworkEvent.NETWORK_MESSAGE_RECEIVED:

            System.out.println("Network Message Received:"
                + ((NetworkEvent)e).message);
            handleNetworkMessage(((NetworkEvent)e).message);
            break;

        case NetworkEvent.NETWORK_DISCONNECTED:
        {
            System.out.println("Network Disconnected");
            exitProgram();
            break;
        }
    }
}

public void handleNetworkMessage(String message)
{
    StringTokenizer st = new StringTokenizer(message, "|");
    int type = Integer.parseInt(st.nextToken());

    switch(type)
    {
        case MSG_INIT_PLAYER:
            player = new Player(Integer.parseInt(st.nextToken()),
                                Integer.parseInt(st.nextToken()),
                                Integer.parseInt(st.nextToken()),
```

```
                          Integer.parseInt(st.nextToken())));

    networkHandler.sendMessage(MSG_SET_NAME+"|"+playerName);
        break;

    case MSG_SET_NAME:
            player.name = st.nextToken();
            playerList.add(player);
            break;

    case MSG_ADD_NEW_PLAYER:
    {
        Player p = new Player(Integer.parseInt
            (st.nextToken()),
                    Integer.parseInt(st.nextToken()),
                    Integer.parseInt(st.nextToken()),
                    Integer.parseInt(st.nextToken())));

    p.name = st.nextToken();
    playerList.add(p);
    break;
    }

    case MSG_MOVE_POSITION:
    {
        Player p;
        int id = Integer.parseInt(st.nextToken());
        for(int i=0; i<playerList.size(); i++)
        {
            p = (Player)playerList.get(i);
            if(p.uniqueId==id)
            {
                p.x = Integer.parseInt(st.nextToken());
                p.y = Integer.parseInt(st.nextToken());
                break;
            }
        }

        break;
    }

    case MSG_REMOVE_PLAYER:
    {
        Player p;
        int id = Integer.parseInt(st.nextToken());
        for(int i=0; i<playerList.size(); i++)
        {
            p = (Player)playerList.get(i);
            if(p.uniqueId==id)
            {
                playerList.remove(i);
                break;
            }
        }
    }
    }
}

public void networkMessageReceived(NetworkEvent e)
{
```

```
        eventProcessor.addEvent(e);
    }


    public void networkDisconnected(NetworkEvent e)
    {
        eventProcessor.addEvent(e);
    }


    public void mousePressed(MouseEvent e)
    {
        eventProcessor.addEvent(e);
    }

    public void mouseReleased(MouseEvent e) {}
    public void mouseClicked(MouseEvent e)  {}
    public void mouseEntered(MouseEvent e)  {}
    public void mouseExited(MouseEvent e)   {}


    public void exitProgram()
    {
        loop = null;
    }

    public static void main(String args[])
    {
        // get the players name...
        playerName = JOptionPane.showInputDialog(null,
            "Please enter your name:");

        // start 'I'm a Circle'!
        SampleClient app = new SampleClient();

        app.loop = new Thread(app);
        app.loop.start();
    }

    private EventProcessor eventProcessor;
    private NetworkHandler networkHandler;

    private Thread loop;
    private BufferedImage backBuffer;
    private Graphics2D bbGraphics;

    private final int DISPLAY_X; // value assigned in constructor
    private final int DISPLAY_Y; // value assigned in constructor
    private static final int DISPLAY_WIDTH = 640;
    private static final int DISPLAY_HEIGHT = 480;

    public Player player;
    public ArrayList playerList;
    public static String playerName;
}
```

So let's look at what we have added to the `ActiveRendering` example
to make it into the absolute best seller "I'm a circle game" (although
"game" might not be the right word here).

First, in the `main` method, we pop up an input dialog to get the player's name, using the static method `showInputDialog` in the `JOption-Pane` class. This can be seen here:

```
// get the players name...
playerName = JOptionPane.showInputDialog(null,
    "Please enter your name:");
```

As you can see, we store the result of this in a static string variable called `playerName`. After we have the player's name, we create our application in the usual manner. Let's look now at what we have added into the constructor.

First, we have initialized an `ArrayList` called `playerList`, which will hold a list of `Player` objects (i.e., all the players that are connected, as well as the client's own player).

Next, we create an `eventProcessor` object using the `EventPro-cessor` class that we created back in Chapter 10, and we add a `MouseListener` to the content pane of our `JFrame`. This can be seen in the following two lines of code:

```
eventProcessor = new EventProcessor(this);
getContentPane().addMouseListener(this);
```

Then we create a new `NetworkHandler` object called `network-Handler`, passing in the IP address and port of the server that we wish to connect to, as well as a reference to our `SampleClient` object that we created, as it implements the `NetworkListener` interface. This can be seen here:

```
networkHandler = new NetworkHandler("127.0.0.1", 9000, this);
```

The `NetworkListener` that we have created works in a similar way to the key and mouse listener methods, notifying our network listener methods when network events occur, as we shall see.

At this point, we should be connected to the server. The client will then proceed into the main game loop, calling the `eventProcessor.pro-cessEventList()` and `render()` methods every loop.

What happens now then? Well, if you remember back to when we created the server, when a client connects, the server sends a `MSG_INIT_PLAYER` message to the client. So the client should look out for the arrival of this message. If you remember back to the `Network-Handler` class, when this message arrives, it will call the `network-MessageReceived` method of the `Listener` object that was passed into the `NetworkHandler` class, which in this example is our main class `SampleClient`; so we need to define the `networkMessageRe-ceived` method in our main class `SampleClient`, as well as the other method of the `NetworkListener` interface, `networkDisconnected`, which receives events if the connection to the server is lost. These two methods can be seen here:

```
public void networkMessageReceived(NetworkEvent e)
{
    eventProcessor.addEvent(e);
```

```
}
public void networkDisconnected(NetworkEvent e)
{
    eventProcessor.addEvent(e);
}
```

All we are doing in these methods is adding the events to our `event-Processor` just as we added other events, such as mouse and keyboard events. Also, notice how we have defined the `mousePressed` method with the following method, as we need to move the player (Circle) through this input:

```
public void mousePressed(MouseEvent e)
{
    eventProcessor.addEvent(e);
}
```

So in this example, our event processor will be receiving both mouse events and network events, although in a more complex example it could also be handling keyboard and focus events. However, we have left these out to keep things as simple as possible.

These events will then be processed when the `processEventList` method of our `eventProcessor` object is called in the main loop thread (nicely synchronizing all our events with the main loop). We now need to define the `handleEvent` method of the `EventProcessable` interface. The entire method that we have created can be seen here:

```
public void handleEvent(AWTEvent e)
{
    switch(e.getID())
    {
        case MouseEvent.MOUSE_PRESSED:
        {
            System.out.println("Mouse Pressed Event");
            MouseEvent mouseEvent = (MouseEvent)e;
            networkHandler.sendMessage(MSG_MOVE_POSITION+"|"
                +mouseEvent.getX()+"|"+mouseEvent.getY());
            break;
        }

        case NetworkEvent.NETWORK_MESSAGE_RECEIVED:

            System.out.println("Network Message Received:"
                + ((NetworkEvent)e).message);
            handleNetworkMessage(((NetworkEvent)e).message);
            break;

        case NetworkEvent.NETWORK_DISCONNECTED:
        {
            System.out.println("Network Disconnected");
            exitProgram();
            break;
        }
    }
}
```

In this method, we simply switch the ID of the message and create cases for each message in which we are interested. For the MOUSE_PRESSED message, we send a message to the server using the sendMessage method of the networkHandler object where the player clicked, so the server can then update the player's position and inform all players as to the new position of the player.

For NETWORK_MESSAGE_RECEIVED events, we have created another method within our SampleClient class to deal with the actual message, as it would be quite messy to put the entire message handling code in here. So all we do is cast the AWTEvent down to being a Network-Event and pass the actual string message into the handleNetwork-Message method, which we will look at in a moment.

Finally, we have the NETWORK_DISCONNECTED message, which means we want to simply quit the application if we receive it. Note here, however, that we could add code to attempt a reconnection to the server by simply creating a new NetworkHandler object again. If the connection failed again, it would send another NETWORK_DISCONNECTED message.

Let's now have a look at the handleNetworkMessage method. In this method, we first tokenize the message and get the type of message as an integer value, as we did in the server code. This can be seen here (note we implement the same Protocol interface in the client as we did in the server so that we have the same message definitions):

```
StringTokenizer st = new StringTokenizer(message, "|");
int type = Integer.parseInt(st.nextToken());
```

Next we create a switch statement for the type of message that we have received. As we mentioned before, once the client has connected to the server, the server will send the client a MSG_INIT_PLAYER message, which contains information such as the initial position of the player, the color ID, and also the unique ID for the player. Therefore, we can create a case for this message as follows:

```
switch(type)
{
    case MSG_INIT_PLAYER:
```

Then, within the case, we want to create a new Player object called player using the values sent from the server. Since we have sent them in the same order from the server as it requires them into the constructor of the player class, we can pass the tokens in directly to the constructor. This can be seen here:

```
player = new Player(Integer.parseInt(st.nextToken()),
                    Integer.parseInt(st.nextToken()),
                    Integer.parseInt(st.nextToken()),
                    Integer.parseInt(st.nextToken()));
```

Once the player object is created, we send the server a MSG_SET_NAME message to set the name of the player. If you remember from when we created the server, the server will send out messages to all the players about the existence of this player and send this player information about

Chapter 17

all of the other players currently connected to the server. The code to send the name of the player can be seen here:

```
networkHandler.sendMessage(MSG_SET_NAME+"|"+playerName);
```

Once this is sent, the server will then send a message back confirming that the name has been set. This will then update it in the `player` object and add the `player` object to the player list, and the rendering code will start drawing your player to the screen (we will look at the `render` method soon). The handling code for the `MSG_SET_NAME` message can be seen here:

```
case MSG_SET_NAME:
    player.name = st.nextToken();
    playerList.add(player);
    break;
```

Note that all of this code does not need to be synchronized explicitly because everything is running in the main loop; so everything is synchronized already.

The next message that we have to handle is when a new player is added to the game. Note that this message is also used when you have sent your name to the server when the server in turn sends you back all of the players that are currently in the game on the server. Let's look at the complete code for the case to handle the `MSG_ADD_NEW_PLAYER` message now.

```
case MSG_ADD_NEW_PLAYER:
{
    Player p = new Player(Integer.parseInt(st.nextToken()),
                          Integer.parseInt(st.nextToken()),
                          Integer.parseInt(st.nextToken()),
                          Integer.parseInt(st.nextToken()));

        p.name = st.nextToken();
        playerList.add(p);
        break;
}
```

As you can see, all we do here is create a new `Player` object from the data contained within the tokens of the string (which also has the player's unique ID), assign the name, and then add the player to the `playerList` `ArrayList`.

The next message that we handle here is the `MSG_MOVE_POSITION`, which is sent whenever any player moves. We can tell which player has actually moved (whether it be ourselves or another player) by looking at the unique ID that was also sent along with the new x and y position of the player that moved.

We first get the `id` (of the player that has moved) from the message using the following line of code:

```
int id = Integer.parseInt(st.nextToken());
```

Then we loop through the `playerList` until we find the player with the matching unique ID. When we find the correct player, we simply set the

new x and y values and then break out of the `for` loop. This can be seen
here:

```
for(int i=0; i<playerList.size(); i++)
{
    p = (Player)playerList.get(i);
    if(p.uniqueId==id)
    {
        p.x = Integer.parseInt(st.nextToken());
        p.y = Integer.parseInt(st.nextToken());
        break;
    }
}
```

The final message that we have to handle is when a player is disconnected
from the server. The server sends this message automatically when it
loses a connection from another client, and it also sends the unique ID of
the player that has disconnected so we can use this to simply remove it
from our `playerList`. The complete case for the `MSG_REMOVE_`
`PLAYER` message can be seen here:

```
case MSG_REMOVE_PLAYER:
{
    Player p;
    int id = Integer.parseInt(st.nextToken());
    for(int i=0; i<playerList.size(); i++)
    {
        p = (Player)playerList.get(i);
        if(p.uniqueId==id)
        {
            playerList.remove(i);
            break;
        }
    }
}
```

All we need to look at now is the `render` method, which is where we
draw all the players to the screen. Here is the complete code for the `ren-`
`der` method:

```
public void render(Graphics g)
{
    g.clearRect(0, 0, DISPLAY_WIDTH, DISPLAY_HEIGHT);

    // render all players...

    Player p;

    for(int i=0; i<playerList.size(); i++)
    {
        p = (Player)playerList.get(i);
        g.setColor(Player.colors[p.colId]);
        g.fillOval(p.x-10, p.y-10, 20, 20);
        g.drawString(p.name, p.x+20, p.y);
    }
}
```

So all we do in the `render` method is loop through `playerList` and set
the color using the color ID (`colId`) in the `Player` object p that was

assigned by the server (by accessing the static `colors` array defined as follows in the `player` class).

```
public static final Color[] colors = {Color.red, Color.green,
    Color.blue, Color.yellow, Color.magenta};
```

Then we draw a circle to represent the player using the `fillOval` method of the `Graphics` object g. Finally, we draw the player name to the right of the player using the `drawString` method.

Note again that we do not need to do any explicit synchronization here, as the rendering is performed actively in the main loop, along with all of the event handling code.

Now here are some images of "I'm a circle" in action!

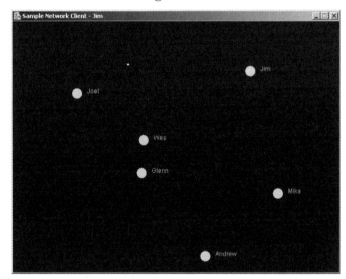

Figure 17-7: Everyone having fun playing "I'm a circle!" or not

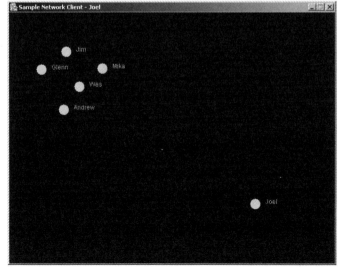

Figure 17-8: Joel then felt lonely as everyone moved away from him.

In general, a multiplayer game will usually have some kind of AI (artificial intelligence), be it enemy computer players or anything that the server needs to control, such as a game timer. The server application that we have made in this chapter did not have a main loop, thus it does not do any real-time processing of its own and is therefore an event-driven server, reacting merely to client messages and processing them when they arrive. For the server to have a main loop itself, simply follow the same steps that we used for the main loop in the client. Having the main loop system in the server will also mean that all event processing would be synchronized, so you would need to perform so much explicit synchronization with the client main loop system. You may also want to add a visual in-game display to the server for debugging purposes.

Summary

In this chapter, you learned the basic theories behind networks, as well as how to create multiplayer games in Java using TCP. There is much to take in here, and it can be difficult to work out what is going on sometimes. The best way to learn is to experiment, so try making your own simple multiplayer game and you will be able to then fully grasp the idea of network programming. However, if you use the network framework that we have created as a base, implementing multiplayer capabilities in your games should be quite feasible. In the next chapter, we will delve into new I/O, which gives us the possibilty of creating non-blocking network code.

Chapter 18

Introduction to NIO Networking

On the subject of C program indentation: "In My Egotistical
Opinion, most people's C programs should be indented six feet
downward and covered with dirt." —Blair P. Houghton

Introduction

Now that you've learned the basics of networking, this chapter will take a
look at the latest networking features available in Java (since the 1.4
release), namely new I/O.

Why Use NIO?

The main advantage of using NIO over standard I/O streams is the fact
that we can now create a non-blocking server, meaning that the server
does not have to sit and wait to read a message from a stream. This also
means that with TCP, we no longer require a separate thread for each individual client that connects to the server.

As you can guess, the main advantage from a games point of view is
massively multiplayer games, where there can be hundreds or even thousands of connections at one time. This would be costly if we had to create
several thousand individual threads to handle each of the players!

Channels

NIO uses what are known as *channels* instead of the normal streams that
the old I/O used. As well as being able to read and write data at the same
time, a channel can also be "non-blocking," meaning that your application
does not have be dedicated to listening for possible network messages.

By using channels, we can use a continuous loop that polls for any
operations to be performed on any of the channels (such as a read or write
operation). This is called selection (i.e., we select any channels that
require an operation to be performed, and then deal with the selection
accordingly).

623

The ByteBuffer Class

A ByteBuffer is a nice wrapper around simple arrays of bytes that makes it really easy for us to send and receive primitive data types, as well as more complex information.

Let's look at a simple example of how we can use ByteBuffer.

Code Listing 18-1: `ByteBufferExample.java`

```java
import java.nio.*;

public class ByteBufferExample
{
    public static void main(String args[])
    {
        String tempString = "Hello";
        byte[] byteText = tempString.getBytes();

        // Create a byte buffer
        ByteBuffer byteBuffer = ByteBuffer.allocate(4 + 4 + 8 +
            byteText.length);
        // int + int + double + 5 character string

        // Add an int to the ByteBuffer...
        byteBuffer.putInt(15);

        // Add a double...
        byteBuffer.putDouble(10.6);

        // Finally add the string...
        byteBuffer.putInt(byteText.length);
        byteBuffer.put(byteText);

        // Rewind the ByteBuffer back to the start...
        byteBuffer.rewind();

        // Now get the info back from the ByteBuffer...
        System.out.println("Integer was "+byteBuffer.getInt());

        System.out.println("Double was "+byteBuffer.getDouble());

        final int MAX_TEXT_LENGTH = 256;
        byte[] buffer = new byte[MAX_TEXT_LENGTH];

        int length = byteBuffer.getInt();
        byteBuffer.get(buffer, 0, Math.min(length, MAX_TEXT_LENGTH));
        System.out.println("String was "+new String(buffer, 0,
            length));
    }
}
```

When you run the example, you should see the following output:

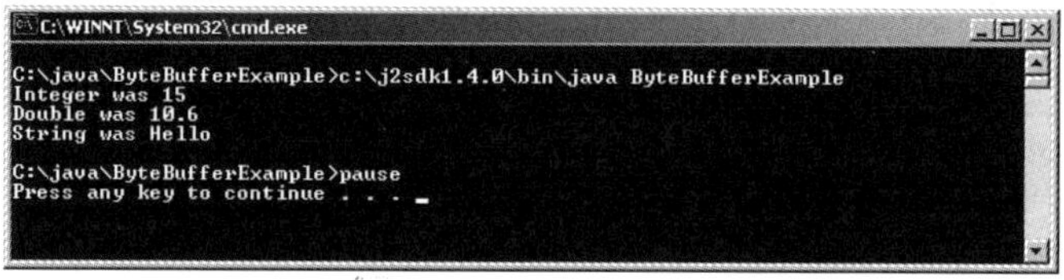

Figure 18-1:
ByteBuffer
example

Let's now look at the source code in detail so we can see how it works. First we include the NIO package, which is `java.nio.*`. This can be seen here:

```
import java.nio.*;
```

Then we create our main class called `ByteBufferExample` and also our `main` method. Once we do this, we assign a `String` object called `tempString` to the value `Hello`. Then we retrieve the string data as bytes and store this in a byte array called `byteText`.

We then allocate a `ByteBuffer` by calling the static `allocate` method, which is a member of the `ByteBuffer` class. This can be seen here:

```
ByteBuffer byteBuffer = ByteBuffer.allocate(4 + 4 + 8 +
    byteText.length);
```

Note that once a `ByteBuffer` has been allocated, it is then not possible to increase its size; however, it is possible to reduce the size by placing a limit on it using the `limit(int)` method. Also, we can obtain the current limit by calling the `limit()` method (with no parameters).

So in this example, we have allocated enough space within the `Byte-Buffer` to hold two `int`s (four bytes each), a `double` (eight bytes), and a five-character string (five bytes). Here is a table of the sizes of primitive data types in bytes:

Data Type	Size in Bytes
byte	1
char	2
short	2
int	4
float	4
long	8
double	8

Once the `ByteBuffer` is allocated, we then use the `putInt` method to place an integer value at the start of the buffer. In this example, we have used the value 15. It will appear in the buffer at the start, which can be seen in the following diagram (note that each square represents one byte):

Next we call the `putDouble` method, which will append a `double` value to the `ByteBuffer`. When the `int` value was added, the current position of the buffer is set to the end of the first four bytes, so when the `double` is added it will look like the following:

Next we add an integer value that represents the length of the string that we are about to add in bytes, which we retrieved from our byte array

byteText using the `length` member. Therefore, after we add this, the
`ByteBuffer` will look as follows:

int	double	int					

Then we finally add our string `Hello` to the `ByteBuffer` using the `put`
method, which can take an array of bytes as a parameter. Therefore, we
can simply pass in our `byteText` byte array and fill the remaining five
bytes; hence, the final `ByteBuffer` will look as follows:

int	double	int	"Hello"

Now all our data is in the `ByteBuffer` and the position of the `Byte-
Buffer` is at the end of it. So to enable us to access any of the data, we
first need to "rewind" it, so the position is at the start. This is done conveniently via the `rewind` method, which can be seen here:

```
byteBuffer.rewind();
```

So the position of the `ByteBuffer` is then back to the start. Now we can
start retrieving information from it using the equivalent get methods.
First, we will get the integer value back by calling the `getInt` method,
which can be seen in the following line of code:

```
System.out.println("Integer was "+byteBuffer.getInt());
```

Then, as with the `put` method, the current position of the `ByteBuffer`
is moved to the end of the `int` value (i.e., four bytes forward), so we can
then extract and print our `double` value using this next line of code:

```
System.out.println("Double was "+byteBuffer.getDouble());
```

Finally, we retrieve our string by first retrieving the length of the string,
which is stored within the `ByteBuffer` as an integer value. Then, once
we have this value, we can call the `get` method, passing in a byte array
and limiting the amount of bytes to retrieve to five. To get our string from
the bytes, we can then create a new `String` object from the array of
bytes by passing the array of bytes into the string's constructor. This can
be seen here:

```
System.out.println("String was "+new String(buffer, 0, length));
```

 NOTE: It is also possible to chain the put methods so instead of having
the four lines as we did in the previous example, we could have the following to add our data into the `ByteBuffer`.

```
byteBuffer.putInt(15).putDouble(10.6).putInt(byteText.length).put
    (byteText);
```

Creating a Blocking Server

Let's now look at a simple blocking server using NIO; when a connection
is made, it will send a predefined string of text to the client. Here is the
complete code for the server and the client:

Code Listing 18-2: `BlockingServer.java`

```java
import java.nio.*;
import java.nio.channels.*;
import java.io.*;
import java.net.*;

public class BlockingServer
{
    public static void main(String[] args)
    {
        try
        {
            ServerSocketChannel serverSocketChannel =
                ServerSocketChannel.open();
            ServerSocket serverSocket = serverSocketChannel.socket();

            serverSocket.bind(new InetSocketAddress(9000));

            while(true)
            {
                System.out.println("Awaiting Client Connection...");
                SocketChannel socketChannel =
                    serverSocketChannel.accept();
                System.out.println("Got Client Connection...");
                // Create a byte buffer...
                String stringToSend = "This is a message";

                int length = stringToSend.length() * 2;
                // * 2 due to size of each char

                ByteBuffer lengthInBytes = ByteBuffer.allocate(4);
                // 4 = size of an 'int'
                lengthInBytes.putInt(length);
                lengthInBytes.rewind();

                ByteBuffer dataToSend = ByteBuffer.allocate(length);
                dataToSend.asCharBuffer().put(stringToSend);
                ByteBuffer sendArray[] = {lengthInBytes, dataToSend};

                socketChannel.write(sendArray);
                System.out.println("Sent Message to Client...");
            }
        }
        catch(IOException e)
        {
            System.out.println(e);
        }
    }
}
```

Code Listing 18-3: `BlockingClient.java`

```java
import java.nio.*;
import java.nio.channels.*;
import java.io.*;
import java.net.*;

public class BlockingClient
{
    public static void main(String[] args)
```

```
{
    try
    {
        SocketChannel socketChannel = SocketChannel.open();
        socketChannel.connect(new InetSocketAddress
            ("127.0.0.1", 9000));

        // wait for the message from the server...
        ByteBuffer incomingLengthInBytes = ByteBuffer.allocate(4);
        // size of an 'int'
        socketChannel.read(incomingLengthInBytes);
        incomingLengthInBytes.rewind();
        int incomingLength = incomingLengthInBytes.getInt();
        System.out.println("Got Incoming Length as:
            "+incomingLength+" bytes, "+incomingLength+" /
            "+2+" = "+incomingLength/2+" characters");

        // now allocate the correct size for the message...
        ByteBuffer incomingData =
            ByteBuffer.allocate(incomingLength);
        socketChannel.read(incomingData);
        incomingData.rewind();
        String string = incomingData.asCharBuffer().toString();

        // Finally print the received message...
        System.out.println("Received: "+string);
    }
    catch(IOException e)
    {
        System.out.println(e);
    }
}
}
```

When we run the server and then a client, we should see the following output:

Figure 18-2:
Blocking
server (after
a client has
connected)

Figure 18-3:
Blocking
client

So it works, but let's see how. First we will look at the server.

We import all the required packages and declare our class and main method. Then we open a `ServerSocketChannel` by calling the static `open` method, which is a member of the `ServerSocketChannel` class. This can be seen in the following line of code:

```
ServerSocketChannel serverSocketChannel = ServerSocketChannel.open();
```

Then we obtain the `ServerSocket` from the channel by calling the `socket` method, which can be seen in the following line of code:

```
ServerSocket serverSocket = serverSocketChannel.socket();
```

Next we bind the socket to port 9000, so the server can begin listening on that port. This can be seen here:

```
serverSocket.bind(new InetSocketAddress(9000));
```

Now we enter an infinite while loop and call the accept method of the serverSocketChannel, which will block until a connection is accepted. This is on par with the networking that we saw in the last chapter, which also blocked waiting for a connection. This can be seen here:

```
while(true)
{
    SocketChannel socketChannel = serverSocketChannel.accept();
```

So when a connection is accepted, it is then stored in the socketChannel reference. We next create a String object, which we are going to send to the client that has just connected. This can be seen in the following line of code:

```
String stringToSend = "This is a message";
```

Once we have assigned this string value, we then retrieve its length in bytes by multiplying the actual length of the string by two, as each (Unicode) character takes up two bytes in memory. We do this and then store the result in a variable called length.

```
int length = stringToSend.length() * 2;
```

Now we create a ByteBuffer to hold the size of the message that we are going to send to the client. The size will be stored as an integer within the ByteBuffer, so we need to allocate four bytes to it to hold the integer value. This can be seen in the following line of code:

```
ByteBuffer lengthInBytes = ByteBuffer.allocate(4);
```

We then place the length of the string in bytes into the lengthInBytes ByteBuffer by means of the putInt method that we saw in the previous example when we looked at ByteBuffers. Then, after we have placed the length value in the lengthInBytes ByteBuffer, we rewind the ByteBuffer so we are ready to send it.

Next we allocate space to our data ByteBuffer, which will be used to hold the actual data that we wish to send to the client (i.e., the actual string data). This will be the length of our string multiplied by two to take into account the size of the char data type (which we have previously stored in the variable length). This can be seen in the following line of code:

```
ByteBuffer dataToSend = ByteBuffer.allocate(length);
```

Next we place the string into the dataToSend ByteBuffer using the following line of code:

```
dataToSend.asCharBuffer().put(stringToSend);
```

We place the string in the ByteBuffer by first viewing it as a CharBuffer, which then has the put method that takes a string as a parameter.

Chapter 18

Next we create an array to store the `ByteBuffer`s that we are sending. This can be seen here:

```
ByteBuffer sendArray[] = {lengthInBytes, dataToSend};
```

Finally we send the `ByteBuffer` array using the following line of code:

```
socketChannel.write(sendArray);
```

Note that this could also be written as:

```
socketChannel.write(lengthInBytes);
socketChannel.write(dataToSend);
```

It really makes no difference which way you do it; it's just a little neater sending an array if you have many `ByteBuffer`s to send at once.

Well, that's the server; let's now take a look at the client code.

In the client, we first open a `SocketChannel` by calling the static open method of the `SocketChannel` class, which can be seen in the following line of code:

```
SocketChannel socketChannel = SocketChannel.open();
```

Then we attempt to connect to the server by calling the `connect` method, which in turn is passed an `InetSocketAddress` that is passed the IP address and port of the server. This can be seen here:

```
socketChannel.connect(new InetSocketAddress("127.0.0.1", 9000));
```

Once we have a connection, we then allocate a `ByteBuffer` called `incomingLengthInBytes` to hold four bytes storing the size of the string message that we need to read in next; this is because we do not know what length the data will be, as it could be a string of any number of characters.

```
ByteBuffer incomingLengthInBytes = ByteBuffer.allocate(4);
```

Next we call the `read` method of the `socketChannel`, which will actually read the four bytes into the `incomingLengthInBytes` Byte-Buffer. This can be seen here:

```
socketChannel.read(incomingLengthInBytes);
```

Once it is read in, we then need to rewind the `ByteBuffer` using the following line of code:

```
incomingLengthInBytes.rewind();
```

Then we can call the `getInt` method to get the length of the string message that is about to be read in. This can be seen in the following line of code:

```
int incomingLength = incomingLengthInBytes.getInt();
```

So now that we know how much memory to allocate, we allocate it using the following line of code:

```
ByteBuffer incomingData = ByteBuffer.allocate(incomingLength);
```

We then proceed by calling the `read` method to read in the data:

```
socketChannel.read(incomingData);
```

Then, as with all `ByteBuffers`, we need to rewind it before we can access the string contained within it. This can be seen here:

```
incomingData.rewind();
```

Then finally, we can get the string out of the `ByteBuffer` and print it to the console window using the following two final lines of code:

```
String string = incomingData.asCharBuffer().toString();
System.out.println("Received: "+string);
```

Creating a Non-Blocking Server

Now that we know how to create a normal blocking server using channels, let's look at the great part of NIO, the non-blocking server. Here is the complete code for a non-blocking server and a slightly modified version of the previous client code, which also returns a message to the server on retrieval of a message:

Code Listing 18-4: `NonBlockingServer.java`

```java
import java.nio.*;
import java.nio.channels.*;
import java.io.*;
import java.net.*;
import java.util.*;

public class NonBlockingServer
{
    public static void main(String[] args)
    {
        try
        {
            Selector selector = Selector.open();

            ServerSocketChannel serverSocketChannel =
                ServerSocketChannel.open();
            serverSocketChannel.configureBlocking(false);

            ServerSocket serverSocket = serverSocketChannel.socket();

            serverSocket.bind(new InetSocketAddress(9000));

            System.out.println("Non-blocking Server created on port
                9000");

            serverSocketChannel.register(selector,
                SelectionKey.OP_ACCEPT);

            System.out.println("Waiting for client connections...");

            int amountToProcess = 0;
            while(true)
            {
                amountToProcess = selector.selectNow();

                if(amountToProcess > 0)
                {
                    try
```

```
{
    Set keys = selector.selectedKeys();

    Iterator iterator = keys.iterator();

    while(iterator.hasNext())
    {
        SelectionKey selectionKey =
            (SelectionKey) iterator.next();
        iterator.remove(); // remove the key

        int operation = selectionKey
            .interestOps();

        if((SelectionKey.OP_ACCEPT & operation)
            != 0)
        {
            // Accept the connection...
            ServerSocketChannel channel =
                (ServerSocketChannel)
                selectionKey.channel();
            SocketChannel socket =
                channel.accept();
            socket.configureBlocking(false);

            // register for a writing operation
            socket.register(selector,
                SelectionKey.OP_WRITE);

            System.out.println("Client
                Connected...");
        }
        else if((SelectionKey.OP_READ &
            operation) != 0)
        {
            // Attempt to read...
            System.out.println("About to read
                from client...");

            SocketChannel socket =
                (SocketChannel) selectionKey
                .channel();

            // get the message from the client...
            ByteBuffer incomingLengthInBytes =
                ByteBuffer.allocate(4);
            // size of an 'int'
            socket.read(incomingLengthInBytes);
            incomingLengthInBytes.rewind();
            int incomingLength =
                incomingLengthInBytes.getInt();
            System.out.println("Got Incoming
                Length as: "+incomingLength+"
                bytes");

            // now allocate the correct size for
            // the message...
            ByteBuffer incomingData = ByteBuffer
                .allocate(incomingLength);
```

```
                            socket.read(incomingData);
                            incomingData.rewind();
                            String string = incomingData
                                .asCharBuffer().toString();


                            // Finally print received message...
                            System.out.println("Received:
                                "+string);

                            // terminate the connection...
                            socket.close();
                        }
                        else if((SelectionKey.OP_WRITE &
                            operation) != 0)
                        {
                            // Attempt to write...


                            System.out.println("Now going to
                                write to client...");

                            SocketChannel socket =
                                (SocketChannel) selectionKey
                                .channel();

                            socket.register(selector,
                                SelectionKey.OP_READ);

                            String stringToSend = "This is a
                                message";

                            int length = stringToSend.length()
                                * 2;

                            ByteBuffer lengthInBytes =
                                ByteBuffer.allocate(4);
                                // 4 = size of a 'int'
                            ByteBuffer dataToSend =
                                ByteBuffer.allocate(length);

                            lengthInBytes.putInt(length);
                            lengthInBytes.rewind();
                            dataToSend.asCharBuffer()
                                .put(stringToSend);

                            ByteBuffer sendArray[] =
                                {lengthInBytes, dataToSend};

                            socket.write(sendArray);
                            //socket.close();
                            System.out.println("Sent Message to
                                Client...");
                        }
                    }
                }
                catch(IOException e)
                {
                    System.out.println(e);
                }
```

```
                    }
                }
            }
        catch(IOException e)
        {
            System.out.println(e);
        }


    }
}
```

Code Listing 18-5: `NonBlockingClient.java`

```java
import java.nio.*;
import java.nio.channels.*;
import java.io.*;
import java.net.*;

public class NonBlockingClient
{
    public static void main(String[] args)
    {
        try
        {
            SocketChannel socketChannel = SocketChannel.open();
            socketChannel.connect(new InetSocketAddress("127.0.0.1",
                9000));

            // wait for the message from the server...
            ByteBuffer incomingLengthInBytes =
                ByteBuffer.allocate(4); // size of an 'int'
            socketChannel.read(incomingLengthInBytes);
            incomingLengthInBytes.rewind();
            int incomingLength = incomingLengthInBytes.getInt();
            System.out.println("Got Incoming Length as: "
                "+incomingLength+" bytes");

            // now allocate the correct size for the message...
            ByteBuffer incomingData =
                ByteBuffer.allocate(incomingLength);
            socketChannel.read(incomingData);
            incomingData.rewind();
            String string = incomingData.asCharBuffer().toString();


            // Finally print the received message...
            System.out.println("Received: "+string);


            // Send a message back to the server...
            String replyMessage = "Message Received - Thank you!";
            int length = replyMessage.length() * 2;

            ByteBuffer replyLength = ByteBuffer.allocate(4);
            replyLength.putInt(length);
            replyLength.rewind();

            ByteBuffer replyText = ByteBuffer.allocate(length);
            replyText.asCharBuffer().put(replyMessage);

            ByteBuffer toSend[] = {replyLength, replyText};
```

```
        socketChannel.write(toSend);


    }
    catch(IOException e)
    {
        System.out.println(e);
    }


    }
}
```

So when we run the non-blocking server, followed by the new client, we
can expect the following output in the console:

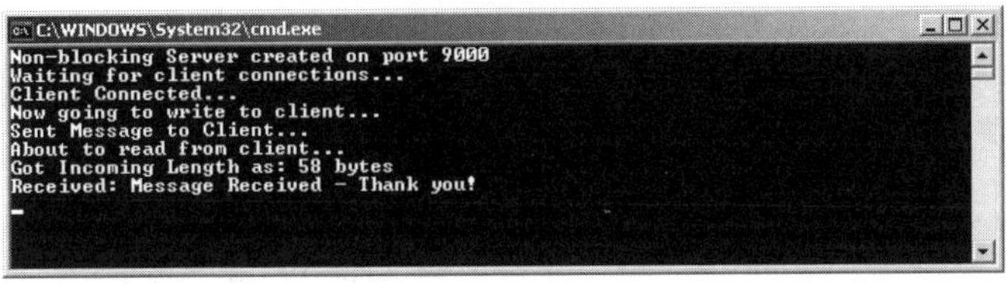

Figure 18-4:
Non-block-
ing server
(after client
has been
executed)

Figure 18-5:
Client

Let's look at how we have changed the server to make it non-blocking.
The first change is that we have added the java.util package to our
import statements at the start. Then, after we declare our main class and
main method, we create a Selector object by calling the static open
method of the Selector class, using the following line of code:

```
Selector selector = Selector.open();
```

A *selector* is used to hold a reference to a "set" of channels and can be
asked to supply a "set" of channels that are ready to have an operation
performed upon them.

Next we create our ServerSocketChannel, as we did for the block-
ing server, but this time, after we create it we call the configure-
Blocking method, passing in false to tell the channel not to block.
This can be seen in the following two lines of code:

```
ServerSocketChannel serverSocketChannel = ServerSocketChannel.open();
serverSocketChannel.configureBlocking(false);
```

Then we create the server, as we did in the previous example, using the
following two lines of code:

```
ServerSocket serverSocket = serverSocketChannel.socket();
serverSocket.bind(new InetSocketAddress(9000));
```

However, this time, we need to "register" our server with the selector so
that when operations are required to be performed, the server channel
will be selected and the operations will be performed.

We do this by calling the register method, which can be seen here:

```
serverSocketChannel.register(selector, SelectionKey.OP_ACCEPT);
```

This registers the `serverSocketChannel` to accept incoming connections (basically, to listen for incoming clients wanted to connect to the server).

Next we create an integer called `amountToProcess` that will store the number of channels that currently require an operation to be performed upon them. This can be seen here:

```
int amountToProcess = 0;
```

Now we enter an infinite `while` loop and then call the `selectNow` method of the selector, which selects a set of keys that are ready to have an operation performed upon them and returns an integer value of how many were selected. This can be seen here:

```
while(true)
{
    amountToProcess = selector.selectNow();
```

Note the `selectNow` method will attempt to select, but if nothing is currently ready, it will continue (i.e., not block). In addition to this method, there is also a `select(long)` method, which will wait the amount of milliseconds you specify for keys to be selected before it continues. Finally, there is the `select` method with no parameters, which will block until there is at least one key ready for an operation.

So we now know how many keys there are to be processed, as the value is stored in `amountToProcess`. We can now check if this value is greater than zero so we know whether any keys are available. This can be seen here:

```
if(amountToProcess > 0)
{
```

We can then get the selected keys (i.e., the ones that require an operation to be performed) by calling the `selectedKeys()` method of the selector, which then returns the keys as a set. This can be seen in the following line of code:

```
Set keys = selector.selectedKeys();
```

From this `Set`, we can then obtain an iterator by calling the `iterator` method, allowing us to easily cycle through all the keys in the set. This can be seen here:

```
Iterator iterator = keys.iterator();
while(iterator.hasNext())
{
```

So for each key, we get the key by calling the `next` method of the iterator and typecast it to type `SelectionKey`. Following that, we remove it from the iterator. This can be seen in the following two lines of code:

```
SelectionKey selectionKey = (SelectionKey) iterator.next();
iterator.remove();
```

We can then find out which operations the key is interested in by calling the `interestOps` method of the `selectionKey` object, which can be seen in the following line of code:

```
int operation = selectionKey.interestOps();
```

Then, once we have the operation in the integer variable (called `opera-tion`), we can compare this to the defined operations (which are static final members of the `SelectionKey` class).

First, we check to see if it is an accept operation (`OP_ACCEPT`). This can be seen here:

```
if((SelectionKey.OP_ACCEPT & operation) > 0)
{
```

If this is true, we get the channel from the `selectionKey` by calling the `channel` method. Then we typecast this to be a `ServerSocketChannel`, as this is the only channel that is registered to accept connections. This process can be seen in the following line of code:

```
ServerSocketChannel channel = (ServerSocketChannel)
    selectionKey.channel();
```

We can then call the `accept` method of the `channel`, which will accept the incoming connection and return a reference to a socket channel that we store in a reference called `socket`. This can be seen here:

```
SocketChannel socket = channel.accept();
```

We then make this socket non-blocking by calling the `configure-Blocking` method, as we did for the server socket. This can be seen in the following line of code:

```
socket.configureBlocking(false);
```

Then, for this example, we will register the socket for a write operation (`OP_WRITE`), since we first want the server to write a string to the client, as we did in the previous example. So here is the line of code required to do this:

```
socket.register(selector, SelectionKey.OP_WRITE);
```

As you can see, we first pass in the `selector`, followed by the operation for which we wish to register the `SocketChannel` (in this case, the `OP_WRITE` operation).

Next we check for a read operation being required (which we will look at in a moment). Then we move on to the write operation. We check the operation variable first using the following `if` statement:

```
else if((SelectionKey.OP_WRITE & operation) != 0)
{
```

Then, once we know it's a write operation, we obtain the `Socket-Channel` by invoking the `channel` method of the `SelectionKey`, which can be seen in the following line of code:

```
SocketChannel socket = (SocketChannel) selectionKey.channel();
```

Next we register the channel for a read operation, as once the client has received the message, it will then send a "thank you" message back to the server. So we do this with the following line of code:

```
socket.register(selector, SelectionKey.OP_READ);
```

We then send the data in exactly the same way as we did in the blocking server.

The client then receives and displays the message from the server in the same way as it did for the previous blocking example; however, this time we also send a message back to the server from the client, using the following block of code defined in the new client:

```
// Send a message back to the server...
String replyMessage = "Message Received - Thank you!";
int length = replyMessage.length() * 2;

ByteBuffer replyLength = ByteBuffer.allocate(4);
replyLength.putInt(length);
replyLength.rewind();

ByteBuffer replyText = ByteBuffer.allocate(length);
replyText.asCharBuffer().put(replyMessage);

ByteBuffer toSend[] = {replyLength, replyText};
socketChannel.write(toSend);
```

This is done in exactly the same way as we sent the message from the server.

When this message is sent to the server, it will read in the message and display it to the screen—using the same code as we used to read in the message on the client—because the channel has been registered with a read operation. Then, finally, it closes the connection to the client by means of the `close` method of the `SocketChannel` object.

Summary

Well, that is it! You've now covered all the aspects of Java that you need to start making your own quality games. Now that you have learned all of the fundamental aspects of creating games using Java, we recommend that you begin making your own reusable game library. It is our hope that we have clarified areas that are often difficult when using Java, most notably those relating to threads, giving you confidence and control over what your program is doing. We hope that you have enjoyed reading this book and gained as much from it as we have writing it. Good luck with your game development in the future, and we hope to see you again for the 1.5 release of Java!

Index

* indicates entry is located in the bonus chapter included on the companion CD

A

abstract classes, 113-115
abstract keyword, 113
abstract methods, 114-115
Abstract Window Toolkit, *see* AWT
access attributes,
    and inheritance, 108-109
    reasons for using, 101
adapter classes, 302
    using, 302-303
addition assignment operator, 26
addition operator, 22
affined transformations, 230-234
.aif format, 339
AlphaComposite class, 247-248
animate method, 263
animation,
    with one-dimensional image sheets,
        373-380
    with two-dimensional image sheets,
        380-386
Animator class, 262
    creating, 262-263
append method, 82-83
applets, 2, 201
    creating, 202-204
    networking with, 574
    running from JAR, 129-131
    security, 207
    signed, 207
    sound example, 339-341
    specifying program arguments, 205-207
    viewing, 204
AppletViewer, using, 204
application, 198
    changing size of, 466
    creating, 199-201
    creating for high scores, 557-565
    running from JAR, 128-129
    sound example, 342-343
arithmetic operators, 22-23

array, 53
    accessing members of, 54-55
    declaring, 53-54
    multi-dimensional, 60-62
    multi-dimensional and multi-length,
        62-65
    passing as parameter, 59-60
    setting values of, 56-57
    using with for loop, 57-59
ArrayIndexOutOfBoundsException, 59,
    143
ArrayList class, 134-135
    using, 135-138
arrays of strings, 69-70
assert keyword, 150-151
assertions, 150-153
assignment operators, 26
associativity, 23-24
.au format, 339
AWT, 198
    components, using, 220-221, 225
    thread, *see* Event Dispatch Thread
    versus Swing, 221, 225-226

B

background, clearing, 250-251
base class, 102
binary numbers, 29
binary operator, 24
bit shifting, 30
bit testing, 31
bitwise assignment operators, 29
bitwise operators, 27
    using, 27-28
blocking, 193
blocking client, creating, 626-631
blocking server, creating, 626-631
boolean data type, 27
bounding box, 408-412
bounding circle, 402-408
break keyword, 40

break statement, 45-46
BufferedImage class, 251-253
BufferStrategy class, 287
buttons,
　adding image to, 6-9*
　setting images for, 477-479
　using, 469-473
byte data type, 16
ByteBuffer class, 624
　using, 624-626

C

case keyword, 37-39
casting, 110-112 *see also* typecasting
　explicit, 18
　implicit, 18
channels, 623
char data type, 32
character escape sequences, 32
　using with string, 67-69
character, changing size of, 465-466
charAt method, 74
check box, adding image to, 22-23*
classes, 8
　creating, 8-9
　implementing, 90
　inheriting, 105-108
　inner, 92-93
　member, 11
　multiple, 97
　nested, 92
　static nested, 95
　top-level, 97
clipping, 230
code blocks, synchronizing, 188-189
code listings,
　ActivelyPassiveRenderingRepaints.java,
　　278-281
　ActiveRendering.java, 273-275
　ActiveRenderingApplet.java, 276-278
　Addition.java, 126
　AdvancedKeyboard.java, 324-326
　AdvancedMouse.java, 315-317
　AffinedTransformer.java, 231-232
　Alien.java, 97-98, 106
　AnimatedNumbers.java, 375-377
　Animator, 322-323
　Animator.java, 329-331
　AppletParam.java, 205-206
　ArrayListExample.java, 134-135
　ArrayListSearchRemove.java, 137

Beings.java, 107
BlendingTest.java, 248-250
BlockingClient.java, 627-628
BlockingServer.java, 627
BoundingBoxIntersection.java, 409-411
BoundingCircleIntersection.java,
　404-406
Box.java, 408-409
BrokenArray.java, 143
BrokenArrayHandled.java, 144
BrokenArrayThrow.java, 148
ByteBufferExample.java, 624
Circle.java, 403-404
ClientHandler.java, 590-595
compile.bat, 126
ConsoleInputExample, 156
Countdown.java, 191-192
Creatures.java, 105-106
DaemonThread.java, 194-195
DatabaseExample1, 550-551
DatabaseExample2, 553
DatabaseExample3, 555
DemoScreen1.java, 430-432
DemoScreen2.java, 432
DemoScreen3.java, 433-435
DrawingShapes.java, 228-230
EventAndFocusHandling.java, 331-334
EventProcessable, 327
EventProcessor, 327-328
ExampleApp, 494-498
FullScreenDemo.java, 288-295
GameFramework.java, 417-424
Globals.java, 414
GUIButton class, 490-491
GUIComponent class, 481-482
GUIContainer class, 484-485
GUISystem class, 488
Highscore class, 557, 558-559, 562-564
HiresTimeExample, 395-396
Human.java, 107
ImageButtonExample, 7-8*, 477-478
ImageCheckBoxExample, 22-23*
ImageIOLoadingApplication.java,
　259-260
ImageRadioButtonExample, 28-32*
JButtonExample, 3-4*, 470-471
JCheckBoxExample, 20-21*
JComboBoxExample, 17-18*
JEditorPaneExample, 49-50*
JLabelExample, 1-2*
JListExample, 34-36*, 37-39*

JMenuExample, 59-60*
JPasswordFieldExample, 11-13*
JProgressBarExample, 33-34*
JRadioButtonExample, 24-26*
JTableExample.java, 40-41*
JTextAreaExample, 13-14*, 15-16*
JTextFieldExample, 9-10*, 474-475
JTreeExample, 45-47*
Keyboard.java, 416
KeyProcessable, 321
KeyProcessor, 321
LinkedListExample.java, 139-140
LookandFeel, 208
MainApp.java, 99
MetaExample1, 565-566
MIDIExample, 354-355
Mouse.java, 416
MouseProcessable, 312
MouseProcessor, 312-313
MyApp.java, 28
MyApplet, 202
MyApplet.java, 129-130
MyApplication, 199
MyException.java, 148
NetworkEvent.java, 605
NetworkHandler.java, 606-609
NetworkListener.java, 605
NonBlockingClient.java, 634-635
NonBlockingServer.java, 631-634
OffScreenSprite.java, 241-242
OptionPanesExample, 52-55*
PassiveRendering.java, 265-268
PauseScreen.java, 436
Player.java, 595-596
PlayerData, 170-171
PreparedStatementExample, 567-568
Protocol.java, 596
RandomImage.java, 251-252
SampleClient.java, 610-614
SampleScreen.java, 415
SampleServer.java, 588-589
SerializationExample, 171-173
Simple Applet Sound (HTML), 340
SimpleMouse.java, 304-305
SimpleRead, 168-169
SimpleSoundApplet, 340
SimpleSoundApplication, 342
SimpleThread1.java, 179
SimpleThread2.java, 180-181
SimpleWrite, 166-167
SoundAPIApplication, 343-345

SoundManager, 364-368
SoundManagerExample, 368-370
StackExample.java, 140-141
StickWalker.java, 382-385
StoppingThread.java, 182-183
StreamingSoundExample, 348-350
Subtraction.java, 126
TableHandler class, 560-561
TableHandler.java, 41-42*
TCPEchoClient, 577-579
TCPEchoServer, 574-575
TemplateGraphicsApplet.java, 219-220
TemplateGraphicsApplication.java,
    215-216
TemplateScreen.java, 413
TestApp.java, 127, 149, 150
TicTacToe, 158-161
Tile Scroller, 439-443
Tile Walker, 449-456
TooltipExample, 63*
TrackerImageLoadingApplet.java,
    257-258
TrackerImageLoadingApplication.java,
    255-256
TransparentSprite.java, 246-247
UDPEchoClient, 584-585
UDPEchoServer, 582
Universe.java, 98
UsingFonts.java, 235-237
view.html, 130-131, 202, 205
VolatileImageRendering.java, 284-286
collision detection, 401-402
    bounding box, 408-412
    bounding circle, 402-408
column types in tables, 520-521
comments, 15
compareTo method, 73
component, 197, 223
    adding, 223-225
    heavyweight, 197-198
    lightweight, 197-198
conditional operator, 37
conditional statements, 34
console game example, 157-166
console input, getting from user, 155-157
console program, 7
console screen, printing to, 14-15
constant, 33
    declaring, 33
constructor, 9
    using, 9-10

container, 197, 469
    top-level, 198
continue statement, 45-46

D
daemon, 513
daemon thread, 194
    using, 194-195
data,
    deleting, 531-532
    importing from Excel, 543-544
    importing from text file, 542-543
    inserting, 528-529
    inserting into table, 552-554
    modifying, 530-531
    reading from file, 168-170
    retrieving from table, 554-556
    storing, 504-506
    writing to file, 166-168
data access, controlling, 100-101
Data Definition Language, *see* DDL
Data Manipulation Language, *see* DML
data types
    boolean, 27
    byte, 16
    char, 32
    double, 20
    float, 20
    int, 16
    long, 16
    numeric, 16
    primitive, 16
    short, 16
database, 503
    backing up, 544-546
    connecting to, 550-552
    creating, 518-519
    dropping, 519-520
    relational, *see* relational database
    restoring, 546-547
database packages, 506-507
datagram socket, 574
DDL, 518
    using, 518-527
deadlock, 195-196
decimal numbers, 29
decrement operator, 25
default keyword, 38
delete method, 83
deleteCharAt method, 83
derived class, 102

dialogs, creating, 52-58*
dimensions, mapping, 386-387
dispose method, 227
division assignment operator, 26
division operator, 22
DML, 518
    using, 527-537
do while loop, 41-42
double buffering, 271-272
double data type, 20
drawImage method, 242-245
drawLine method, 227
drawRect method, 227
drawString method, 228

E
ensureCapacity method, 84-85
equality operator, 34
equals method, 72
error handling, 143-153
errors, 150
escape sequences, 32
    using with string, 67-69
Event Dispatch Thread, 178, 212, 480
event listeners, 297
event processor, creating, 327
Excel, importing data from, 543-544
exceptions, 143
    catching, 144-147
    throwing, 147-150
explicit casting, 18
extends keyword, 105

F
field types in tables, 520-521
file,
    reading data from, 168-170
    writing data to, 166-168
fillRect method, 227
final keyword, 33, 110
finalize method, 401
finally block, 147
flicker, reducing, 270-272
float data type, 20
floating-point data types, 19-20
    conversion, 20-21
focus, 328
    losing, 328-329
font,
    coordinates, 235
    creating, 234
    retrieving, 238-239

Font object, 234
for loop, 42-45
　using with arrays, 57-59
full-screen exclusive mode, 286-287
　using, 288-296

G

game framework,
　creating, 412-429
　demo, 430-438
　integrating screens into, 436-438
garbage collection, 397-398
garbage collector, 398
getDrawGraphics method, 287
GIF format, 253-254
graphical user interface, *see* GUI
Graphics 2D class, 226
Graphics class, 226
　methods, 226-228
GUI, 469
　extending, 479-480
GUI system,
　creating, 480-494
　using, 494-501
GUIButton class, creating, 490-491
GUIComponent class, creating, 481-482
GUIContainer class, creating, 484-485
GUISystem class, creating, 488

H

handleEvent method, 335-336
handles, 13
heavyweight component, 197-198
high-resolution timer, 389
　using, 395-397
high-resolution timing, 389
high-score list sample application, creating,
　557-565
HotSpot class, 261
　creating, 261-262
HTML, using to specify program
　arguments for applet, 205-207

I

"I'm a circle" network game example,
　588-621
IDE, 5
if statement, 34-35
　using with else, 36
Image class, 239-240
image formats, 253-254
ImageIO class, 258

images,
　adding to button, 6-9*
　adding to check box, 22-23*
　adding to radio button, 28-33*
　loading, 253
　loading with ImageIO class, 258-261
　loading with MediaTracker class,
　　254-258
　setting for buttons, 477-479
immutable objects, 234
implements keyword, 117
implicit casting, 18
import keyword, 124-125
increment operator, 25
index, 54
indexOf method, 74-76
inheritance, 102-103
　and access attributes, 108-109
inner class, 92-93
　creating, 93-95
input streams, 155
input, getting from user, 155-157
insert method, 83
instance, 9
instanceof keyword, 119-120
instantiation, 10-11
int data type, 16
integer data types, 16-17
　conversion, 17-19, 21
integrated development environment, *see*
　IDE
interface keyword, 116
interface objects, 118
interfaces, 115
　defining, 115-117
　implementing, 119-120
　using, 117-118
interpolation, 250
interrupt method, 193
invocation chaining, 79-80
IP address, 572-573
isInterrupted method, 193-194

J

JApplet class, 201
JAR, 128
　running applet from, 129-131
　running application from, 128-129
　specifying parameters in, 131
Java,
　and OOP, 8-9

packages, 123-124
platform, 1
using in games programming, 2
web sites, 5-6
Java 2 Standard Edition, 2
installing, 4
Java Database Connectivity, *see* JDBC
Java Native Interface, *see* JNI
Java Sound API, 343
using to play MIDI music, 354-357
using to play sampled sound, 343-347
Java Virtual Machine, *see* JVM
java.lang package classes, 132-134
java.util package classes, 134-142
JButton class, 3-6*, 7-9*, 470, 476
using, 3-9*, 469-473, 477-479
JCheckBox class, 20*, 476
using, 20-23*
JComboBox class, 17*, 476
using, 17-19*
JComponent class, 469-470
JDBC, 549
obtaining MySQL driver for, 549
JEditorPane class, 49*, 477
using, 49-52*
JFrame class, 199
JLabel class, 1*, 476
using, 1-3*
JList class, 34*, 476
using, 34-40*
using with scroll bar, 37-40*
JMenu class, 58-59*, 477
using, 58-62*
JNI, 389
joining, 541
JOptionPane class, 52*, 477
using, 52-58*
JPasswordField class, 11*, 476
using, 11-13*
JPEG format, 254
JProgressBar class, 33*, 476
using, 33-34*
JRadioButton class, 24*, 476
using, 24-33*
JScrollPane class, 15*
using with JTextArea class, 15-17*
JTable class, 40*, 476
using, 40-45*
JTextArea class, 13*, 476
using, 13-17*
using with JScrollPane class, 15-17*

JTextField class, 9*, 474, 476
using, 9-11*, 474-476
JTree class, 45*, 477
using, 45-48*
JVM, 1

K

key input, repetitive, 319-321
keyboard input, reading, 298-302
KeyListener interface, 298, 300
KeyProcessor class, 320
keywords
abstract, 113
assert, 150-151
break, 40, 45-46
case, 37-30
continue, 45-46
default, 38
extends, 105
final, 33, 110
implements, 117
import, 124-125
instance of, 119-120
interface, 116
package, 125-126
private, 100-101
protected, 100-101
public, 100-101
return, 48-49
static, 11-12
super, 106, 109
switch, 37-40
synchronized, 185, 312
this, 91-92, 109
transient, 175
void, 48

L

labels, 46-47
lastIndexOf method, 76
layout manager, 213
disabling, 213-214
length method, 74
lightweight component, 197-198
link table, 505, 537
creating, 537-538
using, 538-541
LinkageError, 150
LinkedList class, 139
using, 139-140
listeners, event, 297
logical operators, 36-37

long data type, 16
look and feel, 208-209
    classes, 209
loops, 34, 40

M

main game loop, 268-270
    implementing, 264
    integrating mouse events with, 310-311
    synchronized drawing in, 272-278
main method, 14, 89
map, changing size of, 466-467
matches method, 78-79
Math class, 133
MediaTracker class, 254-258
memory deallocation, 398
menus, using, 58-62*
metadata, 565
    retrieving, 565-567
method signatures, 50-51
methods, 8, 47
    declaring, 47-48
    overloading, 50-51
    synchronizing, 185-187
MIDI, 354
MIDI music, playing, 354-357
modulus operator, 25
monitor, 187
mouse events, integrating with main loop,
    310-311
mouse input, reading, 303-310
MouseListener interface, 298
MouseMotionListener interface, 298
MouseProcessor class, 312
    adding events to, 314
    processing events in, 314
    using, 314-319
multi-dimensional array, 60-62
multi-dimensional multi-length array, 62-65
multiple classes, 97
multiplication assignment operator, 26
multiplication operator, 22
MySQL, 511
    installing, 512-515
    server versions, 513-514
    starting automatically, 515-517

N

namespace, 95, 123
NativeWinClock class, creating, 392
nested class, 92
network framework, creating, 587-588

network game example, 588-621
    creating client, 604-621
    creating server, 588-604
new I/O, *see* NIO
NIO, 623
non-blocking client, creating, 631-638
non-blocking server, creating, 631-638
notify method, 190
notifyAll method, 190
numeric data types, 16
numeric expression, 22

O

object, 7-8
Object class, 103
    methods of, 104-105
object member, 11
object pool, 399
object pooling, 399-401
object-oriented programming, *see* OOP
off-screen image, 239
    drawing to, 240-241
OOP, 7
    and Java, 8-9
operator precedence, 23-24
operators, 22, 25, 26, 27, 29, 30, 36, 37
option panes, 52*
output streams, 155

P

package, 123
    creating, 125-128
    importing, 124-25
package keyword, 125-126
packages, Java, 123-124
packet, 572
page flipping, 287-288
paintComponent method, 228
parameter passing, 49-50
parameter, passing array as, 59-60
passive rendering, 264-265
pixel coordinates, 214
PNG format, 254
polymorphism, 110
    using, 112-113
port, 573
prepared statements, 567
    using, 567-569
primitive data type wrappers, 132
primitive data types, 16
print method, 43
println method, 14-15

printStackTrace method, 146-147
private keyword, 100-101
program argument, 70-71
   specifying for applet, 205-206
protected keyword, 100-101
protocol, 571
public keyword, 100-101

R
radio button, adding image to, 28-33*
Random class, 142
   methods, 142
random numbers, seeding, 142
record, 503
recordset, 507-508
references, 12-13
regular expression, 78-79, 508
relational database, 503-504, 537-541
remainder assignment operator, 26
render method, 263
rendering, 261
   passive, 264-265
repaint method, 264
replace method, 77, 83
return keyword, 48-49
rotating, 230
Runnable interface, 178, 180-181

S
sampled sound, playing, 343-347
scaling, 231
scope, 51-52
screen management system,
   creating, 412-429
   demo, 430-438
screens, integrating into framework,
   436-438
scroll bar, using with JList class, 37-40*
SELECT statements, using, 533-537
selector, 635
Serializable interface, 171
serialization, 170
   using, 170-175
setColor method, 226-227
setLength method, 84
shapes, drawing, 228-230
shearing, 231
short data type, 16
show method, 287
signed applet, 207
sleep method, 191-192
.snd format, 339

sockets, 573-574
Sound API, *see* Java Sound API
sound example,
   applet, 339-341
   application, 342-343
sound formats, 339
SoundManager class,
   creating, 357-364
   using, 368-371
sprite transparency, creating, 245-250
SQL, 507
   statements, 518
   using, 507-509
Stack class, 140
   using, 140-142
StandardClock class, creating, 391
static block, 101-102
static keyword, 11-12
static methods, synchronizing, 187-188
static nested class, 95
   creating, 95-97
stream socket, 574
streaming audio, 347-348
   using, 348-354
streams, 155
string, 65-66
   concatenation, 66-67
   literal, 66
   using with escape sequences, 67-69
String arrays, 69-70
String class, 72
string data,
   manipulating, 76-78
   retrieving, 74-76
String object, creating, 66
string values, comparing, 72-74
StringBuffer class, 80-81
   constructors, 81
   determining capacity, 84-85
   determining length, 84
   manipulating data in, 82-84
StringTokenizer class, 85-87
Structured Query Language, *see* SQL
subclass, 102
substring method, 74
subtraction assignment operator, 26
subtraction operator, 22
super class, 102
super keyword, 106, 109
Swing, 198
   components, 476-477

versus AWT, 221, 225-226
switch statement, 37-40
synchronization, 183-185
synchronized
    drawing, 272-273
    painting, 278-284
synchronized keyword, 185, 312
System class, 133-134

T
Tab key events, 337
tables, 503
    creating, 521-524
    dropping, 526-527
    inserting data into, 552-554
    joining, 541-542
    modifying, 524-526
    retrieving data from, 554-556
    valid types in, 520-521
TCP, 572
    echo client, creating, 577-581
    echo server, creating, 574-577
    network framework, creating, 587-588
TemplateGraphicsApplication class,
    creating, 213
    declaring, 211-212
    using in applet, 219-220
ternary operator, 24
text fields, using, 474-476
text file, importing data from, 542-543
this keyword, 91-92, 109
ThreadDeath, 150
threads, 177
    creating, 178
    daemon, 194
    extending, 178-180
    interrupting, 193-194
    priority status, 195
    sleeping, 191-193
    stopping, 181-183
    synchronized painting using, 278-284
    synchronizing, 183-185
    user, 194
Tic-Tac-Toe console game example,
    157-166
tile engine, creating, 439-448
tile walker, creating, 449-465
timer,
    creating, 389-393
    native high-resolution, 389

timing, 387-388
    high-resolution, 389
token, 85
toLowerCase method, 77
tool tips, 62*
    creating, 62-64*
top-level
    class, 97
    container, 198
toString method, 81-82, 103-104
toUpperCase method, 77
transient keyword, 175
translating, 230
Transmission Control Protocol, *see* TCP
transparency, 245
trim method, 77
try/catch, 144-147
typecasting, 18

U
UDP, 572
    echo server/client, creating, 581-587
unary operator, 24
Unicode characters, defining, 33
update method, overriding, 270-271
User Datagram Protocol, *see* UDP
user thread, 194

V
valueOf method, 77-78
variable, 8
    declaring, 16-17
    scope, 51-52
VirtualMachineError, 150
void keyword, 48
VolatileImage class, 284
    using, 284-286

W
wait method, 189-191
.wav format, 339
while loop, 40-41
WinClock.dll, creating, 393-394
window border, sizing, 215-219
window, closing, 222
windowed application template, 211-212
wrapper classes, 132
    parse methods, 132

nvSDK

developer.nvidia.com

www.GameInstitute.com
A Superior Way to Learn Computer Game Development

The Game Institute provides a convenient, high-quality game development curriculum at a very affordable tuition. Our expert faculty has developed a series of courses designed to teach you fundamental and advanced game programming techniques so that you can design and develop your own computer games. Best of all, in our unique virtual classrooms you can interact with instructors and fellow students in ways that will ensure you get a firm grasp of the material. Whether you are a beginner or a game development professional, the Game Institute is the superior choice for your game development education.

Quality Courses at a Great Price

○ **Weekly Online Voice Lectures** delivered by your instructor with accompanying slides and other visuals.

○ **Downloadable Electronic Textbook** provides in-depth coverage of the entire curriculum with additional voice-overs from instructors.

○ **Student-Teacher Interaction** both live in weekly chat sessions and via message boards where you can post your questions and solutions to exercises.

○ **Downloadable Certificates** suitable for printing and framing indicate successful completion of your coursework.

○ **Source Code** and sample applications for study and integration into your own gaming projects.

"The leap in required knowledge from competent general-purpose coder to games coder has grown significantly. The Game Institute provides an enormous advantage with a focused curriculum and attention to detail."

–Tom Forsyth
Lead Developer
Muckyfoot Productions, Ltd.

3D Graphics Programming With Direct3D

Examines the premier 3D graphics programming API on the Microsoft Windows platform. Create a complete 3D game engine with animated characters, light maps, special effects, and more.

3D Graphics Programming With OpenGL

An excellent course for newcomers to 3D graphics programming. Also includes advanced topics like shadows, curved surfaces, environment mapping, particle systems, and more.

Advanced BSP/PVS/CSG Techniques

A strong understanding of spatial partitioning algorithms is important for 3D graphics programmers. Learn how to leverage the BSP tree data structure for fast visibility processing and collision detection as well as powerful CSG algorithms.

Real-Time 3D Terrain Rendering

Take your 3D engine into the great outdoors. This course takes a serious look at popular terrain generation and rendering algorithms including ROAM, Rottger, and Lindstrom.

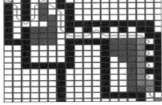

Path Finding Algorithms

Study the fundamental art of maneuver in 2D and 3D environments. Course covers the most popular academic algorithms in use today. Also includes an in-depth look at the venerable A*.

Network Game Programming With DirectPlay

Microsoft DirectPlay takes your games online quickly. Course includes coverage of basic networking, lobbies, matchmaking and session management.

MORE COURSES AVAILABLE AT

www.GameInstitute.com

THIS
CHANGES
EVERYTHING™

NOW WITH 128 MB OF DDR MEMORY!

Brand yourself a warrior with the groundbreaking, high-resolution 3D graphics of RADEON™ 8500 now with 128MB of memory for lightning fast 3D gaming. Get the most out of today's hottest 3D games and experience the most immersive 3D gaming imaginable. RADEON™ 8500 changes everything.

ATI.COM

About the CD

The companion CD includes all the source code discussed in the book, several applications, and a chapter on Swing components.

These are organized in the following folders:

- Apps – The applications in this folder include the Java 2 SDK version 1.4.1 and the Java Runtime for the Linux, Solaris, and Windows platforms; the freeware version of JCreator; and MySQL. Additionally, the MySQL manual is included in PDF format. You will need Adobe Acrobat Reader, which is available for download at http://www.adobe.com/products/acrobat/readermain.html, to read this file.

- Bonus Chapter – The bonus chapter discusses the use of Swing components and is formatted as a PDF file.

- Source – The source code is arranged in folders bearing the name of the chapter in which it is discussed.

The CD contents can be accessed using Windows Explorer.

The MySQL and Cygwin software packages stored on the companion CD are licensed under the terms of the GNU General Public License. For more details, please review the files named README that are stored in the base directory of the mysql-3.23.55-win-src.zip located in the following directory: \Apps\MySQL\File Required for Distribution. The cygwin software readme is in ccygwin-1.3.9-1.tar.tar.out found in the following directory: \Apps\MySQL\File Required for Distribution\cygwin source. You may also check online at http://www.mysql.com/downloads/index.html for licensing information or additional downloads.

Please see the Readme file on the root for more information about the CD contents.

 Warning:

By opening the CD package, you accept the terms and conditions of the CD/Source Code Usage License Agreement.

Additionally, opening the CD package makes this book nonreturnable.

CD/Source Code Usage License Agreement

Please read the following CD/Source Code usage license agreement before opening the CD and using the contents therein:

1. By opening the accompanying software package, you are indicating that you have read and agree to be bound by all terms and conditions of this CD/Source Code usage license agreement.

2. The compilation of code and utilities contained on the CD and in the book are copyrighted and protected by both U.S. copyright law and international copyright treaties, and is owned by Wordware Publishing, Inc. Individual source code, example programs, help files, freeware, shareware, utilities, and evaluation packages, including their copyrights, are owned by the respective authors.

3. No part of the enclosed CD or this book, including all source code, help files, shareware, freeware, utilities, example programs, or evaluation programs, may be made available on a public forum (such as a World Wide Web page, FTP site, bulletin board, or Internet news group) without the express written permission of Wordware Publishing, Inc. or the author of the respective source code, help files, shareware, freeware, utilities, example programs, or evaluation programs.

4. You may not decompile, reverse engineer, disassemble, create a derivative work, or otherwise use the enclosed programs, help files, freeware, shareware, utilities, or evaluation programs except as stated in this agreement.

5. The software, contained on the CD and/or as source code in this book, is sold without warranty of any kind. Wordware Publishing, Inc. and the authors specifically disclaim all other warranties, express or implied, including but not limited to implied warranties of merchantability and fitness for a particular purpose with respect to defects in the disk, the program, source code, sample files, help files, freeware, shareware, utilities, and evaluation programs contained therein, and/or the techniques described in the book and implemented in the example programs. In no event shall Wordware Publishing, Inc., its dealers, its distributors, or the authors be liable or held responsible for any loss of profit or any other alleged or actual private or commercial damage, including but not limited to special, incidental, consequential, or other damages.

6. One (1) copy of the CD or any source code therein may be created for backup purposes. The CD and all accompanying source code, sample files, help files, freeware, shareware, utilities, and evaluation programs may be copied to your hard drive. With the exception of freeware and shareware programs, at no time can any part of the contents of this CD reside on more than one computer at one time. The contents of the CD can be copied to another computer, as long as the contents of the CD contained on the original computer are deleted.

7. You may not include any part of the CD contents, including all source code, example programs, shareware, freeware, help files, utilities, or evaluation programs in any compilation of source code, utilities, help files, example programs, freeware, shareware, or evaluation programs on any media, including but not limited to CD, disk, or Internet distribution, without the express written permission of Wordware Publishing, Inc. or the owner of the individual source code, utilities, help files, example programs, freeware, shareware, or evaluation programs.

8. You may use the source code, techniques, and example programs in your own commercial or private applications unless otherwise noted by additional usage agreements as found on the CD.

Warning:

By opening the CD package, you accept the terms and conditions of the CD/Source Code Usage License Agreement.

Additionally, opening the CD package makes this book nonreturnable.